Warman's
COUNTRY
ANTIQUES & COLLECTIBLES

Second Edition

DANA GEHMAN MORYKAN
HARRY L. RINKER

Wallace-Homestead Book Company
Radnor, Pennsylvania

Volumes in the Encyclopedia of Antiques and Collectibles

Harry L. Rinker, Series Editor

Warman's Americana & Collectibles, 6th Edition,
  edited by Harry L. Rinker

Warman's Country Antiques & Collectibles, 2nd Edition,
  by Dana Gehman Morykan and Harry L. Rinker

Warman's English & Continental Pottery & Porcelain, 2nd Edition,
  by Susan and Al Bagdade

Warman's Furniture,
  edited by Harry L. Rinker

Warman's Glass,
  by Ellen Tischbein Schroy

Warman's Oriental Antiques,
  by Gloria and Robert Mascarelli

Warman's Paper,
  by Norman E. Martinus and Harry L. Rinker

Copyright © 1994 by Rinker Enterprises, Inc.

Second Edition   All rights reserved.
Published in Radnor, Pennsylvania 19089, by Wallace-Homestead, a division of
Chilton Book Company

Manufactured in the United States of America

Library of Congress Cataloging-in-Publication Data
Morykan, Dana Gehman.
    Warman's country antiques & collectibles / Dana Gehman Morykan,
  Harry L. Rinker.—2nd ed.
      p. cm.—(Encyclopedia of antiques and collectibles)
    Includes index.
    ISBN 0-87069-699-8
    1. Antiques—United States. I. Rinker, Harry L.   II. Title.
  III. Title: Warman's country antiques and collectibles. IV. Series.
  NK805.M67   1994
  745.1'0973'075—dc20   93-45256
                                                   CIP

1 2 3 4 5 6 7 8 9 0   3 2 1 0 9 8 7 6 5 4

CONTENTS

INTRODUCTION

Welcome to *Warman's Country Antiques & Collectibles*, a volume in the Warman Encyclopedia of Antiques and Collectibles. While this volume contains all the traditional Warman features—category introductions featuring history, references, periodicals, collectors' clubs, museums, reproduction alerts and detailed, accurate listings—it also represents a significant departure from the usual format.

First, the book focuses on a "style" rather than a group of objects. *Warman's Country Antiques & Collectibles* is one of two style books that will be part of the Warman Encyclopedia series. The other will focus on Victoriana.

Second, because Country marries period pieces with contemporary reproductions and copycats, you will find a listing of contemporary craftspersons and manufacturers in the category introductions. Initial reaction to this innovation has been extremely positive.

COUNTRY

For the purpose of this book, Country is defined as any objects that were part of 19th and early 20th century rural life. This book is more than just a price guide to "farm" collectibles. The agrarian community included both farm and village. Objects from both are included in this book.

Country is part of Americana. Its objects reflect how a major portion of our country's population lived. This book documents a part of their legacy.

However, limiting Country just to American objects in the 1990s is shortsighted. In the 1980s Country collectors expanded their horizons and discovered English Country and French Country. You will find categories relating to each of these movements throughout the book.

There is a strong link between Country and folk art. Many so-called folk art items originated in rural America. Many Country categories, e.g., quilts, have been appropriated by folk art collectors and made part of their movement. This book is concerned only with the objects themselves. If an object is Country in origin, it belongs in this book. Hence, you will find a fair amount of "folk art" within these pages.

Throughout the 1970s and early 1980s, collectors, dealers, and decorators stressed the informal, generic side of Country. In the mid-1980s they discovered that Country had a formal side. *Warman's Country Antiques & Collectibles* has carefully blended the formal and informal. As a result, some categories and listings will challenge your understanding of what does and does not constitute Country.

In the previous section you read that Country on the national level has once again returned to its Early American roots. While some category listings have been changed to reflect this shift, the authors have chosen to continue this book's principal focus on Country as it was defined during the 1970s and 1980s.

Each of us defines Country differently. In a way this reflects the diversity and independent frame of mind that is so much a part of Country. As Country continues to grow, so will the views of the authors and our presentation in subsequent editions. However, first and foremost in selecting the categories and information that appears in this volume is how American collectors and dealers view Country, not how Country periodicals and interior decorators define Country.

FINDING COUNTRY

Country is everywhere. You will find objects at virtually every craft show, flea market, mall, shop, or show that you visit. This is due in part to Country's modern eclecticism and its dualistic nature—formal and informal.

In the past two decades a number of "Country" shows and flea markets have developed. The following list will help you locate them. Because some of the show dates shift, the list is organized by promoter. Check with the promoter for the exact dates of their next Country event.

Jim Burk (3012 Miller Road, Washington Boro, PA 17582). Check the dates for his shows held at Dutch Town & Country Inn on Route 30 east of Lancaster, PA, and at the York County Fairgrounds, York, PA.

Ronald Cox (9411 East 141st Street, Fishers, IA 46038). Cox's Hoosier Antiques Exposition is held at the Indiana State Fairgrounds, Indianapolis, IN, in early April and mid-October each year.

Crutcher-Keighley (PO Box 1267, Hamilton, MT 59840). Antiques Show & Sale, Indiana State Fairgrounds, Indianapolis, IN, held in mid-April and mid-October.

Bruce Knight (PO Box 2429, Springfield, OH 45501). The Springfield Antiques Show & Flea Market is held at the Clark County Fairgrounds, Springfield, OH, the third weekend of the month, year round, excluding July. The December market is held the second weekend of the month.

Britton Knowles (PO Box 6606, South Bend, IN 46660). The Amish Heartland show is held three times a year at the Elkhart County Fairgrounds, Goshen, IN.

Richard E. Kramer (427 Midvale Avenue, St. Louis, MO 63130). Kramer's Heart of Country show held at the Opryland Hotel in Nashville, TN, in early spring each year is the bellwether Country Show in America. Also check out Home in Indiana held in Indianapolis in early fall.

Mrs. J. L. Robinson (PO Box 549, St. Charles, IL 60174). Kane County Antiques Flea Market is held at the Kane County Fairgrounds, St. Charles, IL, the first Sunday of every month and the preceding Saturday.

Sandwich Antiques Market (1510 N. Hoyne, Chicago, IL 60622). The Sandwich Antiques Market is held at The Fairgrounds, Sandwich, IL, one Sunday each month between May and October.

Sha-Dor Shows (PO Box 1400, Rockville, MD 20850). American Classic Antiques Show & Sale held at D.C. Armory, Washington, DC, in mid-May.

As you can see from the above list, Indianapolis, Indiana, is the real "heart" of Country. Almost every weekend there is a show either in or around Indianapolis with a strong Country appeal. Malls in the surrounding area also heavily emphasize Country.

There are many regional Country shows, e.g., the American Country Antiques Show held in Windsor Locks, Connecticut, or the Zoar Antiques Show in Zoar, Ohio. Some communities such as New Oxford, Pennsylvania, and Fairhaven, Ohio, turn their entire town into an outdoor antiques festival one or more times a year. All these shows and antiques festivals advertise in the leading trade papers. Attend as many as possible.

Do not overlook contemporary craft shows. State and regional craft shows abound. Check with your local Council of the Arts to determine the date and location of the shows nearest you. Many have become specialized, e.g., the Mid-Atlantic Quilt Festival held each year in late winter.

Finally, one auction house deserves special mention—Garth's Auctions, Inc. (PO Box 369, Delaware, OH 43015). No one offers a finer selection of Country on a regular basis. An annual subscription to his catalogs is a must for any serious Country collector.

ORGANIZATION OF THE BOOK

General Approach: Warman's has never been wed to tradition. *Warman's Country Antiques & Collectibles* is an excellent case in point. Because Country is a style, it demands a different approach from the straight alphabetical listing of categories found in *Warman's Antiques and Their Prices* or *Warman's Americana & Collectibles*.

After careful consideration, we decided to treat Country topically. In order to do this, a two-fold approach was used for the major categories. One group focuses on general collecting topics, e.g., furniture; the second concentrates on a phase of agrarian life, e.g., the barn. The key was to develop a presentation that corresponds with how YOU collect and deal with Country.

This approach is possible because of our commitment to a strong index. The index ties the book together. Used properly, it will lead you to the correct location for the Country item that you are seeking.

History: Here we discuss the category, describe how the object was made, who are or were the leading manufacturers, and variations of form and style. In many instances a chronology for the objects is established.

Whenever possible, we place the object in a social context—how it was used, for what purpose, etc. We also delve into how the objects are used within a Country setting. An object's decorative use is just as much a part of its history as its utilitarian use.

Where appropriate, we have added some collecting hints such as where cross category collecting and outside factors are critical in pricing, and where to best find some of the objects.

References: A few general references are listed to encourage collectors to learn more about their objects. Included are author, title, most recent edition, publisher (if published by a small firm or individual, we have indicated "published by author"), and a date of publication.

Finding these books may present a problem. The antiques and collectibles field is blessed with a dedicated core of book dealers who stock these specialized publications. You may find them at flea markets, antiques shows, and through their advertisements in leading publications in the field. Many dealers publish annual or semi-annual catalogs. Ask to be put on their mailing lists. Books go out-of-print quickly, yet many books printed over 25 years ago remain the standard work in a field. Also, haunt used book dealers for reference material.

Collectors' Clubs: Collectors' clubs add vitality to any collecting field. Their publications and conventions produce knowledge which often cannot be found anywhere else. Many of these clubs are short lived; others are so strong that they have regional and local chapters. Support those clubs that match your collecting interest.

Periodicals: The Country field is served by a wealth of general and specific publications. You need to be aware of the following:

American Country Collectibles, GCR Publishing Group, 1700 Broadway, New York, NY 10019.
Country, Reiman Publications, 5400 S. 60th Street, Greendale, WI 53129.
Country Accents, GCR Publishing Group, 1700 Broadway, New York, NY 10019.
Country Collectibles, Harris Publications, 1115 Broadway, New York, NY 10010.
Country Folk Art, 8393 East Holly Road, Holly, MI 48442.
Country Home, Meredith Corporation, 1716 Locust Street, Des Moines, IA 50309.
Country Living, Hearst Corporation, 224 West 57th Street, New York, NY 10019.
Country Sampler, Sampler Publications, 707 Kautz Road, St. Charles, IL 60174.
Country Victorian Accents, GCR Publishing Company, 1700 Broadway, New York, NY 10019.
Country Woman, Reiman Publications, 5400 South 60th Street, Greendale, WI 53129.
Early American Life, Cowles Magazines, PO Box 8200, Harrisburg, PA 17105
Farm and Ranch Living, Reiman Publications, 5400 South 60th Street, Greendale, WI 53129.

Articles about Country and Country collectibles are featured regularly in most trade newspapers. Two papers deserve special mention:

AntiqueWeek, PO Box 90, Knightstown, IN 46148.
Maine Antique Digest, PO Box 358, Waldoboro, ME 04572.

Regional papers from New England, the Middle Atlantic, and Midwest stress Country more heavily than those from other parts of the country. You will find a complete list of these papers in David J. Maloney, Jr.'s *Maloney's Antiques & Collectibles Resource Directory, 1994–1995* (Wallace-Homestead Book Company, 1993).

Museums: The best way to study a specific field is to see as many documented examples as possible. For this reason, we have listed museums where significant collections of collectibles are on display. We especially recommend visiting state and regional farm museums.

Reproduction Alert: Reproductions (exact copies) and copycats (stylistic copies) are a major concern. Unfortunately, many of these items are unmarked. Newness of appearance is often the best clue to spotting them. Where "Reproduction Alert" appears, a watchful eye should be kept within the entire category.

Reproductions are only one aspect of the problem. Outright fakes (objects deliberately meant to deceive) are another. Be especially alert for fakes in categories where Country and folk art come together.

Reproduction Craftspersons and Manufacturers: Not everyone can afford period pieces; not everyone wants period pieces. When achieving the "look" is the principal concern, reproductions and copycat items are perfectly acceptable.

Warman's Country Antiques & Collectibles is the first price guide to list contemporary craftspersons and manufacturers side by side with period material. We have done so because we believe these objects can just as effectively provide the Country look as period examples. Further, many are so well made that they will survive and become the collectibles of tomorrow and the antiques of the future.

We gathered the names of craftspersons and manufacturers from existing literature in the field. Some we know personally; others we do not. None paid to have their name or business listed. Before buying from any, we urge you to inspect their merchandise personally and compare their products and prices with others offering similar products.

Listings: We have attempted to make the listings descriptive enough so the specific object can be identified. Most guides limit their descriptions to one line, but not those with the name *Warman's* in the title. We have placed emphasis on those items which are actively being sold in the marketplace. Nevertheless, some harder-to-find objects are included in order to demonstrate the market spread.

Because of the multifaceted nature of the antiques and collectibles field, category overlap will occur within the volumes in the Warman's Encyclopedia of Antiques and Collectibles. When this does happen, all new listings will be provided, with a few minor exceptions.

PRICE NOTES

Most prices within Country categories are relatively stable. This is why we use a "one" price system. When necessary, we will use ranges. But, as you will find in using this book, this is a rarity.

Our pricing is based on an object being in very good condition. If otherwise, we note this in our description. It would be ideal to suggest that mint, or unused, examples of all objects do exist. Objects from the past were used, whether they be glass, china, dolls, or toys. Because of this use, some normal wear must be expected. Furthermore, if the original box is important in establishing a price, it is assumed that the box is present with the article.

As the number of special interest collectors grows, a single object may appeal to more than one buyer, each of whom has his or her own "price" in mind. In preparing prices for this guide we look at the object within the category being considered and price it as though an individual who collects actively within that category is buying it.

Some Country objects have regional interest. However, a national price consensus has formed as a result of the publication of specialized price guides, collectors' club newsletters, and magazines and newspapers. Regional pricing is discounted in favor of the more general national consensus.

RESEARCH

Collectors of Country deserve credit for their attention to scholarship and the skill by which they have assembled their collections. This book attests to how strong and encompassing the Country market has become through their efforts.

We obtain our prices from many key sources—dealers, publications, auctions, collectors, and field work. The generosity with which dealers have given advice is a credit to the field. Everyone recognizes the need for a guide that is specific and has accurate prices. We study newspapers, magazines, newsletters, and other publications in the collectibles and antiques field. All of them are critical in understanding what is available in the market. Special recognition must be given to those collectors' club newsletters and magazines which discuss prices.

Our staff is constantly in the field—from Massachusetts to Florida, Pennsylvania to California. We utilize a Board of Advisors that provides regional as well as specialized information. Each *Warman's* title incorporates information from hundreds of auction catalogs generously furnished by the firms listed in the AUCTION HOUSE section. Finally, private collectors have worked closely with us, sharing their knowledge of price trends and developments unique to their specialties.

BUYER'S GUIDE, NOT SELLER'S GUIDE

Warman's Country Antiques & Collectibles is designed to be a buyer's guide, a guide to what you would have to pay to purchase an object on the open market from a dealer or collector. **It is not a seller's guide to prices.** People frequently make this mistake and are deceiving themselves by doing so.

If you have an object in this book and wish to sell it, you should expect to receive approximately 35 to 40% of the values listed. If the object cannot be resold quickly, expect to receive even less. The truth is simple. Knowing where to sell an object is worth 50% or more of its value. Buyers are very specialized; dealers work for years to assemble a list of collectors who will pay top dollar for an item.

Examine your piece as objectively as possible. If it is something from your childhood, try to step back from the personal memories in evaluating its condition. As an antiques appraiser, I spend a great deal of my time telling people their treasures are not "gold," but items readily available in the marketplace.

When buying and selling, a simple philosophy is that a good purchase occurs when both the buyer and seller are happy with the price. Don't look back. Hindsight has little value in the collectibles field. Given time, things tend to balance out.

COMMENTS INVITED

Warman's Country Antiques & Collectibles is a major effort to deal with a complex field. Our readers are encouraged to send their comments and suggestions to Rinker Enterprises, Inc., 5093 Vera Cruz Road, Emmaus, PA 18049.

COUNTRY IN THE 1990s

Country has come full circle. Mid-1990s Country is now a kissin' cousin to the 1950s Early American look. Midwest rural 19th and early 20th century Country, the look that dominated the 1970s and 1980s, has been replaced by a very formal, traditional Early American style. While there were signs of change toward this direction as Country entered the 1990s, no one expected the transition to be so rapid and complete.

Tracing the evolution of Country in the post-World War II era provides clues to understanding the short and long term significances of this shift. Unless a major refocusing occurs, and there are no indications on the horizon of events that could trigger such a change, Early American will be the decorating style that takes Country into the twenty-first century.

Prior to World War II—in fact through the 1950s—American Country and Early American were synonymous. A Country kitchen or den contained a large open-hearth fireplace with a wood-carved mantel, spider-legged cast iron cooking utensils, trestle table, spinning wheel, and appropriate accessories. Living and bed rooms consisted of a mix of semi-formal Chippendale and Federal pieces with an occasional rustic piece, e.g., a table-chair, thrown in for good measure.

The Early American style is rooted in the prosperous, small, inland coastal village of the eighteenth and early nineteenth century. It is an East Coast style, with a heavy New England presence. It is typified by historic sites such as Historic Deerfield and Old Sturbridge Village in Massachusetts and Colonial Williamsburg. Each site represents a community that has won the struggle with the frontier and is now ready to reap the rewards, i.e., settle down and enjoy the good times.

In the 1960s the dominance of the Early American style was challenged. The social activism of the era stressed a more simplistic, back to nature approach. A major handcraft revival occurred. Foxfire and similar projects moved Country from the village to the frontier.

By the mid-1960s America became deeply engrossed in the preparation of America's Bicentennial. A decision was made to concentrate activities on the local, not national level. America would celebrate all of its history, not just the 150-year period leading up to the American Revolution. As a result the 19th century, not the 18th century became the focal point for celebrations throughout the Midwest and West.

A new Country look was born. Country of the late 1960s through the mid-1980s was rooted in the American heartland of the Midwest of the late 19th century. Country and the rural farmstead became one. The agrarian myth became reality as primitive tools and animal harnesses decorated living room and den walls. The new Country collector chronicled the struggle, not the success of the battle.

A sense of excitement and experimentation swept through Country. Country enjoyed its youthful exuberance. The style was free and open to a vast amount of interpretation. Country was eclectic. There was no emphasis on period, i.e., everything in a room had to be from a fixed historical time period. Country became whatever anyone wanted to make it.

One of the first new approaches to emerge was that of Country primitive. The aged, weathered look was stressed. It was a Country with no electricity or running water. It was a Country style rooted in the earth, its colors linked to nature's seasons.

In the 1970s a kinship was forged between Country and Folk Art. It should come as no surprise that Country and Folk Art evolved at the same time. However, where Folk Art is aesthetic (at least this is what its collectors and dealers would have one believe), Country is utilitarian. Both celebrate life, particularly the life of the "average" American. Where Folk Art emphasizes the individual, Country adds the tempering element of community.

While the linkage between Country and Folk Art served both movements in good stead in the 1970s and early 1980s, it would eventually prove disastrous to Country. The Folk Art market collapsed in the late 1980s. Overexposure, overpricing, numerous fakes and forgeries, and the recession are just some of the reasons for its fall. Unfortunately, it dragged the contemporary Country of the 1980s down with it. While Folk Art is not the sole reason for the shift in emphasis within Country, it is one of the major factors.

In the 1970s interior decorators and Country magazines stole control of Country from the antiques community. Country became the foremost decorating style in America. The Country collecting emphasis was now in the hands of individuals whose survival relied on continual change. One year ducks and redware are in, the next they are out. Country lost its sense of long term continuity.

The effect on Country has been profound. In the early 1980s the interior decorating community attempted to link Country with the prosperous look of late nineteenth century Victorian America. By the mid-1980s this look dominated. Just as collectors were becoming comfortable in the transition, decorators shifted their Country emphasis to the English rural gentry look, bleached look of the Mediterranean, or rural Scandinavian. Country went international just as the recession of the late 1980s struck.

The recession drove the interior decorators from the market. They abandoned ship, leaving Country to sink or swim by itself. Leadership fell exclusively to the periodicals. When in doubt, always retreat to the tried and true. The periodicals did.

Country came full circle. The formal Early American look has returned. Compare any Country periodical with *The Magazine Antiques*. The similarities far outweigh the differences.

The return to dominance of the Early American style has profoundly affected Country. First, since it emphasizes an earlier age, period pieces are much more expensive. Affordability was one of the major keys to the dominance of Country as America's leading decorating style in the 1970s and 1980s. When semi-formal corner cupboards and hutches reach the $5,000 plus range, they are beyond the pocketbook of the average collector.

Second, since period pieces are expensive, individuals interested solely in the look will turn more and more to reproductions, copycats, and fantasy items. Why not? They often sell for less than fifty percent of the price of a period piece.

Third, Early American once again links Country with the formal, upscale antiques show. Differences that were apparent in the 1970s and 1980s are now blurred. On a positive note, this influx of new capital will be most welcome by the antiques community.

Fourth, the handcraft and gift community has responded by shifting its emphasis from the primitive to the formal, from the late 19th to the late 18th and early 19th century. The Country gift show of the mid-1990s is entirely different from its counterpart of the late 1980s. Further, the amount of individually handcrafted products is diminishing, due in part to the recession but also to craftspersons combining their talents into more commercial business consortiums.

Does this mean that the Country look of the 1970s and 1980s is dead? Absolutely not! It is alive and well in America's heartland. The Country show circuit continues. Goods continue to change hands.

Prices have been relatively stable for the past four years. With collectors as the dominant buying force in the market, the annual collecting crazes and trends created by the interior decorators, periodicals, and speculators during the 1970s and 1980s have ceased. Mid-1990s rural Country is trustworthy. Purchasers can be comfortable with what they buy and what they pay for it.

In fact everything about 1980s Country has become comfortable. Leadership remains in the hands of authors, collectors, and dealers who headed the stylistic evolution of Country in the 1970s. Country literature simply rehashes the same material ad nauseam. Given this, it is not surprising that several Country periodicals are facing major declines in subscriptions. Antiques and collectibles publishers have greatly reduced their publication of books about objects that support the Country look. A major Country price guide formerly published annually is now published biennially.

Country needs younger voices—a new generation of leadership. Leadership whose enthusiasm is captivating. Individuals who have the vision to make 1980s Country work in the 1990s through the 21st century. Convincing antiques and collectibles trade leaders to identify, train, and pass the mantle to the next generation is one of the major problems in the antiques and collectibles community.

What must never be forgotten is that combined Country, 1980s Country plus Early American Country, remains the single most important decorating style in America. Country is forever.

Long term collectors have learned to accept the swing of the pendulum of popular taste. It is clear to most that American country is best reflected in the Country look that dominated the late 1970s and early 1980s, not Early American. The pendulum will swing back again. Patience and persistence count.

STATE OF THE MARKET

Country is quiet. In fact, it is so quiet that at first glance it appears to have died. As Mark Twain wrote: "The reports of my death are greatly exaggerated." Country is alive and well. The price stability of the early 1990s continues. Objects continue to sell within a plus or minus five percent range.

Within any stable market, there is an occasional sales burst followed by an extended lull. A surprisingly large number of coverlets sold in late 1993. However, prices remained within established market norms. Ordinary stoneware appears to have undergone a modest decline in 1993. The same is also true for commonly found tools. A quick turnaround in either market would come as no surprise.

Gasoline powered farm equipment, especially tractors, make up one of the "hot" categories in Country collecting. Acquiring and restoring old farm equipment is growing at a rapid rate. Collectors' clubs organized by manufacturer exist for the major producers. Specialized meets occur on a regular basis.

The farm toy market, lead by Ertl, appears to have reached the saturation point. Growth is modest. The market is flooded with new products. Prices are stable, but teetering. Speculators and hoarders continue to hold onto them rather than dump them into the market. As long as this continues, prices will remain steady.

In the first edition of *Warman's Country Antiques & Collectibles,* the article entitled "1990s Country" concluded by recommending divorcing Country from Folk Art. There are signs that this is happening. Much less "old" and new Folk Art has appeared in Country auctions and at Country shows. Country collectors have realized that purchasing Folk Art is one of the most risky investments any purchaser can make.

Country has shifted from a primary to a secondary source of income for many dealers. A large Country dealer whose shop was featured in *Country Living* in the early 1990s reported that he sells more 1920s-40s Colonial Revival furniture now than he does Country pieces. He changed his shop inventory to reflect this trend. He is not alone.

Country collectors have become fussier about condition. Objects showing extensive wear, repairs, or damage (chips, cracks, missing pieces, etc.) are failing to find buyers unless greatly reduced in price. One would have expected just the opposite given the shift to Early American style Country. Since these pieces are older and more subject to the ravages of time, one might assume that collectors would recognize this and forgive some, if not all, of the problems. Collectors now want their 18th and early 19th century pieces in very good or better condition.

There are two reasons for this increased emphasis on condition. Today's collectors are more sophisticated. They recognize that condition is a major hedge against price decline in a falling market. Further, many have had their sights raised by individuals within the collectibles community, especially in the toy sector, where collecting below fine condition is discouraged.

Authenticity also has become a major issue. Major repairs and replacements are no longer acceptable. Furniture constructed from old parts is passé. Collectors now understand how long certain vernacular forms remained in production. Unless adequate provenance is provided, collectors assume late, rather than early production. In the 1980s just the opposite was true.

Unfortunately, the growing emphasis on authenticity and condition does not appear to be accompanied by a similar emphasis on aesthetic quality. In fact, affordability appears to have driven Country collectors to focus more on medium quality, mass-produced utilitarian wares than on older objects with strong aesthetic qualities and quality manufacture.

Nowhere is this more evident than in the rising interest in twentieth century dinner and utilitarian wares. Homer Laughlin, Harker, and Watt are manufacturers whose products were directed toward catalog sales, not the upscale department store. Prices have risen sharply in several collecting categories, often reaching the point of ridiculousness. What happened to the thrifty, practical, common sense side of Country collecting?

Regionalism continues to have a multiplicity of effects. In the case of pottery, decorative accessories, and paper, pieces continue to sell at higher prices in the region from which they originated. A Red Wing stoneware jug with advertising sells best in Minnesota and surrounding states.

However, regional furniture, e.g., Shaker and Pennsylvania German, has fallen on hard times. A major Shaker collection was sold in late 1993. While some pieces did exceptionally well, the real story was the number of pieces in the collection that had been altered (now a no-no) or were not Shaker in origin. A lengthy story about a New York dealer's negative experience with Shaker material appeared in the same issue of *Maine Antique Digest* that reported the Shaker auction. Like so many categories in the antiques and collectibles field, the Shaker market was supported by a relatively small group of big spenders. The absence of two of these individuals depressed prices by over 10 percent.

Pennsylvania German painted case pieces, with the exception of museum quality examples, are depressed more than 25 percent from their late 1970s high. As with most market segments, there are a few high ticket pieces that sell at auction, shows, or privately. However, when one looks at the value of commonly found pieces, the market shows major weakness.

Reproductions (exact copies), copycats (stylistic copies), and fantasy items continue to play a major role in the Country market. In the 1970s and 80s many of these products were made by individual craftspersons or nucleated family groups. Many of these craftspersons have fallen by the wayside, victims of the recession. Some have joined together to reduce overhead. A few have grown into thriving large scale, commercial enterprises. Most have given their products a more formal look.

Early American style Country, despite its handcrafted appearance, lends itself well to commercially produced products. As a result, many large manufacturers in categories ranging from ceramics to textiles have produced product for sale to Country collectors. Most of these goods are made off-shore.

Affordability is the primary reason that reproduction, copycat, and fantasy items are so well received by the Country community. Individuals who simply want to achieve a look have little difficulty buying a new piece at pennies, nickels, or dimes on the dollar when compared to the price of a period original. Collecting areas especially hard hit are ceramics, glass, and textiles.

With Country taking a more formal approach, look for a number of 1930s and 40s traditionalist antiques categories to awake from their slumber of nearly half a century. Romantic Staffordshire patterns and forms are very compatible with the 1990s Country style and surprisingly affordable. Pattern glass, late 19th century art glass, and decorative accessories, e.g., silver-plated napkin rings and toothpick holders, are other revival possibilities.

In the early 1990s Country western emerged as one of the trendy decorating styles. It is best approached by viewing it as four distinct units: (1) the old west (the west of the Indians and early Spanish settlers), (2) the western frontier (the west of the cowboys and wagon trains), (3) dude ranch western (the west of the city slickers), and (4) the TV west (the romanticized west of novels and TV cowboy heroes). Although attempts were made to make the western look a branch of American Country, it emerged in the mid-1990s as a separate entity. While enjoying some popularity in large metropolitan areas, it remains highly regionalized in the Southwest and West Coast regions.

As in the rest of America, the 1990s recession continues to have a negative effect on Country. Everyone, collectors and dealers alike, are taking a conservative tack. Emphasis is on survival, not growth. The good news is that most individuals are surviving. Collectors still find the moneys to add pieces to their collection. Dealers sell enough to encourage them to continue.

Country and survival are inevitably linked. Country collectors and dealers come from hardy stock, accustomed to facing whatever challenges present themselves. Times will change. They always do. Country's future remains bright. It just needs a little polishing.

AUCTION HOUSES

The following auction houses cooperate with Rinker Enterprises, Inc., by providing catalogues of their auctions and price lists. This information is used to prepare *Warman's Antiques and Their Prices*, volumes in the Warman's Encyclopedia of Antiques and Collectibles, and Wallace-Homestead Book Company publications. This support is most appreciated.

Sanford Alderfer Auction
Company
501 Fairgrounds Rd.
Hatfield, PA 19440
(215) 368-5477

Andre Ammelounx
P. O. Box 136
Palatine, IL 60078
(708) 991-5927

Al Anderson
P. O. Box 644
Troy, OH 45373
(513) 339-0850

Ark Antiques
Box 3133
New Haven, CT 06515
(203) 387-3754

Arthur Auctioneering
R. D. 2
Hughesville, PA 17737
(717) 584-3697

Noel Barrett Antiques and
Auctions Ltd.
P. O. Box 1001
Carversville, PA 18913
(215) 297-5109

Robert F. Batchelder
1 West Butler Avenue
Ambler, PA 19002
(215) 643-1430

Biders Antiques, Inc.
241 South Union Street
Lawrence, MA 01843
(508) 688-4347

Butterfield & Butterfield
7601 Sunset Boulevard
Los Angeles, CA 90046
(213) 850-7500

Butterfield & Butterfield
220 San Bruno Ave.
San Francisco, CA 94103
(415) 861-7500

W. E. Channing & Co.
53 Old Santa Fe Trail
Santa Fe, New Mexico
87501
(505) 988-1078

Christie's
502 Park Avenue
New York, NY 10022
(212) 546-1000

Christie's East
219 E. 67th St.
New York, NY 10021
(212) 606-0400

Christmas Morning
1850 Crown Rd. Suite 1111
Dallas, TX 75234
(817) 236-1155

Cincinnati Art Galleries
635 Main Street
Cincinnati, OH 45202
(513) 381-2128

Cohasco, Inc.
Postal 821
Yonkers, NY 10702
(914) 476-8500

Marvin Cohen Auctions
Box 425, Routes 20 & 22
New Lebanon, NY 12125
(518) 794-9333

Collector Auction Services
RR2 Box 431 Oakwood Rd.
Oil City, PA 16301
(814) 677-6070

Marlin G. Denlinger
RR 3, Box 3775
Morrisville, VT 05661
(802) 888-2774

William Doyle Galleries, Inc.
175 E. 87th St.
New York, NY 10128
(212) 427-2730

Early Auction Co.
123 Main St.
Milford, OH 45150
(513) 831-4833

Steve Finer Rare Books
P. O. Box 758
Greenfield, MA 01302
(413) 773-5811

William A. Fox Auctions,
Inc.
676 Morris Ave.
Springfield, NJ 07081
(201)467-2366

Freeman/Fine Arts Co. of
Philadelphia, Inc.
1808 Chestnut St.
Philadelphia, PA 19103
(215) 563-9275

Garth's Auction, Inc.
2690 Stratford Rd.
P. O. Box 369
Delaware, OH 43015
(614) 362-4771 or 369-5085

Glass-Works Auctions
P. O. Box 187-102 Jefferson
St.
East Greenville, PA 18041
(215) 679-5849

Grandma's Trunk
The Millards
P. O. Box 404
Northport, MI 49670
(616) 386-5351

Guerney's
136 East 73rd St.
New York, NY 10021
(212) 794-2280

Ken Farmer Realty &
Auction Co.
1122 Norwood St.
Radford, VA 24141
(703) 639-0939

Hake's Americana and
Collectibles
P. O. Box 1444
York, PA 17405
(717) 848-1333

Harmer Rooke
Numismatists, Inc.
3 East 57th St.
New York, NY 10022
(212) 751-4122

Morton M. Goldberg
Auction Galleries
547 Baronne Street
New Orleans, LA 70113
(504) 592-2300

Norman C. Heckler &
Company
Bradford Corner Rd.
Woodstock Valley, CT 06282
(203) 974-1634

Leslie Hindman, Inc.
215 West Ohio St.
Chicago, IL 60610
(312) 670-0010

Michael Ivankovich Antiques
P. O. Box 2458
Doylestown, PA 18901
(215) 345-6094

James D. Julia, Inc.
P. O. Box 830
Fairfield, ME 04937
(207) 453-7904

Charles E. Kirtley
P. O. Box 2273
Elizabeth City, NC 27906
(919) 335-1262

Howard Lowery
3818 W. Magnolia Blvd.
Burbank, CA 91505
(818) 972-9080

Alex G. Malloy, Inc.
P. O. Box 38
South Salem, NY 10590
(203) 438-0396

Martin Auctioneers, Inc.
Larry L. Martin
P. O. Box 477
Intercourse, PA 17534
(717) 768-8108

Robert Merry Auction
Company
5501 Milburn Road
St. Louis, MO 63129
(314) 487-3992

Mid-Hudson Auction
Galleries
One Idlewild Ave.
Cornwall-On-Hudson, NY
12520
(214) 534-7828

Milwaukee Auction Galleries
318 N. Water
Milwaukee, WI 53202
(414) 271-1105

Neal Auction Company
4038 Magazine St.
New Orleans, LA 70115
(504) 899-5329

New England Auction
Gallery
Box 2273
W. Peabody, MA 01960
(508) 535-3140

New Hampshire Book
Auctions
Woodbury Rd.
Weare, NH 03281
(603) 529-1700

Nostalgia Publications, Inc.
21 South Lake Dr.
Hackensack, NJ 07601
(201) 488-4536

Richard Opfer Auctioneers
Inc.
1919 Greenspring Dr.
Timonium, MD 21093
(410) 252-5035

Pettigrew Auction Company
1645 South Tejon St.
Colorado Springs, CO 80906
(719) 633-7963

Phillips Ltd.
406 East 79th St.
New York, NY 10021
(212) 570-4830

Postcards International
P. O. Box 2930
New Haven, CT 06515-0030
(203) 865-0814

David Rago Arts & Crafts
P. O. Box 3592 Station E
Trenton, NJ 08629
(609) 585-2546

Lloyd Ralston Toys
173 Post Road
Fairfield, CT 06432
(203) 255-1233 or 366-3399

Renzel's Auction Service
P. O. Box 222
Emigsville, PA 17318
(717) 764-6412

R. Niel & Elaine Reynolds
Box 133
Waterford, VA 22190
(703) 882-3574

Roan Bros. Auction Gallery
R.D. 3, Box 118
Cogan Station, PA 17728
(717) 494-0170

Selkirk Gallery
4166 Olive Street
Saint Louis, MO 63108
(314) 533-1700

Robert W. Skinner Inc.
Bolton Gallery
357 Main St.
Bolton, MA 01740
(508) 779-6241

C. G. Sloan & Company, Inc.
4920 Wyaconda Road
North Bethesda, MD 20852
(301) 468-4911

Smith House Toy Sales
26 Adlington Rd.
Eliot, ME 03903
(207) 439-4614

Sotheby's
1334 York Avenue
New York, NY 10021
(212) 606-7000

Rex Stark
49 Wethersfield Rd.
Bellingham, MA 02019
(508) 966-0994

Swann Galleries, Inc.
104 E. 25th St.
New York, NY 10010
(212) 254-4710

Theriault's
P. O. Box 151
Annapolis, MD 21401
(301) 224-3655

Vintage Cover Story
P. O. Box 975
Burlington, NC 27215
(919) 584-6990

Western Glass Auctions
1288 W. 11th St., Suite
  #230
Tracy, CA 95376
(209) 832-4527

Winter Associates
21 Cooke St. Box 823
Plainville, CT 06062
(203) 793-0288

Wolf's Auction Gallery
13015 Larchmere Blvd.
Shaker Heights, OH 44120
(216) 231-3888

Woody Auction
Douglass, KS 67039
(316) 746-2694

ACKNOWLEDGMENTS

We begin by thanking all those individuals who bought a copy of the first edition of *Warman's Country Antiques & Collectibles*. You made the book a success. There would have been no second edition without your support. Hopefully, this second edition not only matches, but exceeds your expectations.

The first edition of *Warman's Country Antiques & Collectibles* officially launched the Warman Encyclopedia of Antiques and Collectibles. There are now seven volumes in the series. By the time the third edition of this book appears, the number will be closer to a dozen. We thank the management, production, and sales personnel at Chilton Books, Wallace-Homestead's parent company, for their continuing efforts to make the Warman Encyclopedia of Antiques and Collectibles the industry's leader.

Country and family are synonymous. So are the "Rinkettes," the Rinker Enterprise, Inc., staff who worked with us to prepare this volume. Although we appear on the cover and title page as authors, the book was truly a joint effort. Since we are a family, there is no reason to keep our adopted sisters and brothers anonymous.

Our very special thanks and appreciation to the following Rinkettes: Ellen T. Schroy, Director of Publications and Research; Terese J. Yeakel, Research Associate, who was married a week before this manuscript was delivered and to whom we wish a joyous, rewarding, and life-long love affair with Peter; Harry L. Rinker, Jr., Art Director; Nancy M. Butt, Librarian; Jocelyn C. Mousley, Diane L. Sterner, and Richard Schmeltzle, Support Staff.

One of my greatest joys as owner of Rinker Enterprises, Inc., is to watch individuals grow. I am blessed to live in a part of the country where the work ethic remains strong and individuals take pride in the product that they produce. While Dana came to Rinker Enterprises, Inc., with a background in antiques and collectibles, I have watched her fine tune her existing knowledge, gain command of a host of new topics, and become committed to making this field better for her involvement in it. *Warman's Country Antiques & Collectibles* is Dana's first book, certainly not her last. As her children grow into young adults (at Rinker Enterprises one's family comes before all else, including the company), releasing her to devote more time to research and writing, additional titles will follow. Personally, I can hardly wait.

The family concept at Rinker Enterprises, Inc., is an extended one. It is common for the children of the Rinkettes to work on company related projects at the office or home. Kristen and Zachary, Dana's two children, assisted throughout the preparation of this book. Numerous objects scheduled for sale through husband Ray's estate and auction activities were detoured to Rinker Enterprises, Inc., for photography. Thanks to our entire extended family for their assistance.

No book of this scope can be written without the cooperation and support of hundreds of individuals within the field. Auction houses, collectors, dealers, mall operators, members of the media, show managers, and many others shared information and opinions about Country. No listing of their names would ever be inclusive. A general thanks to all in print. We will extend our personal thanks the next time we talk.

As authors, we are very possessive about *Warman's County Antiques & Collectibles*. We would like you to feel the same way. Therefore, we ask your help. Let us know what you think—good or bad. Our goal, as it is for all books prepared at Rinker Enterprises, Inc., is to make each edition better than the one that preceded it. Reader response is one of the best tools to achieve this goal.

Finally, we wish you happy hunting. May all the pieces you find be Country treasures.

5093 Vera Cruz Road, Emmaus, PA 18049
Dana Gehman Morykan and Harry L. Rinker
February 1994

ABBREVIATIONS

The following are standard abbreviations which we have used throughout this edition of *Warman's Country Antiques & Collectibles.*

adv = advertisement
C = century
c = circa
cov = cover or covered
d = diameter or depth
dec = decorated or decoration
emb = embossed
ext. = exterior
ftd = footed
gal = gallon
ground = background
h = height
hp = hand painted
illus = illustrated or illustrations
int. = interior
imp = impressed

l = length
lbs = pounds
litho = lithograph
mkd = marked
no. = number
orig = original
oz = ounces
pcs = pieces
pgs = pages
pr = pair
rect = rectangular
sgd = signed
SP = silver plated
sq = square
w = width
# = numbered

COUNTRY BARN

If the Country kitchen is the farm's social center, the barn is the farm's work center. The barn and its supporting structures differ from region to region. Great bank barns are the dominant barn type in Pennsylvania. The lower level housed the animals, the upper level provided equipment storage, and the lofts and attached silo stored feed. Support buildings, e.g., corn cribs, chicken houses, and storage sheds, completed the farm setting.

Much of farm labor is seasonal in nature and requires specific equipment designed for the task at hand. In many instances, equipment usage is limited to a few days or weeks. As a result, farm equipment spends most of its time in storage. Plenty of storage space is a must for any farm.

Like most individuals, farmers tend to fill up space when it is available. Space makes savers. Farmers and individuals in rural communities are driven to saving by two key philosophies–(1) it's too good to throw out and (2)I'll never know when I will need it. If it still works, save it. Best to keep it around in case the new one breaks. If it does not work, but can be repaired easily, save it anyway. It will get fixed the next time work is slow. It is primarily for these reasons that corners and lofts of barns are treasure troves for the Country collector.

The Country barn and outbuildings required continual maintenance, usually drawing the farmer's attention outside the planting and harvesting seasons. An individual farmer's worth in the community was judged on three key points—how he maintained his buildings, equipment, and animals. The condition of the barn was a fair judge of the value of the farm.

The barn also had a developmental and social role. It was a gigantic playground, often an amusement park, for farm youngsters. The hay loft could be a medieval castle one moment, a frontier fort the next. Sneaking behind the barn was a common means of escaping the watchful eyes of parents.

No farm youngster needs a school course on sex education. One learns at a very early age the role of the bull, rooster, and serum injection. The privacy of the barn provides a haven for young lovers. Little wonder there is a strong tradition in rural America of shotgun weddings.

Removing the equipment from the barn created a social hall for functions ranging from an extended family meal to a hoe-down. Social gatherings were extremely important in rural America where the nearest neighbor may be a quarter to half a mile down the road.

Farm museums take pride in their period barn recreations. Since almost every state has one or more farm museums, locating an example should not prove difficult. The fun is to visit a Midwest farm museum shortly after visiting a New England farm museum. One quickly develops an appreciation for the development and differences in farm technology over time and as American agriculture moved west.

References: Joan and David Hagan, *The Farm: An American Living Portrait*, Schiffer Publishing, 1990; Lar Hothem, *Collecting Farm Antiques: Identification and Values*, Books Americana, 1982; R. Douglas Hurt, *Agricultural Technology in the Twentieth Century*, Sunflower University Press: 1991; Stanley Schuler, *American Barns: In A Class by Themselves*, Schiffer Publishing; *Stable & Barn Fixtures Manufactured by J. W. Fiske Iron Works*, Apollo Books, 1987.

Reproduction Manufacturers: Cumberland General Store, Rte 3, Crossville, TN 38555; McClanahan Country, 217 Rockwell Rd, Wilmington, NC 28405.

ANIMAL RELATED

History: When one thinks farm, one thinks animals. Even grain farmers keep a few animals. The domestication of animals and development of agriculture are two of the most important steps in the evolution of humankind.

During the 20th century many of the hand tasks

associated with animals were mechanized. Two transitions that I witnessed as a young boy were the switching of a dairy farm from hand milking to mechanical milking and a chicken farm from nests to individual wire cages. The Country collector is not fascinated by these "newfangled" devices. They prefer a simpler(?) time when there was a one to one contact between farmer and animal. The image is highly myth-oriented, but it persists.

Collectors focus on three types of animal related objects—(1)those used in the care and feeding of animals, (2) those involved in the use of the animal, and (3) those linked to an animal's food value. In almost every instance, the collector wants an object that shows signs of wear, but yet is in good enough condition to display.

The care and feeding category ranges from grain scoops to chicken feeds. Look for objects that contain elaborate stenciling, decoration, and manufacturer information, and/or have an unusual form. Do not overlook veterinarian products. The "Veterinary Collectibles" category in *Warman's Americana & Collectibles, Sixth Edition* will introduce you to the possibilities.

Animals paid for their keep by working or producing a salable product, in some instances, both. The popularity of animal working gear is very craze-oriented. One year ox yokes are in vogue, another year animal harnesses prove popular. Many of these objects do not display well, making this material the least popular of the animal related collectibles.

The most popular items are those involved with processing animal products or the butchering of animals. Hog scrappers, milking stools, sheep shears, and egg crates are just a few of the popular items found in most country decorating schemes. A single type of object is often found in dozens of variations, creating the opportunity for an unusual specialized collection.

Since many individuals utilizing a country decor did not grow up in a farming environment, it is not unusual to find objects whose use is uncertain among the items displayed. These "what's-its" make excellent conversation pieces.

Few country collectors attempt to recreate a barn or equipment shed environment. Instead, animal related items are used indoors and out primarily as decorative accents. A harness set makes an attractive wall display. A stoneware chicken feeder finds a welcome home among a display of stoneware crocks and jugs. A pig carrier with a piece of glass on top functions well as a coffee table. A cast iron scalding kettle serves in the front yard as a planter.

The use of animal related objects in interior and exterior decorating is due in part to the image that they convey of hard, but highly productive, work. Metal objects develop a dark, smooth patina; wood implements have a weathered, worn smooth look. They evoke a strong sense of the unending commitment that a farmer must make.

Reproduction Manufacturers: *Egg Crates*—American Country House, PO Box 317, Davison, MI 48432; *Sleigh Bells*—Conewago Junction, 805 Oxford Rd, New Oxford, PA 17350.

Branding Iron	**45.00**
Bridle rosette, blue ground, gray bridled horse head with pink nose band and pink ribbon rosette	**35.00**
Casting Harness	**150.00**
Chicken Feeder, tin.	**12.00**
Cow Bell, sheet iron, handmade, leather strap, 5" h	**25.00**
Cream Separator, De Laval, full size, gold and black paint, 30" w, 43" h	**100.00**
Egg Candler, tin, kerosene burner, mica window, 8" h	**20.00**
Egg Crate, wire egg holders, wood frame	**35.00**
Feed Box, wood, 18" l	**20.00**
Harness Strap, leather, four decorative brasses, 10" l.	**40.00**
Hog Scraper, tin, circular blade, 6½" h	**18.00**
Hoof Trimmer, compound	**100.00**
Horse Blanket, plaid, horse stamped on inside	**75.00**
Horse Sling, with breast and rump straps	**125.00**
Incubator, wood cabinet, 39" h	**75.00**
Milking Pail, tin, wire bail handle, 2 gallon	**60.00**
Milking Stool, oak, splayed base, three legs	**50.00**
Milk Skimmer, punched tin, hanging loop, c1800	**30.00**
Nesting Box, wood, 14½" h	**15.00**
Scalding Kettle, cast iron, two handles, 27" d.	**350.00**
Sheep Shears, wrought, wool wrapped handle	**35.00**
Shoulder Drop, tack, brass, ornate	**325.00**
Singletree, wood and iron, 15" l	**30.00**

Cream Separator, De Laval, cast iron, yellow, 32" w, 14" d, 48" h, $220.00. Photograph courtesy of James D. Julia, Inc.

Nest Eggs, white milk glass, blown, 2¼ to 2¾" l, price each, $45.00.

Saddle, leather, toolwork dec, early loop seat, 20th C, 16 × 21", $357.50. Photograph courtesy of W. E. Channing & Co, Inc.

Sleigh Bells, 24 bells
Round metal bells, leather strap	**110.00**
Sheep bell shaped brass bells, double row, padded leather strap, buckle, tapered end, 41" l	**260.00**
Tether Weight, cast iron, half round, 18 lbs	**35.00**
Trough, cast iron, 42" l	**25.00**

Sheep Bell, brass, leather strap, $30.00.

LIGHTNING ROD BALLS AND PENDANTS

History: Lightning rod balls and pendants are the ornamental portion of lightning rod systems typically found on the roofs of barns and rural houses from the 1840s to 1930s. The glass balls and pendants served only aesthetic purposes and did not contribute to the operation of the lightning rod system.

Glass balls ranged in color from the common white milk glass and blue milk glass to clear. Some clear glass has turned shades of sun colored amethyst (SCA) through exposure to the sun. Other colors include shades of amber, cobalt, green, and red to the rarer colors of pink, orange, yellow, and marbleized slag. Mercury colored balls were created by silvering the interior surface of balls of different colors to produce silver, gold, cobalt, red, and green mercury colors. Lightning rod balls were colored using several different glass making techniques—flashing, casing, and solid colors.

There are 34 standard shapes or styles of lightning rod balls:

Burgoon, round, covered with rows of dots and dashes, also called "Dot and Dash" ball, scarce.

Chestnut, 4" irregular shaped ball, resembles two ornate glass doorknobs attached face to face, 10 colors, fairly common.

D & S, 10 sided ball resembling Japanese lantern, letters D & S in a diamond in one panel, "Patent Pending" on two lower panels, 15 colors, manufactured exclusively for Dodd and Struthers of Windsor, Ontario, Canada, common.

Diddie Blitzen, 3¾" paneled ball, resembles two lamp shades placed bottom to bottom, embossed letters "DIDDIE BLITZEN" in the panels, 9 colors, fairly common.

Doorknob, 4" ball, resembles two antique ornate glass doorknobs placed face to face with indented equator, 11 colors plus slag glass, fairly common.

Ear of Corn, ovoid ball, panels that resemble kernels of corn on a cob, 6 colors, also known as "Harrisburg" ball because so many were found in the Pennsylvania area, hard to find.

Electra Cone, 5" ball, resembles two funnels with tire bulge at equator of ball, letters "ELECTRA" at bulge, 10 colors, The Electra Protection Co. had offices in Chicago and Cresco, IA, fairly common.

Electra Round, raised letters "ELECTRA" at equator of ball, 11 colors, moderately available.

Hawkeye, resembles a hot air balloon, intaglio poinsettia on the upper portion of canopy, indentations running vertically to form stem, embossed letters "HAWKEYE" found in indentations, 10 colors, made by Hawkeye

Lightning Rod Co. of Cedar Rapids, IA, moderately available.

JFG, 3¾", resembles bottom portion of an hour glass, raised letter "JFG" found on equator, 3 colors, made by Julius F. Gooetz, WI, scarce.

K-Ball, round, 4½", raised initial "K" found at base of the top collar, 9 colors, moderately available.

Maher, 5", detailed ball with raised swirls interrupted with a flat band at equator, "MAHER MANUFACTURING CO., PRESTON, IOWA" on band, 6 colors, difficult to find.

Mast, 5" d, raised swirls from pole to pole, emblem at equator on one side, embossed "Trade MAST Mark Reg US Pat Off," 6 colors, credited to Mast Lightning Rod Co., Ohio, scarce.

Moon & Star, 4½", intaglio of moon and stars over the entire surface, 13 colors, very common.

National, Belted, 5", shaped with a raised band at equator with letters "NATIONAL," 6 colors, made by National Cable and Manufacturing Co., Michigan, hard to find.

National, Round, 4½", raised letters "NATIONAL" on equator, 7 colors, moderately available.

Onion, 3½", shaped like natural onion, vertical indentations originating at necks of ball, 3 colors, non-capped ball used exclusively by the Burkett Lightning Rod Co., Ohio, scarce.

Patent '77, 3½", 4", and 5" d, "PAT'D 77" at equator, sometimes lettering was ghosted, 3 or 4 colors, scarce.

Patent '78, 4", "PAT'D 78" at equator, sometimes lettering was ghosted, 3 or 4 colors, scarce.

Plain, Round, 3", 3½", 4", and 4½" d (most common), 30 colors known, common.

Pleat, Pointed, 3½", 4½", 5", and 5½" d, vertical pleats, 6 colors, moderately available.

Pleated, Round, 4½", vertical pleats that have rounded edges, 7 colors, made by J. Barnett Co., Riverside, IA, also known as "Barnett" ball, moderately available.

Quilt, Flat, 5", quilt effect created with lateral incised lines forming flat diamonds, 13 colors, distributed by G. E. Thompson Lightning Rod Co., Owatonna, MN, moderately available.

Quilt, Raised, 5", quilt effect created with lateral incised lines forming raised diamonds, 8 colors, offered by Kretzer Co., St. Louis, Missouri, moderately available.

R.H.F., 5", raised daisy like petals with one of the initials—"R," "H," or "F"—found in each of three daisy pattern centers, 6 colors, manufactured by Reyburn Hunter Foy Company, Cincinnati, OH, scarce.

Ribbed, Grape, round, equator of raised circles (grapes), raised panels going to each pole, 10 colors, made by several different companies, common.

Ribbed, Horizontal, 3½", resembling two flower pots attached top to top with staircase type concentric circles, 8 colors, known among collectors as "Peewee," moderately available.

S Company, elongated, 5" l, 4" d, window like panels indentations, running vertically at the equator, "S. Co." found in diamond at top of ball, 8 colors, made by Struthers Company, Peoria, IL, moderately available.

Shinn, Belted, resembles two petal bowls facing opening to opening, connected by large bulging equator with raised letters "W. C. SHINN MFG CO.," 8 colors, hard to find.

Shinn, System, 4", "SHINN SYSTEM" embossed at equator, 7 colors, moderately available.

S L R Co., 4½", long necks (collars) with large letters "SLR CO." found on equator, many balls found only with ghosts of the letters, used without metal caps, found in several colors, made by Security Lightning Rod Co., Burlington, WI, scarce.

Staircase, 4", heavy ceramic ball, staircase top and bottom, wide straight panel at equator, 2 colors, common.

Swirl, 5", raised swirls running pole to pole, 9 colors, moderately available.

Thompson, 4½", sharply ribbed ball, raised triangular equator, "GEO. E. THOMPSON LIGHTNING ROD CO., EST 1910" round on equator, 5 colors, ball still in production as reproduction.

Some of these lightning rod balls were made exclusively by a single glass maker, while others were made by several. The Maher Company made the first lightning rod ball in the 1840s. Hawkeye Lightning Rod Company, Cedar Rapids, IA, introduced the Hawkeye ball in the 1940s.

Lightning rod balls have necks or collars at both ends, usually protected by a copper, brass, aluminum, or steel cap. Old necks or collars generally have an irregular or jagged edge, whereas reproduction balls generally have a ground edge. Roofers often replace missing or damaged balls with a modern day plastic ball with a ribbed horizontal pattern.

The value of a lightning rod ball depends on design, color, locality, and condition. Obviously, the scarcer patterns are more valuable and higher in price. Since some lightning rod balls closely resemble lamp parts whose collars often are ground, it is best to avoid any ball that has a ground or etched collar.

The white milk glass balls and the blue milk glass balls are the most common and usually the least expensive. Prices escalate by color beginning with sun color amethyst, amber, and red. The rare colors of orange, pink, and yellow, are at the top of the scale. Mercury balls are higher priced than the clear versions from which they were made.

Pendants were generally installed in sets of four, one dangling from each arm extending from a lightning rod. A metal hook or loop attached to a metal cap held the pendant in place. Rust and the elements often caused the hook or cap to fail, resulting in the loss of a pendant. Cold weather could crack a pendant if water worked its way inside.

Pendants measure 5½" high including cap and hook, 4½" not including cap and hook. They are approximately 3" wide and tear drop in shape. Collectors prefer pendants in mint condition. Loss of the metal loop fastened to the cap or the cap itself reduces value.

References: Mike Brunner and Rod Krupka, *The Complete Book Of Lightning Rod Balls*, published by authors (available from Rod Krupka, 2615 Echo Lane, Ortonville, MI 48462), 1989; Dale Frazier, *Lightning Rod Ball Collector's Guide*, published by author, 1973.

Periodical: *The Crown Point*, 2615 Echo Lane, Ortonville, MI 48462.

Reproduction Alert: Reproductions of the Thompson ball have been found in five colors-white milk glass, amber, cobalt, blue/green, and red. Reports also have been received that some of the rarer colored balls recently have been reproduced using period molds.

BALLS

Diddie Blitzen, clear, emb "Diddie Blitzen Rods", 3¾" w, 4⅛ " h.....	**25.00**
Doorknob, root beer amber, West Dodd Co, 4" w, 4¼" h..........	**175.00**
Ear of Corn, clear, Harrisburg, PA, 2⅞" w, 4⅛ " h...................	**35.00**
Electra, round, cobalt, emb on one side, 4½" w, 5⅛ " h............	**50.00**
JFG, cobalt, emb "PAT," Julius F Goetz Mfg Co, Hartford, WI, 3⅜ " w, 3⅞" h	**45.00**
K Ball, gold mercury, emb "K", 4½" w, 5⅛ " h	**125.00**
Mast, swirl pattern, amber, emb "Trade Mast Mark Reg US Pat Off," West Milton, OH, 4⅞" w, 5¾" h.......	**185.00**

**D & S Co Ball, amber, ten sided, 5 × 3¾",
$25.00.**

**Ribbed Horizontal Ball, white milk glass,
4¼ × 3¼", $20.00.**

National, belted, silver mercury, emb, National Cable and Manufacturing Company, Niles, MI, 4½" w, 5⅛ " h	**125.00**
Onion, blue milk glass, Burkett Lightning Rod Co, Fremont, OH, 3⅜ " w, 4⅛ " h......................	**20.00**
Patent '77, gold mercury, emb "Patd July 77", 5" d.................	**250.00**
Plastiball, plastic, opaque, snap together halves.................	**3.00**
Pleat, round, flashed red, Joseph Barnett & Co, Riverside, IA, 4⅜ " w, 5" h.......................	**90.00**
Quilt, flat, red, George E Thompson Lightning Rod Co, Owatonna, MN, 5" w, 5⅝ " h..................	**80.00**
RHF, amber, emb, Reyburn Hunter Foy Company, Cincinnati, OH, 4⅞" w, 5⅝ " h.......................	**150.00**
Ribbed, horizontal, sun colored amethyst, 3⅜ " w, 4" h.............	**35.00**
S Company, blue milk glass, emb, Struthers Company, Peoria, IL, 4⅛ " w, 5⅛ " h....................	**15.00**
Shinn, round, white milk glass, emb "Shinn System", 4 ½" w, 5⅛ " h	**12.00**
SLR Co, sun colored amethyst, long neck boldly emb, Security Lightning Rod Co, Burlington, WI, 4⅝ " w, 6" h	**200.00**
Swirl, green, 5" w, 5½" h..........	**300.00**
Thompson, cobalt, emb "Geo E Thompson Lightning Rod Co, Est 1910," Owatonna, MN..........	**10.00**

PENDANTS

Acorn, flashed red...............	**175.00**
Flat Quilt, sun colored amethyst.....	**225.00**
Hawkeye, red...................	**380.00**
Ribbed and Paneled, flashed red.....	**175.00**

MILK BOTTLES AND CANS

History: Hervey Thatcher is recognized as the father of the glass milk bottle. By the early 1880s glass milk bottles appeared in New York and New

Jersey. A. V. Whiteman had a milk bottle patent as early as 1880. Patents reveal much about early milk bottle shape and manufacture. Not all patentees were manufacturers. Many individuals engaged others to produce bottles under their patents.

The Golden Age of the glass milk bottle is 1910 to 1950. Leading manufacturers include Lamb Glass Co. (Mt. Vernon, Ohio), Liberty Glass Co. (Sapulpa, Oklahoma), Owens-Illinois Glass Co. (Toledo, Ohio), and Thatcher Glass Co. (New York).

Milk bottles can be found in the following sizes: gill (quarter pint), half pint, 10 ounces (third quart), pint, quart, half gallon (two quart), and gallon.

Paper cartons first appeared in the early 1920s and 30s and achieved popularity after 1950. The late 1950s witnessed the arrival of the plastic bottle. A few dairies still use glass bottles today, but the era has essentially ended.

Many factors influence the price—condition of the bottle, who is selling, the part of the country in which the sale is transacted, and the amount of desire a buyer has for the bottle. Every bottle does not have universal appeal. A sale of a bottle in one area does not mean that it would bring the same amount in another locale. For example, a rare Vermont pyro pint would be looked upon as only another "pint" in Texas.

A painted milk can, often with a regional folk art design, is a commonly used Country decorative accent. When used on the farm, milk cans contained little or no decoration. "Folk Art" milk can painters pay between five and ten dollars for a plain can depending on size and condition. There are milk can collectors, but their number is few, thus keeping prices low.

References: Leigh and Jeff Giarde (eds.), *The Complete, Authentic and Unabridged Milk House Moosletter, Vol. 1*, published by editors, 1993; Don Lord, *California Milks*, published by author; John Tutton, *Udder Delight*, published by author.

Collectors' Club: *National Association of Milk Bottle Collectors*, 4 Ox Bow Road, Westport, CT 06880–2602.

Periodical: The Milk Route, 4 Ox Bow Road, Westport, CT 06880–2602.

Museums: The Farmers Museum, Cooperstown, NY; Southwest Dairy Museum, Arlington, TX; Billings Farm Museum, Woodstock, VT.

MILK BOTTLES

Half Pint, embossed, round
Bellevue Dairy, Syracuse, NY	**22.00**
Brookside Dairies, Inc, Waterbury, CT.	**12.00**
Cooperative Dairy Co, Torrington, CT.	**12.00**
Frasure & Brown, Logan, OH	**14.00**

Half Pint, Rutter Bros, clear glass, pyroglazed label, square, 5½" h, $2.50.

Lackawanna Dairy Co, Inc, Lackawanna, NY	**12.00**
Lott Milk Co, Binghamton, NY, chocolate milk	**36.00**
Sibley Farms, Spencer, MA	**28.00**
Tarbell Guernsey Farms, Smithville Flats, NY, logo on reverse	**12.00**

Half Pint, pyroglazed, round
Alta Crest Farms, Brookfield, MA, maroon, cow head illus.	**16.00**
Consumers Dairy, Westerly, RI, red, "Try our Whipping Cream"	**22.00**
George Poiriers Dairy, Lewiston, ME, red	**16.00**
Hietpas Dairy Farms, Appleton, WI, red	**16.00**
Litchfield Dairy Association, Litchfield, MI, black and orange, "Use Litchfield Butter" on reverse	**18.00**
Peoples Dairy, R & J Peacock, Lake Placid, NY.	**14.00**
Slades Dairy, Santa Fe, NM, maroon, cow's head on reverse.	**22.00**
Tanners Dairy, North Adams, MA, orange, cow in pasture scene . . .	**18.00**
Valley Dairy, Yerington, NV, maroon, "Drink Milk for Health" on reverse	**22.00**

Pint, clear, blown, wire bail, glass lid, emb "Pat. A. For," $12.50.

Windlae Farms, Galena, OH, orange, dairy farm scene **14.00**
Pint, embossed, tall, round
Arizona Creamery, Phoenix Store, Pasteurized, triple V neck treatment **28.00**
F A Sacchi, Marshfield, OR **22.00**
Highland Dairy, Reno, NV **28.00**
John Orr, Wells, NY **18.00**
Russell Creamery Co, Superior, WI, "Tuberculin Tested" in script.... **26.00**
Sunnydale Creamery, Salinas, CA **24.00**
Tomek & Sons Dairy, Trumbull, CT, slug plate with "T" center **18.00**
Willowbrook Creamery, Oakland, CA. **28.00**
Pint, pyroglazed, tall, round
A G Dorr Dairy, Watertown, NY, baby on reverse.............. **22.00**
Butler Dairy, Willmatic, CT, green, milkman illus **24.00**
Kleins Dairy, Farrell, PA, orange and black.................... **18.00**
Old Dominion Creamery, Colville, WA, orange, desserts on reverse **28.00**
Treasure State Dairy, Butte, MT, red, cottage cheese salad on reverse **24.00**
Zeth Weaver-Guernsey A Milk, Greensboro, MD, black, baby in crib on reverse **26.00**
Quart, cream top, embossed, round
Himes Dairy, Eaton, OH **26.00**
Maple Dairies, Tyrone, PA **28.00**
Meadow Gold, silver seal **24.00**
Otto Milk Co, Pittsburg, PA....... **22.00**
Rainier Dairy, Bridgeton, NY **26.00**
Willow Farms/Westminster Farms, MD **28.00**
Quart, cream top, pyroglazed, round
Cloverleaf, red **28.00**
Damascus Cream-Top Milk, Portland, OR, red **28.00**
Indiana Dairy Company, Indiana, PA, Golden Guernsey logo on reverse..................... **28.00**
Producers Dairy, "No substitution for Quality" **26.00**
Shamrock Dairy, Tucson, AZ, maroon, cow's head surrounded by shamrocks................. **48.00**
Quart, embossed, tall, round
Cheyenne Creamery Company **26.00**
Country Maid Dairy, Whites Creek, TN. **18.00**
Fabens Dairy, Fabens, TX **36.00**
Harding Dairy, Magna, UT **28.00**
Jersey Dairy, Jackson, MO........ **22.00**
Meadowland Creamery, Bend, OR, "Gold Medal Milk" **26.00**
Queen City Dairy Inc, Cumberland, MD **26.00**
Robinson Dairy, Boise, ID........ **28.00**

Supreme Dairy Products, Inc, Springfield, TN **26.00**
Quart, pyroglazed, tall, round
Better Farms Dairy Products, Fond Du Lac, WI, orange, dairy logo **38.00**
Clardys Dairy, Roswell, NM, red... **28.00**
Enfield Dairy, Ellensburg, WA, red **28.00**
Golden Rule Dairy, Canon City, CO, orange..................... **36.00**
Hester Dairy, San Jose, CA, maroon **28.00**
Paterson Dairy, Clifton, AZ, green **24.00**
Sardis Creamery, Sardis, MI, green **58.00**
Sunshine Milk, Bridgeport, CT, orange, dairy farm scene........ **32.00**
Supreme Dairy, LaSalle, IL, blue, baby with bottle on reverse **28.00**
Turners Dairy, Sierra City, CA, black, service map on reverse **32.00**
Wehr's Dairy, Mifflinburg, PA, orange, black letters, cow on reverse **34.00**

MILK CANS

Cream, lid, impressed brass plate, Elkin's Dairy, bail handle, 4 qts, 7" d, 10" h...................... **20.00**
Milk
Marked, brass nameplate showing name of shipper, 10 gallon **18.00**
Unmarked, 10 gallon **10.00**

SCALES

History: Prior to 1900, the simple balance scale commonly was used for measuring weights. Since then scales have become more sophisticated in design and more accurate. A variety of styles and types include beam, platform, postal, and pharmaceutical.

Scales were used throughout the farm. Platform scales weighed feed both for sale and use. Hanging scales were used to sell produce at roadside stands and from farm wagons. Grading scales were a necessity if eggs were sold.

Collectors' Club: International Society of Antique Scale Collectors, Suite 1706, 176 W Adams St, Chicago, IL 60603.

Reproduction Manufacturer: Sturbridge Yankee Workshop, Blueberry Rd, Westbrook, ME 04092.

Chatillon #2, balance, 0 to 50 lbs, Jan 26, 1892 pat date **35.00**
Chatillon Milk Scale, dairy, 8" brass dial, 150 lbs **45.00**
Fairbanks, grain, bushel, brass **275.00**
Forschner, spring balance, hanging, brass **65.00**
Hanson Viking, spring balance, #8910, 1 to 100 lbs, steel, painted green...................... **35.00**

Egg Scale, Zenith Egg Grader Scale, O. W. Bedell, Earlville, NY, 1925, $28.00.

Jiffyway, egg grading, brass.........	**90.00**
Oak Manufacturing Co, egg grading	**12.00**
Ohaus, grain, brass..............	**250.00**
Pelouze, dairy, white enamel on brass	**65.00**
PS & T Warranted, balance, 0 to 50 lbs, brass front, July 8, 1889 pat date...	**25.00**
Purina, red, red and white checkered top, blue and cream colored bottom, metal pan, "Purina Feed Saver and Cow Culler" adv..............	**85.00**
Winchester, grain, hanging, bushel, brass......................	**200.00**
Zenith Egg Grader, #1002, red cast iron, weight and balance, blue cast iron base, aluminum egg pan and scale, brass pointer............	**30.00**

TOOLS AND EQUIPMENT

History: The self-reliant aspect of agrarian life required that its members were builders, mechanics, and providers all rolled into one. Farmers and homesteaders were generalists, capable of performing many tasks. In addition, the urgency of time and the state of finances often required "doing things yourself now."

As a result, most rural households and farms contained a wide variety of equipment and tools. Much of the equipment was specialized, designed to perform a specific task such as a corn dryer or stitching horse. Tools were used to keep the equipment in repair, e.g., a hoopsetter or oilstone, or in partnership with the individual to perform a task, e.g., ax or saw.

Equipment and tools are one of the four principal criteria by which others judged individuals in the agrarian environment. The other three are land, buildings, and stock. Most equipment and tools were designed to last for generations, provided they received adequate care and proper use. On most farmsteads, the vast majority of equipment and tools will have been acquired through the secondary market, i.e., passed down through the family or purchased at a farm auction.

Initially farm tools and equipment were made by local craftsmen—the blacksmith, wheelwright, or the farmer himself. Product designs varied greatly. In a large number of instances, the reason a specific tool or piece of equipment was made has been lost. Many collections contain one or more of these "what's-its."

The industrial age and the "golden age" of American agriculture go hand in hand. By 1880–1900 manufacturers saw the farm market as an important source of sales. Farmers demanded quality products capable of withstanding hard use. While Stanley is the most recognized and collected manufacturer, collectors have not ignored the thousands of other firms who concentrated on making equipment and tools for the agrarian community.

In the 1940s urban growth began to draw attention away from the rural areas and consolidation of farms took place. Bigger machinery was developed. Post-World War II farm tools and equipment is just beginning to attract the attention of collectors.

Within the Country community, equipment and tools serve primarily as furniture pieces and wall hangings. Few pieces are displayed in context. Decorators like pieces made wholly or partly of wood with signs of heavy use.

Tool collectors are a breed unto themselves. Although they are found at country auctions, they do much of their trading and buying through the mail, via phone, or at specialized shows and meets. Regional and state collectors' clubs include the Mid-West Tool Collectors Association (808 Fairway Drive, Columbia, MO 65201) and the Ohio Tool Collectors Association (PO Box 261, London, OH 43140).

References: *A Price Guide To Keen Kutter Tools,* L–W Book Sales, 1993 values; Ronald S. Barlow, *The Antique Tool Collector's Guide to Value, Third Edition,* Windmill Publishing Company, 1991; Lar Hothem, *Collecting Farm Antiques: Identification and Values,* Books Americana, 1982; R. Douglas Hurt, *American Farm Tools from Hand-Power to Steam Power,* Sunflower University Press, 1982; Herbert P. Kean and Emil S. Pollak, *A Price Guide To Antique Tools,* The Astragal Press, 1992; Herbert P. Kean and Emil S. Pollak, *Collecting Antique Tools,* The Astragal Press, 1990; Kathryn McNerney, *Antique Tools: Our American Heritage,* Collector Books, 1979, 1993 value update; E. and M. Pollak, *A Guide To American Wood Planes And Their Makers, Second Edition,* The Astragal Press, 1991; Emil and Martyl Pollak, *Prices Realized on Rare Imprinted American Wooden Planes, 1979–1992,* The Astragal Press, 1993; R. A. Salaman, *Dictionary of Tools,* Charles Scribner's Sons, 1974; John Walter, *Antique & Collectible Stanley Tools: A Guide to*

Identity and Value, Tool Merchants, 1990; John Whelan, *The Wooden Plane: Its History, Form, and Function,* The Astragal Press, 1993; Jack P. Wood, *Early 20th Century Stanley Tools: A Price Guide,* L–W Book Sales, 1992 values; Jack P. Wood, *Town-Country Old Tools and Locks, Keys and Closures,* L–W Book Sales, 1990, 1992 value update.

Collectors' Clubs: Cast Iron Seat Collectors Association, PO Box 14, Ionia, MO 65335; Collectors of Rare & Familiar Tools Society, 38 Colony Ct, Murray Hill, NJ 07974; Early American Industries Association, P O Box 2128 Empire State Plaza Station, Albany, NY 12220; New England Tool Collectors Association, 303 Fisher Rd, Fitchburg, MA 01420; Mid-West Tool Collectors Association, 808 Fairway Dr, Columbia, MO 65201; Society of Workers in Early Arts & Trades, 606 Lake Lena Blvd, Auburndale, FL 33823.

Periodical: *Stanley Tool Collector News,* 208 Front St, Marietta, OH 45750; *The Fine Tool Journal,* PO Box 4001, Pittsford, VT 05763; *Tool Ads,* PO Box 33, Hamilton, MT 59840.

Museums: Bucks County Historical Society, Mercer Museum, Doylestown, PA; Pennsylvania Farm Museum, Landis Valley, PA; Shelburne Museum, Shelburne, VT; World O'Tools Museum, Waverly, TN.

Reproduction Craftspersons: Connie Carlton, Shaving Horse Crafts, 1049 Rice Rd, Lawrenceburg, KY 10342; Kevin Riddle, Mountainman Woodshop, P O Box 40, Eagle Rock, VA 24085.

Reproduction Manufacturers: Conewago Junction, 805 Oxford Rd, New Oxford, PA 17350; The Cracker Barrel, 527 Narberth Ave, Haddonfield, NJ 08033; Zimmerman Handcrafts, 254 East Main St, Leola, PA 17540.

Adze
Carpenter's, hammerhead poll	**30.00**
Cooper's, hand forged.	**20.00**
Shipwright's, lipped	**30.00**
Apple Picker, wire cage, wood handle	**25.00**
Archimedean Drill, wood center grip and head, two ball flywheel	**75.00**
Architect's Rule, Stanley, #53½	**30.00**
Bellows, blacksmith's, painted	**225.00**
Bench Knife, hook end, T handle	**75.00**
Block Plane, carriage maker's, tapered, 8" l	**16.00**
Board Rule, octagonal	**60.00**

Brace
Cooper's, birch	**125.00**
Wagon, metal	**15.00**
Breast Auger, brace head, fixed hand forged bit	**175.00**
Broad Axe, wood handle, marked "Hopkins & Co, Hartford, Warranted Cast Steel," 8½" w	**75.00**

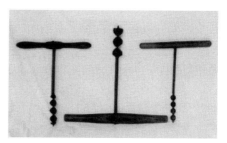

Auger, wood T-handle, price each, $10.00.

Buggy Wrench, brace style, ratchet positioned	**75.00**
Bung Hole Borer, cooper's, 2" d	**10.00**
Caliper	
Dancing Master, brass, human leg shaped.	**80.00**
Double, hand forged, locking circle and wingnuts.	**125.00**
Inside, spring style, 8" l	**10.00**
Outside, friction style, hand forged, 18th C, 7" l	**20.00**
Carpenter's Gimlet, factory made	**5.00**
Carpenter's Rule	
H Chapins Son, folding, #39	**25.00**
Stanley	
#12, boxwood, 2 ft, 2 fold, unbound, with slide	**60.00**
#65, boxwood, ½, 1 ft, 4 fold, brass bound	**45.00**
#78½, boxwood, 2 ft, 4 fold, brass bound	**85.00**
#87, ivory, 2 ft, 4 fold, German silver bound.	**200.00**
C-Clamp, metal, ornate wingnut, painted black	**8.00**
Chamfer Knife, cooper's, 5" w blade	**25.00**
Chisel	
Carving, fishtail gouge, standard handle.	**15.00**
Shipwright's, 2¾" w blade	**60.00**
Clamp	
Furniture, bar type, 60" l	**20.00**
Parallel, wood, 12" jaws	**12.00**
Cobbler's Bench, NH, early 19th C. . .	**600.00**

Beader, Windsor, brass, ebonized wood, marked "Pat. March 10, 1885, June 2, 1885," cutter missing, $150.00.

Jointer Plane, Ogontz Tool Co, pine and maple, 22" l, $30.00.

Pulley Block, iron hook, wood block and wheel, 10¼" h, $30.00.

Compass, surveyor's, brass, engraved "W.I. Young," maker patent, Philadelphia, PA	350.00
Cooper's Axe	50.00
Corn Dryer, wrought iron	15.00
Corn Husking Peg, hand carved, c1900, 5" l	30.00
Corn Sheller, wood case with red wash, iron gears, hand crank, PA, 34" h	60.00
Cranberry Scoop, wood and tin, 18 fingers, factory made, early 20th C	215.00
Divider, wing style	
18" l, wood	65.00
22" l, metal, hand forged, chamfered	45.00
Drawknife, 8" l hand forged blade, reverse curve handles	30.00
Duster, brass cylinder, turned wood handle on brass plunger, labeled "Robt. T. Deakin & Co., Makers, No. O. Philadelphia, Pa.," 17½" l	15.00
Felling Axe, Rockaway pattern	15.00
Fire Axe, embossed	175.00
Goosewing Axe, sgd "Stahler"	300.00
Grain Cradle, four fingers, 41" l	60.00
Grain Shovel, 48½" l, wood, worn patina	75.00
Hammer	
Blacksmith's, top swage	10.00
Cobbler's	5.00
Cooper's, notched end	15.00
Slater's, hand forged	25.00
Strapped eye, hand forged	30.00
Tinsmith's	12.00
Veneer, cast head	75.00
Harrow, arrow shaped, wood frame, iron spikes, mule-drawn	30.00
Hatchet, hewing, one side flat, 8" edge	15.00
Hayfork, metal prongs, wood fork and handle, imp maker's initials, PA	135.00
Hay Rake, wood, 48" l	35.00
Ice Tongs, wrought iron, double handle, 26" l	45.00
Inclinometer	
Davis, iron, level, #4, 24" l	95.00
Warren Knight, orig box	135.00
Mallet	
Carpenter's	8.00
Cooper's, bung starter	25.00
Wheelwright's	15.00
Mortise Chisel, goosenecked	35.00
Mortising Axe, double blade	45.00

Plane	
Alford, NY, narrow bead	75.00
Auburn Tool Co, plow, rosewood, handle	250.00
Beacher & Addis, double beading, boxed	95.00
Colton & B Sheneman, sash	100.00
D P Sanborn, Littleton, NY, cornice	450.00
D R Barton, plow, boxwood, rosewood fence, ivory tips, boxwood arms, handle	1,000.00
E W Carpenter, Lancaster, complex molder	125.00
F Dallicker, large rabbet	175.00
H Albert & Co, astragal	225.00
H H Read, Wilmington, VT, smoothing	65.00
I Lindenberger, Providence, RI, plow, slide arm fence with wood thumbscrews and depth stop	300.00
J H Perry, NY, rabbet	80.00
J L Foster, ship's rabbet, rosewood	175.00
Joseph Titcomb, panel raiser, 14" l, 1½" w iron	400.00
Marley, NY, planemaker's, dovetail	400.00
P A Gladwin & Co, combination tongue and groove, 1856 patent date	175.00
Stanley	
#2, smooth, cast iron, rosewood handle and knob, 7" l	175.00
#5¼, jack, cast iron, rosewood handle and knob, 11½" l	75.00
#13, circular, cast iron, flexible sole, 10½" l	65.00
#120, block, cast iron, rosewood knob, 7½" l	15.00
G27½, gage jack, cast iron frog, beech bottom and handles, lacquered, 15" l	120.00
Plumb Bob	
Conical, brass, 5" l	25.00
Pear shaped, brass, 6¾" l	150.00
Teardrop, iron	35.00
Turnip shaped, brass, 6½" l	125.00
Pocket Level, Davis Level & Tool Co, 3½" l, acorn finials both ends	95.00
Pump Drill, iron flywheel, 14" h	50.00

Race Knife, single blade, curved shank	**18.00**
Rake, wood, twelve prongs, three graduating semi-circular braces, c1850, 77" l	**130.00**
Reamer, cooper's, carved handle, 8" l	**8.00**
Reaping Hook, hand held, hand forged blade, wood handle, sgd, c1870 . . .	**90.00**
Sap Spout, carved wood	**5.00**
Saw	
Bow, 24" l blade, maple	**40.00**
Buck, 30" l blade	**20.00**
Rip, Atkins	**25.00**
Stair, mahogany, fancy	**50.00**
Two-Man	
Cross cut timber, 72"l	**15.00**
Plank, coachmaker's, framed, 72" l, 18" w	**175.00**
Schnitzelbank, hand-hewn oak, co-opering bench for pulling barrel stays while forming barrel, 62" l, 37" h	**100.00**
Scythe, wood handle, hand forged blade	**35.00**
Sickle, iron blade, wood handle, 21" l	**18.00**
Slide Rule, Pickett.	**1,850.00**
Sliding Bevel	
I J Robinson, brass framed, rosewood infill, 6" l.	**225.00**
L D Howard, rosewood, single blade, brass bound	**25.00**
Spiral Auger, turned wood handle, 3" d	**15.00**
Spirit Level, carpenter's	
Akron Eclipse, 12" l, mahogany, brass bound.	**150.00**
Davis Level & Tool Co, 18" l, cast iron	**100.00**
Hall & Knapp, 30" l, mahogany, un-bound	**65.00**
Keen Kutter, 24" l, cherry, unbound	**20.00**
Stanley	
12" l, rosewood, brass bound . . .	**150.00**
24" l, mahogany, brass bound. . .	**50.00**
30" l, cherry, unbound	**20.00**
Stratton Bros	
10" l, rosewood, brass bound . . .	**185.00**
30" l, mahogany, brass bound. . .	**50.00**
Spoke Shave, Stanley #66	**10.00**
Square, hand forged, hand struck num-bers, 18th C	**15.00**
Square and Bevel Combination, F H Coe Mfg	**150.00**
Stitching Horse, hickory, wood screw vise, mortised, hand made, c1840	**145.00**
Tool Chest, paneled lid, brass trim, two trays	**1,200.00**
Transit, surveyor's brass, W & S Jones, Holborn, no tripod	**325.00**
Traveler	
Heart and star wheel, hand forged	**140.00**
Solid wheel, wood	**35.00**
Try Square, Stanley, brass ends.	**10.00**
T-Square, 48" l, mahogany, fixed head	**8.00**
Turnscrew, wide, sculpted, 20" l.	**12.00**
Wheelbarrow, wood, iron wheel and braces, removable sides, sgd	**75.00**
Wheelwright's Reamer, turned wood handle, 3" d, 30" l	**50.00**

WEATHER VANES

History: A weather vane indicates wind direction. The earliest known examples were found on late 17th century structures in the Boston area. The vanes were handcrafted of wood, copper, or tin. By the last half of the 19th century, weather vanes adorned farms and houses throughout the nation. Mass produced vanes of cast iron, copper, and sheet metal were sold through mail order catalogs or at country stores.

In addition to being functional, weather vanes were decorative. Popular forms include horses, Indians, leaping stags, and patriotic emblems. Church vanes were often in the form of a fish or cock. Buildings in coastal towns featured ships or sea creatures. Occasionally a vane doubled as a trade sign.

The champion vane is the rooster. In fact, the name weathercock is synonymous with weather vane. The styles and patterns are endless. Weathering can affect the same vane differently. For this reason, patina is a critical element in collecting vanes.

The two principal forms are silhouette and three dimensional vanes. Silhouette vanes are extremely fragile. Most examples have been repaired with some form of reinforcing strap.

Sportsmen and others frequently used weather-vanes for target practice. Bullet holes decrease the value of a vane. Filled holes usually can be detected with a black light.

References: Robert Bishop and Patricia Coblentz, *A Gallery of American Weathervanes and Whirli-gigs*, E. P. Dutton, 1981; Ken Fitzgerald, *Weathervanes and Whirligigs*, Clarkson N. Potter, 1967.

Museums: Heritage Plantation of Sandwich, Sandwich, MA.

Reproduction Craftsperson: Terrence J Graham, Box 19, Zieglerville, PA 19492.

Reproduction Manufacturers: American Folklore, 330 W Pleasant, Freeport, IL 61032; The Antique Hardware Store, 43 Bridge St, Frenchtown, NJ 08825; Cape Cod Cupola Co, Inc, 78 State Rd, Rte 6, North Dartmouth, MA 02747; The Copper House, RR1 Box 4, Epsom, NH 03234; Country Cupolas, Main St, East Conway, NH 04037; Knot in Vane, 805 N 11th St, DeKalb, IL 60115; Lemee's Fireplace Equipment, 815 Bedford St, Bridgewater, MA 02324; Ricyn Country Collectables, PO Box 577, Twisp, WA 98856; Salt & Chestnut Weathervanes, PO Box 41, West Barnstable, MA 02668; Town and Country, Main St,

East Conway, NH 04037; Unfinished Business, PO Box 246, Wingate, NC 28174.

Reproduction Alert: Reproduction of early models exist, are being aged, and sold as originals. Check provenance and get a written guarantee from any seller.

In the early 1980s the market was flooded with silhouette vanes manufactured in Haiti. These vanes are made from old drums and lack the proper supporting strapwork of an older vane.

Angel Gabriel, copper, molded and gilded, attributed to Cushing & White, Waltham, MA, late 19th C, 30½" l **1,750.00**
Arrow, sheet copper, gilded, pierced geometric dec, late 19th C, 58" l   **750.00**
Banner
  Copper, flower finial, pierced initial "C", verdigris surface, 19th C, 29" l **350.00**
  Copper and Iron, floriform standard, late 19th C, 94" h **440.00**
Bull, copper and zinc, full bodied, 25½" l **3,000.00**
Butterfly, sheet metal, late 19th C, 23" l, 16½" h, imperfections **1,540.00**
Child and Pony Cart, copper, molded and gilded, full bodied figures, shaggy mane and tail pony, pulling little girl in two-wheeled cart, shaped sheet metal finial mounting, J l Mott Ironworks, NY, c1893, 25" l, 35" h **33,000.00**
Cow, copper and zinc, molded, rising horns, copper ears, molded eyes, solid tail, late 19th C, 24" l, 13½" h **3,575.00**
Dove, sheet iron, painted and gilded, folk art design, c1860, 23" h **2,850.00**
Duck, sheet metal, hollow, 36" l **275.00**
Eagle
  Molded Copper, early 20th C, 55" w, 40" h **2,310.00**

Butterfly, sheet metal, late 19th C, 23" l, 16½" h, $1,540.00. Photograph courtesy of Skinner, Inc.

  Molded Gilt Copper, early 20th C, 25" w, 23" d, 19" h **500.00**
Eagle on Ball, copper, old patina, 12¾" w **310.00**
Fish
  Copper, molded, hollow, detailed scales and fins, c1900, 38" l **5,400.00**
  Sheet Iron, silhouette, dorsal fins and tail, drilled eye hole, cut mouth, rod standard mounting on driftwood steeple base, 19th C, 11½" l, 33½" h **1,425.00**
Gamecock, copper and zinc, molded and gilded, standing on arrow, 22" h **2,000.00**
Goddess of Liberty, copper and zinc, molded, full bodied figure, wearing Phrygian cap, five-point stars impressed on sash, full swaying skirt, holding standard with diamond shaped finial, rod mounting with ball point zinc finial and arrow feather tail, directionals, attributed to Cushing and White, Waltham, MA, c1870, 32" l, 39" h **33,000.00**
Goose, flying, plywood core and wings, laminated body, painted, 42" l **1,250.00**
Grasshopper
  Copper, verdigris surface, 20th C, 35" l **775.00**
  Gilded Zinc, 20th C, 20¼" l **360.00**
Hand and Hatchet, pine, carved and painted, full found, realistic hand, red painted and gathered sleeve detail, holding short handled hatchet, traces of polychrome paint, c1850, 26" l, 23½" h **4,675.00**
Henry Hudson's Ship *Half Moon*, molded copper, bears inscription "Half Moon," good surface, early 20th C, 44" h, 45" l **1,870.00**
Hermaphrodite Brig, painted wood and metal, New England, c1930, 16" h, 25" l **715.00**
Horse
  Cast Iron, running, c1900, 23½" w, 30" h **2,650.00**
  Copper, molded, running
    24½" l, 15" h, Black Hawk, attributed to Cushing & White, Waltham, MA, late 19th C **935.00**
    31" l, peaked ears, some facial details, fine verdigris surface, imperfections, 19th C **1,425.00**
    32" l, peaked pushed back ears, head held high, extended mane and tail, fine verdigris surface, 19th C **1,650.00**
    33" l, hollow body, old dark patina, modern base **2,310.00**
    42" l, repousse, cast zinc head, directional arrows **1,320.00**

Horse and Sulky, molded, parcel gilt and painted, full-bodied running horse, minor repairs to horse, 19th C, 48″ l, 20″ h, $4,400.00. Photograph courtesy of Butterfield & Butterfield.

Copper and Zinc, running
  27¼″ l, 18″ h, attributed to A L
    Jewell & Co, Waltham, MA,
    19th C, fine verdigris surface   **1,430.00**
  28″ l, molded, verdigris surface,
    late 19th C. **875.00**
  29″ l, verdigris surface, bullet hole,
    19th C **1,325.00**
  31″ l, 19th C, later gilding **880.00**
  41″ l, molded, full bodied figure of
    Ethan Allen rider, mid 19th C   **1,540.00**
Wood, carved and painted, prancing, old weathered white paint,
  modern base, 1900s, 24″ h **80.00**
Indian
  Copper, molded, Mashamoquet, full
    bodied figure, Indian chief, shaggy
    pony tail, short skirt, repousse detail, drawing bow and arrow,
    standing on arrow headed rod on
    abstract rockwork, c1850, 37″ l,
    35″ h **7,975.00**
  Zinc, cut and molded, silhouette figure, warrior on horseback, scalloped headdress, holding molded
    bow with twisted wire bow string,
    flat horse with molded neck,
    punchmark outlining, rod mounting, 19th C, 35½″ l, 27½″ h **6,600.00**
Logger, sheet metal, silhouette, man
  pushing three logs, traces of polychrome paint, 19th C, 35″ l, 28″ h   **1,100.00**
Mariner, standing, pointing, holding
  spy glass, sheet metal, painted black,
  found in upstate NY, 19th C **615.00**
Merino Sheep, molded copper, verdigris surface, repaired bullet holes,
  early 20th C, 28½″ l **4,125.00**
Moose, zinc and copper, silhouette,
  wooden base, ME, 20th C, 39″ l,
  28½″ h **330.00**

Ox, zinc and copper, regilded, some
  losses to forefront, mid 19th C, 19½″
  h, 34½″ l. **3,850.00**
Peacock, paint dec wood and wire,
  silhouette, early 20th C, 49″ l, 14″ h   **935.00**
Pheasant, copper, molded and painted,
  brown body, cut crown feathers and
  split tail feathers, yellow double neck
  ring, wrought iron rod mounting,
  19th C, 16″ l, 9″ h **2,750.00**
Plow, copper and cast zinc, rod mounting, black metal base, c1860, 52″ l,
  23″ h **5,500.00**
Quill Pen, copper, molded and polychrome painted, yellow, repousse
  feathers, rod mounting, black metal
  base, 19th C, 33″ l **9,900.00**
Rooster
  Cast and Sheet Iron, detailed body,
    flat tail, regilded, 37″ h **1,540.00**
  Copper, traces of bolle, fine verdigris
    surface, old repair, some losses,
    late 18th/early 19th C, 23″ h, 42″ l **3,300.00**
  Steel, silhouette, weathered polychrome paint, old dark finish,
    32¼″ h **400.00**
Schooner, carved and painted wood,
  painted tin sails and wire rigging,
  20th C, wear, 31″ l **1,100.00**
Scroll, gilded copper, zinc, and iron,
  19th C, 55″ w, 7″ d, 47″ h **990.00**
Shore Bird, gilt metal, Long Island, NY,
  20th C, 24″ w, 18½″ h, imperfections **1,210.00**
Sloop, copper, molded, full round hull,
  sheet copper sails hung from bowsprit and main mast, flying pennant and burgee, oval brass
  sternboard plate impressed with
  maker's name and location, Cushing
  & White, Waltham, MA, c1869,
  50″ l, 44″ h **20,900.00**
Stag, copper, polychrome painted, yellow, cast zinc antlers, leaping over
  rockwork and vegetation, rod
  with orb mounting, 19th C, 32″ l,
  26½″ h **18,700.00**

Shore Bird, gilt metal, Long Island, NY, 20th C, 24″ l, 18½″ h, $1,210.00. Photograph courtesy of Skinner, Inc.

Touring Car, molded tin, above orange
  arrow mounted to twisted lightning
  rod, glass Moon and Star patterned
  lightning rod ball above directional
  markers, 1920s **600.00**
Weaver's Shuttle, molded gilt copper,
  fine verdigris surface, 19th C, 64" l   **2,750.00**

WINDMILL WEIGHTS

History: Windmills were an important fixture on
the early prairie landscape of the Midwest. They
pumped underground water for crops, household
use, livestock, and steam locomotives.

Windmill weights counterbalanced the weight
of the large wind wheels which could measure as
much as thirty feet in diameter. They were located
at the end of the arm that ran back from the hub
of the wind wheel. Although simple geometric
shapes such as circles and rectangles were used,
many of the weights were figural. Weight varied
from 10 to 200 pounds. Windmill weights were
painted to match the color of the windmill. Black
was common. Blue, green, and red also were
popular.

Most windmill weights were manufactured in
the Midwest between 1880 and the 1920s. Leading manufacturers include the Dempster Mill
Manufacturing Company (Beatrice, Nebraska), Elgin Wind Power and Pump Company (Elgin, Illinois), and Fairbury Windmill Company (Fairbury,
Nebraska).

In the early 1980s windmill weights joined
weather vanes as a darling of the folk art set.
Although cast in molds and mass-produced, windmill weights were elevated from utilitarian objects
to *objets d'art*. In 1985 the Museum of American
Folk Art sponsored a traveling exhibition on windmill weights.

References: Milton Simpson, *Windmill Weights*,
Johnson & Simpson, 1985; Donald E. Sites, *Wind-
mills and Windmill Weights*, published by author
(P. O. Box 201, Grinnell, KS 67738).

Reproduction Alert: Doug Clemence (Treasure
Chest, 436 North Chicago, Salina, KS 67401) sells

unpainted reproductions of the small chicken,
Hummer #184 chicken with long shaft, Hummer
#184 chicken with short shaft, "barnacle eye"
chicken, short tail horse, buffalo, and squirrel.
Reproductions of the BOSS bull, Fairbury flat bull
(#17 in Site's book), long tail horse, and a chicken
with five tail feathers (#41 in Site's book) have also
been spotted.

New castings often have a finely granulated
orange colored rust, which can be hidden by
new paint, and rough casting edges. Modern
reproductions often are done with pot metal,
rather than cast iron. Finally, reproduction surfaces are rough and grainy, not weathered and
smooth.

Buffalo, Dempster Mfg Co, painted, 16" l	**500.00**
Bull	
Dempster Mfg Co, marked "BOSS" both sides, 18 lbs	**700.00**
Fairbury Windmill Co	**650.00**
Simpson Windmill and Machine Co, Hanchett, bolted halves	**500.00**
Crescent Moon, Fairbanks Morse Co, marked "ECLIPSE," 1900, 27 lbs, 10" l	**150.00**
Halladay Star, US Wind Engine and Pump Co, five points, unpainted, 1890s, 14½" h	**400.00**
Horse	
Dempster Mfg Co, bobtailed	**225.00**
Unknown Maker, 17" h, painted, late 19th or early 20th C	**475.00**
Horse and Jockey, Dempster #4, Dempster Mfg Co, bobtailed horse, jointed sheet metal jockey, painted	**875.00**
Letter "W", Althouse and Wheeler Co, flat back, c1900, 19½" w	**300.00**
Rooster	
Elgin Windmill Power and Pump Co Hummer E184, full bodied, traces of silver paint, mounted on wood base, 12¼" h	**600.00**
Rainbow Tail, painted	**950.00**
Unknown Maker, full bodied, traces of red and white paint, 19" h	**775.00**

COUNTRY STORE

The Country Store is the heart of rural America. Its functions are multifold—supplies,
equipment, drugstore, post office, bank, accounting and bookkeeping services, meeting place,
transportation center, information source, and social arbiter. Although the famed "general"
store has gradually been replaced by shopping centers and mini-malls, many Americans still
have fond memories of spending time around a pot belly wood stove.

One's first country store image is generally the vivid advertising, from broadsides to
products, that graced the counters, shelves, and walls. The counter top equipment is
remembered next, followed by promotional giveaways, some failing to survive because they

were consumable. These are recapturable memories. The individuals, smells, clutter, and grime that were a part of the setting are in the distant past. Most museums and private collection recreations are much too clean and orderly.

Recreating a complete turn-of-the-century country store has been a popular goal of collectors and museums since the 1920s. It was common to buy the entire contents of a country store that was going out of business as a collection base. The advertising craze that started in the 1970s put an end to this practice. Sellers quickly realized that they could obtain far more for their objects by selling them one at a time, rather than in a lot. Rapidly escalating prices, especially for store equipment, makes recreating a complete turn-of-the-century store in the 1990s a very expensive proposition.

For this reason, collectors have begun to focus on recreating Depression era and post-World War II country stores, recognizing that they were very different from their early 1900s counterparts. This corresponds with the new found interest at farm museums in mid-twentieth century farming technology and life.

References: Douglas Congdon-Martin, *Drugstore and Soda Fountain Antiques,* Schiffer Publishing, 1991; Douglas Congdon-Martin with Robert Biondi, *Country Store Antiques: From Cradles to Caskets,* Schiffer Publishing, 1991; Douglas Congdon-Martin with Robert Biondi, *Country Store Collectibles,* Schiffer Publishing, 1990.

ADVERTISING

History: The earliest advertising in America is found in colonial newspapers and printed on broadsides. A large number of the advertisements are rural in nature, often accompanied by a farm related vignette. Rural newspapers were in place by the early 19th century.

By the mid-19th century manufacturers began to examine how a product was packaged. They recognized that the package could convey a message and serve as a source of identification, thus increasing sales. The package logo also could be used effectively in pictorial advertising.

The advent of the high speed, lithograph printing press led to regional and national magazines, resulting in new advertising markets. The lithograph press also brought the element of vivid colors into the advertising spectrum.

Although the "general" store remained a strong force in rural and small town America into the 1950s, it changed with the times. Specialized departments were created. Some product lines branched off as individual stores. The amount and variety of product increased significantly, as did the advertising to go with it.

By 1880 advertising premiums, such as calendars and thermometers, arrived upon the scene. Country store merchants were especially fond of these giveaways. Die-cut point of purchase displays, wall clocks, and signs were introduced and quickly found their way onto walls and shelves.

Advertising continued to respond to changing opportunities and times. The advertising character developed in the early 1900s. By the 1950s the star endorser was established firmly as an advertising vehicle. Advertising became a big business

as specialized firms, many headquartered in New York City, developed to meet manufacturers' needs. Today television programs frequently command well over one hundred thousand dollars a minute for commercial air time.

Many factors affect the price of an advertising collectible—the product and its manufacturer, the objects or persons used in the advertisement, period and aesthetics of design, the designer and/or illustrator, and the form the advertisement takes. Add to this price fluctuations due to the continued use of advertising material as decorative elements in bars, restaurants, and other public places. (The interior decorator purchases at a very different price level than the collector.)

In truth, almost every advertising item is sought by a specialized collector in one or more collectible area. The result is a divergence in pricing, with the price quoted to an advertising collector usually lower than that to a specialized collector, a category into which country store advertising collectors fall.

References: Douglas Congdon-Martin, *America for Sale: A Collector's Guide To Antique Advertising,* Schiffer Publishing, 1991 Jim Cope, *Old Advertising,* Great American Publishing Co., 1980; Sharon and Bob Huxford, *Huxford's Collectible Advertising: An Illustrated Price Guide,* Collector Books, 1993; Robert Joy, *The Trade Card in Nineteenth-Century America,* University of Missouri Press, 1987; Ray Klug, *Antique Advertising Encyclopedia,* Vol. 1 (1978, 1993 value update), Vol. 2 (1985), L–W Book Sales; Ralph and Terry Kovel, *Kovels' Advertising Collectibles Price List,* Crown Publishers, 1986; Tom Morrison, *Root Beer: Advertising and Collectibles,* Schiffer Publishing, 1992.

Collectors' Clubs: Antique Advertising Association, PO Box 1121, Morton Grove, IL 60053; The Ephemera Society of America, PO Box 37, Schoharie, NY 12157; Tin Container Collectors' Association, PO Box 440101, Aurora, CA 80044.

Periodicals: *P.A.C.*, National Association of Paper and Advertising Collectibles, PO Box 500, Mt. Joy, PA 17552; *P.C.M.* (Paper Collectors' Marketplace), PO Box 128, Scandinavia, WI 54977.

Reproduction Manufacturers: AAA Sign Co, 354 S. State Line Rd, Lowellsville, OH 44436; Attic Antiques, 2301 Peach Orchard Rd, Augusta, GA 30906; Design Workshop, PO Box 236, West Barnstable, MA 02668; Desperate Enterprises, PO Box 312, Wadsworth, OH 44281; Lace Wood 'N Tin Tyme, 6496 Summerton, Shepherd, MI 48883; Meadow Breeze, 2010 Wilmington Pk, Cedarville, OH, 45314.

Reproduction Alert

Banner
 DeLaval, cloth, oval vignette of woman using separator, "Sooner or Later You Will Buy A DeLaval Cream Separator, Nearly 2,000,000 In Use," yellow lettering, dark blue ground, 36" w, 8" h   185.00
 Mayo's Plug Tobacco, canvas, rooster standing on tobacco plugs, framed, 18 × 29½" 85.00
 RCA, cotton, symbols and victrola images, 40 × 37½" 55.00
 Walter A Wood Harvesting Machinery, Hoosick Falls, NY, paper and cloth banner mounted on retractable wood rod, black and white wood engravings of farm machinery and factory, 31" w, 23" h . . .   165.00
 Winchester Rifles and Shotguns, silk, cowboy with rifle riding racing horse, white ground, blue, gold, and red image and lettering, yellow fringed bottom, 31" w, 19" h   500.00
Blotter
 American Family Soap, Uncle Sam illus, c1910. . . . .   15.00
 F R Keens Co, Soda Fountain Foods, New Haven, CT, red, yellow and black illus, 1931 . . . .   25.00
 Geo W Engle, Hazelton, PA, Dealer in Flour and Feed, Grain & Hay, Mill Agent For the Famous Ceresota Flour, full color image, c1895 . . . .   25.00
 Goodrich Zipps Shoes, G T Foltz Dept Store, Wyrheville, VA, orange, full color illus, c1935 . . . . .   25.00
 H Gamse & Bros, Food Products Labels of Quality, full color, April, 1923 calendar. 20.00

Blotter, Sugar Creek Creamery, blue and yellow, white ground, 3¼ × 6", $8.00.

J I Case Threshing Machine Co, Racine, WI, full color illus, c1920. . .   25.00
William H Geer Co, Hudson St, NY, representative for canned goods, full color illus, gold highlights, c1900 . . . .   40.00
Booklet
 Buster Brown's Experiences with Pond's Extract, 24 pgs, full color front cov of Buster Brown and Tige, 1904. . . . .   60.00
 Daggett & Ramsdell, Perfect Cold Cream, 16 pgs, full color cov of pretty woman, 1909 copyright. . .   45.00
 Drake's Plantation Bitters, P H Drake & Co, NY, full color cov, black and white illus, 1871 . . . .   50.00
 Dr Fenner's Are Used All Over the World, People's Remedies, 26 pgs, full color cov of Statue of Liberty and ships in lake scene, 1888 . . . .   35.00
 Henry's Cookbook and Household Companion, NY, 32 pgs, full color front and back cov, 1883 . . . . . .   35.00
 Huylers Chocolate & Cocoa, full color cov, 1904 copyright 20.00

Booklet, Metropolitan Life Insurance Co., "All About Milk," color covers, 24 pages, 5¼ × 7¾", $7.50.

Door Push, American Special Flour, litho tin, emb, red, white, and blue, 3½ × 6¾", $50.00.

Jell-O, Genesee Pure Food Co, Leroy, NY, 14 pgs, full color cov, 1920 copyright	20.00
Kickapoo Indian Dream Book, full color cov, testimonials, product information, and dream interpretations, c1888	50.00
No-To-Bac, Don't Tobacco Spit and Smoke Your Life Away, 32 pgs, full color cov, c1895	25.00
Robinson's Patent Barley For Making Infants Food & Barley Water, 8 pgs, full color illus on cov of Thumbelina and baby, c1895 . . .	20.00
The Popular Songster, Rohrer's Expectoral Wild Cherry Tonic, Lancaster, PA, 32 pgs, 1868	45.00

Broadside

C O D Clothing, dated November 1st, 1879, 12 × 4½"	125.00

Folder, Kitchen Magic with Larabee's Best Flour, color covers and illus, recipes, 1920s, 18 × 6" open size, $12.00.

Label, egg crate, Sleepy Eye Brand, A J Pietrus & Sons Co, Sleepy Eye, MN, red, blue, and yellow, 9¼ × 11½", $25.00.

Geo W Smith, Dry Goods, Groceries, Provisions, Mattawamkeag, ME, paper, black lettering, white ground, dry goods store illus	275.00
Splendid Millinery Goods, clothing adv, dated Sept 27, 1865, 10 × 7"	110.00

Calendar

American Chain Co, four female portraits in tire with chains frames, two touring cars, "Weed's Chains on all Four Tires for all Four Seasons," framed, 1916, 13½" w, 34" h	600.00
Collins Baking Co, Buffalo, NY, emb, girl sitting in wicker chair, holding St Bernard puppy, mother dog standing nearby, emb floral border, small calendar pad at bottom right corner, "From painting copyrighted by Kaufman & Strauss Co, Germany," 1911	140.00
Dr Miles' Remedies, Miles Medical Co, Elkhart, IN, little girl holding white rose, full pad at bottom, 1908	50.00
Hood's Sarsaparilla Coupon Calendar, emb, child's portrait, floral border, 1898, unused	70.00
Lautz Brothers & Co, Buffalo, NY, emb, little girl playing with doll-	

Label, fruit crate, Rocky Hill, Sunkist oranges, dark blue ground, 10⅞ × 9½", $2.00.

house made from wood soap crates, Marselle's White Soap and Snow Boy Washing Powder, floral border, 1901 . . . .   135.00

Libby, McNeill & Libby Corned Beef, litho, green ground, red lettering, smiling girl holding flower, corned beef can beside calendar pad at bottom, 1905, 11" w, 16½" h . . .   50.00

National Life and Accident Insurance Co, barnyard animals playing musical instruments, artist H. Twelvetrees, 1935, 10½" w, 13½" h 25.00

Sharples Separator Co, West Chester, PA, Tubular and Jersey Cream Separators, milkmaid holding pail, standing beside separator, cow peering through open window, 1912, full pad, 7" w, 13¾" h . . .   100.00

United States Cream Separators, Vermont Farm Machine Co, Bellows Falls, VT, woman leaning against stone wall, cows in background, inset of cream separator, 1910, 20" w, 30" h 225.00

Carrier, soda, wood
A-Treat, holds 24 bottles. 20.00
Uncle Joe's Soda, 1929. . . . .   75.00

Chalkboard, Vernors, emb and painted tin, top half with yellow ground and green, black, and white lettering "Drink Vernors Deliciously Different," chalkboard bottom half, c1960, 17½" w, 24½" h 30.00

Change Tray, Quick Meal Ranges. . . .   75.00

Clock
Calumet Baking Powder, calendar   675.00
Coca-Cola, wood, drop regulator, paper dial, reverse gold leafed "Coca-Cola In Bottles" on pendulum glass insert, 17½" w, 31" h   650.00

Mirror, pocket, The Invincible Junior, vacuum cleaner, Electric Renovator Mfg Co, Pittsburgh, PA, black-and-white photo image, celluloid back, 1¾ × 2¼", $45.00.

Pamphlet, John Deere No. 999 Corn Planter, 8 pages, black-and-white illus, 8 pages, 1917, 4 × 9", $20.00.

Jolly Tar Pastime Tobacco, wood, figure eight pendulum, reverse gold leafed pendulum glass insert, 18½" w, 31" h 825.00

Mayo's Tobacco, figure eight drop regulator, adv on emb dial border and pendulum door, Baird Clock Co, 18" w, 30½" h 550.00

Nu-Grape, plastic 75.00

Simmon's Liver, regulator 225.00

Display
Bixby's Shoe Polish, diecut, woman holding box of shoe polish, 10 × 32½" 175.00

Dazey Butter Churn, diecut cardboard, housewife with butter churn, 27 × 22' 185.00

Dr Morse's Indian Root Pills, diecut, Indians and native scene, 42 × 27"   375.00

Keil Keys, Charlestown, IN, molded metal, figural key, two sided, red ground, raised ivory lettering, "Keys Made," 1930s, 27½" w, 11¾" h 165.00

Kellogg's Corn Flakes, diecut cardboard, young lady wearing blue and white checkered dress and bonnet, sitting on fence, holding corn stalk and Corn Flakes box, "The Sweetheart of the Corn," 21" w, 45" h 175.00

Liberty Lanterns, diecut cardboard, Liberty Bell replica, two sided, light brown and white lettering, brown ground, "Liberty Lanterns For Sale Here, Simmons Hardware Company Incorporated Manufacturers and Distributors, U.S.A.," c1918 . . . .   50.00

Paper Clip, L F Grammes & Sons, Allentown, PA, brass, 2⅛ × 3⅛ ", $25.00.

Occident Flour, tin, illustrates six stages of wheat processing, encapsulated wheat and flour samples, flour bag illus in upper corners, blue and white lettering, "Russell-Miller Milling Co., Minneapolis-Minnesota," c1935, 14" w, 9" h **350.00**

Redhead Bottle Caps, 1944 .... **18.00**

Skeleton Key, figural, white metal, painted, emb lettering "Independent Lock Co. Fitchburg, Mass." on oval handle, hanging eyelets **55.00**

Towle's Log Cabin Syrup, diecut cardboard, syrup camp and wooded scene, 28 × 22 × 7½" .. **1,600.00**

Uncle John's Syrup, diecut, Uncle John image, 16¾ × 12½" **20.00**

Westinghouse Mazda Lamps, diecut cardboard, stand up, Olive Oyl leaning out window, Popeye with boxes of light bulbs, "Well-ya told me not to forget lamps," reverse with two light bulbs, c1934, 31" h **185.00**

Yara Tobacco, diecut cardboard, stand up, three sections, woman on center section, turned legs, box stretcher base, turned feet, old refinish, restored, New England, 43½" l, 29" d, 27" h **525.00**

Pinback Button, Swift's Premium Hams and Bacon, celluloid, multicolored, paper insert, 1¼" d, $25.00.

Poster
Aultman & Taylor Farm Machinery, busy barnyard scene, 36 × 14½" **350.00**

Barker's Liniment, paper, farm animals and pastoral river scene, 30 × 24" **525.00**

Chase & Sanborn's Teas, color litho, metal border, 27 × 21" **45.00**

Columbus Buggy, paper, Columbus presenting buggy and gifts to King and Queen, 38 × 25" **440.00**

Deering, paper, hunter with spaniel and game, 12 × 15½" **55.00**

Dunlap's Seeds, litho. **175.00**

Hamilton Brown Shoe, paper, lady, metal strip, 20½ × 30" **110.00**

Harvesting Machine, paper, US map with starred manufacturing locations, threshers and agriculture implements border, 58½ × 39½"... **330.00**

Hazlett's Livery, paper, color litho, metal border, wood frame, 19 × 14" **275.00**

Howard Dustless Duster, paper, woman wearing sailor uniform holding dust cloth, 18½ × 27½" **400.00**

International Poultry Food, full color litho, wood frame, 27 × 20"..... **210.00**

International Stock Food, full color litho, cattle yard, wood frame, 27 × 21" **150.00**

John Roots Bitters, paper, wounded man helped by girl, pastoral scene, 21½ × 27¾" **2,100.00**

Lakeside Maple Syrup, paper, horse-drawn sleigh passing winter workers tapping maple trees, skaters in background, 19½ × 13" **850.00**

Rice's Seeds, paper, farm girl and man looking at celery and squash, 20 × 28" **1,050.00**

Poster, Dunlap's Seeds, Nashua, NH, color litho, J Ottmann Litho, 16 × 23½", $605.00. Photograph courtesy of James D. Julia, Inc.

Poster, D. W. Hoegg Canned Goods, Canada, color litho, framed, 22 × 27½", $1,210.00. Photograph courtesy of James D. Julia, Inc.

Runkel Cocoa, paper, couple sampling breakfast cocoa, child holding product, 18 × 24" 700.00
Sweet Orr & Co, cardboard, 20 × 24" **1,600.00**
Yeast Foam, paper, delivery boy handing woman product, child holding doll in background, orig metal strips, 12 × 17½" 450.00
Salesman's Sample
  Bedspring, 5½" l 170.00
  Boots, leather, 4½" h 100.00
  Cookie Cutter, set of 12, tin container 175.00
  Curtain Stretcher, Quaker, orig tag, 26" l, 17" h 45.00
  Fence, Pace Fence Company, chicken wire, cast metal base, 11 × 6 × 1" 75.00
  Furnace, gas boiler, cast iron and brass, orig paint, 3 × 10 ½" 440.00
  Gate, wood and metal, 18" l, 10½" h 200.00
  Horse Harness, leather, 5 × 6" 225.00
  Jackknife, wood, engraved steel blades, brass plate, 30" l **1,800.00**
  Kitchen Cabinet, "Cass," oak, hoosier style, 13¾" w, 15½" h 325.00
  Loom, wood, "Miniature Loom" paper label, "NRA" (National Recovery Act) ink stamp, 9½" w, 15½" d, 12½" h 25.00
  Lunch Pail, Lisk, nickel plated metal, cup and two liners, 4" h 275.00
  Ox Yoke and Buggy Undercarriage, 18" l 70.00
  Pitchfork, True Temper Pitchfork, wood and cast iron, 30" l 350.00
  Plow, cast iron, painted, 13" l: 125.00
  Post Hole Digger, wood and brass, 3 × 29" 220.00
  Rifle Case, Moose Brand leather, brass detail, 16¼ × 5½ × 3" 225.00

Safe, Mosler, cast iron, orig carrying case, 12 × 17 × 6¼" **2,000.00**
Screen Door Set, Griffin Perfection Screen Door Set, 8¾" w, 12½" h 20.00
Stove
  Karr, blue porcelainized steel and nickel plated cast iron, 14 × 21 × 9" **4,500.00**
  Quick Meal, cast iron, includes pots and pans, 17 × 26 × 16" **1,300.00**
  Royal, 10½" w, 5" h 60.00
Table
  Drop Leaf, walnut, round leaves, turned legs, 9¼" h 175.00
  Pedestal, Victorian, square top, turned vasiform column, square base with paw feet, 10" h 225.00
  Thrasher, wood and tin, 19" l, 9" h 110.00
  Trash Canister, galvanized tin, hand-painted adv panels, 12" h 100.00
  Umbrella, cloth and wood, 1½ × 10" 65.00
Windmill, Model 12B, Aero Mfg Co, aluminum, 16¾" h 130.00
Wringer
  Gem, cast iron and wood, 16" l 90.00
  Lovell Manufacturing Co., Erie, PA, 7¼" w, 8" h 30.00
Sign
  Adriance Farm Machinery, wood, sanded, double sided, 13 × 31" 125.00
  Arm & Hammer Brand Soda, color litho on paperboard, product and lettering with black background, 12 × 16" 25.00
  Big Ben's Smoking Tobacco, paper, man riding champion stallion and tobacco tin illus, 20 × 14" 125.00
  Brookfield Pork Sausage, cardboard, boy running with package under arm, 15 × 20" 175.00

Sign, Dover Egg Beater, color litho, 1870s, 9 × 12", $1,540.00. Photograph courtesy of James D. Julia, Inc.

Trade Card, McCormick Reaping Machines, 6¼ × 4¹⁄₁₆″, $12.00.

Bunte Bros Candies, paper, mountain climbers and eagles protecting nest, 15½ × 21″ **650.00**

Campbell's Tomato Soup, sheet metal, figural soup can, red, black, yellow, and white, 22½ × 14″ . . .   **85.00**

Carhartt's Clothing, porcelain, railroad car emblem over heart, blue, white, and red, orig bracket, 22½ × 28 × 5½″ **750.00**

Carter's Little Liver Pills, reverse painted glass, 11½ × 10¼″ **225.00**

Catlin's Smoking Tobacco, arched hissing cat standing on product carton, cat sitting in window smoking pipe, 9 × 12″ **450.00**

C F & I Coals, porcelainized steel, red and black lettering, three devils running, 9 × 20″ **250.00**

Chase's Liquid Glue, reverse painted glass, blue, red, and yellow, silver lettering, gilt wood frame, 25½ × 17½″ **110.00**

Coca-Cola, porcelainized steel, red, white, and black logo, yellow and green border, 10 × 30″ **725.00**

Columbus Buggy, ostrich pulling buggy, 40 × 26″ **3,000.00**

Cow Brand Baking Soda, cocker spaniel in field and product illus, framed, 16½ × 25″ **325.00**

Crisco, porcelain, can shape, 14 × 20″ **1,250.00**

DeLaval, girl with feathered hat holding separator, 13½ × 18″ . . .   **625.00**

Derby Boot and Shoe Polish, paper, man wearing costume sees reflection in boot, 7¾ × 9¾″, c1859 . . . .   **330.00**

Diamond Wedding Rye, tin, woman holding shot glass, 12″ d **330.00**

Dixon's Stove Polish, paper, girl wearing green dress and paper hat with product adv, 12½ × 29″ . . .   **175.00**

Drink Rochelle Club, tin, emb, 12 × 24″ **90.00**

Eagle Brand Condensed Milk, paperboard, color litho, young girl with raised finger, matted and framed, 13 × 10″ **300.00**

Ebbert Wagon, tin, farmer helping girl with basket of apples, 27½ × 25½″ **800.00**

Eisemann's Klondike Head Rub, cardboard, emb, litho, colorful bottle image, 8½ × 11″ **75.00**

Enjoy Hires, It's Always Pure, litho tin, emb, green and yellow lettering, blue background, wood frame, 9½ × 27½″ **660.00**

Enjoy Orange Crush, plastic, emb, painted, orange and white, blue background, 9 × 11″ **35.00**

Enterprise Stoves & Ranges, litho tin, emb, white lettering, dark blue background **45.00**

Erickson's Pure Rye Whiskey, tin, full color litho, submarine being attacked, surrounded by floating whiskey bottles, wood frame, 22 × 32″ **660.00**

Eskimo Pie, red and blue image, textured imitation foil background, 9½ × 19½″ **175.00**

Fairbanks Scales, wood, relief carved letters, 40½ × 18¾″ **450.00**

Fatima Cigarettes, tin, veiled Turkish girl, wood stretcher frame, 37½ × 25½″ **550.00**

Fehr's Malt Tonic, tin, oval, bare chested nude maid holding bottle, cherubs, 22 × 28″ **1,500.00**

Foster Hose Supporters, celluloid over cardboard, corset center with women, wood frame, 16½ × 8½″   **275.00**

Francisco Auto Heater, tin, color litho, framed, 18 × 40″ **375.00**

Trade Card, Phelps, Dodge & Palmer, Chicago, Children's fine sewed shoes, full color, 3 × 4¼″, $5.00.

Granger Tobacco, Keeps the Smoker Happy, paperboard, color litho, Sam Snead, 19 × 14½" **165.00**

Granite Iron Ware, paper, cow and girl holding bucket, 12 × 28". . . . **1,450.00**

Grape-Nuts, little girl with dog carrying lunch, 20 × 30". **1,600.00**

Handy Package Dyes, paper, litho, 17 × 13½" **110.00**

Horsford's Baking Powder, paper, double image of little girl wearing bowed bonnet, 32½ × 23½". . . .   **700.00**

Household Sewing Machines, paper, woman at sewing machine, child playing with cats and kittens, 25¾ × 18¾" **770.00**

Ivory Soap, cardboard, little girl washing doll's clothing, Maud Humphrey illus, 17 × 24½". **450.00**

J & P Coats, paper, man fishing with spools of thread and woman sewing, 22½ × 17½". **125.00**

Kennedy's Chimmie Fadden Biscuit, paper, arrogant Irish boy, 14 × 20".   **900.00**

Kirk Soap, tin, diecut, American shield with soap adv, 19½ x 20"   **3,750.00**

Lipton's Teas, paperboard, color litho, woman of the world in rising steam, gold and yellow lettering, blue background, matted and framed, 21 × 14". **485.00**

Long Wear Shoes, porcelainized steel, double sided, red and white, 17 × 16" **275.00**

Masury's Paint, tin, man mixing color, merchant pointing to can of paint, paint mixing machine background, 23½ × 17½" **440.00**

Milwaukee Harvester, paper, horse-drawn threshing machine and hay rakes, 24 × 36" **550.00**

Montag Furnaces, porcelainized steel, flanged, red and white, 10 × 18" **110.00**

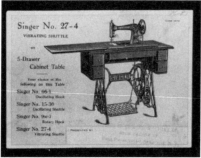

Trade Card, Singer Sewing Machine, text on back, 5⁹⁄₁₆ × 4¹⁄₁₆", $8.00.

Nehi In This Bottle Only, paper, litho, mounted on artist board, 39¾ × 18¾" **130.00**

Noonan's Hair Petrole, porcelainized steel, flanged, double sided, red, white, and blue, 12 × 16" **375.00**

Oleo Margarine, tin, girl riding on cow, 13 × 9" **2,700.00**

Orcherade, paperboard, full color litho, two women, one holding glass, other pouring from bottle, 14½ × 11½" **200.00**

Otto F Ernst Saddles, litho tin, emb, black lettering, yellow ground, 9 × 20" **75.00**

Pal Ade, Your Pals Drink Pal Ade, tin, emb, stenciled, orange, yellow, and red image, blue background, 16 × 16" **90.00**

PDF Plow Shapes, porcelainized steel, double sided, white lettering, green ground, 8 × 24". **175.00**

Penn Esther Kitchen Range, paper transfer between glass, woman cooking, 7½ × 8½" **175.00**

Piper-Heidsieck Chewing Tobacco, paper, color litho, emb, orig wood frame, 12½ × 15" **210.00**

Polo Club Beverages, litho tin, emb, green and white, 3 × 20". **150.00**

Rice's Flower Seeds, paper, girl with rake surrounded by flowers, 13¾ × 29". **1,450.00**

Rising Sun Stove Polish, paper, Victorian woman looking out window, 18 × 29½" **1,850.00**

Royal Crown Cola, sheet metal, flanged, stenciled, green, red, yellow, and blue, 10½ × 17½" **125.00**

Sparrow's Chocolates, tin, emb central sq, crowned Empress served box of candy, 13 × 19" **550.00**

Splendid Plug Tobacco, paper, five pretty women portraits, 26 x 40" **1,100.00**

Swift's Premium Oleomargarine, paperboard, color litho, matted and framed, 19 × 14". **475.00**

Tru Ade, sheet metal, flanged, stenciled, red, blue, and orange, yellow background, 14 × 20". **110.00**

Tulip Soap, paper, woman surrounded by tulips and various other vignette scenes, framed, 21½ × 27½" **55.00**

Van Houten's Cocoa, paperboard, color litho, Dutch woman and man, orig wood frame, 27 × 16" .   **250.00**

Victor Talking Machine, tin, dog and Victrola, 19 × 13½". **550.00**

Walter A Wood's Mowing and Reaping Machine Company, Hoosick

Falls, NY, paper, color litho, mounted on wood scrolls, 28 × 22" **525.00**

Walter Baker & Co Cocoa, tin, girl serving cocoa on tray, framed, 13½ × 19½" **550.00**

Washburn Flouring Mills, paper, multiple buildings and train scene, 36½ × 26½" **400.00**

We Sell Star Tobacco, porcelainized steel, flanged, blue and white, 8 × 18" **250.00**

Westinghouse Threshing Machines, steam powered equipment running threshing machines, 26½ × 21" **330.00**

White Label Soup, tin, knight with can on shield, 20 × 14" **225.00**

Wilson Sewing Machine, paper, litho, Mr Wilson image surrounded by factories and machines, 19 × 24" **350.00**

Woonsocket Rubber Boots, paper, child standing on ocean pier wearing rubber boots, 15 × 22" **475.00**

Ye Old Country Store, wood, double sided, stenciled, gold lettering, 36" h **275.00**

Yukon's Self-Rising Flour, sheet metal, stenciled, 22½ × 13½" **200.00**

String Holder

Post Toasties, tin, 11½" d **725.00**

Red Goose Shoes, figural, goose, cast iron, painted, red, yellow lettering, green base, 14½" l **475.00**

SSS For The Blood, cast iron, reticulated insert, painted, raised letters, 4⅞" h **140.00**

Thermometer

Arbuckles Coffee, litho tin, red, black, and yellow, 19" h **125.00**

Buster Brown Shoes, printed paper dial, brown and white, 9" d **175.00**

C E Hidlebaugh Saddlery Co, wood, stenciled, black and white, 47" **210.00**

Clown Cigarettes, litho paper dial, black and yellow illus, white background, 9" d **60.00**

Coca-Cola, litho tin, girl silhouette, green, red, and silver, 16" h **180.00**

Doan's Kidney Pills, wood, diecut, man holding his back, 5 × 21". .. **110.00**

Dr Pepper, litho tin, green and red bottle, white and black lettering, yellow background, 1939, 17¼" h **440.00**

Exlax, The Chocolate Laxative, porcelainized steel, black lettering, light and dark blue and orange, 36" h **125.00**

Folger's Coffee, tin, red and black illus, white background, 9" d **220.00**

Thermometer, Braun's Town Talk Brand Bread, porcelain, 38¾" h, $45.00.

Hamlin's Wizard Oil, wood, impressed lettering, lacquer finish, 21" h **75.00**

Joan of Arc Red Kidney Beans, wood, painted and stenciled, black lettering, white background, 15" h ... **45.00**

Northrup, King & Co, Clover and Alfalfa Seed, steel, black lettering, yellow background, 27" h **90.00**

Pepsi Cola, sheet metal, litho and stenciled, multicolored bottle image, blue and white background, 27" h **275.00**

Ramon's Pills, A Real Laxative for Adults, wood, stenciled, green and red illus, mustard background, 21" h **135.00**

Red Seal, porcelainized steel, red and blue, white background, 27" h **70.00**

Rock Island Plow Co, Better Farm Implements, wood, impressed lettering, lacquered finish, 21" h ... **100.00**

Wesson Oil & Snowdrift, paper dial, black and red illus, white background, 9" d **55.00**

Trade Card

Acher Co Coffee, pretty girl, 1904 **18.00**

American Standard Corn Planter, Victorian girl illus **26.00**

Anthony Wayne Washers, folder type, "Ye Old and Ye New"..... **32.00**

B A Hadsell Ready Made Plain Clothing...................... **28.00**

Barbours Irish Flax Thread **10.00**

Bay State Lawn Mower, Old Homestead **40.00**

Belding Bros Spool Silk **34.00**

Bixby's Royal Polish, NY, full color, 1880 .... **30.00**

Black Cat Hosiery, diecut, cat	20.00
Buffalo Scale Co	34.00
Bush Hill Creamery Butter, red and green illus, cream background	10.00
California Brand Condensed Milk	12.00
Calkins Champion Washer, red background	28.00
C Riessner Co, Queen Oil Range, turkey cooking scene	20.00
D M Osborne Mowers, Reapers, folder type	22.00
Doty's Washer, folder type, red, black, and buff, 1873 price list int	15.00
Edw K Tryon, Jr & Co, Firearms, Philadelphia, c1880	40.00
F Mayer Boot & Shoe Co, multicolored, boys playing leap frog	8.00
Frishmuth Bro & Co Fine Cut & Smoking Tobacco, Philadelphia, reverse with buildings illus	15.00
Geo Edwards Leaf Tobacco & Cigars, black and white, brown logo. . . .	44.00
Geo Hubbard Co Wholesale Groceries, black and white	12.00
Gold Coin Stoves & Ranges, stove vignette	10.00
Henderson's Red School House Shoes	20.00
J I Case, Racine, WI, black and white illus	34.00
Joe Michl's Fifty Little Orphans Cigar, hanging string	15.00
Lenox Soap, diecut, standup	10.00
Levering's Roasted Coffee, diecut . .	18.00
Luzianne Coffee, diecut	14.00
Model Grand Portable Range, Uncle Sam being fed by black man	26.00
Moline Plow, American Royalty, King Corn & Queen Wheat	55.00
Monarch Teenie Weenie Sweets, diecut, pickle barrel	10.00
New Process Soap, multicolored	15.00
Reliance Corset Co, "Imperial Corset," blue reverse with corset vignettes	12.00
Schuttler Wagon, farm scene	40.00
Shaker and New Tariff Ranges, Lt Greeley arriving at North Pole. . .	55.00
Standard Sewing Machine, stitched cloth border	18.00
Sunshine Stoves and Ranges, folder type, 1898 calendar	8.00
Swift's Premium Ham & Bacon, multicolored	15.00
Tyson's Montgomery County Milk	55.00
Wheatlet Breakfast Food, diecut, standup	40.00
White Sewing Machine, Cleveland, OH, full color, c1890	10.00
Williams Poultry Food, "Makes Hens Lay"	8.00
Wool Soap, diecut, "My Mamma used Wool Soap"	14.00

CABINETS, COUNTERS, SHELVING, AND ACCESSORIES

History: When a building was built specifically as a country store building, it was customary to build-in shelving, cabinets, and counters. Much of the interior architecture was utilitarian, not ornately decorative or elaborately trimmed. A surprising number of these buildings survive. Attempting to remove and relocate these fixtures poses a major problem.

The key merchandising technique utilized by the country store was open storage. Glass cases, visible from front, top, and sides and with a back featuring a stepped shelf interior, were common. The main counter was the exception, usually containing a plank board top and solid side with shelves or bins accessible only from the back.

The main counter usually contained several small and medium size, special purpose glass cabinets. The three most prevalent uses were for candy, cheese, and notions. In addition, companies, especially thread companies, provided the country store merchant with cabinets designed to store, promote, and sell their products. Many of these featured brightly lithographed tin fronts.

In addition to the fixed pieces, the country store was home to a host of other point of purchase display units, ranging from the cracker barrel to the broom rack. Large floor bins held coffee, flour, and grains. Many of these contained stenciled advertisements.

The universal country store look is eclectic. Occasionally a merchant remodeling his store would install a matched set of counters, cabinets, and shelves. These matched sets bring a handsome premium when sold. However, carefully check the provenance of any matched set offered. The same fixtures would be used in a jewelry or small department store. Country Store collectors prefer a country store provenance.

Keep your eyes open for photographs of country store interiors. They are important research sources for collectors and museums. Value ranges from $5 to $25. Add 10 to 25 percent if the store and town are identified and the photograph dated.

Reproduction Manufacturer: J P Bartholomew Co, 170 Pearson Lane, McCall, ID 83639.

Apothecary Chest, spruce, 24 drawers, turned wood pulls, stenciled labels, England, early 19th C, 49" w, 9¼" d, 23½" h	1,100.00

Cabinet

Best Quality Sewing Needles, wood, three drawers, emb tin front, 17½" l 75.00

Bolts, oak, two sections, revolving octagonal top with column of 10 drawers on each side, square base with 12 drawers, bolt sizes stamped on drawer fronts, porcelain knobs, 1880s, 30" w, 64 ½" h 1,500.00

Christie's Biscuits, ash, 16 drawers each with glass pane drawer front with stenciled label "Christie's Biscuits," c1900, 47" w, 12½" d, 54" h 1,200.00

Diamond Dyes, litho tin and wood, door panel with woman using product, 30" h 750.00

High Class Biscuits, wood, marble top, three glass-fronted bins, shoe feet, 43" w, 52½" h 775.00

Jaques Flavoring Extracts, glass, wood frame, reverse stenciled lettering, 35"h 600.00

J P Privley's Gum, wood, reverse painted gold lettering, 18½" l . . . 575.00

Lion Brand Shirts, Collars & Cuffs, wood, stained, glass door, nickel plated trim, pedestal base, 66" h . 750.00

Our Best Snuffs, George W Helme Co, wood, stained, side door, twenty sealed tins, 19¼" h 225.00

Peerless Dyes, wood, paper front, roll back top, orig stenciled back, 19 × 32 × 11" 660.00

Putnam Dyes, wood case, hinged front, double sided tin front and back, General Putnam on horse escaping Red Coats illus, paper int., 21" w, 8½" d, 10" h 225.00

Rainbow Dye, metal, wood base, orig dye packets, 13¼" w, 14" h 145.00

Rice Seed Company, wood and metal, shelves unfold accordion style to hold seed packets, c1909 . . . . 28.00

Rit Dye, wood and tin, slant top, litho slogan, 64 compartment drawers, three orig handles, 14" w, 10" d, 16" h 225.00

Seed, oak, stained, eighteen illuminated glass panels, nineteen drawers, 12" l 990.00

Shumate Razors & Strops, wood and glass, decal, 23" h 880.00

Ceiling Fan

General Electric, four blades, plain cast iron housing, wood paddles, 36" d, 84" drop 65.00

Western Electric, four blades, ornate cast iron housing, wood paddles, 36" d, 66" drop 130.00

Display Case

Blackman's Medicated Salt Bricks, wood, painted yellow, open front, two shelves, slatted back, boot jack ends, yellow and black tin marquee, "Every Animal Its Own Doctor," 16½" w, 31 ½" h 50.00

Eveready, emb tin, rows of figural emb batteries on door, battery displays on sides, "Extra Long Life Flashlight Batteries, 10¢ Each," on marquee, 9½" w, 16" h 25.00

Johnson Nut Co, Cleveland and Minneapolis, wood frame, glass top,

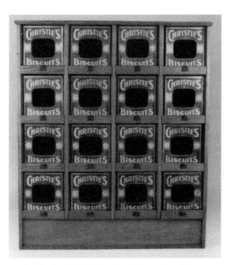

Cabinet, Christie's Biscuits, ash, sixteen compartments each with glass pane and label, c1900, 47" w, 12½" d, 54" h, $1,210.00. Photograph courtesy of Skinner, Inc.

Display Case, Boye Needle Company Rotary Needle Case, Chicago, holds flanged tubes of needles and shuttles, metal, last patent date July 9, 1907, 16" d, $75.00.

sides, and front, name plate and "Temptingly Fresh, Deliciously Crisp" on frame, four separate compartments held peanuts and candy, brass scoop, 1910–20, 24" w, 13" h **325.00**

Lighter Fluid Dispenser, Van-lite Lighter Fluid, metal and plastic, locking, circular base, Van Lansing Co, Pittsburgh, PA, c1930, 19" h. **350.00**

Sanford's Inks, wood, shaped marquee with gold leaf shadow letters, glass door, three int. shelves, molded base, 21½" w, 36" h . . .   **550.00**

Hanging Display

Pretzel, figural, composition, 20" w, 14" h. **550.00**

Safety Razor, brass, gnarled handles, oversized, 16" h, 8" w **600.00**

Mannequin, child size, Stockman, Paris   **375.00**

Peanut Roaster, Royal No. 5 Roaster, Planter's Nut and Chocolate Co, A J Deer Co, copper drum, cast iron base, ornate brass dec, 45 x 41" . . .   **1,320.00**

Pickle Dispenser, Monarch, sheet metal, litho lion images inside logos, four removable ceramic containers, octagonal glass lids, four legs with casters, 43" l.   **825.00**

Platform Scale, coin operated

Royal Crown Cola, figural soda bottle, red and yellow label, platform base, drop coins in yellow bottle cap, 1950s, 45½" h. **2,100.00**

Watling Fortune Scale, Watling Scale Co, Chicago, IL, porcelain, over 2,000 different response cards with fortunes, dreams, and quiz questions, c1935, 66" h **225.00**

Register Cabinet, McCaskey Register Co, Alliance, OH, wood, top with locking roll-top door enclosing vertical metal files, large drawer in bottom, early 20th C, 19" w, 24" d, 19" h **175.00**

Showcase, oak frame, glass panels, hinged top, 71" w, 27" d, 14" h . . .   **80.00**

Spice Bin, spice, wood, six drawers, hp red, gold, and black dec, oval inset with pastoral scene, 24 × 13½ × 13" **660.00**

Spool Cabinet

Belding's Silk, mahogany, stained, revolving, gold and black lettering, 32½" h. **880.00**

Brainerd & Armstrong Co, Victorian, walnut, glass drawer fronts, mirror side panels **1,000.00**

Corticelli Silk, twelve glass-front drawers, mirrored sides, orig stenciled dec, 33" h **675.00**

Gutermann's Sewing Silk, wood, stenciled, hinged glass doors, 19" l   **325.00**

J P Coats, oak, four sided, revolving, hinged panels, ornate dec, 22¾" h   **1,250.00**

Merrick's, oak, cylindrical, adv on curved glass panels, revolving interior, 18" d, 23" h **500.00**

CATALOGS

History: Catalogs played an important role in Country living. First, they broadened the farmer's knowledge of what was available beyond his local community. Second, they provided a way to keep abreast of changing technology. Finally, they decreased the sense of isolation that is part of farming.

Catalogs serve as excellent research sources. The complete manufacturing line of a given item is often described and pictured in a wide variety of styles, colors, etc. Catalogs provide an excellent method to date objects.

Many old catalogs are reprinted for use by collectors as an aid to identification of items within their collecting interest, e.g., reprints of Heisey and Hubley catalogs. The photocopy machine also contributes to the distribution of information among friends.

References: Don Fredgant, *American Trade Catalogs*, Collector Books, 1984, out-of-print; Norman E. Martinus and Harry L. Rinker, *Warman's Paper*, Wallace-Homestead, 1994.

Abernathy Furniture Co, Kansas City, MO, 1919, 504 pages **195.00**

Albert Jordan Co, NY, 1929, 32 pages, Agents for "Dick" and "Wusthof" brand of butcher's and cook's cutlery, diamond steels, steel hand forged cleavers, splitters, knives, 8 × 11" **28.00**

American Range Corp, Shakopee, MA, c1930, 26 pages, Sanico Ranges Presents Their "Tu-Tone" Ranges, 7½ × 10½" **18.00**

Armstrong & Co, 1909, 57 pages, firearms and accessories. **20.00**

A W Hastings & Co, Boston, MA, 1914, 78 pages, doors, windows, frames, and blinds. **30.00**

Baltimore Bargain House, Baltimore, MD, 1918, 32 pages, men, women, and children's coats **20.00**

Barnard & Leas Mfg Co, Moline, IL, 1914, 235 pages, farm equipment. .   **45.00**

Beethoven Piano & Organ, Washington, NJ, 1905, 12 pages, boudoir, parlor, and grand pianos **48.00**

Burnap & Burnap, Toledo, OH, 1900, 224 pages, dairy supplies **110.00**

The Franklin Merchandise Co, Chicago, Buyer's Guide No. 5, 352 pages, illus, 1900s, 8½ × 11″, $18.00.

Columbia Records, Jan, 1922	**15.00**
E H Scott Radio Labs, Chicago, IL, 1932, 10 pages, custom built consoles	**25.00**
Excelsior Stove Mfg Co, Quincy, IL, c1924, Supplement No. 1 to Catalog 41 of National Stove & Ranges For Gas and Electric, 8 × 10 ½″	**24.00**
Forbes Silver Plate Co, c1932, 22 pages, dinnerware	**35.00**
Frick Co, Inc, Waynesboro, PA, c1934, 20 pages, steel threshers	**36.00**
Gearhart Knitting Machine, Clearfield, PA, 1906, 48 pages	**20.00**
Hagerstown Shoe & Legging, Hagerstown, MD, 41 pages	**22.00**
Haricon Clothes, Inc, New York, NY, 1940, 8 pages, formal fashions	**12.00**
Hummer Plow Works, Springfield, OH, 1928, 24 pages, farm tools	**35.00**
Iver Johnson Arms Works, Fitchburg, MA, 1929, 20 pages, firearms	**30.00**
James Manufacturing Co, Ft Atkinson, WI, 1936, 192 pages, barn equipment	**45.00**
J I Case Threshing Machine, Racine, WI, 1927, 44 pages	**35.00**
Joseph Breck & Sons, Boston, MA, 1912, 300 pages, agricultural hardware and implements	**68.00**
Kalamazoo Stove Co, Kalamazoo, MI, 1931, 36 pages, Kalamazoo Sales Book, color illus of stones, ranges, etc., 8½ × 11″	**20.00**
Keene's Watch Store, New York, NY, 1900, 96 pages, watches and jewelry	**40.00**
Kemp & Burpee Mfg Co, Syracuse, NY, 1895, 8 pages, Kemp Manure Spreader	**18.00**
Keystone Driller Co, Beaver Falls, PA, 1925, 94 pages, well pumps	**22.00**

Knapp Brothers Mfg Co, Chicago, IL, 1934, 18 pages, wood floors	**12.00**
Leroy Plow Co, Leroy, NY, 1925, 12 pages, walking and riding plows	**15.00**
Lucius C Pardee, Chicago, IL, 1875, 64 pages, groceries and importers of wines, liquors, and cigars	**60.00**
L W Cushing and Sons, Waltham, MA, Catalogue of Weather Vanes, No. 8, 1883, Grinn Curtis Co Printers, Boston, 20 pages, 12¼ × 8¾″	**200.00**
Manchester Silver Co, Providence, RI, 1940, 48 pages, sterling silver hollow ware	**25.00**
May Hardware, 1915, 128 pages, enamel ware, tin ware, and kitchen items	**30.00**
McCormick Machinery, 1900	**75.00**
Metropolitan Sewing Machine, New York, NY, c1927, 71 pages	**12.00**
Millwork Supply Corp, Seattle, WA, 34 pages	**35.00**
Mishawaka Woolen Mfg Co, Mishawaka, IN, 1922, 40 pages, Ball brand rubber and woolen footwear	**18.00**
National Cash Register, 1902	**150.00**
National Lock Co, c1932, 196 pages, furniture hardware	**85.00**
N Shure Co, 1907, 588 pages, carnival equipment and supplies	**45.00**
Richardson Mfg Co, Worcester, MA, 1923, 24 pages, Kemp manure spreader	**30.00**
Smith American Organ Co, Boston, MA, 1882, 12 pages	**35.00**
St Johnsville Agricultural Works, 1881, 16 pages, horse-drawn plows and threshers	**46.00**
The Sahlin Mfg Co, Chicago, IL, 1918, 16 pages, corsets	**28.00**

The Larkin Plan, No. 94, 50th Anniversary, 240 pages, illus, Fall and Winter, 1925, 8 × 11″, $20.00.

McKinley Music Co, No. 25, 64 pages, sheet music, 6 × 9½", $25.00.

The Sheldon Mfg Co, New York, NY, 1894, 32 pages, gas cooking and heating stoves and water heaters... **40.00**
Victor and Bluebird Records, 1943... **20.00**
Victor Records, Nov 1912 .... **25.00**
Walker-Turner Co, Inc, Plainfield, NJ, 1936, 40 pages, power tools...... **24.00**
W E Beckman Bakers, St Louis, MO, 1936, 32 pages, baker's and confectioner's supplies **30.00**

COUNTER TOP ITEMS

History: The Country Store counter top was home to a number of items that supplemented the counters and larger display units. Attractive lithograph tin bins housed products ranging from coffee and tea to spices and tobacco. The cast iron decorative elements on cash registers turned them into stylish works of art. Coffee grinders, glass jars, paper dispensers, and string holders are just a few of the additional items that can be found.

The Country store collector competes with the advertising tin collector and specialized theme collector for much of this material. Since the vast majority was mass-produced and used in a variety of settings other than the country store, Country Store collectors place a premium on pieces with a country store provenance.

References: Henry Bartsch and Larry Sanchez, *Antique Cash Registers, 1880–1920: The Yellow Book*, published by authors, 1987; Al Bergevin, *Tobacco Tins and Their Prices*, Wallace-Homestead, 1986; Richard Crandall and Sam Robins, *The Incorruptible Cashier, Volume I: The formation of an industry, 1876–1890* (1988) and *Volume II: The Brass Era, 1888–1915* (1991), Vestal Press; Terry Friend, *Coffee Mills*, Collector Books, 1982, out-of-print.

Reproduction Manufacturer: *Coffee Grinders—* Cumberland General Store, Rte 3, Crossville, TN 38555.

Museum: John Conti Coffee Museum, Louisville, KY.

Battery Dispenser, Bright Star Flashlights, Bright Star Battery Co, Hoboken, NJ, Chicago, San Francisco, six sided, revolving, red, black, and white, 6" w, 20" h **250.00**
Bell, rect, soldered spring, tempered metal shaft **32.50**
Canister, cov
  La Paloma 5¢ Cigar, glass **30.00**
  Sunflower Tobacco, wood, label with black men dancing around tobacco container, 12" d, 11½" h **440.00**
Cash Register, National
  #7, detail adder............... **275.00**
  #35, nickel plated, allover raised ornate vine design, c1935, 17" h **500.00**
  #313, brass................... **450.00**
  #332, brass, ornate emb design, marble tray, 1913, 16½" w, 16½" h **350.00**
  #542–5E, standing model **450.00**
Cigar Cutter
  Brunhoff Mfg Co, cast iron, ornate, emb, dual arms, 7¼" h **225.00**
  Silas Pierce & Co's Nine Cigar, blue glass globe and lighter font above circular cast iron base, key wound cutter, match striking base...... **650.00**
  Sir Roger de Coverley Cigar, key wound, cast iron, coal oil lighter font and wick holders attached to ornate cutter, paper label under glass plate, 5" w, 12" d, 9½" h **250.00**
Coffee Bean Dispenser, wall mount, half-round cylinder, brass case, glass window, measuring spout attached, 16½" w, 41" h **180.00**

Cigar Cutter, Don Equestro Havana Cigars, cast metal, oval mirror, 8" w, 8½" h, $132.00. Photograph courtesy of James D. Julia, Inc.

Coffee Grinder
  Arcade, #25, wall mount **115.00**
  Cole Mfg Co, Philadelphia, PA, dou-
    ble wheel, painted blue, red, and
    gold, 10" h **375.00**
  Crescent, Rutland, VT, cast iron,
    double wheel **190.00**
  Enterprise, cast iron, wood handles
    and drawer, painted, raised gold
    lettering, stenciled floral dec, 27" h   **850.00**
Display, cigar store figure, chalkware,
  Ohio Indian chief, reclining position,
  wearing feathered headdress, hold-
  ing peace pipe, 24" w, 12" h. **185.00**
Grain Scale, brass. **180.00**
Gum Dispenser, Wrigley's Gum, re-
  volving cylinder, five sided, nickel
  plated brass cylinder, iron base, 8"
  w, 14" h **110.00**
Gum Vendor
  Gum Vendor Centasmoke, 1¢. **275.00**
  Pepsin Gum, square, glass top and
    sides, metal base, metal sign on
    top reads "Pepsin Gum Mans-
    field's Choice Has No Equal De-
    posit A Nickel," winter green and
    blood orange flavors, Automatic
    Clerk Co, Newark, NJ, early
    1900s, 15¾" h **900.00**
Jar, glass, clear
  Apothecary, pear shaped, ground
    faceted stopper, blown pontil bot-
    tom, 12" d, 22" h **190.00**
  Beich's Candy, raised letters, 14" h .   **230.00**
  Candy, vertical cylinder shape, spiral
    stopper and collar, three mold
    foot, spiral design at collar and
    foot, ground neck and stopper, 5"
    d, 22½" h **135.00**
  Dakota Candy, globular, three mold
    foot, geometric design at collar
    and foot, ground neck and stop-
    per, 8" d, 17" h **250.00**
  Planters Salted Peanuts, glass cov
    with finial, flattened front and
    back, emb lettering, c1950, 6½" h   **65.00**
Soap, Glory Cocoanut Oil Soap,
  glass, clear, metal lid, 10" h **125.00**

Match Vendor
  Advance, 1¢, glass cylinder enclos-
    ing cast iron mechanical vendor
    with four columns, 9" d, 18" h. . .   **350.00**
  Northwestern, 1¢, cast iron, ornate
    dolphin design, square, two col-
    umns, cigar cutter on base, 6" w,
    13½" h **650.00**
  Pix, 1¢, wood case, dovetailed,
    black painted cast iron front, red
    lettering, 14½" h **330.00**
Peanut Vendor, Hanse, 1¢, tapered
  globe, cast iron base, 14" h **375.00**
Popcorn Roaster, metal top-mounted
  roasting unit, wood frame, glass pane
  sides, "Popcorn" decals on sides,
  17½" sq, 26" h **200.00**
Root Beer Dispenser, oak barrel
  Richardson's Liberty Root Beer, cov,
    spigot front, multicolored foaming
    root beer mugs and man drinking
    root beer, decals on front and
    sides, 16" d, 27" h **1,075.00**
  Veribest Root Beer, cov with finial,
    metal spigot, metal claw feet, gold
    and black lettering, c1900,
    25½" h **650.00**
Scale
  Dayton, barrel cylinder, platform,
    money weight marquee, 19 × 32 ×
    20" **880.00**
  Honest Weight, brass pan, 16 × 15 ×
    12" **110.00**
  Jacobs, Brooklyn, hardware, 8" dial,
    20 lbs, scoop type weighing pan,
    suspension chains **48.00**
  National Store Specialty Co, candy,
    4 lb, nickel plated cast iron, ftd
    base, dial ornamentation, 14" h   **275.00**

Pop Corn Roaster, top roasting unit, decal glass panels, wood frame, 17½" sq, 26" h, $192.50. Photograph courtesy of James D. Julia, Inc.

Display Figure, Ohio Indian Chief, chalkware, 24" l, 12" h, $192.50. Photograph courtesy of James D. Julia, Inc.

The Micrometer, rect marble and cast iron base, The Dodge Scale Co, 11th Ave & 20th St., New York, patented March 22, 1898/July 21, 1903, 11¾" h **200.00**

The National, National Scale Corp, Chicopee Falls, MA, cast iron, painted black **165.00**

Straw Holder, glass, clear
 11" h, nickel plated top and base .. **145.00**
 11⅝ " h, notched ridges, brass top **225.00**

Syrup Dispenser
 Grape Kola Syrup, ceramic, gold leaf lettering, grape cluster dec, 9" d, 19" h.................... **650.00**
 Orange Julep, orange, white lettering, flared white base, orig pump, 13½" h **375.00**
 Prall's Root Beer, frosted glass, lift-off lid, stenciled letters, sheet metal base, four glass claw and ball feet, 19½" h **210.00**
 Ward's Lime Crush, figural lime, 10" w, 7" h **875.00**

Trade Stimulator
 Ball Gum, ornate cast white metal case, three reels, vending mechanism, c1930, 9½" w, 12" h..... **325.00**
 Horse Race, A W Hoechin, "The Honest Race," wood frame, diecut litho tin horses on revolving tin disc top, operator spins disc manually from underside of frame, patented 1887, 13" w, 11½" h..... **375.00**

PACKAGES AND TINS

History: Factory processed food revolutionized life in the second half of the 19th century. Although it would be several decades before the majority of the food that constituted an American's daily diet would be "store bought" and not "fresh," factory processed food was eagerly embraced by most Americans.

The number of factory processed food products was limited initially. Manufacturers quickly realized that packaging was the key to sales and the development of brand loyalty. The evolution of processed food also corresponded to the golden age of American lithography. The country store's shelves were lined with brightly colored lithographed paper and tin packages.

Unlike their historical antecedents whose shelves contained several dozen of each item, few Country Store collectors have more than one example of a product on their shelves. Cost is the prohibiting factor.

Although condition and scarcity are two important value considerations, the pizzazz of the piece is the most critical value element. Many packages contain images that cross over into other collecting categories, e.g., a movie star collector is as strong or stronger a competitor than a Country Store collector for a Jackie Coogan Peanut Butter pail.

References: Al Bergevin, *Drugstore Tins and Their Prices*, Wallace-Homestead, 1990; Al Bergevin, *Food and Drink Containers and Their Prices*, Wallace-Homestead, 1978; Al Bergevin, *Tobacco Tins and Their Prices*, Wallace-Homestead, 1986; Douglas Congdon-Martin, *Tobacco Tins: A Collector's Guide*, Schiffer Publishing, 1992; M. J. Franklin, *British Biscuit Tins 1868–1939: An Aspect of Decorative Packaging*, Schiffer Publishing, 1979; Vivian and Jim Karsnitz, *Oyster Cans*, Schiffer Publishing, 1993; James H. Stahl, *Key Wind Coffee Tins: A Collector's Guide to Short One Pound Coffee Cans Including Slip Lid and Pry Top Varieties*, L–W Book Sales, 1991; Robert and Harriet Swedberg, *Tins 'N Bins*, Wallace-Homestead, 1985.

Reproduction Manufacturer: The Country Lane, RD #1, Box 100 Ericsson Rd, Kennedy, NY 14747.

Box
 Bossie's Best Brand Butter, 1 lb **4.50**
 Chase's Ice Cream, cardboard, female skier illus,½ pint **12.00**
 Cross-Cut Cigarettes, cardboard, men sawing illus, eight female photo cards inside........... **82.00**
 Fairbank's Santa Claus Soap, wood, 14 × 10 × 20½".............. **250.00**
 Frank Miller's Blacking, Uncle Sam shaving on lid int., 3 × 11 × 9" **350.00**
 Hoosier Poet Brand Rolled Oats, cardboard, 4" d, 7½" h **55.00**
 Huston's Biscuits, wood, paper label, lift lid, 8 × 22 × 14" **20.00**
 Log Cabin Brownies, cardboard, cabin shape, Palmer Cox Brownies illus, 3 × 4 × 3" **50.00**

Box, Aunt Lydia's Carpet & Button Thread, American Thread Co, red, cardboard, holds 12 spools, 3¼ × 9⅜ × 2⅛ ", $8.00.

Box, Goblin Soap, Cudahy Soap Works, $8.00.

Box, Quick Mother's Oats, cardboard canister, The Quaker Oats Company, $20.00.

Magnolia Brand Condensed Milk, wood, black painted letters, 7 x 19 x 13".	30.00
Maillard Chocolates, cardboard, cloth and linen appliques	65.00
Marksman Cigars, cardboard, two men shooting guns, 3 x 5 x 1". . .	25.00
Montgomery Ward Tea, 5 lb, cardboard, tin lid, 1913	40.00
M P Holt's Cough/Candy, mahogany, dovetailed, 11" l	200.00
National Biscuit Co, polished brass front, tin logo insert.	95.00
Robinson Bros Bakery Crackers and Fine Cakes, wood, paper label, 23½ x 14 x 13".	80.00
Royal Baking Powder, wood, black lettering, paper label on end, 8½ x 14¾ x 7¾".	25.00
Seal of North Carolina Plug Cut Tobacco, wood, paper label, 2 x 5 x 4"	55.00
Slade's Mustard, wood, blue, red, and white paper labels, 2 x 20"	55.00
Smith Brothers Cough Drops, tin litho, three images, 11 x 3"	450.00

Box, National Biscuit Company Shredded Wheat, cardboard, multicolored, 14⅝ × 7¾ × 11¾", $15.00.

Tootsie Roll, cardboard	15.00
Van Houten's Cocoa, wood, paper label, stamped lettering, 4 x 14 x 10"	75.00
Vaseline, tin and wood, colorful illus, hinged, 16 x 7 x 7".	240.00
Warner's Safe Yeast, wood, dovetailed, 1890–1900, 7 x 13 x 7"	38.00
Washington Crisps Toasted Corn Flakes, patriotic oval with Washington, white lettering, red and white striped background, 9 x 6"	100.00
Pail, tin	
Armour's Peanut Butter, litho, blue and yellow, Nursery Rhyme figures, wire and bail handle, 4" h	70.00
Aurora Coffee, 1 lb, paper label, goddess with four horses	150.00
Bagley's Burley Boy, child boxer, 6½ x 4 x 5".	2,200.00
Bowes Peanut Butter, 1 lb, slip lid, bail handle	500.00
Campbell Brand Coffee, 4 lb, desert scene.	55.00
CD Kenny Coffee, milkmaid on front	200.00
Clark's Peanut Butter, moose hunter, Indian canoe, and man with dog sled, snowy mountain scene background, orig slip lid and bail handle, 3¾ x 3½".	550.00
Ellis & Helfer H.H. Tablets Confections, round, red ground, log cabin in center, red and black lettering, gold and black highlights, bail handle, c1940, 5¾" d, 6½" h	15.00
Fashion Cut Plug Tobacco, rect, elegantly dressed man and woman, old auto in background, wire handle, 7¾" w, 4½" d, 5¼" h	175.00
Forster's Peanut Butter, circular logo, slip lid, bail handle	55.00

Pail, Frontenac Peanut Butter, 12 oz, 3¾″ h, $28.00.

Foss & Deering Mustard,½ lb, black and yellow **180.00**

Giant Salted Peanuts, giant with club and circus parade illus **125.00**

Happiness Candy, 1 lb, rect, elephants on lid, outdoor animal circus around sides, "Happiness in Every Box," sgd "H. Cady," United Happiness Candy Stores, bail handle, c1925, 6″ w, 3¾″ d, 3¼″ h **300.00**

Hoody's Peanut Butter, two girls on see-saw, 3½″ d, 4″ h **125.00**

Iten Biscuit Co Animal Cookies, rect, animals on wheeled platforms parading around sides, clown and animals on lid, bail handle **55.00**

Jack and Jill Peanut Butter, product name over Jack & Jill, slip lid, bail handle. **110.00**

Kid Kandy, round, yellow ground, black and white Jackie Coogan portrait on front, policeman chasing boy on back, sgd "Henry Clive," bail handle, c1935, 3¼″ d, 3½″ h **275.00**

Light House Peanut Butter, boat and lighthouse, rope border, slip lid, bail handle **150.00**

Lipton Tea, workers picking tea. . . . **70.00**

Lovell & Covel Candies, Little Red Riding Hood and wolf illus, orig slip lid, 3″ d, 3″ h **85.00**

Master Guard Cigars, dog with pail, slip lid, bail handle **325.00**

Miners and Puddlers Smoking Tobacco, red ground, red, black, and ivory lettering, three miners at center, "B. Leidersdorf Co., Milwaukee, The American Tobacco Co. Successor, Incorporated," bail handle, c1930, 6¾″ h **70.00**

Mosemann's Peanut Butter, yellow, animals and product name, press lid **150.00**

Nigger Hair Tobacco, litho **175.00**

Ontario Brand Peanut Butter, lake with lettering, checked border, press lid. **65.00**

Parke's Newport Coffee, 5 lb. **50.00**

Pony Brand Sugar Butter, two ponies **360.00**

Red Bell Tobacco, paper label, red, white, and black **15.00**

Red Feather Peanut Butter, 1 lb, red feather image with logo **500.00**

Red Indian Tobacco, black and red, full feathered Indian logo, 8 × 4¼ × 5¼″ **650.00**

Scudder's Brownie Brand Syrup, litho, blue, yellow, and red, bail handle, 3½″ h **25.00**

Squirrel Peanut Butter, 15 lb, gold, squirrel illus **225.00**

Sultana Peanut Butter, litho, yellow, red, and black, wire handle, 4″ h **40.00**

Sunshine Kisses, round, light blue ground, yellow and orange sunrise scene, red, black, and yellow accents, bail handle, c1930, 9¾″ d, 7″ h **60.00**

Seed Packet, Danvers Half Long Carrot, Card Seed Co, Fredonia, NY, orange and green, 3¼ × 5″, $5.00.

Seed Packet, Clematis, Huth Seed Co, San Antonio, TX, purple and gold, 2¾ × 3½″, $8.00.

Sweet Mist Chewing Tobacco, children at fountain, yellow background, 6" d **100.00**
Taylor's Homemade Peanut Butter, 1 lb, white and blue illus **400.00**
Tiger Tobacco, tiger logo, red and black, 10 × 7¾ × 5½" **65.00**
Virgin Smoking Tobacco, paper label. **850.00**
White Goose Coffee, 5 lb, goose illus **550.00**
White Swan Peanut Butter, red, white, and blue **180.00**
Winner Cut Plug Smoke and Chew, rect, motor car race, wire handle, 7¾" w, 4½" d, 5¼" h **350.00**
Yum Yum Smoking Tobacco, boy smoking, blue background **100.00**
Tin
Adams Honey Chewing Gum, peacocks illus, 1 × 9 × 6" **50.00**
ADVO Gold Medal coffee, round, white, blue, red, and gold lettering and dec **35.00**
Airee Renewal Flints **18.00**
Allouette Tobacco, grouse illus, 9" d **35.00**
American Ace Coffee, 1 lb, aviator holding cup of coffee illus, key-wind lid, 5" d **120.00**
Ammen's Powder, paper label, baby's face **12.00**
Angelus Marshmallows, 5 lb, cream, gold, green, and red **30.00**
A & P Tea, oval with elderly woman, slip lid, 1880s, 11 × 7 × 7" **175.00**
Arco Coffee, 1 lb, key-wind lid **45.00**
Bagshaw's Brilliantone Phonograph Needles. **20.00**
Bar B Q Coffee, 1 lb, slip lid **40.00**
Barbour's Salted Peanuts, 10 lb, red, yellow, and black letters, slip lid **150.00**
Battleship Coffee, 3 lb, battleship illus, c1920 . . . . **50.00**
Betteryet Salted Peanuts, 5 lb, orange and blue, two boys holding giant peanuts, press lid. **375.00**
Blue Ribbon Tea, 3 lb, red, green, yellow, and black **65.00**
Bone, Eagle & Co Cough Drops, slip lid, 8 × 5" **65.00**
Bonnette Coffee, 1 lb, Dutch children at table, white and black, 4¼" d, 5¾" h **220.00**
Brach's Candies of Quality, 5 lbs, square, gold, colorful candies on two sides, factory scene other two sides, c1940, 4½" sq, 10⅛" h **60.00**
Bridal Brand Coffee, 1 lb, oval, man with donkeys and harbor scene, 4¾ × 5¾ × 3½" **250.00**
Buster Brown All Spice, paper label, press lid. **25.00**
Canova Coffee, 1 lb, paper label . . . **35.00**

Tin, Bon Ami Powder, 12 oz, $16.00.

Clubb's Perique Mixture Tobacco, club logo with three portraits, 4 × 7 × 2" **35.00**
Colgate's Baby Talc, oval with baby illus, c1910 . . . . **85.00**
Columbia Ideal 200 Phonograph Needles. **15.00**
Cottage Peanut Butter, yellow, blue, red, and white **45.00**
Countess Cookies, 1 lb, children playing **80.00**
Country Club Coffee, 1 lb, clubhouse illus **80.00**
Crescent Peanuts, 10 lb, two children carrying crescent, blue, white, and red, 8½ × 9¾" **175.00**
Darby's Swan Tolu, black and red, 2 × 4 × 4" **35.00**
Dead Shot Gun Powder, MA Powder Works, rect, red, paper label, dog lying beside rifle, 4" h **20.00**
Dixie Kid Cut Plug, litho, hinged lid with handle, black boy on cotton images on front and back, 7¾" l **175.00**
Djer Kiss Talc **12.00**
Eagle Brand Dry Cleaner, American Shoe Polish Co, 5 × 3" **125.00**
E–J Workers Coffee, 1 lb, scrolled design **75.00**
Ex-Cel-Cis Talc **15.00**
Express Tobacco, 1 lb, round, railroad engine and cars, 8¼" d **350.00**
Fort Pitt Coffee, 3 lb, fort illus, press lid, 6" d, 8" h **350.00**
F W McNess Fine Confections, 3 lbs, square, blue and white plaid ground, red lettering, dish of candy, Furst-McNess Co, Freeport, IL, c1930, 4" sq, 7⅝" h **12.00**
Game Fine Cut Tobacco, orange and black lettering, 11½" w, 8" d, 6½" h **285.00**
Gibson's Lozenge, floral dec, 9 × 6 × 6" **250.00**

Gold Dust Scouring Cleanser, Gold Dust twins illus, paper label **65.00**

Grand Union Hard Candies, 5 lbs, rect, red ground, blue bands at top and bottom, blue and white lettering, Grand Union Tea Co, Brooklyn, NY, c1930, 6" w, 8⅝ " h . . . **27.50**

Gumbert's Cream Dessert, 8 lb **50.00**

Happiness Candy Stores, animals in sporting events, slip lid **80.00**

Harvard Jumbo Peanuts, 10 lb, 10 × 8" **60.00**

Hero Coffee, 1 lb, octagonal, hero illus, wood knob slip lid, 4¼" d, 7" h **175.00**

Hoadley Blood Orange Pellets, square, red ground, black lettering and orange, E J Hoadley, 236 Asylum St. Hartford, Conn.," c1930, 5" w, 8½" h **50.00**

Honeysuckle Tobacco, honeysuckle blossom with bees illus, slip lid, 5 × 5" **110.00**

Hope Denture Powder **35.00**

Hoyt's Selected Sweets, 5 lbs, round, black and white grid ground, boy holding candy jar, girl holding hand out, Howard H Hoyt Candy Co, Chicago, raised lettering on lid, 1920s, 5" d, 9¾" h **70.00**

Huntley and Palmer Biscuit, pocket book form, emb lizard. **65.00**

Ivins Big Show Cookies, drum shape, circus parade around sides, cloth strap, 7¼" d, 3¾" h **12.00**

Jewel Tea Orange Spice **15.00**

Kemp Golden Glow Peanuts, 10 lb, label with logo **45.00**

Lewis's Family Size Teaflake Biscuits, litho, 9 × 6½" **25.00**

Libby's Corned Beef **45.00**

Log Cabin Syrup, log cabin shape. . **55.00**

Lower Canada Maple Syrup, maple leaves and portrait, red and black **115.00**

Tin, Huyler's Cocoa, Irving Place, NY, yellow-brown ground, black lettering, ½ lb, 2⅝ × 2⅝ × 4¼", $12.00.

Luden's Menthol Cough Drops, 8 × 6 × 4" **50.00**

Luzianne Coffee, red, handle, 3 lb, 1928 . . . . **90.00**

Mammoth Salted Nuts, 10 lb, black and white, elephant illus, 11 × 8" **125.00**

Manhattan Sugar Cones, 20 lb, round, cone and name **65.00**

Maryland Club Tobacco, circle with building illus, orange, blue, and white, 3½ × 4" **350.00**

Matlby's Cocoanut **55.00**

Mohican Coffee, 1 lb, slip lid **200.00**

Monarch Cocoa, sample size **65.00**

Moonlight Mellos Candy, angel dec **35.00**

Nabob Baking Powder, cake with product name **10.00**

Ne-Gro Cleanser, man seated on ledge, press lid **140.00**

Normodust, Normodust girl illus. . . **15.00**

Northpole Tobacco, North Pole scene, red, white, and blue, 6 × 6 × 4" **330.00**

Oak Hill Coffee, 1 lb, cup of coffee in large oval **40.00**

Old Fire Side Tea, couple by hearth, slip lid, 5 × 5 × 3" **10.00**

Old Glory Tobacco, pocket size, rect, eagle with shield surrounded by ornate filigree on lid, two people discussing benefits of chewing tobacco on bottom, Spaulding & Merrick, Chicago, IL, 3½" l, 2½" w **275.00**

O-So-Good Coffee, red, white, and blue, 10" h **145.00**

Pedro Tobacco, red and black designs, orange-yellow background, hinged lid, 7½" l **175.00**

Peerless Maid Confections, 5 lbs, square, yellow, red and white candy cane striped corners, colorful candies on two sides, lady with parasol other two sides, c1940, 4½" sq, 10¼" h **45.00**

Pheasant Pure Lard, paper label, two pheasants and lettering **140.00**

Planter's Novola Brand Peanut Oil, 5 gal, images on four sides, 14" h **70.00**

Postmaster Smokers Cigar, orange, white lettering, 5" h, 5¼" w **30.00**

Power Candy Mineralized, round, green ground, white lettering, black and white photo illus of boy standing in front of house, "Made at Granger Farms Buskirk, N.Y., U.S.A.," c1930, 3¾" d, 6¼" h. . . **40.00**

Quaker Maid Golden Table Syrup, maid illus **60.00**

Reception Java Mocha, litho **100.00**

Red Feather Coffee, large center feather. **65.00**

Red Seal Peanut Butter, litho, nursery
rhymes **55.00**
Royal Crown Pomade **12.00**
Runkel Brothers Chocolate, 5 lb . . .   **125.00**
Schepp's Coconut, monkey with let-
tering. **70.00**
Sharp's Toffee, barrel shape, emb   **105.00**
Silvertone 200 Phonograph Need-
les. **20.00**
Staples Prepared Wax, beehive illus,
3" d. **8.00**
Star Maid Salted Peanuts, 10 lb. . . .   **25.00**
Stillboma Oriental Polish, deer illus,
6 × 2" **10.00**
Sultana Spice, round, yellow, black
lettering. **20.00**
Sunshine Biscuit, litho, girl, 12" h   **20.00**
Supreme Dental Powder **12.00**
Towle's Log Cabin Syrup, log cabin
shape **55.00**

Victrola   Tungstone   Phonograph
Needles. **18.00**
Walter   Baker   &   Co   Cocoa,   sq,
Chocolate girl, ornate pattern on
sides, screw lid, 6 × 3". **75.00**
Williams Baby Talc, litho, blue and
yellow, red accents, images on
both sides, 5" h **90.00**
Winner   Cut   Plug,   racing   scene,
brown and blue lettering, 4" h . . .   **60.00**
Yankee Boy Tobacco, red and white
check design, boy wearing base-
ball uniform, 3½ × 4" **550.00**
Yankee Doodle Dandy Candy, 8 oz,
drum shaped, children parading
around sides, cloth strap, Floriana
Candy   Co,   Philadelphia,   PA,
1920s, 5⅝ " d, 2⅜ " h. **45.00**
Zanol Baby Mine Talc, baby with
blocks **140.00**

FOLK ART

History: Although there was a folk art consciousness among a few collectors and museum professionals prior to the 1960s, it was largely ignored by most collectors and dealers. All that changed in the late 1960s and early 1970s as museum exhibits and other events leading up to the celebration of the American Bicentennial seized upon folk art as the popular art of the American people.

The definition of what constitutes folk art is still being vigorously debated among collectors, dealers, museum curators, and scholars. Some want to confine folk art to non-academic, hand made objects. Others are willing to include manufactured material. In truth, the term is used to cover objects ranging from crude drawings by obviously untalented children to academically trained artists' paintings of "common" people and scenery.

Since this book wishes to avoid this brouhaha altogether, it has adopted the widest definition possible. If one or more groups within the field have designed a category or item as part of the folk art movement, it is listed. Since the Country community tends to emphasize the primitive, naive, and painted rather than the more formal, these pieces are more heavily weighted in the listings.

A major development in the folk art renaissance of the 1970s was the revival of the folk art craftsperson. Across the United States individuals and manufacturers began to copy pieces from the past, often using the same tools and techniques to produce them as was done originally. You will find more craftspersons and manufacturers listed in this section of the book than any other.

Collect pieces from individuals and manufacturers who are introducing new design and form in the vocabulary of their chosen category, rather than on those who merely copy the past. These pieces have potential long term value. While exact copies have immediate and decorative value, they will be the least sought examples in the future.

Because so many objects are being copied exactly, collectors and dealers have been fooled by them. This resulted in a slowing down of the folk art market in the late 1980s. Reproductions, copycats, and fantasy folk art pieces continue to grow in numbers. Until all these forms are documented with detailed information as to how to distinguish them from the original, the folk art market will remain a perilous place.

In addition to being plagued with the problem of confusing contemporary copies, the folk art market is subject to hype and manipulation. Weather vanes, cigar store figures, and quilts are just a few of the categories that were actively hyped and manipulated in the 1970s and 80s. Neophyte collectors are encouraged to read Edie Clark's "What Really Is Folk Art?" in the December 1986 *Yankee*. Clark's article provides a refreshingly honest look at the folk art market.

Finally, the folk art market is extremely trendy and fickle. What is hot today can become cool and passé tomorrow. Late 19th century quilts are cool, 20th century quilts such as the Double Wedding Ring are hot. Whirligigs are cool, painted firemen's hats are hot.

Finally, in the 1980s, the American market began to look seriously at European material that closely resembled American folk art forms. Much was brought into the United States and sold. By the second and third transaction, many European pieces wound up with an American attribution. Today's folk art collector needs a thorough background in both American and European folk art to collect effectively.

All in all, collecting folk art is not for the faint-of-heart or the cautious investor.

References: Kenneth L. Ames, *Beyond Necessity: Art In The Folk Tradition,* W. W. Norton, 1977; Robert Bishop and Judith Rieter Weissman, *Folk Art: The Knopf Collectors' Guides To American Antiques,* Alfred A. Knopf, 1983; Jean Lipman and Alice Winchester, *The Flowering of American Folk Art 1776–1876,* Penguin Books, 1977; Henry Niemann and Helaine Fendelman, *The Official Identification and Price Guide To American Folk Art,* House of Collectibles, 1988; Beatrix T. Rumford and Carolyn J. Weekley, *Treasures of American Folk Art from The Abby Aldrich Rockefeller Folk Art Center,* Little, Brown and Company, 1989.

Collectors' Club: Folk Art Society of America, PO Box 17041, Richmond, VA 23226.

Periodicals: *Folk Art,* Museum of American Folk Art, 61 W 62nd St, New York, NY 10023; *Folk Art Finder,* 117 N Main St, Essex, CT 06426.

Museums: Abby Aldrich Rockefeller Folk Art Center, Williamsburg, VA; Boston Museum of Fine Arts, Boston, MA; Cooper-Hewitt Museum, New York, NY; Crafts & Folk Art Museum, Los Angeles, CA; Fruitlands Museum, Harvard, MA; Landis Valley Farm Museum, Lancaster, PA; Museum of American Folk Art, New York, NY; Museum of Early Southern Decorative Arts, Winston-Salem, NC; Museum of International Folk Art, Sante Fe, NM.

Reproduction Manufacturers: The Calico Corner, 513 E Bowman St, South Bend, IN 46613; Conewago Junction, 805 Oxford Rd, New Oxford, PA 17350; Country Bouquet, PO Box 200, Kellogg, MN 55945; Country Loft, 1506 South Shore Park, Hingham, MA 02043; Country Wicker, 2238–D Bluemound Rd, Waukesha, WI 53186; Folk Art Emporium, 3591 Forest Haven Lane, Chesapeake, VA 23321; Good Things, PO Box 2452, Chino, CA 91708; Gray's Attic, Box 532, Manson, IA 50563; Honk 'N Quax, Ltd, PO Box 15155, 1500 Main St, Springfield, MA 01115; Mulberry Magic, PO Box 62, Ruckersville, VA 22968; The Painted Pony, 8392 West M–72, Traverse City, MI 49684; Southern Manner, Inc, 106 N Trade St, Matthews, NC 28106; Traditions, RD #4, Box 191, Hudson, NY 12534; The Vine and Cupboard, PO Box 309, George Wright Rd, Woolwich, ME 04579; Woodbee's, RR #1, Poseyville, IN 47633; Woodpenny's, 27 Hammatt St, Epswich, MA 01938.

CARVINGS

History: Carving and whittling were common pastimes in rural America. In many cases, the end product was a whimsical item or simply a pile of shavings (skills varied tremendously).

Figures, especially those used for store displays and ship's mastheads, were professionally done. Better local carvers developed a regional reputation. Unfortunately, few carvers trained a succes-

sor. Nonetheless, earlier works have influenced later generations, e.g., Schimmel's influence on Mountz.

Much of the "folk" carving in modern collections dates from the last half of the 19th through the first half of the 20th centuries. Age is not as critical a factor in this sector as in other "folk art" categories; identification of the carver is. Since many of the pieces are unsigned, identification is done primarily by attribution.

Many attributions are loosely made and should be questioned.

Modern folklorists, such as Bishop and Hemphill, have been instrumental in the identification and promotion of contemporary carvers. Recent auction results have proven that much of the value attributed to these pieces is speculative.

References: Robert Bishop, *American Folk Sculpture*, E. P. Dutton, 1974; Jack T. Ericson, *Folk Art in America: Painting and Sculpture*, Mayflower Books, 1979; Herbert W. Hemphill, *Folk Sculpture U.S.A.*, Universe Books, 1976; Jean Lipman, *American Folk Art in Wood, Metal, and Stone*, Dover Publications, 1972; Richard and Rosemarie Machmer, *Just For Nice: Carving and Whittling Magic of Southeastern Pennsylvania*, Historical Society of Berks County (PA), 1991; George H. Meyer, *American Folk Art Canes: Personal Sculpture*, Sandringham Press in association with Museum of American Folk Art and University of Washington Press, 1992; John J. Stoudt, *Early Pennsylvania Arts and Crafts*, A. S. Barnes and Co., 1964.

Reproduction Craftspersons: Eileen and Dennis Aresta, Arestacraft, Brady Lane, Plymouth, MA 02360; John Jeffrey Barto, PO Box 127, Kintnersville, PA 18930; Jonathan K. Bastian, Pennsylvania German Woodcarvings, Rte 2, Box 240, Robesonia, PA 19551; Ed Boggis, Woodcarver, Old Church Rd, Box 387, Claremont, NH 03743; Connie Carlton, Shaving Horse Crafts, 1049 Rice Rd, Lawrenceburg, KY 40342; William J. Cooey, 248 Van Horn Rd, Milton, FL 32570; Sande & Steven Elkins, S. Elkins Folk Art, RR 1, Box 147A, Loudon, TN 37774; Jonathan Graves, 13708 Kenwanda Dr, Snohomish, WA 98290; Christopher Gurshin, Itinerant Painter, PO Box 616, Newburyport, MA 01950; Bill Henry, 111 N Tampa Ln, Oak Ridge, TN 37830; Sherman Hensal, The Lion & The Lamb, Box 278, Sharon Center, OH 44274; Jay V. Irwin, Wood Carver, RR 2, Box 354, Auburn Rd, Avondale, PA 19311; Paul W. Jeffries, 1158 Putnam Blvd, Wallingford, PA 19086; Thomas A Kloss, 321 Keneagy Hill Rd, Paradise, PA 17562; Alan Kohr, 144 Krause Rd, RD 2, Schwenksville, PA 19473; Christopher LaMontagne, 900 Joslin Rd, Harrisville, RI 02830; Donna Long, 1 Third St, Fair Haven, VT 05743; Eleanor Meadowcroft, 25 Flint St, Salem, MA 01970; Don Mounter, Rte 1, Box 54, Fayette, MO 65248; John T. Nicholas & Son, 704 N Michigan Ave, Howell, MI 48843; Clark Pearson, 21515 Raymond Rd, Marysville, OH 43040; Donna H. Pierce, 522 Meadowpark La, Media, PA 19063; Bush Prisby, Prisby's Country, 388 Ingomar St, Pittsburgh, PA 15216; Les Ramsay, Linden Tree Gallery, 137 S Broad St, Grove City, PA 16127; Vaughn & Stephanie Rawson, The Whimsical Whittler, 1745 W Columbia Rd, Mason, MI 48854; Philip A. Sbraccia, 174 Emerald St, Maiden, MA 02148; S. Arthur Shoemaker, 2025 Plymouth Rd, Lancaster, PA

17603; Tom Smith, Olde Kantucke Wolken Stik's Inc, 1280 Old U.S. 60, Frankfort, KY 40601; Daniel G. Strawser, 2741 Buckner Rd, Thompson Station, TN 37179; Randy & Pam Tate, Knot in Vane, 805 N 11th St, DeKalb, IL 60115; Carolyn E Taylor, 300 Artillery Rd, Yorktown, VA 23692; Roberta Taylor, 1717 Maywood Dr, West Lafayette, IN 47906; Criss Zimmerman, RD 4, Box 2268, Lebanon, PA 17042.

Reproduction Manufacturers: Bay Built Ship Models, 227 Second St, Lewes, DE 19958; Big Sky Carvers, P O Box 507, 308 S Railroad, Manhattan, MT 59741; Country Corner Collectibles, PO Box 422, Pitman, NJ 08071; Country House, 5939 Trails End, Three Oaks, MI 49128; Faith Mountain Country Fare, Main St, Box 199, Sperryville, VA 22740; Flying Pig Artworks, PO Box 474, Milford, MI 48042; J J Decoy Co, P O Box 60, Fairfield, ME 04937; Lace Wood 'N Tyme, 6496 Summerton, Shepherd, MI 48883; Lamb and Lanterns, 902 N Walnut St, Dover, OH 44622; Maggie MacKenzie's, PO Box 148, Beloit, KS 67420; The Magic Cottage, Inc, PO Box 438, East Meadow, NY 11554; Maine Woods, Main St, PO Box 270, Bowdoinham, ME 04008; Meadow Craft, PO Box 100, Rose Hill, NC 28458; On the Countryside, PO Box 722, Forsyth, MO 65653; My Home Towne, Snyder Marketing Group, 49 Jonathan St, Hagerstown, MD 21740; Noah's Ark, P O Box 1050, Salisbury, MD 21802-1050; Our Home, Articles of Wood, 666 Perry St, Vermilion, OH 44089; Ozark Cottage Crafts, PO Box 157, Galena, MO 65656; Pesta's Country Charm, 300 Standard Ave, Mingo Junction, OH 43938; Plantation Characters, Box 896, Painesville, OH 44077; Schopfungen, 71 South St, Pittsford, NY 14534; A Special Blend of Country, RD #1, Box 56, Fabius, NY 13063; Wesson Trading Co, PO Box 669984, Marietta, GA 30066.

Reproduction Alert: Fakes—pieces deliberately meant to deceive—abound. In the early 1970s, I (Harry L. Rinker) visited a York County carver who was aging a garage full of Schimmel copies. I believe several of these have entered the market in the intervening years as Schimmel originals.

The August, 1991, issue of *Maine Antique Digest* contained David Hewitt's "Jacob Joyner: Mississippi Wood Carver or The Man Who Never Was?" An entire school of carvings, sold by some of America's most prominent folk art dealers and purchased by some of America's leading collectors, turned out to be forgeries. There are many who question whether the Joyner incident is an isolated example.

Bank, nodding black man wearing high
    hat, seated on box, dark paint, 8½" h   **45.00**
Cigar Store Figure, painted
    Indian Brave, standing, right hand
      raised above head, left hand holding knife, wearing single feather

headband, bear tooth necklace and arm bracelet, buckskin pants and moccasins, blanket draped over shoulder, trapezoidal platform 775.00

Indian Maiden, standing, raised right hand holding bunch of cigars, wearing feathered headdress, simple belted dress, and moccasins, square platform 600.00

Figure

Baltimore Oriole, painted, chips, repair to bill, 6½" l 125.00

Bird on Nest, natural finish, base sgd "David Arther Myers," 5¾" l 75.00

Blue Jay

Balsa, twig base, orig paint, wire feet, bead eyes, 3¾" h 45.00

Carved wood body, tin wings, orig paint, wire legs, loose wire feet, beak glued, 8¾" l 105.00

Cardinal, balsa, twig base, orig paint, loose wire feet, bead eyes, 4¾" h 45.00

Chain Gang with Guard, convicts in striped prison uniforms marching single file behind guard, guard carrying rifle, convicts include Indian, Chinese, black man, Mexican, and white man, first four convicts carry sledgehammers, last man pushing wheelbarrow and shovel, oblong platform, sgd "C. Oakley," 1940s 550.00

Cow, old black paint, 3⅛ " h 100.00

Eagle

42" w, attributed to John Hales Bellamy (1836–1914,) Kittery Point, ME, painted, some retouch, losses 5,500.00

26" w, 24" h, outstretched wings, gilt painted, old repairs, age cracks, 19th C 225.00

King Fisher, painted, imperfections, late 19th C, 20" h 825.00

Lamb, carved, walnut, alligatored finish, rect base, 6½" l 325.00

Lion, old brown finish, 5¾" l 175.00

Man's Head, vestiges of paint dec, iron support mount, repaired, 19th C, 24" h 450.00

Cigar Store Figure, American Indian Maiden, polychrome painted brown and gray fringed dress with beaded necklace, black moccasins, right arm restored, 19th C, 69" h, $4,675.00. Photograph courtesy of Butterfield & Butterfield.

Peafowl, nodder, polychrome paint, 5" h 75.00

Robin, painted, chips, repair to bill, 8" l 125.00

Soldier, painted blue, black, white, mustard, and red, articulated arms, some paint wear, chips, 19th C, 17" h 8,250.00

Squirrel, sitting on stump, three color brown stain, small edge chips, 20th C, 5" h 25.00

Two Birds, perched facing in stylized trees, rect base, orig polychrome dec, contemporary, 7" h 40.00

Uncle Sam, standing, white top hat, white stars on blue swallowtail coat, flying tails, pink vest, striped pants, black shoes, gray stirrups, holding fabric American flag, yellow pyramid base, late 19th/early 20th C, 17¼" h 12,100.00

Woman

6⅛ " h, blue dress, orig polychrome paint 25.00

11½" h, glass eyes, old paint 95.00

16¾" h, glass eyes, polychrome paint 100.00

20½" l, carved, glass marble eyes 140.00

Woodpecker, balsa, wood base, orig paint, wire feet, bead eyes, loose feet, 6" h 80.00

Wren, balsa, twig base, orig paint, wire feet, bead eyes, 4½" h 45.00

Puzzle Cane, walnut, ball and trap handle, entwining tapered shaft, 35" l, $100.00.

Figure, man, arms raised above head, painted, 19th C, 38½" h, estimated price $3,000.00–5,000.00. Photograph courtesy of Skinner, Inc.

Figurehead, painted, figure of young woman, right arm across chest to left shoulder, facing upward, some losses, repainted, found on Martha's Vineyard Island, mid 19th C, 47½" h **16,500.00**

Model

Nautical

Cased Model, *Flying Cloud of Boston,* painted wood, fully rigged, labeled "by E. F. Tanner," 20th C, 91" l, 14" d, 29⅝ " h, glass case **3,190.00**

Class Model for Pond Racing, New England, early 20th C *M.M.F. Emileo,* painted hull, paper label on cradle "M.M.F. Emileo on Lowell St., Peabody, Mass," 50" l, 76" h **1,540.00**

Display Model

Brig *Truxton,* painted, imperfections, 20th C, 16" l **525.00**

Whale Boat, painted, fully rigged, sails, tubs of line and harpoons, mounted on display stand, 20th C, 18½" **935.00**

Scale Model, two masted Pinky, rigged, 20th C, 21" l **470.00**

Railroad, engine and tender on tracks, "Cornwall" name plate, painted, late 19th, early 20th C, 40" l, 17½" h **1,100.00**

Pilot House Figure, Columbia, half round, relief carved, golden tresses, corkscrew curls, draped robes, left hand holding gold sphere, right hand

holding elongated US shield, stars and stripes on shield, pendant spray of wheat sheaves at her side, mid 19th C, 22½" w, 64" h **24,200.00**

Plaque

15" w, 8½" h, brass, hinged, painted and gilded, Massachusetts state seal **660.00**

44½" l, carved eagle, gold paint, red, white, and blue shield, 20th C . . . **600.00**

Puzzle Cane

33½" l

Rifle shape, butt handle, openwork carved flat shaft contains two balls, incised hunting dog, late 19th C **275.00**

Snake, flat headed, incised and chip carved scales, red glass eyes, late 19th C **495.00**

37" l

Ball handle, openwork cage contains second ball, relief carved snake entwining tapered shaft, incised leaf carving on base, dated 1861 . . . . **325.00**

Stars and Stripes motif, cut and peeled bark technique, incised stars, stripes, herringbones, and diamonds, late 19th C **450.00**

Walking Stick

31" l, round knob, diamond design shaft **35.00**

32¾" l, pine, bone, ebonized finish **40.00**

34" l, shaft carved with serpent with man's head, identified as "Rockeffer," figures of men identified as "the people" over figures of cattle, train car, and chicken laying egg, inscription "Beef trust" and "profit," another male figure identified as "Lawson" at serpent's back, flag inscribed "frenzied finance," inscribed name "W. H. Lawson," deer foot handle, c1905 **2,310.00**

Adam and Eve motif, 1866 nickel 3¢ piece set in top **225.00**

Whimsey, polychrome paint, two carved wooden bead handles, center cage with free rolling bead **75.00**

DECOYS

History: Carved wooden decoys, used to lure ducks and geese to the hunter, have become widely recognized as an indigenous American folk art form in the past several years.

Many decoys are from the 1880–1930 period when commercial gunners commonly hunted using rigs of several hundred decoys. Many fine carvers also worked through the 1930s and 1940s.

The value of a decoy is based on several factors: (1) fame of the carver, (2) quality of the carving, (3) species of wild fowl-the most desirable are herons, swans, mergansers, and shorebirds, and (4) condition of the original paint.

The inexperienced collector should be aware of several facts. The age of a decoy, per se, is usually of no importance in determining value. Since very few decoys were ever signed, it will be quite difficult to attribute most decoys to known carvers. Anyone who has not examined a known carver's work will be hard pressed to determine if the paint on one of his decoys is indeed original.

Repainting severely decreases a decoy's value. In addition, there are many fakes and reproductions on the market and even experienced collectors are occasionally fooled.

Decoys listed here are of average wear unless otherwise noted.

References: Joel Barber, Wild Fowl Decoys, Dover Publications, 1954; Joe Engers (general editor), The Great Book of Wildfowl Decoys, Thunder Bay Press, 1990; Henry A. Fleckenstein, Jr., American Factory Decoys, Schiffer Publishing; Ronald J. Fritz, Michigan's Master Carver Oscar W. Peterson, 1887–1951, Aardvark Publications, 1988; Bob and Sharon Huxford, Collector's Guide to Decoys, Vol. I (1990), Vol. II (1992), Collector Books; Gene and Linda Kangas, Decoys, Collector Books, 1991; Gene and Linda Kangas, Decoys: A North American Survey, Hillcrest Publications, 1983; Linda and Gene Kangas, Collector's Guide to Decoys, Wallace-Homestead, 1992; Art, Brad and Scott Kimball, The Fish Decoy, Aardvark Publications, Inc., 1986; Carl F. Luckey, Collecting Antique Bird Decoys: An Identification & Value Guide, Books Americana, 1983; William Mackey, Jr., American Bird Decoys, E. P. Dutton, 1965.

Periodicals: Decoy Hunter Magazine, 901 North 9th, Clinton, IN 47842; Decoy Magazine, PO Box 277, Burtonsville, MD 20866; Sporting Collector's Monthly, RW Publishing, PO Box 305, Camden, DE 19934; Wildfowl Art, Ward Foundation, 909 S Schumaker Dr, Salisbury, MD 21801.

Reproduction Craftspersons: Frank O'Brien Decoys, PO Box 522, Bryn Athyn, PA 19009; K Kautz & Sons, RR 1, Box 156B, Hartland, VT 05048; James Long, 1 Third St, Fair Haven, VT 05743; Richard Morgan, The Painted Bird, 770 Route 47, Woodbury, CT 06798.

Reproduction Manufacturers: Back Bay Decoys, 684 Princess Anne Rd, Virginia Beach, VA 23457; Briere Design, 229 N Race St, Statesville, NC 28677; Lamplighter Antiques, 615 Silver Bluff Rd, Aiken, SC 29801; McClanahan Country, 217 Rockwell Rd, Wilmington, NC 28405; Maine Woods, Main St, P O Box 270, Bowdoinham, ME 04008; Tidewater Shorebirds, 2818 Lancelot Dr, Baton Rouge, LA 70816; Unfinished Business, PO Box 246, Wingate, NC 28174.

Black Duck
  Hendrickson, Gene, NY, orig paint, good condition **125.00**
  Sullivan, Gene, orig paint, carved Salisbury style **385.00**
  Updike, John, orig paint, worn **110.00**
Bluebill, Addie Nichol, Smith Falls, Ontario, drake, professionally restored **275.00**
Blue Goose, unknown maker, MI, good detail, orig paint, glass eyes, mid 20th C, 24½" l **225.00**
Bluewing Teal
  Serigny, Joseph, LA, drake, hand carved cypress root, raised detail and tail feathers, orig paint **210.00**
  Spiron, Charles, Winston Salem, NC, hen, carved, raised detail, branded name on bottom **200.00**
Brandt
  Corliss, Rube, old repaint, good condition **175.00**
  Predmore, Cooper, NJ, repainted, replaced bill **90.00**
Broadbill
  Barnegat Bay Decoy Company, Point Pleasant, NJ, drake, orig paint . . .   **210.00**
  Corliss, Rube, drake, orig paint, gouges to body **60.00**
Buffleheads, pr, Jim VanBrunt, orig paint, glass eyes, labeled "Carved by Jim VanBrunt, Setauket, N.Y., gunned over Long Island Sound in the 1950s," 8½" l **350.00**
Canada Goose
  Attributed to Lowell Strayer, Monroe, MI, alert posture, cork body wood head, glass eyes, orig paint, mid 20th C, 21" l **55.00**
  Soukup, Phil, northern OH, swimming posture, cork body, wood head, glass eyes, orig paint, 21" l **180.00**
Coot
  Attributed to Bill Goenne, glass eyes, worn paint, 11½" l **85.00**
  Unknown Maker, glass eyes, orig paint, 11¼" l **100.00**

Broadbill Drake, Mason Decoy Co, Detroit, MI, standard grade, glass eye, $185.00.

Left: Canada Goose, Ward Brothers, Crisfield, MD, working decoy, c1930, $1,550.00; right: Duck, Sam Barnes, Havre de Grace, MD, c1898, $350.00. Photograph courtesy of Freeman Fine Arts of Philadelphia.

Curlew, Elmer Crowell, MA, turned neck, orig paint, maker's stamp on base 16,500.00
Goldeneye, Orel LaBoeuf, Quebec, drake, branded on bottom, two fine hairline cracks 650.00
Goose, canvas, straw stuffed. 100.00
Green Winged Teal, D W Nichol, Ontario, mated pair, orig condition . . . 1,325.00
Loon, Byron Bruffee, orig paint, name stamped on base 325.00
Mallard
   Mason Decoy Company, drake, premiere grade, orig paint 610.00
   Soukup, Phil, northern OH, set of six, swimming posture, cork body, wood head with hunched neck, glass eyes, orig paint, three hens, three drakes, orig canvas carryall, 15" l 275.00
   Verdin, Joseph, LA, drake, hand carved cypress root 225.00
Merganser
   Hamilton, John, drake, hooded, hollow and hand carved, inletted weight bottom, branded on bottom 125.00
   Sprankle, James, NY, drake, hooded, orig blue ribbon carving, sgd on bottom 200.00
   Unknown Maker, glass eyes, orig paint, glued crack in neck, minor wear, 17½" l 500.00
Owl, confidence decoy, papier mâché, four glass eyes, marked "Souler Swicher, Decatur, Illinois, Pat. Pen," orig paint, 14¼" h. 105.00
Pintail, Lou Reineri, VA, drake, flying posture, c1960s 325.00
Redbreasted Merganser
   Conklin, Harry, NJ, mated pair, orig paint, some exposed wood 1,210.00
   Meekens, Alvin, VA, mated pair, orig paint, shot scarring and bare wood. 385.00
   Unknown Maker, drake, bare wood   825.00

Redhead, unknown maker, Maumee River Bay area, drake, tack eyes, inset head, worn working repaint, neck repairs, 13" l 75.00
Sanderling, Elmer Crowell, MA, preening posture, raised wing carving, orig paint, maker's stamp under base . . . 4,400.00
Widgeon, Wildfowler Decoy Company, CT, drake, orig paint, normal wear 150.00
Wood Duck, drake, miniature, glass eyes, orig paint, 8" l 110.00

FRAKTUR

History: Fraktur, the calligraphy associated with the Pennsylvania Germans, is named for the elaborate first letter found in many of the hand drawn examples. Throughout its history, printed, partially printed-hand drawn, and fully hand drawn works existed side by side. Frakturs often were made by the school teachers or ministers living in rural areas of Pennsylvania, Maryland, and Virginia. Many artists are unknown.

   Fraktur exists in several forms—geburts and taufschein (birth and baptismal certificates), vorschrift (writing example, often with alphabet), haus sagen (house blessing), bookplates, bookmarks, rewards of merit, illuminated religious text, valentines, and drawings. Although collected for decoration, the key element in fraktur is the text.

   Fraktur prices rise and fall along with the American folk art market. The key market place is Pennsylvania, the Middle Atlantic states, and Ontario, Canada.

References: Michael S. Bird, *Ontario Fraktur: A Pennsylvania-German Folk Tradition in Early Canada*, M. F. Feheley Publishers, 1977; Donald A. Shelley, *The Fraktur-Writings of Illuminated Manuscripts of the Pennsylvania Germans*, Pennsylvania German Society, 1961; Frederick S. Weiser and Howell J. Heaney (compilers), *The Pennsylvania German Fraktur of the Free Library* *of Philadelphia*, two volume set, Pennsylvania German Society, 1976.

Museum: The Free Library of Philadelphia, Philadelphia, PA.

Reproduction Craftspersons: Sally Greene Bunce, 4826 Mays Ave, Reading, PA 19606; Jacquelyn Trone Butera, Colonial Yard, 500 S Park Ave, Audubon, PA 19403; Terence J Graham, Box 19, Zieglerville, PA 19492; Ceil Cox & Kathy Hendrix, Primitives 'n' Paper, 4932 Baylor Dr, Charlotte, NC 28210; Sandra K Gilpin, 509 Baer Ave., Hanover, PA 17331; Mary Lou Harris, Aunt Sukey's Choice, 514 E Main St, Annville, PA 17003; Ruthanne Kramer Hartung, 1138 Greenwich St, Reading, PA 19604; Tom Kelly, 3 Liberty St, Mineral Point, WI 53565; Michael S Kriebel, 1756 Breneman Rd., Manheim, PA 17545; K Kerchner McConlogue, Snibbles, 701 Hunting Pl, Baltimore, MD 21229; Cheryl Ann Nash, 100 Summer St, Kennebunk, ME 04043; Sharon Schaich, 411 Woodcrest Ave, Lititz, PA 17543.

Reproduction Manufacturers: Anthony House, PO Box 235, Newville, PA 17241; Harwell Graphics, P O Box 8, Napoleon, IN 47034; Pine Cone Primitives, P O Box 682, Troutman, NC 28166.

Birth and Baptismal Certificate
  1806, Freiderich Krebs, Northampton County, PA, hand drawn and printed, pen and ink and watercolor on laid paper, parrots, tulips, flowers, and hearts, red, yellow, green, brown, and black, printed label "F. Krebs," some fading, portions of one parrot restored, framed, 12½ × 15½". **1,250.00**
  1810, Manheim Township, York County, PA, pen and ink and watercolor, dates 1794 and 1810, pin pricked hearts, flowers, and pair of parrots, period frame, 13¼ × 16" **2,000.00**
  1811, Schuylkill County, PA, hand drawn, pen and ink and watercolor on wove paper, Berks County artist, pair of parrots with striped necks, scalloped feathered bodies, herringbone tails, period painted frame, 8⅛ × 12" **4,500.00**
  1826, Johanna Adam Eyer, hand drawn, pen and ink and watercolor, pair of trumpeting red angels above apple tree with serpent, black painted period ogee frame, 9 × 6½" **9,500.00**
  1848, Blumer & Busch, Allentown, PA, printed, angels, birds, and eagle, minor creases, framed, 14¼ × 17¼". **125.00**

Religious Text, Southeastern Pennsylvania, German script, 1802, 7⅞ × 6⁵⁄₁₆", $500.00.

Birth and Christening Record, 1812, Berks County, PA, printed, hand colored, 15½ × 12¾" **650.00**
Birth Record
  1814, unknown artist, hand drawn, pen and ink and watercolor, Jacob Becter birth, geometric border design, compass stars and designs, orange, yellow, and olive green, curly maple frame, 14 × 17¾". . . **1,320.00**
  1818, Henrich Ebner, Allentown, PA, Cumberland County, hand drawn and printed, handcolored, olive, yellow, and purple, matted and framed, 20 × 16½" **225.00**
  Peters, Harrisburg, Berks County, PA, hand drawn and printed, handcolored, molded walnut frame, 19¼ × 16". **165.00**
  1840, pen and ink and watercolor on wove paper, English text, May 30, 1840 Oley Township, Berks County, PA birth of Mahlon B Spang, floral design, bright red, yellow, green, orange, blue, and black, minor damage on fold line, 9⅝" w, 11⅝" h **1,210.00**
Bookplate
  1827, pen and watercolor, stylized tulip and flowers, red, blue, green, black, and yellow, framed, 8⅝" h, 5¾" w. **1,375.00**
  1831, pen and ink and watercolor on woven paper, "Miss Roxy Hyde, when this you see remember me, Aruba Baker, April 25, 1831," floral designs and circle, black, brown, and blue, 9¼" w, 6⅝" h. **1,150.00**
  1849, pen and ink and watercolor on paper, black and red, framed, red has bled and stained paper, 7½" w, 10½" **110.00**
  1854, pen and ink and watercolor on paper, red, yellow, and green

roses, black ink inscription, matted and framed, 11″ w, 11″ h . . . **95.00**
Drawing
  1806, pen and ink and watercolor on laid paper, Johanes Schmidt, Baterland, pair of birds, red, orange, green, and black, 9″ w, 7″ h, framed. **500.00**
  1847, Mary Thornton, pencil, pen and ink, and watercolor, wove paper, stylized flowers, birds, and "M S M K 1847," 11½″ h, 91½″ w. **650.00**
Geburts und Taufschein (birth and baptism)
  1877, pen and ink and watercolor, wove paper, primitive angel in brown ink, green polka dots, holding upside down rose, Wullimann family births from 1840 to 1877, wear, stains, and fading, framed, 13½″ w, 15½″ h **450.00**
  1823, printed, hand colored, recording 1823 Montgomery County, PA, birth, printed by "H. Ebner, Allentown," faded colors, creases, and tears, modern painted frame, 16¼″ w, 19¼″ h **115.00**
Haus Sagen (House Blessing), printed, Ritter, Reading, PA **150.00**
Memorial, pencil, pen and ink, and watercolor, "In Memory of Freedom Ransdell who died at Watertown, Oct 11, 1817 aged 23," dried leaves and paper cut outs, stylized flower and geometric architectural elements designs **330.00**
Reward of Merit, 1827, PA, hand drawn, bird in floral bush with stylized tulip and daisy above heart reserve inscribed "Das Hertze mein ist dir allein," sgd "Anna, 1827, Tier" in script on bottom, 4¼ × 3¼″ **350.00**
Taufschein (baptism), 1789, Lykens Valley Artist, hand drawn, pen and ink and watercolor, baptismal record for Johann Frederick Lupold, June 6, 1789, framed, 8¼ × 13¼″ **2,500.00**
Valentine, hand drawn, pen and ink and watercolor
  1800, Quaker, folding, central heart with initials "SN" (possibly for Sarah Newlin of southern Chester County) surrounded by four circles enclosed in a diamond, each corner with a three block motif, extensive text interwoven throughout, folds into an envelope with a central heart on outer surface and text around edges, 13½ x 13½″ **1,200.00**
  1835, cutout heart, interlaced with red ribbon, translated text reads

"Being acquainted, I want to send you greetings and to add that I am of nobody fonder. Since I have sat with thee I cannot forget thee . . .," 5¼ × 5½″ **5,600.00**
Vorschrift, 1808, pen and ink and watercolor on laid paper, "World Interest speaks all sort languages, and acts all sorts morels, Rhode Adams, Aged 13 years, Holiston, 1808," simple floral dec, red, green, and black, 7¾″ w, 9½″ h **135.00**

LAWN ORNAMENTS AND ACCESSORIES

History: Farmers enjoyed relaxing as much as working in the outdoors. It was common to find a cast iron bench or an ornamental statue under the shade of a large tree as part of a farmyard setting. Ornamental pieces also were used in garden and entrance settings.

Most lawn ornaments were cast from metal or concrete and were often painted to provide protection from the elements. Finding an example with original paint is unusual. Hitching posts are a favorite form among collectors.

The 1980s witnessed renewed collecting interest in lawn ornaments and accessories, due in part to the Victorian decorating craze. Prices rose dramatically. Often outside ornaments became part of inside decorating schemes.

Many individuals failed to realize that excellent reproductions and copycats of nineteenth century examples were made in the 1930s and 1940s by a number of firms, e.g., Virginia Metalcrafters. Ruth Webb Lee's "Ironworks" chapter in *Antique Fakes & Reproductions: Enlarged and Revised, Seventh Edition* (Lee Publications: 1950) is well worth reading.

References: Margaret Lindquist and Judith Wells, *The Official Identification and Price Guide To Garden Furniture and Accessories,* House of Collectibles, 1992; Alan Robertson, *Architectural Antiques,* Chronicle Books, 1987; J. P. Whyte's Pyghtle Works (Bedford England), *Garden Furniture,* Apollo Books, 1987.

Reproduction Craftspersons: Michael Dutcher, 415 W Market St, West Chester, PA 19380; Susan Gardiner, 12 Brookway Dr, Greenville, SC 29605; Larry R Hanapole, PO Box 175, Marblehead, MA 01945; Julie and Lance Huber, 13939 Cuba Rd, Hunt Valley, MD 21030; Joseph Hutchison, Hearthstone House, 1600 Hilltop Rd, Xenia, OH 45385; Mark Kuzio, 175 High St, Belfast, ME 04915; Bob and Charlotte Lauier, Big Bear on Cosby, 777 Big Bear Rd, Cosby, TN 37722; Greg Leavitt, 476 Valleybrook Rd, Wawa, PA 19063; Doug and Carol Lockhart, 4515 Twp Rd 430,

Logan, OH 43138; Fred B Odell, 6209 Upper York Rd, New Hope, PA 18938; Stephen and Mary Petlitz, The Owl's Nest, 350 Sparger Rd, Mt Airy, NC 27030; Sandra McKenzie Schmitt, 12770 Kain Rd, Glen Allen, VA 23060; C Thomas Wright, Hoosier Barnwood Village, 10455 Collingswood Ln, Fishers, IN 46038.

Reproduction Manufacturers: Ala Bamma Folk Art, 210 W Commerce St, Greenville, AL 36037; Barb & Co, 16314 Martincoit Rd, Poway, CA 92064; Bird N Tree Pholk, M Dallas & Co, 28864 Newcastle Rd, Howard, OH 43028; Cabin Fever, 5770 S Meridian, Laingsburg, MI 48848; Cape Cod Cupola Co, Inc, 78 State Rd, Rte 6, North Dartmouth, MA 02747; Country Accents, RD #2, Box 293, Stockton, NJ 08559; Country Is . . . Country Castings, PO Box 824, Jacksonville, AL 36265; The Country Stippler, Rte 2, Box 1540, Pine Mountain, GA 31822; Designs In Wood, PO Box 788, Sparta, NC 28675; House of Graham, PO Box 309, 100 Wildwood Dr, Adamsville, TN 38310; J R Bird Company, 1207 Park Terrace, Greensboro, NC 27403; Moultrie Mfg Co, P O Drawer 1179, Moultrie, GA 31776; Nathan's Forge, Ltd, 3476 Uniontown Rd, Uniontown, MD 21158; Nature's Niche, PO Box 261, Anderson, MO 64831; S. Chris Rheinschild, 2220 Carlton Way, Santa Barbara, CA 93109; Town and Country, Main St, East Conway, NH 04037; The Woodman, 102 Callecita, San Clemente, CA 92672.

Note: This category also includes items from around the farm that are used as lawn decorating accessories in modern suburbia. Good sense and a respect for the sublime has caused us to fail to list and price old cast iron, porcelain lined bathtubs, used by some in an upright position (the lower third buried in the earth) as a grotto for a religious statue.

Birdhouse
    Sewer Tile, cylindrical, tooled bark-
      like surface, 8½" h **525.00**
    Wood, barn shaped, painted red,
      20" h.   **250.00**
Chair, wood slat seat, painted black and white, each with different back, anvil, initials, and "1931," 36" h, price for set of three **660.00**
Farmyard Bell and Yoke, cast iron, painted black **60.00**
Fencing, cast iron, single panel, three posts, extra finials and hardware . . .   **225.00**
Garden Stake, wood cutout, painted, black boy, fishing, c1950, 28" h . . .   **55.00**
Garden Statue, Newfoundland Dog, cast, detailed coat, 52" l, 35½" h, mid 19th C **24,200.00**
Gate
    Cast Iron, Victorian, dated "1856," cast "Thing" and "No 235," 45" h   **375.00**

Garden Statue, dog, cast iron, painted, 19th C, 49" l, 28½" h, $3,025.00. Photograph courtesy of Skinner, Inc.

Wood, picket, New England, gray painted weathered surface, 19th C, 35¼" w, 49" h **225.00**
Hitching Post, cast iron
    Horse head, stylized detail, black repaint, repair, 15" h **415.00**
    Whip shape, round base with fastening holes, 40" h. **275.00**
Kettle, cast iron, bail handle, 28" d . . .   **85.00**
Lawn Jockey, cast iron, painted, holding lantern, lantern added, 26" h. . .   **450.00**
Lawn Ornaments, wood, cutout, painted
    Squirrel, begging, wearing high collared shirt and checked pants . . .   **90.00**
    Turtle, standing, wearing top hat, modern steel bases, 25½" h. **85.00**
Planter
    Cast Iron, tulip shaped, worn green paint, 8½" h **50.00**
    Cement, urn shaped, painted white, square base, 24" h. **20.00**
Signal Cannon, cast iron, ornate, painted black, 17¾" l **385.00**
Statue
    Dog, cast iron, painted, long thin tail, 19th C, 40" l, 28½" h **3,100.00**
    Stag, standing, cast metal, painted. .   **1,200.00**
Sundial, lead, 9¼ × 9¼". **95.00**
Wagon Wheel, wood, painted red . . .   **45.00**
Water Pump, cast iron, painted white   **50.00**

PAINTINGS

Note: Three major types of paintings play important roles in the agrarian community—portraits, town and homestead views, and landscapes. Each provides a valuable record of the past. Their highly personal nature was both a plus and minus. The personal and local nature of the paintings meant that they would be handed down from generation to generation. However, as tastes changed or individuals moved, the importance of many of these paintings diminished. As a result there are often more paintings found in a rural homestead's attic than hanging on the walls.

The individual portrait helped preserve the sense of family continuance. The portraitist survived in rural America until the end of the 19th century. The talents of the artists varied widely. However, a portrait by a less skilled artist was better than no portrait at all. Today, knowing the name of the subject, date of the painting, and identity of the artist are value pluses when examining any work. By 1900 the camera replaced the portrait artist. It is worth noting that many late 19th and early 20th century photographs meant to hang on the wall duplicated the size and poses of early oil and watercolor portraits.

Rural America loved landscapes, evident by the large number of oils, watercolors, and prints that survive. Many are extremely large in size, meant to occupy the major portion of a wall in a rural parlor. Most were done by academically trained artists. Alas, the location, if painted from real life, has all too often been lost. Today the frame is often more valuable than the painting or watercolor that it contains.

Farm homestead and townscapes were done in few numbers. They are valued not only as works of art, but as historical documents. Many were done by amateurs and crudely drawn. A small majority were done by semi-professional and professional artists. Some of these artists have reached legendary status, e.g., the Pennsylvania Alms House painters of the mid-19th century.

Many members of the rural community could not afford original works of art; instead, they relied on mass-produced etchings and prints that copied the works of popular painters of the period to decorate their walls. This is one of the most overlooked areas of collecting. Many examples sell for less than one hundred dollars.

There is no way a listing of less than several hundred paintings can accurately represent the breadth and depth of the folk painting examples sold during the last few years. This listing merely serves as an introduction to the wealth of material that is viewed as folk painting.

The art community assigns a broad definition to folk painting. The itinerant limners of the colonial period are viewed as kin to Grandma Moses. In the 1970s and 1980s ethnicity was introduced as a key element in 19th and 20th century examples.

In the final analysis, what constitutes a "folk" painting is a judgment call. Since attaching a "folk" attribution to a painting usually results in a significant increase in value, learn to question the motives of individuals making such an attribution.

References: The principal purpose of this section is to help users identify and value their paintings. The section begins with general reference books on artist identification and folk paintings in particular. Price guide listings follow. Many specialized studies exist, such as Barbara and Lawrence Holdridge's *Ammi Phillips: Portrait of a Painter, 1788–1865* (Crown, 1969). Check with the librarian at your local art museum for help in locating them.

Artist Dictionaries: Emmanuel Benezit, *Dictionnaire Critique et Documentaire des Peintres, Sculpteurs, Dessinateurs et Graveurs*, 10 volumes, third edition, Grund, 1976; Mantle Fielding, *Dictionary of American Painters, Sculptors and Engravers*, Apollo Books, 1983; J. Johnson and A. Greutzner, *Dictionary of British Artists, 1880–1940: An Antique Collector's Club Research Project Listing 41,000 Artists*, Antique Collector's Club, 1976; Les Krantz, *American Artists*, Facts on File, 1985.

Folk Painting References: Robert Bishop, *Folk Painters of America*, E. P. Dutton, 1981; Mary Black and Jean Lipman, *American Folk Painting*, Clarkson N. Potter, 1966; C. Kurt Dewhurst, Betty MacDowell, and Marsha MacDowell, *Artists in Aprons: Folk Art by American Women*, E. P. Dutton, 1979; John and Katherine Ebert, *American Folk Painters*, Charles Scribner's Sons, 1975; Jack T. Ericson, *Folk Art in America: Painting and Sculpture*, Mayflower Books, 1979; Herbert W. Hemphill, Jr., and Julia Weissman, *Twentieth Century American Folk Art and Artists*, E. P. Dutton, 1974; Sidney Janis, *They Taught Themselves: American Primitive Painters of the 20th Century*, Dial Press, 1942; Jean Lipman and Tom Armstrong, *American Folk Painters of Three Centuries*, Hudson Hills Press, 1980; Beatrix T. Rumford, *American Folk Portraits: Paintings and Drawings from The Abby Aldrich Rockefeller Folk Art Center*, New York Graphic Society Books, 1981.

Price Guide References, Basic: *Art At Auction in America, 1993 Edition*, Krexpress, 1993; William T. Currier (compiler), *Currier's Price Guide To American Artists 1645–1945 at Auction, Fifth Edition*, Currier Publications, 1991; William T. Currier (compiler), *Currier's Price Guide To European Artists 1545–1945 at Auction, Third Edition*, Currier Publications, 1991; *Huxford's Fine Art Value Guide, Volume III*, Collector Books, 1992; Rosemary and Michael McKittrick, *The Official Price Guide To Fine Art, Second Edition*, House of Collectibles, 1993; Susan Theran, *Fine Art: Identification and Price Guide, Second Edition*, Avon Books, 1992.

Price Guide References, Advanced: Richard Hislop (editor), *The Annual Art Sales Index*, Weybridge, Surrey, England, Art Sales Index, Ltd., since 1969; Enrique Mayer, *International Auction Record: Engravings, Drawings, Watercolors, Paintings, Sculpture*, Paris, Editions Enrique Mayer, since 1967; Susan Theran (editor), *Leonard's Price Index of Art Auctions*, Auction Index, Inc., since 1980.

Museum Directories: *American Art Directory*, R. R. Bowker Co.; American Association of Museums, *The Official Museum Directory: United States and Canada*, updated periodically.

Reproduction Craftspersons: Arlene Strader Folk Art, 100 S Montgomery St, Union, OH 45322; Cate Mandigo Editions, PO Box 221, Hadley, NY 12835; Kacey Sydnor Carneal, Rte 3, Box 988, Gloucester, VA 23061; Elizabeth F. Gilkey, 3000 Coleridge Rd, Cleveland Heights, OH 44118; Terrence J Graham, Box 19, Zieglerville, PA 19492; Betsy Hoyt, Butternut Hill Gallery, 3751 State St W, N. Canton, OH 44720; Warren L. Kimble, RR 3, Box 3038, Brandon, VT 05773; D. Masters Kriebel, 7560 Cerro Gordo Rd, Gainesville, VA 22065; Donna Lacey-Derstine, Richardson Hollow Artworks, RR 1, Box 500, West Paris, ME 04289; Jeanne Marston, 811 S Park Ave, Audubon, PA 19407; Carol Martell, Designs Unlimited, 13401 Chestnut Oak Dr, Gaithersburg, MD 20878; Eleanor Meadowcroft, 25 Flint St, Salem, MA 01970; Diane Ulmer Pedersen, 15 Avery Rd, Holden, MA 01520; Christine L Smith, 110 Graham Way, Devon, PA 19333; Sandra Somers, PO Box 246, New Boston, MI 48164;

Reproduction Manufacturers: The Battered Brush, 228 Dogwood Ave., Quitman, MS 39355; Sheepscot Stenciling, RFD #1, Box 613, Wiscasset, ME 04578.

Reproduction Alert: Unless you are thoroughly familiar with the artist, you are advised to have any folk painting that you are considering buying authenticated by an independent source. In Samuel Pennington's "The Folk Art Forger," an article about Robert Trotter's forgeries in the March 1990 *Maine Antique Digest*, he states: "No amount of money or hard time in prison, however, is likely to heal the scars his schemes inflicted on an industry that often all too readily absorbed his artistic frauds." Trotter is not the only art forger around; he just happened to get caught.

Anderson, J W, oil on canvas, winter landscape and ice skaters, sgd "Painted by J W Anderson, 115 West 11th St NY 1884," framed, 23" h, 37¼" w **990.00**
Branchard, Enyle, oil on canvas, landscape, avenue of trees, primitive, sgd "Enyle Branchard," 14½" w, 18½" h   **150.00**
Davis, Joseph H, watercolor and ink on paper, "Portrait of Eleanor Jane Jones, Aged 10 Years 1835," unsigned, 9¾ × 6½", framed **5,500.00**
Reinhart, B F, oil on canvas, portrait, seated lady, subject is reputed to be Normanda Workman Larwill, wife of John Christmas Larwill, founder of Wooster, OH, sgd "B. F. Reinhart, N.Y. 1870," 51¼" w, 61" h **1,100.00**

Stock, Joseph Whiting, (1815–55), Springfield, MA, oil on canvas, woman, primitive, well detailed setting of green curtain, red couch, and landscape, black dress, white lace trimmed bodice, holding a red book, rebacked and cleaned, minor restoration, 32" h, 27" w, modern 37½"×32¼" veneer frame **2,860.00**
Street, Robert, oil on canvas, portrait, woman wearing lace collar and gold jewelry, landscape in background, rebacked, cleaned and restored, gild frame, 25" w, 30" h **1,325.00**
Unknown Artist
   Drawing, black and white on sandpaper, "Great Elm Tree, Penn. Society AD 1827," landscape with monument, framed, tears in margins, 25½" w, 19" h **850.00**
   Oil on Academy Board
      Dog with bird, gilt frame, 12⅞" h, 15" w **1,045.00**
      Landscape, mill, primitive, mahogany veneer beveled frame, 12½" w, 10" h **165.00**
   Oil on Canvas
      Landscape
         Barnyard scene, cat, chicks, and bird, strip frame, 15" h, 19¼" w **1,100.00**
         Portrait of a Yellow Farm House, American School, unsgd, 19th C, 14 × 18", framed . . .   **475.00**
         Lakeside cabin, two men and dogs, primitive, 16⅓" h, 29" w, 19" h × 34¼" frame **175.00**
      Portrait
         Boy wearing black coat, high white collar, holding whip, forest landscape background, American School, old poorly executed restoration, patched tears, 19th C, 25" h, 30" w, gold repainted 37" h × 32" w frame **580.00**

Side-Wheeler Seneca, James Bard, oil on canvas, sgd, 50 × 30", $100,000.00. Photograph courtesy of James D Julia, Inc.

Boy wearing red coat, with hoop, American School, period frame, scattered punctures, retouched, craquelure, 19th C, 45½ × 37" **4,675.00**

Children, two little girls and toddler, all wearing coral and gold jewelry, primitive, American School, cleaned and restored, 19th C, 25" h, 31" w, 30¾" h × 35¼" gilt frame **2,100.00**

Couple, man wearing black coat, gold pin and watch chain, heart shaped mark on one finger, woman seated in armchair, holding book, wearing black dress, white lace collar and trim, gold jewelry, lace bonnet with flowers, primitive, American School, orig unrestored good condition, chestnut stretchers, 19th C, 28" h, 23" w, modern silver gilt 31¾" h × 26¾" frames, price for pair   **3,800.00**

Couple, man with cello, woman with book "Mother At Home," Rochester, NY, primitive, American School, rebacked on masonite, repairs, restoration, 28½' h, 23¼" w, modern 31¾" h × 26½" w gilt frames, price for pair . . .   **1,430.00**

Gentleman wearing black frock coat, holding rolled paper, red curtain and classical urn background, gilt frame, 32½" h, 27½" w **1,210.00**

Pencil, Ink, and Watercolor
Portrait
Gentleman, miniature profile, worn gilt frame, 5⅜" h, 4½" w   **250.00**

Woman, miniature profile, woman in lace bonnet, dark stains, cracked glass, gilt frame, 7" h, 6" w **175.00**

Young girl, writing, stains, edge tear, oval gilded frame, 7" w, 8¼" h **60.00**

Squirrel in tree, primitive, worn gilt frame, 5¾" h, 4½" w **85.00**

Pinprick and Watercolor on Paper, woman and child with drum, elaborate floral wreath, wear, stains, fold lines, some damage, framed, 11⅝" h, 7⅞" w **305.00**

Watercolor
Bird in tree, yellow bird, sgd in pencil, early 20th C, matted, old gilt frames, 11⅝" h, 9⅝" w, price for pair **100.00**

Die Natur Lehre (Cat's Nature), Lewis Miller, watercolor, 7½ × 9½", framed, $1,250.00.

Equestrian, orange, green, gray, and black, framed, 12¼" h, 9½" w **225.00**

Landscape
Estate guarded by stone wall and soldiers, titled "The Gate of Ellerslie by Anjulene Barney AD 1823," artist reputed to have been student in NC Seminary, stains, minor surface damage, repair to edge tears, 14½" h, 17½" w, old gilt 17¾" h × 21¾" w frame   **2,700.00**

Two houses and log cabin, 8¼" h, 8¾" w **95.00**

Portrait
Child, miniature portrait, blond hair, blue eyes, salmon dress, holding rose, some wear, faded colors, black lacquered frame with minor damage, 6¾" h, 5½" w **165.00**

Seated child, large red cushion, blue dress, holding whip, sgd and dated "1889," matted and framed, 18¼" h, 16½" w   **150.00**

Seascape, three masted ship, moonlit seas, titled "H.M.S. Doris off Jamaica," back titled and labeled "Christmas Eve 1806," matted and framed, round, opaque, 7½" d **150.00**

Watercolor and Ink on Paper, memorial, female figure standing beside memorial with urn, willow tree and buildings in background, "Sacred to the Memory of Mrs. Rebecca Barber who Departed this Life, September the 4th, 1828, Aged 48 Years," some discoloration, 18½ × 15" **2,200.00**

Watercolor, Ink, and Hair on Paper, memorial, American School, grieving woman standing beside tomb inscribed "Sacred to the memory of Amos Tyler who died Jan 15, 1829 Aug. 37 . . .", weeping willow in background, 8½″ w, 6½″ h, framed. **4,125.00**

SCHERENSCHNITTE

History: Scherenschnitte, translated as scissor-cut, is the art of decorative paper cutting. It was brought to America by German-speaking immigrants.

Scherenschnitte is found in two basic forms—complete picture and supplemental decoration. While a silhouette is technically a scissor-cutting, the term is generally reserved for full size pictures of landscape and forest scenes. As a decorative element, scherenschnitte is found on objects such as birth certificates, marriage certificates, memorial pictures, and valentines.

The term "scherenschnitte" is generally reserved for examples cut in the late 18th and early 19th centuries. Some were cut on gilded paper. Most were mounted against a cloth or paper of contrasting background.

Scissor-cutting is a continuing tradition. Late 19th and early 20th century Victorian examples do not command the same value as early examples. In Europe the tradition is especially strong in Slavic regions, especially Czechoslovakia. Many of these examples have worked their way into the American market.

Finally, some contemporary scherenschnitte artists are experimenting with cutting techniques other than scissors, e.g., lasers. When buying a contemporary example make certain that you know how the piece was cut.

Reproduction Craftspersons: Pamela Dalton, RD 2, Box 266A, Harlemville, Ghent, NY 12075; Faye and Bernie DuPlessis, Traditional Papercutting, 101 Blue Rock Rd, Edgewood Hills, Wilmington, DE 19809; Judy Garges, 2886 Ridge Rd, Perkasie, PA 18944; Elizabeth Lee Gaul, Rt 1, Box 122, Waterford, OH 45786; Sandra Gilpin, 509 Baer Avenue, Hanover, PA 17331; Claudia and Carroll J. Hopf, 13 Mechanic Street, Kennebunk, ME 04043; Melissa Pottenger, Sabbath Toys, 11800 Jason Ave, Concord Twp, OH 44077; Nancy G Shelly, 45 Wall St, Bethlehem, PA 18018.

Reproduction Manufacturers: Southern Scribe, 515 E Taylor, Griffin, GA 30223; Tree Toys, Inc, Box 492, Hinsdale, IL 60521.

Card, cut work, people, animals, and hearts **3,500.00**

Picture

7¾ × 9″, vignettes, "Man's Abuse of Animals" and "The Hunted's Revenge," first grouping illustrates abuse by man of animals in hunting, farming, and playing, second grouping depicts hunted birds and deer stringing up their persecutors, scissor-cut black paper on gray-green paper ground, 19th C, price for pair **875.00**

11½ × 16″, landscapes, one with church, mill, houses, animals, and trees, other with manor house, swan pond, outbuildings, gate, animals, and trees, scissor-cut white paper on turquoise blue paper ground, 19th C, price for pair **1,100.00**

13½ × 11½″, birds, chickens, and peafowl, scissor-cut white paper on faded black paper backing, framed. **80.00**

22¼ × 18½″, collection of twenty-five individual designs, includes horse-drawn vehicles, trees, birds, and flowers, scissor-cut white paper mounted on black ground cloth, shadow box frame **575.00**

Valentine

13″ d, round, hex sign type cuttings, hearts and other borders, pen and ink inscription, scissor-cut white paper mounted on olive green ground, dated 1842 . . . . **2,000.00**

14¾ × 15″

8-point star surrounded by eight hearts and birds on vines, heart border, verses inscribed on all hearts, scissor-cut white paper, c1840 . . . . **1,000.00**

16 point star surrounded by eight hearts, verses inscribed on hearts, busts of 19th C garbed man and woman over each heart, pairs of birds flanking small heart in each corner, scissor-cut white paper, dated 1850 **1,200.00**

SEWER TILE ART

History: The sewer tile factories in the area of eastern Ohio, near Akron, produced utilitarian objects made of clay. These companies made a number of advertising giveaways featuring miniature examples of their products or decorative items such as plaques, paperweights, and horseshoes. At day's end, workers fashioned left over clay into a myriad of objects for personal enjoyment. Molds also were available, and miscellaneous figures from cats to pigs were made.

Although sewer tile materials date from the 1800s to the 1950s, the golden age of this folk art form dates from 1900 to 1940. Focus on the hand sculpted pieces. Research has identified many of the artisans who produced these materials.

Since pieces are highly individualistic, artistic consideration is a large factor in determining price. Damage causes serious problems for the collector. One-of-a-kind items need to be carefully restored if damaged. Collectors prefer items in very good or better condition. Prices do fluctuate; the market is still seeking a level of stability. Whenever a collecting category attracts the folk art collectors, it is difficult to find an accurate pricing level. Design, style, and even the whimsical nature of the piece determine the price, as well as how much the collector is willing to pay.

Reference: Jack E. Adamson, *Illustrated Handbook of Ohio Sewer Pipe Folk Art*, privately printed, 1973.

Bank
    Cat, white clay, colored glass eyes, 6⅜" h **85.00**
    Pig, seated, molded, simple tooled detail, green-brown salt glaze, missing plug, 9¼" h **425.00**
    Rabbit, crouching, incised "AL," 10½" l **415.00**
Bookend
    Minerva Head, minor chips, 7¾"   **28.00**
    Semi-circular, pr, tooled line dec, small chips, 4½" h **72.00**
Brick, relief bust of Abraham Lincoln, unglazed dark patina, chips, 4 × 8¼"   **180.00**
Desk Organizer
    Brick Barbecue, incised "Louis Staley 1946," small flakes, 8¼" l **75.00**
    Pig, standing by tree stump, tan glaze, chips, 5½" h **28.00**
    Three Stumps, boat shaped base, chips, 10" l **30.00**

Eagle, E W Nurenburg, Somers, NY, 1930–40, 12½" h, $800.00.

Sewer Tile Face, artist E W Nurenburg, Somers, NY, c1935, 8" h, $400.00.

Figure
    Basset Hound, long face with sad expression, hole in back, small chips, 9½" h **165.00**
    Cat, colored glass eyes, 6¾" h **45.00**
    Cherub, paper label "Made by John H Crosley, Mar 31, 1906, Brazil, Ind," 4¾" h **385.00**
    Dog, seated
        6" h, orig red, green, and brown paint, wear, minor edge damage   **365.00**
        9½" h, molded front, flat back, simple tooled details, bottom incised "Arnold" **110.00**
        10" h, orange-tan glaze, molded, simple tooled detail, indistinct incised name on bottom. **55.00**
        10¼" h, head points forward, simple hand tooled details. **275.00**
        10½" h, dark glaze, molded, simple tooled detail **325.00**
        10½" h, molded, bored tooled details, incised "Swaldd" on bottom   **465.00**
        11¾" h, half relief, flat back, molded detail, edge chips **110.00**
    Frog, 7" l **250.00**
    Horse Head
        5½" h, sq base, incised inscription "Jack Finck, Aug. 25, 1861," firing cracks. **225.00**
        7" h, hand molded and tooled . . .   **235.00**
    Lion
        5" l, minor edge damage from kiln adhesion **450.00**
        8½" l, rect scalloped base, incised "L E Sr, #16, 9–16–52, Wadsworth, Ohio". **275.00**
        10" l, rect scalloped base. **385.00**
        14" l, crouching, rect base **275.00**
    Man's Head, unglazed buff clay, firing crack in forehead, 20th C, 8" h   **105.00**

Owl, unglazed, chips, 8½" h	**25.00**
Pig, sitting, incised "E.R.," 9" h	**165.00**
Squirrel, sitting up, holding nut, hand molded, tooled detail, green painted eyes, 11" h	**300.00**
Paperweight, sardine can, glazed, 9½" l, 6½" w	**600.00**
Planter, tree stump shape	
24" h, imp label "C C P Co Uhriches-ville"	**225.00**
33" h, glazed, chipped edges	**110.00**
Plaque, crane, old polychrome paint, 11" l, 6¼" h	**130.00**
Shoe, 5" l	
Daisy and button with cat pattern, small chip	**35.00**
Plain, small chip	**25.00**

SILHOUETTES

History: Silhouettes (shades) are shadow profiles, produced by hollow cutting, mechanical tracing, or painting. They were popular in the 18th and 19th centuries.

The name came from Etienne de Silhouette, a French Minister of Finance, who tended to be tight with money and cut "shades" as a pastime. In America the Peale family was one of the leading silhouette makers. An impressed stamp marked "PEALE" or "Peale Museum" identifies their work.

Silhouette portraiture lost popularity with the introduction of the daguerreotype prior to the Civil War. In the 1920s and 30s a brief revival occurred when tourists to Atlantic City and Paris had their profiles cut as souvenirs.

References: Shirley Mace, *Encyclopedia of Silhouette Collectibles On Glass,* Shadow Enterprises, 1992; Blume J. Rifken, *Silhouettes in America, 1790–1840, A Collectors' Guide,* Paradigm Press, 1987.

Museums: Essex Institute, Salem, MA; National Portrait Gallery, Washington, DC.

Reproduction Craftpersons: Susan B Anderson, SBA Silhouettes, 145 N Laurel St, Hazleton, PA 18201; Judy Garges, 2886 Ridge Rd, Perkasie, PA 18944; Ellen Mischo, Profiles, PO Box 412, Leesburg, VA 22075.

Reproduction Manufacturers: Olde Virginea Floorcloth and Trading Co, PO Box 3305, Portsmouth, VA 23707; *Silhouette Patterns*—Mill Pond Designs, PO Box 390, East Longmeadow, MA 01028.

Boy	
3⅝" w, 4½" h, reverse cut, white paper, black cloth backing, old gilt frame	**65.00**

Gentleman, ink details, artist sgd "White," 6½ × 10½", $275.00.

5⅝" w, 4⅝" h, hollow cut paper, black cloth backing, marked "Charles —," emb letter "M," fold line, edge tears, framed	**85.00**
Couple, unidentified	
3¾" w, 4¾" h, hollow cut paper, good detail, ink details on man, stains and insect damage, orig frames, price for pair	**325.00**
4½" w, 5⅛" h, hollow cut paper, ink and watercolor details, emb brass frames, price for pair	**715.00**
8" w, 5¾" h, eglomise glass and black molded frames, minor tear in woman, price for pair	**400.00**
10" w, 6½" h, hollow cut paper, ink and watercolor details, pair framed together, sgd "Doyle," eglomise glass with two ovals and gilded frame	**415.00**
10" w, 7" h, hollow cut, gilt frame	**175.00**
Dearborn, General Henry, 8" w, 10½" h, full length, gilt highlights, imperfections	**165.00**
Gentleman, unidentified	
4½" w, 5¼" h, ink and gold wash on paper, black lacquer frame with gilded trim	**475.00**
4½" w, 5½" h, cut, gilt highlights, gilt frame	**150.00**
4½" w, 5¾" h, hollow cut, orig folding cardboard case with printed wallpaper, black cloth backing	**410.00**
4¾" w, 5½" h, black painted silhouette on chalk, fine detail, orig black lacquered frame with gilded trim, convex glass	**450.00**
4⅞" w, 5¾" h, watercolor on paper, black lacquered frame, damaged gilded liner	**225.00**

Lady, hollow cut, sgd and dated "Elizabeth Baker, Boston, 1824," 5 × 6", $200.00.

5¼" d, ink, pencil and ink wash on paper, stains and faded pencil inscription, orig round turned frame, convex glass 75.00

6⅝ " w, 7½" h, hollow cut, wig, frilly shirt front, laid paper emb "Peale Museum," fold line, rosewood grained frame 150.00

7" w, 10" h, hollow cut, gilt frame 175.00

7¼" w, 12¾" h, full length, wearing top hat, cut black paper, edges ragged, blue stains, framed 200.00

10" w, 14" h, full length cut figure, lithographed scenic background, framed................... 415.00

13¾" w, 15¾" h, standing, full length, cut, white brushed detail, ink wash river landscape background, bird's eye veneer frame with gilded liner 525.00

Hamilton, Alexander, 5½" w, 6¾" h, hollow cut, identified on reverse, imp stamp "Peale's Museum," oval, minor imperfections 225.00

Kerr, William, Esq., 7½" w, 13½" h, label inscribed "by Forrest St. Muray Howe 19th March," discoloration 275.00

Knox, Brigadier General Henry, 4" w, 5" h, watercolor and ink on paper, unsigned, framed 450.00

Lewis, Charles, 2¾" w, 4¼" h, hollow cut, sgd "Cut out with scissors by Fredrick Smith, aged 14," dated September 1833................. 45.00

McNair, Alexander, (1776–1826), 12½" w, 16½" h, full length cut, top hat, riding crop, black and white lithographed background, brief biography on back of mahogany veneered beveled frame, minor stains 775.00

McNeil, Alexander and Isabel Loomis, 4" w, 5¼" h, cut, with black paper

backing, ink highlights, eglomise mats, orig gilt frames, identified on reverse in pencil, accompanied by further genealogical information, price for pair 650.00

Military Officers, 6" w, 7⅜ " h, ink and watercolor on paper, orange and gold uniforms, marked "F. Perring 1840" and "C.C.–1804," repainted black and gold frames, price for pair 325.00

Warner, Philinda M, 5½" w, hollow cut, wood block printed torso, black cloth backing, gilt frame, paper label "Philinda M Warner, Roxburg, Vt 1831" 200.00

Webster, Daniel and Franklin Pierce, Lloyd N Rogers, and Millard Fillmore, 11½" w, 13" h, reverse painted glass, set of four in single rosewood veneer framed with gilded liner and eglomise mat 415.00

Woman, unidentified

4" w, 5¼" h, hollow cut, ink details, black cloth backing, gilt frame... 60.00

4¼" w, 5½" h, young features, hollow cut, black cloth backing, ink details, black molded frame..... 275.00

5" w, 5¾" h, young features, hollow cut paper, faded pen and ink detail, flaking eglomise glass, black frame.................... 55.00

5" w, 6" h, elderly features, ink on paper, elaborately coiffed hair, stains, old black reeded frame, gilded liner 120.00

5" w, 6¾" h, young features, hollow cut paper, braided hair in bun, framed.................... 140.00

5¾" w, 7½" h, elderly features, hollow cut, black cloth backing, emb "Peale Museum," dark paper, silver gilt frame 150.00

5⅞" w, 6⅞" h, young features, hollow cut, black paper backing, stained and minor damage, old gilt frame.................... 100.00

6" w, 7¾" h, young features, hollow cut paper, black cloth backing, high collar, stains and fold line, mahogany veneer frame 90.00

6" w, 8" h, ink, wearing opaque white shawl and bonnet, convex glass, black wood frame, brass liner.................... 175.00

6⅜ " w, 6¾" h, hollow cut, black cloth backing, gilt frame 70.00

8½" w, 11½" h, full length, cut, holding a book, gilt highlights, giltwood frame, some foxing, imperfections 220.00

10½" w, light yellowed satin backing, lacquered frame labeled "W.
Hill, Birmh" **150.00**

THEOREM

History: Theorem describes the creation of art
through the use of stencils, one for each color. As
a form it was extremely popular in the early 19th
century, especially in New England and Pennsylvania. The technique was used by furniture manufacturers as well as artists. However, when this
term is used by the antiques community, it means
a work of art executed as a watercolor on paper
or oils on velvet or cloth.

Still lifes of fruits and flowers in bowls and vases
were the most popular subject. Many of the patterns were based upon examples in instruction
manuals or popular prints. Although some individuals cut their own stencils and mixed their own
colors, many of the young female academy stu-
dents and women at home that painted theorems
relied on pre-cut and ready mixed colors.

Dating theorems can often be accomplished by
noting the style of the basket or container used in
the still life. Pressed glass compotes were first
produced in the 1830s. Another aid is to note the
stencil pattern and compare it with dated examples found in carpets, fabrics (bedspreads, curtains, pillow shams, and tablecloths), and floors.
Patterns did cross over.

Two keys to value are design and originality.
Add extra for the inclusion of animals, such as a
bird or butterfly. Most collectors assign a 50 percent premium to a watercolor on paper theorem.
However, oils on velvet theorem often acquire a
mellow palette that is stunning.

Two contemporary theorem painters deserve
special mention—David Ellinger (active between
1940 and 1980) and William Rank. Ellinger's
works appear on velvet, cotton, and paper and are
often confused with period examples. Not all his
works are signed. Rank's theorems are much more
vivid in color than those of Ellinger.

Reproduction Craftspersons: Donna W Albro,
Strawberry Vine, 6677 Hayhurst St, Worthington,
OH 43085; Hope R Angier, Sheepscot Stenciling,
RFD 1, Box 613, Wiscasset, ME 04578; Linda
Brubaker, 916 May Rd, Lititz, PA 17543; Terence
J Graham, Box 19, Zieglerville, PA 19492; Petra
& Thomas Haas, P O Box 20, Oley, PA 19547;
Sharon J Mason, Olde Virginia Floorcloth & Trad-
ing Co., P O Box 438, Williamsburg, VA 23185;
Nancy Rosier, Rosier Period Art, 2366 Rocking-
ham Dr, Troy, OH 45373; Jean Smith, Stenciler,
1300 Westwood Ave, Columbus, OH 43212; Bar-
bara Strawser, P O Box 165, Schaefferstown, PA
17088; Barbara Strickland, 728 Hawthorne, El
Cajon, CA 92020; Carolyn Lloyd Swain, Folke
Artstyles, Rte 3, Box 1175, Gloucester, VA 23061.

Reproduction Manufacturers: Basye-Bomber-
ger/Fabian House, P O Box 86, W Bowie, MD
20715; Country Accents, RD #2, Box 293, Stockton, NJ 08559; Heritage Designs, 7816 Laurel
Ave, Cincinnati, OH 45243; Sheepscot Stenciling,
RFD #1 Box 613, Wiscasset, ME 04578.

"A Primrose," watercolor and ink on
paper, sgd and dated "Painted by
Sally Stearns 1857," light staining,
tears lower edge, 6¾ x 8¼", framed   **825.00**
Basket of Flowers, painted on velvet,
blue, beige, and brown, minor wear
to velvet on upper and lower corners, grain painted frame, 19th C, 18
× 18". **1,000.00**
Basket of Flowers and Fruit, watercolor
on paper, sgd "Maria Robinson,"
good color, old shadow box frame,
12¼ × 9⅜ " **550.00**
Basket of Fruit
    Watercolor on Paper
    9¾" w, 7½" h, light staining, tear
    at left, framed **2,100.00**
    18½ × 14½", primitive, initialed
    "A.E.M.," slightly trimmed,
    framed **200.00**
Watercolor on Velvet, attributed to
David Ellinger, sgd on background
"D. Y. Ellinger," minor discolora-
tion, framed, 21 × 15½" **875.00**
Bird, watercolor on paper, brown, yel-
low, and green, modern frame, 7¾ ×
5⅜ " **75.00**
Bowl of Flowers, watercolor, pencil,
and mica on paper, yellow and red
tulips, roses, chrysanthemums, and
pansies, glittering bowl, c1830,
11¼ × 8¾" **1,425.00**
Compote of Flowers, polychrome
paints on velvet, small stains to lower
background, 19th C, 17½ × 23½"   **1,750.00**

**Basket of Fruit, watercolor on paper, un-
signed, light staining, small tear lower left,
19th C, 9¾×7½", $2,090.00. Photograph
courtesy of Skinner, Inc.**

Fruit, soft colors, white ground, matted, old gilt frame, 11 ½ × 9¼", price for pair **875.00**

Horse, eagle, shield, and flag, watercolor and graphite on paper, 26½ × 20½" **2,850.00**

Landscape, watercolor on velvet, buildings, trees, and deer, red, yellow, green, brown, and blue, 13⅛ × 12¼" **4,800.00**

Parrot, watercolor on velvet, soft colors, perched on grapevine, eating strawberries from overflowing basket of fruit, 26 × 22" **3,050.00**

Pot of Flowers, watercolor on velvet, sgd Jessie N Boyer, 14 × 12¼" **500.00**

"Summer's Bounty," watercolor, pen, and ink on paper, fruits and leaves, 19th C, 15 × 12" **875.00**

TRAMP ART

History: Tramp art was prevalent in the United States from 1875 to the 1930s. Items were made by itinerant artists who left no record of their identity. They used old cigar boxes and fruit and vegetable crates. The edges of items were chip-carved and layered, creating the "Tramp Art" effect. Finished items usually were given an overall stain.

Reference: Helaine Fendelman, *Tramp Art: An Itinerant's Folk Art Guide*, E. P. Dutton & Co., 1975.

Box
  8" h, drawer, sliding lid. **150.00**
  9½" l, hinged lid. **95.00**
  10" l, worn finish, white porcelain buttons **110.00**
  13½" l, worn maroon velvet panels, gilded tin trim, lid mirror and int. lining missing, some edge damage. **115.00**
  14½" l, chip carved, multi-layered lid, paneled sides, secret compartment in lid, old label reads "Made by Gus C. Leyerle 10–30–57," minor edge damage. **65.00**

Chest of Drawers, miniature, 13" h, three drawers, porcelain pulls, old alligatored finish, back labeled "I bought this July 2, 1955," old repairs to crest **140.00**

Clock
  21" h, cuckoo, polychrome dec, birds perched on arched crest inscribed and cutout to read "Made in Brookfield, Mass Aderlarl Courville," losses and repairs, early 20th C. **925.00**

Tramp Art Sewing Box, three drawers, pin cushion, heart and star appliques, 9½ × 5¾ × 6¼", $250.00.

  27" h, chip carved, portrait medallion below clock face **500.00**

Cosmetic Box, chip carved, mirror and red lined int., 10½" l. **85.00**

Desk, miniature, pine, multi-layered chip carved stars, compasses, circles, and geometric shapes, slant front hinged lid, blue paper lined int., six drawers, c1930, 21 × 15" **1,000.00**

Jardiniere, painted, early 20th C, 13¼" h **110.00**

Jewelry Box, poplar, bird finial, floral dec, carved name "Addie," four swing out trays, center compartment, scrolled feet, old dark finish, 12¼" h   **200.00**

Magazine Rack, hanging, brass tack dec, dark finish, 15" w **75.00**

Mirror, pine, chip carved, multi-layered moons, circles, hearts, and geometric designs, c1930, 12¼" w, 20½" h **925.00**

Picture Frame
  8 × 10" opening, applied dec, hearts at corners with points extending outward, elongated diamond on each side, losses, late 19th C **250.00**
  8½ × 10" opening, chip carved, floral design, four rect slats overlapping at corners, early 20th C **110.00**
  9 × 10¾", star shape, old brown paint **325.00**

Sewing Box, pincushion frame top, drawer, dark finish, 9½" l **30.00**

Wall Pocket, multi-layered strip dec, 11 × 16½".   **125.00**

WHIRLIGIGS

History: Whirligigs are a type of whimsical wind toy. Their origins are uncertain. Some claim that they began as a "Sabbath day toy" in Pennsylvania's German regions; others see them as a weather vane variation. In 1819 Washington Irving mentions whirligigs in his famous story "The Legend of Sleepy Hollow." Whirligigs enjoyed great popularity in the rural areas of New England, Middle Atlantic states, and the Midwest.

Whirligigs often contain more than one material in their construction. Wood and wire are the most commonly found. Since most were made by amateurs, a primitive appearance dominates. Single-figures usually feature rotating paddle-like arms. Multifigure examples employ a propeller that drives a series of gears and rods to make the figures move. The variety of subjects is endless.

Collectors place a premium on 19th century examples, many of which featured three dimensional figures. The use of plywood and silhouette figures are signs of a twentieth century example.

Many whirligigs have been reproduced and faked. Since whirligigs were used outdoors, there should be strong evidence of weathering as well as wear where the movable parts rubbed against the body. Look for signs of rust and corrosion. Contemporary whirligig makers copy older designs. Placed outside, they can age quickly. Thus, relying solely on condition to date a whirligig is risky.

References: Robert Bishop and Patricia Coblentz, *A Gallery of American Weathervanes and Whirligigs*, E. P. Dutton, 1979; Ken Fitzgerald, *Weathervanes and Whirligigs*, Clarkson N. Potter, 1967.

Reproduction Craftspersons: Bill Muehling, 440 Yemmerdall Rd, Lititz, PA 17543; Len Norman's Whirligig Creations, 5726 North Mobile, Chicago, IL 60646.

Reproduction Manufacturers: Maine Woods, Main St, PO Box 270, Bowdoinham, ME 04008; Plantation Characters, Box 896, Painesville, OH 44077

Bird, wood, polychrome paint, 7½" h   **125.00**
Boy, wood, painted, black cap, nail
    eyes, red jacket with steel tack but-
    tons, blue pants, aluminum colored
    arm paddles and boots, 13¼" h plus
    burl plinth base, 19" h overall. **1,100.00**

Directional Arrow, pine, 12¼" l, 10½" h, $50.00.

Dutch Windmill, wood, painted, black trim, gray ground, 16½" h, $150.00.

Carousel, wood and tin, carved and painted, bicycle wheel base, horses, chariots, toy soldiers, red, white, and blue tin base and scalloped awning roof, topped by flag and brass lamp finial, four conical metal cups mounted under base catch wind and turn carousel, carved wood lamp stand base, c1900, 24" d, 51" h . . . **6,500.00**
Dewey Boy, carved and painted, c1900, 12" h. **925.00**
Dirigible, pine and tin, carved and painted, silhouette of man on wood rod suspended by thin metal wires from flattened cigar-shaped balloon, green tin propellers and tail, early 20th C, 25½" l, 22 ½" h **4,125.00**
George Washington, on horseback, pine, carved and painted, stylized

American Indian, standing in birchbark canoe, carved and polychrome painted, 12" l, 10" h, $2,750.00. Photograph courtesy of James D Julia, Inc.

design, wearing military uniform, dappled gray horse, cannon, red, white, and blue propeller, green base, figures move when activated, late 19th/early 20th C, 47½″ l, 26¼″ h **7,150.00**

Horse, worn polychrome paint, 20th C, 15″ l **225.00**

Indian in Canoe

One Indian, dark skin, feathered headdress, white skirts, canoe paddles attached to arm baffles, green turned baluster and sphere base, late 19th/early 20th C, 16½″ h **950.00**

Two Indians, carved wood, polychrome dec, imperfections, New England, c1900, 21″ w, 3″ d, 11″ h **650.00**

Indian Warrior, gilded, relief carved facial features, glass bead eyes, red gilt-trimmed leather headdress and costume, black metal high boots, revolving arms extend to tapering gilded paddles, early 19th C, 16½″ h **35,200.00**

Jogger, wood and metal, old polychrome paint, 11″ h **250.00**

Kicking Mule, painted wood, imperfections, 20th C, 48″ l **275.00**

Man, carved, metal cap, vestiges of orig paint, 19th C, imperfections, 14¾″ h **500.00**

Man Sawing Log, tin and pine, carved and painted, wooden man holding tin saw above log, standing beneath black umbrella-propeller, figure saws log as umbrella spins, late 19th/early 20th C, 9½″ l, 14″ h **4,500.00**

Roman Soldier, carved, c1900, 12″ h **225.00**

Rudder, primitive, wood and metal, painted red, olive, and white, new oval base with stars dec, Adams County, OH, 20th C, 25½″ h **100.00**

Sailor, pine, carved and painted, relief carved facial features, painted hair, blue hat, metal brim, navy blue short jacket, nail head buttons, white shirt and pants, relief carved fingers and thumbs, hands extend to paddles, square black base, early 19th C, 14″ h **38,500.00**

Soldier, wood, very worn two tone blue paint, tin hat, belt, buttons, sword, and medal, Prince Albert Tobacco adv on hat, replaced applied facial features, 15¾″ h plus old wooden stool base, 31″ h overall **1,155.00**

Uncle Sam, pine, carved and painted, relief carved facial features and goatee, black top hat, blue swallowtail coat and vest, red and white striped trousers, paddle arms, round black base, 19th C, 11″ h **1,650.00**

FURNITURE

The Country look divides into three major categories—primitive, vernacular, and formal. A typical rural home contained all three types. Primitive work benches, shelves, and cabinets were found in the pantry, back porch, wash area, and sheds. Vernacular furniture dominated the kitchen, guest bedrooms, and living room. The parlor and master bedroom contained more formal pieces.

Not only was the Country home an eclectic mixture of furniture types, styles were mixed as well. Pieces were passed down from generation to generation. Family heirlooms comprised much of a Country home's furnishings. Further, members of the agrarian community practiced thrift. Many household furnishings and equipment were bought second hand at country auctions.

Rural America was not isolated from the formal furniture styles of the large metropolitan areas. However, they worked their way slowly into the countryside. Further, only styles whose architecture conveyed ruggedness and a long lasting quality were favored.

In the formal area, two major currents dominate the American furniture marketplace-furniture made in Great Britain and furniture made in the United States. American buyers continue to show a strong prejudice for objects manufactured in the United States. They will pay a premium for such pieces and accept them above technically superior and more aesthetic English examples.

Until the last half of the 19th century, formal American styles were dictated by English examples and design books. Regional furniture, such as the Hudson River Valley [Dutch] and the Pennsylvania German styles, did develop. A less formal furniture, designated as vernacular, developed throughout the 19th and early 20th centuries. Vernacular furniture deviates from the accepted formal styles and has a genre charm that many collectors find irresistible.

America did contribute a number of unique decorative elements to English styles. The American Federal period is a reaction to the English Hepplewhite period. American designers created furniture which influenced, rather than reacted to, world taste in the Gothic Revival style, Arts and Craft Furniture, Art Deco, and Modern International movement.

The following chart introduces you to the formal American design styles. Note that dates are approximate.

FURNITURE STYLES [APPROX. DATES]

William and Mary	1690–1730	Louis XIV	1850–1914
Queen Anne	1720–1760	Naturalistic	1850–1914
Chippendale	1755–1790	Renaissance Revival	1850–1880
Federal [Hepplewhite]	1790–1815	Neo-Greek	1855–1885
Sheraton	1790–1810	Eastlake	1870–1890
Empire [Classical]	1805–1830	Art Furniture	1880–1914
Victorian		Arts and Crafts	1895–1915
French Restauration	1830–1850	Art Nouveau	1896–1914
Gothic Revival	1840–1860	Art Deco	1920–1945
Rococo Revival	1845–1870	International Movement	1940–Present
Elizabethan	1850–1915		

American Country pieces, with the exception of Windsor chairs, stabilized and even dropped off slightly in value. This is due to two major market developments. First, the country-designer-look no longer enjoys the popularity it did during the American Bicentennial period in the late 1970s. Second, American decorators have focused more recently on the regional and European Country look.

Furniture is one of the few antiques fields where regional preferences are a factor in pricing. Victorian furniture is popular in New Orleans, and unpopular in New England. Oak is in demand in the Northwest, but not so much in the Middle Atlantic states.

References: Joseph T. Butler, *Field Guide To American Furniture*, Facts on File Publications, 1985; E & R Dubrow *Furniture, Made In America, 1875–1905*, Schiffer Publishing, 1982; Eileen and Richard Dubrow, *American Furniture of the 19th Century, 1840–1880*, Schiffer Publishing, 1983; Rachael Feild, *Macdonald Guide To Buying Antique Furniture*, Wallace-Homestead, 1989; Benno M. Forman, *American Seating Furniture, 1630–1730*, Winterthur Museum, W. W. Norton & Company, 1988; *Furniture Dealers' Reference Book, Zone 3, 1928–29*, reprint by Schiffer Publishing as *American Manufactured Furniture*, 1988; Myrna Kaye, *Fake, Fraud, Or Genuine, Identifying Authentic American Antique Furniture*, New York Graphic Society Book, 1987; William C. Ketchum, Jr., *Furniture, Volume 2: Chests, Cupboards, Desks, & Other Pieces*, Knopf Collectors' Guides To American Antiques, Alfred A. Knopf, 1982; Lew Larason, *Buying Antique Furniture: An Advisory*, Scorpio Publications, 1992; David P. Linquist and Caroline C. Warren, *Colonial Revival Furniture With Prices*, Wallace-Homestead, 1993.

Kathryn McNerney, *American Oak Furniture*, Book I (1984, 1992 value update), Book II (1994), Collector Books; *Pine Furniture, Our American Heritage*, Collector Books, 1989, 1994 value update; Kathryn McNerney, *Victorian Furniture*, Collector Books, 1981, 1994 value update; Milo M. Naeve, *Identifying American Furniture: A Pictorial Guide To Styles and Terms, Colonial to Contemporary, Second Edition*, American Association for State and Local History, 1989; George C. Neumann, *Early American Antique Country Furnishings: Northeastern America, 1650–1800's*, L–W Book Sales, 1984, 1993 reprint; Ellen M. Plante, *Country*

Furniture, Wallace-Homestead, 1993; Don and Carol Raycraft, *Collector's Guide to Country Furniture,* Book I (1984, 1991 value update), Book II (1988, 1991 value update), Collector Books; Harry L. Rinker, (ed.), *Warman's Furniture,* Wallace-Homestead, 1993; Marvin D. Schwartz, *Furniture: Volume 1: Chairs, Tables, Sofas & Beds,* Knopf Collector's Guides To American Antiques, Alfred A. Knopf, 1982; Tim Scott, *Fine Wicker Furniture, 1870–1930,* Schiffer Publishing, 1990.

Robert W. and Harriett Swedberg, *American Oak Furniture, Style and Prices, Book III, Second Edition,* Wallace-Homestead, 1991; —*Country Furniture and Accessories with Prices, Book 1* (1983) and *Book II,* (1984), Wallace-Homestead; —*Collector's Encyclopedia of American Furniture,* Volume 1 (1990, 1993 value update), Volume 2 (1992), Volume 3 (1994), Collector Books; —*Country Pine Furniture,* Wallace-Homestead, 1983; —*Furniture of the Depression Era,* Collector Books, 1987, 1992 value update; —*Swedberg's Price Guide To Antique Oak Furniture, First Series,* Collector Books, 1994; —*Victorian Furniture, Book I* (1976), *Book II* (1983), and *Book III* (1985), Wallace-Homestead; —*Wicker Furniture,* Wallace-Homestead, 1983; Gerald W. R. Ward, *American Case Furniture,* Yale University Art Gallery, 1988; Derita Coleman Williams and Nathan Harsh, *The Art and Mystery of Tennessee Furniture,* Tennessee Historical Society, 1988; Norman Vandal, *Queen Anne Furniture,* The Taunton Press, 1990; Lyndon C. Viel, *Antique Ethnic Furniture,* Wallace-Homestead, 1983.

There are hundreds of specialized books on individual furniture forms and styles. Two examples of note are: Monroe H. Fabian, *The Pennsylvania-German Decorated Chest,* Universe Books, 1978, and Charles Santore, *The Windsor Style in America, 1739–1830, Revised, Volumes I and II,* Running Press, 1992.

References, Clocks: Robert W. D. Ball, *American Shelf and Wall Clocks: A Pictorial History for Collectors,* Schiffer Publishing, 1992; Roy Ehrhardt, *Clock Identification and Price Guide,* Book I (rev. ed. 1979), Book II (1979), Heart of America Press; Roy Ehrhardt (ed.), *The Official Price Guide To Antique Clocks,* House of Collectibles, 1985; Tran Duy Ly, *American Clocks: A Guide To Identification and Prices,* Arlington Book Co, 1989, 1991 value update; Rick Ortenurger, *Vienna Regulators and Factory Clocks,* Schiffer Publishing, 1990.

Reproduction Craftspersons: *Beds*—Charles E Thibeau, The Country Bed Shop, PO Box 222, Groton, MA 01450; *Clocks*—Thomas & H W Blumenfeld, 10262 Raleigh Tavern Ln, Ellicott City, MD 21042; Clocks by Foster Campos, 213 Schoosett St, Pembroke, MA 02359; Edward H Stone, C–3 Company, 13200 Forest Dr, Bowie, MD 20715; Patrick J Terry, Terry Clocks, 2669 N Lakeview Dr, Warsaw, IN 46580; *Frames*—William Adair, Gold Leaf Studios, PO Box 50156 NW, Washington, DC 20004; John Morgan Baker, Framer, Reed Arts and Crafts, 233 West Fifth Ave, Columbus, OH 43201; Carolyn Fankhauser, Heartwood, PO Box 458, Canfield, OH 44406; Sally Greene Bunce, 4826 Mays Ave, Reading, Pa 19606; Ted Van Valin, The Scarlet Letter, PO Box 397, Sullivan, WI 53178; *Furniture Hardware*—Charles Euston, Woodbury Blacksmith & Forge Co, PO Box 268, Woodbury, CT 06798; James W Faust, 488 Porters Mill Rd, Pottstown, PA 19464; Steve Kayne, Kayne & Son Custom Forged Hardware, 76 Daniel Ridge Rd, Candler, NC 28715; Peter Renzetti, 301 Brinton's Bridge Rd, West Chester, PA 19382; Elmer Roush, Jr, Roush Forged Metals, Rte 2, Box 13, Cleveland, VA 24225.

General—Gary S Adriance, Adriance Heritage Collection, 5 N Pleasant St, South Dartmouth, MA 02748; Walter Ambrosch, RD 2, Box 311 Leona Rd, Troy, PA 16947; The Antique Catalog, Virginia Dowd Oberlin, 207 N Bowman Ave, Merion Station, PA 19066; Tom Bainbridge, Oley Valley Reproductions, RD 1, Box 207A, Oley, PA 19547; Michael Barba, 425 Old Ironhill Rd, Doylestown, PA 18901; John Conrad Bernstein, 5900 Green Spring Ave, Baltimore, MD 21209; Brian Boggs, Chairmaker, PO Box 4041, Berea, KY 40403; Joseph B Brannen & Co, 145 West 2nd St, Maysville, KY 41056; Gordon & Christopher Bretschneider, Bretschneider & Bretschneider, Box 12, School St, Shoreham, VT, 05770; Teri M Browning, The Wentworth Collection, PO Box 131, Wentworth, NH 03282; John W Bunker

& Son, 411 E Lincoln Hwy, Exton, PA 19341; Michael Camp, Cabinetmaker, 636 Starkweather Rd, Plymouth, MI 48170; Steven Cherry & Peter Deen, 1214 Goshen Mill Rd, Peach Bottom, PA 17563; Gene Cosloy, Great Meadows Joinery, PO Box 392, Wayland, MA 01778; Lawrence Crouse, PO Box 606, Kearneysville, WV 25430; Ted Curtin & Rob Tarule, Heart of the Wood, PO Box 3031, Plymouth, MA 02361; Peter J DiScala, Strafford House, 43 Van Sant Rd, New Hope, PA 18938; Donald A Dunlap, Cabinetmaker, Goodell Rd, RR 2, Box 39, Antrim, NH 03440; Clint Edwards, Cabinetmaker, 5208 Brook Rd, Richmond, VA 23227; Craig Farrow, PO Box 534, Watertown, CT 06795; Dennis Fly, 17th & 18th Century Ltd, 1440 Pineville Rd, New Hope, PA 18938; James A Frank, Box 55, Baldwin, MD 21013; Jim Fuller and Dolores Wood, The Craft Cove, 1516 Olive St, Coatesville, PA 19320; Robert Ian Gale-Sinex, Gale-Sinex Restorations, Ltd, 100 S Baldwin St #306, Madison, WI 53703; Joe and Lois Ann Gardner, Highway 91, Saratoga, NC 27873; Jeffrey P Greene, Furnituremaker, 1 W Main St, Wickford, RI 02852; D T Gutzwiller & Son, 777 Mason Morrow Rd, Lebanon, OH 45036; Chris Harter, The Country Furniture Shop, Box 125, Rte 20E, Madison, NY 13402; Jeff L Headley & Steve Hamilton, Mack S Headley & Sons, Rte 1, Senseny Rd, Berryville, VA 22611; Kenneth W Heiser, 195 E Yellow Breeches Rd, Carlisle, PA 17013; Van Heyneker, Rte 52, Box 314, Mendenhall, PA 19357; Benjamin C Hobbs, Rte 1, Box 517, Hertford, NC 27944; Robert Treate Hogg, 4500 Union School Rd, Oxford, PA 19363; Michael E Houle, Traditional Woodworking, PO Box 1089, Marstons Mills, MA 02648; Lenore Howe & Brian Braskie, North Woods Chair Shop, 237 Old Tilton Rd, Canterbury, NH 03224; Ian Ingersoll Cabinetmakers, Main St, West Cornwall, CT 06796; Irion Company Furniture Makers, 1 South Bridge St, Christiana, PA 17509; William Kidd, Cabinetmaker, 104 Jackson Ave, Morgantown, WV 26505; Jim Kirkpatrick, 9473 Perry Rd, Graham, NC 27253; R LaMontagne & Sons, 900 Joslin Rd, Harrisville, RI 02830; James Lea, Cabinetmaker, 9 West St, Rockport, ME 04856; David LeFort & Co, 293 Winter St, Hanover, MA 02339; Terri Lipman, 437 Lombard St, Dallastown, PA 17313; Jeffry Lohr Woodworking, Inc, 242 N Limerick Rd, Schwenksville, PA 19473; Pam Long and Steve Greene, PS Collection, Inc, 1294 Credle Rd, Virginia Beach, VA 23454; Thomas Lord, PO Box 194, Canterbury, CT 06331; Roger Z Mason, Olde Virginea Trading Co, PO Box 438, Williamsburg, VA 23187; Michael A McCullough, 1634 Chambersburg Rd, Gettysburg, PA 17325; Paula McDaniel, Jeff McFarlane, 1001 Election Rd, Oxford, PA 19363; Robert L McKeown III, 227 Gallaher Rd, Elkton, MD 21921; Meredith and Chris Miller, The Copper Rooster, RD #4, Country Place, Export, PA 15632; Paul S Miller, Chestnut Hill, PO Box 703, East Berlin, PA 17316; William H Miller, III, The Miller's, Box 562, Hatfield, PA 19440; Thomas B Morton Cabinetmakers, The Artworks, Studio 128, 100 N State St, Ephrata, PA 17522; Robert W Mouland, Colonial Designs, Box 1429, Havertown, PA 19083; John T Nicholas & Son, 704 N Michigan Ave, Howell, MI 48843; Robert J Nunn, PO Box 247, Unionville, PA 19375; Alan W Pease, The Country Bed Shop, RR 1, Box 65, Richardson Rd, Ashby, MA 01431; William A Pease, Cabinetmaker, 17 Fresh Meadow Dr, Lancaster, PA 17603; David and Emily Quinn, Olde Town Originals, 35 East 7th St, Bloomsburg, PA 17815; William J Ralston, Ralston Furniture Reproductions, Box 144, Cooperstown, NY 13326; Walter Raynes Cabinetmakers, 4900 Wetheredsville Rd, Baltimore, MD 21207; C W Riggs, Hannah's House, PO Box 158, St Marys, WV 26170; Bryce M Ritter, 100 Milford Rd, Downingtown, PA 19335; Jack B Robinson, American Country Reproductions, 8760 Beatty St NW, Massillon, OH 44646; Brian Rondeau, Brian's Country Cupboard, 2621 F York Rd, Gettysburg, PA 17325; William James Roth, PO Box 355, Yarmouth Port, MA 02675; Kirk Rush Reproductions, 406 Kirkwood Ln, Camden, SC 29020; Lee & Cynthia Sawyer, L Sawyer Fine Painted Furniture, 2304 Carolina Rd, Chesapeake, VA 23322; Roger W Scheffer, Straw Hill Chairs, Straw Hill, R 1, West Unity, NH 03743; Edward J Schoen, Signature Gallery, Depot Shoppes, Plank & Lancaster Aves, Paoli, PA 19301; K Alan Styer, Cabinetmaker, PO Box 50, Greenford, OH 44422; John R Sullivan, Starling Furniture, 50 Allen St, Braintree, MA 02184;

Ted Sypher, 69 Richards Rd, Chenango Forks, NY 13746; William Tillman, RD 3, Box 93, Stewartstown, PA 17363; Thomas W Timm, 213 West 5th St, Summerville, SC 29483; Michael B Timmins, PO Box 95, 140 Valleybrook Rd, Chester Heights, PA 19017; Norman Vandal, Cabinetmaker, PO Box 67, Roxbury, VT 05669; Gregory Vasileff Reproductions, 740 North St, Greenwich, CT 06831; Herman Woolfrey Furnituremakers, 1433 Whitford Rd, West Chester, PA 19380.

Grain Painting—Margorie Akin, Akin/D'Lamater Studio, Inc, 61 W Chapel Ave, Carlisle, PA 17013; Rebecca A Erb, 706 Brownsville Rd, Sinking Spring, PA 19608; Dorothy Fillmore Studio, 84 Pilgrim Dr, Windsor, CT 06095; David and Marie Gottshall, Gottshall's Folk Art, 210 E High St, Womelsdorf, PA 19467; Petra & Thomas Haas, PO Box 20, Oley, PA 19547; Dorothy Wood Hamblett, PO Box 295, Millbury, MA 01527; Carol Martell, Designs Unlimited, 13401 Chestnut Oak Dr, Gaithersburg, MD 20878; Virginia Jacobs McLaughlin, Antique Cupboard, 812 W Main St, Emmettsburg, MD 21727; Larry Plummer, 329 E Piccadilly St, Winchester, VA 22601; Sherry A Ringler, Ringler Design Associates, 2812 Poplar Dr, Springfield, OH 45504; Barbara Strawser, PO Box 165, Schaefferstown, PA 17088; David Bradstreet Wiggins, Itinerant Painter, Hale Rd, Box 420, Tilton, NH 03276.

Ladderback Chairs—David Barrett, Barretts Bottoms, Rt 2, Box 231, Bower Rd, Kearneysville, WV 25430; Rick & Susan Steingress, Candlertown Chairworks, PO Box 1630, Candler, NC 28715; *Miniatures*—Michael A McCullough, 1634 Chambersburg Rd, Gettysburg, PA 17325; L H Peavey, 41 Wagonwheel Rd, Sudbury, MA 017876; *Pennsylvania German*—Dan Backenstose, Jr, Spring House Classics, PO Box 541, Schaefferstown, PA 17088; Jan Switzer, Painted Pony Folk Art, 8392 M–72 West, Traverse City, MI 49684; *Shelves*—Douglas and Karen Jones, Missouri Pine Co, PO Box 31, Seneca, MO 64865; Jeff and Sandy Jones, Black River Woodworks, 47777 Griggs Rd, Wellington, OH 44090; *Tin Pie Safe Panels*—Gerald Fellers, The Tin Man by Gerald Fellers, 2025 Seneca Dr, Troy, OH 45373; *Trunks*—Steven Lalloff, Traditional Leatherwork Co, 14311 Bryn Mawr Dr, Noblesville, IN 46060; *Twig Furniture*—Jane and Don Miles, The Willow Place, 374 S Atlanta St, Roswell, GA 30075; *Upholstered Furniture*—Alexandra Pifer, 1817 Shoppe, Inc, 5606 E State Rt 37, Delaware, OH 43015; Betty Urquhart, The Maynard House, 11 Maynard St, Westborough, MA 01581.

Windsor—Robert Barrow, 412 Thames St, Bristol, RI 02809; Curtis Buchanan, 208 E Main St, Jonesborough, TN 37659; Jeffrey M Fiant, 260 Golf Rd, Reinholds, PA 17569; Rolf A Hofer, 1077 Ellis Woods Rd, Pottstown, PA 19464; Samuel J Laity, II, RE 11, Accomac Rd, York, PA 17406; Brendan Murphy, 2757 Lydius St W, Schenectady, NY 12306; Olde Virginia Floorcloth & Trading Co, Sharon and Roger Mason, PO Box 438, Williamsburg, VA 23185; Kai Pedersen, RD 3, Box 3088A, Mohnton, PA 19540; Jim Rantala, Windsor Wood Works, 8909 Toad Lake Rd, Ellsworth, MI 49729; Vince Rygelis, PO Box 231, Williams, OR 97544; David Sawyer, RD 1, Box 107, East Calais, VT 05650; Roger W Scheffer, Straw Hill Chairs, RFD 1, Straw Hill, West Unity, NH 03743; Woody Scoville, Box 65, E. Calais, VT 05650; Mark Soukup, Rte 1, Box 27A1, Gap Mills, WV 24941; Windsors by Bill Wallick, 41 N 7th St, Wrightsville, PA 17368; Max Wardlow, RR 1, Fillmore, MO 64449.

Reproduction Manufacturers: *Adirondack & Rustic Furniture*—Adirondack Store and Gallery, 109 Saranac Avenue, Lake Placid, NY 12946; Amish Country Collection, RD 5, Sunset Valley Rd, New Castle, PA 16105; Ptarmigan Willow, PO Box 551, Fall City, WA 98024; Wood-Lot Farms, Star Rte 1, Shady, NY 12479; *Benches*—American Country House, PO Box 317, Davison, MI 48423; *Brass Beds*—Bedlam Brass, 137 Rte 4 Westbound, Paramus, NJ 07652; *Cane and Rush Supplies*—The Country Seat, RD #2, Box 24, Kempton, PA 19529, Frank's Cane and Rush Supply, 7252 Heil Ave, Huntington Beach, CA 92647; *Chairs*—Hummingbird Hill Chairmakers, PO Box 322, Millville, PA 17846; *Children's Furniture*—Nap Brothers Parlor Frame Co, Inc, 122 Naubuc Ave, Glastonbury, CT 06033; Ricyn: Country Collectables, PO Box 577, Twisp, WA 98856; Woodbee's, RR #1, Poseyville, IN 47633.

Clocks—Riverside Time, 1 Fado Ln, Cos Cob, CT 06807; Van Dommelen Clocks, 9–A Church St, Lambertville, NJ 08530; Cupboards—Ohio Painted Furniture, Rte 4, Box 200 B, Athens, OH 45701; Cut Nails—The Tremont Nail Co, 8 Elm St, PO Box 111, Wareham, MA 02571; Doors—Old 'N Ornate, PO Box 10493 H, Eugene, OR 97440; Furniture Finishes— Stulb's Old Village Paint, PO Box 297, 618 W Washington St, Norristown, PA 19404; Furniture Hardware—The Antique Hardware Store, 43 Bridge St, Frenchtown, NJ 08825; Old Smithy Shop, Box 336, Milford, NH 03055; Town and Country, Main St, East Conway, NH 04037; Williamsburg, Blacksmiths, Inc, Goshen Rd, Williamsburg, MA 01096.

General—Amanda Wilder Collection, 500 Bowman Dr, Sidney, OH 45365; American Country Reproductions, 8760 Beatty St NW, Massillon, OH 44646; Basye-Bomberger/Fabian House, PO Box 86, W Bowie, MD 20715–0086; Bathroom Machineries, 495 Main St, PO Box 1020, Murphys, CA 95247; Bucks County Furniture Ltd, 174 Keystone Dr, Telford, PA 18969; Carolina Leather House, Inc, PO Box 2468, Hickory, NC 28603; Chairmakers, Box 67, Melrose, WI 54642; Chestnut Tree Studio, 100 Summer St, Kennebunk, ME 04043; Chinaberry General Store, 1846 Winfield Dunn Highway, Sevierville, TN 38762; Classic Furniture, Box 1544, Kansas City, MO 64141; Classics in Wood, 82 Lisbon Rd, Canterbury, CT 06331; The Colonial Keeping Room, 16 Ridge Rd, RFD #1, Box 704, Fairfield, ME 04937; Colonial Woodworks, PO Box 10612, Raleigh, NC 27605; Country Is . . ., PO Box 824, Jacksonville, AL 36265; Country Loft, 1506 South Shore Park, Hingham, MA 02043; Country Workshop, 41-A Bacon St, Westminster, MA 01473; Cumberland General Store, Rte 3, Crossville, TN 38555; Decker Antique Reproductions, PO Box 5688, Knoxville, TN 37918; Ezra G, 1120 Sandusky St, Fostoria, OH 44830; Goodwood, PO Box 426, Plainfield, VT 05667; Hammermark Associates, 10 Jericho Turnpike, Floral Park, NY 11001; H C Gulden Mfg Co, Legacy Lane, PO Box 66, Aspers, PA 17304; Heartwood, PO Box 458, Canfield, OH 44406; House of Vermillion, PO Box 18642, Kearns, UT 84118; Ingrid's Handcraft Cross-roads, 8 Randall Rd, Rochester, MA 02770; The Joinery Company, PO Box 518, Tarboro, NC 27886; Lace Wood 'N Tin Tyme, 6496 Summerton, Shepherd, MI 48883; Mailwagon Gifts, Box 378, Bowmansville, PA 17507; McFarland & Conroy Furniture & Collectibles, 923 Broad St, Shrewsbury, NJ 07702; McGuire Family, PO Box 124, Esle La Motte, VT 05463; Mount Royal Reproductions, 23 Greylock Rd, Bristol, RI 02809; Muff's Antiques, 135 S Glassell St, Orange, CA 92666; Olde Mill House Shoppe, 105 Strasburg Pike, Lancaster, PA 17602; Out of the Woods, 38 Pinehurst Rd, Marshfield, MA 02050; Pine Tree Reproductions, 88160 Celery Court Rd, Decatur, MI 49045; Pure and Simple, PO Box 535, 117 W Hempstead, Nashville, AR 71852; James Redway Furniture Makers, 93 Porter Hill, Middlebury, CT 06762; Thomas Schwenke Inc, 219 East 60th St, New York, NY 10022; Sturbridge Yankee Workshop, Blueberry Rd, Westbrook, ME 04092; J L Treharn & Co, 1024 Mahoning Ave, Youngstown, OH 44502; Van Sinderen, Box 498, West Lebanon, ME 04027; The Warmth of Wood, 540 McCombs Road, Venetia, PA 15367; Woodstock Furniture Co, Inc, 1100 W Beardsley Ave, PO Box 2401, Elkhart, IN 46515; The Workshops of David T Smith, 3600 Shawhan Rd, Morrow, OH 45152; Yield House, North Conway, NH 03860.

Jelly Cupboards-Five Trails Antiques and Country Accents, 116 E Water St, Circleville, OH 43113; Miniatures—River Bend Miniatures, PO Box 856, West Chester, OH 45071; Toncoss Miniatures, PO Box 15146, Riverside, RI 02915; Mirrors— Williams Cabinetry, PO Box 39, Hog Bay, North Sullivan, ME 04664; Mission—Black Oak Industries Ltd, PO Box 64, Cayuta, NY 14824; Pie Safes—The Vine and Cupboard, PO Box 309, George Wright Rd, Woowich, ME 04579; Porcelain Reglazing—Guaranteed Porcelain Services, 3568 Western Branch Blvd, Portsmouth, VA 23707; Shelves—Old South Craftsman, Inc, 1477 Rowe Rd, Lexington, NC 27292; Weese's Woodshop, 3619 Walton Ave, Cleveland, OH 44113; Shutters—Historic Windows, PO Box 1172, Harrisonburg, VA 22801; Stenciling Supplies— Gail Grisi Stenciling, Inc, PO Box 1263, Haddonfield, NJ 08033; StenArt, Inc, PO Box 114,

Pitman, NJ 08071; Stencil School, PO Box 94, Shrewsbury, MA 01545; *Tin Pie Safe Panels*—Clark Manufacturing Co, 1611 Southwind Dr, Raymore, MO 64083; Country Accents, RD #2, Box 293, Stockton, NJ 08559; *Trunks*—Lamb and Lanterns, 902 N Walnut St, Dover, OH 44622.

Upholstered Furniture—Hunt Galleries, Inc, PO Box 2324, 2920 Highway 127 North, Hickory, NC 28603; The Seraph, PO Box 500, Sturbridge, MA 01566; *Wicker*—Ellenburg's Wicker & Casual, I-40 & Stamey Farm Rd, PO Box 5628, Statesville, NC 28677; *Windsor*— The Guild of Gulden Cabinetmakers, Gulden Gallery Investment Replicas, PO Box 66, Aspers, PA 17304; Rustic Reproductions, PO Box 1966, Gulf Shores, AL 36547; Warren Chair Works, 79 Joyce St, Warren, RI 02885.

Reproduction Alert: Beware of the large number of reproductions. During the twenty-five years following the American Centennial of 1876, there was a great revival in copying furniture styles and manufacturing techniques of earlier eras. These centennial pieces now are over one hundred years old. They confuse many dealers and collectors.

Note: Prices vary considerably on furniture. Shop around. Furniture is plentiful unless you are after a truly rare example. Examine all pieces thoroughly. Too many furniture pieces are bought on impulse. Turn furniture upside down; take it apart. The amount of repairs and restoration to a piece has a strong influence on price. Make certain you know about all repairs and changes before buying.

The prices listed below are "average" prices. They are only a guide.

AMERICAN COUNTRY

BEDS

Folk Art, hardwood, red and brown grain painting, turned posts, applied moldings, harlequin scratch carved dec, zig-zag details highlighted in black paint with white striping, some wear and age cracks, removable plates cover holes for bed bolts, sgd "Biekman," one orig plate, others old replacements, expertly replaced finials, replaced side rails, Harrisburg, PA, 45" w, 74" l mattress size, 78" h **2,700.00**

Bed, cannonball, maple, paneled headboard, turned posts with ball finials, early 19th C, 40" w, 84" d, 42" h, $1,320.000. Photograph courtesy of Leslie Hindman

Hired Man's, maple, ring and block turned posts with turned finials, turned head and foot rails, refinished, side rails replaced, 24" w, 73" d, 28" h **250.00**
Mission, Frank Lloyd Wright, designed for Evans Residence, Chicago, oak, heavy crest rail on solid headboard and footboard, twin size, 1909 . . . . **7,000.00**
Pencil Post, birch, tapered posts with chamfered corners, shaped headboard, old nut brown finish, replaced side rails and canopy frame, 50" w, 70" d, 73" h **1,475.00**
Quarter Tester, cherry, octagonal shaped posts, shaped headboard, foot posts with acorn finials, baluster turned legs, 59½" d, 78" h **725.00**
Rope
Birch and Pine, cannonball finials, turned posts, scrolled headboard, old honey colored refinishing, replaced side rails, 53" w, 74" d, 48" h **250.00**
Cherry and Poplar, cannonball finials, similarly shaped head and foot boards, replaced side rails, refinished, 54" w, 72½" d, 48" h **385.00**
Curly Maple
Bottle-like finials, turned posts, shaped headboard and footboard, turned tapered feet, refinished, footboard and side rails replaced, 56" w, 74" d, 52" h **990.00**

Mushroom and ball finials, turned posts, scrolled headboard with turned crest, turned blanket rail, raised ball feet, 53" w, 69" d, 60" h **1,750.00**

Grain Painted, fancy turned posts with mushroom finials and raised ball feet, paneled headboard and footboard with shaped crest, PA or OH, 19th C, 51½" w, 47½" h . . . **1,325.00**

Poplar

Flattened ball finials, turned posts, curved headboard and footboard, old replaced side rails, gray repaint over earlier paint layers, 42" w, 57" d, 32½" h   **150.00**

Spool shaped finials, turned posts, shaped headboard and footboard, raised flattened ball feet, 50" w, 73" d, 47½" h **100.00**

Settle, pine, paneled back with applied molding at top, shaped ends, bench folds out into bed, finish cleaned down to old red, minor repairs, 73½" w, 48¾" h **700.00**

Tall Post

Mahogany

Chippendale, carved, fluted tapered posts, shaped headboard, cabriole legs, claw and ball feet, restored, MA, 56¾" w, 76" d, 81¾" h **3,250.00**

Federal, carved, tester, two fluted and vasiform and ring turned posts, two plain posts, New England, c1800, 82" h **1,975.00**

Federal, turned and reeded bulbous posts, highly arched headboard, turned legs, old faded finish, rails replaced, headboard altered to make bed narrower, 44" w, 73" d, 89½" h **1,275.00**

Maple, bird's eye maple, and poplar, massive ball turned post with mushroom finials, paneled headboard, ball feet, old refinishing, replaced headboard, rails extended, age cracks in posts, replaced tester frame, 53" w, 76" d, 85" h **375.00**

Walnut, carved and turned posts, flat tester, refinished, with linens, southeastern US, c1825, 93" h   **3,575.00**

Vernacular, oak, paneled headboard with applied feather and fan moldings, flat rail on paneled footboard, square legs, 40" w, 76" d **300.00**

BENCHES

Amish, pine, legs mortised through top, simple apron, rounded ends, old red paint, wear and edge damage, 80" l   **110.00**

Bucket, ash, mortised construction, rect top, two shelves, one board bootjack ends, old varnish finish, OH, 37" w, 14" d, 32" h **250.00**

Hall, oak

Mission

Attributed to Brooks or Imperial, slightly canted ends with four square cutouts, triangular back boards, long lift top seat, deep apron, recent medium brown finish, 84" w, 19½" d, 24" h   **900.00**

Gustav Stickley, Model No. 205, five broad slats across back, one broad slat each side, exposed tenons, red decal mark, some orig finish, 55¾" w, 22" d, 30" h **2,500.00**

Straight crest rail and lower rail with exposed mortise and tenon construction, five flat arrow form spindles, square stiles with arched tops, shaped arms, flat arrow form arm supports, hinged lift lid seat, straight apron, square legs, 39" w, 17" d, 38" h, matching hanging wall mirror with arched crest, double hat hooks on each corner, exposed mortise and tenon construction, and beveled mirror plate, c1900, price for 2 pcs **800.00**

Shaped crest with applied C-scroll moldings, scrolled finials on rect stiles, crest shaped beveled mirror panel above vasiform splat, straight arms, curved arm supports, hinged lift lid seat, scalloped apron, cabriole legs, four double hat hooks, 80" h **600.00**

Kneeling, Windsor, rect top with reeded edge, splayed base, bamboo turned legs, gray repaint over earlier olive green and red layers, 36¾" w, 6¾" d, 6" h **325.00**

Mammy, Windsor, bamboo turnings, flat crest rail, double seat back with sixteen turned spindles, scrolled arms, plank seat, flat board stretchers front and back, rockers, refinished, holes in seat for baby guard plugged, 54" l **600.00**

Piano, oak, rounded corners on rect overhanging seat, straight skirt, square tapered legs, flared feet, 39" w, 19" d, 21" h **125.00**

Porch, pine

Plank top, shaped apron, bootjack legs, trestle stretcher, old brown graining, minor wear and edge damage, 55½" l, 15½" d, 18" h   **135.00**

Weathered top with molded apron, bootjack feet mortised through top, old dark finish, 96" l, 10½" d, 18" h **175.00**

Settle

Decorated

Brown and black striping, angel wing, fruit, and foliage dec, grayish-yellow ground, shaped crest, triple seat back with three fat vase splats separated by turned spindles, scrolled arms, S-scrolled seat, turned legs, flat board stretchers front and back, 80½" w **1,375.00**

Polychrome stenciled birds and fruit on shaped two part crest rail, turned half spindle back, shaped arms, rolled plank seat, turned legs and front stretchers, white and yellow striping on arms, seat, and turnings, dark ground, striping may be old repaint, 73" w **900.00**

Hardwood, arrow back

Straight crest, triple seat back, scrolled arms, turned tapered legs, refinished, repairs and replacements, 76" w **385.00**

Wide board crest, triple seat back with twenty-one arrow spindles, scrolled arms, shaped seat, splayed base with eight turned tapered legs and wide board stretchers, refinished, repairs and replacements, 76" w **385.00**

Pine

Paneled back, shaped ends and arms, shoe feet, minor age cracks, worn finish, 60½" w, 16" d, 55" h **2,425.00**

Vermont, cutout ends form armrests, random board back, plank seat, straight apron, bootjack feet, old refinishing, 66½" w, 13" d, 61" h **650.00**

Poplar and Hardwood, arrow back, plank seat, highly refinished, 72" w **325.00**

Windsor style, bamboo turnings, straight crest, twenty-four spindle back, plank seat, ten bamboo turned legs, black repaint, repaired break in seat, 96" w **650.00**

Water

Pine

Rectangular overhanging top, bootjack ends, rect base shelf, one board top, ends, and shelf, square nail construction, 48" w, 17 ½" d, 27" h **150.00**

Rectangular top, bootjack ends are canted and dovetailed into top, old worn green repaint, 32" l, 11¾" d **275.00**

Pine and Poplar, scalloped crest, shaped brackets, upper shelf with three bevel edged dovetailed drawers, shaped ends, open back with straight backsplash, pair of paneled cupboard doors, cutout feet, refinished, 42" w, 18" d, 54" h **1,750.00**

Poplar

Stepback upper shelf with peaked crest and two dovetailed drawers, shaped one board ends, base with open shelf, two paneled doors, and cutout feet, old cast iron pulls, old varnish finish, door latches replaced with turnbuckles, 48" w, 15" d, 47½" h **1,000.00**

Three quarter gallery, two shelves, bootjack ends, old worn olive gray repaint, 48½" w, 14" d, 29" h **450.00**

Windsor, bowed back rail, thirty-nine bamboo turned back spindles, scrolled arms, turned arm supports, shaped seat, splayed base with bulbous turned legs and H-form stretchers, old repaired split in one end of seat at arm post, minor repairs, Philadelphia, PA, 72½" w, 16¼" h seat, 35" h **5,500.00**

BLANKET CHESTS

Curly Maple, poplar, walnut, and cherry secondary woods, molded edge lid, dovetailed case, dovetailed drawer, dovetailed bracket feet, refinished, lid rehinged, front edge molding replaced, 39¾" w, 19½" d, 27½" h **1,750.00**

Decorated

Black brush stamped polka dots on red ground, pine, six board construction, edge molded lid, dovetailed case, till, base molding, lid hinge rail repaired, end piece of base molding replaced, base cut down, 38½" w, 17½" d, 18¼" h   **225.00**

Black sponged spots on gray ground, pine, applied edge molding on lid, dovetailed case, painted top, front, and ends, New England, early 19th C, 48½" w, 19" h **1,425.00**

Blue sponged paint, pine, paneled construction, lidded till, single drawer with applied edge beading and turned pulls, corner posts with turned flattened ball feet, some old paint touch up, lid repainted, one drawer pull replaced, 38¾" w, 20" d, 31¼" h **2,200.00**

Grained and putty dec, Federal, brass escutcheon, two drawers, glass knobs, bracket feet, central MA, c1820, 38" w, 17½" d, 41" h . . . **4,290.00**

Ochre and mustard putty dec, pine, six board, bracket feet, New England, c1820, 42" w, 17⅛ " d, 22½" h **3,200.00**

Red and black paint dec, pine, scalloped bracket feet, New England, c1800, 42½" w, 20½" d, 28" h . . **1,760.00**

Figured Walnut, Country Sheraton, mortised and pinned construction, applied lid edge molding, lidded till, paneled sides and ends, applied base molding, high turned feet on casters, old mellow finish, KY or TN, 43½" w, 22" d, 31¼" h **600.00**

Grain Painted

Brown and yellow vinegar graining, bootjack ends, minor wear and edge damage, feet repaired on one end, 48½" w, 20½" d, 29 ¾" h. . **715.00**

Brown comb graining over yellow ground, poplar, dovetailed case, large lidded till, dovetailed bracket feet with scroll design apron all four sides, 47½" w, 23" d, 28" h **685.00**

Dark brown graining, pine, molded edge lid, dovetailed case, lidded till, base molding, turned feet, 43" w, 21" d, 26" h **275.00**

Red and black graining over earlier dark brown finish, poplar, dovetailed case with relief carved arched front and end panels, lidded till, molded base, ogee bracket feet, yellow painted initials, date, and trim on panels, added underside braces to lid, repair to till lid, 48½" w, 22½" d, 29" h. **1,650.00**

Reddish-brown flame graining, poplar, molded edge lid, dovetailed case, molded edge base, turned feet, till removed, 45¾" w, 20" d, 24" h. **1,000.00**

Red flame graining, poplar, pine secondary wood, molded edge lid, paneled case with square corner posts, lidded till, turned ball feet, minor molding damage, 36¾" w, 18¼" d, 24¾" h **850.00**

Red graining, pine, hinged breadboard type lid, dovetailed case with till, turned feet, 38" w, 19" d, 24¼" h **715.00**

Red vinegar graining on yellow ground with black trim, poplar, molded edged lid, lidded till, dovetailed case, molded edge base, turned legs, orig porcelain escutcheon, 44" w, 22½" d, 24½" h **1,825.00**

Salmon graining, maple and pine, two false drawers, single base drawer, MA, c1750, 41¾" w, 18" d, 34½" h **1,540.00**

Pine

Putty green paint, single long drawer, New England, 42" w, 20" d, 32" h   **925.00**

Red Paint, Queen Anne, old finish, MA, c1740, 36" w, 17" d, 31 ¾" h **1,980.00**

Poplar and Pine, dovetailed case, till, molded base, bracket feet, wrought iron strap hinges, refinished, glued repair to one foot, 46" w, 20¾" d, 25" h **450.00**

Walnut, Country Chippendale, molded edge lid, till, dovetailed case, molded base, two dovetailed and cockbeaded drawers flanked by carved rope twist quarter columns, ogee bracket feet, orig oval brasses, varnished int., traces of red and yellow paint, minor repair to one foot, old faded refinishing, 44" w, 21¾" d, 28¼" h **2,035.00**

Walnut and Poplar, Country Chippendale, molded edge lid, dovetailed case, till with three dovetailed drawers, three dovetailed overlapping base drawers, base molding, dovetailed ogee feet including center foot, wrought iron strap hinges, old worn soft finish, feet replaced, some edge damage to drawers, drawer pulls missing, 50" w, 22¾" d, 27¾" h . . . **1,100.00**

BOOKCASE

Cherry, Chippendale, on frame, molded cornice, three glazed doors each with ten panes, three short drawers in base, shaped bracket feet, two shaped center feet, NY, c1800, 72" w, 19" d, 86½" h **6,000.00**

Oak

Mission

Lifetime Co, Grand Rapids, MI, rect top, three glazed doors each with eight panes, corner posts with through tenons, iron pulls, sgd metal tag, c1912, 61½" w, 13" d, 49¼" h **4,000.00**

Skandia Furniture Co, Rockford, IL, sectional, four graduated sections, hinged glass fronts, Viking trademark **575.00**

Bookstand, oak, mortised construction, Roycroft, 26" w, 14" d, 26½" h, $495.00. Photograph courtesy of Leslie Hindman Auctioneers.

Stacking, quarter sawn, five sections, swelled ogee cornice, three graduated bookcase sections with retractable glass doors, false drawer in base, brass knobs, orig paper label "Manufactured by the Globe-Wernicke Co., Cincinnati, O," 34" w, 12" d, 47" h **525.00**

Two glazed doors, divided shelved int., cabriole legs with center leg, 48" w, 13" d, 51" h **750.00**

Walnut, poplar secondary wood, Country Hepplewhite, molded cornice, glazed double doors each with eight wavy glass panes, beaded door frames, cloth lined int., four dovetailed overlapping drawers, slightly curved apron, high cutout feet, old refinishing, replaced brasses, minor pieced repairs in feet and cornice, 63" w, 12¾" d, 84¼" h **4,625.00**

BOOKCASE DESKS

Larkin, oak, bombe shaped cornice supported by beveled mirrored back panel and front columns with scrolled capitals, bowed top shelf, bowed bookcase with convex glass door panel, recessed beveled mirror over fall front writing flap, three graduated short drawers, column posts, scroll feet, turned wood pulls, 42" w, 14" d, 67" h **1,500.00**

Side by Side, oak, asymmetrical, shaped crest, full length bookcase with glazed door, shelved int., square beveled mirror, paneled fall front writing flap, three overlapping short drawers, shaped apron, bracket feet, bail handle drawer pulls, 38" w, 14" d, 65" h **475.00**

CABINET

China, oak
  Bow front, shaped top with molded back, rect center glazed door with single pane, convex glass side panels flanked by scrolled columns, scrolled bracket feet, 38" w, 58" h   **600.00**
  Mission, Lifetime Co, Grand Rapids, MI, rect top with inset corner posts, two plain glazed doors, adjustable shelves, 43" w, 14½" d, 57" h . . .   **650.00**
  Quarter sawn veneer, flat cornice, two full length glazed doors, int. shelves, base molding, cabriole legs on casters, 40" w, 12" d, 63" h   **500.00**
  Filing, oak, four drawers with brass handles and label frames, paneled ends, 20" w, 25" d, 53" h **350.00**
  Kitchen, oak, Hoosier style, two pieces
    Ingram Richardson Manufacturing Co, Frankfort, IN, top with shaped crest, four three-paneled cupboard doors, and pull down tambour door, base with porcelain pullout work surface, large paneled cupboard door, bank of three graduated overlapping drawers, paneled ends, and square feet on casters, floral dec on upper doors, white factory finish, 40" w, 25" d, 71" h **350.00**
    Sellers, Elwood, IN, top with full length paneled door enclosing flour sifter, pair of double paneled cupboard doors, and pull down tambour door, base with porcelain pullout work surface, int. pullout cutting board and wire rack shelf, overlapping drawer over paneled cupboard door, bank of three graduated overlapping short drawers, third drawer is tin lined bread drawer, paneled ends, and square legs, metal tag "Sellers The Better Kitchen Cabinet Kitchen Maid, Elwood, Ind., U.S.A. Trademark registered," 41" w, 27" d, 70" h **750.00**
  Medicine, oak, incised lines on straight crest and base rail, shaped ends, glazed door, shelved int., 17" w, 6" d, 28" h **125.00**
  Music, oak, rect top with rounded corners, single door with scalloped lower edge, cabriole legs, 18" w, 16" d, 34" h **175.00**

CANDLESTANDS

Birch, Country Hepplewhite
  Rectangular top with cut corners, turned column, scimitar legs, refinished with traces of old red fin-

ish, legs have some damage where they join column, one leg nailed, stained top, 31¼" w, 13½" d, 26¼" h **200.00**

Square one board top, turned column, tripod base with spider legs, legs repaired at base juncture, one leg replaced, 16½" sq, 27½" h **300.00**

Cherry

Chippendale

Square one board top with scalloped edge, turned column with simple chip carved dec, tripod base, snake feet, 15¾" sq, 26" h **2,200.00**

Square one board top, sculptural bracket with cutout for drawer, turned column, tripod base with shaped legs, old black paint on base, dark finish on top, replaced drawer, 16¾" sq, 25" h   **650.00**

Country Chippendale, square top, turned column, tripod base with snake feet, old soft finish, repairs, two feet ended out, patch and age cracks to top, 16½" sq, 27" h . . .   **425.00**

Federal, inlaid, square top, turned column, CT, c1800, 12½" sq, 27¼" h **3,190.00**

Mathew Allen, one board top with cut corners, turned column, tripod base with spider legs, underside of top sgd "Mathew Allen," one leg with edge damage at column, glued break at column base, refinished, 18" w, 17¾" d, 28¾" h   **525.00**

Curly Maple

Country, octagonal top with applied gallery, turned two part laminated column, tripod base with snake feet, old finish, small crack in one leg at post, one section of gallery molding damaged, 14" w top, 28½" h **1,550.00**

Hepplewhite, two board top with cutout ovolo corners, turned column, tripod base with spider legs, mellow refinishing, replaced top, 16" w, 15½" d, 26" h **875.00**

Curly Maple and Birch, Country Hepplewhite, elongated octagonal curly maple tilt top, birch tripod base with turned column and spider legs and spade feet, old mellow finish, age cracks in column, one leg repaired, New England, 20¼" w, 12½" d, 27½" h **385.00**

Mahogany, Country Federal

Round top, turned column, cabriole legs, pad feet, refinished, top reset, RI, 1790–1800, 19½" d, 26" h   **775.00**

Candlestand, Federal, tiger maple, oblong top, three out-curving legs, circular medial shelf, first quarter 19th C, 24" w, 18" d, 28" h, $1,320.00. Photograph courtesy of Leslie Hindman Auctioneers.

Tilt top, octagonal shaped top with band inlaid edge, tripod base with ring turned baluster column and spider legs, New England, 1800–15, 28½" h **650.00**

Mahogany and Cherry, Federal, circular tilt top, New England, c1810, 19¾" d, 29½" h **1,320.00**

Maple, one board top with decorative cutout corners, turned column, tripod base with highly arched cutout feet, old dark reddish brown varnish stain, old repairs to column base, one leg loose, 17½" w, 16¼" d, 27¾" h **350.00**

Maple or Cherry, Country Chippendale, sq two board top with rounded corners, turned column with chip carved dec, tripod base with snake feet, refinished, repairs to legs and column base, 16¾" sq, 27" h **550.00**

Maple and Birch, Country Federal, tilt top, line inlaid octagonal top, ring and baluster turned column, cabriole legs, pad feet, one foot restored, New England, 1810–20, 20" w, 26" h . . .   **825.00**

Poplar and Oak, round adjustable shelf on turned and threaded post, round base with three splayed legs, old dark patina, cracked top braced on underside, 32½" h **400.00**

Walnut

Chippendale, circular dished top, turned column, tripod base with snake feet, refinished, PA, c1770, 18¼" d, 27" h **1,050.00**

Round one board tilt top, turned column, four part base with wide arched feet, old refinishing, repaired crack in top, 18" d, 26 ¼" h   **200.00**

Turtle back top, turned column, tripod base with short cutout legs and snake feet, old worn green repaint, two legs have repaired breaks, 15¼" w, 15" d, 25¼" h. .   **500.00**

Walnut and Cherry, Country Chippendale, circular walnut top, cherry tripod base with turned column and padded snake feet, 18⅛ " w, 17⅜ " d, 25¼" h **465.00**

CHAIRS

Arrow Back, side, decorated, original dark brown paint, yellow striping and floral decoration on crest, some wear, 17½" seat, 33¾" h, price for set of six **1,485.00**

Banister Back, side, curly maple, shaped arched crest, block and baluster turned posts with urn shape finials, four shaped vertical slats, rush seat, bulbous turned front stretcher, refinished, replaced seat, 44" h **550.00**

Corner, shaped crest and arms, turned posts, shaped splats, replaced rush seat, double box stretchers, old worn black paint over earlier dark green, damaged seat, 33" h **600.00**

Country Empire, dining, straight crest with stenciled rose dec, five turned spindles, arched back posts, scrolled seat, turned legs and front stretcher, ball feet, red flame graining and black ground with yellow striping, 33" h, price for set of six **1,200.00**

Ladderback Chair, New England, maple, sausage-turned stiles with ring and button finials, arched slats, shaped and turned arms, rush seat, ring and baluster turned box stretchers, feet restored, one slat reshaped, $770.00. Photograph courtesy of Butterfield & Butterfield.

Country Queen Anne, side
Decorated, hardwood, yoke crest, vasiform splat, rush seat, old black paint with gold striping and chinoiserie dec on splat, 42¾" h . . .   **220.00**

Yoke crest, vasiform splat, turned posts with flared finials, rush seat, turned legs and stretchers, old black repaint, replaced seat, wear and damage, Connecticut River Valley, 39¼" h **100.00**

Country Sheraton, side, hardwood and curly maple, turned arched crest rail, shaped center slat, narrow lower slat, heavily ring turned front legs and stretcher, tapered legs with button feet, old mellow refinishing, price for pair **385.00**

Country Windsor, bow back, molded crest rail, seven spindle back, saddle seat, splayed base with bamboo turned legs, H-form stretcher, refinished, traces of red paint on seat, age cracks, 15¾" h seat, 38" h. **250.00**

Decorated, side
Half spindle, rabbit ear posts, shaped crest, narrow slat, four turned half spindles, plank seat, turned legs and front stretcher, worn orig red and black graining with yellow and pale blue striping and stylized fruit and foliage dec, 17½" h seat, 32¼" h, price for set of eight **450.00**

Wide crest with stenciled and freehand fruit and foliage dec, plank seat, old yellow-green repaint over earlier colors, striping, minor damage, 33" h, price for set of six. . . .   **575.00**

Dining
Queen Anne style, one armchair, six side chairs, shaped crest rail with carved ears, shaped splat, rush seat, block turned front posts, turned stretchers, slipper feet, armchair with scrolled arms, worn brown paint, 42¾" h, price for set of seven **1,735.00**

Oak, plain crest rail, narrow rect back splat, pressed cane seat, rope carved front legs, H-form stretcher, 1910, 37" h **35.00**

Easy, Chippendale, mahogany, reupholstered in silk brocade, Newport, RI, 1770–90, 15" h seat rail, 44½" h   **11,000.00**

Hitchcock style, yellow striping, polychrome floral dec slats, dark ground, balloon seats with old rush, turned legs, 34" h, price for pair **145.00**

Ladder Back, hardwood, turned spire shaped finials
Four arched graduated slats, rush seat, reddish varnish finish, four

side and one armchair with scrolled arms, some replaced seats, 42¾″ h, price for set of five **685.00**

Three arched graduated slats, paper rush seat, turned feet, old mellow refinishing, replaced seat, 38¾″ h **135.00**

Lolling, Hepplewhite, mahogany, inlaid, serpentine upholstered back, shaped arms, outline stringing on down curving arm supports, upholstered seat, outline stringing on square tapered legs, casters, yellow upholstery, refinished, restored, New England, early 19th C, 18″ h seat, 46″ h **1,975.00**

Martha Washington, Chippendale style, mahogany frame, worn gold striped upholstery, worn finish, 38″ h   **100.00**

Mission, oak

Harden Co, Camden, NY, slat back, double crest rail, five vertical slats, curved arms, four vertical slat arm supports, spring cushion, orig paper label, 30″ w, 38¼″ h. **500.00**

Phoenix Furniture Co, Grand Rapids, MI, caned back and seat, wide flat arms, 1894–1920 . . . . **1,500.00**

Morris, oak, Mission, Gustav Stickley, No. 369, adjustable back with curved crest rail and four narrower horizontal slats, shaped slanted arms with corbels, five vertical side slats, spring cushion seat, casters, brand mark, refinished, c1912, 32½″ w, 41½″ h **4,750.00**

Overstuffed, mahogany frame, foliate carved apron, carved scrolling legs, animal paw front feet, new cut velvet floral upholstery, 36½″ h, matching ottoman, price for two pieces **50.00**

Queen Anne, side, maple, shaped yoke crest, curved back posts, vasiform splat, slip seat, cabriole legs, turned H-form stretcher, padded slipper feet, old red finish on underside of seat frame and bottoms of stretchers, minor repair to seat frame and one foot, 17 ½″ h seat, 40″ h. **990.00**

Rabbit Ear, side, decorated, stenciled crest, four turned spindles, shaped seat, bamboo turned legs, red and black with yellow striping, 17″ h seat, 34″ h **65.00**

Windsor

Bamboo turnings, side, decorated, straight crest with polychrome painted floral dec, bamboo turned posts, spindles, legs, and stretchers, shaped seat, yellow ground, black striping, PA, c1820, 33″ h, price for set of six **1,650.00**

Windsor Chair, brace back, shaped crest with carved ears, turned posts and legs, saddle seat, H-form stretcher, $750.00.

Bow back

35½″ h, eleven spindles, shaped arms, bulbous turned arm posts, saddle seat, splayed base with bulbous turned legs and H-form stretcher, old refinishing, small split in back of arm rail, 16½″ h seat **825.00**

36½″ h, eleven spindles, shaped arms, turned arm posts, saddle seat, splayed base with turned legs and H-form stretcher, old refinishing, cracks and repairs in seat, 16½″ h seat **550.00**

37½″ h, molded crest rail, seven spindle back, shaped seat, splayed base with bulbous turned legs, H-form stretcher, old worn black repaint with yellow striping, 17¾″ h seat, price for set of six **5,275.00**

38¼″ h, bamboo turnings, seven spindle back, scrolled arms, shaped seat, splayed base, H-form stretcher, old red repaint over other colors, 17″ h seat . . **465.00**

Brace back, maple and pine, molded hoop back, seven spindles, supporting brace behind, incised edge on saddle seat, ring and baluster turned tapered legs, H-form stretcher, gold striping, black ground, RI, 1780–1805, 34″ h, price for set of five. **23,000.00**

Comb back, shaped crest, bowed crest rail, shaped arm rail, five spindle back, turned arm supports, saddle seat, splayed base with bulbous turned legs and H-form stretcher, worn old red repaint, re-

pair in back edge of seat, arm rail with split at curve, 18" h seat, 48½" h **1,500.00**
Continuous arm, molded bowed crest rail, seven spindle back, shaped arms, turned arm supports, shaped saddle seat, splayed base with turned legs and H-form stretcher, old brown finish, old breaks in rail, 16½" h seat, 38¼" h **1,375.00**
Fan back, serpentine crest rail, seven turned spindles, baluster turned posts, saddle seat, splayed base with ring and baluster turned legs, bulbous turned H-form stretcher, painted black, New England, 1780–1800, 17" h seat, 35¾" h **325.00**
Sack back
 Arched crest rail, spindle back, U-shaped arm rail continuing to scrolled arms, canted baluster turned arm supports, oval saddle seat, splayed base with baluster turned legs, H-form stretcher, painted dark green, PA, c1780 . . . . **1,425.00**
 Knuckle arm, old red varnish, New England, c1780, 28" h **3,850.00**
 Stepdown crest, seven slender spindles, shaped seat, splayed base, plain legs and stretchers, old worn dark reddish brown repaint over earlier colors, 17¼" h seat, 34¼" h **325.00**
Wing
 Chippendale, shaped wings, out scrolled arms, upholstered with

Wing Chair, Queen Anne, New England, walnut, upholstered frame, cabriole legs, pad feet, block turned H-form stretcher, c1750, $4,125.00. Photograph courtesy of Butterfield & Butterfield.

brass tack trim around bottom, molded front legs, straight stretchers, refinished, restored, PA, 1770–90, 17½" h seat, 48" h **2,550.00**
Hepplewhite, mahogany, serpentine upholstered back flanked by shaped wings, out scrolled arms, upholstered seat, square tapering legs, straight stretchers, refinished, pumpkin colored 20th C upholstery, New England, early 19th C, 17½" h seat, 46½" h **1,100.00**
Writing, arm, shaped crest, spindle back, scrolled arm, large leather cov writing arm with two underside drawers, turned posts and legs, plank seat with drawer beneath, stretchers, old black repaint, gold striping, some edge damage, one drawer replaced, 17½" h seat, 47" h **225.00**

CHESTS OF DRAWERS

Birch
 Chippendale, tall chest, molded cornice, six graduated drawers with eagle brasses, scalloped long bracket foot, NH, c1780, 36" w, 18" d, 51" h **3,300.00**
 Country Federal, rect top, four cockbeaded drawers, shaped apron continuing to French feet, oval brasses, restoration to back edge of top, New England, 1810–20, 41" w, 41½" h **1,100.00**
Cherry
 Chippendale
  Molded edge top, four graduated overlapping dovetailed drawers, bracket feet with rounded returns, bottom sgd, "B.I. Lord," restored returns, replaced brasses, 42½" w, 20¼" d, 34" h **2,100.00**
  Serpentine thumb molded top, conforming dovetailed case with fluted quarter columns, four graduated dovetailed drawers with applied beading, ogee bracket feet, pine secondary wood, old brasses, replaced feet, CT, 39¾" w, 19½" d, 34" h **3,300.00**
 Country, rounded corner top, two short over four graduated long drawers, rounded corner stiles, solid ends, deeply scalloped apron, refinished, filled age cracks in ends, replaced brass pulls and escutcheons, 38¾" w, 18" d, 43¾" h **1,000.00**
 Country Empire, four dovetailed cockbeaded drawers, large projecting drawer supported on

turned and rope carved pilasters, three recessed graduated drawers, turned feet and pulls, old worn finish, 42¼" w, 20" d, 47" h **525.00**

Country Federal, mahogany veneer, bow front, conforming top with inlaid edge, four graduated cockbeaded drawers, scrolled skirt, French feet, refinished, replaced oval brasses, Connecticut River Valley, 1790–1810, 41" w, 23" d, 38" h.   **2,300.00**

Country Hepplewhite

Four graduated dovetailed drawers with line inlaid drawer fronts, extra deep top drawer over three graduated drawers, one board ends, shaped apron, cutout feet, refinished, replaced eagle brasses, edge damage, front feet replaced, drawer runner need repair, 46¾" w, 20" d, 46" h. **475.00**

Tall chest, poplar secondary wood, inlaid band below cove molded cornice, five short drawers over five graduated long drawers, cockbeaded drawers, orig acorn brasses, band inlaid base, curved apron, straight cutout legs, inlaid diamond shield escutcheons, feet poorly ended out, edge damage, old repairs, 45¼" w, 23¾" d, 75" h. **3,850.00**

Country Sheraton, poplar secondary wood, shaped crest, four dovetailed drawers with applied edge beading, crossbanded walnut veneer and surface beading with inlaid diamond escutcheons, paneled ends, turned legs, refinished, split in one back post, 45½" w, 20" d, 41" h **605.00**

Hepplewhite, inlaid, oblong top with band inlaid edge, four cockbeaded graduated drawers, stringing on stiles, band inlaid scalloped apron, French feet, inlaid diamond escutcheons, replaced oval brasses, old refinish, feed ended out with replaced brackets, 38¾" w, 20½" d, 43¼" h. **2,200.00**

Cherry and Mahogany, Country Formal, rect top, four cockbeaded drawers, shaped skirt, French feet, old refinishing, replaced oval brasses, NH, 1790–1810, 36" w, 18¾" d, 37½" h. **1,975.00**

Cherry and Poplar, slightly overhanging rect top with molded edge, two short drawers over four graduated long drawers, dovetailed drawers, shaped apron, cutout feet, repairs to top edge molding, front feet, and apron, replaced pulls, 40¾" w, 16½" d, 41½" h **450.00**

Curly Maple and Walnut, Country Sheraton, tall chest, walnut top, dovetailed drawers, two short drawers flanked by two bonnet drawers over three graduated long drawers, scalloped apron, turned feet, walnut edging on drawer fronts, old mellow refinishing, back boards replaced, top may be old replacement, replaced oval brasses, 43½" w, 22½" d, 50¾" h. **1,700.00**

Curly Walnut, Hepplewhite, poplar secondary wood, four graduated cockbeaded drawers with line inlay, shaped apron, French feet, oval lion brasses, refinished, 38½" w, 18¼" d, 38" h. **2,525.00**

Decorated

Hepplewhite style, red and black flame graining, yellow and green striping, birch, four dovetailed drawers, beaded frame, scalloped apron, cutout feet, turned wood pulls, embossed brass escutcheons, 36⅜ " h **3,400.00**

Painted diamond and swirl pattern, one extra deep drawer over three graduated drawers, cutout feet, turned wood pulls, PA, c1825, 44" w, 17" d, 41½" h. **2,750.00**

Mahogany Veneer, Country Federal, bow front, conforming case with four cockbeaded drawers, shaped bracket feet, oval brasses, refinished, New England, 1800–20, 38¾" w, 19¾" d, 40½" h **1,875.00**

Chest, three-masted clipper ship painted on lid int., lidded till, rope handles, molded base, 41½" w, 15" d, 15" h, $1,100.00. Photograph courtesy of James D Julia, Inc.

Maple

Chippendale, tall chest, painted red, molded cornice, six graduated drawers, eagle brasses, scalloped bracket feet, New England, c1780, 36" w, 17¾" d, 53" h **7,150.00**

Country Chippendale, tall chest

Molded cornice, seven graduated drawers with bail handled pulls, molded base with bracket feet, refinished, imperfections, RI, c1770, 35½" w, 17¼" d, 63" h **4,125.00**

Molded cornice with secret drawer, six graduated overlapping dovetailed drawers, dovetailed case, high cutout dovetailed bracket feet, pine and poplar secondary wood, refinished, minor edge repairs, replaced brasses, 39¾" w, 20¾" d, 56½" h **4,500.00**

Maple and Bird's Eye Maple Veneer, bow front, slightly overhanging top, four drawers with bird's eye maple veneer drawer fronts, fluted three-quarter column stiles, scalloped skirt front and ends, ring turned tapered legs, ball feet, refinished, replaced turned wood pulls, northern New England, 1820s, 44½" w, 18½" d, 43" h **1,325.00**

Oak, quarter sawn

Mission, Stickley Brothers, rect swivel mirror, overhanging top, two narrow short drawers over two graduated long drawers, arched skirt, wood knobs **800.00**

Pine

Country Empire, rect top with rounded corners, four graduated drawers with ogee drawer fronts, rounded corner posts, block feet, turned pulls, refinished, age cracks in top, replaced pulls, repairs and replacements to feet, 36½" w, 22" d, 35½" h **350.00**

Tall chest, cornice with applied edge molding, five graduated drawers with dovetailed back joints and groove joinery in front, bracket feet, red stain finish, replaced feet and edge molding, 28½" w, 20½" d, 56" h **1,250.00**

Poplar, Country Chippendale, tall chest, molded cornice, two short over four long graduated overlapping drawers, bracket feet, old medium brown refinishing, repairs to backboards, some edge damage, replaced feet and brasses, 38¾" w, 20¾" d, 55¾" h **1,100.00**

Chest of Drawers, pine, painted dec, possibly Pennsylvania, c1825, 44" w, 17" d, 41½" h, $2,750.00. Photograph courtesy of Skinner, Inc.

Walnut

Country Hepplewhite, four graduated dovetailed drawers with applied edge beading and inlaid diamond escutcheons, scalloped apron, cutout feet, old worn refinishing, some edge damage, old repair, 39¾" w, 19¾" d, 41¼" h   **1,000.00**

Queen Anne, chest on frame, period chest with molded top and eight dovetailed overlapping drawers, frame with shaped apron, cabriole legs, and slipper feet, base is modern restoration made from old wood, replaced brasses, PA, 41½" w, 23" d, 56½" h **825.00**

CHESTS, OTHER

Apothecary

Pine, sixteen nailed overlapping drawers with porcelain pulls, chamfered corner posts, scrolled apron, cutout feet, square nail construction, old mellow refinishing, feet reworked, front apron added, drawers have repairs to overlap, 33" w, 18¼" d, 36" h. . . **2,300.00**

Pine, poplar, and mahogany, old red flame graining over white undercoat, molded mahogany top, beveled frames around dovetailed drawers, 24 small drawers over six larger drawers, replaced brass pulls, some drawers with edge damage and repairs, 38" w, 13" d, 40¼" h **4,175.00**

Chest Over Drawers

Grain Painted, Queen Anne, pine, molded lid, two false drawers over two working drawers, molded base, bracket feet, teardrop pulls, 34½" w, 17½" d, 36¼" h **1,500.00**

Pine

Joined, rounded corners on rect cleated top, three raised panels on chest front, two long drawers with raised panel fronts, paneled sides, old refinish, western MA, 17th C, 41½" w, 19½" d, 43" h **4,125.00**

Molded lid, two false drawers over two working drawers, bracket feet, later 19th C ochre grain painting, New England, 18th C, 37½" w, 20¼" d, 41¾" h **715.00**

Dower's, decorated and grain painted, pine, edge molded lid, dovetailed case, till, dovetailed bracket feet, wrought iron strap hinges, yellow, black, and white polka dots, stylized potted flowers, eagles, names of couple, and date "September 21, 1826," red ground, faint signature inside lid, till lid and lock missing, feet repaired, lid molding replaced one end, lid dec very worn, dec on chest may be old repaint, PA, 47" w, 21" d, 22½" h **1,650.00**

Immigrant's

Decorated, pine, paneled lid and ends, dovetailed case, iron bear trap lock and key, blue ground, red trim, polychrome flowers, name, and date on light blue panels on front, traces of paint on lid panels, old repairs, turned feet missing, iron strapping added to front and ends, 1820, 50½" w, 23" d, 21" h   **650.00**

Pine, iron bound, white painted label, blue ground, 31½" l **325.00**

Mule

Cherry, Country Chippendale, six board type construction, lift lid with applied edge molding, graduated dovetailed drawers with two false drawers over two working drawers, wide edge beading, dovetailed bracket feet, refinished, replaced batwing brasses, minor repairs to feet, 44" w, 19½" d, 42½" h **2,200.00**

Grain Painted, dark brown flame graining, pine, poplar secondary wood, six board type construction, two false drawers over two dovetailed working drawers, drawers with beaded edges and frames, high cutout feet, small loose knot in lid, 43¼" w, 18½" d, 44¾" h   **1,100.00**

Pine

Cleated lid with scrolled edge, two drawers with wide early dove-

tailing, molded base, turned ball feet, refinished with traces of old dark paint, 40¼" w, 19" d, 38" h **550.00**

Country Chippendale, six board type construction, two false drawers over three graduated dovetailed overlapping working drawers, bracket feet, old worn yellow grained repaint, one back foot facing incomplete, locks removed, 39½" w, 19¾" d, 40¾" h **1,325.00**

Single dovetailed overlapping drawer, six board type construction, cutout feet, staple hinges, refinished, replaced brass pulls, repairs to feet and drawer lip, one backboard replaced, 41½" w, 17¾" d, 32¾" h **450.00**

Two dovetailed overlapping drawers, six board type construction, bootjack feet, old dark repaint, replaced brasses, 44½" w, 18" d, 44½" h **600.00**

Two false drawers over two dovetailed working drawers, six board type construction, bootjack ends, refinished, added or replaced molding on base and lid, filled cracks in lid, 39" w, 17" d, 43½" h **500.00**

Spice

Grain Painted, William and Mary, single hinged door, int. drawers arranged as two over three over single base drawer, ball feet, molded top and base, MA, early 18th C, 18¾" w, 12½" d, 18" h **10,450.00**

Yellow Pine, mortised and pinned construction, rect two board top, ten dovetailed drawers, square posts extending to turned feet, old mellow refinishing, age cracks in top, replaced turned wood pulls, southern US, 59¼" w, 25" d, 33½" h **3,200.00**

Sugar, cherry, lift off lid, dovetailed case with inlaid stars, lines, and circles, large till, single dovetailed drawer in frame, square tapered legs, cutout leg brackets, old finish, old repairs, replaced moldings, NC, 31¼" w, 15¾" d, 36" h **11,000.00**

CHILDREN'S

Bed, tall post, maple and cherry, canopy, urn finials, turned and tapered posts, shaped headboard, turned feet, restored, New England, 38" w, 72¼" d, 50" h **1,650.00**

Blanket Chest, six board, old blue paint, New England, 34" w, 15½" d, 20½" h 775.00

Chair

Ladder back

Arm, acorn finials, three shaped slats, woven cane seat, turned arm posts, tapered feet, old black repaint, broken seat, 25¼" h 80.00

Side, rabbit ear posts, three narrow slats, woven splint seat, tapered feet, box stretchers, refinished, replaced seat, 28" h 80.00

Windsor

Flat crest, rabbit ear posts, three arrow shaped spindles, shaped plank seat, bamboo turned legs, tretchers, black and red striping, red-brown flame graining on crest and seat, yellow ground, 17½" h seat, 29½" h 175.00

Side, old refinishing, branded "E P Rose," 12¼" h seat, 25½" h. . . 100.00

Cradle

Bentwood, oval bentwood basket, extended ornate scrolled supports, trestle base, c1900, 52" l, 36" h 750.00

Cherry, dovetailed, four cutout heart handles, wide shaped rockers, worn red paint, age cracks, nailed edge repairs, 42" l 300.00

Galvanized sheet metal, hooded, shaped wood rockers, old worn red and blue paint, 26 /12" l 115.00

Hardwood, Windsor, hooped bentwood ends with three turned spindles, upper and lower flat rails on sides joined by ten short rods, pinned mortise construction, old green paint, nailed reinforcement to joints, some spindles are old replacements, 36" l 250.00

Pine

Hooded top, shaped sides, scrolled rockers, red, yellow, and green fruit border on brown ground, New England, c1830, 29" l, 19 ½" w, 28" h 650.00

Primitive, hardwood spindles, traces of old brown paint, 39" l 95.00

Walnut, dovetailed, scrolled headboard, shaped sides and rockers, refinished, old replaced bottom, rockers reset, 39" l 275.00

Desk

Pedestal, hardwood and pine, wire nail construction, chip carved detail, two banks of three drawers, old dark varnish finish, 22¾" w, 8¾" d, 15½" h 350.00

Cradle, Pennsylvania, trestle base, painted red, late 18th C, 39½" w, 24" d, 37" h, $525.00. Photograph courtesy of Skinner, Inc.

Roll Top, oak, C-curve tambour sliding door, slightly overhanging rect writing surface, single drawer, square legs, stretchers at sides and back, turned wood pulls, 26" w, 16" d, 37" h 225.00

Slant Front, oak, arched crest, fall front writing flap with applied foliate moldings, single drawer, recessed base shelf, shaped bootjack ends with cutout tulip dec, turned wood pulls, 22" w, 11" d, 33" h 200.00

Highchair

Bentwood, caned back panel and seat, stationary food tray, footrest with punched board panel, out curving legs, c1890 .... 275.00

Country Sheraton, hard and soft woods, rabbit ear posts, three narrow slats, scrolled arms, sausage turned front posts, woven splint seat, worn footrest, ring turned front stretchers, small flanged feet, chipped feet, 32½" h 825.00

Ladder back

Hardwood, turned finials and posts, three shaped slats, rush seat, footrest, refinished, 38¾" h 300.00

Lemon finials, turned back posts, three shaped slats, flattened ball handholds, woven rush seat, well worn front stretchers, New England, 18th C, 34" h 1,210.00

Two shaped slats, splint seat, splayed base, natural finish, 31" h 250.00

Press Back, oak, stroller type, shaped crest rail with pressed arch, leaf, and fan dec, pressed foliate design on splat, turned stiles, hinged shaped food tray, turned arm supports, caned seat, shaped footrest, turned legs, ring turned stretchers, iron spoked wheels, 42" h. **450.00**

T Back, oak, hinged bowed front food tray, square arm supports, shaped seat, out curving legs with ring and baluster turnings, rect footrest, box stretchers, 39" h . . . **175.00**

Windsor

Rod Back, straight crest rail, open arms, saddle seat, splayed base with ring turned legs, stretchers, footrest replaced, early 19th C **225.00**

Spindle Back, flat crest rail, bamboo turned spindles, shaped plank seat with rolled front rail, splayed base, shaped footrest, bamboo turned legs, orig yellow paint with olive green stencil dec and black striping, PA or OH, 24" h seat, 36½" h. **925.00**

Potty Chair

Decorated, shaped crest with stenciled floral dec, six spindle back, scrolled arms, turned arm posts, shaped seat with round cutout, turned legs, old brown paint with black and yellow striping, door missing from compartment back, ironstone chamber pot, 39" h . . . **50.00**

Pine, high back with cutout handle in shaped crest, shaped sides and arms, scrolled apron, rockers, painted **125.00**

Crib, pine, turned posts and spindles, shaped crest rail and foot rail, turned and tapered feet on castors, $357.50. Photograph courtesy of Morton M Goldberg Galleries.

Rocker

Ladder back, turned posts with ball finials, three shaped slats, turned arms, splint seat, ring turned front posts, refinished, replaced seat, 25" h. **135.00**

Windsor, bamboo turnings, youth size, stepped crest, five spindle back, center spindle with dec tablet, shaped seat, splayed base, front stretcher with center tablet footrest, shaped rockers, old yellowed white repaint with black and gold striping and foliage scrolls, 28 ½" h. **250.00**

Table, drop leaf, six leg, cherry, rect 10" w leaves, turned legs, ball feet, handmade reproduction, 32" w, 14½" d, 18" h. **450.00**

Trunk, grain painted, mid 19th C, 19¾" w, 8¾" d, 8¾" h **110.00**

CLOCKS

Banjo, hanging

Howard & Davis, #4 size, fine grained case, 8 day time only weight driven brass movement, two replaced glue blocks, bottom board removed, c1860, 32" h . . . **450.00**

Levi Hutchins, Concord, NH, gold front, painted iron dial, 8 day time movement with T-bridge and step train, pendulum, 1820, 42" h. **800.00**

New Haven Clock Co, mahogany case, 8 day time and strike movement, replaced eagle finial, c1920 **165.00**

Unknown Maker, Federal, NH, painted and stencil dec, c1830, 33½" h **3,400.00**

Beehive

Chelsea, brass, porcelain dial, c1900, 5¼" h **50.00**

Seth Thomas, inlaid mahogany case, 8 day brass time and strike movement, quarter hour Sonora chimes, 14½" h **400.00**

Calendar

Ansonia, hanging, drop octagon, rosewood veneer, gilt molding, 8 day strike, 24" h **300.00**

Welch Spring & Co, shelf, rosewood veneer case, 8 day time and strike, B B Lewis calendar movement, old replacement base, part of lower bezel missing, replaced glass, c1870, 19¼" h **325.00**

Cottage

J C Brown, rosewood veneer case, 8 day brass time and strike movement, 1850–60, 14¾" h **400.00**

S B Terry, mahogany case, 30 hour time and alarm ladder brass movement, c1840, 11" h **175.00**

Figure 8, hanging, Seth Thomas, regulator, cherry case, 8 day time only movement, refinished, orig dial, tablet, and label, c1880, 28¾" h **825.00**

Gingerbread

Ansonia, X-O.6, oak case, 8 day time, hour, and half hour strike, 22½" h **175.00**

F Kroeber Clock Co, Wanderer, walnut case, elaborate geometric tablet, 6" fancy dial, 8 day gong strike, 23" h **300.00**

New Haven Clock Co, pressed oak case, 8 day time, strike, and alarm movement, c1915, 24½" h **75.00**

Half Column

Boardman & Wells, veneer, glass panel with boy fishing from boat while St Bernard dog watches illus, 30 hour wooden time and strike movement, Maine clock dealer label, 1830–40, 32" h **125.00**

Eli Terry & Sons, carved columns, splat, and feet, 8 day wood time and strike movement, c1825, 37" h **900.00**

Kitchen, New Haven Clock Co, white painted case, 8 day time movement, c1825, 11¾" h **60.00**

Mantel

A Stowell & Co, Boston, mahogany, rect case, arched top, engraved face, 8 day time and strike movement, Westminster chimes, key and pendulum, 12⅞" w, 18½" h **600.00**

Russell & Jones, marbleized wood, Tennessee marble columns, 8 day time movement, 5" dial, 10" h .. **125.00**

Pillar and Splat, E Thayer, carved pillars and splat, 30 hour wood Groner movement, c1830, 35" h **300.00**

Regulator, hanging

Boston Clock Co, painted cherry case, 8 day time movement, 1880–90, 34" h **800.00**

E Howard & Co, model #58, store box, cherry case, 8 day time only weight driven movement, c1880, 39" h **1,925.00**

Little & Eastman Co, Boston, MA, quarter sawn oak case, sgd 8 day time movement, c1890, 35¼" h **650.00**

Waltham Clock Co, Waterbury, CT, oak case, Regulator tablet, painted zinc dial, 8 day time and strike movement and half hour strike, pendulum, 1910, 32" h **375.00**

Schoolhouse, hanging

Ingraham, pressed oak case, 8 day time, strike, and calendar movement, c1900, 18¾" h **325.00**

Sessions, Century model, short drop, pressed oak case, 8 day time, strike, and calendar movement, orig label, replaced calendar hand, c1900, 26½" h **425.00**

Seth Thomas, Globe model, long drop, rosewood veneer case, 8 day time only movement, orig label, c1875, 31½" h **725.00**

Ship

Chelsea, brass, clock and Waterbury barometer with thermometer mounted on ftd rect base, 8 day time and ship's bells, door button latch missing, c1890, 12¾" w, 7¼" h **275.00**

Seth Thomas, brass, hanging, 8 day time and strike movement, outside bell, orig label, late 19th C, 6¼" d **575.00**

Steeple

Brewster & Ingraham, rosewood veneer case, frosted and cut door glass, c1840, 19¼" h **350.00**

Unknown Maker, mahogany veneer, brass works, worn painted metal face, worn paper label, reverse painted transfer scene of "Washington's Rock, N.J.," some veneer damage, 20" h **135.00**

Tall Case

Chandler, cherry, bonnet top with cove molded cornice and freestanding front columns, cove molding between sections, shaped apron, bracket feet, brass works with second hand, calendar movement and painted face with faint label "..Chandler," with weights and pendulum, old finish, bracket feet replaced, overlapping molded edge door warped and with some edge damage, 79½" h **4,500.00**

Riley Whiting, Winchester, CT, pine, arched pediment with fretwork crest, floral and ball finials, reeded half pillars, thumb molded door, molded base, shaped apron, bracket feet, thirty hour wooden movement, refinished, c1830, 88" h **2,200.00**

Unknown Maker

Cherry, dovetailed bonnet with broken arch pediment and free standing columns above wide cove molding, chamfered corners, paneled base with cove molding and flattened ball feet, refinished, minor repairs, replaced feet and waist door,

Tall Case Clock, Maine, red, ochre, and cream sponge dec case, works marked "Silas Hoadley," 86" h, $8,250.00. Photograph courtesy of James D Julia, Inc.

backboards incomplete, formerly in the Butler Mansion Museum, Carrollton, KY, 93½" h   1,100.00

Cherry, simple bonnet with molded cornice, cove molded between sections, ogee feet, brass works and painted metal face with moon phases dial, second hand, and calendar movement, with weights and pendulum, case is later than works and has some old reconstruction and renailing, 93" h   2,375.00

Walnut, PA, molded cornice, turned half columns, arched door, shaped bracket feet, brass pull-up movement, c1750, 91" h 3,025.00

Wag-On-The-Wall, hanging, sgd "Gabrie Constant, A Orleans," brass and iron case, 8 day time and strike brass weight driven movement, small repair on crest, c1860, 58" h 450.00

Wall Master, hanging, Standard Electric Time Co, electric
Mahogany case, simulated mercury pendulum, c1920, 65" h 500.00
Pressed quarter sawn oak case, mercury pendulum, c1915, 73" h . . .   1,210.00

CUPBOARDS

Chimney
Pine, corner, one piece, open top, single board door, angled back, old finish, modern hinges, 24" w, 15" d, 84½" h 525.00

Walnut and poplar, decorated, simple cornice, single door with four recessed panels, int. shelves, old brownish-yellow graining over earlier brighter yellow, orig built-in, front edge moldings removed, OH, 26¾" w, 18¼" d, 83½" h   450.00

Corner
Cherry, one piece, molded cornice, pair of glazed doors each with six panes, shelved int., pair of cupboard doors each with two tin pie safe panels with punched circular designs, cast iron latches, bottom latch damaged, 54" w, 77" h 1,875.00

Cherry and Poplar, barrel back, molded cornice, pair of full length raised panel doors, int. shelves, edge beading on stiles and rails, cutout feet, water damaged feet, OH, 62" w, 84½" h 990.00

Grain Painted, red flame graining, pine, one piece, single paneled door, reeded detail on door and stiles, some edge damage, 31½" w, 54" h 900.00

Pine
Barrel back, crown molded cornice, open top with two shelves, pair of raised double panel

Corner Cupboard, Chippendale, Pennsylvania or Ohio Valley, carved pine, two sections: upper: chip carved swag and fluted molded cornice, twelve-panel glazed door, shelved int.; lower: molded waist, two paneled cupboard doors, chip carved and reeded center post, shelved int., ogee bracket feet, feet restored; late 18th C, 43" w, 87" h, $1,980.00. Photograph courtesy of Butterfield & Butterfield.

doors, molded base, butterfly hinges, old dark patina, old repairs, edge damage, bottom boards and base molding replaced, repaired hinges are old replacements, 63" w, 75 ½" h **800.00**

One piece, molded cornice, pair of raised panel doors enclosing top shelves with butterfly cutouts, two shorter raised panel doors in base, base molding, repairs, replaced "H" hinges, base moldings and bottoms of stiles restored, 45" w, 85½" h...... **1,325.00**

One piece, cleaned down to traces of old blue paint, perimeter molding with unusual applied scalloping, pair of glazed doors each with eight panes, int. with butterfly scalloped shelves and arched baffle with cutout pinwheels, reeded and relief carved mid section panel, single paneled cupboard door flanked by two stationary panels, old glass, minor edge damage, PA, 54½" w, 89¼" h............... **6,500.00**

Two piece, cove molded cornice, single glazed door with nine panes of old wavy glass, molded waist, pair of paneled cupboard doors, beaded edge door frames, old dark finish, cornice ends replaced, 44 ½" w, 74½" h...................... **2,100.00**

Poplar, two piece

Cove molded cornice, single glazed door with twelve panes and arched top lights, base with two paneled doors, scalloped apron, and bracket feet, cast iron thumb latches, porcelain knobs, refinished, two glass panes broken, locks and drilled keyholes added to doors, top door missing latch, base marked "Mrs. Amanda Bobb, Bristol, Ind.," 40½" w, 85½" h...... **2,750.00**

Molded cornice, very wide top rail, two glazed doors each with six panes of wavy glass, int. serpentine shelves with spoon cutouts, base with pair of paneled cupboard doors and stubs of old feet, old red repaint, feet cut down, replaced cast iron latches, one glass cracked, 55" w, 77¾" h............... **775.00**

Poplar and Cherry, one piece, molded cornice, pr of paneled doors, int. shelves, pr paneled cupboard doors, scalloped apron,

worn down feet, cornice repaired, one hinge with broken pin, 48" w, 80" h.................... **1,500.00**

Hanging

Cherry, paneled door, pigeonholed int., dovetailed base drawer, old finish, 13½" w, 13" d, 20¾" h... **325.00**

Pine

Beveled cornice, single door, shelved int., old worn red repaint, wear, damage, and enlarged keyhole, 21¼" w, 12½" d, 26½" h.............. **500.00**

Corner, worn brown graining over red, two paneled doors with iron latches, wire nail construction, 26" w, 41½" h......... **675.00**

Reeded frame, dovetailed case, two raised panel doors, int. with shelves and two dovetailed drawers, old worn red paint, 22½" w, 16¾" d, 28½" h.... **950.00**

Shaped crest, single glazed door, three int. shelves, molded base, old reddish brown graining over earlier green, blue int., 13" w, 17¾" h.................. **175.00**

Poplar, orig red paint, one piece, dovetailed case with cornice and base, board and batten door, two int. nailed drawers, added turnbuckle latch, 23¼ × 11½ × 36½" h.................. **1,125.00**

Walnut, single paneled door, plain stiles and rails, refinished, 34" w, 43" h..................... **225.00**

Yellow Pine and Poplar, broken arch crest, single paneled door, base molding, 25" w, 9¾" d, 41¼" h **300.00**

Jelly

Grain Painted, poplar, brown burl grained door panels and drawer fronts, two nailed drawers over pair of raised panel doors, cutout feet, wood pulls, nailed repair to one door, 41" w, 14½" d, 54¼" h................... **400.00**

Painted, single door, turned feet, restored, PA, 19th C, 35" w, 17¾" d, 58" h..................... **550.00**

Pine

Federal, shaped splashboard, straight front fitted with two small drawers and a pair of paneled doors, turned wood pulls, straight bracket feet, c1800, 36" w, 19" d, 54" h........... **975.00**

Single narrow paneled door, similarly paneled ends, turned feet, brass latch with porcelain knob, old mellow finish, 43½" w, 20 ¾" d, 60" h.............. **325.00**

Slightly overhanging top, single long drawer, pair of paneled cupboard doors, pegged doors, plank ends, turned wood pulls, 41" w, 15½" d, 54½" h **425.00**

Poplar

Country Empire, regionally known as a Jackson press, rect overhanging top, projecting dovetailed long drawer supported on half column pilasters, two paneled cupboard doors, applied half turned feet, old worn red repaint, 45" w, 21¼" d, 50½" h **275.00**

Slightly overhanging rect top, two paneled cupboard doors, molded stiles, simple cutout feet, old green repaint over earlier colors, 42" w, 17¾" d, 49" h **775.00**

Yellow Pine, primitive, decorated, painted yellow stylized trees and diamond latticework design on green ground, rough sawn wood with wire nail construction, single door with wood turnbuckle, cutout feet, found in a barn in Catawba County, NC, 36" w, 17" d, 73" h **3,200.00**

Kas

Painted, pine, molded cornice, paneled doors set in beaded frames, open int. with cast iron hooks, solid ends, base molding, orig red paint, 64" w, 21½" d, 76¾" h . . . **1,500.00**

Pine, break down, molded cornice, pair of paneled doors with beaded frames, one board ends, molded edge base, cast iron hooks inside, orig red paint, several hooks broken, 64" w, 21½" d, 76¾" h **1,500.00**

Linen Press, mahogany, two pieces, top with molded edge top, two paneled doors, and three int. drawers, base with two short over three long beaded edge drawers, shaped skirt, and flaring French feet, small chips to front feet and skirt, brasses replaced with turned wood pulls, New England, 1800–10, 54" w, 89" h . . . **4,000.00**

On Frame, Country Empire, paint grained, walnut and poplar, dark redbrown flame graining, two sections, top: simple cornice and base moldings, paneled door with int. stenciled label "Jah Hart Jan the 4, 1847"; base: single dovetailed drawer with turned pulls, turned legs, flattened ball feet; 39" w, 24" d, 57¾" h **1,705.00**

Pewter

Pine, corner, one piece, molded cornice open butterfly shelves, paneled door in base, old mellow refinishing, some old alterations, base worn down and repaired, 43" w, 82½" h **2,200.00**

Walnut, one piece, perimeter molding top and bottom, molded cornice, open top with beaded stiles and rail and three shelves, pr of paneled doors in beaded frame in base, some edge damage, missing moldings, 47" w, 22" d, 86" h . . . **2,525.00**

Stepback

Cherry, Country Sheraton, poplar secondary wood, one piece, triple arched pediment with center broken arch with goosenecks above carved oval sunbursts, pair of small paneled doors with carved oval sunbursts flanked by banks of five graduated drawers and separated by applied half turned columns, single shelf and secret compartment int., base with four dovetailed and cockbeaded graduated long drawers, figured walnut inlaid stiles, short turned feet, secret compartment later addition, one front post with poorly repaired break at foot, 41½" w, 19" d, 72½" h **3,000.00**

Pine, one piece, two tiered cornice, pair of paneled cupboard doors top and bottom, stepback shelf, two short waist drawers, wood turnbuckle latches, refinished, age cracks in door panels, 44" w, 16" d **750.00**

Stepback Cupboard, Federal, Pennsylvania, cherrywood and pine, two sections, upper: molded cornice, two glazed doors, shelved int.; lower: four large drawers, ball feet, early 19th C, 63" w, 85½" h, $1,650.00. Photograph courtesy of Butterfield & Butterfield.

Poplar, two piece

Beveled cornice, pair of glazed doors each with six panes, shelved int., pie shelf, base with two nailed short drawers over pair of raised panel cupboard doors with molded center stile, simple cutout feet, orig brown flame graining, old wavy glass, bottom door has added brass thumb latch, some paint touch-up, 47" w, 19½" d, 84" h **3,100.00**

Cove molded cornice, pair of raised panel doors, shelved int., low pie shelf, base with center stack of drawers with two small drawers between two larger drawers, flanked by a pair of raised panel cupboard doors, simple cutout feet, dovetailed case, mortised construction, turned pulls, some edge damage, nailed repair to one top stile at hinge, int. with modern yellow paint, 55" w, 15½" d, 81½" h **2,100.00**

Cove molded cornice, paneled doors, shelved int., pie shelf, three short drawers over pair of paneled cupboard doors, shaped apron, cutout feet, applied moldings at tops of stiles, old dark refinishing, 54" w, 17¼" d, 90½" h **650.00**

Molded cornice, dovetailed construction, pair of glazed doors each with six panes, shelved int., three short drawers over pair of raised panel cupboard doors, dovetailed bracket feet, turned wood pulls, some replaced and added moldings, hardware replaced, top cut down to eliminate pie shelf, 53½" w, 14¾" d, 74¾" h **1,425.00**

Walnut and Poplar, beveled cornice, pair of paneled doors top and bottom set in beaded frames, high pie shelf, shelved int., deeply scalloped apron, high cutout feet, refinished, small repair to one corner of bottom door, base has some reconstruction, southern US, 48¼" w, 13¼" d, 79" h **1,400.00**

Utility, pine and hardwood, handmade, two full length doors with three recessed panels, bootjack ends, five shelf int., worn refinishing, 30" w, 14¾" d, 75" h **325.00**

Wall

Grain Painted, poplar, one piece, two cupboard doors, two long drawers, bootjack ends, imperfections, New England, 39" w, 17½" d, 39½" h **450.00**

Pine, one piece

Crown molded cornice, reeded frame, paneled doors, scrolled base, refinished, repairs, replaced cornice, 39¾ × 15¾ × 39¾ × 84¾" **400.00**

Perimeter molding, single paneled door top and bottom, old refinishing, moldings partially replaced, 27½" w, 16¼" d, 79" h **1,325.00**

Pine and Poplar, one piece, old green and red paint, primitive, six small shelves, age cracks in backboards, 10 × 6 × 41¼" **525.00**

Poplar, one piece, red repaint, single board cornice, four paneled doors, two nailed drawers, damage to base, nailed repair to back foot, edge damage to one drawer, 40½ × 20 × 71" **1,210.00**

DAY BEDS

Cherry, block and baluster turned posts with urn like finials, head and foot boards with three horizontal turned rails, tapered feet, orig rope rails, grayish blue ribbed upholstery back and seat cushions, board back added to support back cushion, 72½" w **550.00**

Cherry and Hardwood, shaped side rails slightly elevated at head end, dovetailed frame, shaped cutout feet on casters, 72" w, 24¾" d, 16" h. . . **100.00**

Curly Maple, block and turned posts with triple ring turned finials, shaped walnut headboard, tick cushion, old mellow finish, 77" w, 24" d **510.00**

Maple, some curl, turned posts and legs, webbed with canvas covering, 25" w, 62½" d, 31" h **300.00**

Oak, Mission, Frank Lloyd Wright, headboard and footboard connected by broad sideboards with applied moldings, 1902, 79" w, 25" d, 40" h**17,500.00**

Windsor, triple seat back, three rails over eighteen half spindles, turned arms, baluster turned arm posts, upholstered seat cushion, foldout hinged sleeping area supported by four pinned legs, orig yellow paint with gold and black stenciled fruit and leaf dec, seat replaced, New England, 84" w, 26" d, 19½" h seat, 36½" h, 49½ × 80 ⅝ " open size . . **1,750.00**

DESKS

Bookcase, cherry, Country Federal, molded broken scroll pediment, cast brass ball finials, pair of raised panel doors, shelved int., hinged writing flap, fitted int. with small drawers and center prospect door, pullout slides, four graduated overlapping drawers, shaped skirt, French feet, refinished, replaced brasses, southern New England, early 19th C, 41½" w, 20¼" d, 85½" h **3,250.00**

Carpenter's, pine, rect top with lift lid, hinged slant front, pair of wainscoted cupboard doors, square feet on casters, painted red, 43" w, 19" d, 42" h **275.00**

Cylinder, burl walnut and mahogany, shaped pediment with carved flowerheads, pair of glazed cabinet doors, cylinder door enclosing writing surface over two doors, long drawer above recessed cupboard doors, shaped apron, 27" w, 22" d, 66" h **1,000.00**

Lady's, oak, fall front writing surface with applied moldings and carved dec, shaped mirrored back, two swelled drawers, cabriole legs, claw and ball feet, 29" w, 55" h **600.00**

Library, walnut, rect top with inset brown leather writing surface and gadrooned edge, straight front, single wide thumb molded drawer flanked by four small drawers, cabriole legs, claw and ball feet, brass bail handled pulls, 28½" w, 31½" d, 30½" h . . . **775.00**

Lift Lid, cherry and poplar, Country Sheraton, three quarter gallery with scrolled crest and turned spindle rails, slant top lift lid, fitted int. with three dovetailed drawers and pigeonholes, single dovetailed long drawer, turned legs, button feet, old mellow refinishing, some edge damage, replaced pulls, hinges reset, 31" w, 25½" d, 32¼" h plus gallery . . . **500.00**

On Frame

Butternut, Country Hepplewhite, dovetailed gallery with scrolled ends, slant top lift lid on dovetailed case, base stand with two dovetailed short drawers and square tapered legs, turned pulls, refinished, repairs, reeded edge molding added to base, lid hinge broken, 30¼" w, 29 ½" d, 36" h **385.00**

Pine, Country Hepplewhite, slant top desk compartment with wide early dovetailing, overlapping drop lid, fitted int. with pigeonholes with arched top baffles, base with single

Roll Top Desk, oak, S-form roll, fitted int., paneled ends, double pedestal base with center long drawer flanked by banks of short drawers, 54" w, 31" d, 50" h, $1,100.00. Photograph courtesy of Morton M Goldberg Galleries.

dovetailed drawer and square tapered legs, refinished, base reconstructed, lid replaced, 37¾" w, 19¾" d, 37¾" h **425.00**

Parlor, oak, quarter sawn veneer, brass gallery, molded rect top, applied C-scroll moldings on fall front writing flap, single drawer, shaped apron, cabriole legs, brass ring drop pulls, 26" w, 17" d, 38" h **525.00**

Roll Top, oak

C-curve tambour sliding door, fitted int., single drawer over bracketed kneehole, pullout writing board over bank of four drawers, paneled ends, 36" w, 28" d, 44" h **750.00**

S-curve tambour sliding door, fitted int. with prospect door, small drawers, shelves, and file slots, slightly overhanging desk top, center drawer and kneehole flanked by banks of drawers with pullout writing boards, paneled ends, quarter sawn oak, 50" w, 34" d, 46" h **2,500.00**

School, pine, Country Hepplewhite, slant top lift lid, square tapered legs, old worn mellow refinishing, int. corner braces added, hinges replaced, gallery removed, 25" w, 21" d, 31" h. **125.00**

Schoolmaster's, low arched crest, slant top lift lid, nailed case, one int. shelf, square tapered legs, old yellow paint graining over earlier red, 28 12" w, 24¾" d, 34" h **185.00**

Desk/Bookcase Combination, carved oak, bookcase with leaded glass door and shelved int., slant front desk with fitted int. over three short drawers, Rockford Desk Co, c1890, 44" w, 16" d, 82" h, $1,320.00. Photograph courtesy of Morton M Goldberg Galleries.

Slant Front

Cherry, Country Federal, thumb molded edge on slant lid, fitted int. with eight small drawers centering a prospect door opening to five graduated small drawers, pullout slides, four graduated drawers with thumb molded edges, shaped apron, flaring French feet, PA, 19th C, 39¾" w, 47" h **1,875.00**

Maple

Chippendale, fitted int. with pigeonholes and small drawers, drop front writing surface, pull-out slides, three graduated drawers with bail handle pulls, bracket feet, refinished, New England, c1770, 36¼" w, 17¼" d, 44" h **3,575.00**

Queen Anne, high back with whale's tail pediment, circular inlay, and rect beveled glass mirror, row of five small drawers, fitted int. with valanced pigeonholes and drawers, four graduated drawers in base, bracket feet, New England, c1760, 35¼" w, 19" d, 66¾" h **9,350.00**

Oak, Mission, Lifetime Co, Grand Rapids, MI, Model No. 8548, gallery, fall front lid, fitted int., two long drawers,

arched apron, round copper pulls, missing escutcheon plate, decal on lower side stretcher, c1910 . . . . **600.00**

Pine

One piece, open shelf over two short drawers, hinged fold down writing surface, fitted int. with pigeonholes, pullout slides, one board door in base, shaped apron, nut brown finish, reconstructed, 24" w, 16" d, 56½" h **715.00**

Rectangular top with single drawer frieze, fall front writing surface with int. small drawers, three graduated drawers, reeded stiles, shaped apron, bracket feet, early 19th C, 41½" w, 21" d, 52" h **1,500.00**

Tiger Maple, fall front lid, fitted int. with leather writing surface, pull-out slides, four graduated overlapping drawers, molded base, bracket feet, early 19th C, 36½" w, 17½" d, 41" h **4,000.00**

Walnut

Country Formal, rect top, fall front lid, fitted int. with six short drawers, six valanced pigeonholes, two fluted document drawers, and a paneled prospect door opening to three drawers, four graduated long

Dresser, Federal, pine, projecting molded cornice, scalloped and floral carved frieze, three open shelves with scalloped ends, rect top, single raised panel cupboard door, H-form hinges, second quarter 19th C, 58" w, 18½" d, 83" h, $1,210.00. Photograph courtesy of Leslie Hindman Auctioneers.

drawers, ogee bracket feet, feet replaced, New England, 1800–15, 38½" w, 44½" h **1,100.00**

Country Sheraton, drop front writing surface, fitted int. with pigeonholes, nine small drawers with curly maple veneer fronts, and center door with bird's eye maple veneer, dovetailed case, three graduated cockbeaded long drawers, reeded stiles, turned feet, 42" w, 21" d, 45" h. **2,300.00**

Walnut and Figured Walnut, pine and poplar secondary wood, drop front writing surface, fitted int. with five dovetailed drawers, two vertical letter drawers, center prospect door, and pigeonholes, pull-out slides, four dovetailed graduated drawers with applied edge beading and inlaid escutcheons, cutout feet, old refinishing, some damage, old repairs, age cracks in ends and lid, replaced oval brasses, 39 ½" w, 19" d, 43" h. **1,925.00**

Table Top, mahogany, folding, dovetailed construction, pop-up compartment, fitted int. with pigeonholes and four dovetailed drawers, lift up writing surface with replaced green felt covering, old dark finish, folds to 10 × 16 × 22". **400.00**

DRY SINKS

Decorated

Pine, top with straight crest, three aligned drawers, horizontal random board back, and shaped ends, base with drain board, single short drawer, open well, pair of paneled cupboard doors, two shelf int., and scalloped apron, turned wood pulls, polychrome pineapples and feathery dec on red and green ground, some height loss, PA, 44" w, 17¼" d, 57½" h **825.00**

Poplar and other secondary wood, red vinegar graining on yellow ground with sunbursts, fans, and X's, open well, single dovetailed drawer, paneled doors, worn int. shelf, well shaped bracket feet, 42 × 19¼ × 31¾" **11,500.00**

Grain Painted, poplar

Brown flame graining, one piece, hutch top with peaked crest, two paneled doors, chamfered corner posts, three short drawers, shaped ends, and vertical board back,

base with zinc lined well, pair of paneled cupboard doors, chamfered corner posts, and cutout feet, cast iron and brass thumb latches, white porcelain pulls, wire nail construction, damaged liner, 36" w, 19" d, 74¼" h. **1,650.00**

Imitation oak graining over earlier red paint, shaped crest, overhanging well with zinc liner and one dovetailed drawer, pair of paneled cupboard doors, cutout feet, Lancaster County, PA, 45¾" w, 20½" d, 32¾" h plus crest **715.00**

Pine

Central well flanked by two dovetailed drawers, pair of raised panel doors set in reeded frames, apron drop on center stile, cutout feet, int. and well painted blue, ext. with old mellow refinishing, 58¾ × 22 × 32". **925.00**

Flat cornice, shaped ends, single narrow shelf, rect well, pair of one board cupboard doors separated by center stile, straight apron, 39" w, 16" d, 51" h **625.00**

Rectangular well, pair of paneled cupboard doors, straight base, 36" w, 19" d, 28" h **425.00**

Straight crest, projected rect tin lined well, pair of paneled cupboard doors separated by center stile, missing feet, 56" w, 25" d, 34" h   **550.00**

Pine and Poplar, two pieces, top with flat cornice, center shelf flanked by two small drawers, and shaped ends, base with shallow rect well, pair of paneled cupboard doors separated by center stile, straight apron, and bracket feet, 48" w, 17" d, 48" h . . .   **650.00**

Poplar

Hutch top with shelf and two dovetailed drawers, zinc lined well, two dovetailed base drawers, pair of paneled doors, well-shaped cutout feet, old dark finish, 61¾" w, 21½" d, 51" **2,200.00**

Shaped crest, molded edge well, pair of paneled cupboard doors, base molding, turned raised ball feet, refinished, bottom board of well replaced, feet replaced, damage to base and base molding, 49" w, 22" d, 34¼" h plus crest **450.00**

Poplar and Walnut, decorated, recessed well, pair of paneled doors flanking center stile, cutout feet, turnbuckle latches, old worn red repaint with black brushed graining and black door panels over earlier dark blue, 39¼" w, 19" d, 36" h. **625.00**

FOOTSTOOLS

Decorated
Cherry, shaped aprons, bootjack ends, primitive village landscape on top, sponging, old repaint, 13½" w **225.00**
Pine, rect top with diamond cutout handle, polychrome dec of two dogs, loving couple, and lovebirds on top, two dogs on one apron, green ground, 14¼" w, 6½" d, 8" h **175.00**
Poplar, rect top, splayed legs, stylized floral design, red, green, and yellow, dark ground, dark varnish over orig finish, 13 ¾" l, 7" h ... **105.00**
Hardwood, thick oval top, splayed legs, old dark worn paint, 11½" l, 8" w, 6" h **75.00**
Pine, book shaped top, cutout legs, old green paint, wear and edge damage, 15" l **290.00**
Poplar, rect molded top, straight skirt, square legs, old worn red repaint, age crack in top, two molding pieces missing, 14" l **80.00**
Upholstered
Oval top with floral design on hooked rag covering, red, olive, and gold on dark ground, brown fringe, dec base with red and yellow striping and yellow tree-like designs on each turned leg, green ground, bottom initialed "S.G.," worn fringe, some wear, 12½" l **350.00**
Rectangular pine frame top with modern reupholstery, hardwood pencil post legs, old alligatored finish, 13½" w, 8½" d **30.00**
Windsor, pine, oval top, turned splayed legs, underside of top branded "A.W. Pratt," old black paint with striping on legs, worn red overpaint on top, worn top, 13½" w, 8" d, 7" h **225.00**

HIGHBOYS

Curly Maple, Queen Anne, top with cove molded cornice, dovetailed case, and five graduated dovetailed overlapping drawers, base with two graduated dovetailed overlapping drawers, scrolled apron, cabriole legs, and padded duck feet, old mellow refinishing, replaced batwing brasses, CT, 38½" w, 20½" d, 73½" h **13,750.00**
Maple, Queen Anne, top with molded cornice, dovetailed case, and four graduated dovetailed overlapping drawers, base with two graduated dovetailed long drawers, bottom drawer with three false fronts and

carved sunburst, scalloped apron, cabriole legs, padded duck feet, deep honey colored finish, old brasses, one bail missing, minor repair to drawer overlap and feet, knee returns replaced, CT, 39¾" w, 20½" d, 72¾" h **9,350.00**
Walnut, Country Queen Anne, pine secondary wood, top with molded cornice, dovetailed case, and eight dovetailed overlapping drawers, base with three dovetailed overlapping drawers, scalloped apron, and cabriole legs, orig engraved brasses, orig finish, 41¾" w, 22¾" d, 69¾" h ... **18,700.00**

ICEBOXES

Oak
Lapland Monitor, Ramey Refrigerator Co, Greenville, MI, three doors, double paneled full length door beside pair of two paneled doors, paneled ends, straight apron, square feet, orig label, 35" w, 20" d, 48" h **575.00**
North Pole, two doors, applied dec on paneled doors, paneled ends, bracket feet, metal tag, zinc lined, orig hardware, 25" w, 19" d, 55" h **475.00**
Victor, Challenge Refrigerator Co, Grand Haven, MI, one door, double raised panel door, paneled ends, metal tag, zinc lined, orig hardware, 22" w, 15" d, 40" h ... **500.00**

MINIATURES

Bench, settle, decorated, double chair back, shaped crest rail, spindles, turned posts, legs, and stretchers, brown, white, and yellow fruit and foliage dec crests, yellow and brown striping, old green repainted ground, late 18th C, one back leg and stretcher poorly reglued, 26" l **500.00**
Blanket Chest
Pine, molded edge lid, paneled sides and ends, turned feet, old dark reddish alligatored finish, 24½" w, 14½" d, 19" h **925.00**
Pine and Poplar, lid with applied edge molding, dovetailed case, lidded till, molded base, shaped apron, bracket feet, presentation inscription on till lid underside, one side foot incomplete, damaged lid, repaired hinge rail, one hinge reset, 24¾" l **375.00**
Poplar, molded edge lid, dovetailed case with lidded till, base molding, turned feet, orig reddish brown flame graining, 19¾" w **600.00**

Chest of Drawers

Cherry, Empire, figured mahogany veneer, rect top, projecting ogee drawer above two lower drawers, stripe inlaid posts over S-form pilasters, 12¾" w, 7" d, 13¼" h . . .   **465.00**

Cherry and Curly Maple, Country Sheraton, dovetailed drawers, two short over three long graduated drawers with curly maple drawer fronts and brass pulls, paneled ends, turned feet, refinished, replaced pulls, repairs, back feet and top replaced, 14" w, 11" d, 17¾" h **775.00**

Curly Maple, Hepplewhite Style, slightly overhanging top, four dovetailed drawers with oval eagle brasses, scalloped apron, French feet, 20¼" w, 12" d, 22½" h **2,200.00**

Grain Painted, red-brown graining, pine, thumb molded top, two short over two long drawers, molded base, turned feet, wrought nail construction, wooden pulls, 13½" w, 7½" d, 17½" h **725.00**

Walnut and Curly Maple, poplar secondary wood, rect top, three dovetailed drawers, cutout feet, turned pulls, backboards replaced, notch cut in back top edge, 13¼" w, 12¾" d, 14½" h **325.00**

Cupboard

Corner, curly maple, two piece, single glazed door in top, two glazed doors in base, single pane each door, light natural finish, handmade reproduction, 27¾" w, 38" h. **465.00**

Jelly, pine, paneled doors, one drawer, corner and edge molding, turned front and tapered back feet, 20¼" w, 9" d, 24½" h **385.00**

Wall

Grain Painted, red flame graining, pine, scrolled crest, molded cornice, pair of paneled doors, adjustable int. shelves, cutout feet, end pieces of cornice molding missing, repaired crest, 18½" w, 8½" d, 24¼" h **550.00**

Pine, molded cornice, open top shelf, pair of paneled cupboard doors, dovetailed case, scalloped apron, old dark finish, 21¾" w, 7" d, 21¾" h **275.00**

Desk, slant front

Curly maple, Chippendale Style, fall front lid with pullout slides, fitted int. with seven drawers and pigeon holes, four graduated overlapping long drawers, shaped bracket feet,

long drawer have dovetailed front and nailed back joints, handmade reproduction, 18¾" w, 10" d, 23¾" h **1,350.00**

Pine, mahogany fall front lid with pullout slides, three dovetailed drawers, old dark finish, old repairs, 10" w, 7¼" d, 10½" h **200.00**

MIRRORS

Bull's Eye, hanging, carved and ebonized giltwood, circular convex mirror plate, molded frame, foliate and shell crest dec, foliate pendant, 28" w, 48" h **1,750.00**

Hall, oak, hanging, diamond shaped, applied beading on outer and inner edges, beveled mirror plate, three ornate iron double hat hooks at lower corners, 18" sq **225.00**

Scroll, hanging

Cherry, Country Chippendale, scrolled crest and pendant, molded mirror frame, old glass, old finish, 11" w, 18" h **525.00**

Pine, Country Queen Anne, scrolled crest, molded frame, old dark finish, discolored and flaked orig glass, 8½" w, 14½" h **575.00**

Walnut

Chippendale, scrolled crest and pendant, replaced glass, one ear incomplete, 12¼" w, 20¼" h **195.00**

Country Chippendale, scrolled crest and pendant, old glass, old finish, two ears damaged, 11¾" w, 18" h. **95.00**

Country Queen Anne, scrolled crest and pendant, molded frame, old mirror plate with worn silvering, pendant scroll incomplete, 8⅜" w, 14½" h   **75.00**

Shaving

Pine and Mahogany Veneer, rect swivel mirror on plain square posts, bowfront base with conforming dovetailed drawer, ball feet, 14½" w, 6¾" d, 16½" h . . .   **150.00**

Walnut and Cherry, inlaid, turned posts, swivel mirror in inlaid frame, single dovetailed drawer, turned feet, old refinish, repairs, 17½" w, 7¾" d, 26" h **110.00**

PIE SAFES

Oak, flat cornice over two short drawers, pair of doors each with three punched tin panels, concentric circle and diamond design, paneled ends, French feet, 41" w, 15" d, 56" h . . .   **525.00**

Pie Safe, Wythe County, VA, walnut, molded cornice, six tin door panels with pierced floral dec, six tin side panels with tulip dec and dated 1868, bootjack ends, 47″ w, 14″ d, 58″ h, $2,600.00. Photograph courtesy of James D Julia, Inc.

Pine
   Hanging
      Single door, five punched tin panels attached to form single large panel on door and back, dovetailed case, wrought iron hooks along end top edges, tin panels with concentric circles design, refinished, 39″ w, 23½″ d, 30¼″ h 350.00
      Two doors, single full length tin panel on each side and door, punched concentric circle design, pegged construction, mortise and tenon joints, hand planed, PA, 36″ w, 19½″ d, 34¾″ h 725.00
   On stand, pair of doors, two punched tin panels both doors and ends, punched diamond design with stylized tulip and stars, mortised and pinned frame on high square legs, NC, 42″ w, 17″ d, 60″ h . . .   1,500.00
   Stepped gallery with cutout dec, rect cornice, pair of doors with screen panels, three int. shelves, block feet, 30½″ w, 15″ d, 44″ h 350.00
   Three quarter gallery with shaped stepdown ends, two short drawers over two doors each with three punched tin panels, shaped apron, bracket feet, mellow refinishing, tin panels painted black, repairs and restoration, 42″ w, 14″ d, 57″ h plus gallery. 500.00

Poplar
   One piece, two doors, twelve tin panels with punched star designs, one dovetailed drawer, square legs, refinished dark brown cherry color, some rust damage, one front leg and drawer front repaired, 39″ w, 16½″ d, 54″ h 385.00
   Two piece, step back top with beveled cornice and two doors, one tin panel each door, base with two dovetailed short drawers above pair of doors, two tin panels each door, square corner posts extend to tapered legs, three tin panels each end, punched diamond and concentric circle designs, int. strips holding tins replaced, tin panels may be replacements, 44″ w, 19½″ d, 78″ h 875.00
Walnut, pair of doors with three punched tin panels each door and three each end, panels with circle and pinwheel design, slightly tapered legs are extensions of square corner posts, panels rusted and damaged, one front leg broken at tenon, 41¼″ w, 18″ d, 49¾″ h 1,000.00
Yellow Pine, molded cornice, double top doors each with two punched tin panels, two dovetailed short drawers, pair of raised panel cupboard doors, paneled ends each with two upper and one lower punched tin panels and one raised panel at drawer level, corner posts extend to square legs, applied molding around base, punched pinwheel design, minor repairs, replaced tins, GA, 43¾″ w, 19½″ d, 70¾″ h 2,100.00

ROCKERS

Bentwood, arched back with conforming caned panel, caned seat, broad sweeping supports, elongated S-form rockers, early 20th C 2,200.00
Country Chippendale, maple, arm, shaped crest, pierced vasiform splat, turned posts, legs, and front stretcher, old rush seat, added rockers, old refinish, 40½″ h 110.00
Country Windsor, crest with painted blue and yellow floral dec, spindle back, scrolled arms, plank seat, yellow striping on black ground, heavily alligatored repaint, 30¼″ h 100.00
Ladder Back
   Five arched graduated slats, turned finials and arm posts, shaped arms, woven splint seat, old mellow refinishing, one slat and seat

replaced, minor age cracks, 44½" h 250.00
Three shaped slats, turned finials and posts, scrolled arms, woven splint seat, shaped rockers, refinished, replaced seat, 39" h 150.00
Lady's, decorated, shaped crest, five narrow turned spindles, scrolled arms, S-scroll seat, ring turned legs, worn and flaking orig red and black graining with yellow striping, 37" h   75.00
Mission Style, oak, straight crest rail, three vertical slats, flat arms with rounded corners, six board seat, 26" h 165.00
Platform, oak, applied leaf and vine dec on shaped crest, square posts, upholstered back panel, scrolled arms, baluster turned arm supports, overstuffed seat, platform base, rect front stretcher with incised lines, casters, 22" w, 38" h 200.00
Pressed Back, oak
Flower and bead design, straight crest rail, bulbous turned finials on tapered posts, seven rod spindles, bentwood arms, splayed base with turned legs and box stretchers, 38" h 150.00
Man of the North Wind design, shaped crest rail, ball finials on ring turned posts, six ring and baluster turned spindles, hip brackets, shaped seat, ring turned front legs and front stretchers, rod stretchers on ends and back, 39" h 200.00
Windsor Style
Bow Back, hooped crest rail, seven tapered rods, U-shaped arm rail with knuckle hand holds, baluster turned arm posts, oval dished seat, splayed base, baluster turned legs,

Child's Rocker, shaped crest rail, scrolled arms, cane back and seat, 24" h, estimated price $100.00–200.00. Photograph courtesy of James D Julia, Inc.

similarly turned H-form stretcher, repaired split in seat, arms ended out, rockers are later addition, 34" h 150.00
Comb back, birch, Colonial Furniture Co, Grand Rapids, MI, turned legs, mahogany finish 175.00

SETTEES

Chippendale Style, walnut, shaped crest rail, rolled arms and seat, salmon upholstered back, seat, and sides, chamfered legs, 59" l 425.00
Decorated
Federal, yellow, green, and brown stenciled fruit dec on straight crest rail, triple back splat, plank seat, ring turned tapered legs, stretcher, c1820, 75" w 725.00
Sheraton, black, red, and gold shell and vintage dec crest, pierced rail back, scrolled arms, turned arm supports, balloon shaped rush seat, turned legs, outward curved feet, white ground, repainted 2,250.00
Windsor, New England
Arrow back, flat crest rail, 26 arrow shaped spindles, splayed base, bamboo turned legs, double arrow shaped front stretchers, red and black striping, red, green and black floral dec, mustard ground   3,000.00
Rod back, nine bamboo turned spindles, bamboo turned posts, arms, and arm supports, shaped incised seat, splayed base with bamboo turned legs, H-form stretcher with central tablet, refinished, repairs, early 19th C, 25" w, 10¼" h seat, 24" h 3,500.00

SHELVES

Folk Art, hanging, spool, three graduated shelves with scalloped front edge, spool turned posts, old reddish finish, 28" w, 18" h 25.00
Hardwood, hanging, four shelves, frame-like facade with half turned pilasters, closed back, reddish brown stain ext., natural varnish int., 12¼" w, 4¾" d, 13¼" h 40.00
Oak, Mission Style, hanging, four shelves, reticulated plank ends, D-shaped handles, exposed keyed tenons, 27¼" w, 6¼" d, 36" h 125.00
Painted, corner, 5 shelves, top three shelves graduated in size with stepped scalloped sides, bottom two shelves same size as third shelf, worn dark red paint, late wire nail construction, 60" h 750.00

Shelf, wall mounted, chip carved edges, carved spruce trees on back and sides, painted green and brown, varnish finish, 17" w, 9½" d, 16" h, $1,430.00. Photograph courtesy of James D Julia, Inc.

Pine
1 Shelf, hanging, dovetailed drawer under shelf, decorative cutout brackets, old red paint, 24¼" w, 6¾" d, 13" h **1,100.00**
2 Shelves, hanging, scalloped ends, old refinishing, 20" w, 23 ¾" h . . **225.00**
3 Shelves, hanging, cutout ends, old yellow repaint, 28½" w, 6¾" d, 29" h **125.00**
4 Shelves, hanging, plate rack, plate bars on two center shelves, cutout ends, gray repaint, 68½" w, 11" d, 37" h **150.00**
6 Shelves, rect, straight ends, painted green, 1800–50, 9¾" w, 6½" d, 21¼" h **725.00**
Pine and Poplar, 6 shelves, rect top, one board ends, scrolled upper edge on front base board, old green and red paint, blackboards with age cracks, 10" w, 6" d, 41¼" h **525.00**
Poplar, four graduated shelves, scalloped ends, weathered gray finish with traces of white paint, 49" w, 59" h **1,600.00**
Walnut, hanging, three scalloped shelves, turned posts and finials, refinished, 23½" w, 7¼" d, 25½" h **95.00**

SIDEBOARDS

Curly Maple, poplar secondary wood, scalloped crest, three dovetailed drawers, base shelf, turned legs and feet, turned curly maple pulls, light natural refinishing, 36½" w, 36½" h **3,750.00**
Oak
Empire Style, rect molded top, two drawers, center section with glazed center door flanked by bowed glass end panels, demilune

carved stiles, swelled base drawer, carved paw feet, 44" w, 38" h . . . **400.00**
Mission Style, two pieces, top with rect shelf supported by shaped brackets and rect beveled mirror plate flanked by outset etagere shelves, base with row of two drawers, two center drawers flanked by two glazed doors with geometric fretwork, single long base drawer, shaped apron, and paneled bootjack ends, 55" w, 18" d, 51" h **400.00**
Naturalistic Revival, quarter sawn, applied moldings, two pieces, top with center grotesque face flanked by gadrooned ram's horns and leafy dec, beveled mirror plate flanked by rect etagere shelves, shaped backboard, and ornate reeded and spiral turned columns, base with ovolo edge on overhanging rect top, two short drawers over single long drawer over two cupboard doors, molded bottom edge, paneled feet, and paw feet on casters, carved shell motif on short drawer fronts, wood inverted shell pulls, applied conch shell dec on cupboard doors, applied scroll dec on top and bottom of stiles, 48" w, 24" d, 77" h **1,750.00**
Pine, thumb molded rect top with rounded corners, two short drawers with molded edges, pair of paneled cupboard doors separated by center stile, scalloped apron, bracket feet, turned walnut drawer pulls **450.00**

SOFAS

Cabriole, Country Formal, upholstered back and curving sides, loose seat cushion, carved mahogany square tapered legs with molded edges, straight front legs, curved back legs, MA or NY, 1790–1810, 80½" w . . .**13,200.00**
Chippendale, mahogany, camel back, upholstered arched back, out scrolled arms, upholstered seat with loose cushion, square molded legs, stretchers, Philadelphia, PA, 1760–70, 97" l **2,200.00**
Chippendale Style
Camel back, scrolled sides, loose seat cushion, carved mahogany base with square legs and box stretchers, pale gold floral damask upholstery, light stains, 85" l **850.00**
Shaped back, rolled arms, yellow velvet upholstered seat, mahogany frame, gadrooned apron, cab-

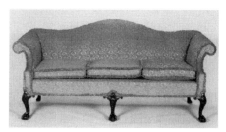

Sofa, Chippendale style, carved mahogany, arched back, cabriole legs with carved knees, claw and ball feet, Scalamandre, 84″ l, $880.00. Photograph courtesy of C G Sloan & Co, Inc.

riole legs with carved knees, claw and ball feet, late 19th C, 62″ w **1,400.00**

Couch, oak, shaped crest rail with applied foliate moldings, upholstered scrolled arms fold down, overstuffed seat, straight seat rail, carved paw feet, c1890, 55″ w, 31″ d, 34″ h ... **500.00**

Country, walnut, turned posts with acorn finials, slightly arched crest rail, upholstered cushion back and seat, turned arms and feet, ogee seat rail, some edge damage, old worn blue and white reupholstery, 77″ l . **525.00**

STANDS

Crock

Oak, four tiers, molded edge shelves, scalloped legs, old green repaint, 39″ w, 19″ d, 43¾″ h **375.00**

Pine

2 Tiers, wire nail construction, rect shelves with cove molded brackets, bootjack ends, old worn green paint, 34½″ w, 12″ d, 14½″ h **325.00**

3 Tiers, graduated half round shelves, three part stepped scalloped frame, dark finish, 34½″ w, 38¾″ h **300.00**

Drop Leaf

Birch, Country Hepplewhite Style, rect top, 8″ w leaves, nailed drawer, square tapered legs, turned drawer pull, refinished, 25¾″ w, 19½″ d, 27¾″ h **95.00**

Cherry, bird's eye veneer drawer fronts, one board top, 9″ w drop leaves with decorative cutout corners, two graduated dovetailed drawers with turned wood pulls, boldly turned legs, raised ball feet, refinished, flange on one back leg chipped, 23¼″ w, 15¼″ d, 27¼″ h **725.00**

Night

Cherry, Country Sheraton

Rectangular two board top, single dovetailed drawer with turned wood pull, turned legs, old mellow refinish, 21¼″ w, 20¾″ d, 29¼″ h **325.00**

Rectangular two board top, two dovetailed drawers, turned legs, refinished, 22¾″ w, 17¾″ d, 28¾″ h **500.00**

Square overhanging top, straight apron, turned posts, base shelf with dovetailed drawer, turned legs, old dark finish, replaced top, 18″ sq, 30½″ h **135.00**

Square overhanging two board top, dovetailed drawer with under lip pull, slender ring turned legs, raised ball feet, old worn red finish, worn and stained top, chip on back corner, one front foot has edge damage, PA, 16¼″ sq, 30″ h **650.00**

Cherry and Curly Maple, Country Sheraton, rect top, two graduated dovetailed drawers, turned legs, old mellow refinishing, repaired breaks in reattached top, replaced brass pull, 22″ w, 18¼″ d, 28 ½″ h **875.00**

Curly Maple

Rectangular, overhanging one board top, dovetailed drawer, turned legs, tapered feet, old refinishing, reattached top braced on underside, replaced glass pull, 20½″ w, 17½″ d, 28¾″ h **450.00**

Square top, two dovetailed drawers, square tapered legs with turned detail, refinished, 20″ sq, 28¾″ h **770.00**

Curly Maple and Walnut, Country Hepplewhite, walnut legs, three board rect top, single dovetailed drawer with fiery opalescent lacy pull, square tapered legs with corner beading, drawer rebuilt, apron missing, 19½″ w, 17½″ d, 28″ h **525.00**

Pine, Sheraton, grain painted, one board top with outset rounded corners, two dovetailed drawers, turned legs, raised ring turned feet, red flame graining, emb gilded brass pulls, one pull dented, 21¼″ w, 17½″ d, 28½″ h **1,925.00**

Pine and Poplar, rect one board top, single dovetailed drawer with turned pull, ring turned legs, ball feet, old red paint, 19″ w, 18½″ d, 26¾″ h **500.00**

Poplar and Cherry, rect top, two dovetailed drawers with curly maple veneer fronts, turned legs, cherry finish, resurfaced drawer fronts, repairs, 27¾" w, 20" d, 28½" h **182.00**

Walnut

Country Empire, rect one board top with rounded corners, two dovetailed drawers, turned half columns applied to corner posts, block and turned legs, turned feet, curly maple pulls with inlaid diamonds, diamond shaped pearl inlays on drawers and rails, one pull replaced, one inlay missing, top flipped and reattached, 22" w, 19 ¾" d, 30" h **150.00**

Square top, single overlapping drawer, turned legs, handmade reproduction, old worn finish, 20½" sq, 24½" h **72.00**

Walnut and Poplar

Country Hepplewhite, rect two board top, mortised and pinned apron, pencil post legs, old dark finish, 20½" w, 19¼" d, 28¾" h **75.00**

Country Sheraton, rect overhanging one board top, two dovetailed drawers, ring turned legs, turned feet, refinished, top reattached and probably replaced, 16⅜ " w, 19" h **275.00**

Parlor, cherry and poplar

Round two board top, splayed base with turned legs and ball feet, attributed to Zoar, OH, warped top, 24" d, 24" h **415.00**

Turtle shaped top, four down curving legs join at center and flare to feet, refinished, stained top, 19" w, 17" d, 27¾" h **200.00**

Pedestal

Grain Painted, brown, round top, octagonal column, square base, some wear, age cracks in top, 15½" d, 31½" h **65.00**

Primitive, soft wood, round top, four board box type pedestal, shaped brackets, beveled base, old worn orange and blue repaint, 30" h   **100.00**

Plant

Hardwood, square well with copper liner, cabriole legs, duck feet, 20th C, 30" h **200.00**

Mahogany veneer, three tier, solid mahogany frame with acanthus and reeded carving, bottom tier with flowerpot cutouts, outswept feet **85.00**

Oak

Square top, splayed base with ring and baluster turned legs, square medial shelf, 16" sq, 31" h **80.00**

Round top, turned and reeded baluster pedestal, circular base, four scroll feet, 12" d, 34" h . . .   **125.00**

Sewing

Martha Washington Style, mahogany, three drawers, shaped ends, ring turned legs, 1920, 28" w, 14" d, 29" h **100.00**

Priscilla type, painted red, dark trim, floral decal, turned rod handle, 1930, 13" w, 11" d, 25" h **30.00**

Smoking

Oak, Mission, Charles Rohlfs, square top, paneled cupboard doors and ends, plinth base, 1900, 30" h . . .   **800.00**

Walnut veneer, William and Mary Style, rect top, figured walnut veneer door, painted base, 18" w, 11" d, 30" h **95.00**

Work, walnut, Country Hepplewhite, removable two board top with cleated underside, single dovetailed drawer, square tapered legs, old shiny varnish finish, drawer front has repaired split and some edge damage, 25½" w, 21¼" d, 29¼" h **875.00**

STOOLS

Country Windsor, round top, splayed base with turned and tapered legs, double box stretchers, underside of seat branded "P. Mitchell," traces of old paint, 15¾" h **95.00**

Mission, oak, rect top with spring cushion seat, legs with corbel supports, lower side stretcher, medial stretcher

Footstool, Lebanon Valley, PA, oak and pine, upholstered lift-top, sides inlaid with angels, birds, and trees, turned legs, late 19th C, 17" w, 12" d, 16" h, $330.00. Photograph courtesy of James D Julia, Inc.

tenoned through side, 1910, 23" l, 17" d, 18" h **300.00**

Piano, oak, adjustable round seat on threaded rod, base with circular top, reeded bulbous pedestal, and splayed legs with reeded bulbous turnings, stretchers, and claw and glass ball feet, 12" d, 20" h **175.00**

Upholstered, mahogany, square top with floral upholstery, turned legs, box stretcher, turned feet, old dark finish, 17" sq, 20" h **115.00**

TABLES

Breakfast, cherry, rect top, rounded corners on drop leaves, single beaded drawer, square double tapered legs with inlaid cuffs, New England, 1810–20, 18½" w, 36" d, 29" h **650.00**

Butterfly, William and Mary, elongated oval leaves, splayed base, single drawer frieze with trapezoid shaped drawer front, turned knob pull, turned legs, box stretchers, block feet, old refinish, imperfections, height loss, 43" w open, 27" d, 25" h   **1,210.00**

Dining

Cherry, Sheraton Style, drop leaf, rect top, 23" w leaves, six turned and rope carved legs, 49¼" w, 22" d, 26½" h **275.00**

Cherry and Maple, Queen Anne, drop leaf, demilune leaves, straight apron, square tapering slightly curving legs, slipper feet, New England, c1770, 45½" l, 45" w open, 27½" h **1,750.00**

Mahogany, Queen Anne, rect top, D-shaped drop leaves, cabriole legs, spade feet, Long Island, NY, c1770, 51½" w, 40½" d, 28" h   **4,400.00**

Oak

Mission, Gustav Stickley, round overhanging top, wide apron, five tapered legs, recent shellac finish over orig medium brown color, 48" d, 30½" h **750.00**

Round extension top, raised square beading on straight apron, turned pedestal base, four cabriole legs, carved paw feet on casters, 45" d, 30" h. . .   **850.00**

Square extension top, incised lines on straight aprons, five reeded ring and ball turned legs, ball feet on casters, 42" sq, 30" h   **425.00**

Walnut, Chippendale, two thumb molded end drawers, squared legs, block feet, PA, 1770–90, 49¼" w, 52¼" d, 29¾" h **4,290.00**

Dressing, oak, adjustable side mirrors, arched center mirror, two small drawers, scalloped apron, high legs, cabriole front legs, straight back legs, 1925 . . . .   **250.00**

Drop Leaf

Cherry

One board top, 15¼" w rect leaves with cut corners, swing legs support leaves, well turned legs, refinished, minor repairs to rule joints, 40" w, 17¼" d, 29" h **550.00**

Two board top, 13¼" w rect one board leaves, slender turned legs, button feet, minor wear, legs have some edge damage, mellow refinishing, 37¼" w, 18¾" d, 28¾" h **350.00**

Cherry and Birch, Country Sheraton, rect top, single rect 18 ½" w drop leaf, wide board apron, two dovetailed frieze drawers, turned and rope carved legs with brass casters, brass ring pulls, age cracks in top, 72" w, 22¾" d, 28½" h **650.00**

Curly Maple, two board top, single board drop leaves, shaped end apron, turned legs, castors, refinished, opens to 47" d, 28¼" h . . .   **470.00**

Maple, Queen Anne, rect top, one board rect drop leaves with rounded corners, round tapered swing legs, small duck feet, old nut brown color, reattached top, top underside scored, leaves slightly warped, one leaf repaired, 52¼" w, 15½" d, 17" leaves, 27½" h **1,650.00**

Drop Leaf Table, Chippendale, Rhode Island, mahogany, rect top, two hinged rect drop leaves, shaped frieze, six chamfered square legs, 18th C, 47¾" w, 62" open l, 28" h, $2,475.00. Photograph courtesy of Butterfield & Butterfield.

Gateleg Table William and Mary, New England, oval top with two drop leaves, single short-drawer frieze, ring squashed ball turned legs, squashed ball feet, top restored, 18th C, 48″ w, 28½″ h, $2,750.00. Photograph courtesy of Butterfield & Butterfield.

Walnut, Country Federal, rect leaves, single drawer, turned tapered legs, raised ball feet, refinished, PA, c1810, 44¼″ w open, 29 ¾″ d, 29½″ h **875.00**

Harvest

Bird's Eye Maple and Ash, refinished, New England, 60½″ w, 17″ d, 28¾″ h **900.00**

Pine

Drop leaf, two board top, 11¾″ w leaves with rounded corners and square butt joints, square tapered legs, gold graining on yellow ground, old repaint, corners possibly recut, 62½″ w, 19¾″ d, 28¾″ h **1,000.00**

Rectangular overhanging two board top with applied edge molding, nailed apron, turned legs and feet, old brownish gray repaint, 105″ w, 29″ d, 33¼″ h **550.00**

Pine and Poplar, two board top, single drawer, square tapered legs, old brown grained repaint, 144″ l, 25½″ d, 31″ h **200.00**

Huntboard

Decorated, pine, Country Hepplewhite, mortised and pinned construction, rect top with applied edge molding and old gray over yellowed marbleized dec, pullout shelf between two dovetailed long drawers, square tapered legs, alligatored brown finish with black and gold painted dec, replaced pulls, molding around bottom edge of case replaced, 30¾″ w, 19½″ d, 38″ h **2,200.00**

Yellow Pine, rect top, three small drawers with wide early dovetailing, molding applied to top and bottom of apron, high square tapered legs, repairs to drawer fronts, SC, 52½″ w, 25½″ d, 42″ h **4,750.00**

Hutch

Cherry, round top, cleated, shaped ends, shoe feet, NY, 18th C, 29″ d, 47½″ h **2,975.00**

Pine, removable two board top, box compartment, one board ends, shoe feet, layers of old worn reddish brown and blue paint, wear and age cracks, top boards warped, orig wrought iron nails with old renailing, 48″ w, 35″ d, 27½″ h **700.00**

Pine and Maple, round top, straight ends, rect boxed seat, shoe feet, New England, late 18th C, 45¾″ d, 27⅛ ″ h **2,100.00**

Poplar and Pine, rect two board pine top, hinged lid seat, poplar base with single board ends and cutout feet, old brown graining over orig red, 37″ w, 28″ d, 28″ h **1,050.00**

Library

Mahogany, Mission, George Washington Maher, Chicago, IL, rect overhanging top, wide apron, massive square legs, base shelf, molded feet, 66″ l, 30″ d, 36″ h **2,700.00**

Oak

Empire Style, oblong top, pillar base, scroll feet, 1920, 48″ w, 28″ d, 28″ h **400.00**

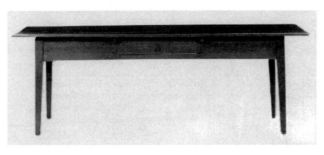

Harvest Table, Country Federal, Virginia, walnut, overhanging rectangular top, conforming recessed single-drawer frieze, square tapered legs, late 18th C 86″ w, 34½″ d, 29½ h, $4,620.00. Photograph courtesy of William Doyle Galleries.

Hutch Table, rounded corners on square top, carved handholds, square seat, box stretcher base, block turned legs, old green paint, 42" sq top, 29" h, $2,750.00. Photograph courtesy of James D Julia, Inc.

Mission Style, Imperial Furniture Co, Grand Rapids, MI, quarter sawn, rect top, two short drawers with triangular copper pulls, square legs, three vertical slats each side, side stretchers, medial shelf, applied tenons on legs and side stretchers, 50" w, 32" d, 30" h 450.00

Parlor
Oak
Octagonal top, beaded apron, splayed base, slender spiral turned legs continuing to ring and baluster turnings, flattened ball feet, scalloped medial shelf, 26" w, 29" h 275.00

Square top with scalloped edge, conforming apron, splayed base with spiral, ring, and baluster turned legs, scalloped medial shelf with metal brackets, ball feet, 23" sq, 29" h 175.00

Poplar, round two board top, square tapered legs with chamfered tops, old worn black paint, repaired crack and edge damaged top, 26¼" d, 26½" h 110.00

Pembroke
Cherry, Country Sheraton, 12½" w rect drop leaves, simple turned and tapered legs, ball feet, old red finish, minor edge damage, 40" w, 17¼" d, 28¾" h 500.00

Mahogany, Country Hepplewhite, inlaid, serpentine top, 9¼" serpentine leaves, square tapered legs with corner beading, old worn finish, minor inlay damage, 35" w, 16" d, 28½" h **1,900.00**

Pine, Country Hepplewhite, rect top with 12½" w leaves, square tapered legs, old dark natural finish on top, old red finish on base, top is old replacement, NY, 43¾" w, 19¼" d, 28½" h **250.00**

Sawbuck
Pine
Cleated two board top, X-form legs with wide board stretchers, traces of old paint under red wash finish, age cracks in top, 31½" w, 23" d, 20" h **415.00**

One board top with some stains and use scars, refinished, 43 x 21 × 26½" **500.00**

Pine and Hardwood, one board breadboard top, old mellow refinishing, one end of cleat is ended out, 90 × 25 × 29½" **1,000.00**

Poplar, one board breadboard top, straight apron, X-form legs, orig dark mustard painted base, old natural finish top, VT, 43" w, 21¼" d, 33¾" h **775.00**

Tavern
Hardwood, Country Queen Anne, two board breadboard top, single overlapping drawer, turned legs, mortised and pinned stretchers, old worn soft patina, replaced batwing brass, drawer joints loose, screws added to top, 41" w, 26" d, 28" h **1,550.00**

Maple
Pilgrim Style, old reproduction, two board breadboard top, scalloped apron, turned legs,

Tavern Table, Country Chippendale, maple, rect overhanging rect breadboard top, conforming recessed single-drawer frieze, turned legs, box stretcher, $550.00. Photograph courtesy of William Doyle Galleries.

stretcher base, worn dark brown finish, 42" l, 24¾" d, 26½" h **500.00**

Rectangular overhanging top, single overlapping drawer, turned wood pull, turned legs, box stretcher base, turned feet, old refinish, restored, New England, 43½" l, 29" d, 27" h **525.00**

Oak, William and Mary Style, oval top, recessed frieze, turned splayed legs, box stretcher, 34" w, 25" d, 25" h **675.00**

Pine, Country Chippendale, oval two board top, deeply scalloped apron, splayed base, square legs with molded edge, top with natural finish and age cracks, layers of old paint on base, 31¾" w, 24 ¾" d, 26½" h **1,650.00**

Pine and Maple, red stain finish, New England, mid 18th C, 41" w, 23" d, 24" h **1,425.00**

Pine and Poplar, Country Hepplewhite, poplar breadboard top, red painted pine splayed base with reeded apron and square tapered legs, old breadboard top with edge damage, 31" w, 23" d, 29¾" h   **600.00**

Tea

Cherry, Chippendale, scalloped top, turned vasiform standard, tripod base terminating in claw and ball feet, attributed to MA, c1780, 33" w, 30½" d, 27¾" h **925.00**

Mahogany, Chippendale

Circular dished top, shaped column, tripod base with padded snake feet, New England, c1780, 28" d, 25⅛ " h **2,100.00**

Tilt top, round cleated three board top, turned column, tripod base with snake feet, refinished, latch holding top missing, age crack in column, repaired column base, replaced top, 33" d, 28" h   **800.00**

Mahogany, Oak, and Cherry, tilt top, circular two board top with diagonal cross grain splice, turned column, tripod base, cutout feet, 35" d, 28" h **275.00**

Maple

Chippendale, tilt top, three board with serpentine edges, square top tilts to diamond, turned column, tripod base with slipper feet, shim added to one foot, 36" w, 35" d, 27¼" h **725.00**

Queen Anne, rect top with thumb molded edge, shaped skirt with half moon pendants, turned tapered legs, raised flattened ball feet, refinished, minor imperfec-

tions, RI, late 18th C, 27" w, 19¼" d, 27¾" h **3,750.00**

Maple and Cherry, Country Hepplewhite, round cherry tilt top, maple tripod base with turned column, spider legs, and spade feet, 25" d, 28¾" h **525.00**

Walnut, Chippendale, circular dished tilt top, turned column, tripod base with padded snake feet, refinished, repairs, PA, 22" d, 31" h **600.00**

Walnut and Curly Maple, tilt top, round three board top with reeded edge and round center inlay, small underside drawer, short turned column, tripod base, arched cutout legs with reeded edge and scrolled feet, old mellow refinishing, age crack in top, attributed to Zoar, OH, 23½" d, 28" h **225.00**

Trestle, oak, oblong top with rounded corners, wedged trestle base, shoe feet, old patina, 30" w, 8½" d, 26½" h **75.00**

Work

Curly Maple, Country Chippendale, rect overhanging two board top with molded edge, dovetailed drawer, square molded legs, old refinishing, top reattached, reconstruction to drawer and parts of apron, 29½" w, 20" d, 25½" h   **875.00**

Decorated, poplar, removable rect top painted red, red paint grained apron with two dovetailed overlapping drawers, turned legs painted black, legs have plugged holes, 48" w, 35¾" d, 28¼" h ... **1,000.00**

Hardwood and Pine, Country Hepplewhite, rect overhanging two board top, wide board apron, splayed base, square tapered legs with molded corner beading, orangish-red repainted base, slightly warped top, 33½" w, 20" d, 28¼" h **525.00**

Pine, Country Hepplewhite

Rectangular overhanging three board top, mortised and pinned wide board apron, square tapered legs, old worn dark finish, 35½" w, 30" d, 29" h **325.00**

Removable overhanging four board top with rounded corners, mortised and pinned apron with dovetailed drawer, square tapered legs, refinished with traces of blue and white paint, two legs with edge damage, one leg with old nailed repair, 49" w, 31" d, 29½" h **300.00**

Poplar, three board top, square tapered legs, refinished, red repaint on base, $37\frac{1}{2} \times 56\frac{1}{2} \times 29''$ **200.00**

Walnut, Country Hepplewhite

Rectangular overhanging two board top, mortised and pinned beaded apron with two nailed drawers, squared chamfered corner legs and H-form stretcher, minor water damage to feet, one back foot ended out, edge damage to drawers, age cracks in top, PA, $72\frac{1}{2}''$ w, 36" d, $29\frac{3}{4}''$ h **1,150.00**

Rectangular overhanging two board breadboard top, mortised and pinned wide board apron with inlaid initials "A.H.", square tapered legs, worn and scrubbed finish, $34\frac{3}{4}''$ w, 25" d, $26\frac{1}{2}''$ h **415.00**

Walnut and Pine, Country Hepplewhite, removable three board overhanging top, two dovetailed cockbeaded drawers, square tapered legs, old mellow refinishing, replaced top, replaced turned drawer pulls, 59" w, 33 $\frac{1}{4}''$ d, 29" h. **650.00**

TRUNKS

Decorated, dome top, green and salmon putty dec, imperfections, New England, early 19th C, $32 \times 16\frac{1}{2} \times 13\frac{3}{4}''$. **525.00**

Grain Painted, dome top

Initialed "DH" in top, MA, c1830, $26\frac{1}{2}''$ w, 13" d, 11 $\frac{1}{2}''$ h **250.00**

Red and yellow graining, dovetailed, iron lock with shield shaped escutcheon, replaced hasp, edge damage, age cracks, $40\frac{3}{4}''$ w. **90.00**

Yellow ochre and burnt umber graining, minor surface mars, New England, 19th C, $30\frac{1}{2}''$ w, 15" d, 14" h. **150.00**

Pine, rect hinged lid, dovetailed case, bail handles, bracket base, 36" w, 19" d, 22" h **175.00**

WARDROBES

Grain Painted, pine and poplar, beveled cornice, single paneled door, cutout feet, worn varnish over old red flame graining, top rail over door cracked, $44\frac{1}{4}''$ w, $19\frac{1}{4}''$ d, 79" h   **385.00**

Oak

Break down, molded cornice, applied scrolled dec on frieze, pair of paneled cupboard doors over two short base drawers, scalloped apron, square legs on casters, 43" w, 17" d, 83" h **950.00**

Spoon carved dec on arched pediment, molded cornice, pair of double paneled cupboard doors, base drawer, 39" w, 16" d, 80" h   **750.00**

Pine, break down, molded cornice, pair of paneled doors with molded frames, single base drawer, shaped apron, bracket feet, pegged construction, turned wood pulls, 46" w, $18\frac{1}{2}''$ d, $77\frac{1}{2}''$ h **750.00**

Yellow Pine, molded cornice, two raised panel doors in molded frames, one board ends, bracket feet, old mellow refinishing, feet ended out, age cracks, some edge damage, moldings between doors replaced, some renailing, southern US, $52\frac{1}{2}''$ w, $20\frac{1}{4}''$ d, 77" h **400.00**

WASHSTANDS

Cherry and Hardwood, Folk Art, late wire nail construction, scrolled crest, turned towel bars both sides, single drawer, turned posts, base shelf with inlaid running horse, drawer front with laminated strips of cherry and walnut, $28\frac{1}{2}''$ w, $14\frac{1}{4}''$ d, $35\frac{1}{2}''$ h **375.00**

Grain Painted, bowed high back with shelf, scalloped supports, rect top with outset corners, two drawers, bamboo legs, shaped medial shelf, New England, c1830, 39" w, 23" d, 46" h. **415.00**

Hard and Soft Woods, Country Sheraton, three quarter gallery with shaped ends, scalloped apron, turned posts, base shelf with drawer, turned feet, reddish repaint, reconstructed, $23\frac{1}{2}''$ w, $15\frac{1}{2}''$ d, 35" h **190.00**

Mahogany, Country Hepplewhite, lift lid, int. seat and turned lid, square tapered legs, chamber pot missing, 17" sq, $18\frac{1}{2}''$ h **135.00**

Maple, rect molded top, harp shaped towel rack, swivel mirror with shell carved crest, ogee top drawer, serpentine shaped case with single cupboard door and two small drawers, 36" w, 76" h **375.00**

Oak

Eastlake Style, spoon carved dec, circles and incised lines on shaped backsplash, slightly overhanging top, single long drawer over paneled cupboard door and two graduated short drawers, acorn spoon carved designs and incised lines on drawer and door fronts, incised lines on stiles, brass bail handle pulls, 32" w, 19" d, 36" h   **350.00**

Lyre shaped towel bar with applied feather moldings and molded base, serpentine shaped top with conforming long drawer above recessed paneled cupboard door and bank of two short drawers, shaped apron, square legs on casters, 34" w, 20" d, 53" h **350.00**

Pine

Country Sheraton, three quarter gallery with wide board crest and shaped ends, rect top with bowl cutout, turned posts, medial shelf with false drawer front, slender turned legs, refinished, 16½" w, 16¼" d, 30½" h plus gallery **185.00**

Scalloped splashboard, rounded corners on slightly overhanging top, single long drawer over pair of cupboard doors with tombstone shaped panels, shaped apron, bracket feet, turned wood pulls, 39" w, 15" d, 29" h **325.00**

Three quarter gallery with shaped ends, square top with bowl cutout, straight apron, square tapered legs, square medial shelf with single drawer frieze, turned walnut pull, 14½" sq, 28½" h **200.00**

Poplar, rect top, dovetailed three quarter gallery with wide board crest and rounded corners, dovetailed drawer, block and baluster turned posts, base shelf, turned feet, stenciled label "Wm Brown, Successor to Brown & Tate, Manufacturer, Lawrenceburgh,

Ind. Warranted" inside drawer, replaced porcelain pulls, 24½" w, 16½" d, 37 ¾" h plus gallery **350.00**

Walnut, Hepplewhite, corner, line inlaid edges, arched dovetailed gallery, top shelf with bowl and accessory cutouts, medial shelf with dovetailed drawer flanked by false drawers, base shelf, square out curving legs, refinished, minor old repairs, drawer pull incomplete, 24½" w, 16" d, 41" h **575.00**

WICKER

Bench, window, tightly woven rolled arms, curlicue design on sides, rect pressed-in seat, wrapped legs, three stretcher front and back with S-scrolled curlicues above and below, natural color, 34" w, 18" d, 29½" h **350.00**

Bookcase, ring turned spire type finials on front and back spiral turned posts, arched crest with turned baluster spindles surmounted by balls, seven spindles with curlicue top form back, four wood shelves, open sides, ball feet, natural color, 19½" w, 14" d, 42" h **350.00**

Chair

Desk, arched crest rail, square back, central tightly woven panel on open work splat, wrapped posts and hip brackets, upholstered seat cushion in woven seat, tightly woven seat rail, open work skirt, wrapped legs joined by X-form stretcher, white, 36" h **175.00**

Wicker Parlor Set, sofa, table, rocker, and armchair, metal label "Fogle," estimated price $600.00–1,000.00. Photograph courtesy of Morton M Goldberg Galleries.

Photographer's, oval panel with tightly woven radiating design supported by posts and central spindle flanked by curlicues, tightly woven S-scrolled rolled down curving arms continue to long skirt with diamond design over open work and braid, pressed-in round seat, wrapped legs, white, 20" w, 42" h **425.00**

Wing, braided edges, open work back, wings, and sides, magazine pockets both sides, hinged lids serve as armrests, tightly woven seat rail, arched open work skirt, tightly woven bulbous feet, 33" w, 40" h **400.00**

Chaise Lounge, tightly woven crest continuing to braced armrests, one arm shorter, open work back, tightly woven seat and seat rail, upholstered seat cushion, arched open work skirt, wrapped tapered legs, white, 58" l, 35" w, 36" h **875.00**

Divan, tightly woven heart shaped back with curlicue dec at top and double diamond design over a lyre shaped splat with curlicues and stick and ball dec, rolled curved arms with tightly woven armrests above similar inverted lyre shaped arm supports, pressed-in seat, tightly woven cabriole legs, X-form stretchers, natural color, 1900–05, 34" w, 18" d, 38" h **575.00**

Fernery, tightly woven rect well, front of well shorter than back, wrapped braced legs, X-form stretcher, white, 25½" w, 18 ½" d, 32" h **100.00**

Rocker, Heywood Brothers, willow, paper label, No. W59D, c1910, 32 ½" w, 23" d, 38" h, $225.00. Photograph courtesy of Skinner, Inc.

Footstool, round, tightly woven pattern radiated from center top and continues to skirt with open weave edge design, four wrapped out curving ball turned legs with brackets, X-form stretchers, white, 16" d, 23" h **200.00**

Rocker, hooped back with tightly woven roll continuing to arms, trapezoidal caned back panel surrounded by open work C- and S-scrolls, stick and ball arm supports, round seat with pierced design, S-scrolled cabriole legs, natural color, 23½" w, 37" h **375.00**

Sofa, tightly woven crest with diamond designs continuing to rolled arms, open work double chair back and sides, upholstered seat cushion, braided seat rail, tightly woven scalloped apron, wrapped legs, two X-form stretchers, white, 58" w, 31¼" h **475.00**

Table

Library, slightly overhanging rect wood top, tightly woven straight skirt, boxed legs, rect medial shelf, white, 42" w, 26" d, 30" h **300.00**

Parlor, oval wood top with braided edge, turned straight legs, square medial shelf with braided edge, open work demilune magazine pockets attached to legs on both sides, white, 30" w, 20½" d, 30" h   **250.00**

ADIRONDACK AND RUSTIC

History: The use of natural materials, ranging from tree branches to rattan, in furniture construction enjoyed great popularity in the latter half of the 19th century and first quarter of the 20th. The rustic look was found in cottage, porch, and some garden furniture.

It is extremely important to differentiate between rustic and primitive furniture. Although much rustic furniture appears primitive in form and construction, factory and craftsperson examples dominate. Among the catalogs in the collection at Rinker Enterprises is *Rustic Furniture—Rustic Bird Houses* of the Ye Olde Rustic Furniture Company of Philadelphia which advertises its products for "porches, lawns, summer homes, parks, country clubs, gardens, pavilions, theaters, hotels, dens, sanatoriums, etc."

One of the best known manufacturers of rustic furniture is the Old Hickory Furniture Company of Martinsville, Indiana, which celebrated its 40th anniversary in 1931. Their "Pioneer" suite of porch furniture featured a chair, rocker, rocker settee, settee, stool, swing and chains, and table. Note the use of the term "Pioneer." Rustic furniture is sold as part of the Western as well as the Country look.

Adirondack furniture is a type of rustic furniture. It features a number of unusual designs and painted decoration. As a result, it became a darling of the folk art set in the 1980s. The collecting ardor for Adirondack furniture quickly cooled in the late 1980s when a large number of reproductions, copycats, and fakes arrived upon the scene. Beware of small end tables featuring a bird house motif.

References: Ralph Kylloe (ed.), *The Collected Works of Indiana Hickory Furniture Makers,* Rustic Publications, 1989; Victor M. Linoff (ed.), *Porch Lawn, and Cottage Furniture: Two Complete Catalogs, ca. 1904 and 1926, Rustic Hickory Furniture Co.,* Dover Publications, 1991.

Reproduction Craftpersons: Rick and Denise Pratt, Around The Bend, 3436 Co Rd 959, Loudonville, OH 44842.

Reproduction Manufacturers: Adirondack Store and Gallery, 109 Saranac Ave, Lake Placid, NY 12946; Genesee River Trading Co, PO Box 126, New Wilmington, PA 16142; Ptarmigan Willow, PO Box 551, Fall City, WA 98024; Wood-Lot Farms, Star Rte 1, Shady, NY 12479; Vermont Crafted Classics, RD 3, Box 690, Upper Barnett Rd, Montpelier, VT 05602.

Bed, bunk, set, arched rails and three
   spindles over fiber woven headboard
   and footboard, fiber woven side rails,
   woven diamond designs, casters, detachable ladder, twin mattress size,
   39" w, 68" h 500.00
Bench
   Corner, cedar, straight upper rails,
      three posts, smooth planed thirty-
      five board seat, diamond shaped
      braces between upper and lower
      stretchers, c1915 . . . .   225.00
   Garden, bark covered cedar, straight
      rails, geometric and random twig
      designed back, twig braces, wide
      armrests with spindle supports,
      fourteen board seat, c1920 . . . . .   275.00
   Tennis, bark covered cedar, no
      back, X-form braces between front
      and back arm posts, nine board
      seat 225.00
   Tete-a-tete, bark covered cedar, two
      seats opening to opposite sides,
      straight rails, four spindles on
      backs and arms, six board seats,
      double stretchers front and back,
      1910s 300.00
Bookshelf, Jasper Hickory Furniture Co,
   Jasper, IN, spindled gallery and sides,
   five shelves with back rails, 1930s,
   36" w, 12" d, 54" h 185.00
Breakfront, pine, stripped bark, four
   doors, oak and walnut geometric

wood facings, one initial "J," "O,"
   "H," and "N" over each door, 87" w,
   94½" h, 1875–1900 . . . .   250.00
Chair
   Indiana Hickory Furniture Co, dining, hickory, woven seat, Paine
      Furniture Boston metal retailers
      tag, set of four 800.00
   Indiana Willow Products Co,
      Martinsville, IN, high square fiber
      woven back with rect headrest
      panel, open barrel shaped arm
      rails, splayed arm posts, fiber
      woven seat, box stretchers, 1948   250.00
   New York, log, stripped bark,
      painted, straight crest, sloping
      arms, dark green, 19th C, 30¼" h   175.00
   Old Hickory Furniture Co, Martinsville, IN
      Andrew Jackson style, bark covered, woven splint back and
         seat, continuous arms, 20" w,
         18" deep, 21" h, 1930s 225.00
      Morris chair, straight shawl rail,
         adjustable reclining woven
         splint back, seven spindle arm
         supports each side, woven
         splint seat, box stretchers, 1912,
         20" w seat, 21" d, 48" h 275.00
   Rustic Hickory Furniture Co, IN, central woven splint panel in square
      back, woven splint seat, box
      stretchers, 1904, 17" w seat, 15" d,
      40" h 95.00
Chest of Drawers, Indiana Willow
   Products Co, IN, rect overhanging
   top, five drawers, paneled ends,
   square legs on casters, 1948, 39" w,
   18" d, 49" h 275.00
Clothes Tree, State of Indiana Farm Industries, Putnamville, IN, hickory,
   eight pegs, four arched legs joined to
   column by stretchers, 1930s, 66" h   150.00
Cupboard, Old Hickory Furniture Co,
   Martinsville, IN, corner, oak and
   hickory, spindled gallery, two glazed
   doors, interior shelf, two paneled
   cupboard doors, ftd, dark oak finish,
   wooden pulls, 1930s, 66" h, 20" w   775.00
Desk, Old Hickory Furniture Co,
   Martinsville, IN, hickory and oak,
   arched spindled rail, oak top and two
   medial shelves each side, spindles on
   curved shelf supports, drawer, dark
   oak finish, 1930s, 36" l, 24" w,
   30¼" h 475.00
Divan, Old Hickory Furniture Co,
   Martinsville, IN, spindled back,
   arms, and base, wrapped woven
   splint rail, arms, and seat, checkered
   diamond design on cushions, 1930s,
   64" l, 22" deep, 18" h back 500.00

Fainting Couch, Old Hickory Furniture Co, Martinsville, IN, raised curved backrest, continuous woven splint top reinforced with coil springs under weaving, 1930s, 29" w, 82" l   **450.00**

Fern Stand, NY, twig, stripped bark, painted, black and silver, 14" square top   **65.00**

Flower Box, bark covered cedar, two rows of eight upright logs, joined together, cutout rect planting area, 1910s, 8" d well, 33" l, 12" w   **45.00**

Footstool
Upholstered top, NY, worn blue and white cloth upholstery, 13" w, 10½" d, 9" h   **100.00**
Woven splint top, splayed base, 10" sq, 12" h   **65.00**

High Chair, State of Indiana Farm Industries, Putnamville, IN, hickory, four spindle back, rect food tray on hinged arms, woven splint seat, splayed base, shaped footrest, pair of box stretchers, 1930s, 13" w seat, 14" d, 40" h   **275.00**

Lawn Seat, bark covered cedar, straight rails, geometric and random twig designed back, twig braces, wide spindled arm rests, fourteen board seat, c1910   **275.00**

Magazine Stand, Old Hickory Furniture Co, Martinsville, IN, square oak top and three shelves, four hickory legs, woven splint panels sides and back, dark oak finish, 1930s   **100.00**

Planter, ftd, painted
Bark covered cedar, upright pickets surrounding square well, 24" l   **35.00**
Decorated, NY
Black and silver paint dec, 36" l   **50.00**
Orange and lime green ornate paint dec, 51" l   **450.00**

Planter Stand, bark covered cedar, twelve upright pickets form circular planter, tripod column, random logs form base, c1915   **50.00**

Porch Swing, Rustic Hickory Furniture Co, La Porte, IN, three rect woven splint panels in back, flared arm posts, rect woven splint seat, spindled skirt, four suspension chains, 60" w   **275.00**

Rocker
Child's, NY, black, red, and silver paint decorated, 30" h   **120.00**
Andrew Jackson style, Old Hickory Furniture Co, Martinsville, IN, bark covered, continuous arms, woven splint back and seat, c1930, 20" w seat, 18" d, 21" h   **275.00**
Barrel Back, Old Hickory Chair Co, Martinsville, IN, rect woven splint headrest panel above woven splint back and sides, woven splint seat, box stretchers, 17" w seat, 15" d, 47" h   **250.00**
Porch, bark covered cedar, straight upper and lower rails, five straight spindles, six board seat, double stretchers, 1910s, 40" h   **200.00**

Settee
Indiana Willow Products Co, Martinsville, IN, double chair back, open barrel shaped arms, fiber woven back, sides, and set with diamond designs, box stretchers, 1948, 42" w seat, 18" d   **300.00**
Old Hickory Furniture Co, Martinsville, IN, bark covered, arched rail, woven splint back and seat, 1930s, 43" w seat, 19" d, 25" h   **350.00**

Plant Stand, Old Hickory Furniture Co, Martinsville, IN, round well, crossed tripod base, X-form stretchers, 1930s, 11" d, 31" h, $65.00.

Settee, Old Hickory Furniture Co, Martinsville, IN, double chair back with woven splint panels and seat, 1930s, 42" w, 19" d, $275.00.

Rustic Hickory Furniture Co, La Porte, IN, rocking, double barrel back, woven splint back curves around to sides, flared arm posts, rect woven seat, legs joined by box stretchers, 1913, 40" w seat, 16" d   **375.00**

Stand

Pedestal, bark covered cedar, hexagonal top, tripod table top support and base, stretchers, 1910–20   **125.00**

Plant, Jasper Hickory Furniture Co, Jasper, IN, oak and hickory, sq oak top, four legs, box stretchers top and bottom joined by vertical spindles, 1930s, 16" sq, 21" h . . .   **75.00**

Whatnot, NY, corner, oak and thornwood, stripped bark, six tiers, late 19th C, 55½" h **325.00**

Steamer Chair, Old Hickory Furniture Co, Martinsville, IN, woven splint back and seat, 12 × 24" writing table arm, spindled base, 1930s, 22" w, 48" deep, 30" h **425.00**

Stool, Old Hickory Furniture Co, Martinsville, IN, woven splint saddle seat, 1930s, 18" w, 15" d, 15" h . . .   **75.00**

Table

Drop Leaf, Rustic Hickory Furniture Co, La Porte, IN, rect golden oak top, rounded corners on 11" w leaves, splayed base, legs joined by X-form stretchers, 1926, 33" w, 22" d, 31" h **175.00**

Gateleg, NY, oak and hickory, stripped bark, rect top, rounded corners, rounded edges on two triangular leaves, thick legs, 22 spindles supported by stretchers and rails, two swing-out legs, cast iron hinges, c1915, 43½" w, 40" d, 33½" h **350.00**

Lamp, Old Hickory Furniture Co, Martinsville, IN, bark covered hickory and oak, octagonal oak top, splayed hickory legs, double stretchers, dark oak finish, c1932, 24" d, 30" h **225.00**

Trestle, Old Hickory Furniture Co, Martinsville, IN, oak top, pinned trestle, hickory base, dark oak finish, 1930–35, 42" 2, 24" d, 30" h   **475.00**

ENGLISH COUNTRY

History: The role of the English gentry is glorified in fact and fiction. The concept of the "gentleman farmer" enjoys great popularity in America. Although American views about life in the English countryside are mythical and idealistic, their influence on American Country collecting is very strong.

Among early "antiques" collectors, there was a strong prejudice for things English. The concepts of England as the source for American design and that somehow English goods were simply superior resulted in English pieces occupying positions of prominence in many American collections.

English country is found in both formal and vernacular styles. Formal was reserved for the manor house; vernacular suited the common folk and local tavern crowd. In the 1930s and 1940s English vernacular furniture (from Welsh dressers to Windsor chairs) was eagerly sought by American collectors. In the 1960s and 1970s emphasis was placed on things American; English country vernacular lost favor.

The return to the formal look in the 1980s and the desire to replace the American Country look that evolved during the Bicentennial era resulted in the rediscovery of English Country by collectors and decorators. In essence, the market has come full cycle. Pieces that were popular in the 1930s and 1940s are popular again in the 1990s.

The lack of adequate reference and decorating texts makes collecting English Country a hodgepodge operation. It is highly recommended that anyone wishing to focus on English Country travel to Great Britain and visit regional and local museums and historic sites.

References: Bernard D. Cotton, *The English Regional Chair*, Antique Collector's Club, 1990; Howard Pain, *The Heritage of Country Furniture: A Study in the Survival of Formal and Vernacular Styles from the United States, Britain, and Europe Found in Upper Canada, 1780–1900*, Van Nostrand Reinhold, 1978.

Reproduction Alert: A fair amount of English Country enters the American market via preassembled containers. Buyers should be aware that great liberties are taken in respect to rebuilding and reconstructing this furniture. Have any "period" piece authenticated by an expert.

Bench

Settle, oak, vertical board back, shaped wings, scrolled arms, plank seat, paneled base with two drawers, old worn finish with some graining, bottom boards missing, old repairs, 72" w, 20" d, 56½" h **1,100.00**

Chair

Armchair, hardwood, curved crest rail, rabbit ear posts, turned slat with rect tablet, shaped arms, turned arm posts, shaped yew wood seat, turned legs, H-form stretcher, old worn finish, 35¾" h   **55.00**

Ladderback, armchair, curved square crest rail, four graduated arched slats, shaped arms, turned arm posts and front stretcher, rush seat, hoof front feet, old worn finish, seat needs replacement, feet ended out, 42" h 250.00

Windsor, molded bowed crest rail, nine back spindles, shaped arm rail, shaped saddle seat, splayed base with turned legs, X-form stretcher, old worn dark finish, breaks and age cracks in crest and arm rails, 17½" h seat, 42" h 875.00

Chest of Drawers, quarter sawed oak, dovetailed drawers, three short over three long drawers, bracket feet, orig bail handle brasses, old worn finish, brass name plates on two drawers, late 19th/early 20th C, 41" w, 22" d, 43" h 500.00

Cupboard

Chimney, hanging, curly oak, cove molded top, single full length paneled door, molded base, old worn finish, 16¾" w, 18" d, 41" h 250.00

Corner, pine, one piece, blocked front, molded dentilated cornice, open top with fan carved upper corners, tombstone shaped opening with fretwork border, and butterfly shelves, reeded stiles, pair of paneled cupboard doors, scalloped apron, molded base, refinished and restored, 50" w, 87" h **1,650.00**

Display, pine, molded cornice, carved brackets, sliding paneled doors in top and base, top doors each with single glass pane, refinished, 72" w, 20" d, 70" h 250.00

Pewter, pine, two piece

Molded cornice, vertical board back, three open shelves with beaded edges, base with four short drawers in beaded frames over a bank of three false drawers flanked by two paneled doors, turned wood pulls, refinished, putty filled cracks in top, 65" w, 20½" d, 80 ¾" h **1,050.00**

Apothecary Chest, spruce, twenty-four drawers, early 19th C, 49" w, 9¼" d, 23½" h, $1,100.00. Photograph courtesy of Skinner, Inc.

Corner Cupboard, Georgian, pine, projecting molded cornice, two pairs of paneled cupboard doors, c1800, 53" w, 23" d, 92" h, estimated price $2,000.00–3,000.00. Photograph courtesy of Leslie Hindman Auctioneers.

Molded cornice with scalloped frieze, four open shelves with plate bars, pie shelf, base with three dovetailed short drawers flanked by two raised panel cupboard doors, square legs, old red repaint, back feet and cornice replaced, some wear and edge damage, 52" w, 20" d, 75½" h **1,650.00**

Open top with scalloped shelves and opening, base with two drawers and two paneled cupboard doors, refinished, repairs and insect damage, 49½" w, 16¾" d, 80" h 225.00

Wall, pine, one piece, crown molded cornice, four paneled doors, molded base, refinished, replaced porcelain knobs, water marks, 58" w, 17¾" d, 90" h 500.00

Dresser, sea captain's, mahogany, pine secondary wood, center adjustable mirror on turned posts flanked by pair of dovetailed short drawers, three graduated dovetailed long drawers, short turned feet, inset brass hardware, faded finish, 42" w, 24½" d, 40" h plus mirror. 300.00

Fire Screen, Sheraton, mahogany, rosewood graining, delicate turnings, trestle base with carved feet, petit point floral panel, folding spindled shelf, 40" h 225.00

Huntboard, Late Georgian, oak, rect top, center drawer above cupboard door flanked by three graduated drawers on one side, three faux drawers facing a cupboard on other side, bracket feet, bail handles, 19th C, 82″ w, 23½″ d, 35″ h, $4,620.00. Photograph courtesy of Leslie Hindman Auctioneers.

Footstool, Queen Anne style, mahogany, upholstered rect slip seat, cabriole legs, turned H-form stretcher, duck feet, old finish, one knee bracket replaced and one missing, minor repair, 22″ w, 15″ d, 19″ h **415.00**

Mirror, Queen Anne, walnut veneer on pine, scrolled crest, ogee frame, refinished, 11½″ w, 20½″ h **550.00**

Sideboard, Arts and Crafts, oak, molded top, four paneled doors, molded base, 72″ w, 21½″ d, 45″ h **450.00**

Table

Dressing, Country Sheraton, pine and hardwood, red flame graining, scrolled three sided gallery, two drawers, scalloped apron, turned tapered legs, replaced brasses, worm holes, 36″ w, 19″ d, 37″ h **775.00**

Drop Leaf, Queen Anne, mahogany, 17″ rect leaves, swing legs support top, turned tapered legs, duck feet, refinished, minor damage to rule joints at hinges, 41″ w, 14½″ d, 27¼″ h **325.00**

Tea, Chippendale, tilt top, mahogany, round one board top, turned column with birdcage, tripod base with snake feet, refinished, minor old repairs, small age crack in top, 32″ d, 27½″ h **990.00**

Work

Oak and pine, rect tongue and groove constructed top, turned legs on casters, dark refinishing, reconstructed, 78″ w, 26¾″ d, 30″ h **275.00**

Pine, rect two board top

One drawer, mortised stretcher base, square legs, refinished, some insect damage, drawer replaced, 72″ l, 29″ d, 30¾″ h   **325.00**

Two dovetailed frieze drawers, base shelf, square legs, refinished, 57″ w, 24″ d, 30½″ h   **195.00**

Washstand

Pine, shaped three quarter gallery with shelf, single drawer frieze, turned legs, shaped medial shelf, ball feet, refinished, insect damage, gallery replaced, 30½″ w, 15″ d, 41¾″ h **195.00**

Pine and oak, wide board three quarter gallery, rect top with bowl cutout, square tapered legs, round base shelf, refinished, 19″ w, 16″ d, 30½″ h **110.00**

FRENCH COUNTRY

History: Like its English counterpart, French Country furniture is found in formal and vernacular styles. Formal French Country tends toward the high style. Its American popularity is confined to collectors and decorators living in metropolitan areas.

French vernacular pieces, especially the bleached examples from Southern France, were discovered by collectors and decorators in the mid-1980s. As the 1990s progress, their popularity appears to be waning. This is due in part to the large number of reproductions, copycats, and fakes that flooded the American market.

French Canadian furniture is attracting the strong attention of American country collectors and decorators. It recently was revealed that a large amount of furniture that sold in the market from the 1960s through the 1980s as painted rural New England country furniture was actually from the rural regions of French Canada.

Reference: Warren Johansson, *Country Furniture and Accessories from Quebec*, Schiffer Publishing, 1991; Howard Pain, *The Heritage of Country Furniture: A Study in the Survival of Formal and Vernacular Styles from the United States, Britain, and Europe Found in Upper Canada, 1789–1900*, Van Nostrand Reinhold, 1978.

Reproduction Alert.

Armoire
    Burl Elm, Louis Philippe, pair of doors, straight grained stiles and rails, carved apron, stylized paw feet, shrinkage gaps in panels, c1840, 44″ w, 24″ d, 80″ h **6,500.00**
    Pine, Louis Philippe, projecting molded cornice, pair of paneled doors, painted int. with shelves over two aligned drawers and two paneled cupboard doors, bracket feet, 52″ w, 20″ d, 98″ h **1,600.00**
    Walnut, Second Empire, deeply molded cornice, single full length paneled door, chamfered and paneled ends, shaped block feet, 1860, 36″ w, 22″ d, 90″ h **900.00**
Bench, window, fruitwood, Louis XV style, scrolled voluted arms, pale gray and dusty rose striped silk upholstery, cabriole legs, 41 ½″ w . . . **250.00**
Bookcase, oak, Louis XV style, thumb molded cornice, central grilled door, opposing foliate scroll carved frame on top and mid-section, grilled panels, plinth base, late 19th C, 60″ w, 87″ h **3,300.00**
Cabinet, curio, walnut, Louis XV style, single serpentine glazed cabinet door with painted armorial panel, mounted ormolu dec, 26″ w, 14″ d, 59½″ h **475.00**
Candlestand, mahogany, Louis XVI style, circular top with pieced brass border, paneled column, shaped tripod base, 14½″ d, 26½″ h **1,200.00**
Chair, walnut, Louis XV style, shaped crest rail, bird, figural, and floral petit-point and needlepoint upholstered back and seat, matching upholstered loose cushions, shell carved apron, cabriole legs, 35″ w **2,000.00**
Chaise Lounge, walnut, Louis XV style, floral carved crest rail, yellow and ivory striped upholstered back and seat, shell carved seat rail, cabriole legs, price for pair. **385.00**

Stepback Cupboard, Louis Philippe, chestnut, two sections: upper: molded cornice, raised panel cupboard doors; lower: pair of short drawers over pair of raised panel cupboard doors: c1840, 43″ w, 97″ h, $1,540.00. Photograph courtesy of Morton M Goldberg Galleries.

Commode, walnut, Second Empire, rect marble top, single drawer, single cupboard door faced with faux drawers, 15″ w, 12″ d, 33½″ h **200.00**
Daybed, mahogany, Restauration, slightly bowed rect upholstered back, upholstered seat, turned tapered legs, ball feet, crimson silk upholstery **525.00**
Footstool, walnut, Louis XVI style, petit-point upholstered top, 4″ h **200.00**
Mirror, pier, walnut, Louis XV style, foliate pierced carved crest, scalloped beveled rect mirror plate surrounded by molded carved foliate dec, 34″ w, 92″ h **2,750.00**
Secretary Desk, walnut, Louis Philippe, projecting cornice, single drawer, fall front writing surface, three drawers, turned feet, 40″ w, 20″ d, 65″ h **1,300.00**
Sofa, mahogany, Restauration, asymmetrical shape, rolled ends, loose cushion seat, plain straight apron, turned legs, bell shaped feet, 66″ w **750.00**
Table
    Dining, mahogany, Louis XVI style, circular top with brass banding, straight tapered legs, brass toe caps, 54″ w, 82″ l extended, 27½″ h **1,500.00**
    Game, oak, Louis XV style, square top, red leather inset surface with gilt dec, shallow gallery, scalloped

apron, cabriole legs, 32 ¼" w,
28¾" h **2,000.00**
Library, Louis XV style, rect top with
gilt tooled leather writing surface,
central ribbon inlaid frieze
drawer, two shaped drawers with
parquetry inlay in front, back with
similar false drawers, slight cabriole legs with foliate cast gilt
bronze knees and feet, scuffed
leather, minor losses and repairs,
late 19th C, 59" w, 29½" h **4,950.00**
Sewing, mahogany, Restauration,
square lift lid top, fitted int. with
14 compartments, turned column
with scrolled supports, square
carved base, four scrolled feet,
c1830, 29¼" h **1,750.00**
Writing, pine, Louis Philippe, rect
top, paneled apron, reeded ta-
pered legs, 54½" w, 27½" d, 28" h **1,750.00**

PENNSYLVANIA GERMAN

History: The first German settlers arrived in Pennsylvania in 1683. With Philadelphia as a hub, they
spread north, west (to Harrisburg, PA, then south),
and east. The initial period of immigration ended
in the 1740s at which time Pennsylvania communities dotted southeast Pennsylvania, the Shenandoah Valley from Hagerstown, Maryland, to the
Southern back country, and portions of Ontario in
Canada.

The Germans brought with them a strong craft
tradition. Next to Shaker, Pennsylvania-German is
the most widely collected form of American regional furniture. Although Pennsylvania-German
painted furniture has received the most attention
in exhibit and print, there is also a strong tradition
of unpainted formal pieces as well.

Pennsylvania-German vernacular forms survived for centuries. One of the most valuable
reference sources is Henry Lapp's handbook. This
book illustrates vernacular forms made by Lapp
well into the 20th century.

Pennsylvania-German furniture was meant to
be used—and survive. Its sturdy construction and
vertical lines make it easy to distinguish from other
regional forms. Most examples were made by
furniture craftsmen. The Pennsylvania-German
farmer as maker of his own furniture is largely a
myth.

References: Bernard Deneke, *Bauernmobel: Ein
Handbuck Fur Sammler and Liebhaber*, Deutsche
Taschenbuck Verlag, 1983; Monroe Fabian, *The
Pennsylvania-German Decorated Blanket Chest*,
Universe Books, 1978; Beatrice Garvan, *The
Pennsylvania German Collection*, Philadelphia
Museum of Art, 1982; Alan Keyser, Larry Neff, and
Frederick S. Weiser (trans. and eds.), *The Accounts*

*of Two Pennsylvania German Furniture Makers—
Abraham Overholt, Bucks County, 1790–1833,
and Peter Ranck, Lebanon County, 1794–1817*,
Sources and Documents of the Pennsylvania Ger-
mans III, Pennsylvania German Society, 1978;
Henry Lapp, *A Craftsman's Handbook*, Good
Books, 1975.

Bench
Bucket, pine and poplar, overhanging top, two mortised shelves with
gallery backs, bootjack ends, worn
blue paint, 1830–40 .... **1,900.00**
Wash, poplar, mortised one board
top, straight aprons, scalloped
bootjack ends, painted red, minor
repairs, 1830–40 .... **725.00**
Blanket Chest
Curly Walnut, lift lid, dovetailed
case, till with secret drawer, two
base drawers, dovetailed bracket
feet, brass fishtail hinges and crab
lock, 1790–1800 .... **7,000.00**
Pine
Berks County, molded lid, till, two
beaded drawers with brass bail
handles, wrought iron lock,
heart strap hinges, lid with
two stylized potted flowers in
tombstone arched panels, front
with central tombstone arched
panel with potted tree and two
stylized birds below partially
legible inscription "Michael . . .
Den 19 Daig, Mertz and 1773,"
flanked by two adjoining symmetrical panels containing a
stylized potted flower, four birds
perched on corners of arched

**Blanket Chest, pine, painted and deco-
rated, rect hinged lid with cleated ends,
lidded till, bracket feet, dec with arched
reserves with scrolling foliage and flowerheads issuing from flowerpots and pitcher,
early 19th C, later decoration, 44" w, 27"
h, $1,650.00. Photograph courtesy of But-
terfield & Butterfield.**

panels, stylized tulips on drawer fronts, hearts and flowers on ends, scroll cut dovetailed bracket feet, 55½" w, 22¼" d, 29" h....................**13,200.00**

Somerset County, miniature, molded lid, dovetailed case, polychrome painted stylized tulips, floral designs, initials, and date "1844" on front panel, red ground, molded base, turned feet, 25" w, 13" d, 17¼" h.... **5,200.00**

Pine and Poplar, edge molded lid, square corner posts with mortised and pinned single board sides and ends, lidded till with secret drawer, base molding, turned feet, hinges marked "Philada," red-brown flame graining, repair in edge of lid at hinge, some edge damage, casters added, 50¾" w, 21¼" d, 24½" h............ **250.00**

Poplar

Phillip Dutrer, hinged lid, two overlapping drawers, yellow hearts inscribed "Phillip Dutrer 1775," green ground, dovetailed bracket feet, minor repairs................... **5,000.00**

Soap Hollow, dovetailed case, lidded till, two dovetailed drawers, reeded trim, white porcelain pulls, black trim, yellow striping, gold stenciled initials and date "J. B. 1878" on red ground, bracket feet, 48" w, 21" d, 26½" h................ **3,400.00**

Chair, New Oxford, straight crest rail, vasiform splat, turned posts, shaped plank seat, splayed base, turned front legs and stretcher, brown ground, dark red and yellow striping, polychrome rose dec on crest rail, one chair sgd "Peter Geisen, New Oxford, Pa" on seat underside, one with minor repairs and reglued, one replaced leg, 33" h, price for set of six........................ **480.00**

Chest, dower, pine, Centre County, attributed to Titus Geesey, dovetailed case with till, wrought iron bear trap lock and strap hinges, diagonal braces on front feet, black, brown, and white eagle, shield, banner, pinwheels, tulips, and compass stars in framed central front panel, "Catarina Klinglibe 1816" on banner, traces of compass dec on lid and ends, dovetailed bracket feet, escutcheon replaced, minor edge damage, minor touch up to eagle, 51½" w, 22½" d, 27" h **3,500.00**

Cupboard

Corner

Cherry, hanging, molded cornice, carved potted tulip on molded paneled door, carved ferns on case, spiral inset corner columns, reeding, scalloped apron, cutout feet, refinished **10,000.00**

Pine, thumb molded cornice above stylized flowerhead carved dentil frieze, two arched paneled doors enclosing red painted shelved int., fluted columnar stiles, base with pair of cupboard doors with single shelf int., red and black grain painting, 53" w, 96" h **6,600.00**

Pine and Poplar, two sections, top with pair of glazed doors each with three panes and shelved int., base with single drawer, two paneled doors, and cutout feet, orange and red geometric stripe design **6,500.00**

Dutch, two sections

Butternut and Cherry, Soap Hollow, top with molded cornice, pair of glazed doors each with six panes, and shelved int., base with two small waist drawers, turned quarter columns, raised panel cupboard doors, and applied bracket feet, refinished, c1850 .... **3,750.00**

Cherry, top with molded cornice, pair of glazed doors each with six panes, and scalloped opening around pie shelf, base with three small overlapping waist drawers, chamfered corners, paneled cupboard doors, paneled ends, and turned feet, refinished, c1830 .... **7,750.00**

Pine and Poplar, top with molded cornice, single glazed door with nine panes, and shelved int., base with two small waist drawers, paneled cupboard doors, and turned feet, old red finish, int. painted white, c1835, 42" w **4,250.00**

Jelly, pine and poplar, molded cornice, pair of raised panel doors, chamfered corners on stiles, turned feet, brown grain painted finish, c1830............... **2,400.00**

Stepback

Pine, molded cornice, pair of glazed doors each with six panes, spoon holder shelf, three small waist drawers over two paneled cupboard doors, refinished, replaced pulls, 44¼" w, 78½" h **1,500.00**

Poplar, blind, two sections, top with molded cornice, pair of glazed doors each with sixteen panes, and shelved int., base with five overlapping waist drawers, four paneled cupboard doors, scalloped apron, and cut-out feet, grain painted, 48" w, 84" h **4,200.00**

Wall, straight front, pine and poplar, blind, molded flaring cornice, pair of paneled doors, shelved int., three small molded waist drawers, pair of paneled cupboard doors, paneled ends, old refinishing, traces of old red paint, molding loss, early 19th C, 83" h **3,000.00**

Cradle, walnut, heart cutout on headboard and footboard, scrolled headboard, arched footboard, dovetailed case, shaped rockers, c1830 . . . . . . **650.00**

Dry Sink

Grain Painted, high back with scalloped crest, overhanging top, and three drawers, base with raised panel cupboard doors and cutout feet, yellow grain painting, c1860 . . . . **1,800.00**

Pine and Poplar, dovetailed gallery, two drawers, two paneled doors,

paneled ends, turned feet, yellow and brown stippled panels, c1820 **4,200.00**

Poplar, open well, single dovetailed drawer, two paneled doors, shaped bracket feet, wood pulls, red vinegar graining on yellow ground, sunbursts, fans, and X designs, 42" w, 19¼" d, 31¾" h . . .**11,500.00**

Pie Safe, pine and poplar

Hanging, single door, four tin panels with punched diamond and floral design, refinished, c1840 . . . . . . **1,500.00**

Single door with three tin panels flanked by three tin panels on each side, two tin panels on ends, punched star design, square posts and legs, brown finish, c1835 . . . **5,500.00**

Schrank

Pine and Poplar, large blocked cornice, two raised panel doors, fluted pilasters, two overlapping base drawers, repainted, missing ball feet, c1870 . . . . **2,000.00**

Walnut, molded cornice above dentil molded and fluted frieze, pair of molded raised panel doors, fluted quarter columns, five overlapping base drawers, chamfered corners, ogee bracket feet, H-form hinges, refinished, c1795 . . . .**18,000.00**

GLASS

Glass serves two key functions in Country—utilitarian and decorative. Glass used in rural America was manufactured to last. Most pieces were thickly made to last a long time when handled carefully. Glass had a permanence attached to it that was easily understood by the agrarian housewife.

Glass was recyclable. It could serve the same purpose over and over again. Every agrarian home had a place in the pantry or basement where jars and other glassware were stored awaiting reuse. Further, manufacturers of food products quickly realized the value placed upon glass by the agrarian housewife. Sales increased when prepackaged foods were placed in reusable glass.

The arrival of inexpensive glassware revolutionized Country life. Storage possibilities increased considerably. Home canning became a seasonal activity. Inexpensive pattern glass added a touch of elegance to everyday life. The level of sanitation increased.

The Country housewife classified her glassware in three categories: (1) storage vessels, (2) everyday glassware, and (3) special occasion glass. Glass storage vessels were limited until the arrival of the refrigerator. The most common glass storage vessel was the fruit jar. The fruit jar along with the cold cellar were the principal means of food storage in rural America until the arrival of electricity and the refrigerator. Although some farmsteads had icehouses, most did not. Individuals living in towns fared better, albeit ceramic and tin storage dominated in an ice box.

Everyday glassware consisted primarily of drinking glasses and table accessories such as spoon holders and salt and pepper shakers. The kitchen and Depression era glasswares of the 1920 to 1950 period found favor among the rural housewife. It was colorful and affordable.

Although more glass forms appeared throughout the house, the most heavily used items, e.g., dinner plates, still tended to be ceramic.

Cut glass was the most highly prized glassware in rural America. It graced the dining room buffet and was used only for special occasions. It was passed down from generation to generation more than any other glass type. Those who were unable to afford cut glass turned to pattern glass that imitated cut glass patterns.

Glass played a major role in lighting. See the "Lighting" section for more detailed information.

Practicality aside, the agrarian housewife loved the decorative nature of glass. Leaded cut glass sparkled with brilliance on a dining room buffet. Shelves were installed in a kitchen window so light could reflect through a host of colored glassware. A surprising amount of early American glass and flasks survived because they fulfilled this latter role.

One final glass form deserves mention—souvenir glass. Since farming is primarily a seven-day-a-week occupation, individuals who traveled loved to bring home souvenirs from the places that they visited. Glass souvenirs were especially popular. Whether a ruby stained mug acid-etched with the name of the place and date or a milk glass canoe with a decal of the site, these glass souvenirs enjoyed a place of honor in the Country home.

References: Corning Museum of Glass and The American Committee of the International Association for the History of Glass, *Glass Collections in Museums in the United States and Canada*, The Corning Museum of Glass, 1982; Harold Newman, *An Illustrated Dictionary of Glass*, Thames and Hudson, 1977; Ellen Tischbein Schroy, *Warman's Glass*, Wallace-Homestead, 1992; Jane Spillman, *Glass*, The Knopf Collectors' Guides to American Antiques, *Volume 1: Tableware, Bowls & Vases* (1982) and *Volume 2: Bottles, Lamps & Other Objects* (1983), Alfred A. Knopf.

Periodicals: *Antique Bottle & Glass Collector*, PO Box 187, East Greenville, PA 18041; *Glass Collector's Digest*, PO Box 553, Marietta, OH 45750; *The Daze*, PO Box 57, Otisville, MI 48463.

Museums: Corning Museum of Glass, Corning, NY; Toledo Museum of Art, Toledo, OH; Chrysler Museum, Norfolk, VA; Bennington Museum, Bennington, VT.

20TH CENTURY UTILITARIAN HOUSEHOLD GLASSWARE, aka DEPRESSION GLASS

History: The Country housewife welcomed utilitarian glassware for the Country table; by the post-World War I period it was readily available, durable, and inexpensive. Many patterns were produced in full table settings and often in a variety of colors.

When interest developed in collecting glass stemware and tableware from the post-World War I era in the early 1950s, a select group of patterns were classified as "Depression Glass." The label stuck. Unfortunately, such a designation contains more problems than it resolves.

First, many of the patterns were introduced long before the 1929 Depression. Second, many of the patterns continued in production long after the Great Depression ended. Third, the pattern selection was narrow, ignoring hundreds of patterns that were also produced during that period. Finally, antiques dealers used the "Depression Glass" label against these popular 20th century glass patterns. "Depression Glass" in their minds became that cheap junk that was sold in the five and dime or given away as premiums.

The Depression Era label continues to create more negatives than positives in the collecting of twentieth century glassware. It is time to abandon the concept. The dates simply are no longer meaningful as we move further and further away from the 1929 to 1940 period and glassware collecting interests expand into the 1950s and 60s.

A much better designation for this glassware is *Twentieth Century Utilitarian Household Glassware*, a term used to cover mass produced, mass marketed glass manufactured from the 1920s through the present. The date is based on the assumption that for collecting purposes, the 20th century actually started after World War I. Admittedly, the designation is a mouthful; but, it reflects the reality of the current collecting situation.

Such an approach puts the emphasis where it belongs—identity of major and minor patterns and allows prices to dictate which are the most desired. Collecting popularity is the key.

References: Gene Florence, *Collectible Glassware from the 40's, 50's, 60's: An Illustrated Value Guide, Seventh Edition*, Collector Books, 1994; Gene Florence, *The Collector's Encyclopedia of Depression Glass, Eleventh Edition*, Collector Books, 1994; Gene Florence, *Elegant Glassware of the Depression Era, Fifth Edition*, Collector Books, 1993; Gene Florence, *Very Rare Glassware of the Depression Era*, First Series (1988, 1991 value update), Second Series (1991), and Third Series (1993), Collector Books; Carl F. Luckey and Mary Burris, *An Identification & Value Guide to Depression Era Glassware, Third Edition*, Books Americana, 1993; Hazel Marie Weatherman, *1984 Supplement & Price Trends for Colored Glassware Of The Depression Era, Book 1*, published by author, 1984.

Collectors' Club: National Depression Glass Association, Inc., PO Box 69843, Odessa, TX 79769.

Periodical: *The Daze*, Box 57, Otisville, MI 48463; *The Society Page*, PO Box 856, LaGrange, IL 60525.

Reproduction Alert: Reproductions and fantasy items abound. Period molds have survived and, after changing ownership several times, are owned by modern reproduction glass manufacturers. Fortunately, many of these examples are made in colors not used during the initial period of pattern production and can be easily spotted. In some instances color is identical, but the modern mold slightly different. Thorough knowledge of patterns, colors, and markings is very important.

Send a self addressed stamped business envelope to *The Daze* and request a copy of their glass reproduction list. It is one of the best bargains in the antiques business.

Ashtray

Caprice, pink, round	**12.50**
Florentine No. 2, yellow	**20.00**
Forest Green, 5¾" d	**6.50**
Manhattan, crystal, 4" d	**10.00**
Moderntone, cobalt blue, concentric rings	**30.00**
Moroccan, amethyst, triangular, 6⅞" w	**15.00**
Pineapple and Floral, crystal	**12.50**
Sandwich, crystal, spade shape	**3.00**

Bowl

Adam, cov, pink, 9" d	**5.00**
Aunt Polly, blue, oval, 7¼" l	**35.00**
Avocado, green, oval, two handles, 8" l	**20.00**
Block Optic, green, 4¼" d	**7.00**
Cherryberry, green, 7½" d	**19.00**
Colonial, green	**14.50**

Butter Dish,¼ lb, cobalt blue, Criss Cross, Hazel Atlas, 6¾" l, $75.00.

Columbia, crystal, 8½" d	**16.00**
Forest Green, mixing	**18.00**
Iris and Herringbone, irid, 4½" d. . .	**7.50**
Madrid, amber, 5" d	**7.00**
Miss America, pink, 6¼" d	**22.50**
Moroccan, amethyst, 6" d	**11.00**
Normandie, irid, 5" d	**5.00**
Patrician, amber, 8½" d	**44.00**
Rosepoint, crystal, two handles, 9½" d	**62.00**
Sierra, pink, 5½" d	**16.50**
Swirl, ultramarine, 10½" d	**25.00**
Windsor, crystal, 12½" d	**22.50**

Butter Dish, cov

Chinex Classic, blue trim, castle decal	**120.00**
Colonial Knife and Fork, crystal. . . .	**35.00**
Florentine No. 2, yellow	**145.00**
Iris and Herringbone, irid	**40.00**
Lace Edge, pink.	**57.50**
Mayfair, blue.	**270.00**
Patrician, amber	**85.00**
Rosepoint, crystal	**150.00**
Wildflower, crystal, 5½" d	**135.00**

Cake Plate

Adam, pink	**25.00**
Harp, crystal, gold trim	**24.00**
Jubilee, yellow	**60.00**
Miss America, crystal	**28.00**
Princess, green	**22.50**
Radiance, crystal	**28.00**
Sunflower, green	**14.00**

Candlesticks, pr

Block Optic, pink	**75.00**
English Hobnail, pink	**65.00**
June, blue	**75.00**

Bowl, Royal Ruby, Coronation, Anchor Hocking, 1938–40, 6½" w handle to handle, $10.00.

Laurel, French ivory	24.00
Madrid, amber	25.00
Candy Dish, cov	
Aunt Polly, green	60.00
Block Optic, green	42.00
Caprice, pink, 3 ftd............	295.00
English Hobnail, crystal, ruby stain, cone	50.00
Moroccan, amethyst	30.00
Queen Mary, crystal	18.00
Cereal Bowl	
American Sweetheart, Monax.....	14.50
Block Optic, green	12.50
Chinex Classic, blue trim, castle decal.	12.50
Georgian Lovebirds, green	22.00
Hobnail, crystal	4.00
Lace Edge, crystal	5.00
Newport, cobalt blue	30.00
Normandie, irid, 6½" d	11.00
Pineapple and Floral, crystal......	23.00
Champagne	
Della Robbia, crystal, pale stain ...	25.00
Diamond Quilted, green.........	10.00
Heather, crystal	19.50
June, blue...................	47.50
Rock Crystal, crystal	15.00
Wildflower, crystal	27.50
Coaster	
Cherry Blossom, green	12.00
Florentine No. 2, green.........	13.00
Miss America, crystal	17.50
Waterford, crystal	3.50
Compote	
Cameo, green.................	28.00
Cherryberry, pink	25.00
Della Robbia, crystal, dark stain, 6½" d	32.50
Rock Crystal, crystal	32.50
Cookie Jar, cov	
Cameo, green.................	48.00
Sandwich, crystal	45.00
Creamer	
Cherry Blossom, delphite	16.00
Hobnail, crystal	3.50

Creamer, pink, Beaded Block, Imperial, 4⅞" h, $15.00.

Horseshoe, yellow	15.00
Iris and Herringbone, irid, ftd	10.00
Katy Blue, blue with opalescent edge	38.00
Madrid, amber	10.00
Mt Pleasant, black.............	17.00
Queen Mary, crystal	5.00
Swirl, ultramarine	12.00
Windsor, crystal	5.00
Cream Soup	
Apple Blossom, yellow	45.00
Cameo, green	100.00
Florentine No. 2, green.........	13.00
Patrician, amber	15.00
Royal Lace, crystal	11.00
Cup and Saucer	
American Sweetheart, monax	18.00
Block Optic, green	12.50
Cameo, green	18.50
Chinex Classic, blue trim, castle decal.	14.00
Cloverleaf, yellow.............	13.50
Crow's Foot, red	17.50
Diamond Quilted, green.........	13.00
Dogwood, pink................	23.00
Fairfax, pink	12.50
Florentine No. 2, yellow	14.00
Horseshoe, green	13.00
Iris and Herringbone, irid	19.00
Jane Ray, jadite...............	3.00
Lafayette, wisteria	24.00
Miss America, pink	26.00
Patrician, amber	17.00
Sandwich, crystal	7.50
Swirl, ultramarine	16.00
Waterford, crystal	9.50
Fruit Bowl	
American, crystal, 12" d	55.00
Cherry Blossom, pink, 10½" d	75.00
Floragold Louisa, irid	8.00
Goblet	
Cameo, green	48.00
Colonial, green	22.00
Hobnail, crystal	6.50
Jamestown, amber	10.00
Jubilee, yellow, 6½" h	45.00
Miss America, pink	45.00

Candy Dish, cov, pink, Cube, Jeannette, 1929–33, 6⅜ " h, $25.00.

Ice Bucket
    Block Optic, green **55.00**
    Cleo, green **60.00**
    Diamond Quilted, pink. **45.00**
Iced Tea Tumbler
    Block Optic, green, 4¾" h **22.50**
    Cameo, green **60.00**
    English Hobnail, crystal **17.00**
    Forest Green **7.00**
    Hobnail, crystal **7.50**
Juice Tumbler
    Boople, green **4.00**
    Cameo, pink. **80.00**
    Fairfax, pink **12.50**
    Forest Green **4.00**
    June, crystal **22.50**
    Moondrops, cobalt blue, ftd **12.00**
Lemon Plate, handle
    Della Robbia, crystal, pale stain . . .   **10.00**
    Fairfax, pink **18.00**
    Versailles, blue **32.50**
Mayonnaise, cov, underplate
    American, crystal **40.00**
    Apple Blossom, yellow **95.00**
    English Hobnail, pink **35.00**
    Katy Blue, blue with opalescent edge   **130.00**
    Wildflower, crystal **95.00**
Pickle Dish
    Apple Blossom, yellow, 9" l **45.00**
    Cherryberry, green **9.00**
    Gloria, yellow, 9" l **40.00**
Pitcher
    Cherry Blossom, pink **65.00**
    Della Robbia, crystal, dark stain . . .   **195.00**
    English Hobnail, pink, straight sides   **150.00**
    Floral Poinsettia, pink, cone, ftd, 8" h   **30.00**
    Hobnail, crystal, 67 oz **25.00**
    June, crystal **395.00**
    Roulette, green **35.00**
    Strawberry, green **210.00**
    Windsor, pink, 6¾" h **28.00**
Plate
    American Sweetheart, monax, 8" d.   **8.00**
    Apple Blossom, yellow, 10½" d . . .   **95.00**
    Block Optic, green, lunch **4.00**
    Cherry Blossom, pink, 9" d **25.00**
    Colonial, green, grill **27.50**
    Crow's Foot, red **19.50**
    Diamond Quilted, green. **4.00**
    Florentine No. 2, yellow, 6" d. **5.50**
    Hobnail, crystal, 8½" d. **3.50**
    Horseshoe, green, 8⅜ " d **9.00**
    Iris and Herringbone, irid, 9" d **35.00**
    Janice, light blue, 8⅞" d **20.00**
    Katy Blue, blue with opalescent
      edge, 8" d **32.00**
    Lafayette, wisteria, 8" d. **20.00**
    Laurel, French ivory, grill **9.00**
    Miss America, pink, 5¾" d **9.50**
    Newport, cobalt blue, 8½" d **12.00**
    Patrician, amber, 9" d **11.00**
    Princess, green, 9" d **22.50**

    Royal Lace, crystal, 8½" d **9.00**
    Waterford, crystal, 7⅛ " d **5.00**
Platter
    Cameo, green, 12" l **27.50**
    Florentine No. 2, yellow **16.00**
    Horseshoe, green **22.00**
    Jane Ray, jadite **12.00**
    Katy Blue, blue with opalescent
      edge, 13" l. **145.00**
    Lace Edge, pink. **25.00**
    Madrid, amber **18.00**
    Miss America, pink **30.00**
Punch Bowl, Forest Green **45.00**
Relish
    Fairfax, pink, three part **18.00**
    Florentine No. 2, green, three part. .   **22.00**
    June, blue, divided, 8½" l **54.00**
    Miss America, pink, four part **24.00**
    Portia, crystal, two part, 6" l **30.00**
Salt and Pepper Shakers, pr
    Apple Blossom, yellow **150.00**
    Della Robbia, crystal, dark stain . . .   **45.00**
    June, blue **250.00**
    Normandie, amber **45.00**
    Waterford, crystal, small **8.50**
    Windsor, pink **38.00**
Sandwich Server, center handle
    June, blue **85.00**
    Mayfair, blue. **75.00**
    Rock Crystal, crystal **25.00**
Sherbet
    American Sweetheart, pink **15.00**
    Block Optic, green **12.50**
    Cloverleaf, green. **6.50**
    Colonial Knife and Fork, crystal. . . .   **6.00**
    Diamond Quilted, pink. **7.00**
    Hobnail, crystal. **3.00**
    Iris and Herringbone, irid **11.00**
    Madrid, amber **8.00**
    Patrician, amber **9.50**
    Pineapple and Floral, crystal **18.50**
    Popeye and Olive, red, 8¼" h. **18.00**
    Princess, green **18.00**
    Waterford, crystal **3.50**
Soup Bowl
    Bubble, blue **14.50**
    Cherry Blossom, pink **50.00**
    Chinex Classic, blue trim, castle de-
      cal. **27.50**
    Iris and Herringbone, irid, 7½" d. . .   **50.00**
    Katy Blue, blue with opalescent
      edge, 7" d **75.00**
Sugar, cov
    English Hobnail, crystal. **12.00**
    Georgian Lovebirds, green, ftd **12.00**
    Horseshoe, green **10.00**
    Iris and Herringbone, irid **18.00**
    Katy Blue, blue with opalescent
      edge **38.00**
    Miss America, pink **18.50**
    Moonstone **6.00**
    Newport, white. **5.00**

Swirl, ultramarine	**12.50**
Tearoom, pink	**13.00**
Waterford, crystal	**4.00**
Tumbler	
Block Optic, green, 4" h	**16.50**
Dogwood, pink	**60.00**
Florentine No. 2, green	**12.50**
Iris and Herringbone, irid, 6" h	**14.00**
Katy Blue, blue with opalescent edge	**58.00**
Miss America, crystal	**25.00**
Pineapple and Floral, crystal	**40.00**
Sharon Cabbage Rose, amber	**23.00**
Waterford, crystal	**10.00**
Windsor, crystal	**7.00**
Vase	
Adam, green, 7½" h	**50.00**
Harp, crystal, gold trim	**18.50**
Moonstone, bud	**13.00**
Pineapple and Floral, crystal	**40.00**
Silvercrest, fan, 12" h	**95.00**
Tearoom, green, ruffled, 6½" d	**145.00**
Vegetable Bowl	
Chinex Classic, blue trim, castle decal	**27.50**
Katy Blue, blue with opalescent edge	**85.00**
Madrid, amber, 10" oval	**18.00**
Sierra, pink, oval	**65.00**
Water Bottle, Cameo, dark green	**17.50**
Wine	
American, crystal	**12.50**
Della Robbia, crystal, pale stain . . .	**20.00**
English Hobnail, crystal	**25.00**
Hobnail, crystal	**6.00**
Iris, crystal, 4½" h	**16.00**
Manhattan, crystal	**5.00**
Royal Ruby	**12.00**

CUT GLASS

History: Cut glass provided the rural homestead with a touch of elegance. It was the center of attraction in many china cabinets and prominently featured on the dining room table and in the parlor when special guests arrived. A typical Country home averaged between six and a dozen pieces, mostly accessory pieces, e.g., candy dishes, celery dishes, pitchers, vases, etc.

Cut glass was a favorite wedding and anniversary gift. These pieces were supplemented by those received through inheritance. As a result, most cut glass pieces had a highly personal provenance and quickly achieved heirloom status. This helps explain why damaged pieces remained in use rather than being discarded.

Glass is cut by the process of grinding decoration into the glass by means of abrasive-carrying metal wheels or stone wheels. A very ancient craft, it was revived in 1600 by Bohemians and spread through Europe, to Great Britain, and finally to America.

American cut glass came of age at the Centennial Exposition in 1876 and the World Columbian Exposition in 1893. The American public recognized American cut glass to be exceptional in quality and workmanship. America's most significant output of this high quality glass occurred from 1880 to 1917, a period now known as the "Brilliant Period."

About the 1890s some companies began adding an acid-etched "signature" to their glass. This signature may be the actual company name, its logo, or chosen symbol. Today, signed pieces command a premium over unsigned pieces since the signature clearly establishes the origin.

However, caution should be exercised in regard to signature identification. Objects with forged signatures have been in existence for some time. To check for authenticity, run your fingertip or fingernail lightly over the area with the signature. As a general rule, a genuine signature cannot be felt; a forged signature exhibits a raised surface.

Many companies never used the acid-etched signature on the glass and may or may not have affixed paper labels to the items originally. Dorflinger Glass and the Meriden Glass Company made cut glass of the highest quality, yet never acid-etched a signature on the glass. Furthermore, cut glass made before the 1890s was not signed. Many of these wood polished items, cut on blown blanks, were of excellent quality and often won awards at exhibitions. Consequently, if collectors restrict themselves to signed pieces only, many beautiful pieces of the highest quality glass and workmanship will be missed.

References: E. S. Farrar & J. S. Spillman, *The Complete Cut & Engraved Glass Of Corning*, Crown Publishers, Corning Museum of Glass monograph, 1979; John Feller, *Dorflinger: America's Finest Glass, 1852–1921*, Antique Publications, 1988; J. Michael Pearson, *Encyclopedia Of American Cut & Engraved Glass*, Volumes I to III, published by author, 1975; Albert C. Revi, *American Cut & Engraved Glass*, Schiffer Publishing, 1965; Ellen T. Schroy, *Warman's Glass*, Wallace-Homestead, 1992; Martha Louise Swan, *American and Engraved Glass*, Wallace-Homestead, 1986, 1994 value update; H. Weiner & F. Lipkowitz, *Rarities In American Cut Glass*, Collectors House of Books, 1975.

Collectors' Club: American Cut Glass Association, 36 Crosstie Lane, Batesville, IN 47006.

Museums: The Corning Museum of Glass, Corning, NY; High Museum of Art, Atlanta, GA; Huntington Galleries, Huntington, WV; Lightner Museum, St. Augustine, FL; Toledo Museum Of Art, Toledo, OH.

Atomizer, De Vilbiss, allover cutting, Brilliant Period, 6" h	**125.00**

Banana Bowl, Hunt, Royal pattern, 11½ × 8" **550.00**

Bell, hobstar diamond point fan, 5½" d **225.00**

Berry Set, master bowl, six serving bowls, Eggington, Cluster pattern, hobnail, hobstar, star, and strawberry diamond, price for seven pc set. ... **495.00**

Bonbon, Huntly, Broadway pattern, minor flakes, 8" d, 2" h **125.00**

Bowl
Hobstar diamond point fan, blown out, 8" d **525.00**
Russian hobstar diamond cuttings, cut buttons, two handles, sectional, low, 12" d **225.00**
Well cut border of flowers and leaves, 1¾" w diamond border, fluted, 7¾" d, 4" h **125.00**

Bread Tray, Clark, hobstars, sgd, 11 × 5" **275.00**

Butter Dish, cov, Libbey, hobstars and fans, 5" h, 8" d **425.00**

Candlesticks, pr, Pairpoint, Adelaide, amber, 12" h................. **365.00**

Candy Dish, cov
Hawkes, Devonshire pattern, pedestal base, sgd **245.00**
Pairpoint, vintage cutting, dark canary................... **150.00**

Carafe, Hawkes, Cypress pattern, large hobstars separated by smaller fans, clear centers, blown blank, wood polished, sgd............... **145.00**

Celery Tray, Harvard pattern sides, two large flowers and leaves on base, 10½" l **95.00**

Champagne, Dorflinger, cranberry cut to clear, Panel and Flute cut bowl, clear stem with ring in center **160.00**

Cheese and Cracker Dish, cross cut diamond, fan, and large star, 9" d **140.00**

Cigar Jar, Hoare, Monarch pattern, hobstar base, hollow for sponge in lid........................ **625.00**

Pitcher, Cluster pattern, O F Eggington, Corning, NY, c1910, 10" h, $300.00.

Cologne Bottle, Dorflinger, Parisian pattern, sq, 7½ × 2¾", price for pair....................... **620.00**

Compote, Sinclaire, Forty and Grapes pattern, amber, faceted horizontally stepped cutting, engraved leaf and vine border, 3⅝" h, 8½" d, price for pair....................... **200.00**

Compote Serving Set, master compote, seven matching smaller compotes, Brilliant Period allover cutting, pointed rims, price for eight pc set **325.00**

Creamer and Sugar, hobstars, nailhead, and fan, triple cut handles....... **250.00**

Cream Pitcher, bulbous, notched fluted rim, Persian, clear hobstar center, triple notched handles, 5¼" h..... **150.00**

Cruet, Hawkes, Chrysanthemum pattern, tri-pour spout, cut handle and stopper, 6" h **350.00**

Decanter
American, Russian pattern, three ringed faceted neck, bulbous body, starred base, conforming teardrop stopper, 11½" h....... **935.00**
Hawkes, deep intaglio thistles and leaves, top becomes shot glass, trifolio Hawkes signature **275.00**

Dresser Tray, hobstar and diamond, fan border, 12 × 8" **325.00**

Eggnog Punch Set, bowl, stand, four matching punch cups, hobstars **2,750.00**

Finger Bowl and Underplate, Dorflinger, 4½" d bowl, 6" d underplate, blown blank, wood polished...... **150.00**

Flower Center, hobstars in diamond shaped fields, fans, strawberry diamond, honeycomb neck, 7½" h, 10" d...................... **750.00**

Ice Tub, Mount Washington, c1870, Russian pattern, single star, Russian cut tab handles, blown blank wood polished **425.00**

Knife Rest, barbell shape, pinwheel cut ends, 5" l..................... **90.00**

Orange Bowl, Eggington, Lotus pattern, 7½" d **275.00**

Plate
Arcadia type pattern, square, 7" w **225.00**
Swirls of notched prisms and hobstars, 7" d **125.00**

Punch Bowl, two pcs, Hunt, Royal pattern, 12" d.................... **1,500.00**

Relish, Russian pattern, clear buttons, leaf shape, 13" l **315.00**

Salad Set, Russian pattern, starred buttons, silver mountings by Gorham and Sons, c1890 .... **375.00**

Salt, open
Dorflinger, wood polished, price for set of six **175.00**

Punch Bowl on Stand, American Brilliant period, 15½″ h, $2,420.00. Photograph courtesy of William Doyle Galleries.

Hoare, Monarch pattern, blown blank, wood polished	95.00
Spooner, Eggington, Lotus cutting, 4 × 8″.	80.00
Syrup Pitcher, Russian cutting, hinged silverplate top, cut handle.	770.00
Tankard, Averbeck, Genoa pattern, 11″ h	395.00
Tumbler	
Dorflinger, Renaissance Exact, price for set of six.	180.00
Unknown maker, Russian cutting, cut buttons, price for set of nine	325.00
Vase	
Brunswick, Brilliant Period, 14″ h	550.00
Hawkes, Brazilian pattern, trumpet, 5″ h.	175.00
Tuthill, Vintage pattern, two handles, Brilliant Period, urn shape, 11″ h	475.00
Unknown maker, green cut to clear, 8½″ h, price for pair	350.00
Water Set, pitcher, matching tumbler, Greek Key with hobstars, caning. . .	595.00
Whiskey, attributed to Hawkes, Russian pattern, single star centers, wood polished	85.00
Wine	
Dorflinger	
Cranberry cut to clear, Old Colony pattern.	195.00
Solid green cut to clear, strawberry, diamond, and fan cutting, clear stem	275.00
Libbey, cranberry bowl cut to clear, concentric circle in single stars, clear knob stem, c1890	210.00
New England Glass Co, Rhine, apricot cut to clear, canes, fans, oval vesicias, nailhead diamonds, clear stem, rayed base, c1890	225.00

EARLY AMERICAN GLASS

History: Early American glass covers glass made in America from the colonial period through the mid-19th century. As such, it includes the early pressed glass and lacy glass made between 1827 and 1840.

Major glass producing centers prior to 1850 were: Massachusetts with the New England Glass Company and the Boston and Sandwich Glass Company; South Jersey; Pennsylvania with Stiegel's Manheim factory and Pittsburgh; and Ohio with Kent, Mantua, and Zanesville.

Early American glass was collected heavily during the 1920 to 1950 period, regaining some of its earlier popularity in the mid-1980s. In the Country movement, its role is largely as a decorative accessory.

Leading sources for the sale of early American glass are the mail auctions of Collectors Sales and Services and Glass Works Auctions and the auctions of Richard A. Bourne, Early Auction Company, Garth's, Norman C. Heckler & Company, and Skinners.

References: William E. Covill, *Ink Bottles and Inkwells,* 1971; Lowell Inness, *Pittsburgh Glass: 1797–1891,* Houghton Mifflin Company, 1976; George and Helen McKearin, *American Glass,* Crown, 1975; George and Helen McKearin, *Two Hundred Years of American Blown Glass,* Doubleday and Company, 1950; Helen McKearin and Kenneth Wilson, *American Bottles And Flasks,* Crown, 1978; Adeline Pepper, *Glass Gaffers of New Jersey,* Scribners, 1971; Jane S. Spillman, *American and European Pressed Glass,* Corning Museum of Glass, 1981; Kenneth Wilson, *New England Glass And Glassmaking,* Crowell, 1972.

Collectors' Club: The National Early American Glass Club, PO Box 8489, Silver Spring, MD 20907. [j19]Museum: Sandwich Glass Museum, Sandwich, MA.

Reproduction Craftsperson: Art Reed, Sweetwater Glass, RD 1, Box 88, DeLancey, NY 13752.

Reproduction Manufacturer: The Ebenezer Averill Co., PO Box 156, Milford, NH 03055.

Bottle	
Aqua	
Club shape, blown, 24 swirled ribs, wear and light stain, 8⅝″ h	160.00
Tapered, 20 molded ribs, slightly swirled to right, flanged lip, pontil, Kent, OH, 7⅛″ h	100.00
Clear, lavender tint	40.00
Cobalt Blue, tam o' shanter stopper, pint	325.00
Deep Amethyst, smelling salts, flattened globular body, applied side	

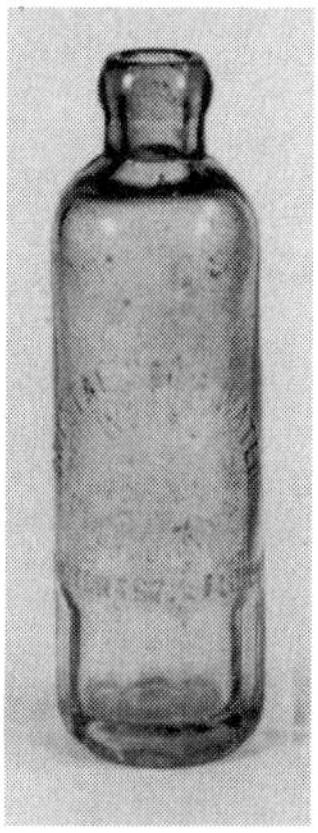

Bottle, Soda Water Works, Uniontown, PA, 7½ fluid oz, $10.00.

quilling, sheared mouth, pontil, Marlboro Street Glassworks, Keene, NH, c1815–20, 1⅞″ h . . . **1,300.00**
Olive Amber, pint **245.00**
Peacock Blue, smelling salts, ovoid, 26 vertical molded ribs, sheared mouth and pontil, Kent OH, 3″ h **225.00**

Bowl
Aqua, folded rim, wear, star in flared rim, NY, 14″ d, 4¼″ h. **225.00**
Clear, gray tint, geometric design, Mount Vernon Glassworks, NY, c1840, 5½″ d, 2⅜″ h **700.00**
Cobalt Blue, clear foot, wide flaring rim, rough pontil, Pittsburgh, 4⅜″ d, 3⅞″ h **600.00**

Candlesticks, pr,clear
Blown three mold, shaped standard, 7″ h. **55.00**
Flint, hexagonal, Pittsburgh **145.00**

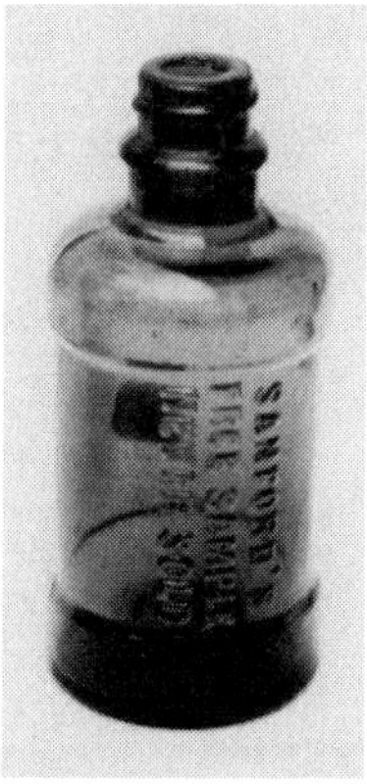

Ink Bottle, Sanford's Free Sample, amber, round, 1½″ d, 3½″ h, $30.00.

Compote
Clear, blown, engraved with wreaths and tassels, sq stepped base, rounded corners, pontil scar, attributed to New England, 1825–35, 9″ w, 8¼″ h. **1,325.00**
Cranberry cased bowl, clear solid knop stem, thick heavy base, Pittsburgh, c1850, 8¾″ d, 5¼″ h **425.00**

Cordial, clear, blown three mold **135.00**

Creamer, brilliant yellow amber, blown, Jacob Relyea, Ellenville, NY, 3¾″ h **500.00**

Creamer and Sugar, medium sapphire blue, 17 swirled ribs, drawn base, hollow foot, flared, folded rim, applied handle, Midwestern, 3½″ h **425.00**

Cruet, purple-blue, tapered, 24 molded ribs, swirled to left, slightly flared, rolled lip, 6⅜″ h. **2,300.00**

Decanter, clear
Baroque pattern, blown three mold, some stains, no stopper, 8¼″ h **50.00**
Miniature, blown three mold. **160.00**
Pillar molded, 8 blue ribs, thick sloping lip and pouring ring, polished pontil, 8½″ h. **1,200.00**
Three applied rigaree rings, blown three mold, chips on lid, mismatched stopper, 8¼″ h **40.00**
Vintage Pattern, orig stopper **75.00**

Flask
Chestnut, blown
Aqua
16 swirled ribs, some wear, stain, light residue, Mantua, OH, 6″ h **165.00**
16 vertical ribs, slightly misshapen, some int. stain, 5⅝″ h. **135.00**
21 vertical ribs, heavy glass with wear and scratches, Midwestern, 6″ h **165.00**
Pale Green, 18 swirled ribs, Midwestern, 6½″ h **190.00**
Pitkin
Aqua, vertical ribs, half pint. **30.00**
Medium Olive Green, swirled shoulder, vertical ribs, pint. . . . **450.00**
Scroll, aqua
Half pint, 6″ h **75.00**
Pint, 7″ h, iron pontil **40.00**
Quart, shallow flake at pontil, 8¾″ h **28.00**

Flip, clear, blown three mold
3¾″ h, etched rim **80.00**
4⅞″ h, engraved band. **165.00**
5⅜″ h, pontil scar, New England Glass Co, 1825–40 . . . . **135.00**

Inkwell, blown three mold
Green, Keene Marlboro Street Glassworks, Keene, NH, 1815–30, 1¾″ w, 1½″ h **150.00**

Olive Amber. **110.00**
Olive Green, expanded diamond
patterned band, 2⅜ " d **140.00**
Lamp, clear
Blown font and hollow stem, pressed
base, wafers, cut foliage, panels,
strawberry diamonds, and fans,
pewter collar, minor chips on
base, Pittsburgh, 12¼" h **575.00**
Flattened diamond font, hexagonal
base, flint, pewter collar, chips,
10" h. **85.00**
Free blown font, grape pattern en-
graving, attached by wafer to
elaborate round stepped standard,
sq ripple edge base, double pewter
burner, New England, 1835–40,
10¼" h **325.00**
Pan, pale green, 16 ribs, folded over
rim, Mantua, OH, 6" d **375.00**
Salt
Light Green, 16 vertical ribs, petaled
foot, double ogee form, Midwest-
ern, 1820–40, 2⅞" h. **250.00**
Smoky Blue, 16 vertical ribs, pontil
scar, Pittsburgh, 3" d **325.00**
Shot Glass, clear, blown three mold   **100.00**
Tumbler,   yellowish-green,   plain
sheared rim, large polished pontil,
New Geneva, PA, 4½" h **275.00**
Vase
Canary, Three Printie Block, hexagonal standard and foot, no wafer,
pressed, New England Glass Co,
1840–60, 9¼" h **225.00**
Clear, flint, Honeycomb pattern, 10"
h, pr **125.00**

HISTORICAL FLASKS

History: A flask is a container for liquids. Early
American glass companies frequently formed
them in molds which left a relief design on the
front and/or back. Historical flasks with a portrait,
building, scene, or name are the most desirable.

Most flasks have a narrow neck. A chestnut is
hand blown, small, and has a flattened bulbous
body. The pitkin has a blown globular body with
vertical ribs with a spiral rib overlay. Teardrop
flasks are generally fiddle shaped and have a scroll
or geometric design.

Dimensions can differ for the same flask because of variations in the molding process. Color
is important, with scarcer colors demanding more
money. Aqua and amber are the most common
colors. Bottles with "sickness," an opalescent scal-
ing which eliminates clarity, are worth much less.

Relief decorated flasks, especially those featuring patriotic or historical themes, are the most
popular among Country collectors. Although aqua
is the most common color, it is favored because

of its ability to blend well into any Country decorating scheme.

Reference: George L. and Helen McKearin,
American Glass, Crown Publishers, 1941 and
1948.

Collectors' Club: The National Early American
Glass Club, PO Box 8489, Silver Spring, MD
20907.

Reproduction Manufacturer: The Ebenezer Averill Co., PO Box 156, Milford, NH 03055.

Cornucopia-Urn
Emerald Green
Half Pint **110.00**
Pint **325.00**
Gold Amber **55.00**
Olive Amber, chip on medial rib,
half pint, 5¼" h. **50.00**
Olive Green, pint **45.00**
Pale Aqua, half pint, 5½" h. **125.00**
Eagle-Anchor, iron pontil, Ravenna
Glass Co, pint, 7⅞" h **115.00**
Eagle-Cornucopia, olive amber. **75.00**
Eagle-Eagle with Banner, aqua, pint,
7⅜ " h **40.00**
Eagle-Masonic
Amber, half pint **100.00**
Clear, pint. **350.00**
Golden Amber, vertically ribbed,
flared and rolled lip, pontil mark,
J Shepard & Co, White Glass
Works, Zanesville, OH, 1830–40,
pint **1,200.00**
Eagle-Railroad, gold amber, pint. **110.00**
Eagle-Union, aqua, clasped hands,
small chip on lip, half pint, 6" h . . .   **50.00**
Flora Temple, amber, applied handle,
attributed to Whitney Glass Works,
Glassboro, NJ, 1860–80, pint **80.00**

**Cornucopia/Eagle, aqua, half pint, 7" h,
$375.00.**

For Pike's Peak, aqua, rough lip, half
  pint, 6½" h **50.00**
General Taylor, aqua, "A Little More
  Grape" and "General Taylor Never
  Surrenders," pint, 7¼" h **300.00**
General Washington-Eagle, aqua, pint,
  6¾" h **220.00**
Jenny Lind, deep emerald, calabash,
  broad sloping collar, pontil mark, S
  Huffsey Glass Works, 1850–60,
  quart **685.00**
Kossuth, aqua, calabash, fluted edges,
  sloping collar, pontil mark, S Huffsey
  Glass Works, 1850–60, quart **250.00**
Lafayette-Liberty, olive, half pint. **225.00**
Masonic, aqua, Shepards & Co, pint,
  6¾" h **225.00**
Ship and Star, aqua, half pint, 5⅝ " h .   **225.00**
Success to the Railroad, aqua, three
  vertical ribs, sheared lip, pontil mark,
  two reversed numeral "5"s on base,
  Lancaster, NY Glass Works, 1830–
  40, pint **415.00**
Success to the Railroad-Eagle, olive
  green, pint **110.00**
Washington and Taylor, aqua, pint,
  7" h **72.00**

KITCHEN GLASSWARE

History: The first quarter of the 20th century
brought inexpensive kitchen and table products to
center stage. Hocking, Hazel Atlas, McKee, U. S.
Glass, and Westmoreland were companies which
led in the production of these items.

    Utilitarian kitchen glassware complements De-
pression Glass tableware. Many items were produced in the same color and style. Because the
glass was molded, added decorative elements
included ribs, fluting, arches and thumbprint patterns. Kitchen Glassware was thick to achieve
durability, which resulted in forms which were
awkward looking and difficult to handle at times.
After World War II, aluminum products began to
replace Kitchen Glassware.

    Kitchen Glassware was made in large numbers.
Although collectors do tolerate signs of use, they
will not accept pieces with heavy damage. Many
of the products contain applied decals; these
should be in good condition. A collection can be
built inexpensively by concentrating on one form
such as canister sets, measuring cups, reamers,
etc.

References: Gene Florence, *Kitchen Glassware of
the Depression Years, Fourth Edition*, Collector
Books, 1990, 1992 value update; Shirley Glyn-
don, *The Miracle In Grandmother's Kitchen*, privately printed, 1983; Garry Kilgo et al., *A
Collectors Guide To Anchor Hocking's Fire-King
Glassware*, K & W Collectibles Publisher, 1991;

April M. Tvorak, *Fire-King II*, published by author,
1993; April M. Tvorak, *History and Price Guide to
Fire-King*, VAL Enterprises, 1992; April M. Tvorak,
Pyrex Price Guide, published by author, 1992;
Susan Tobier Rogove and Marcia Buan Stein-
hauer, *Pyrex By Corning: A Collector's Guide*,
Antique Publications, 1993; Mary Walker, *Ream-
ers-200 Years* (1980, separate price guide) and
The Second Book, More Reamers—200 Years
(1983), Muski Publishers.

Collectors' Club: National Reamer Collectors Association, 405 Benson Road N., Frederic, WI
54837; The Glass Knife Collectors Club, PO Box
342, Los Alamitos, CA 90720.

Batter Bowl
  Green Transparent, spiraled, Anchor
    Hocking **25.00**
  Mayfair Blue, ribbed, Anchor Hock-
    ing. **100.00**
  White, peaches and grapes, Fire-
    King. **12.00**
Batter Jug
  Black, metal handle with lid, McKee   **60.00**
  Crystal, cobalt blue lid, Paden City   **35.00**
  Green Transparent, melon ribbed,
    Jenkins.   **275.00**
  Jadite, rect, Jeannette. **175.00**
  Pink, Cambridge **65.00**
Batter Set, cov batter jug, cov syrup,
  tray
  Black, Paden City **200.00**
  Cobalt Blue, New Martinsville. **250.00**
Butter Dish, cov
  Amber, ¼ lb, Federal **30.00**
  Cobalt Blue, emb "BUTTER
    COVER," 1 lb, Hazel Atlas. **150.00**
  Custard, 1 lb, McKee. **35.00**
  Delphite, emb "BUTTER," 1 lb, Jean-
    nette **150.00**
  Pink, emb "B", 2 lb, Jeannette **100.00**
  White, red Ships, 1 lb, McKee. **20.00**
Cake Server, amber flattened handle,
  crystal spatula **45.00**
Cheese Dish, cov, crystal, square, emb
  "Sanitary Preserver," Hazel Atlas . . .   **35.00**

**Batter Bowl, Skokie Green, flanged rim
with spout, McKee, 7⅛ " d, $12.00.**

Canister, cov, clear, red, white, and yellow dec, 4¾″ d, 6″ h, $18.00.

Knife, Vitex-Glas, pink, stars and diamonds on handle, 9⅛ ″ l, $18.00.

Coffeepot, cov

Crystal, ribbed, large, Silex	95.00
Ring Decorated, Glasbake	30.00
Crock, jadite, 40 oz, Jeannette	40.00

Cruet

Amber, Cambridge	30.00
Green Transparent, US Glass	38.00
Jadite, black lettering "Vinegar" . . .	115.00
Janice Blue, New Martinsville.	45.00
Yellow, Lancaster Glass Co.	70.00

Drawer Knobs

Crystal, ribbed	8.75
Moonstone, screw through, 1½″ d, six sided	4.75
Peacock Blue, single.	12.00

Drip Jar, cov, round, flattened front and back, black circle with flowers on white, black lid. 20.00

Funnel

Crystal

Embossed "Tufglas".	80.00
Ribbed, 9″ h	12.00
Green Transparent, ribbed, 4½″ h .	35.00

Gravy Boat

Blue, double, Cambridge	20.00
Pink, Imperial	18.00

Ice Bucket

Green Frosted, tab handles, emb "Frigidaire Ice Server," Hocking	10.00
Green Transparent, bail handle, McKee	20.00
Jadite, cov, emb circles, wrapped bail handle, Fenton	80.00
Pink, bail handle, Fostoria	25.00
Ring, Hocking, tab handles.	15.00

Knife

Aer-Flo, pink.	75.00
Durex, Three Leaves, crystal, 9¼″ l	12.00

Three Star

Blue, 8½″ l	40.00
Crystal, 9″ l, orig box	30.00
Pink	38.00

Ladle

Black	60.00
Crystal, Fostoria	10.00
Moonlight Blue, Cambridge	30.00
White, Imperial.	35.00

Measuring Cup

Advertising, crystal

Capital B Band, Handy Cup Measure.	28.00
Use S S Sleeper's, Best of all Spices, Westmoreland	20.00
Amber, Federal	32.00
Blue, three spout, Fire-King.	15.00
Crystal, stippled bottom, unembossed, Glasbake, McKee	10.00
Delphite, set of four, Jeannette	125.00
White, red trim, three spout, Hazel Atlas	60.00

Measuring Pitcher

Crystal, 1 quart, Umpire Glass Co, Pittsburgh	20.00

Fired-on color

Green, 2 cup, McKee	10.00
Green, 2 cup, Hazel Atlas	38.00
Frosted Green, 4 cup, Hazel Atlas. .	18.00
Jadite, dark, sunflower in bottom, 2 cup, Jeannette	45.00
Seville Yellow, 2 cup, McKee	40.00
Vitrock White, cov	35.00
White, black bow, 2 cup, McKee . .	25.00

Napkin Holder

Black, Nar-O-Fold.	30.00
Green Clambroth, emb "Serv-All". .	125.00
Green Transparent, Paden City	75.00
White, emb "Fan Fold, Property of Diana Mfg., Green Bay"	60.00

Reamer

Amber, ribbed, loop handle, Federal	18.00

Baby, 2 pc set

Amber, Westmoreland.	175.00
Blue	425.00
Crystal, elephant dec, Fenton . . .	70.00

Frosted

Crystal, floral dec.	90.00
Pink.	110.00
Green Transparent, Jenkins	100.00
Pink, L E Smith	225.00
Black, emb "Saunders"	900.00
Butterscotch, emb "Sunkist"	550.00
Canary Vaseline, straight sides, tab handle, Fry	40.00
Caramel, light, emb "Sunkist"	225.00

Reamer, Sunkist, yellow, No. 330, $50.00.

Chalaine Blue, grapefruit	400.00
Cobalt Blue, Crisscross, loop handle, Hazel Atlas	200.00
Crystal	
Crisscross, tab handle, Hazel Atlas	5.00
Glasbake, McKee on handle	90.00
Lemons branch dec, flattened loop handle, Westmoreland.	85.00
Custard, grapefruit	325.00
Delphite, small, Jeannette	60.00
Forest Green, emb "Sunkist"	375.00
Green Opalescent, emb "Sunkist"	140.00
Green Transparent	
Paneled, loop handle, Federal . . .	25.00
Silver Rockwell dec, loop handle, Cambridge.	325.00
Jadite, Jeannette	
Large, dark	25.00
Small, light	20.00
Mustard Slag, emb fleur-de-lis.	400.00
Olive Green Milk Glass, emb "Sunkist"	550.00
Pearl, flute sides, loop handle, Fry	32.00
Pink	
Indiana Glass, six sided cone, vertical handle	125.00
US Glass, slick handle.	90.00
Seville Yellow, grapefruit	200.00
Skokie Green, pointed cone, emb "Sunkist," McKee	50.00
Ultra-marine, Jennyware, small, Jeannette	75.00
White, emb "Valencia"	95.00
Reamer Pitcher Set, 2 pcs	
Black, Fenton	900.00
Blue Dot, 2 cup, Hazel Atlas.	30.00
Cobalt Blue, 2 cup, Hazel Atlas . . .	225.00
Crystal	
2 Cup, decorated, U S Glass	20.00
4 Cup, marked "A & J"	20.00
Fired-on Red 2 cup pitcher, white reamer with red trim, Hazel Atlas	35.00
Frosted Green, 2 cup, US Glass. . . .	30.00
Green Transparent	
2 Cup, Jeannette	18.00
4 Cup, ftd, Anchor Hocking	35.00
2 Quart, 3 pcs, reamer, pitcher, and lid, US Glass.	225.00

Jadite, 2 cup, Jeannette	
Dark	80.00
Light	20.00
Pink	
2 Cup, emb lemon, Westmoreland	130.00
4 Cup, Party Line, Paden City . . .	125.00
Westmoreland	125.00
Turquoise Blue, Party Line, Paden City	275.00
Vitrock White, 2 cup, Anchor Hocking.	85.00
Refrigerator Dish, cov	
Chalaine Blue, 5 × 8", rect, Hazel Atlas	60.00
Cobalt Blue	
5¼" d, round, flat knob, Hazel Atlas	55.00
8 × 8", square, Crisscross, Hazel Atlas	80.00
Delphite	
4 × 4", square, Jeannette	25.00
32 oz, round	40.00
Fired-on Blue, 7" l, oval, Hocking . .	18.00
Jadite, 5 × 9", rect, Fire-King	12.00
Pink, 4 × 4", square, ribbed, Federal	6.00
Seville Yellow, 7¼", square, Hazel Atlas	35.00
Ultra-marine, 4 × 8", rect, Jeannette	20.00
White, 4¼ × 6¼", rect, blue rooster dec, Pyrex	12.00
Yellow, 4½ × 4½", square, flat knob, Hazel Atlas	35.00
Rolling Pin	
Amber, blown.	100.00
Amethyst, blown	90.00
Chalaine Blue, blown	300.00
Clambroth, screw-on wood handles	85.00
Cobalt Blue, wood handles attached to metal rod	325.00
Crystal, screw-on cap	12.00
Delphite, screw-on cap, smooth handle	350.00
Green Transparent, handles attached to wood dowel pin	300.00

Refrigerator Dish, clear, raised vegetable design on lid, ribbed sides, 8⅜ " sq, 3" h, $12.00.

Jadite, screw-on cap, circular band on opposite handle, McKee	250.00
Peacock blue	
Blown	135.00
Wood handles attached to metal rod	175.00
Pink, wood screw-on handles	300.00
Seville Yellow, screw-on cap, smooth handle, McKee	225.00
Salad Set, fork and spoon	
Amber flattened striped handle, crystal fork and bowl	35.00
Black hexagonal handle, crystal fork and bowl	60.00
Blue-green, ribbed handle flared at end, Imperial	65.00
Cobalt blue, slender round vertically ribbed handle, crystal fork and bowl	40.00
Crystal, slender round vertically ribbed handle	18.00
Green pointed handles, crystal fork and bowl	35.00
Light Blue, ribbed handle, Cambridge	90.00
Pink flattened handle, crystal fork and bowl	45.00
Red, vertically ribbed handle, Cambridge	135.00
Salt Box	
Chalaine Blue, hinged metal lid, McKee	160.00
Crystal, round, emb "SALT"	12.00
Green	
Rectangular, emb "SALT," Sneath	200.00
Round, emb "SALT" on lid, Jeannette	150.00
Jadite, hanging, rect, wood lid, black lettering, Jeannette	185.00
White, hanging, half round, emb "SALT"	70.00
Shakers	
Black, square, white lettering, McKee	15.00
Blue Circle, round, blue design on white	8.00
Cattails, square, red and black design on white	5.00
Chalaine Blue, square, emb block letters, McKee	65.00
Custard, Roman Arches shape, red dots and lettering, McKee	15.00
Delphite, round, horizontal ribs, black lettering, Jeannette	
Paprika	40.00
Salt	18.00
Sugar	35.00
Dutch Girl, square, blue design on white	12.00
Fired-on Yellow, square, black lettering, Hocking	5.00
Green Clambroth, square, paneled, paper label, Hocking	15.00

Shakers, Skokie Green, Roman Arch sides, McKee, set of four, $80.00.

Green Transparent, ovoid, vertical ribs, black and gold label, Owens-Illinois	10.00
Jadite, light, square, black lettering, Jeannette	
Flour	12.00
Pepper	8.00
Pink, square, emb design, Hazel Atlas	45.00
Scotty Dog, square, ribbed corners, black design on white, black lid	7.00
Ships, Roman Arches shape, red design on white, McKee	8.00
Skokie Green, Roman Arches, black script lettering, McKee	
Cinnamon	30.00
Flour	15.00
Salt	20.00
Tulips, red, yellow, green, and blue design on white, red, white, and blue lid, Hocking	6.00
White, round, vertical ribs, paper label, Frank Tea & Spice Co, Cincinnati	5.00
Straw Holder	
Cobalt Blue, metal lid	250.00
Crystal, metal lid and base	175.00
Sugar Shaker, pour top	
Amber, hour glass shape, Paden City	125.00
Cobalt Blue, conical top	325.00
Crystal, indented dots at top, metal screw-on base, McKee	20.00
Green, paneled, Hocking	60.00
Syrup Pitcher	
Amber, glass lid, Cambridge	30.00
Black, glass lid, Fenton	45.00
Blue, Caribbean, horizontal ribs, metal lid, Duncan & Miller	115.00
Green, metal lid, Paden City	25.00
Pink, metal lid, Hazel Atlas	40.00
Towel Bar	
Jadite, 17" l	25.00
Skokie Green, McKee	25.00
White, slick handle, US Glass	50.00
Water Bottle	
Dark Green, emb "Juice" and "Water," screw-on lid, Owens-Illinois	4.00
Royal Ruby, horizontal ribs, glass lid, Hocking	60.00

Water Dispenser, cov, refrigerator type
  Cobalt Blue, rect, spirals, L E
  Smith. **325.00**
  Custard, McKee **115.00**
  Green Clambroth, crystal lid, Sneath
  Glass Co **50.00**
  White, McKee. **100.00**

PATTERN GLASS

History: Pattern glass often marked a Country family's first introduction to utilitarian household glassware. Replacement of horn, tin, and wooden tableware occurred gradually. Initial glassware purchases often were reserved for Sundays, holidays, and special occasions.

Some patterns imitated cut glass patterns. It was common to find the two mixed together in a table setting. While clear (crystal) was the most popular, colored lines were available in many patterns. It also was common practice to mix patterns, especially in accessory pieces.

Pattern glass is clear or colored glass pressed into one of hundreds of patterns. Deming Jarves of the Boston and Sandwich Glass Company invented the first successful pressing machine in 1828. By the 1860s glass pressing machinery had been improved, and mass production of good quality matched tableware sets began. The idea of a matched glassware table service (including goblets, tumblers, creamers, sugars, compotes, cruets, etc.) quickly caught on in America. Many pattern glass table services had numerous accessory pieces among which were banana stands, molasses cans, water bottles, etc.

Early pattern glass (flint) was made with a lead formula, giving it a ringing quality. During the Civil War lead became too valuable to be used in glass manufacturing. In 1864 Hobbs, Brockunier & Company, West Virginia, developed a soda lime (non-flint) formula. Pattern glass also was produced in colors, milk glass, opalescent glass, slag glass, and custard glass.

The hundreds of companies which produced pattern glass experienced periods of development, expansion, personnel problems, material and supply demands, fires, and mergers. In 1899 the National Glass Co. was formed as a combination of 19 glass companies in Pennsylvania, Ohio, Indiana, West Virginia, and Maryland. U. S. Glass, another consortium, was founded in 1891. These combines resulted as an attempt to save small companies by pooling talents, resources, and patterns. Because of this pooling, the same pattern can be attributed to several companies.

Sometimes the pattern name of a piece was changed from one company to the next to reflect current fashion trends. U. S. Glass created the States series by issuing patterns named for a particular state. Several of these patterns were new issues, others were former patterns renamed.

References: Bill Edwards, *Opalescent Glass,* Collector Books, 1992; Elaine Ezell and George Newhouse, *Cruets, Cruets, Cruets, Volume I,* Antique Publications, 1991; Regis F. and Mary F. Ferson, *Yesterday's Milk Glass Today,* published by author, 1981; Joyce Ann Hicks, *Just Jenkins,* printed by author, 1988; Kyle Husfloen, *Collector's Guide To American Pressed Glass, 1825–1915,* Wallace-Homestead Book Co., 1992

Bill Jenks and Jerry Luna, *Early American Pattern Glass–1850 to 1910: Major Collectible Table Settings with Prices,* Wallace-Homestead, 1990; Bill Jenks, Jerry Luna, and Darryl Reilly, *Identifying Pattern Glass Reproductions,* Wallace-Homestead, 1993; Minnie Watson Kamm, *Pattern Glass Pitchers, Books 1 through 8,* published by author, 1970, 4th printing; Lorraine Kovar, *Westmoreland Glass: 1950–1984,* Antique Publications, 1991; Lorraine Kovar, *Westmoreland Glass: 1950–1984, Vol. II,* Antique Publications, 1991; Thelma Ladd and Laurence Ladd, *Portland Glass: Legacy of a Glass House Down East,* Collector Books, 1992; Ruth Webb Lee, *Early American Pressed Glass,* Lee Publications, 1966, 36th edition; Ruth Webb Lee, *Victorian Glass,* Lee Publications, 1944, 13th edition; Bessie M. Lindsey, *American Historical Glass,* Charles E. Tuttle Co., 1967; Robert Irwin Lucas, *Tarentum Pattern Glass,* privately printed, 1981;

Mollie H. McCain, *The Collector's Encyclopedia of Pattern Glass,* Collector Books, 1982, 1992 value update; James Measell, *Greentown Glass,* Grand Rapids Public Museum Association, distributed by Antique Publications, 1979, 1992–93 value update; James Measell and Don E. Smith, *Findlay Glass: The Glass Tableware Manufacturers, 1886–1902,* Antique Publications, Inc, 1986; Alice Hulett Metz, *Early American Pattern Glass,* published by author, 1958; Alice Hulett Metz, *Much More Early American Pattern Glass,* published by author, 1965; S. T. Millard, *Goblets I,* privately printed, 1938, reprinted Wallace-Homestead, 1975; S. T. Millard, *Goblets II,* privately printed, 1940, reprinted Wallace-Homestead, 1975; Arthur G. Peterson, *Glass Salt Shakers: 1,000 Patterns,* Wallace- Homestead, 1970;

Ellen T. Schroy, *Warman's Glass,* Wallace-Homestead Book Co., 1992; Ellen T. Schroy, *Warman's Pattern Glass,* Wallace-Homestead, 1993; Jane Shadel Spillman, *American and European Pressed Glass in the Corning Museum of Glass,* Corning Museum of Glass, 1981; Jane Shadel Spillman, *The Knopf Collectors Guides to American Antiques, Glass Volumes 1 and 2,* Alfred A. Knopf, Inc., 1982, 1983; Doris and Peter Unitt, *American and Canadian Goblets,* Clock House, 1970; Doris and Peter Unitt, *Treasury of Canadian Glass,* Clock House, 1969, 2nd edition; Peter Unitt and Anne Worrall, *Canadian Handbook, Pressed Glass Tableware,* Clock House Productions, 1983.

Museums: Corning Museum of Glass, Corning, NY; National Museum of Man, Ottawa, Ontario, Canada; Sandwich Glass Museum, Sandwich, MA; Schminck Memorial Museum, Lakeview, OR.

Periodical: *Glass Collector's Digest,* Richardson Printing, PO Box 663, Marietta, OH 45750.

Reproduction Alert: Pattern glass has been widely reproduced.

Ale Glass
  Ashburton, 5" h 90.00
  Honeycomb, flint 50.00
Banana Stand, high standard
  Art, ruby stained 175.00
  Eyewinker................... 100.00
  Moon and Star 90.00
  Snail...................... 145.00
  Wisconsin.................. 75.00
Berry Set, master bowl, matching serving bowls
  Cherry Thumbprint, ruby stain, gold trim, four pcs. 125.00
  Flower with Cane, pink stain, gold trim, seven pcs. 125.00
  Peach, green, Northwood, "N" mark, seven pcs 150.00
Biscuit Jar, cov
  Broken Column 85.00
  Pennsylvania, emerald green 100.00
Bowl, open
  Beaded Swirl with Disc Band, 8" d ... 60.00
  Feather, 8 × 6" oval 25.00
  King's #500, Dewey Blue, gold trim, 7" d..................... 30.00
  Plum and Cherry, 9" d 65.00
  Plume, 8" d 15.00
  Regent, gold trim, 9½" d 50.00
  Utah...................... 18.00
Bread Plate
  Actress, HMS Pinafore 90.00
  Chain and Shield 15.00
  Clear Diagonal Band, Eureka 40.00
  Deer and Pine Tree, amber....... 145.00
  Jeweled Band 20.00
  Koyak 15.00
Bride's Basket, Delaware, emerald green, gold trim, silverplated frame. 115.00
Butter Dish, cov
  Beaded Tulip 50.00
  Cherry Thumbprint, ruby stain, gold trim...................... 100.00
  Esther, emerald green 100.00
  Horseshoe 125.00
  Maryland, gold trim 65.00
  Peach, Northwood, "N" mark..... 95.00
  Pressed Diamond, blue.......... 55.00
  Ruby Thumbprint, etched 85.00
  Strawberry and Cable 110.00
  Yale 45.00

Cake Stand
  Artichoke 42.00
  Deer and Pine Tree, apple green... 115.00
  Feather, 8⅜ " d 50.00
  Paneled Thistle 35.00
  Reverse Torpedo............... 85.00
  Shoshone, amber stained 135.00
  Willow Oak, amber, 10" d 60.00
Carafe
  Bull's Eye 45.00
  Minnesota................... 35.00
  New Hampshire 60.00
Castor Set
  Alabama, green, shakers, cruet, mustard, orig frame 275.00
  Daisy and Button, vaseline, four bottles, glass stand 75.00
Celery Tray
  Beaded Grape................. 45.00
  Broken Column............... 35.00
  Wisconsin................... 40.00
Celery Vase
  Barberry, 7" h 60.00
  Beaded Swag 45.00
  Canadian 65.00
  Diamond Point, flint, 8" h........ 95.00
  Feather 45.00
  Florida 30.00
  Frosted Flower Band, base polished 35.00
  Horseshoe................... 85.00
  Paneled Forget Me Not 45.00
  Snail 35.00
  Willow Oak, 8" h 90.00
Champagne
  Bull's Eye 95.00
  Diamond Point, flint 85.00
  Fancy Loop................... 55.00
  Paneled Thistle 40.00
Cheese Dish, cov
  Flamingo Habitat 110.00
  Magnet and Grape with Stippled Leaf 45.00
  Zipper..................... 55.00
Compote, cov
  Canadian, low standard, 7" d 125.00
  Carolina, dome cov, 13½" h...... 125.00
  Jacob's Ladder, high standard, 9½" d 125.00
  Portland, gold trim, high standard, 6" d..................... 60.00
  Three Face, high standard, 8" d 175.00
Compote, open
  Austrian, low standard, canary yellow 150.00
  Bow Tie, flared, high standard, 8" d 65.00
  Crystal Wedding, sq, 8" h 55.00
  Diamond Thumbprint, flint, low standard, 8" d 50.00
  Kansas, low standard, 6½" d 45.00
  Scroll With Cane Band, ruby stained, 8½ x 8¼" 220.00
  Sheaf and Diamond, 7" h 45.00
  Strawberry and Fan, 9" h 100.00

Cordial
Almond Thumbprint, flint	**45.00**
Bellflower, single vine, fine ribbed, knob stem, rayed base	**115.00**
King's Crown	**45.00**
Sawtooth, flint	**50.00**

Creamer
Atlanta	**50.00**
Button Arches, ruby stained	**40.00**
Cherry Thumbprint, ruby stain, gold trim	**45.00**
Cupid and Venus	**55.00**
Feather	**45.00**
Iowa	**30.00**
Peach, green, Northwood, "N" mark	**75.00**
Ruby Thumbprint, etched	**85.00**
Truncated Cube, ruby stained, individual size	**30.00**
Vermont, gold trim	**30.00**

Cruet, orig stopper
Beaded Grape	**65.00**
Broken Column	**65.00**
Massachusetts	**45.00**
Medallion Sunburst	**75.00**
Wisconsin	**80.00**

Cup and Saucer
Cornell, green, gold trim	**25.00**
King's Crown	**55.00**
Stippled Forget Me Not	**30.00**

Decanter
Banded Portland	**50.00**
Georgia	**70.00**

Doughnut Stand
Horseshoe	**75.00**
Paneled Thistle	**25.00**

Egg Cup
Budded Ivy	**25.00**
Lily of the Valley	**40.00**
Morning Glory, flint, tiny base nick	**225.00**
Open Rose	**12.00**

Finger Bowl
Chandelier, etched	**40.00**
Heart with Thumbprint	**45.00**
Snail	**50.00**
Fruit Bowl, Three Panel, blue, ftd, 10" d	**55.00**

Goblet
All Over Diamond	**25.00**
Beautiful Lady	**35.00**
Block & Circle	**30.00**

Cruet, Bull's Eye, no stopper, New England Glass Co, 1850s, 5" h, $95.00.

Cape Cod	**55.00**
Excelsior, barrel shape, flint	**75.00**
Feather	**65.00**
Giant Prisms with Thumbprint Band, flint	**145.00**
Greek Key	**45.00**
Herringbone	**45.00**
King's Crown, ruby stained	**45.00**
Liberty Bell	**30.00**
Loganberry and Grape	**20.00**
Minerva	**120.00**
Mitred Diamond Point	**28.00**
New England Pineapple, flint	**65.00**
New Jersey, gold trim	**40.00**
Pennsylvania, gold trim	**30.00**
Pleat and Panel	**35.00**
Red Block, set of eight	**300.00**
Rose in Snow, amber	**45.00**
Shell and Tassel	**70.00**
Stippled Peppers	**45.00**
Twisted Stem	**30.00**

Goblet, Dakota pattern, States Series, etched floral design, US Glass, early 1890s, $35.00.

Creamer, Pillow in Oval, c1890, $25.00.

Westward Ho!	95.00
Wildflower, amber	40.00
Yale	35.00
Zig-Zag.	28.00

Honey Dish

Bull's Eye with Diamond Point	25.00
Inverted Fern, flint, 3½" d.	35.00
Oregon #1	10.00

Ice Bucket

Block and Fan.	45.00
Champion.	40.00

Ice Cream Dish, Esther, individual size,

green, gold trim	55.00

Jelly Compote

Feather	35.00
Jewel and Loop.	30.00
Pennsylvania, gold trim	50.00

Lamp, oil

Cable, glass base	135.00
Heart and Thumbprint, green	275.00
Moon and Star	140.00
Torpedo, finger.	125.00

Lemonade Pitcher

Bull's Eye and Fan	55.00
Pavonia	125.00

Marmalade Jar, cov

Butterfly and Spray	75.00
Classic.	350.00
Log Cabin.	275.00
Viking.	175.00

Milk Pitcher

Cape Cod	65.00
Dahlia, vaseline	70.00
Eyewinker.	70.00
Rose Sprig, amber.	80.00
Torpedo	95.00

Mug

Basketweave, apple green.	40.00
Bird and Owl	80.00
Heart Band, ruby stained, Oxford, MI, souvenir	40.00

Nappy

Bird and Strawberry, colored	65.00
Galloway, rose stained	50.00

Olive Dish

Beaded Grape.	20.00
Illinois	18.00
Thousand Eye, amber	40.00

Pickle Dish

Aegis	18.00
Lily of the Valley, scoop shape	20.00
Maryland	15.00
Utah	15.00

Pickle Castor, silverplated frame

Daisy and Button with V Ornament, vaseline.	100.00
Feather	145.00
Shell and Tassel, orig Tufts sq dec frame, sq cover, and tongs	165.00

Plate

Dahlia, handles, amber, 9" d	35.00
Dart, 7" d	35.00

Fleur de Lis and Drape, 8" d	12.00
Horseshoe, 8" d	75.00
Marsh Pink, 10" sq	65.00
Wheat and Barley, handles, 9" d. . .	22.50
Willow Oak, amber, 9" d	36.00
Platter, Deer and Pine Tree, apple green, 8 × 13".	85.00

Punch Cup

Fandango	12.00
Kentucky.	7.00
Memphis, gold trim.	10.00
Paneled Thistle	20.00
Wisconsin.	10.00

Relish

Bull's Eye	25.00
Rose Sprig, boat shape, amber	35.00

Salt and Pepper Shakers, pr

Austrian, dredge lids	175.00
Beaded Grape.	48.00
Missouri, emerald green	90.00

Salt, master

Bull's Eye with Diamond Point, cov	100.00
Eureka, flint.	18.00
Jacob's Ladder	20.00

Sauce

Bull's Eye and Daisy	20.00
Cherry.	15.00
Dahlia, amber.	15.00
King's #500, Dewey Blue, gold trim	35.00
Zipper.	12.00

Spooner

Aegis.	15.00
Cherry Thumbprint, ruby stain, gold trim	75.00
Feather	35.00
Flying Swan, Challinor's, butter-scotch slag	125.00
Ohio, etched.	40.00
Ruby Thumbprint, etched	65.00
Thousand Eye, amber	52.00
Sugar, open, Bleeding Heart, purpling	35.00

Sugar, cov

Anthemion	25.00
Bull's Eye and Daisy, handled.	25.00
Cherry Thumbprint, ruby stain, gold trim	45.00
Flying Swan, Challinor's, butter-scotch slag	185.00
Lacy Valance	25.00
Magnolia, frosted	45.00
Memphis, green, gold trim	80.00
Nestor, amethyst.	75.00
Spirea Band, etching	25.00
Three Story	25.00
Torpedo	95.00
Syrup, Adonis, canary yellow	150.00

Table Set, four pieces, cov butter, creamer, spooner, and sugar

Beaded Swag, milk glass, pink flow-ers.	365.00
Egyptian	295.00
Liberty Bell	355.00

Toothpick Holder
  Beaded Grape, green **75.00**
  Delaware, rose, gold trim **75.00**
  Giant Bull's Eye **35.00**
  Medallion Sunburst. **42.50**
  National's Eureka, ruby stained. . . . **110.00**
  Quartered Block **35.00**
  Shoshone, gold trim **45.00**
Tray, Daisy and Button with Amber
  Panels, 11 × 9" oval **135.00**
Tumbler
  Bleeding Heart **37.50**
  Cherry and Plum. **30.00**
  Cherry Thumbprint, ruby stain, gold
  trim **30.00**
  Horn of Plenty, flint **85.00**
  Leaf Medallion, green, gold trim . . . **35.00**
  Peach, green, Northwood, "N" mark **30.00**
  Red Block **35.00**
  Strawberry and Cable **35.00**
  Teardrop and Tassel **55.00**
Tumble-Up, Bull's Eye with Diamond
  Point. **165.00**
Vase
  Cut Log, 16" h **55.00**
  Mardi Gras, trumpet shape, scal-
  loped rim, amber, 8" h **35.00**
  Paneled Thistle, 9¼" h **25.00**
Water Pitcher
  Basketweave, amber **70.00**
  Cane, amber. **85.00**
  Cherry and Plum. **120.00**
  Daisy and Button with "V" Orna-
  ment, amber **95.00**
  Deer Alert. **250.00**
  Flamingo Habitat **125.00**
  Mascotte, etched. **110.00**
  Medallion, amber **70.00**
  Memphis, gold trim. **175.00**
  Teardrop and Tassel, tankard, pur-
  pling, mold mark. **85.00**
  Wildflower, amber **80.00**
Water Set, pitcher and six tumblers
  Cherry Thumbprint, ruby stain, gold
  trim. **225.00**
  Shell and Jewel, sapphire blue **235.00**
Water Tray
  Artichoke **45.00**
  Basketweave, scenic, amber **55.00**
Whiskey
  Ashburton, applied handle **125.00**
  Diamond Point, applied handle . . . **85.00**
Wine
  Arched Ovals **12.00**
  Banded Portland **28.50**
  Bull's Eye and Daisy, emerald green **25.00**
  Cornell, green, gold trim **45.00**
  Currier and Ives **24.00**
  Dewdrop and Rain **12.00**
  Floral Oval **12.00**
  Lady Hamilton **24.00**
  Lattice. **12.00**

Maryland **35.00**
Primrose, amber **25.00**
Sedan **12.00**
The States **32.00**
Three Face **150.00**
Wyoming **85.00**

VICTORIAN GLASSWARE

History: Glassware was popular during the Victorian era for a variety of reasons. First, a wealth of new utilitarian forms ranging from cruets to spooners were introduced. They were adopted universally.

Second, the glass industry utilized mass-production. Glass items were no longer a prerogative of the upper class; they were affordable by everyone.

Third, glass manufacturers produced glass in a wide range of patterns and colors. You did not have to have the same type of glass as your neighbors. Glassware allowed the Victorians to introduce individuality into their home.

Finally, combining glass with inexpensive silver plated frames allowed the creation of a wide variety of elegant pieces, such as pickle castors, that were modest in cost. As a result, a touch of class could be introduced to even the poorest household.

During the Victorian era, the glass industry also produced some of the finest art glass ever made in America. Mount Washington Glass Company (New Bedford, Massachusetts) introduced Burmese, Crown Milano, and Royal Flemish. The New England Glass Works (Boston, Massachusetts) and Hobbs, Brochunier & Co. (Wheeling, West Virginia) manufactured Peachblow. Amberina, cosmos, cranberry, Mary Gregory type, pomona, and satin glass are just a few of the other highly collectible styles of Victorian glassware.

References: William Heacock, Encyclopedia of Victorian Colored Pattern Glass, Antique Publications—*Toothpick Holders from A to Z, Book 1, Second Edition*, (1976, 1992 value update); *Opalescent Glass from A to Z, Book 2* (1981); *Syrups, Sugar Shakers & Cruets, Book 3* (1981); *Custard Glass from A to Z, Book 4* (1980); *U. S. Glass from A to Z, Book 5* (1980); *Oil Cruets from A to Z, Book 6* (1981); *Ruby Stained Glass from A to Z, Book 7* (1986); and, *More Ruby Stained Glass, Book 8* (1987); *1000 Toothpick Holders: A Collector's Guide*, 1977; *Rare and Unlisted Toothpick Holders*, 1984; William Heacock and William Gamble, *Cranberry Opalescent from A to Z, Book 9*, Encyclopedia of Victorian Colored Pattern Glass, Antique Publications, 1981; William Heacock, James Measell, and Berry Wiggins, *Harry Northwood: The Early Years 1881–1900*, Antique Publications, 1990; William Heacock, James Measell, and Berry Wiggins, *Harry Northwood: The*

Wheeling Years 1901–1925, Antique Publications, 1991; William Heacock, James Measell, and Berry Wiggins, *Dugan/Diamond: The Story of Indiana, Pennsylvania, Glass,* Antique Publications, 1993. John A. Shuman III, *The Collector's Encyclopedia of American Art Glass,* Collector Books, 1988, 1991 value update.

Periodical: *Glass Collector's Digest,* PO Box 553, Marietta, OH 45750.

Banana Boat, Grape and Cable, Carnival Glass, marigold, Fenton and Northwood	140.00
Berry Bowl, master	
Chrysanthemum Sprig, Custard Glass, blue, Northwood	595.00
Geneva, Custard Glass, Northwood	135.00
Intaglio, Custard Glass, green, Northwood	195.00
Louis XV, Custard Glass, Northwood	160.00
Berry Set, master bowl, matching serving bowls, Atlas, clear, Northwood, three pcs	90.00
Biscuit Jar, Wavecrest, pale pink ground, multicolored flowers, silverplated handle and cover	200.00
Bonbon, Prisms, Carnival Glass, marigold	60.00
Bowl	
Cherry Chain, Carnival Glass, white, 10½" d	125.00
Good Luck, Carnival Glass, green, piecrust edge, Northwood, 9" d	425.00
Peacock and Grape, Carnival Glass, amethyst, ruffled, Fenton	85.00
Stag and Holly, Carnival Glass, ice green, 10" d, 3 ftd, fluted, Fenton	350.00
Windflower, Carnival Glass, blue, ruffled	65.00
Bread Plate, Last Supper, Goofus Glass, red and gold, grapes and foliage border, 7" w, 11"l	60.00
Bride's Basket	
Peachblow, crimped undulating rim, enameled white flowers, yellow centers, gold-tan branches, ornate silverplate stand, 11" h	550.00
Satin, emerald green, shaded light to dark, enameled dec, ornate ftd silverplate frame, 11¼" h	285.00
Butter Dish, cov	
Argonaut Shell, Custard Glass, Northwood	375.00
Beaded Circle, Custard Glass, Northwood	485.00
Intaglio, Custard Glass, green, Northwood	295.00
Candlesticks, pr	
Crystal, Baccarat, clear, leaf design, Museum collection, reissue of 1860s design, limited to 250 prs, orig box, 10⅞" h	500.00

Grape and Cable, Carnival Glass, marigold, Fenton and Northwood	235.00
Celery Tray, Alaska, Opalescent Glass, vaseline	150.00
Condiment Set, Cranberry Glass, open salt, pepper shaker, mustard pot, silverplated holder, 5½" h	175.00
Cracker Jar, Grape and Cable, Carnival Glass, marigold, Fenton and Northwood	225.00
Creamer	
Atlas, clear, gold trim, Northwood	30.00
Beaded Circle, Custard Glass, Northwood	190.00
Chrysanthemum Sprig, Custard Glass, blue, Northwood	385.00
Louis XV, Custard Glass, Northwood	85.00
Maple Leaf, Custard Glass, Northwood	160.00
Cruet	
Cranberry Glass, enameled white flowers and leaves, applied clear handle, clear bubble stopper, 7½" h	175.00
Diamond Quilted, Satin Glass, yellow, raised pattern, applied frosted handle, faceted clear stopper, 7" h	250.00
Louis XV, Custard Glass, Northwood, orig stopper missing, plastic replacement	175.00
Epergne, Baccarat, four flower holders with cranberry overlay cut to clear, gilt metal holder, 10¾" h	550.00
Finger Bowl, Diamond Quilted, amberina, trefoil rim, 4½" d, Midwestern	125.00
Fruit Bowl, Orange Tree, Carnival Glass, white, ftd, Fenton, 10" d	200.00
Goblet	
Camphor Glass, butterscotch bowl, gold dec, blue ring, red jewels	90.00

Castor Set, five bottles, Gothic Arches pattern, flint glass, pewter standard, attributed to Sandwich Glass, c1860, 10½" h, $235.00.

Pickle Castor, pigeon blood insert, silver-plated frame marked "Quadruple Empire Mfg Co," $275.00.

Diamond Spearhead, Opalescent Glass, vaseline **115.00**
Early American, Duncan **20.00**
Plantation Ivy etch, Heisey **25.00**
Hair Receiver, Camphor Glass, white body, gold scroll dec **50.00**
Jack In The Pulpit Vase, Burmese Glass, rich color, crimped rim, Mt Washington, 7¼" h **345.00**
Jelly Compote, Geneva, Custard Glass, Northwood **80.00**
Lemonade Set, Cranberry Glass, 10¾" h pitcher, six matching glasses, 13¼" d undertray, polychrome floral dec, applied angular amber handles, attributed to Mt Washington **665.00**
Mug
Mary Gregory Glass, white enameled figure of praying girl, amber ribbed ground, applied handle **135.00**
Singing Birds, Carnival Glass, marigold, Northwood, "N" mark **125.00**
Nappy, Cherries, Goofus Glass, red cherries, gold foliage, clear ground **35.00**
Orange Bowl, Rose Marie, Nucut, Imperial, 12" d **48.00**
Pickle Castor
Coin Spot, Cranberry Glass, enamel dec, silverplated holder **225.00**
Hobnail pattern insert, amberina, fancy silverplated frame and cov, Mt Washington **1,100.00**
Plate
Grape and Cable, Carnival Glass, purple, Fenton and Northwood **165.00**
Holly, Carnival Glass
Blue **275.00**
White **180.00**
Powder Jar, Grape and Cable, Carnival Glass, purple, Fenton and Northwood **145.00**

Punch Cup, Grape and Cable, Carnival Glass, marigold, Fenton and Northwood **100.00**
Rose Bowl, Burmese Glass, bronze and gold tinted chrysanthemum blossoms and leaves, gold outlines, rose colored enameled tinted turned in rim with gold accents, Thomas Webb, 3⅜ " d, 3⅜ " h **650.00**
Salt and Pepper Shakers, pr
Chrysanthemum Sprig, Custard Glass, blue, Northwood **395.00**
Geneva, Custard Glass, Northwood **225.00**
Grape and Leaf, Goofus Glass, 4" h **40.00**
Sandwich Server, Diamond Quilted, Black Glass, Imperial, c1930 . . . . . . **40.00**
Sauce Dish
Chrysanthemum Sprig, Custard Glass, blue, Northwood **225.00**
Geneva, Custard Glass, Northwood **40.00**
Gonterman Swirl, Opalescent, blue top **45.00**
Intaglio, Custard Glass, green, Northwood **55.00**
Louis XV, Custard Glass, Northwood **45.00**
Spooner
Beaded Circle, Custard Glass, Northwood **190.00**
Chrysanthemum Sprig, Custard Glass, blue, Northwood **275.00**
Geneva, Custard Glass, Northwood **100.00**
Grape and Gothic Arches, green, gold trim, Northwood **40.00**
Hobnail Opalescent, lavender, ruffled top, ftd **95.00**
Intaglio, Custard Glass, green, Northwood **135.00**
Maple Leaf, Custard Glass, Northwood **160.00**
Sugar Bowl, cov
Chrysanthemum Sprig, Custard Glass, blue, Northwood **465.00**
Intaglio, Custard Glass, green, Northwood **190.00**
Maple Leaf, Custard Glass, Northwood **235.00**
Sugar Shaker, Inverted Thumbprint, amberina, globular, emb floral and butterfly lid, 4" h **400.00**
Syrup Pitcher
Cosmos, Consolidated, 6½" h **120.00**
Swirl and Dot, blue, orig brass top, 6" h **145.00**
Sweet Pea Vase, Black Glass, Cambridge, 7" h, 8½" d **55.00**
Table Set, cov butter, creamer, cov sugar, spooner, Ring Band, Custard Glass, rose dec, Heisey **470.00**
Toothpick Holder
Burmese Glass, two bold blossoms on front, smaller blossom on back, urn shape, Mt Washington, 2¾" h **535.00**

Diamond Quilted, amberina, triple plated holder with pond lilies and leafy stems, 4½" h. **325.00**
Geneva, Custard Glass, Northwood   **300.00**
Ring and Beads, Custard Glass, souvenir **45.00**
Tumbler
  Burmese Glass, shiny finish, eggshell thin body, shading to 1" w band of pastel yellow at base, Mt Washington **375.00**
  Geneva, Custard Glass, Northwood   **55.00**
  Intaglio, Custard Glass, green, Northwood **85.00**
  Palm Beach, Opalescent Glass, vaseline **80.00**
  Stork and Rushes, Carnival Glass, blue **50.00**
Tumble-Up, Mary Gregory Glass, white enameled girl on carafe, boy on tumbler, cranberry ground **400.00**
Vase
  Amberina, deep red shading to rose to yellow, 10" h **195.00**
  Overshot, crimped top, lavender shaded to clear base, applied feet, 7½" h **130.00**
Water Pitcher
  Argonaut Shell, Custard Glass, Northwood **475.00**
  Diamond Peg, Custard Glass, US Glass, hp rose dec **395.00**
  Diamonds, Carnival Glass, marigold **150.00**
  Interior Swirl, Carnival Glass, marigold **175.00**
  Inverted Fan and Feather, Custard Glass, Northwood **650.00**
  Jackson, Custard Glass, Northwood   **275.00**
  Tree Bark, Carnival Glass, smoky marigold **45.00**
  Winged Scroll, Custard Glass, bulbous, Heisey **375.00**
Water Set, pitcher and six tumblers, Grape and Cable, Carnival Glass, pastel, Fenton and Northwood **625.00**

WHIMSIES

History: Glass workers occasionally spent time during lunch or after completing their regular work schedule creating unusual glass objects, known as whimsies, e.g. candy striped canes, darners, hats, paperweights, pipes, witch balls, etc. Whimsies were taken home and given as gifts to family and friends.

Because of their uniqueness and infinite variety, whimsies can rarely be attributed to a specific glass house or glass worker. Whimsies appeared wherever glass was made, from New Jersey to Ohio and westward. Some have suggested that style and color can be used to pinpoint a region or factory, but no one has yet developed an identification key that is adequate.

Glass canes are one of the most collectible types of whimsies. Glass canes range from very short, under one foot, to lengths of ten feet and beyond. They come in both hollow and solid forms. Hollow canes can have a bulb type handle or the rarer "C" or "L" shaped handle. Canes are found in many fascinating colors, with the candy striped being a regular favorite with collectors. Many canes are also filled with varied colored powders, gold and white being the most common, silver being harder to find. Many canes were made to be carried in regional parades organized to display craftsmen's wares. Others were used as candy containers.

References: Joyce E. Blake, *Glasshouse Whimsies*, printed by author, 1984; Joyce E. Blake and Dale Murschell, *Glasshouse Whimsies: An Enhanced Reference*, printed by author, 1989.

Collectors' Club: The Whimsey Club, 4544 Cairo Drive, Whitehall, PA 18052.

Cane
  Aqua, S-curved handle, twisted shaft, 54½" l **75.00**
  Clear
    Alternating close red, white, and blue spirals, 50" l **175.00**
    Mahogany spiral, int. gilding, 58¾" l **85.00**
    Red, white, and blue twisted spirals, crook handle, England, 47" l **100.00**

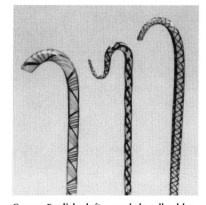

Canes, English, left: crook handle, blue, green, and yellow spirals, crystal casing, 41" h, $110.00; center: twisted crook handle, red, white, and blue spirals, crystal casing, 42" h, $99.00; right: crook handle, red and blue spirals, crystal casing, 43" h, $88.00. Photograph courtesy of Leslie Hindman Auctioneers.

Red, white, and green twisted spirals, crook handle, England,
41" l **85.00**
White, yellow, and mahogany
looping, 59" l **150.00**
Dark Amethyst, hollow, simulated
branch body, raised spirals, right
angle bulbous handle, 36" l..... **135.00**
Gilt Casing, red, white, and blue spi-
rals, knop finial, England, 40" l **120.00**
Darner
Peachblow, glossy finish, c1900, 6" l **225.00**
White Milk Glass, blue loopings,
straight sheared open end **175.00**
Egg, milk glass, cobalt blue and pink
spattering, 2⅜ " h **75.00**
Hatchet
Clear, 8⅝ " l twisted handle, 5⅛ " l
blade.................... **120.00**
Vaseline, raised molded letters
"World's Fair 1893" and "George
Washington Father of this Coun-
try," George Washington relief
bust, sgd "Libbey Glass Co Toledo
Ohio," 7" l **485.00**
Hat Stand, blown, blue-white base,
pink top, pontiled, England, c1850,
14¾" h..................... **215.00**
Muddler, crystal rod, duck crest, 1939
New York World's Fair, 4½" l..... **20.00**
Pear, amber, 5½" h **85.00**
Pipe
Aqua, white spirals entire length,
souvenir of 1876 Philadelphia Ex-
position, 40" l.............. **165.00**
Cranberry, one large band flanked by
two smaller bands on deep

Goblet and Witch Ball, Lutz-type lattice glass, pink, white, and gold design, 7" h goblet, 4" d witch ball, $375.00.

bended stem, white bordered
bowl, c1800, 15" l........... **250.00**
Powder Flask, clear, milk glass loopings, 13" l **225.00**
Rolling Pin, medium sapphire blue,
painted red floral dec and gold inscription "A Present from Newcastle," freeblown, knobbed ends,
c1850, 15" l **175.00**
Witch Ball
Aqua, freeblown, contains paper
flower, leaf, butterfly, and people
cutouts, red, blue, green, and
white int. powder, New England,
1850–80, 9½" d **450.00**
Clear, milk glass loopings, 4" d.... **185.00**
Cobalt Blue, clear blown pedestal
base, 11" h **450.00**

KITCHEN COLLECTIBLES

Family life in rural America focuses around the kitchen. A substantial breakfast at the break of dawn and a robust meal at the end of a day's hard work are standard fare. At the conclusion of the evening meal, it was not uncommon to sit around the table and converse, often for hours. In an agrarian environment, the kitchen table is as important a social center as the living room or parlor.

The kitchen remained a central focal point in the family environment until frozen foods, TV dinners, and microwave ovens freed the family to congregate in other areas of the house during meal time. Initially, food preparation involved both the long and short term. Home canning remained popular through the early 1950s.

Many early kitchen utensils were handmade and prized by their owners. Next came a period of utilitarian products manufactured of tin and other metals. Design began to serve both an aesthetic and functional purpose. Brightly enameled handles and knobs were made to appeal to the busy housewife. With the advent of bakelite and plastic even more color found its way into the kitchen.

Multicolored enameled matchsafes, pot scrubbers, and string holders were not only functional, but advertised a product or service. These early advertising giveaways are prized by country collectors.

The newfangled gadgets and early electrical appliances changed the type and style of kitchen products. Many products became faddish. Electric waffle makers were popular in the 1930s and breakfast was served on special waffle dinnerware sets, complete with serving platters and syrup pitchers. Old hand operated egg beaters were replaced by aerators and mixers.

References: Jane H. Celehar, *Kitchens and Gadgets, 1920 To 1950,* Wallace-Homestead, 1982; Linda Campbell Franklin, *300 Years Of Kitchen Collectibles: An Identification and Value Guide, 3rd Edition,* Books Americana, 1991; *Griswold Cast Iron: A Price Guide,* L–W Book Sales, 1993; Bill and Denise Harned, *Griswold Cast Collectibles: History & Values,* privately printed, 1988; Jan Lindenberger, *Black Memorabilia For The Kitchen: A Handbook and Price Guide,* Schiffer Publishing, 1992; Mary Lou Matthews, *American Kitchen And Country Collectibles,* L–W Promotions, 1984; Kathryn McNerney, *Kitchen Antiques: 1790–1940,* Collector Books, 1991, 1993 value update; Gary Miller and K. M. Scotty Mitchell, *Price Guide To Collectible Kitchen Appliances: From Aerators to Waffle Irons, 1900–1950,* Wallace-Homestead, 1991; Ellen M. Plante, *Kitchen Collectibles: An Illustrated Price Guide,* Wallace-Homestead, 1991; Diane Stoneback, *Kitchen Collectibles: The Essential Buyer's Guide,* Wallace-Homestead, 1994.

Periodicals: *Cast Iron Cookware News,* 28 Angela Ave, San Anselmo, CA 94960; *Kettles n' Cookware,* Drawer B, Perrysburg, NY 14129; *Kitchen Antiques & Collectibles News,* 4645 Laurel Ridge Drive, Harrisburg, PA, 17110.

Reproduction Manufacturers: American Country House, PO Box 317, Davison, MI 48423; Conewago Junction, 805 Oxford Rd, New Oxford, PA 17350; Cumberland General Store, Rte 3, Crossville, TN 38555; Lemee's Fireplace Equipment, 815 Bedford St, Bridgewater, MA 02324; Mathew's Wire & Wood, 654 W Morrison, Frankfort, IN 46041; Matthews Emporium, PO Box 1038, Matthews, NC 28106; McClanahan Country, 217 Rockwell Rd, Wilmington, NC 28405; Old Smithy Shop, Box 336, Milford, NH 03055; Our Home, Articles of Wood, 666 Perry St, Vermillion, OH 44089; Town and Country, Main St, East Conway, NH 04037.

BAKING

History: The Country kitchen is readily acknowledged as the source of nourishing, hearty meals. A Country kitchen isn't complete without a freshly baked pie cooling on the window sill. The smell of freshly baked goods lingers in the minds of many individuals. Homemade bread is a must. Dessert is an integral part of dinner. In fact, dessert products have a habit of showing up at breakfast as well as in the lunch box.

All items associated with baking are collectible, from ingredient packaging to utensils used to serve the end product. Collectors concentrate on three distinct periods: 1850 to 1915, 1915 to 1940, and 1940 to the present. The presence of the original box is extremely important for items made after 1915.

Pieces containing a manufacturer's or patent date marking and highly decorated pieces, either painted or lithographed, are more highly valued than unmarked or plain examples. Many collectors like to use these old implements. Hence, the desirability of pieces that are in working condition. Finally, the category is subject to crazes. Pie birds are the "hot" collectible of the moment.

Collectors' Club: Cookie Cutter Collectors Club, 1167 Teal Road SW, Dellroy, OH 44620; International Society of Apple Parer Enthusiasts, 3911 Morgan Center Road, Utica, OH 43080.

Periodical: *Cookies,* 5426 27th St NW, Washington DC 20015.

Reproduction Craftspersons: *Cookie Cutters—* Michael Bonne, Copper Smith, 11044 N Carthage Pike, Box 177, Carthage, IN 46115; Robert and Sylvia Gerlack, PO Box 213, Emmaus, PA 18049.

Reproduction Manufacturer: *Cookie Cutters—* Gooseberry Patch, PO Box 634, Delaware, OH 43015.

Apple Peeler, wood, hand crank, old dark finish, 7 × 31½"	**140.00**
Apple Slicer, wood and iron, six blades, 19th C, 42" l	**150.00**
Beater, Chicago, motor on top, measuring glass bottom	**25.00**
Biscuit Cutter, tin	
Mennonite, cuts 14 rolls each revolution, 11" l	**25.00**
Rumford Baking Powder adv, single biscuit	**15.00**

Cake Pan, tin, 8½" d, $8.00.

Bread Board, wood, round, carved motto "Give Us This Day Our Daily," 9½" d	50.00
Bread Maker, White House Bread Maker, table clamp, 1902	125.00
Bread Pan, Ideal, tin, two tubes	30.00
Bread Raiser, tin, stamped, ventilated dome lid, 8 quart	40.00
Bread Slicing Box, wood, varnished, 19th C, 13½" l, 5¾" h	65.00
Bridge Pan, Little Slam, cast iron	100.00
Cake Decorator, aluminum and copper, eight design attachments	10.00
Cake Filler, Jaburg Bros, tin, table mount, 1908	30.00
Cake Mold, lamb, cast iron, two pcs, 13" l	95.00
Cake Pan, angel food, darkened tin, faceted sides, Star of David shape	30.00

Cherry Pitter

Enterprise, #16	35.00
Watt, #15	60.00

Chocolate Mold

Hen, folding, tin, two part, 2½"h	105.00
Jack-O-Lantern, marked "U.S.A.," 3¼" h	55.00
Rabbit, standing, 11¼" h	45.00
Rabbits, sitting, three, tin plated steel, folding, two part, 10½" l	50.00
Santa, 7½" h	95.00

Chocolate Mold, stork, #2055, tin, clamp style, 5½" h, $35.00.

Coconut Grater, turned iron shaft, serrated blades, brass and wood handle, mid 19th C, 7" h	95.00

Cookie Board, wood

Animal, simple relief carving, round, refinished, 14½" d	50.00
Animals, fish, fruit, birds, man, and mermaid, fourteen designs, elongated, dark patina, 20 × 5"	360.00
Cat on one side, equestrian figure on other, primitive, worn, age cracks are scarred by old iron repairs on ends, 6½ × 10"	80.00
Grape Clusters, four bunches, elongated, hardwood, dark patina, 19¼ × 3½"	425.00
Man, full figure, carved beech, primitive, metal edging, old patina, minor age cracks, 6¾" w, 18" h	360.00

Cookie Cutter, tin

Bird, long neck, 5" h	40.00
Hoop, hearts, crown, flower, and crescent all contained in circle, 6" d	95.00
Horse, 6½" l	175.00
Stag, stylized, 6½" l	95.00
Cookie Press, tin, star, wood plunger, 10½" l	35.00
Cookie Roller, Guirier, tin, wire, three rollers, orig box, c1930	40.00

Cookie Sheet

Advertising, Betty Crocker Bisquick	10.00
Springerle	110.00
Corn Stick Pan, seven cavities, Griswold #79	35.00
Dough Box, poplar, dovetailed box, mortised and pinned frame, turned legs, 35 × 19 × 27"	660.00

Dough Scraper, wrought iron

Short conical rattle handle, 3½" l	30.00
Heart cutout in blade, minor damage to iron handle, 4" l	110.00
Flour Dredger, tin, domed pierced lid, ftd, strap handle, c1825, 6" h	20.00
Flour Grinder, cast iron, graniteware hopper, wood pusher, late 19th C	65.00

Cookie Cutter, horse, tin, Davis Baking Powder adv, c1920, 3⅝ " l, 3" h, $8.00.

Pie Crimper, brass, 5½" l, $12.00.

Flour Sifter, Kwik, tin, 5 cup, double ended, yellow wood handle	**18.00**
Fruit Baller, hinged cutting ring, red handle, 1920s, 5¼" l	**5.00**
Fruit Press, Enterprise Mfg Co, Philadelphia, cast iron, nickel plated, bowl shaped hopper, table mount, Sept 30, 1879 patent date, 12" h, 11" l	**60.00**
Maple Candy Mold	
Fruit and Foliage design, hardwood, two part, 5½ × 8"	**28.00**
Two Hearts, varnished wood, 3⅛"	**125.00**
Measuring Cup, spun aluminum, Swans Down Cake Flour adv, 1 cup	**15.00**
Measuring Spoons, Towles Log Cabin adv, set of four	**45.00**
Mixing Spoon, metal, slotted bowl, green wood handle, Rumford Baking Powder adv, 10¾" l	**15.00**
Muffin Pan, G F Filley No. 3, cast iron	**100.00**
Nut Grinder, Climax, cast iron and tin, glass jar, screw-on tin hopper, 1940s	**12.00**
Nutmeg Grater, tin cylinder and barrel, wood plunger, 4" l	**85.00**
Pastry Blender, wire, Omar Wonder Flour adv	**8.00**
Pastry Brush, Shaker, turned wood handle, 8¼" l	**120.00**
Pastry Crimper	
Aluminum, Just Right Pie Sealer . . .	**8.00**
Brass, black wood handle	**12.00**
Pastry Cutter, two blades, one wheel, one wedge, red handle	**12.00**
Pastry Roller, turned wood, vining design, soft patina, minor chips on edge of cylinder, 14" l	**225.00**
Peach Parer, David H Whittemore, cast iron, wood board base, two opposing forks, 1860s	**95.00**
Pie Bird	
Big Mouth Bird, white	**30.00**
Chicken	**50.00**

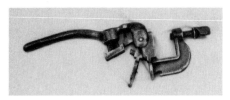

Raisin Seeder, clamp grip, 6¾" l, $225.00.

Duck, pink	**24.00**
Woman, holding pie	**50.00**
Pie Lifter, Shaker, brass ferule, turned wood handle	**50.00**
Pie Pan, tin, adv	
Bowie Pies	**5.00**
Knotts Berry Farm	**6.00**
Mrs Smith's	**5.00**
Popover Pan, Erie, cast iron	**20.00**
Poppyseed Mill, Standard, cast iron, painted turquoise green, spun brass hopper, table clamp, 1890s, 9¼" h	**35.00**
Pudding Mold	
Acorn, two part	**18.00**
Melon, flat lid, c1890	**40.00**
Raisin Seeder, cast iron, marked "Ezy Raisin Seeder, Pat May 21, 1895" and "Scald the Raisins," 6" l	**110.00**
Rolling Pin	
Curly Maple	
15¼" l	**50.00**
21" l	**150.00**
Springerle, 16" l	**30.00**
Spatula, Rumford Baking Powder adv .	**6.00**
Strawberry Huller, A S Bunker, Lawrence, MA, tweezer type, folded spring steel, c1877	**4.00**
Tart Sealer, Tart Master, tin and cast aluminum, wood knob handle, spring loaded, 1938 patent date . . .	**18.00**
Wafer Iron, cast and forged iron, heart shaped wafer, 29½" l	**250.00**

CANNING

History: The bountiful harvest is a common theme in Country collecting. However, a bountiful harvest meant plenty of hard work, especially for the Country housewife. The products of one harvest had to last until the next. Further, one had to plan ahead, laying away extra in case the next year's returns were insufficient.

Canning, also known as jarring, is labor intensive. Time passed quicker and more was accomplished when extra hands were available. Canning bees, similar to quilting bees, were common occurrences. Most canning parties consisted of the women from one's extended family. Often the group moved from one home to another during a harvest season.

An innovative Philadelphia glass maker, Thomas W. Dyott, began promoting glass canning jars in 1829. John Landis Mason patented the screw type canning jar on November 30, 1858. The progress of the American glass industry and manufacturing processes can be studied through fruit jars. Early handmade jars show bits of local history.

Many ways were devised to close the jars securely. Lids of fruit jars can be a separate collectible, but most collectors feel it is more desirous to have a complete fruit jar. Closures can be as simple as a cork or wax seal. Other closures include zinc or glass lids, wire bails, metal screw bands, and today's rubber sealed metal lids.

Many fruit jar collectors base their collections on a specific geographical area, others on one manufacturer or one color. Another way to collect fruit jars is by patent date. Over 50 different types bear a patent date of 1858. Note: The patent date does not mean the jar was made in that year.

Most canning collectors do not limit their focus to fruit jars. Canners, funnels, sealing equipment, and cooking thermometers also are sought.

References: Alice M. Creswick, *The Fruit Jar Works, Volume I* and *Volume 2,* published by author; Alice M. Creswick, *Red Book No. 6: The Collector's Guide To Old Fruit Jars,* published by author, 1990; Dick Roller, *Standard Fruit Jar Reference,* published by author, 1987; Dick Roller, *Supplementary Price Guide to Standard Fruit Jar Reference,* published by author,1987; Bill Schroeder, *1000 Fruit Jars: Priced And Illustrated,* 5th Edition, Collector Books, 1987.

Collectors' Clubs: Ball Collectors Club, 22203 Doncaster, Riverview, MI 48192; Midwest Antique Fruit Jar & Bottle Club, PO Box 38, Flat Rock, IN 47234.

Periodicals: *Bottles & Extras,* PO Box 154, Happy Camp, CA 96039; *Fruit Jar Newsletter,* 364 Gregory Avenue, West Orange, NJ 07052.

Note: Fruit Jars listed are machine made unless otherwise noted.

Canner, Mudge's Patent Canner, tin and copper, Biddle-Gaumer Co, late 1880s 225.00
Canning Rack, wire, rect, used in two-hole boiler 12.00
Corn Dryer, twisted wire, hanging ring at top, c1910 .... 12.00
Fruit Dryer, tin frame, wire screen, three shelves, removable trays, Arlington Oven Dryer, 9" h 135.00
Fruit Jar
American Fruit Jar, light green, handmade, glass lid, wire bail, 1 quart 100.00
Atlas E–Z Seal, cornflower blue, 1 pint 10.00
Atlas Mason, aqua, handmade, zinc lid, 1 quart 25.00
Ball, Sure Seal, blue, smooth lip, lightning beaded neck seal 4.00
BBGM Co, green, glass lid, wire bail, Patent Nov 30, 1858, 1 quart ... 35.00
Blue Ribbon, clear, glass lid, wire clip, 1 quart................. 7.50
Clark Fruit Jar Co, blue, handmade, glass lid emb "Clark Fruit Jar Cleveland," 1 quart 7.50

Fruit Jar, 1½ qt, clear, emb "Whitney, Mason, Pat'd 1858," $4.50.

Crown Cordial & Extract Co, New York, clear, ½ pint 10.00
Dexter, aqua, ground lip glass insert and screw band, patented Aug 8, 1865 .... 35.00
Eagle, green, handmade, wax seal, 1 quart 75.00
Economy, amber, metal lid, spring clip, 1 pint................. 5.00
Empire, aqua, handmade, stopper neck, name emb in arch, 1 quart 215.00
Faxon, blue, 1 quart 8.00
Forster Jar, clear, smooth lip, glass insert and screw band 8.00
Garden Queen, 1 quart 4.00
Good House Keepers, clear, machine made, zinc lid, 2 quart.... 2.00
Green Mountain Ga Co, green, glass lid, wire bail, 1 pint......... 15.00
Hazel Atlas E Z Seal, clear, smooth lip 10.00
Hoosier, aqua, handmade, threaded glass lid, emb "Hoosier Jar," 1 quart 315.00
Independent, aqua, handmade, glass screw lid, 1 quart............ 40.00
Ivanhoe, clear, metal lid, name on bottom, 1 quart 4.00
Kerr, sky blue, smooth lip, two pc lid, 1 pint..................... 25.00
Lamont Glass Co, aqua, glass lid, 1 pint 35.00
Lightning Putnam #31, aqua, bail handle.................... 10.00
Lyon Jar, clear, patented Apr 10, 1900 .... 2.00
Mason
Aqua, Midget, 1858.......... 25.00
Green, handmade, zinc lid, emb "S Mason's Patent 1858," 1 quart 4.50
Mason's Improved, light green, 1 quart 15.00

Millville Atmospheric, aqua, 1861, 1 quart **40.00**
Mother Jar, aqua, emb "Mother Jar, Trade Mark, R E Tonque & Bros Inc, Phila Pa," 1 quart **35.00**
Ohio, clear, handmade, zinc lid, emb "Ohio Quality Mason," 2 1 quart **12.00**
Pearl, aqua, handmade, emb "The Pearl," 1 quart **25.00**
Protector, aqua, six-sided, name emb vertically, 1 quart **40.00**
Putnam, amber, 1 quart **15.00**
Regal, clear, handmade, glass lid, emb "Regal" in oval, 1 quart **3.00**
Reverse Ball, aqua, 1 quart **5.00**
Schram Automatic Sealer, aqua, name emb in script, 1 quart **10.00**
Smalley & Co, amber, rect, arched shoulders, tin lid, patented Apr 7, 1896, 2 quart **38.00**
Smalley's Royal Trademark Nu-Seal, 1 pint **10.00**
Swayzee's Improved, green. **12.00**
Texas Mason, clear, 1 quart **15.00**
Tropical, clear, machine made, zinc lid, name emb in script, 1 quart **2.75**
Wan-Eta Cocoa, Boston, amber, zinc lid, 1 pint **6.00**
Yeoman's Fruit Bottle, aqua, wax cork closure **45.00**
Fruit Jar Holder, wire, 6" h **6.00**
Fruit Jar Lifter
E–Z Lift, iron **4.00**
Mason Jar Sealer and Opener, cast iron frame, steel blade, adjustable leather strap, c1912 . . . . **18.00**
Simplex, metal, Gorman Mfg Co, late 19th C. **15.00**
Fruit Jar Wrench
Presto, iron, Cupples Co, orig box, 20th C. **7.50**
Speedo, cast metal, geared mechanical, c1900. . . . . **10.00**
Wilson's, cast iron, Wilson Mfg Co, early 20th C **12.00**
Funnel
Enamelware, wide untapered neck, 5" l, c1900 . . . . **12.00**
Tin, ring handle, large mouth, c1900 **8.00**
Herb Drying Rack, wood, orig blue paint, 28" l, 19th C **425.00**
Jelly Glass, pressed glass, clear **3.00**
Scale, spring, cast iron and stamped sheet iron, Simmons Hardware Co, 20th C **28.00**
Soldering Iron, copper, bullet shaped head, iron wire shaft, wooden handle, 8" l, late 19th C **8.00**
Thermometer, jelly, knife shaped, calibrated metal plate, glass tube, ta-

pered turned wooden handle, hanging loop, Taylor Instrument Co, NY, mid 1930s. **7.50**

CLEANING AND WASHDAY

History: Living and working in a rural environment was dirty business. Field work and feeding the animals generated large amounts of dust. Wet weather meant mud and plenty of it.

The housewife faced a never-ending battle to keep things clean. Dusting was a daily chore. Washday was not limited to Mondays on most farms. Rural society always has judged wives on how they kept house and family. Women's liberation may have changed some things, but not this.

Many individuals who decorate in Country favor the weathered look. Cleaning and washday material fills the bill. These implements were meant to be used, used hard, and to last. Try beating a rug with a carpet beater.

Because electricity came late to many rural areas, most pre-1940 implements are hand powered. The number of variants within each product are overwhelming. Mail order catalogs are a great research source to determine what was available during a given time period.

Reference: Linda Campbell Franklin, *300 Years of Housekeeping Collectibles*, Books Americana, 1992.

Reproduction Craftspersons: *Brooms*—Bill Case, Mellow Mtn Broom Co, 3190 Raulerson Rd E, St Augustine, FL 32092; Kenelm Winslow III, 252 Clover Hill Rd, Newburg, PA 17240; *Wood Ironing Boards*—John and Naomi Olivera, 201 Crest Dr, Havelock, NC 28532.

Reproduction Manufacturers: Ogle's Broom Shop, 808 Crest View Dr, Gatlinburg, TN 37738.

Carpet Beater
Wicker, knot design, 35" l **28.00**
Wire, braided loop, turned wood handle, c1905, 30" l **25.00**
Clothes Dasher
Rapid Vacuum Washer, heavy tin, wood handle, c1920 . . . . **45.00**
Ward Vacuum Washer **35.00**
Clothes Dryer, wood, folding **20.00**
Drying Rack, pine, two mortised and pinned bars, block feet with some damage, old dark green repaint, 20" w, 33" h **150.00**
Dusting Brush, horsehair, turned wood handle, 9" l **20.00**
Dust Pan
Graniteware, gray, speckled **100.00**
Pine, lollipop handle, tapered lip, painted gray-blue, c1840, 14" w **130.00**
Fly Trap, Sus-Ket-Vim, orig instructions **28.00**

Sad Iron, round back, 5¾" l, 4½" h, $20.00.

Iron
Fluter, Empire Fluter, Heinz & Munschauer, Buffalo, NY, nickel plated cast iron, wood handle, hinged base plate, two heating plates, 2½" d roller, 6¾" l base **110.00**
Goffering, iron and brass, heavy metal, good detail, 12¾" h **110.00**
Ironing Board, poplar, folding, one board top, four turned legs, old green paint on base, 59½" l, 30" h **150.00**
Laundry Basket, woven splint
Oblong, ribbed, open rim handles, damage, 24" l, 20" w, 11" h **95.00**
Rectangular, 31" l, 21" w, 10" h ... **75.00**
Laundry Dryer, wood, rect press trestle, driven by metal gears, X-shaped stretcher base, worn leather straps, early 20th C, 15" l, 11" h **800.00**
Mouse Trap, wire mesh, 9" l **45.00**
Soap Box, Fun-To-Wash, full color illus, black Mammy wearing red bandanna, early 1900s, 3¼" h **25.00**
Soap Saver, tin frame, twisted wire handle, hanging loop, wire mesh container, 3½ × 2½", 7" l handle **20.00**
Sprinkler Bottle
Chinaman, Cleminson **45.00**
Dog, white and black **60.00**

Wash Boiler, cov, copper, orig paper label with Lisk adv, wood handles, 26" w, 12" d, 16" h, $82.50. Photograph courtesy of James D Julia, Inc.

Elephant **45.00**
Glass, clear, mold blown........ **18.00**
Myrtle..................... **75.00**
Siamese Cat, ceramic **30.00**
Turtle, McCoy................ **25.00**
Tin, Johnson's Wax, powdered wax **30.00**
Washboard
Glass
Cupples Co, wood frame....... **25.00**
Midget-Washer, wood frame, orig label, 6" w, 8½" h **12.00**
Tin, bentwood frame........... **55.00**
Zinc, The Zinc King, wood frame **15.00**
Washing Machine, tin tub, wood dasher, iron crank, 1883 .... **175.00**
Wash Stick, wood, 36" l **12.00**
Whisk Broom
Advertising, Whiskbroom Cigars, cigar shaped................. **30.00**
Mammy Handle, wood, 4½" l..... **18.00**
Wringer Washer, copper bottom tub **180.00**

COOKBOOKS

History: Among the earliest Americana cookbooks are *The Frugal Housewife; or, Complete Woman Cook* by Susanna Carter, published in Philadelphia in 1796 and *American Cookery* by Amelia Simmons, published in Hartford, Connecticut in 1796. Cookbooks of this era are crudely written, for most cooks could not read well and measuring devices were not yet refined.

Other types of collectible cookbooks include those used as premiums or advertisements. This type is much less expensive than the rare 18th century books.

References: Bob Allen, *A Guide to Collecting Cookbooks and Advertising Cookbooks: A History of People, Companies, and Cooking*, Collector Books, 1990, 1993 value update; Mary Barile, *Cookbooks Worth Collecting*, Wallace-Homestead, 1993; Mary-Margaret Barile, *Just Cookbooks!—The only directory for cookbook collectors*, Heritage Publications (PO Box 335, Arkville, NY 12406); Linda J. Dickinson, *Price Guide to Cookbooks and Recipe Leaflets*, Collector Books, 1990, 1993 value update; Linda Campbell Franklin, *300 Years of Kitchen Collectibles, 3rd Edition*, Books Americana, 1991.

Collectors' Club: Cook Book Collectors Club of America, PO Box 56, St James, MO 65559.

Periodicals: *Cookbook Collectors' Exchange*, PO Box 32369, San Jose, CA 95152; *Just Cookbooks!* PO Box 642, Arkville, NY 12406.

Adirondack Country Cookbook, Colton, NY, 1987, 206 pgs **5.00**
All About Baking, 1937, 144 pgs, hard cov **12.00**

Aladdin's Lamp at Mealtimes, Premier Coffee, 1927, 47 pgs 2.00
Arm & Hammer Soda Valuable Recipes, 1900, 32 pgs 6.00
Art of Cookery Made Plain & Easy, Glasse, 1799 . . . .   170.00
Art of Making Bread at Home, NW Yeast, c1930, 28 pgs, black and white cov 4.00
Aunt Ellen, Griswold, 1928 . . . .   15.00
Berks County Cookbook, Pennsylvania Dutch Recipes, c1945, 48 pgs 6.00
Bewley's Best Bakes Better 10.00
Biscuits for Salads, National Biscuit, 1926, 8 pgs 2.00
Butterick Book of Recipes & Household Helps, 1927, 256 pgs, hard cov . . .   5.00
Calumet Baking Powder Baking Book, 1931 . . . .   4.00
Central Adirondack Cook Book, American Legion Auxiliary, 1934 . . . .   5.00
Ceresota Flour, 1930s, 32 pgs 18.00
Choice Cookery, F Owen, 1889 . . . . .   40.00
Choice Recipes, Miss Parola, 1895 . . .   15.00
Compendium of Cooking & Knowledge, 1890 . . . .   15.00
Congress Cookbook, Congress Yeast Powder, 1899, 80 pgs 5.00
Continental Cookery for the English Table, Siepen, 1915, 1st ed 22.00
Cook Not Mad, or Rational Cookery, Watertown, 1831 . . . .   200.00
Cookbook of Useful Household Hints, F Owens, 1883 . . . .   25.00
Cook's Book, KC Baking Powder, 1933   3.00
Cottolene Shortening Recipes, 1905 . .   15.00
Crown Cork & Seal Canning Book, 1936 . . . .   5.00
Dairy Cookbook, R Berolzheimer, 1941 . . . .   5.00
Davis Cookbook, Davis Baking Powder, 1904, 62 pgs 6.00
Delineator Cookbook, Delineator Home Institute, 1928, 788 pgs, hard cov 28.00
Down on the Farm Cookbook, H Worth, 1943, 322 pgs 10.00
Dr King's New Discovery Electric Bitters Prize Cookbook, 1900 . . . .   15.00
Durkee Famous Food Cookbook, Century of Progress, 1933 . . . .   5.00
Economical Cook Book — All-Round Cookery & Hints, C Doring, 1929 . .   15.00
Economy in Food, M Wellman, 1918, 36 pgs, hard cov 5.00
Edna Eby Heller's Dutch Cookbook, 1953, 64 pgs 5.00
18 Unusual Recipes, Jack Frost Sugar, 1930 . . . .   2.00
Eline's Old Style Cocoa, c1910 . . . . .   5.00
Elsie's Cookbook, Borden's, 374 pgs, hard cov 9.00

My Meat Recipes, The National Live Stock and Meat Board, 48 pages, color cov, black and white illus, 1926, 5½ × 8", $15.00.

Encyclopedia of Practical Cookery, T Garrett, c1890, hard cov 180.00
Feeding the Child from Crib to College, Wheatena, 1928, 44 pgs 12.00
Ficher's Blend Baking Book, 1941, 164 pgs 4.00
55 Ways to Save Eggs, Royal Baking, 1917, 22 pgs 3.00
Fruit and Their Cookery, H Nelson, 1921 . . . .   18.00
Gold Medal Flour Cook Book, 1917, 74 pgs 10.00
Good Housekeeping — New Ways to Handle Housework, 1924 . . . .   8.00
Grand National, 1928 . . . .   10.00
Grand Union Cookbook, M Compton, 1902, 322 pgs 22.00
Granite Ironware Cookbook, 1887 . . .   90.00
How's & Why's of Cooking, 1936, 252 pgs 6.00
Jell-o — Polly Put the Kettle On, 1923, Maxfield Parrish illus 50.00
Karo Syrup, 1910, 47 pgs, Leyendecker cov 25.00
Kerr Home Canning, Kerr, 1943, 56 pgs   15.00
Kickapoo Indian Medicine Co. Cookbook, 1891 . . . .   9.00
Larkin Company Cookbook, 1908 . . .   12.00
Lippincott's Housewifery, L Balderston, 1919 . . . .   35.00
Magic Baking Powder, 32 pgs 16.00
Mary Dunbar's Favorite Recipes, Jewel Tea, 1936, 78 pgs 8.00
Maxwell House Coffee, 1927, 22 pgs .   7.00
Maytag Dutch Oven Cookbook, 49 pgs   5.00
Milk and Its Place in Good Cookery, Borden, 1926, 92 pgs, hard cov . . .   5.00
Monarch Cookbook, 1905, hard cov   12.00
Nunsuch Mincemeat, c1915, 28 pgs   3.00
Occident Flour, 1936, 24 pgs 5.00

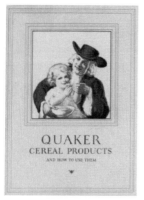

Quaker Cereal Products And How To Use Them, 56 pages, color cov and illus, 1927, 5 × 7", $17.50.

100 Centennial Recipes, Flour Mills Texas Centennial Expo, 1936, 32 pgs	**4.00**
100 Tested Crisco Recipes, Crisco, 1906	**6.00**
Our Favorite Recipes, LFP Church, Washington, c1950, 65 pgs	**5.00**
Pillsbury Cookbook, 1914, 122 pgs	**25.00**
Prudence Penny's Cookbook, 1939, hard cov	**8.00**
Pure Food, 1907	**8.00**
Pyrex Prize Recipes, 1953, 128 pgs	**5.00**
Quality Grocer, March 1931, 24 pgs	**11.00**
Ransom's Family Receipt Book, 1904, 32 pgs	**6.00**
Rockie Mountain Cookery, Norton, 1903	**40.00**
Royal Baker & Pastry, 1911	**20.00**
Rumford Baking Powder Cookbook, 1911, 32 pgs, girl in green	**17.00**
Rumford Cookbook, Fannie Farmer, 1922, plain red and black cov, 46 pgs	**8.00**
Science of Food & Cookery, H Anderson, c1926, hard cov	**18.00**
Secrets of the Jam Cupboard, Certo, 1932, 23 pgs	**3.00**
Sleepy Eye Flour Mills Cookbook, Old Sleepy Eye in center	**300.00**
Spry Shortening Cookbook, Aunt Jenny's Favorite Recipes, 1930s, 50 pgs, color illus	**12.00**
Successful Preserving with Kold-pak Rubber Jars, 1917, 16 pgs	**5.00**
Teddy Bear Baking School, Fleischmann, 1906	**25.00**
Text-book of Cooking, C Greer, 1915, 431 pgs	**15.00**
13 Colonies Cookbook, A Donovan, 1975, 270 pgs, hard cov	**8.00**
Treaties on Cake Making, Standard Brands, 1935, 468 pgs	**12.00**

Universal Cookbook, J Taylor, 1888, 185 pgs	**10.00**
Vaughn Feed Store — Vegetable Cookbook, 1919	**7.00**
Virginia Housewife Methodical Cook, Randolph, 1831, 1st ed	**300.00**
Watkin's Almanac Home Doctor and Cookbook, Watkins, 1932, 92 pgs	**5.00**
White House Cookbook, F Gillette, 1889	**100.00**
Whole Wheat Way to Better Meals, Shredded Wheat, 1940	**5.00**
Women's Temperance Kitchen Wall Cookbook, 1888, 27 pgs	**45.00**

COOKIE JARS

History: Cookie jars, colorful and often whimsical, are one of the fastest growing categories in the collectibles field. Many cookie jars have been made by more than one company and as a result can be found with different marks. This resulted from mergers or splits of manufacturers, e.g., Brush-McCoy which is now Nelson McCoy. Molds were also traded and sold among companies.

Cookie jars often were redesigned to reflect newer tastes. Hence, the same jar may be found in several different style variations.

Cookie jars are subject to chips and flaking paint. Collectors should concentrate on jars which have their original lid and are in very good condition or better. Learn to identify makers' marks and codes. Do not fail to include some of the contemporary manufacturers in your collection.

Above all, ignore the prices and hype associated with the cookie jars sold at the Andy Warhol sale in 1988. Neither is realistic.

References: John W. Humphries, *Humphries Price Guide To Cookie Jars,* published by author, 1992; Harold Nichols, *McCoy Cookie Jars: From The First To The Last,* Nichols Publishing, 1991; Fred and Joyce Roerig, *Collector's Encyclopedia of Cookie Jars,* Book I (1990, 1993 value update), Book II (1994), Collector Books; Mike Schneider, *The Complete Cookie Jar Book,* Schiffer Publishing, 1991; Ermagene Westfall, *An Illustrated Value Guide To Cookie Jars,* Book I (1983, 1993 value update), Book II (1993), Collector Books.

Periodicals: *Cookie Jarrin',* RR2, Box 504, Walterboro, SC 29488; *Crazed Over Cookie Jars,* PO Box 254, Savanna, IL 61074.

Museum: The Cookie Jar Museum, Lemont, IL.

Abingdon Pottery	
Hobby Horse	**250.00**
Jack-O-Lantern, #674	**200.00**
Little Miss Muffet, #622	**200.00**
Little Old Lady, green, #471	**175.00**

Train, #651 . . . .   100.00
Wigwam 950.00
Windmill, #678 . . . .   230.00
American Bisque
    Basket of Cookies 50.00
    Bear and Beehive, #804 . . . .   135.00
    Boy Pig 60.00
    Cat 65.00
    Chick, yellow 65.00
    Churn Boy 125.00
    Cow Jumped Over the Moon, #806   140.00
    Dutch Boy with sail boat, gold but-
        tons 200.00
    Feed Sack 40.00
    Jack-In-The-Box 95.00
    Kittens on Yarn 65.00
    Lady Pig, gold trim 80.00
    Lantern, black and yellow 50.00
    Oak Bucket, yellow dipper finial . .   35.00
    Paddle Boat 130.00
    Pennsylvania Dutch Girl 145.00
    Pig-in-Poke 65.00
    Pig, strawberries 95.00
    Recipe Jar 135.00
    Saddle 100.00
    Tortoise and Hare, #803 . . . .   125.00
    Train 40.00
Brayton
    Animal Cookies 65.00
    Calico Dog, red 100.00
Brayton Laguna
    Dutch Lady 180.00
    Gingerbread House 60.00
    Grandma 165.00
    Gypsy Woman 150.00
    Mammy, red dress, #8 . . . .   600.00
Brush
    Davy Crockett 195.00
    Clown, yellow pants, #W22 . . . . . .   140.00
    Cow, black and white, #W10 . . . . .   475.00
    Crock, green
        "Cookies" 40.00
        Raised tulip design 50.00
    Formal Pig, black 120.00
    Granny, holding rolling pin, #W19   115.00
    Hen on Nest 100.00
    Hobby Horse 375.00
    House, gray, #W31 . . . .   65.00
    Humpty Dumpty, wearing beanie . .   245.00
    Lantern 65.00
    Owl, gray and white 100.00
    Raggedy Ann, #W16 . . . .   150.00
    Squirrel on Log 80.00
California Originals
    Christmas Tree, #873 . . . .   115.00
    Coffee Grinder, #861 . . . .   30.00
    Cottage, #2754 . . . .   35.00
    Dog 35.00
    Frog, sitting, #2645 . . . .   50.00
    Hen, brown, #1127 . . . .   35.00
    Little Red School House, #869 . . . .   60.00
    Rabbit on Stump 28.00

Raggedy Ann, #859 . . . .   65.00
Scarecrow, #871 . . . .   80.00
Shoe House, #874 . . . .   35.00
Tea Kettle, #737 . . . .   30.00
Cardinal China
    Cookie Sack 30.00
    Old Fashioned Telephone, #311 . . .   50.00
DeForest of California
    Bird House, white roof, 1959 . . . . .   55.00
    Granny Rabbit 35.00
    Owl, wearing night cap, #5537 . . . .   40.00
    Pig Head 45.00
    Pot O Cookies 30.00
    Teddy Bear, 1960 . . . .   30.00
Doranne of California
    Bear, bee finial 45.00
    Cow Jumped Over the Moon, green   100.00
    Eggplant, #CJ31 . . . .   45.00
    Ketchup Bottle, #CJ68 . . . .   45.00
    Milk Carton 40.00
    Mother Goose, yellow, gold trim,
        #CJ16 . . . .   90.00
    Pig with Barrel, white, gold trim,
        #CJ105 . . . .   50.00
    Pumpkin 30.00
    Rocking Horse, white, green and yel-
        low dots, yellow saddle, #J63 . . .   50.00
    Squash, #CJ37 . . . .   35.00
Enesco
    Betsy Ross 165.00
    Little Bo Peep 225.00
    Little Red Riding Hood 225.00
    Snow White 775.00
F & F Mold & Die Works
    Keebler Elf 125.00
    Mammy, black face, red dress 200.00
Five Bridges Inc, Pepperidge Farm
    cookie bag 75.00
Gilner
    Gingerbread Boy 70.00
    Rooster, crowing, brown, #G622   40.00
    Tree Stump, green, squirrel finial . . .   40.00

Doranne, Farmyard Follies, hen, blue and white body, marked "CJ-100 of U.S.A. Doranne" on bottom, 10¾" h, $30.00.

Haeger Potteries, Inc.

Cookie Barrel, brown, #R1657	**15.00**
Keebler Tree House, molded elf in window, unmarked	**90.00**

Hall China Co, Eva Ziesel design, Golden Clover pattern, gold trim **70.00**

Harker Pottery Co, Ruffled Tulip pattern **70.00**

Holiday Designs

Almost Home, white house, red roof and trim, 1986	**70.00**
Nestle Toll House Cookie	**125.00**
Orange, #9045	**18.00**
Pillsbury Doughboy, 1973	**75.00**
Pumpkin	**20.00**

Homer Laughlin, ball shape, Pastel Tulips pattern **50.00**

Hull Pottery

Apple, yellow and pink, green leaf	**45.00**
Daisy	**30.00**
Gingerbread Boy, brown.	**95.00**
Little Red Riding Hood, gold trim, #967	**175.00**

Lane and Company

Butter Churn, brown	**30.00**
Indian Chief, 1950	**550.00**

Lefton, Santa. **75.00**

Los Angeles Pottery

Apple, yellow	**30.00**
Bakery, 1956, #XX95	**40.00**

Maddux

Apple Barrel, girl and boy finial, #2112	**65.00**
Cat, going to market	**60.00**
Rabbit, going to market.	**75.00**
Raggedy Ann, #2108	**50.00**

Marcia Ceramics

Mushroom House, red roof.	**30.00**
Tortoise and Hare, brown	**20.00**
Tree Stump, bear with beehive finial	**35.00**

Maurice of California

Basket of Fruit, #FR211	**25.00**
Raggedy Ann, #WD33	**50.00**
Shoe House, green and white	**40.00**

Hull, Big Apple, red and yellow, green leaves, 8″ h, $35.00.

McCoy

Apple, white, #261	**30.00**
Barn, cow in doorway.	**225.00**
Barnum's Animals.	**60.00**
Bean Pot, white, floral dec	**35.00**
Coal Bucket, sleeping cat finial	**125.00**
Coffee Cup	**40.00**
Coffeepot, blue, Pennsylvania Dutch tulips	**40.00**
Cookie Jug, brown and white	**20.00**
Cook Stove, white	**40.00**
Covered Wagon	**75.00**
Ears of Corn, yellow, #275	**35.00**
Fireplace	**90.00**
Flowerpot, red tulips	**70.00**
Grandfather Clock.	**115.00**
Lamb, basketweave	**55.00**
Lantern, black	**60.00**
Mammy	**175.00**
Milk Can, brown, Bicentennial, #7019	**30.00**
Picnic Basket.	**50.00**
Potbelly Stove, black.	**60.00**
Puppy with Sign	**85.00**
Raggedy Ann.	**70.00**
Rooster, yellow and brown	**125.00**
Strawberry, red	**40.00**
Tea Kettle, hammered copper look	**50.00**
Touring Car.	**75.00**
Wishing Well	**40.00**

Metlox

Apple	**35.00**
Bundle of Corn	**40.00**
Calf Head	**80.00**
Clown	**65.00**
Head of Cabbage, rabbit finial.	**70.00**
Humpty Dumpty	**40.00**
Katy Cat, white	**50.00**
Lamb, white, flower necklace	**40.00**
Mammy, white dress with blue trim	**150.00**
Rooster, blue.	**65.00**
Scottie Dog, black.	**175.00**
Sheaf of Wheat	**40.00**
Sir Francis Drake.	**40.00**
Tulip, yellow, green leaves	**55.00**

Morton

Basket of Fruit, #3720	**35.00**
Coffeepot, white, multicolored "Cookies," #3721	**35.00**
Hen, chick finial, green	**50.00**
Pineapple, #3719	**25.00**
Turkey.	**80.00**

Mosaic Tile, Mammy, blue **500.00**

Napco, Little Bo Peep **195.00**

National Silver Co, black chef. **250.00**

N S Gustin

Cat, sleeping, white, floral dec	**45.00**
Granny, holding rolling pin.	**80.00**

Pottery Guild

Balloon Lady.	**85.00**
Dutch Girl.	**50.00**
Red Riding Hood	**125.00**

Purinton Pottery
Apple pattern	**30.00**
Rooster	**120.00**

Randsburg
Asters	**35.00**
Davy Crockett	**125.00**

Red Wing
Banana Bunch, yellow	**40.00**
Barrel Jar, yellow, red flowers and trim	**75.00**
Chef, yellow	**60.00**
Rooster, green, #249	**75.00**
Stoneware Jar, salt glazed, cattails and "Cookies"	**135.00**

Regal China
Cat, white, gold trim	**150.00**
Dutch Girl, red hat, blue dress	**150.00**
Hobby Horse	**275.00**
Quaker Oats	**170.00**
Tulip Jar, gold trim	**50.00**

Robinson Ransbottom
Hootie Owl	**75.00**
Dutch Boy, #423	**80.00**
Old King Cole	**100.00**

Roseville
Clematis, brown, #3–8	**135.00**
Freesia, green, #3–8	**175.00**

Shawnee
Basket of Fruit, #84	**120.00**
Corn King, #66	**100.00**
Corn Queen, #66	**135.00**
Cottage, #6	**200.00**
Drummer Boy	**150.00**
Kraft Marshmallow Bear	**175.00**
Puss N' Boots	**150.00**
Smiley Pig, sweet clover	**165.00**
Winnie Pig, gold trim	**200.00**

Sierra Vista
Rooster, 1958	**75.00**
Toadstools, 1952	**35.00**
Tug Boat	**100.00**
Stanford Pottery, red tomato, green worm finial	**30.00**

Robinson-Ransbottom, Sheriff Pig, brown hat, unmarked, 12½" h, $40.00.

Starnes of California
Noah's Ark	**120.00**
Old Fashioned Telephone, white and black	**60.00**

Treasure Craft
Cactus, green	**45.00**
Cookie Barn	**30.00**
Cookie Chef	**50.00**
Covered Wagon, brown	**35.00**
Grandma, blue dress	**50.00**
Hobo	**45.00**
Kitten with Goldfish Bowl, gray and white	**35.00**
Noah's Ark	**40.00**
Old Radio	**45.00**
Potbelly Stove, brown	**35.00**
Rooster	**40.00**
Stagecoach	**65.00**
Watering Can, white, roses dec	**50.00**

Twin Winton
Bucket, #59	**40.00**
Butter Churn	**35.00**
Cook Stove	**85.00**
Covered Wagon, "Cookie Wagon"	**75.00**
Mammy	**95.00**
Mother Goose, 1964	**45.00**
Persian Kitten, #63	**45.00**
Potbelly Stove	**40.00**
Raggedy Andy, sitting on drum	**60.00**

Watt Pottery
Apple pattern, bean pot shaped, #503	**85.00**
Bleeding Heart pattern, bean pot shaped, #76	**75.00**
"Goodies," white jar with green bands and red lettering, #72	**120.00**

EGG AND DAIRY

History: Most farms were self-sufficient. Even grain farmers kept a cow and flock of chickens to meet their need for dairy products. What was not used on the farm was sold for extra income. Many a farming wife bought Christmas presents with the egg money.

Egg and dairy products were both primary and secondary food stuffs. They were an important ingredient in baking. It was necessary to process many products before use. Churning butter was an after-dinner task that often fell to young children. Of course, there was a pleasurable side, especially when the ice cream freezer was brought out.

Butter prints are divided into two categories: butter molds and butter stamps. Butter molds are generally of three-piece construction—the design, the screw-in handle, and the case. Molds both mold and stamp the butter at the same time. Butter stamps are of one-piece construction, sometimes two pieces if the handle is from a separate piece of wood. Stamps are used to decorate the top of butter after it is molded.

References: Paul Dickson, *The Great American Ice Cream Book*, Galahad Books, 1972; Paul Kindig, *Butter Prints and Molds*, Schiffer Publishing, 1986; Ralph Pomery, *The Ice Cream Connection*, Paddington Press, 1975; Wayne Smith, *Ice Cream Dippers: An Illustrated History and Collector's Guide to Early Ice Cream Dippers*, published by author, 1986.

Collectors' Club: The Ice Screamers, PO Box 5387, 1042 Olde Hickory Road, Lancaster, PA 17601.

Periodical: *Creamers*, PO Box 11, Lake Villa, IL 60046; *Cream Separator News*, Rte 3, Box 189, Arcadia, WI 54612; *Eggcup Collectors' Corner*, 67 Stevens Ave., Old Bridge, NJ 08857; *The Udder Collectibles*, HC 73, Box 1, Smithville Flats, NY 13841.

Reproduction Manufacturers: *Butter Churns*—Zimmerman Handcrafts, 254 E Main St, Leola, PA 17540; *General*—Chinaberry General Store, 1846 Winfield Dunn Highway, Sevierville, TN 38762; *Molds*—Holcraft, PO Box 792, Davis, CA 95616; M & M Enterprises, PO Box 185, Atkins, VA, 24311; Olde Mill House Shoppe, Box H, Lancaster, PA 17602.

Butter
  Churn
    Dasher type
      18½" h, mixed woods, brass hoops, North Andover, MA, 19th C **200.00**
      24" h, stave constructed, steel bands, lid and dasher, old red paint **175.00**
      26" h, barrel shape, stave construction, metal bands, turned lid, old dark finish, dasher, some edge damage, 26" h plus handle **225.00**
    Electric, Dazey, 4 quart **85.00**
    Rocker type, wood churn and cradle, red milk paint **250.00**
  Cutter, cast iron, nickel plated, painted, table mount, wire cutter, early 20th C **50.00**
  Fork, wood, painted, five tines, "Mrs Bragg's Butter Fork," late 19th C, 6" l **15.00**
  Merger, Mak-Mor Butter Machine, tabletop glass jar, cast iron frame and gears, metal blades, NY, May 30, 1911 patent date **60.00**
  Mold
    Compote with Fruit, foliage, and vegetables, rect, old varnish, one foot replaced, 4 × 5" **250.00**
    Fish, round, scrubbed finish, cracked case, 3¾" d **350.00**

    Floral, rect, treen, simple four part floral design, removable frame, brass fittings, 5½ × 6" **25.00**
    Pomegranate, 4¾" d, round, cased **45.00**
    Rose, 5 × 8", rect, old varnish finish **75.00**
    Roses and Cherries, rect, old patina, age cracks, 4 × 7" **95.00**
    Swan, 5" d, round, cased, old finish **110.00**
  Paddle
    9½" l, curly maple, key type handle, refinished **165.00**
    10" l, maple, shaped handle with bird's head hook end, scrubbed patina **500.00**
  Print
    Basket of Fruit, round, turned elongated handle, scrubbed with dark stains, 4" d **325.00**
    Bird head hook, curly maple, old finish, 11" l **100.00**
    Bowl of Flowers, round, no handle, stylized flowers in cross hatched crescent shaped bowl, scrubbed, 4" d **50.00**
    Cow, round, one piece turned handle, old patina, 3" d **275.00**
    Eagle, round, one piece turned handle, scrubbed, old small edge repair, 4⅜" d **225.00**
    Flower, round, one piece turned handle, stylized design, old patina, 3½" d **110.00**
    Hook handle, curly maple, worn finish, 11" l.............. **75.00**
    Leaf, round, stylized design, old patina, inserted handle missing, 4⅞" d **85.00**
    Pineapple, round, one piece turned handle, stylized design, scrubbed, 4½" d **165.00**
    Pomegranate and Foliage, round, one piece turned handle, concave surface, old patina, 5⅛" d **250.00**

Butter Stamp, scallop, reeded border, 3½" d, 2⅝" h, $95.00.

Starflower
Paddle shaped, lollipop handle,
primitive design, 9" l **110.00**
Round, lollipop handle, good
worn patina, 7⅜" l **300.00**
Star Hexagon, round, turned fat
handle, scrubbed, wear and
short hairlines, 5½" d **60.00**
Stylized Tulip, scrubbed, 3½" w,
5½" h **110.00**
Tulip, round, turned, scrubbed soft
finish, handle, 4½" d **350.00**
Wheat Sheaf, round, one piece
turned handle, deeply carved,
old yellow patina, 4¼" d **325.00**
Scoop, curly maple, horse head han-
dle, refinished, age crack, 10¼" l   **390.00**
Slicer, Elgin #48, nickel plated iron,
11 cutting wires, enameled base,
c1911, 8½" l, 8½" h **50.00**
Worker, tabletop, wood frame and
gears, bentwood holder, iron
crank handle, 19th C, 13½" h . . .   **300.00**
Cheese
Curd Whipper, spring steel blades,
wood handle, c1880, 24½" l . . .   **75.00**
Drainer, basket, round top, tightly
woven sides, square bottom, two
handles, 19th C, 12½" d, 6" h . . .   **250.00**
Mold, round, wood, carved, pig,
19th C, 12" d **75.00**
Press
Tin cylinder, three legs, pierced
bottom and lower sides, ring
handle, handmade, 19th C,
6⅜" d, 7⅛" h **125.00**
Wood, old green repaint, shoe
feet, 28" l, 31½" h **75.00**
Sieve, heart shaped, punched tin, ftd,
late 19th C, 5¾" w **200.00**
Egg
Basket, wire, c1905, 8" d **25.00**
Beater, Holt, Aug 22, 1899 patent
date. **65.00**
Candler, The Family Egg-Tester, tin
cylinder, pierced, strap handle,
Mar 13, 1876 patent date **30.00**
Lifter, wire **6.00**
Scale
Oakes Mfg Co, painted tin, 7" h   **25.00**
Zenith Egg Grader, #1002, cast
iron, weight and balance, red
and blue, aluminum pan, brass
pointer, early 20th C **30.00**
Timer, Alarm Whistle, aluminum in-
sert, orig box and instructions . . .   **15.00**
Whisk, wire **6.00**
Ice Cream
Carrier, Bradley Ice Cream Cabinet,
oak box, zinc lining, side door for
ice cream storage, lift-off top for
ice, late 19th C, 8½" **250.00**

Egg Beater, transparent green measuring cup, Vidrio Prod. Company, Chicago, IL, $18.00.

Dipper, Mosteller #79 . . . .   **195.00**
Disher, Mayer, adjustable shank . . .   **250.00**
Freezer, Kwik Freeze, galvanized tin,
blue, paper label **50.00**
Mold, pewter
Bride and Groom, Krauss, #627–
K, 20th C **45.00**
Daisy, two part, hinged, late 19th
C, 2½" d **45.00**
George Washington, S & Co #336,
bust profile on hatchet shaped
mold, two part, hinged, early
20th C, 4" h **60.00**
Straw Basket, #598, three part,
early 20th C **35.00**
Turkey, dressed, 5" l **20.00**
Scoop
Dover #20, nickel plated brass,
round bowl, turned wood han-
dle, lever-activated scraper,
1930s, 10½" l **40.00**
Gilchrist #33 . . . .   **145.00**
Indestructo #30, Benedict Mfg
Co, nickel plated brass, round
bowl, wood handle, 1920s,
10½" l **50.00**

Ice Cream Mold, standing Uncle Sam, pewter, E & Co, #1073, $65.00.

Quick and Easy #486, Erie Specialty Co, nickel plated brass, cone shaped bowl, thumb lever, turned wood handle, c1910 .... **75.00**

FOOD PREPARATION

History: A Country housewife cooked, and cooked, and cooked. Just as farming was a seven day a week occupation, so too was cooking. The Country cook was willing to try any labor saving device at least once. This explains why so many mint examples remain with their original box. Not every device worked well.

Many of these implements were mechanical. Collectors prefer examples in working order. Value decreases rapidly if an object is rusted or pitted.

Look for unusual shapes, highly decorated pieces, and examples that obviously have been used but carefully cared for. A marked piece is a plus. Most collections focus on one form and its many variations.

Reproduction Craftspersons: *Utensils*—Horwood's Country House, 4307 Gotfredson Rd, Plymouth, MI 48170; Jonathan Marshall, Blacksmithing, 1310 Westview, East Lansing, MI 48823; Virginia Petty, Whistlin' Whittler, 1684 Three Forks-Flatrock Rd, Oakland, KY 42159; Ronald Potts, Blacksmith, Chriswill Forge, 2255 Manchester Rd, North Lawrence, OH 44666; Roush Forged Metals, Rte 2, Box 13, Cleveland, VA 24255; *Wooden Spoons*—Richard McCollum, White Forest Spoons, Box 687, Bryn Athyn, PA 19009.

Reproduction Manufacturers: *Utensils*—Applecore Creations, PO Box 29696, Columbus, OH 43229; *Wooden Spoons*—Kentucky Hills Industries, Box 186, Pine Knot, KY 42635.

Asparagus Cutter, Ward's Keen Edge, wood **85.00**
Asparagus Tongs................ **4.00**
Bean Dryer, tin, rect **8.00**
Bean Slicer/Pea Huller, green handle, table mount **25.00**
Cabbage Cutter
16¾" l, walnut, heart shaped crest with large heart cutout, old refinishing **175.00**
17¾" l, walnut, round crest with heart cutout, chip carving and traces of scratch carved compass designs highlighted in black, old worn patina, age crack in crest, screw holding blade incomplete **200.00**
18" l, walnut, cutout star in circle crest, old scrubbed patina, broken crest, no blade.............. **70.00**

19¼" l
Pine, red finish, scratch carved date "1801" **95.00**
Walnut, curved crest with hole hanger, found in Zoar, OH, old worn patina **60.00**
21¼" l, pine, heart shaped crest with heart cutout, chip carved bottom edge, old red paint............ **3,300.00**
22½" l, 7¼" w, walnut, heart cutout, old finish **170.00**
25½" l, cherry and walnut, curved crest with heart cutout, branded "A. J. Kuhn" in three places, double blade, old dark patina **110.00**
Chopper
5¼" w, well curved wrought steel handle.................... **35.00**
6" h, wood and steel, unusual swivel blade, marked "Potts & Co"..... **45.00**
6¼" w, wood and steel, marked "Eton & Marsdens" **30.00**
6¾" w, 7¾" h, wrought steel blade, burl handle **60.00**
7" h, wrought iron blade, bone and composition inlaid handle, 19th C..................... **350.00**
9" w, crescent blade, turned double handles, original maker's label **60.00**
14½" l, wood and steel, long curved blade, turned handle at each end **40.00**
Cider Press, Buckeye, Dewey and Able Bros, Buffalo, NY, late 19th C, 32" l, 45" h....................... **415.00**
Coffee Grinder, Enterprise Mfg Co, Philadelphia, PA, cast iron
11½" h, Oct 21, 1873 patent date, drawer.................... **85.00**
33" h, painted and decorated, late 19th C.................... **875.00**
Coffee Mill, table top model, cherry, pewter hopper, dovetailed drawer with porcelain knob, scalloped base, wrought iron crank, marked "E. Nagle, Maker," 10" h.............. **165.00**
Cutting Board
16½" l, 8½" w, wood, rect with rounded corners, lollipop handle **20.00**
17½" l, 10" w, butternut, worn surface....................... **75.00**
Deep Fryer, Griswold #1003, basket.. **90.00**

Lemon Squeezer, Griswold Mfg Co, Erie, PA, $145.00.

Dipper
  13" l, 3¼" d brass bowl, wrought iron
    handle, pitted handle **40.00**
  13½" l, wrought iron and brass, han-
    dle marked "FBS Canton, O Pat Jan
    26, 86" **180.00**
  14" l, 5½" d brass bowl, wrought iron
    handle. **45.00**
  15" l, wrought iron and brass, simple
    tooled handle **30.00**
Dutch Oven, cov, Griswold, cast iron
  #6, large emblem **40.00**
  #8, small emblem. **45.00**
  #10, trivet, large emblem **80.00**
Fireplace Crane, sawtooth trammel,
  primitive wrought iron, 24" l. **210.00**
Food Grinder, Keen Kutter, Simmons
  Hardware, model K110, tinned cast
  iron. **25.00**
Food Mill, Foley, tin and steel **75.00**
Food Mold
  Copper, swirl design, 6⅝ " d **85.00**
  Copper and Tin
    Ear of corn, tin wash, 4 × 6" **110.00**
    Pears, battered, minor repair, 6½" l   **35.00**
    Sheaf of wheat, tin wash, 4½ × 6"   **95.00**
  Rockingham, tulip design on bottom
    of bowl, brown sponged glaze,
    wear and minor hairlines, 9" d   **30.00**
  Tin
    Fish shape, 12" l **28.00**
    Lion, oval, 5¼" l **45.00**
Fork, wrought iron
  16½" l **30.00**
  18¼" l, marked "J. Metzger". **125.00**
  23" l, three tine, tooling, brass han-
    dle, slightly battered **160.00**
  23½" l, ram's horn handle **75.00**
French Fry Cutter, Maid of Honor, tin,
  stamped, 1930s **6.00**
Garlic Press, wood **30.00**
Grater
  Brass, scratched initials and mark,
    4½ × 12½" **165.00**
  Punched Tin, 17" l **40.00**
Gypsy Kettle, Wagner, cast iron, ftd,
  wire bail handle, 5" d **30.00**
Kitchen Saw, Keen Kutter, Simmons
  Hardware, carbon steel blade, wood
  handle, 13½" l **12.00**
Kitchen Scale, Hanson **25.00**
Ladle, brass bowl, wrought iron handle,
  18" l **35.00**
Meat Grinder, Russvin, 1903 . . . .   **15.00**
Meat Slicer, Dandy, tin, wood handle   **12.00**
Meat Tenderizer, stoneware, wood
  handle, marked "Pat'd Dec 25,
  1877," 9½" l **75.00**
Muddler, maple, turned, 7" l **35.00**
Noodle Cutter, The Ideal, Toledo
  Cooker Co, rolling type, wire handle
  and frame, 14 blades, c1910 . . . . .   **15.00**

Meat Slicer, Improved, Enterprise Mfg Co, Philadelphia, PA, cast iron, painted black, 1881 patent date, 19½ × 12 × 18", $95.00.

Peel, poplar, old refinishing, 33½" l   **95.00**
Pestle
  11¾" l, curly maple, turned, soft pat-
    ina. **70.00**
  12¼" l, curly chestnut, turned, soft
    patina, burned spot on end **12.00**
Potato Masher
  Blue Onion. **120.00**
  Double grid **50.00**
Potato Ricer, Handy Things, Ludington,
  MI, tinned metal presser and cup,
  iron handles painted red, c1940,
  12" l. **10.00**
Pot Holder Hanger, hanging, chalk-
  ware, black children eating water-
  melon **20.00**
Roaster, Mi Pet, cast iron **35.00**
Sausage Stuffer, cherry and other hard-
  woods, metal teeth, refinished, 17" l   **40.00**
Skillet
  Griswold, cast iron, large emblem
    #3 . . . .   **20.00**
    #4 . . . .   **35.00**
    #5 . . . .   **25.00**
    #6, cov **35.00**
    #7 . . . .   **25.00**

Stove Lid Lifter, cast iron, $5.00.

#8, cov	35.00
#9, smoke ring	35.00
#10, smoke ring	35.00
#12, smoke ring	45.00
Martin Stove Co	15.00

Wagner

#3	20.00
#4, smoke ring	24.00
#5	20.00

Skimmer

Wrought iron, large flat bowl, 12" d	40.00
Wrought iron and brass, large flat bowl, shaped handle, 25¼" l	185.00

Spatula

11" l, offset blade	35.00
14½" l, brass turner, wrought iron handle	45.00

Spoon

11" l, wood, handle carved "1828," worn patina	225.00
26" l, primitive, hardwood, chip carved detail, old worn dark finish	40.00

Sugar Nippers, wrought steel

8¼" l	200.00
9" l, tooled designs	100.00

Tea Kettle

Griswold, aluminum	15.00
Wagner, 5 quart	25.00
Vegetable Slicer, A & J, Binghamton, NY, wood handle, twisted wire blade, c1930, 16" l	18.00
Waffle Iron, cast iron, double handles, 22" l	45.00

GRANITEWARE

History: Graniteware is the name commonly given to iron or steel kitchenware covered with an enamel coating.

The first graniteware was made in Germany in the 1830s. It was not produced in the United States until the 1860s. At the start of World War I, when European manufacturers turned to the making of war weapons, American producers took over the market.

Colors commonly marketed were white and gray. Each company made their own special colors, including shades of blue, green, brown, violet, cream, and red. Graniteware still is manufactured with the earliest pieces in greatest demand among collectors.

Old graniteware is heavier than new. Pieces with cast iron handles date from 1870 to 1890; wood handles date from 1900 to 1910. Other dating clues are seams, wood knobs, and tin lids.

References: Helen Greguire, *The Collector's Encyclopedia of Graniteware: Colors, Shapes & Values*, Book 1, (1990, 1992 value update), Book 2 (1993), Collector Books; Vernagene Vogelzang and Evelyn Welch, *Graniteware, Collectors' Guide With Prices, Volume 1* (1981) and *Volume 2* (1986) Wallace-Homestead.

Collectors' Club: National Graniteware Society, PO Box 10013, Cedar Rapids, IA 52410.

Reproduction Manufacturer: Faith Mountain Country Fare, Box 199, Sperryville, VA 22740.

Baking Pan

Cobalt Blue and White, large swirl	**195.00**
Gray, mottled, oblong	**10.00**
Basin, dark green and white	**125.00**

Batter Jug, cobalt blue and white, tin

lid, bail handle	**275.00**
Bedpan, cov, gray and white, speckled	**30.00**

Berry Bucket, blue and white, large

swirl, tin lid	**165.00**
Biscuit Cutter, gray	**300.00**

Bowl

Blue and White

Mottled, 7" d	**25.00**
Speckled, 11" d	**10.00**

Brown and White, mottled, Onyx

Ware, 7½" d, 3¼" h	**20.00**
Cream and Green	**12.00**

Bread Box, white, black letters and

trim, round, vented top	**125.00**
Bread Pan, gray, mottled	**15.00**

Bread Riser, cov

Blue and White, swirl, tin lid, large	**175.00**
Cobalt Blue and White, mottled, black trim, ftd, small	**475.00**

Bucket, aqua and white, swirl, 2 quart,

bail handle	**20.00**

Butter Carrier, aqua and white, swirl,

cobalt blue trim, oval	**300.00**

Cake Pan

Blue and White, swirl, 10" d	**25.00**
Gray, mottled, angel food, fluted, 11" d	**25.00**
Robin's Egg Blue and White, marbleized, 7½" d	**45.00**

Chamber Pot, cov

Blue-green, swirl	**245.00**
Green and White, mottled	**135.00**
Gray, small	**50.00**
Cocoa Dipper, gray, hollow handle	**225.00**

Basin, green and white swirled ext., white int., cobalt rim and riveted handles, 20" w handle to handle, 5½" h, $85.00.

Chamberstick, marbleized pink and green, 6″ d base, $70.00.

Colander, gray mottled, applied strap handles, ftd, 9½″ d, 3¾″ h, $18.00.

Coffee Boiler
  Brown, swirl 100.00
  Chrysolite, swirl 175.00
  Cobalt Blue and White, swirl 175.00
  Gray 25.00
  Iris, swirl 285.00
  Coffee Flask, gray 450.00
Coffeepot
  Blue and White
    Medium swirl 95.00
    Spatter, gooseneck 100.00
  Brown and White, swirl 145.00
  Chrysolite 140.00
  Cobalt Blue and White, chicken wire
    pattern 95.00
  Gray, Columbian label 85.00
Coffee Roaster, black and white, mottled, screen drum 425.00
Colander
  Blue and White, large swirl inside and out 125.00
  Brown and White, swirl 265.00
  Emerald and White, swirl 150.00
  Gray
    Round 75.00
    Starburst 60.00
Cream Bucket, gray
  Mottled, tin lid, orig label 100.00
  Swirl, ½ gallon, tin lid, bail handle 115.00

Coffeepot, gray speckled, orig paper label "Savory Sterling Enameled Nickled Steelware, No. 901, Newark, NJ," 2½ gal, 13″ h, $85.00.

Creamer, turquoise and white, swirl, 5″ h. 12.00
Cup
  Blue and White, swirl 30.00
  Gray, mottled 12.00
Cup and Saucer, cream and green . . . 7.00
Custard, cobalt blue and white, large swirl 65.00
Dipper
  Cobalt Blue and White, swirl 25.00
  Dark Brown and White, mottled, Onyx Ware 40.00
Dish Pan, blue and white 55.00
Double Boiler, cov
  Cobalt Blue and White, large swirl, Brilliant Belle 295.00
  Gray, mottled 15.00
Dust Pan
  Blue, 6 × 4½″ 75.00
  Cream and Green 100.00
  Gray, speckled 100.00
Eggcup, blue, cobalt blue and white checkerboard trim, pr 95.00
Fry Pan, gray. 75.00
Funnel
  Blue Diamond Ware, 9″ d. 95.00
  Gray, fruit jar type. 40.00
  Robin's Egg Blue 50.00
  White, 3″ d, squatty 20.00
Grater
  Blue, flat 95.00
  Cream and Green, flat. 95.00
  Red, small 75.00
Gravy Boat, blue and white, mottled 195.00
Jelly Roll Pan, blue and white, large swirl 40.00
Kettle, cov, gray, mottled, 11½″ d, 9″ h 45.00
Ladle
  Blue and White, large swirl 70.00
  Brown and White, swirl 75.00
  Gray, slotted 40.00
  White 30.00
Loaf Pan, gray. 25.00
Lunch Box and Cup, gray 195.00
Measuring Cup, gray. 50.00
Milk Can
  Black and White, speckled, lock top, wire bail handle, 8″ h 35.00

Emerald and White, swirl, blue trim,
Emerald Ware 350.00
Milk Pan, blue and white 35.00
Milk Pitcher, blue and white, large swirl 175.00
Mixing Bowl, blue 30.00
Molasses Jug, white, large, tin lid 35.00
Mold
  Turquoise and White, swirl, Turk's
    head 200.00
  White, fluted. 40.00
Muffin Pan
  Cobalt Blue and White, mottled, 8
    cup 85.00
  Gray, 12 cup. 60.00
Mug, child's
  Cobalt Blue and White, large swirl,
    pr 100.00
  Gray, set of four 70.00
Mush Mug
  Blue and White, swirl, black trim . . 185.00
  Emerald and White, swirl, black trim,
    Emerald Ware, large 115.00
Mustard Pot, cov, white, handle,
  3½" h 45.00
Pan, blue and white, heart shaped . . . 125.00
Pie Plate, child's, gray 45.00
Pitcher
  Blue and White, mottled, blue trim . 140.00
  Gray, ice lip, 11" h 110.00
Pitcher and Bowl, gray 125.00
Plate
  Gray, mottled 40.00
  Red and White, mottled, white int.,
    12 sided 45.00
Platter, blue and white, mottled, large 70.00
Preserving Kettle, blue and white, mot-
  tled, seamless, bail handle 140.00
Pudding Pan, cobalt blue and white,
  swirl, 8" d 40.00
Refrigerator Dish, blue 30.00
Roaster, cov
  Cobalt Blue, round 18.00
  Cobalt Blue and White, speckled,
    oval, small. 10.00
  Gray
    Savory. 50.00
    Thistle 160.00
Salt Box, light blue, hanging 125.00
Sauce Pan, green and white, swirl,
  white int. 195.00
Scoop, blue ext., white int., 3½" 165.00
Sink Strainer, cobalt blue and white,
  mottled, triangular, wire feet 125.00
Skimmer
  Gray, mottled, 10" l 25.00
  White, pierced diamond pattern
    bowl 120.00
Soap Dish, blue and white, swirl, hang-
  ing 65.00
Soup Tureen, cov, gray, flat bottom . . 300.00
Spatula, gray. 85.00
Spittoon, green and white, swirl 80.00

Spoon
  Blue Diamond Ware, long handle 48.00
  Gray 30.00
Strainer, light blue and white, mottled,
  black trim, squatty. 275.00
Sugar Bowl, gray, tin lid, L & G. 295.00
Syrup Pitcher, brown, Onyx Ware, bul-
  bous 365.00
Teapot
  Blue and White, swirl 145.00
  Brown and White, swirl, gooseneck
    spout 145.00
  Cream and Green, gooseneck spout,
    8½" w 75.00
  Gray, gooseneck spout, L & G 95.00
  Green and White, swirl 325.00
Tea Strainer
  Blue, star perforations 55.00
  Cream, circular hole pattern 40.00
  Gray 45.00
  White, circles 30.00
Tray, blue and white, mottled, corru-
  gated, 25 × 19" 125.00
Tumbler
  Blue and White, mottled, 5" d 65.00
  White, small 10.00
Water Bucket, cobalt blue and white,
  large swirl 125.00
Water Pitcher, brown and white, swirl 285.00

STRING HOLDERS

History: The string holder developed as a utilitarian tool to assist the merchant or manufacturer who needed tangle-free string or twine to tie packages. Early holders were made of cast iron, with some patents dating to the 1860s.

When the string holder moved to the household, lighter and more attractive forms developed, many made of chalkware. The string holder remained a key kitchen element until the early 1950s.

Reproduction Manufacturer: Bullfrog Hollow, Keeny Rd, Lyme, CT 06371.

Apple
  China, red 20.00
  Tin, marked "Shenandoah Valley Ap-
    ple Candy, Winchester, VA," 4" h 150.00
Ball
  Nickle Plated Brass, pedestal stand,
    c1910 . . . . 115.00
  Cast Iron, wire hanger, 6" d 8.00
Ball of Twine, cast iron, painted black,
  5" h 50.00
Beehive, cast iron, dated Apr 1865, 6" h 55.00
Bust, lady with curly hair, redware . . . 95.00
Cat, china 15.00
Cylinder, cardboard, pink, olive green
  polka dot dec, imp label "Sealright,"
  3½" d, 2¼" h 50.00

Cast Iron, beehive, 6½" d, 4½" h, $30.00.

Plaster, French Chef, painted, red hat, green collar, 8" h, $45.00.

Dutch Girl, cast iron.............	**20.00**
Elderly Lady, sitting in rocking chair, chalkware...................	**20.00**
Fish, cast iron..................	**60.00**
Girl's Head, chalkware, wearing blue bonnet	**45.00**
Gypsy Kettle, cast iron	**145.00**
Jack-O-Lantern, china	**50.00**
Mammy, pottery, 6¾" h	
Blue turban, blue and white dress and apron, holding flowers, marked "Japan, Fred Hirode," 1940s	**65.00**

Red turban, red and white checkered dress	**110.00**
Mammy's Head, chalkware, wearing white turban with red polka dots, 1910–20, 5" h.................	**135.00**
Peach, chalkware	**30.00**
Pear, chalkware	**20.00**
Teapot, wood, chef decal	**25.00**
Woman, tin, knitting, cat playing with yarn	**18.00**
Woman's Head, plaster	**60.00**

LEISURE AND PLAY

Life in rural America is harsh and repetitive. Members of the agrarian community work hard and play hard. They are believers in the adage "All work and no play makes Jack a dull boy."

Farming is a seven-day-a-week occupation. It is difficult to escape for an extended vacation. As a result, leisure activity often centered around day-long or half-day events. Extended leisure time was possible only when someone stayed behind to do the chores.

Leisure activities and social interaction are closely linked. Rural America is held together by its strong sense of community. It is only natural to spend time with family and friends during holidays, outings, and religious events.

A day away from the daily routine is a day from which memories are created. Souvenirs, mementos, and photographs document and rekindle the event. These treasured keepsakes grace the parlor or a favored corner of the bedroom chest or drawers.

Not all leisure and play is socially interactive. Some allows individuals a little time to themselves. Until the post-World War II era, rural families were large, often nucleated. Finding one's own space (to use a modern phrase) was difficult. The means to achieve that space, whether toy or hunting rifle, is among the most cherished of possessions.

The Country decorator too often misses the leisure and play side of Country life. The tendency is to stress decorative elements that convey hard work and products derived from that work. A true Country decorating scheme never fails to illustrate the agrarians' ability to celebrate life itself.

AMUSEMENT PARKS, CARNIVALS, CIRCUSES, AND COUNTRY FAIRS

History: The biggest social events in the lives of most agrarians were the county and state fairs.

Participation often occurred on two levels—through membership in a local agrarian organization, usually The Grange, and individually. Families planned for the fair for a year. For many, it was their one trip away from home.

A trip to the fair usually resulted in many keepsakes. First, there were the prizes ranging from trophies and ribbons that were won. Second, manufacturers often handed out premiums such as bookmarks, calendars, and sewing implements to help remind individuals of their products. Finally, there were the souvenirs from a pinback button to a pennant.

Although most county and state fairs contained a midway, the primary reason for going was business and education. Pleasure came only after the business was concluded. Rest assured that entering a pie in the pie contest was serious business. Local reputation stood or fell on the results of the judging.

When the agrarian family simply wanted to get away from it all, they went to an amusement park, carnival, or circus. These were purely social events.

Carnivals normally were sponsored by a local group, ranging from the church to a fire company. Often they contracted with professional groups to provide rides and booths featuring games of chance. Food was provided locally. The most commonly found memento is a piece of carnival chalkware.

Carnival chalkware, cheerfully painted plaster of paris figures, was a cheap, decorative, art form. Doll and novelty companies mass produced and sold chalkware pieces for as little as a dollar a dozen. Many independents, mostly immigrants, molded chalkware figures in their garages. They sold directly to carnival booth owners.

Carnival chalkware was marketed for a nominal price at dime stores. However, its prime popularity was as a prize at games of chance located along carnival midways. Some pieces are marked and dated; most are not. The soft nature of chalkware means it is easily chipped or broken.

By the mid-19th century the tent circus with accompanying side shows and menagerie became popular throughout America. There were hundreds of circus companies, varying in size from one to three rings. The golden age of the tent circus was the 1920s to the 1940s when a large circus would consist of over 100 railroad cars.

Almost every rural town of any size was visited by a circus. It was a day eagerly anticipated by the local youth who would gather at the rail siding to watch the circus unload, follow it to the field where it set up, and hang around until performance time.

The most commonly found circus souvenir is the program. A few individuals saved the large promotional broadsides. Country collectors often incorporate the circus theme into their settings through games, puzzles, and toys. Although not obtained at a circus, they capture the excitement that the circus creates.

A trip to the amusement park meant a trip to the big city. It was quite common for a town or township to have "community" or "church" day at an amusement park. Mothers and their children arrived in the morning; fathers joined the festivities

when work was done. Of all the features, it is the amusement park carousel which is best remembered.

By the late 17th century carousels were found in most capital cities of Europe. In 1867 Gustav Dentzel carved America's first carousel. Other leading American manufacturers include Charles I. D. Looff, Allan Herschell, Charles Parker, and William F. Mangels. The price of carousel figures skyrocketed in the 1980s when folk art collectors took the market for themselves. Today most Country collectors who want a carousel figure as an accent piece utilize a modern reproduction.

References: Charlotte Dinger, *Art Of The Carousel*, Carousel Art, Inc., 1983; Tobin Fraley, *The Carousel Animal*, Tobin Fraley Studios, 1983; Frederick Fried, *The Pictorial History Of The Carousel*, Vestal Press, 1964; William Manns, Peggy Shank, and Marianne Stevens, *Painted Ponies: American Carousel Art*, Zon International Publishing, 1986; Thomas G. Morris, *The Carnival Chalk Prize*, Prize Publishers, 1985; Ted Sroufe, *Midway Mania*, L-W, Inc., 1985.

Periodicals: *Carousel Art Magazine*, PO Box 992, Garden Grove, CA 92642; *The Carousel News & Trader*, 87 Park Avenue West, Suite 206, Mansfield, OH 44902.

Collectors' Clubs: American Carousel Society, 3845 Telegraph Rd, Elkton, MD 21921; Circus Fans Association of America, PO Box 59710, Potomac, MD 20859; The Circus Historical Society, 3477 Vienna Court, Westerville, OH 43081; National Amusement Park Historical Association, PO Box 83, Mount Prospect, IL 60056; National Carousel Association, PO Box 4333, Evansville, IN 47724.

Museums: The Barnum Museum, Bridgeport, CT; Circus World Museum, Baraboo, WI; Ringling Circus Museum, Sarasota, FL.

Reproduction Craftsperson: *Carousel Horses*—J T Nicholas & Son, 704 N Michigan Ave, Howell, MI 48843.

Reproduction Manufacturer: *Carousel Horses*—Ed Boggis, Box 287, Claremont, NH 03743.

Advertising Trade Card, Jumbo the elephant, arrival at Castle Garden, Clark's ONT Spool Cotton, copyright 1889 . . . . **8.00**
Ball Toss Targets, canvas, black screened cats, lambswool fringe, wood base, wear and damage, 22" h, pr **100.00**
Banner, circus freak, "Eeka the Cannibal" **1,000.00**
Carousel Figures, carved wood
   Cat, Dentzel, finely carved fur detail, fish clamped in jaws, 54" l, President's Park, Carlsbad, NM, c1903 **27,500.00**

Deer, Herschell-Spillman, outside row, standing pose, elaborately decorated trappings, dog's head at cantle, deeply carved fur, real antlers, 58" l, Newtown Lake Park, Carbondale, PA, c1910 . . . . **23,100.00**

Dog, Herschell-Spillman, jumping, sweet expressive face, 54" l, portable carousel, c1905 . . . . **6,875.00**

Elephant, unknown artist, realistic proportions, expressive face, scalloped blanket, 52" l, c1880 . . . . . **11,550.00**

Giraffe
Dentzel, outside row, whimsical expression, elaborately deeply carved trappings include large leaves and draped blanket, 70" h, Fun City Park, Johnstown, PA **42,900.00**

Looff, expressive face, criss-cross blanket, twin eagles' heads at saddle cantle, 48" l, c1895 . . . **13,200.00**

Goat, PTC, jumping, animated pose, heavily carved fur detail, layered trappings, 45" l, c1906 . . . . **5,500.00**

Horse
Armitage Herschell, track horse, jumper, pleasing expression, parallel leg position, suggestion of bird at saddle cantle, orig paint, mounted on rocking mechanism, 54" l, c1895 . . . . . **6,600.00**

Charles Carmel
Lead Stander, outside row, wildly flowing mane, draped forelock, elaborately jeweled trappings, full sword and scabbard, fish-scale armor,

Carousel Horse, stander, Philadelphia Toboggan Co, carved and painted, c1918, 70" l, 65" h, $11,000.00. Photograph courtesy of C G Sloan & Co, Inc.

fringed fabric, layered straps, 64" l, Sherman's Park, Caroga Lake, NY, c1915 . . . . **29,700.00**

Stander, alert expression, long windswept mane, jeweled scalloped trappings, 43" l, c1905 . . . . **8,800.00**

Dentzel
Mare Prancer, inner row, expressive face, long flowing mane, parted forelock, scalloped straps, draped blanket, period body paint, 54" l, c1900 . . . . **16,500.00**

Prancer, alert expression, full intricately carved mane, layered straps, rippled blanket, western saddle, 64" l, c1900 **13,200.00**

Illions
Jumper, slim tapered head, spirited expression, full reverse swept mane, 52" l, c1910 **5,500.00**

Stander, outside row, gentle expression, protruding peek-a-boo mane, ornately carved jeweled trappings and blanket, buckle on girth strap, 62" l, Supreme Carousel, c1921 **45,100.00**

Looff, prancer, gentle expression, full mane, checkered blanket, two eagles' heads with glass eyes at saddle cantle, 66" l, c1895 . . . . **7,700.00**

Parker, jumper, armored, upright pose, lattice work on blanket, jeweled trappings, large medallion on breastplate, 50" l, c1905 **6,600.00**

PTC
Jumper, Muller period, sensitive expressive face, parted and curled mane, fancy forelock, jeweled straps and blanket, c1905 . . . . **9,625.00**

Stander, outside row, reverse flowing windswept mane, raised forelock, layered jeweled trappings, large detailed rifle from saddle cantle to front leg, 60" l, c1914 . . . . . **22,000.00**

Stander, outside row, Zalar style, gentle expression, full flowing mane, long draped forelock, tucked head, multilayered strap decoration with star motif and large jewel at bridle rosette, 65" l, PTC Carousel #49, Clementon Park, NJ, c1919 . . . . **22,000.00**

Spillman, jumper, jeweled layered trappings, fringed blanket, large single rose on breast strap, 58" l, c1924 . . . . **5,500.00**

Stein and Goldstein, jumper, roached mane, criss-cross bridle, wide decorated breast strap, 44" l, c1905 . . . . **3,300.00**

Mule, Herschell-Spillman, jumping, animated pose, pleasant expression, folded blanket, 52" l, Rocky Point Park, RI, c1914 . . . . **6,600.00**

Pig, Herschell-Spillman, jumping, elaborate trappings, deeply rippled blanket, huge ribbon and bow at neck, curly metal tail, 44" l, c1914 . . . . **16,500.00**

Rounding Board, E Joy Morris, ornately carved, scrolls and foliage motif, central mirror, 90" l, Lake Quassy, Middletown, CT **2,200.00**

Sea Dragon, Looff, fierce expression, bared teeth, shell-like saddle, jeweled straps and blanket, fish scale tail, 66" l, c1900 . . . . **20,900.00**

Wild Boar, Parker, aggressive expression, bared tusks, scalloped layered blankets, 52" l, c1895 . . . . . **2,200.00**

Zebra, PTC/E Joy Morris, outside row, proud stance, layered blanket, elaborately fringed straps, 56" l, Lakemont Park, Altoona, PA, c1903 . . . . **22,000.00**

Carousel Band Organ, Wurlitzer, style 146A, approx 40 keys, cymbals, pair of drums, elaborately carved and painted facade with foliage motifs and painted panels, 3' d, 6' h, 8' l, c1922 . . . . **17,600.00**

Carousel Platform Panel

Coney Island, NY, mirrored, Illions signature **600.00**

Daniel Muller, jester head wearing garland of bells, 50" h, c1912 . . . **1,540.00**

Circus Wagon Wheel, sunburst. **525.00**

Pinback Button

Annual Fair, lettering on banner above farm animal heads, horse race below, multicolored, 1¼" d, c1900 . . . . **4.00**

Clyde Beatty Circus, photo illus, lion tamer Beatty and lion, black and white on blue ground, 1¾" d, 1940s **10.00**

Coney Island, NY, "The Great Coal Mine/Coney Island," mule pulling cart and miner swinging axe at mine shaft, multicolored, 1¼" d, c1905 . . . . **18.00**

Dreamland Park, NY, "Meet Me at Dreamland Park," white lettering, red ground, 1" l oval, 1900s **5.00**

Elks Carnival & Midway, small girl sitting in bird cage inscribed "A Bird in a Gilded Cage" and "Baby Vera," gold colored, 1¾" d, c1905 **15.00**

Hershey Park, PA, "Hershey Park," child holding candy bar, sitting in cocoa bean, multicolored, 1¼" d, c1908 . . . . **35.00**

Long Beach, CA, "Aviator/I Flew on the Air Ship/Spiralway/Long Beach, Cal," red and blue lettering and ride illus, white ground, 1¼" d, 1910s **20.00**

Luna Park, Washington, DC, "New Virginia Reel/Luna Park," six adults on amusement park ride, multicolored, 1¼" d, 1910s **35.00**

Midway Amusement Park, FL, "7115/$2,000,000 Playground," red and blue lettering, white ground, ⅞" d, 1930s **3.00**

Moxahala Park, "I Rode the Swooper/Gee It's Great/Moxahala Park," black lettering, white ground, ⅞" d, 1930s **5.00**

Ringling Bros, "Souvenir Ringling Bros./World's Greatest Shows," black lettering, black and white Ringling Bros' photo, white ground, 1½" d, 1910s **35.00**

Royal-Adams Circus, "Broadway Arsenal Dec. 12–17th," caricature clown illus, red, white, and black, 1¾" d, 1900s **20.00**

Steeplechase Park, NY, "Steeplechase Funny Place," smiling man illus, multicolored, ⅞" d, 1910s **20.00**

Texas State Fair, state flag illus, multicolored, ⅞" d, c1905 . . . . **2.50**

Plate, Ocean Pier & Fun Chase, Wildwood, NJ, pierced border, 4" d **8.00**

Post Card

The Great Allentown Fair, Allentown, PA, Dan Patch race horse illus, undivided back, 1906 . . . . . **75.00**

Atlantic City, NJ, "Famous Old Landmark/The Elephant at South Atlantic City," photograph, #9, Chilton Publishing Co **4.00**

Circus Performer, photo, snake handler Millie Leatrice, copyright Campbell's Photo Art Shop, Richmond, IN **30.00**

Poster

Christy Bros Big 5 Ring Wild Animal Shows, "The Wonder Show," litho, camels in foreground with trained bison, oxen, and deer, Christy Bros in vignette at upper left, 27 × 41", c1925 . . . . **150.00**

C W Parker, Leavenworth, Kansas, U.S.A., paper, vignettes of double cylinder steam engine and military band organ in sky above large double horse carousel illus, 27½ × 20½" **250.00**

Poster, Christy Bros 5 Ring Wild Animal Show, Riverside Print Company, 42 × 28", $495.00. Photograph courtesy of James D Julia, Inc.

Downey Bros Big 3 Ring Circus "Leaps-Revival of that Astounding and Sensational Exhibition," group of elephants, camels, and horses in line, aerial artist leaping overhead, audience background, 41 × 27", c1925 . . . .   125.00

Ringling Bros Barnum & Bailey, "Rudy Rudynoff, Peerless Equestrian," Rudynoff in Cossack-like costume flanked by steed and Great Dane, 28 × 41" 200.00

Sells Bros Circus, 1893 . . . .   775.00

Ruby-Stained Souvenir Glass
Bell, Elkhorn Fair, Button Arches pattern, clear paneled handle, 6½" h, 1913 . . . .   65.00
Butter Dish, cov, Lancaster Fair, Button Arches pattern, 1916 . . . .   150.00
Syracuse Fair, cordial, 1905 . . . . . .   45.00
Tumbler, etched "Carnival, July 29, 1904," and "J. M. Craig," Button Arches pattern, 3⅞" h, 2⅞" d . . .   30.00

Sign, Greater Bucks County Fair, cardboard, color, The Fair Publishing House, Norwalk, OH, 1963, 13 × 21", $25.00.

Shooting Gallery Target, cast iron
Bird, 4¼" l 40.00
Duck, 5½" l 65.00
Muskrat, worn repaint, 9" h 25.00
Spoon, "Goin' to the Fair," Chicago Children's Home, young girl, 1892   40.00
Stereograph
Asbury Park, NJ, buildings, G W Pach, 1870s 10.00
Bostock Wild Animal Show, tamer and lions, #74, whiting 25.00
Coney Island, NY, #501, trained bears riding carousel pulled by pony, H C White 18.00
Costello's Circus, Sacramento, CA, #1119, The Educated Elephant, Soule, 1870 . . . .   65.00
Wheel of Fortune
24" d, wood, painted, horses and jockeys, mounting hardware 175.00
30" d, wood, thirty numbers, mounting hardware, marked "Will & Finck, San Francisco" 400.00

BIRD CAGES

History: During the Victorian era, the keeping of exotic pets, such as parrots and other types of birds, was common among the middle and upper class. A standing bird cage often graced a solarium or living room. Well-to-do farmers and small town merchants imitated their big city counterparts.

Bird cages were constructed from a variety of materials ranging from wire and wood to wicker. Few period cages survive in good condition.

Bird cages became a "hot" decorator item in the late 1980s. Although primarily associated with the Victorian revival, they quickly found a place in the Country community. The most decorative examples made from natural materials also attracted the attention of the folk art collector.

Reference: Leslie Garisto, *Birdcage Book: Antique Birdcages for the Contemporary Collector,* Simon & Schuster, 1992.

Reproduction Manufacturer: Guemes Arts & Crafts, PO Box 3700, Edinburg, TX 78540.

Reproduction Alert: The vast majority of the bird cages being offered for sale today are reproductions. Before buying any bird cage become familiar with the Victorian Fantasies catalog from J. K. Reed, 1805 SE Union Ave, Portland, OR 97214.

Bamboo, center peaked top flanked by two smaller peaks, some damage, 16" h 50.00
Brass Plated, dome shaped, 24" d, 66" h gooseneck floor stand, replated   525.00

Rococo-Style Bird Cage, carved wood, wire screen top, C-scroll carved molding, domed projections with grillwork, scroll carved apron, short cabriole legs, metal perches and swings, 20¼" w, 14" d, 24¼" h, $715.00. Photograph courtesy of Butterfield & Butterfield.

Tin
  Crown shaped top, upright posts, pitted, rust, some damage, 19¼" h   50.00
  Dome shaped, old blue paint, 13½" d, 20½" h 195.00
Wire and Wood
  Arched top, posts topped with white porcelain buttons, rust, tray missing, bottom board damaged, 12¾ × 21¼ × 20" 160.00
  Arched top, old brownish-red paint   325.00
  Rococo Style, rect, serpentine shaped wire screen top, grillwork sides, arching foliate and C-scroll carved molding, four short cabriole legs, metal perches and swings, 20¼" w, 14" d, 24¼" h   715.00
  Tramp Art, chip carved and painted, gold and silver, 26" h 600.00
  Wrought Iron, dome shaped,⅛ " w vertical strips, four horizontal braces, hanging ring, 17" d, 30" h 225.00

CHILDREN'S RIDE-ON TOYS

History: Many toys found in agrarian homesteads were handmade. Among the most common were children's ride-on toys, especially rocking horses. Since rural families were large, especially during the 19th and first half of the 20th centuries, ride-on toys were made to survive. Repainted and repaired examples are typical.

During the late 19th century, mass produced riding vehicles and wagons arrived on the scene. Many were made by the same companies that manufactured larger vehicles. Wood was the most commonly found construction element.

By the 1920s pressed metal riding vehicles appeared. Many of these automobiles, fire trucks, and planes mimicked their real-life counterparts. Pedal cars from the 1920s through the 1950s are one of the "hot" collectibles in today's market.

References: Marguerite Fawdry, *An International Survey of Rocking Horse Manufacture,* New Cavendish Books, 1992; Patricia Mullins, *The Rocking Horse: A History of Moving Toy Horses,* New Cavendish Books, 1992; L–W Book Sales (ed.), *Riding Toys With Price Guide,* L–W Book Sales, 1992; Neil S. Wood (ed.), *Evolution of The Pedal Car and Other Riding Toys, 1884–1970's,* L–W Book Sales, 1989; Neil S. Wood (ed.), *Evolution of the Pedal Car, Vol. 2,* L–W Book Sales, 1990; Neil S. Wood (ed.), *Evolution of the Pedal Car, Vol. 3,* L–W Book Sales, 1992.

Collectors' Club: National Pedal Vehicle Association, 1720 Rupert, NE, Grand Rapids, MI 49505.

Periodicals: *The Peddler,* 6464 North Rucker Rd, Indianapolis, IN 46220; *The Wheel Goods Trader,* PO Box 435, Fraser, MI 48026-0435.

Reproduction Craftspersons: John T Nicholas & Son, 704 N Michigan Ave, Howell, MI 48843.

Reproduction Manufacturers: The Colonial Keeping Room, RFD 1, Box 704, Fairfield, ME 04937; Woodshed Originals, Box 3, Itasca, IL 60143.

Baby Carriage, 42½" h, 56" w, wood carriage and wheels, fringed top supported by iron framework, painted and dec, white ground, blue and yellow pinstriping, polychrome swans, late 19th C 550.00

High Wheeler, wire spoke wheels, c1800, $1,650.00. Photograph courtesy of Morton M Goldberg Galleries.

Bear, 30¾" h, 38" l, brown mohair, tan muzzle, glass eyes, steel frame, wheels, Steiff, c1940 . . . . **2,800.00**
Bicycle, Monarch Super Deluxe, boy's **850.00**
Carriage, 45" h, wicker, ivory colored umbrella style canopy, metal and rubber spoke wheels, large rear wheels, small front wheels, upholstered seat, 1880–1900 . . . . **700.00**
Hobby Horse, on frame
24½" h, 51" l, dapple gray, green saddle, heart shaped supports, New England, early 19th C **1,200.00**
26½" h, 48½" l, solid head mounted on bentwood frame, yellow pinstriping, red ground, 19th C **10,500.00**
34½" h, 56¾" l, bouncing, brown and white calfskin, glass eyes, horsehair mane and tail, fringed cut velvet and leather saddle, leather tack, wooden frame, red, pinstriping, late 19th C **1,550.00**
36" h, bouncing, wood, carved, painted, white, galloping, glass eyes, horsehair mane and tail, leather ears and tack, painted wooden arched base, cast iron fittings, black, gold, and white pinstriping and dec on red painted platform, c1900 . . . . **725.00**
Horse
27" h, wooden platform, lever action stirrups **1,500.00**
36" h, 45" l, wood, hide cover, glass eyes, horsehair mane and tail . . . **1,300.00**
Mail Cart, 37" l, paint decorated, raised panel on side reads "U. S. Mail," eagle dec on front, 19th C **3,520.00**
Pedal Car
Airplane, 48" l, sheet metal, painted, gray, short wings, rubber rims on three wide metal wheels, repainted, rust and pitting **500.00**

Wicker Carriage, ball and curlicue dec, 32" l, 27" h, $385.00. Photograph courtesy of James D Julia, Inc.

Pedal Car, Packard, spotlight mounted on running board, headlights, siren, 50" l, 24" w, 28" h, $5,500.00. Photograph courtesy of James D Julia, Inc.

City Fire Dept, 35" l, metal, red and white, ball bearing drive **150.00**
Chrysler Air Flow, 1937, restored **3,750.00**
Dump Truck, 46" l, sheet metal, painted, yellow and black, Murray Ohio Mfg Co, 1950s **475.00**
Hook & Ladder Pumper, 45" l, sheet metal, worn metallic red paint. . . **85.00**
Hudson, wood and steel, folding windshield **150.00**
Packard Dual Cowl Phaeton, 72" l, American National **3,300.00**
Race Car, 51" l, metal, painted, hinged hood, Eureka, c1940 . . . . **600.00**
Roadster, 34" l, yellow and black trim, green ground. **600.00**
Scout Master Airplane, 44" l, wood and sheet metal, painted **750.00**
Station Wagon, 44" l, pressed steel, painted **150.00**
Rocking Horse, wood
21" h, primitive, painted, carved body, straight legs, dapple gray, painted mane, horsehair tail, leather type harness and saddle, polychrome floral dec and brown pinstriping on cream colored rockers and center base platform **950.00**
32" l, painted, two horse cutouts on rockers, center seat **250.00**
33" l, black plush velvet seat, c1880 **650.00**
41½" l, 23½" h, stylized, pine, carved, painted, incised eyes, sides form rockers, yellow, red, and black outline and feather painting, black leather bridle, black and white printed oil cloth cushioned saddle seat, c1840 . . . **1,325.00**
42" l, painted, dapple gray, leather saddle **1,100.00**
45" l, 23" h, wood, painted, gray, black mane and horsehair tail, leatherette saddle, brown stained rockers, 19th C **650.00**

Wagon, wood, painted and stenciled, 22" l, $143.00. Photograph courtesy of James D Julia, Inc.

Rocking Horse, cloth-covered wood, saddle, wood swivel rocker base with yellow stenciling on red ground, 34" l, 30" h, $330.00. Photograph courtesy of James D Julia, Inc.

50" l, painted, turned legs, pinstriping. 550.00
51" l, 30½" h, full figured, pine, carved, painted, white horse, leather star and shield stitched saddle and bridle, cast iron stirrups, brass button eyes, real horsehair tail, yellow pinstriping on red rockers, sailboat motif on platform, 1875–1900 . . . . .17,600.00
54" l, carved wooden body, beige repaint, leather saddle and harness, replaced mane and tail, arched wooden rockers painted red, rockers repaired 375.00
Sled
37½" l, wood, painted, oblong platform, red and black, "Grant," pinstriping and floral dec, iron tipped looped fronts on wooden runners, missing one brace 450.00
39" l, wood, steel runners, stenciled "King of the Hill," striping, orig red paint and varnish. 275.00
40" l, iron tips on wood runners, old yellow repaint 100.00
41" l, 11" w, 4" h, child riding high wheeler illus, late 19th C. 415.00
45" l, horse head, scrolls, and pinstripes on red ground. 650.00
49" l, running horse dec, brown and beige "Chester" inscription, black and yellow pinstriping, red painted deck, late 19th C 325.00
72" l, oak and walnut, no dec, iron runners 115.00
Sleigh, wood
40" l, 24" h, painted red, pinstripe detail, hide covered horse head with glass eyes and leather trim 500.00

43" l, painted, tufted upholstered seat 650.00
Tricycle
Thunderbolt, 34" l, pulley type, wooden seat 200.00
Wood, spoke wheels, wooden pedals, cast iron fittings 400.00
Velocipede
35" l, steel, spoked wheels, incomplete seat. 165.00
36" l, 31½" h, wood and metal, horse-form, glass eyes, carved and painted horse, repaired, remnants of mane and tail 375.00
40" l, 32" h, wood, carved, painted, dapple gray, glass eyes, horsehair mane and tail, tricycle base, black striping on red wheels, wrought iron pedals, filigreed cast iron hardware, late 19th C 6,875.00
Wagon
22" l, sheet metal, Hy-Speed, red and white. 200.00
28" l, wood bed, painted, red and green, cast iron wheels 250.00
31" l, wood, Hibbard Playmate 175.00
33" l plus tongue, wood, steel fittings, wood spoke wheels with steel rims, old worn white repaint 375.00
42" l, Lightning Wheel Coaster, wood, wooden spoke wheels. . . . 385.009
43" l, Pioneer Coaster, wood artillery wheels, 1900 . . . . 450.00

FIREPLACE EQUIPMENT

History: The fireplace was a gathering point in the colonial home for heat, meals, and social interaction. In the urban environment, it maintained its dominant position until the introduction of central heating in the mid-19th century. In the countryside, the fireplace as a heat source remained dominant well into the 20th century.

Even after central heating was introduced, the rural farm house retained working fireplaces.

There was something nostalgic, comfortable about a roaring fire.

The open fireplace was one of the most popular decorating motifs of the early American decorating revival of the 1920s and 1930s. When Country became popular in the 1970s and 1980s, the living room and parlor fireplace became a major decorative focus. Because of the continued popularity of the fireplace, accessories still are manufactured, usually in an early American motif. In the 1970s the folk art community developed a strong interest in fireboards, a device put in front of the fireplace to hide the opening when it was not in use during the late spring, summer, and early fall. It was not long before several reproduction craftspersons began providing contemporary copies of old fireboards.

Reference: George C. Neumann, *Early American Antique Country Furnishings: Northeastern America, 1650–1800's,* L–W Book Sales, 1984, 1993 reprint.

Reproduction Alert: Modern blacksmiths are reproducing many old iron implements.

Reproduction Craftspersons: *Firebacks*—Patricia Euston, New England Firebacks, PO Box 268, Woodbury, CT 06798; Kurt P Strehl, Orpheus Coppersmith, 52 Clematis Rd, Agawam, MA 01001; *Fireboards*—Hope R Angier, Sheepscot Stenciling, RFD 1, Box 613, Wiscasset, ME 04578; Art by Marianne, Box 122, Amherst, NH 03031; Dorothy Fillmore Studio, 84 Pilgrim Dr, Windsor, CT 06095; Betsy Hoyt, Butternut Hill Gallery, 3751 State St W, N Canton, OH 44720; Sharon J Mason, Olde Virginea Floorcloth & Trading Co, PO Box 438, Williamsburg, VA 23185; Christine L Smith, 110 Graham Way, Devon, PA 19333; *Fire Buckets*—Russel A Bigelow, Bigelow Harness, 212 Richmond Rd, Winchester, NH 03470; *Fireplace*—Charles W Euston, Woodbury Blacksmith & Forge Co, PO Box 268, Woodbury, CT 06798; James W Faust, 488 Porters Mill Rd, Pottstown, PA 19464; James A Hoffman, Hoffman's Forge, 2272 Youngstown Lockport Rd #1, Ransomville, NY 14131; Steve Kayne, Kayne & Son Custom Forged Hardware, 76 Daniel Ridge Rd, Candler, NC 28715; Jonathan Marshall, Blacksmith, 1310 Westview, E Lansing, MI 48823; Charles R Messner, Colonial Lighting and Tinware Reproductions, 316 Franklin St, Denver, PA 17517; Ronald Potts, Blacksmith, Chriswill Forge, 2255 Manchester Rd, N Lawrence, OH 44666; Kurt P Strehl, Orpheus Coppersmith, 52 Clematis Rd, Agawam MA 01001; Virginia Metalcrafters, 1010 East Main St, Waynesboro, VA 22980.

Reproduction Manufacturers: *Firebacks*—The Country Iron Foundry, PO Box 600, Paoli, PA 19301; *Fireboards*—The Country Hand, PO Box 212, West Terre Haute, IN 47885; Heritage Designs, 7816 Laurel Ave, Cincinnati, OH 45243; The Prairie Stenciler, 7215 Nobel Court,

Shawnee, KS 66218; *Fireplace*—Conner Prairie Blacksmithing, 13400 Allisonville Rd, Fishers, IN 46038; Lemee's Fireplace Equipment, 815 Bedford St, Bridgewater, MA 02324; The Reggio Register Co, PO Box 511, Ayer, MA 01432; *Mantels*—Maurer & Shepherd Joyners, Inc, 122 Naubuc Ave, Glastonbury, CT 06033; Williams Cabinetry, PO Box 39, Hog Bay Rd, North Sullivan, ME 04664.

Andirons, pr

Bell Metal, 13½" h, lemon finial, round plinth, slipper feet, 19th C	**225.00**
Brass	
11½" h, acorn finial, faceted plinth, spurred arched legs, penny feet, c1800	**450.00**
14½" h, ball finial, turned standard	
Arched spurred legs, slipper feet, early 19th C	**190.00**
Scrolled legs, ball feet	**425.00**
15¼" h, ball finial, turned standard, spurred legs, slipper feet, 19th C	**200.00**
17" h, belted ball finial, minor imperfections, early 19th C	**275.00**
18" h, lemon finial, conforming log stops, early 19th.	**440.00**
20" h	
Double urn finial, spurred arched supports, ball feet, back rods replaced.	**450.00**
Lemon finial, sgd "John Molineux founder Boston, c1800	**1,975.00**
21" h, ball finial, turned standard, spurred legs, spade feet, CT, c1800	**350.00**
22" h, Colonial Revival, urn finial, fluted standard, spurred legs, ball and claw feet	**3,575.00**
24" h, Federal, lemon finial, paneled standard, spurred legs, ball feet, early 19th C	**825.00**
28" h, Colonial Revival, urn finial, slender standard, spurred legs, ball feet	**145.00**
Brass finial, wrought iron shaft	
13½" h, mushroom finial, tall stems, broad base with center crown pendant and ball feet, spit rests.	**415.00**
19½" h, belted ball finial, knife blade shaft, early 19th C	**715.00**
20½" h, urn finial, knife blade stems, penny feet.	**325.00**
24" h, lemon finial, Chippendale, c1790	**800.00**
Urn finial, brass details, knife blade shaft, penny feet, marked "IC"	**550.00**

Cast Iron
  12½" h, heart finial **400.00**
  15" h, 8½" w, 15" d, painted, George Washington form, stamped "pat. desig'd 1837," 19th C **325.00**
  16" h
    Owl, glass eyes, dated 1887 **375.00**
    Snake, intertwined, late 19th C **135.00**
    17" h, sitting cat, yellow glass eyes **120.00**
    Hessian Soldier, hand on hip, walking to left **225.00**
Polished Brass, 20" h, urn finial, ring turned stems, spurred legs, ball feet, "Griffiths & Morgan" label, one leg repaired at stem **450.00**
Wrought Iron
  13½" h, gooseneck finial, penny feet, old black repaint over rust **50.00**
  17½" h, knob finial, open cage style scrolled design, knob feet **200.00**
  20½" h, gooseneck finial. **650.00**
  23" h, scrolled design, c1910 . . . **55.00**
Apple Roaster, 34¼" l, wrought iron, hinged apple support, heart-pierced end on slightly twisted projecting handle, late 18th C **1,650.00**
Bellows
  10" l, miniature, turned face, old black paint, yellow striping, gold stenciling, tin nozzle, old worn leather. **75.00**
  17" l, turtle back, orig painted dec, brass nozzle
    Bowl of flowers, stenciled and freehand, red, gilt, and black, striping, yellow ground, old worn leather **215.00**
    Cornucopia, gold, green, and black, red ground, very worn old leather. **85.00**
    Fruit and foliage, stenciled and freehand, green, gold, black, and yellow, red ground, old worn leather, back handle damaged **75.00**

Bellows, wood, iron nozzle, leather trim, adv "Bellows Made and Repaired," 13¾" w, 24¾" l, $165.00.

17¼" l, grain painted and stenciled dec, leather trim, some leather deterioration, 19th C **165.00**
17¾" l, leather, brass nozzle
  Basket of stylized fruit and foliage, yellow, green, gold, and black, yellow striping, gold and black stenciled border, red and black rosewood graining, some wear, old releathering **250.00**
  Floral design, red, black, and brown, yellow ground **200.00**
18" l, leather, turtle back, brass nozzle, stenciled and freehand dec, black, bronze, and silver gilt, cream colored ground, brass nozzle. . . . **140.00**
Bird Roaster, tin reflector, four hooks, 1870s **175.00**
Broiler, wrought iron
  9" d, 16" l, rotary **125.00**
  14" d, 26½" l, twistwork grill, 18th C **225.00**
  15" d, 22¾" l, serpentine grillwork, 18th C **325.00**
  15" w, 14" h, scroll design, hinged arm back rest. **100.00**
  28" h, adjustable heart shaped rack with five sets of tines to hold small game, decorative diamond shaped rivet on sprint, tripod base, penny feet **1,100.00**
Chestnut Roaster, 28½" l, pierced iron, heart shaped, long twisted handle, 18th C. **900.00**
Coals Carrier, 31" l, wrought iron, sliding lid **225.00**
Coffee Roaster, 51" l, down-hearth, sheet metal, iron rod, wood handle, late 18th-early 19th C **125.00**
Crane, wrought iron
  26" l **100.00**
  27" l, 17" h **45.00**
  38½" l, scrolled detail. **85.00**
Dutch Oven, 19" l, tin, iron spit **200.00**
Ember Tongs, 14½" l, wrought iron, scissor extension **125.00**
Fire Back, cast iron
  16" w, 22" h, floral dec, rose and portcullis, arched. **1,550.00**
  17" w, 23" h, man and horse, inscription at top, foliage **200.00**
  24" w, 21" h, Tree of Life, Lancaster, PA, 18th C. **300.00**
Fire Board, 22¾ × 36¼", geometric pattern, painted blue, yellow, green, sienna, black, and white **2,000.00**
Fire Cover, 9½" h, wrought iron, gooseneck, penny feet, 18th C **140.00**
Fire Fender
  39" w, 12" d, 8½" h, brass and iron, pierced, New England, 19th C. . . **110.00**
  48" l, wrought iron, decorative spindles **225.00**

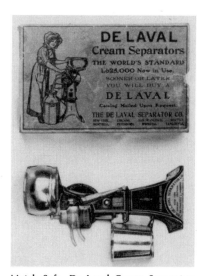

Match Safe, De Laval Cream Separator, litho tin, orig box, $65.00.

56" w, 23" d, 24" h, wire, brass rail, scrolled wire designs	375.00
Fire Mark, cast iron	
3¹⁄₁₆" h, oval, eagle, "1792," traces of old paint	45.00
7³⁄₈ × 11½", hydrant and hose, marked "F A," polychrome paint, pitted	210.00
Flue Cover	
Cast Iron, plain	20.00
Tin, emb, painted, paper litho farm scene, c1900.	15.00
Fork, 32½" l, wrought iron, long handled with open cage spiral finial . . .	60.00
Hearth Brush	
22" l, turned wood handle, traces of old black paint	70.00
27" l, baluster turned wood handle, grain painted, smoke dec, leaves and flowers, gray and yellow ground, c1830	450.00
Jamb Hooks, brass, steeple top, England, early 19th C, price for pair . . .	450.00
Kettle Shelf, 16½" h, hanging, wrought iron, very pitted	65.00
Kettle Tilter, 14" w, wrought iron, acorn finial on swivel ring, c1810	375.00
Mantel, 73½" w, 50" h, Federal, attributed to Salem, MA, c1800, wood, carved florals and swags, 51½" w opening	1,325.00
Match Holder, wood, Scottie dog	15.00
Match Safe, hanging	
Brass, milk pail, figural	185.00
Cast Iron, horseshoe shaped, antlered stag crest, knob finial on cov box base	35.00

Tin, advertising,	
American Steel Farm Fences, 3½ × 5", fence illus, "Made In All Heights"	70.00
DeLaval Cream Separators, 4 × 6¼", diecut, emb, figural separator, orig box	300.00
Sharples Cream Separator, 2 × 7", diecut, mother and child using separator, "The Pet of the Dairy"	115.00
Wood, 5¼" h, heart shaped, chip carved edges, angled pocket, white sanded paint, gold trim . . .	60.00
Peel, wrought iron	
38" l, primitive, attributed to Shakertown, Pleasant Hill, KY, edge wear and damage to blade	60.00
53" l, ram's horn handle	225.00
Roaster, 30" l, screen mesh, wooden handle, tin lid, emb eagle	60.00
Roasting Spit, 12" l, brass and wrought iron	40.00
Screen, 19" w, 30" h, brass and mesh, spindled gallery, arched feet	75.00
Skewer, 10½" l, wrought iron, twisted handle, delicate hanger	75.00
Skewer Rack, 11½" l, wrought iron, four twisted skewers	150.00
Skillet, down-hearth, iron, long handle, hook hanger	165.00
Spit Rack, 19½" w, 13½" h, wrought iron, spike end, three hooks to adjust end of spit, good detail	55.00
Stove Plate, cast iron	
25½" w, 23½" h, stylized floral designs with hearts in double arch, emb "Henrich Wilhelm, Elisabeth Furnace," H W Stiegel Foundry, very pitted, crack in right side . . .	225.00
26¼" w, 24½" h, Biblical scene of Potiphar's wife under bed canopy clutching the cloak of Joseph, German inscription "Das. Weib. Des. Svcht. Joseph. Zv. Entzvnde. Im. I. B. Mose. 13C. 1749," pitted from rust, black repaint, PA, right side of five plate jamb stove	200.00
Toaster, wrought iron	
15" l,	
Shaped handle	110.00
Twisted detail	250.00
16" l, stylized tree designs with spiral arches, down-hearth	275.00
26" l, turned wood handle, double jaws end in scrollwork.	140.00
Toasting Fork, adjustable, brass, weighted conical base, stamped "Patent No.—," dents in base	165.00
Tongs, 26" l, brass handle.	160.00
Tool Set	
Brass, tongs, hearth brush, ash shovel, and poker, matching stand	120.00

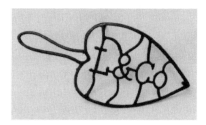

Trivet, cast iron, heart shape, loop handle, "L & Co" in center, tripod ftd, 8⅛ " l, $50.00.

Wrought Iron, hammered finish, sailing ship on tripod stand, knobs hold tongs, hearth brush, ash shovel, and poker, Heather, NYC, NY, c1925 . . . . 60.00

Trammel, sawtooth
Brass, simple detail, adjusts from 18" l 305.00
Wrought Iron
12¾" l 95.00
15" h, with four spout grease lamp 330.00
19½" l 150.00
23" l, with three prong hook at end 115.00
40½" l, three part, large sawtooth adjustable trammel on top, two smaller side trammels with animal head dec, allover tooled dec 385.00

Trivet
Brass, 6½" d, octagonal, engraved star design, four short feet 60.00
Wrought Iron
10½" l, penny feet 175.00
Primitive, fork rest, pitted 95.00
Waffle Iron, 29½" l, down-hearth, heart shape, late 18th-early 19th C 325.00

FISHING

History: Water is a precious commodity in rural America. The location of a stream often dictated the site of a town or farmstead. The farm pond, usually stocked with a variety of fish, provides a hedge against drought.

Fishing was more a means of relaxation than sport for the farmer. Many a cartoon of "the lazy farmer" pictured him asleep with his back against a tree while fishing along the bank of a stream that ran through his farm.

Early man caught fish with crude spears and hooks made of bone, horn, and flint. By the middle 1800s metal lures with hooks attached were produced in New York State. Later, the metal was curved and glass beads added for greater attraction. Spinners with wood-painted bodies and glass eyes appeared around 1890. Soon after, wood

plugs with glass eyes were being produced by many different makers. A large number of patents were issued in this time period covering developments of hook hangers, body styles, and devices to add movement to the plug as it was drawn through the water. The wood plug era lasted up to the mid-1930s when plugs constructed of plastic were introduced.

With the development of casting plugs, it became necessary to produce fishing reels capable of accomplishing that task with ease. Reels first appeared as a simple device to hold a fishing line. Improvements included multiplying gears, retrieving line levelers, drags, clicks, and a variety of construction materials. The range of quality in reel manufacture varied considerably. Collectors are mainly interested in reels made with quality materials and workmanship, or those exhibiting unusual features.

Early fishing rods were made of solid wood which were heavy and prone to break easily. By gluing together strips of tapered pieces of split bamboo, a rod was fashioned lighter in weight and with greatly improved strength. The early split bamboo rods were round with silk wrappings to hold the bamboo strips together. With improvements in glue, fewer wrappings were needed, and rods became slim and lightweight. Rods were built in various lengths and thicknesses, depending upon the type of fishing and bait used. Rod makers' names and models can usually be found on the metal parts of the handle or on the rod near the handle.

The fishing collectibles category has broadened significantly beyond rod, reel, and lure to include landing nets, minnow traps, bait boxes, advertising signs, catalogs, and fish decoys used in ice spearing. Items in original containers and in mint condition command top prices. Lures that have been painted over the original decoration or rods that have been refinished or broken have little collector value.

References: Bruce Boyden, *Fishing Collectibles: Identification and Price Guide,* Avon Books, 1994; Jim Brown, *Fishing Reel Patents of The US, 1838–1940,* published by author; Silvio Calabi, *The Collector's Guide To Antique Fishing Tackle,* Wellfleet Press, 1989; Ralf Coykendall, Jr., *Coykendall's Second Sporting Collectibles Price Guide,* Lyons & Burford, 1992; Ralf Coykendall, Jr., *Coykendall's Sporting Collectibles Price Guide,* Lyons & Burford, 1991; Clyde A. Harbin, *James Heddon's Sons Catalogues,* CAH Enterprises, 1977; Art and Scott Kimball, *Collecting Old Fishing Tackle,* Aardvark Publications, 1980; Art and Scott Kimball, *Early Fishing Plugs of the U. S. A.,* Aardvark Publications, 1985; Art and Scott Kimball, *The Fish Decoy,* Aardvark Publications; Carl F. Luckey, *Old Fishing Lures and Tackle: Identification and Value Guide, Volume I and II,* Books Americana; Albert J. Munger, *Those Old*

Fishing Reels, privately printed, 1982; J. L. Smith, *Antique Rods and Reels,* Gowe Printing, 1986; Richard L. Streater, *Streater's Reference Catalog of Old Fishing Lures, Volume I and II*; Steven K. Vernon, *Antique Fishing Reels,* Stackpole Books, 1984; Karl T. White, *Fishing Tackle Antiques and Collectables: Reference and Evaluation of Pre-1960 Tackle,* Holli Enterprises, 1990.

Collectors' Club: National Fishing Lure Collectors Club, PO Box 0814, Chicago, IL 60690.

Periodicals: *Fishing Collectibles Magazine,* 2005 Tree House Lane, Plano, TX 75023.

Museums: American Fishing Tackle Mfg. Assn. Museum, Arlington Heights, IL; American Museum of Fly Fishing, Manchester, VT; National Fishing Tackle Museum, Arcadia, OK; National Fresh Water Fishing Hall of Fame, Hayward, WI; Sayner Museum, Sayner, WI.

Reproduction Manufacturer: *Lobster Traps and Accessories*—The Cracker Barrel, 527 Narberth Ave, Haddonfield, NJ 08033.

Reproduction Alert: Lures and fish decoys.

Bait Bucket, round
    Punched hole fish design, homemade, orig wooden latch **28.00**
    Stenciled "St Lawrence Bucket," gold lettering, green ground, lift-out bait compartment, 8 × 9" **120.00**
Basket, trout
    Birch Bark, center hole in tin lid . . .   **525.00**
    Splint, high neck, web strap **495.00**
    Willow, loops on sides, small lid opening, replaced hinge and latch loop **120.00**
Bobber, float
    Panfish, hp, black, red, and white stripes, 5" l **10.00**
    Pike, hp, yellow, green, and red stripes, 12" l **24.00**
Book
    Camp, Samuel G, *Taking Trout With The Dry Fly,* NY, 1930, dj **24.00**
    Griswold, Frank Gray, *Fish Facts & Fancies,* Norwood, 1923, sgd . . .   **75.00**
    Hewitt, Edward R, *Hewitt's Handbook of Fly Fishing,* NY, 1933 . . .   **50.00**
    Loller, Larry, *The Treasury of Angling,* 1963, 251 pgs **16.00**
    Robinson, Ben C, *Pond, Lake & Stream Fishing,* Philadelphia, 1941, dj **12.50**
    Stevens, Charles W, *Fishing in Maine Lakes,* Boston, 1881 . . . .   **85.00**
Box, fishing tackle salesman's, lettered, 5' l, 2' w, from buggy of Thomas Kenyon, Gladding Co, New England, late 19th C **550.00**
Canoe, 17½' l, 35" w, light blue canvas covered, yellow trim, two cane seats   **150.00**

Booklet, "Where to fish in Western Michigan," The Grand Rapids Herald, 64 pages, soft cov, black and white maps, folded "Official Michigan Service Map," 6 × 9", $8.00.

Canoe Seat, folding, rattan **360.00**
Catalog
    Bristol Rod Company, #39, fishing rods, reels, and lines **130.00**
    Heddon, 1952, fishing tackle **38.00**
    H W Hawes & Co, fishing rods, 26 pgs **70.00**
    Shakespeare, 1909, tackle, 64 pgs. .   **120.00**
Creel
    Birchbark, sewn, leather hinges, wooden toggle latch, sgd on interior "Paul Reading, Narrow Lake, June, 1927" **350.00**
    Crushed Willow, form fit, leather bound, curved back, carrying strap, printed ruler on back, 14" l, 7" w, 9" h **25.00**
    Mahogany, copper hinges **950.00**
    Whole Willow, woven rim, center hole, orig latch, strap and loop, leather harness, wire hinges **330.00**
    Wicker, ribbed bow front, straight back, 12" l, 6" d, 8" h **18.00**
Decoy
    Bass, Bud Stewart, wood and aluminum, worn paint, 6½" l **95.00**

Creel, wicker, leather straps, 14" w, 9" h, $30.00.

Crayfish, Bud Stewart, 6¼" l **160.00**
Fish
  5¼" l, glass eyes, bright paint, initialed "MM" **35.00**
  6" l, cast aluminum body, sheet
  aluminum fins and tail **18.00**
  7¼" l, spinner, wood and tin,
  curved tail, orig paint. **16.50**
  12¼" l, primitive, glass eyes, worn
  paint, fins rusted **50.00**
  15¼" l, eating a smaller fish, glass
  eyes, bright paint **115.00**
  17" l, tubular, primitive, tack eyes,
  worn and weathered paint **50.00**
  Muskie, Bud Stewart, wood and aluminum, worn paint, 11½" l **75.00**
  Pike
  6¾" l, Bud Stewart, wood and aluminum, worn paint **85.00**
  15" l, wood, glass eyes **75.00**
Fishing License
  1922, Resident Citizen's, paper,
  white, black printing, 5½ x 7" . . . **30.00**
  1929, Resident Citizen's, paper,
  blue, black letters, 2½ x 4" **6.00**
  1930, Non-Resident, pinback but-
  ton, gray and black **15.00**
Line Dryer
  Edward Vom Hofe, sgd **250.00**
  L T Weiss **200.00**
Lure
  Abbey & Imbrie
  Basser, #8500, 1922, 4¼" l **35.00**
  Spoon-Fish #590, aluminum,
  1930, 4¼" l **300.00**
  Arbogast
  Jitterbug, wood, 1937, 2¾" l **25.00**
  Sputter Bug, 1955, 3¾" l **4.00**
  Bucktail Jigs, six white, nine yellow,
  orig packets **30.00**
  Carters Bestever, wood, white and
  red, pressed eyes, 3" l **8.00**
  Creek Chub Bait Co
  River Rustler, 1930, 2⅝" l **125.00**
  Wagtail Chub Deluxe, wood, mul-
  let finish, smooth tail, glass
  eyes **22.00**
  Edkins, minnow, silver tinsel inside
  clear hollow glass body, painted
  brass head, painted eyes, German
  silver tail stamped "C. Edkins-Pat-
  ent," five clear glass beads between treble hook and tail,
  spinner, 3½" l **400.00**
  Foss, Frog Wiggler, brass, 1926,
  1¾" l **75.00**
  Heddon
  Crab Wiggler #1800, 1915, 4" l **50.00**
  Dowagiac Minnow #100, yellow
  sides, black and red stripes, L-rig **85.00**
  River Runt Spook, jointed, floater,
  4" l **10.00**

Spin-Diver, #3000 series, glass
  eyes, three triple hooks **45.00**
Jamison
  Muskie Coaxer, surface trolling,
  tail mounted single hook **15.00**
  Winged Weedless Mascot #2,
  double belly hook, trailing double hook, luminous painted
  body, red head **20.00**
Keeling, Expert Minnow, wood, five
  hooks, 1919, 4" l **250.00**
Kingfisher, Wood Minnow, Series
  101, glass eyes, green, orange, and
  red body, orig box, 3" l **30.00**
K & K, Minnowette, jointed body,
  silver shiner finish plug, green top,
  silver bottom with scales, metal
  tail, 3½" l **325.00**
Lane, Wagtail Wobbler, brown and
  gold, 3⅞" l **125.00**
Moonlight Bait Co
  Baby Bass Seeker, tack eyes, 2½" l **65.00**
  Muskie Pikaroon, yellow body,
  black and red on back, glass
  eyes, 1922 . . . . **80.00**
  Pikaroon, spotted, red and yellow,
  glass eyes **45.00**
  Wilson Wobbler, three hooks,
  4¼" l **45.00**
Paw Paw Bait Co
  Great Injured Minnow #3400,
  glass eyes, 4" l **125.00**
  Muskie Hair Mouse, deer hair, red
  head, black eyes, 4¼" l **125.00**
Pflueger
  Daisy Spinner #200, 1898 . . . . . . **35.00**
  Monarch, three hooks, glass eyes,
  1908, 2¾" l **75.00**
  Neverfail Minnow, decal eyes,
  1927, 3" l **50.00**
  Pearl Minnow, saltwater, 3½" l **25.00**
  Self Striker Spoon, large, 4¼" l **15.00**
  Riley Haskell, minnow, handmade,
  silver plated copper body, brass
  tail and fins, wire wrapped double
  hook, marked "R. Haskell, Paines-
  ville, O. Pat'd Sep. 20, 1859,"
  4½" **8,500.00**
Shakespeare
  Frog Skin Bait, glass eyes, 3¾" l **65.00**
  Sea Witch, saltwater, spotted
  body, glass eyes **100.00**
  Surface Minnow, emb eyes, 2¾" l **75.00**
  Tarpalunge #6640, 5¾" l **400.00**
South Bend Bait Co
  Bass-Oreno, glass eyes, 1923,
  3½" l **25.00**
  Minnow, five hooks, 1910, 3¾" l **350.00**
  Pike Oreno, green scale finish,
  glass eyes, boxed **25.00**
Winchester, Minnow #9216, five
  hooks **275.00**

Minnow Trap
  Handmade, metal and mesh, hinged
    door, 12 × 10 × 10″ **32.00**
  Orvis, glass **88.00**
  Shakespeare, glass, pale green, metal
    lid, emb name, 1 gal **85.00**
Net
  Kosmic, sgd, 62″ l **55.00**
  Telescoping, brass and copper, fold-
    ing **125.00**
Reel
  Abbie & Imbrie
    Casting Reel, latch stop, 1880s   **150.00**
    Sea Bright, bakelite, 1920s **35.00**
  Appleton & Litchfield, fly reel, Ger-
    man silver and black hard rubber,
    built-in click, Boston, MA **500.00**
  Bogdan, Baby Bogdan, orig leather
    case, 2¼″ d **1,300.00**
  Bradford & Anthony, casting, silver,
    1870s **175.00**
  Hardy Bros
    The Perfect, salmon reel, hard rub-
      ber handle, no ring guide, brass
      foot, adjustable drag, 4¼″ d   **225.00**
    The Uniqua, black handle, en-
      forced crescent latch, ridged
      brass foot, 3⅛″ d **55.00**
  Heddon
    Casting Reel 4–18, 1920s **750.00**
    Chief Dowagiac, 1920s **65.00**
    Lone Eagle, 1930s **45.00**
  Hendryx, raised pillar type, multiply-
    ing, fancy handle, horn knob, two
    button back plate, drag, click,
    nickel over brass **25.00**
  L A Kiefer, bait casting, slide and pull
    drag, pat Aug 23, 1881/Feb 21,
    1882, missing rear bearing cap   **500.00**
  Langley, Streamlite Deluxe, 1940s   **45.00**
  Meisselbach, casting reel, bakelite,
    1896 . . . .   **125.00**
  Orvis, Orvis Fly Reel, aluminum,
    1920 . . . .   **450.00**
  Pennell Reel Co, Philadelphia, cast-
    ing, brass, 40 yard line capacity,
    1½″ d **15.00**
  Pflueger
    Four-Brothers Eclipse, 1917 . . . .   **35.00**
    Sal Trout Fly Reel, 1915 . . . .   **25.00**
  Rochester Reel Co, Quick-A-Part,
    nine multiplier, 1909 . . . .   **175.00**
  Shakespeare
    Automatic Fly Reel, 1926 . . . . . .   **15.00**
    Champion, 1914 . . . .   **25.00**
    Special Tournament #1744, 1940   **250.00**
  South Bend Bait Co, Super Reel
    #1300, aluminum, 1931 . . . .   **250.00**
  Uslan 500, Model 1, line grab and
    under spool tension adjustment. .   **50.00**
  Vom Hofe, Julius, trout, #5, German
    silver and hard rubber **375.00**

Winchester
  Casting Reel, 1920s **125.00**
  Single Action Reel, 1920 . . . . . .   **50.00**
Rod
  Andrus, 3 pcs, two tips, red and black
    intermediates, wood reel seat,
    "Made by H. Andrus-1918-Hart-
    ford, CT." engraved on nickel-sil-
    ver butt cap, 8′ l **150.00**
  Barney & Berry, trout fly, 3 pcs, two
    tips, honey wraps, black interme-
    diate winds, German silver and
    screw-down reel seat, orig cane
    case and bag, 8½′ l **160.00**
  Carpenter, Brownstone, 7′ 9″ l **1,200.00**
  Forest, Maker & Kelso, 2 pcs, one tip,
    salmon, wood, dark brown finish,
    brass sliding reel bands, cork butt,
    rubber butt cap, 10′ l **10.00**
  Granger Special, fly, split bamboo,
    green wraps, dark colored cane,
    cork reel seat, featherweight, 8′ l   **175.00**
  Hardy, salmon, 3 pcs, two tips, cane,
    dark maroon wrap and intermedi-
    ates, patent steel center, cork grip
    butt, ferrule plugs, old rod bag and
    65″ wood rod box, 16′ l **150.00**
  Heddon
    Blue Water, fly, 3 pcs, split bam-
      boo, 9′ l **125.00**
    Pal, casting, 1 pc, steel, 5½′ l . . .   **20.00**
  H L Leonard
    Special Tournament, 3 pcs, two
      tips, salmon dry fly, honey wraps,
      red tip, German silver reel seat,
      orig bag, tag, and tube, 9′ l . . .   **175.00**
    Trout, 3 pcs, two tips, engraved,
      8′ l **5,500.00**
  Horrocks & Ibbotson, 3 pcs, two tips,
    fly, split bamboo, maroon wraps,
    9′ l **40.00**
  Montague, trout, 3 pcs, two tips,
    black and maroon wraps and in-
    termediates, silver screw-down
    reel band, fitted case, 9′ l **35.00**
  Orvis, 3 pcs, two tips, red wraps,
    screw-down reel band, cedar foot,
    orig bag and tube, 8½′ l **225.00**
  Payne, bait casting, 5′ l **935.00**
  Powell, trout, orig bag and tube, 7′
    2″ l **400.00**
  South Bend
    Casting, 2 pcs, split bamboo, 5½′ l   **50.00**
    Spinning, Joe Bates #569, 2 pcs,
      split bamboo, 7′ l **75.00**
  Salmon Fly
    Col Esmond Drury, double hook,
      General Practitioner **275.00**
    Jimmy Younger, Wilkinson **132.00**
  Spring Graff, MSA Co, Gladstone, MI,
    pat June 1900, wooden handle,
    37½″ l **275.00**

Tackle Box
  Heddon Outing, fitted interior, fish
    measure, c1930. . . . .   **100.00**
  Leather, fitted metal interior, con-
    tains assorted weights, small vise,
    one reel, hooks, hardware, and old
    floats **60.00**
  Wooden, canvas covered, contents
    include one each small S handled
    Multiplier, unmarked reel, 2⅝
    Multiplier Trout reel, Pepper-type
    spinner-fly lure, and hooks,
    leather fly keeper, two Phantoms,
    and assortment of flies **90.00**

HOLIDAYS

History: Holidays provided a welcome break from the tedious daily chores that were a constant in Country living. Work could not be totally ignored, however; the cows had to be milked and the animals fed, holiday or not. The rural community followed a Sunday, rather than a weekday, schedule.

Religious holidays tended to be family-oriented and personal. Coming together was achieved at the traditional church service. Patriotic holidays were community celebrations, a time when frivolity prevailed.

Many holidays have both religious and secular overtones such as Christmas, St. Patrick's Day, Easter, and Halloween. National holidays such as the Fourth of July and Thanksgiving are part of one's yearly planning. There are also regional holidays; Fastnacht Day in Pennsylvania-German country is just one example.

Some holidays are the creation of the merchandising industry, e.g., Valentine's Day, Mother's Day, Father's Day, etc. The two leading forces in the perpetuation of holiday gift giving are the card industry and the floral industry. Through slick promotional campaigns they constantly create new occasions to give their products. Other marketing aspects follow quickly. Holiday items change annually. Manufacturers constantly must appeal to the same buyer.

Collectors tend to specialize in one holiday; Christmas, Halloween, and Easter are the most popular. Christmas collectors split into two groups—those who collect material associated with the Christmas tree and those who collect Santa Claus-related material. Halloween and Easter collectors tend to be generalists, albeit some Easter collectors limit their collection to Easter bunnies. New collectors still can find bargains, especially in the Thanksgiving and Valentine's Day collectibles.

Many holiday collectibles were manufactured abroad. Germany and Japan are two of the leading exporters of holiday items to the United States. German items from the turn of the century are highly prized.

It is possible to build a holiday collection around a single type of object. Two possibilities are post cards and papier mâché candy containers. Among contemporary material, it is possible to find one or more limited edition collectors' plates issued for most holidays.

One of the most overlooked holiday collectibles is the greeting card. A greeting card's message and artwork is an important reflection of the values of the time the card was printed. With the exception of Valentines, most examples, even those from the early decades of the twentieth century, are priced under two dollars.

References: Robert Brenner, *Christmas Past,* Schiffer Publishing, 1985; Robert Brenner, *Christmas Through The Decades,* Schiffer Publishing, 1993; Juanita Burnett, *A Guide To Easter Collectibles,* Collector Books, 1992; Helaine Fendelman and Jeri Schwartz, *The Official Price Guide Holiday Collectibles,* House of Collectibles, 1991; L–W Book Sales (pub.), *Favors & Novelties: Wholesale Trade List No. 26, 1924–1925,* price list available; Polly and Pam Judd, *Santa Dolls and Figurines Price Guide: Antique to Contemporary,* Hobby House Press, 1992; Ruth Webb Lee, *A History of Valentines,* reprinted by the National Valentine Collectors Association; Robert M. Merck, *Deck The Halls,* Abbeville Press, 1992; Margaret Schiffer, *Christmas Ornaments: A Festive Study,* Schiffer Publishing, 1984; Margaret Schiffer, *Holiday Toys and Decorations,* Schiffer Publishing, 1985; Lissa Bryan-Smith and Richard Smith, *Christmas Collectibles: A Guide To Selecting, Collecting, and Enjoying The Treasures Of Christmas Past,* Chartwell Books, 1993; Margaret and Kenn Whitmyer, *Christmas Collectibles, Second Edition,* Collector Books, 1994.

Collectors' Clubs: Del-Mar-Pa Ornament Kollector's Klub, 131 South Tartan Dr, Elkton, MD 21921; Enesco Treasury of Christmas Ornaments Collectors' Club, One Enesco Plaza, PO Box 773, Elk Grove Village, IL 60009–0073; Golden Glow of Christmas Past, 6401 Winsdale St, Golden Valley, MN 55427; Hallmark Collectors Club Connection, PO Box 110, Fenton, MI 48430; Hallmark Keepsake Ornament Collectors Club, PO Box 412734, Kansas City, MO 64141–2734; National Valentine Collectors Association, Box 1404, Santa Ana, CA 92702.

Periodicals: *Golden Glow of Christmas Past,* 6401 Winsdale St, Golden Valley, MN 55427; *I Love Christmas,* PO Box 5708, Coralville, IA 52241; *Ornament Trader Magazine,* PO Box 7908, Clearwater, FL 34618–7908 *Starlight,* Planetarium Station, PO Box 770, New York, NY 10024; *Trick or Treat Trader,* PO Box 499, 4 Lawrence St, Winchester, NH 03470; *Twelve Months of Christmas,* PO Box 97172, Pittsburgh, PA 15229.

Museum: Hallmark Visitors Center, PO Box 580, Kansas City, MO 64141.

Reproduction Craftspersons: *Christmas*—Linda and John Beazley, Parsley Junction Paperworks, 183 Sylvan Dr, Pottstown, PA 19464; Rob and Dianna Carlson, Carlson's Christmas Collectibles, Rt 4, 30997 Gerken Rd, Defiance, OH 43512; Yvonne Carpenter, Snickles and Kringles, 123 Chestnut St, Haddonfield, NJ 08033; James A Frank, Box 55, Baldwin, MD 21013; Donald and Janice Hobart, 614 Geneva Dr, Westminster, MD 21157; Cheryl Jones, Timeless Treasures, 52411 St Rt 513, Summerfield, OH 43788; Cynthia Jones, 1515 Meadow Creek Dr, Pacific, MO 63069; Bush Prisby, 163 Camp Meeting Road Ext, Sewickley, PA 15143; Marie Nelson-Kidd, 324 Brown St, Santa Rosa, CA 95404; Ronnie and Clark Pearson, Delights of the Past, 21515 Raymond Rd, Marysville, OH 43040; Alice Strom, Spirit of America, R2, Box 358A, Nevis, MN 56467; Roberta Taylor, Box 336, Jeromesville, OH 44840; Lana Testa, 42 Camp St, Milford, MA 01757; Elizabeth Werner, 9781 Bluebird St, NW, Coon Rapids, MN 55433; Julia Mary Williams, Sweet William Studio, 15265 Thirty Mile Rd, Romeo-Ray, MI 48096.

Dummy Boards—Boardwalk Originals, PO Box 358, Bristol, IN 46507; *Figures*—Pat Broyles, Rte 1, Box 494-C, Weyers Cave, VA 24486; Carolyn E Taylor, 300 Artillery Rd, Yorktown, VA 23692; *Easter Eggs*—John J Hejna, 4529–289th St, Toledo, OH 43611; Valerie M Martz, Eggstrordinaire!, PO Box 118, Doylestown, PA 18901; Elizabeth Mayer, RR 3, Box 290, Langhorne, PA 19047; *General*—Johathan K. Bastian, Pennsylvania German Woodcarvings, Rte 2, Box 240, Robesonia, PA 19551; William Boyer, 5249 Angling Rd, Wooster, OH 44691; Will Carlton, Carlton Studio, 2925 McMillan Rd, San Luis Obispo, CA 92401; Bruce Catt, C & V Emporium, PO Box 985 Planetarium Sta, New York, NY 10024; Lois Clarkson, Snowdin Studios, Box 28, Buckingham, PA 18912; Ruth Clotfelter Camenisch, Clotfelter Creations, Rte 2, Box 207-A, Monett, MO 65708; Sandra Coker, A Visit From St Nicholas, 1213 W Mulberry St, Salem, IN 47167; Glenn F Hale, Star Route, Harmonyville Rd, Pottstown, PA 19464; Joretta & Ron Headlee, 22 Downing Circle, Downingtown, PA 19335; Gerard Lavoie, Glassblower, Gerard Originals, PO Box 531, Methuen, MA 01844; Lydia Withington Holmes, Pewterer, Barton Hill, Stow, MA 01775; David & Sharon Jones, Three Feathers Pewter, Box 232, Shreve, OH 44676; Ed & Amy Pennebaker, Red Fern Handblown Glass, HCR 68, Box 19A, Salem, AR 72576; Pamela F Pizzichil, RD 2, Pottstown, PA 19464; Randy & Pam Tate, Knot in Vane, 805 N 11th St, DeKalb, IL 60115; Roberta Taylor, PO Box 336, Jeromesville, OH 44840.

Reproduction Manufacturers: *Christmas*—Cloar's Store, PO Box 5, 113 East Huntington, Trenton, TN 38382; C & V Emporium, Box 985, Planetarium Station, New York, NY 10024-0541; Keepsakes, 4 Old Fishing Pond Rd, Sanford,

ME 04073; *Feather Trees*—Twins Feather Trees, 1543 Pullan Ave, Cinti, OH 45223; *Figures*—Arestacraft, Brady Lane, Plymouth, MA 02360; Wooden Images, 861 Main St, Hingham, MA 02043.

General—Amazon Vinegar & Pickling Works Drygoods, 2218 E 11th St, Davenport, IA 52803; Applecore Creations, PO Box 29696, Columbus, OH 43229; Briere Design, 229 North Race St, Statesville, NC 28677; Cabin Fever, 5770 S Meridian, Laingsburg, MI 48848; Checkerberry Hill, 253 Westridge Ave, Daly City, CA 94015; Country at Heart Creations, PO Box 67-B, Forest City, PA 18421; Country Bouquet, PO Box 200, Kellogg, MN 55945; Country House, 5939 Trails End, Three Oaks, MI 49128; Country Lady, PO Box 68, 201 E. Main St, Larwill, IN 46764; The Crafty Attic, 1107 Copeland School Rd, West Chester, PA 19380; Designs in Copper, 7541 Emery Rd, Portland, MI 48875; The Evergreen Press, Inc, 3380 Vincent Rd, Pleasant Hill, CA 94523; Faith Mountain Country Fare, Main St, Box 199, Sperryville, VA 22740; Fernswood Strawwork, Box 26, R.D. 2, New London, OH 44851; Five Trails Antiques and Country Accents, 116 E Water St, Circleville, OH 43113; Gooseberry Patch, PO Box 634, Delaware, OH 43015; Gray's Attic, Box 532, Manson, IA 50453; Lamplighter Antiques, 615 Silver Bluff Rd, Aiden, SC 29801; Lancaster Collection, PO Box 6074, Lancaster, PA 17603; Mathew's Wire & Wood, 654 W Morrison, Frankfort, IN 46041; Matthews Emporium, 157 N Trade St, PO Box 1038, Matthews, NC 28106; McLeach, Box 575, Fitchburg, MA 01420; Mulberry Magic, PO Box 62, Ruckersville, VA 22968; The Painted Pony, 8392 West M-72, Traverse City, MI 49684; Pure and Simple, PO Box 535, 117 W Hempstead, Nashville, AR 71852; The Roos Collection, PO Box 20668, New York, NY 10025; Rustique Designs, Rte 4, Box 295, Parsons, KS 67357; The Tinhorn, 9610 W 190th, Lowwell, IN 46356; Unfinished Business, PO Box 246X, Wingate, NC 28174; Woodpenny's, 27 Hammatt St, Ipswich, MA 01938; You & Me Inc, Rte 1, Box 179, Owalonna, MN 55060; *Ornaments*—Joyeana's, 9792 Edmonds Way, Edmonds, WA 98020; Timbered Ridge, 2921 Pebble Creek, Ann Arbor, MI 48108; *Santas*—Attic Treasures, 419 East Third St, Madison, IN 47250; Beaumont Pottery, PO Box 15, Seagrove, NC 27341; Briercroft, Rte 3, Box 262, Winchester, IN 47394; Knobstone Studio, RR 3, Box 168 A, Scottsburg, IN 47170; Maine Woods, Main St, PO Box 270, Bowdoinham, ME 04008; Merrytymes, PO Box 4699, Pagosa Springs, CO 81147; Ray's, 134 Volunteer Dr, Hendersonville, TN 37075; Schrimsher Originals, 308 Woodlawn Dr, Longview, TX 75604; Springfield Potteryworks, 3346 Murray Rd, Finksburg, MD 21048; St Nicholas Collection, 5260 Old Salem Rd, Clayton, OH 45315; Stone Soup Designs, Inc, 42 Summit Dr, Corte Madera, CA 94925; Uniquely Yours, PO Box 16861, Philadelphia, PA 19142; Vaillancourt, 145 Armsby Rd, Sutton, MA 01590; D Wesson and Co, Inc, 4075 Monroe Rd, Kennesaw, GA 30144.

Christmas

Apron, organdy, applied berries and mistletoe, early 20th C **35.00**

Bank, chalkware, Santa, early 20th C   **95.00**

Building

House, cardboard, white mica, cellophane windows, 4" h **5.00**

Village, litho paper, five buildings, USA, 5" h **25.00**

Calendar, 1912, litho paper, family around Christmas tree **35.00**

Candy Box, cardboard, Santa on zeppelin holding stars and stripes   **225.00**

Candy Container

Reindeer, papier mâché, blown glass eyes, neck closure, 6" h   **350.00**

Santa

Climbing into chimney, glass, c1920, 5" h **125.00**

Holding feather tree, papier mâché, Germany, 11" h **950.00**

On rooftop, litho cardboard, mid 20th C, 9" h **75.00**

Snowman, papier mâché, wearing top hat, holding branch, Germany, early 20th C **110.00**

Chocolate Mold, Santa, tin, four cavities, Germany **225.00**

Cookie Cutter, Father Christmas, tin, 19th C **600.00**

Doorstop, Santa, cast iron, early 20th C, 10½" h **350.00**

Figure, Santa, papier mâché and cloth, felt costume, rabbit fur beard, Germany, 20th C, 9½" h   **525.00**

Flask, "A Merry Christmas/Happy New Year," smoky aqua, half barrel shape, woman sitting on barrel, tooled lip, smooth base, 1880–1900 . . . .   **135.00**

Light Bulb

Bell, milk glass, Santa face dec, red, green, blue, and black, c1930, 2½" h **125.00**

Santa, red suit, green pants, orange bag, c1930, 3" h **110.00**

Light Set

Bubble, orig box, mid 20th C . . .   **75.00**

Fruit, orig box, early 1920s **300.00**

Nativity Figure, composition

Camel, hide covering, wooden legs, Germany, 5" l **38.00**

Donkey, hide covering, wooden legs, Germany, 3" h **20.00**

Mary, kneeling, Japan, 2" h **2.00**

Sheep, white wool coat, wooden legs, marked "Germany" on red ribbon collar, 5" h **60.00**

Shepherd, kneeling, Germany, 5¼" h **10.00**

Ornament

Bisque, doll, human hair **75.00**

Chromolithograph

Father Christmas, cotton batting coat, flat, 9" h **150.00**

Three Children, wearing winter clothing, tinsel trim, 4" h . . .   **15.00**

Composition, dog **25.00**

Cotton Batting

Girl with basket **175.00**

Santa, diecut scrap **125.00**

Snowman **75.00**

Dresden

Baby Buggy, silver **150.00**

Bear with stick, gold **125.00**

Bird Cage **125.00**

Cross, gold **150.00**

Duck **225.00**

Elephant, silver **400.00**

Fox **225.00**

Frog, sitting **150.00**

Rooster, white **350.00**

Santa in sleigh **75.00**

Vase **100.00**

Glass

Angel, gold hair, red cheeks . . .   **125.00**

Bell, "Merry Christmas" **35.00**

Boy, wearing red jacket and hat   **125.00**

Candle Cup, glass, red **35.00**

Candy Cane, white, red stripes, 7¼" l **6.00**

Clown and begging dog, c1910   **225.00**

Grape Cluster **35.00**

Santa, windup, walking, plaster face and arms, cotton beard and mustache, red felt coat, metal legs, holding feather tree and basket, Germany, 7¼" h, $750.00.

Icicle	50.00
Mandolin.	75.00
Pig, pink	145.00
Pine Cone, blow, orig blue paint, c1910, 2½" h.	125.00
Rose and leaf, white, clip-on	55.00
Santa in sleigh	75.00
Snowman, wearing green hat, holding broom.	65.00
Teddy Bear, yellow	175.00
Tree, red garland	75.00
Vase, blue and pink flower dec, wire-wrapped	110.00
Metal	
Basket, 3" h	35.00
Wreath, painted.	35.00
Tin, wheelbarrow	75.00
Post Card	
Christmas winter scene, hold-to-light type, early 20th C	35.00
Santa Claus, holding mistletoe wreath, early 20th C	10.00
Santa	
Cardboard, holding sack, red and white, c1930, 5" h.	15.00
Celluloid, sleigh, red and white, c1930, 10½" l.	125.00
Composition, red cloth robe, black boots, white beard, c1910	450.00
Cotton Batting, white body, scrap paper face, red buttons, 10" h	200.00
Stocking	
Fabric, 30" l, cut and sewn, St Nicholas with toys on one side, smiling moon over city on reverse, "T'was the Night Before Christmas" verse	130.00
Paper, chromolithograph, Germany, early 20th C	250.00
Tablecloth, paper, Santa in sleigh with toys and reindeer, orig cellophane package	15.00
Toy	
Battery Operated, Santa with scooter, orig box, mid 20th C	150.00
Pull, composition, Santa with reindeer, Germany, c1890, 9⅞" l	300.00
Windup, tin, celluloid head, rings bell, orig box, mid 20th C	50.00
Tree	
Chenille, green, orig box, 1920, 7' h	300.00
Feather	
18" h, white, early 20th C	300.00
38" h, sq wood base with stenciled holly dec, Germany, mid 20th C.	175.00
39" h, red berries, tin candle sockets, turned wood base with old white paint, marked "Made in Germany".	200.00

Tree Stand	
Cast Iron	
8" h, Father Christmas, Germany, early 20th C.	125.00
11" d, cast iron, relief Santa's head and beard, orig red, green, and gold paint	265.00
Wood, Germany, early 20th C. . .	40.00
Wreath	
Felt holly leaves, composition berries, wire frame, homemade, 12" d	35.00
Plastic, Santa dec, electrified, mid 20th C, 26" d	65.00
Easter	
Basket	
Cardboard, woven, cellophane grass, cotton batting chicks . . .	25.00
Twig, grass and chenille chicks, early 20th C.	75.00
Wood, painted flowers, paper label on base marked "Made in Germany," 6" d, 10" handle	18.00
Candy Box, sq, litho cardboard, bunnies and carrots	10.00
Candy Container	
Chick, glass eyes, wire spring feet, c1930	175.00
Chicken Man, composition, dressed, 4" h	140.00
Duck, composition, 1920s	125.00
Egg, papier mâché, litho of boy golfer on front, separates in middle, marked "Germany," 4" l	35.00
Gentleman Rabbit, composition, yellow jacket, Germany, 4" h	140.00
Rabbit	
Composition, fur covered, carrot in mouth, c1900	225.00
Papier mâché, white, open back, Germany.	35.00
Rooster, composition, bright colors, fine detail, metal feet, removable head, marked "Germany," 5" h	60.00
Cookie Cutter, tin, egg shape, late 19th C.	5.00
Figure	
Chick in Egg, celluloid.	20.00
Rabbit, sitting, glass eyes, West Germany, 2" h	15.00
Nodder, rabbit, chalk, brown flocking, marked "USA," 1950s, 5" h	12.00
Post Card	
"Easter Greetings," emb, boy and girl carrying flowers	5.00
"Happy Easter," chick emerging from shell, four chicks, and flowers.	10.00
Roly Poly, rabbit, celluloid, dressed in purple, standing on ball, Japan, 4½" h	25.00

Sheet Music, *Easter Parade* **10.00**
Toy, windup, rabbit, fur covered, hops, marked "Japan," 5" h **55.00**

Halloween
Apron, crepe paper, orange and black, ruffled edge. **25.00**
Candy Box, cardboard, Halloween dec, 1930s **15.00**
Candy Container
 Boot, cardboard, pumpkin face, 4" h **40.00**
 Cat, papier mâché, standing, blown glass eyes, Germany, early 20th C **195.00**
 Pumpkin, cardboard, molded, 1940 . . . .   **65.00**
 Witch, composition, Germany, 4" h **245.00**
Chocolate Mold, witch, four cavities, Germany, early 20th C **150.00**
Diecut, black cat face, emb **22.50**
Figures, set of 3, devil, cat, and pumpkin, chenille, 3" h, price for set . .   **17.50**
Jack-O-Lantern Insert, 4" h **55.00**
Lantern
 Black Cat. **160.00**
 Goblin, pumpkin head, papier mâché, cloth dec, 5¼" h **220.00**
 Jack-O-Lantern, tin, paint touch-ups, 1900–08. . . . .   **400.00**
Post Card, "Happy Halloween," witch riding broom, early 20th C   **10.00**
Tambourine, black Halloween cat face.   **40.00**
Trick-Or-Treat Bag, litho paper, pumpkin head and "Happy Halloween," 1940 . . . .   **18.00**

Independence Day
American Flag
 28 Stars, cotton, hand sewn, stars arranged in a star pattern on blue field, 34 × 52" **225.00**
 35 Stars, homespun, hand sewn, stencil marked in three places "Jam Van Dyk" **275.00**
Bank, mechanical, Uncle Sam, late 19th C. **1,550.00**

Diecut, mechanical cat, black with orange outline, 1940s, $15.00.

Candy Container
 Independence Hall, glass, dated   **150.00**
 Liberty Bell, glass, blue, early 20th C **75.00**
 Uncle Sam, composition, removable base, 1930s **175.00**
Ice Cream Mold, pewter, flag, hinged, 1930. . . . .   **75.00**
Sheet Music, *Stars & Stripes Forever*   **10.00**

New Year's Day
Banner, fabric, "Out With the Old-In With the New," 1935 . . . .   **22.00**
Candy Container, champagne bottle, cardboard, paper label, 1920. . . .   **125.00**
Handkerchief, cotton, bell dec and "Happy New Year Greetings," 1940 . . . .   **6.00**
Hat
 Cone shape, cardboard, crepe paper and cut-out silver foil dec, 1928 . . . .   **12.00**
 Headband, tissue paper, silver foil, and feather dec, early 20th C **10.00**
Menu, January 1, 1906, open house, handpainted pen and ink design   **25.00**
Noisemaker
 Horn, litho tin, New Year's baby, red, yellow, and blue, wood mouthpiece, 1920 . . . .   **10.00**
 Snapper, cardboard, crepe paper dec, glitter "Happy New Year"   **5.00**
 Whistle, paper and cardboard, feather blow-out, 1930. . . . . . .   **6.00**
Post Card, "Happy New Year," emb, 1912 surrounded by flowers **10.00**

President's Day
Abraham Lincoln
 Bank, bottle, glass, tin closure . . .   **25.00**
 Plate, blue jasperware, Wedgwood, mid 20th C **95.00**
George Washington
 Candy Container
  Hat, cardboard, tri-cornered, cloth cherries **30.00**
  Tree Stump, papier mâché, surrounded by composition cherries, marked "Germany," 3" h **45.00**
 Diecut, Washington with hatchet and cherry, flanked by stump with hatchet, 2½" h, set of 3   **8.00**
 Ice Cream Mold, cast iron, Washington chopping cherry tree, early 20th C **75.00**

St. Patrick's Day
Candy Container, figural
 Bust, Irishman, molded cardboard, handpainted **75.00**
 Top Hat, cardboard, green and white, shamrock in band, early 20th C **75.00**

Turkey Platter, Barnyard King, transfer, multicolored, Johnson Brothers, England, 20½" l, 16" w, $50.00.

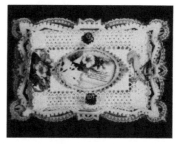

Valentine, lacy pull-out, diecuts and stamped lace, decal-edge, early 1900s, 4½ × 7", $35.00.

Diecut
  Leprechaun, green top hat, smoking clay pipe, marked "Germany," set of 42 . . . .   15.00
  Shamrock, Irish lass center, marked "Germany," set of 40   20.00
Doll, boy, composition, green and white felt clothing, white felt hat with shamrock trim, marked "Japan," 4½" h 35.00
Handkerchief, linen, embroidered shamrock, crocheted green border   8.00
Sheet Music, *When Irish Eyes Are Smiling*, 1930s 10.00
Tablecloth, linen, embroidered shamrocks, early 20th C 75.00
Thanksgiving
  Candy Container, turkey
    Cardboard, orange, 1930 . . . . . .   35.00
    Chalk, metal feet, Germany. 25.00
    Composition
      Fantail, horsehair beard, metal feet, marked "Germany," 12" h   85.00
      Folded tail, glass eyes, metal feet, removable head, marked "Germany," 6" h 45.00
      Papier Mâché, green, black, red, 4½" h 20.00
  Chocolate Mold, turkey, Germany, 8" h. 30.00
  Figure, turkey
    Celluloid, white, pink, and blue, weighted bottom, marked "Irwin, USA," 4" h 25.00
    Composition, folded tail, green base, marked "Japan," 6" h . . .   35.00
    Rubber, black, red and green trim, USA, 1½" h. 7.50
  Greeting Card, turkey with feather tail, 1930s. 8.00
  Place Card, turkey, cardboard, emb, stand-up, USA, 3" h 5.00
Valentine's Day
  Candy Box, cardboard, couple riding in car illus, unused, 5 x 8". 15.00

Ice Cream Mold, pewter, entwined hearts and "Love," early 20th C   25.00
Post Card
  Children wearing clown costumes with hearts. 10.00
  Kewpies holding hearts 35.00
  Mailman with Valentines, hold-to-light type, early 20th C. 35.00
Valentine
  Card Style
    Child, verse inside, 4½ × 6". . .   6.00
    Colonial dancers, emb, poem inside, 2¾ × 4¼" 6.00
    Cupid with baby, cut paper lace, emb, orig envelope, 3¼ × 4½" 10.00
    Girl wearing green dress and hat, "To My Sweetheart," red wild rose border, verse inside, 6½" h. 10.00
  Easel Back
    Children ice skating, winter scene, Grace Drayton, early 20th C 25.00
    Girl, carrying red honeycomb paper parasol, 8½" h 50.00
    Girl with basket, Twelvetrees, 1917 . . . .   12.00
  Fold-out
    Carriage, children, and flowers, three dimensional tissue, 1910 . . . .   150.00
    Cupids and flower swags, tissue dec, 1925. . . . .   35.00
    Honeycomb heart, carriage, c1920 . . . .   50.00
  Mechanical
    Black boy, emb cardboard, wearing soldier uniform, 1930s. 50.00
    Cherubs, movable faces and heart festoons, Tuck, 1910   35.00
    Girl on roller skates, emb cardboard, 1930 . . . .   15.00
    Heart, diecut, girl emerging from flower, Tuck, 5½" 15.00

Stand-Up

    Delivery boy on motorbike, holding red hearts, "A Valentine Specially For You," marked "Germany," 4" h . . .   **7.00**

    Girl holding doves, diecut, Germany, 6¾" h **8.00**

Wall Hanging, 4 pcs, Valentine, Clapsaddle type design **25.00**

HUNTING

History: There is a strong link between the Country community and firearms. Almost every farmer owns one or more rifle. These weapons provide self preservation and sport.

Varmints from rats to groundhogs plague the farmer. Some attack small domesticated animals, eat harvested grain, or cause damage that can lead to accidents. The standard means of ridding the farm of varmints is to shoot them.

Hunting also plays an important role in the agrarian community. In lean times, it provides all-important food for the table. In good times, it provides sport and a means of escape from daily chores.

The 15th century arquebus was the forerunner of the modern firearm. The Germans refined the wheelock firing mechanism during the 16th and 17th centuries. English settlers arrived in America with the smoothbore musket; German settlers had rifled arms. Both used the new flintlock firing mechanism.

A major advance was achieved when Whitney introduced interchangeable parts into the manufacturing of rifles. The warfare of the 19th century brought continued refinements in firearms. The percussion ignition system was developed by the 1840s. Minie, a French military officer, produced a viable projectile. By the end of the 19th century cartridge weapons dominated the field.

Two factors control pricing firearms-condition and rarity. The value of any particular antique firearm covers a very wide range. For instance, a Colt 1849 pocket model revolver with a 5" barrel can be priced from $150.00 to $750.00, depending on whether or not all the component parts are original, whether some are missing, how much of the original finish (bluing) remains on the barrel and frame, how much silver plating remains on the brass trigger guard and back strap, and the condition and finish of the walnut grips. Be careful to note any weapon's negative qualities. Know the production run of a firearm before buying it.

Muzzle loading weapons of the 18th and early 19th centuries varied in caliber and required the owner to carry a variety of equipment with him, including a powder horn or flask, patches, flints or percussion caps, bullets, and bullet molds. In addition, military personnel were responsible for bayonets, slings, and miscellaneous cleaning equipment and spare parts.

In the mid-19th century, cartridge weapons replaced their black powder ancestors. Collectors seek anything associated with early ammunition from the cartridges themselves to advertising material. Handling old ammunition can be extremely dangerous due to decomposition of compounds. Seek advice from an experienced collector before becoming involved in this area.

References: Ralf Coykendall, Jr., *Coykendall's Second Sporting Collectibles Price Guide,* Lyons & Burford, 1992; Ralf Coykendall, Jr., *Coykendall's Sporting Collectibles Price Guide,* Lyons & Burford, 1991; Norman Flayderman, *Flayderman's Guide To Antique American Firearms . . . And Their Values,* 5th ed., DBI Books, 1991; Jim and Vivian Karsnitz, *Sporting Collectibles,* Schiffer Publishing, 1992; Joseph Kindig, Jr., *Thoughts On The Kentucky Rifle In Its Golden Age,* 1960, available in reprint; Russell and Steve Quetermous, *Modern Guns: Identification & Values, Revised 8th Edition,* Collector Books, 1991; Gordon L. Stetser, Jr., *The Compleat Muzzleloader,* Mountain Press, 1992.

Periodicals: *Gun List,* 700 State Street, Iola, WI 54990; *Gun Week,* PO Box 488, Buffalo, NY 14209; *The Gun Report,* PO Box 38, Aldeo, IL 61231.

Museums: National Firearms Museum, Washington, DC; Springfield Armory National Historic Site, Springfield, MA.

Reproduction Alert: The amount of reproduction and fake powder horns is large. Be very cautious!

Reproduction Craftspersons: *Firearms*—William J Cooey, 248 Van Horn Rd, Milton, FL 32570; Daniel Winkler, PO Box 255 DTS, Boone, NC 28607; *General*—Mark Odle, Rte 1, Box 40, Reedy, WV 25270; *Powderhorns*—Robert Miller, Golden Age Powderhorns, 100 Summer St, Kennebunk, ME 04043; Michelle Ochonicky, Stone Hollow Scrimshaw Studio, 4059 Toenges Ave, St Louis, MO 63116; Mark Odle, Rte 1, Box 40, Reedy, WV 25270; Scott & Cathy Sibley, Sibley's Engraved Powderhorns, 3224 Wyatt Rd, North Pole, AK 99705.

Reproduction Manufacturers: *Firearms*—Log Cabin Shop, Box 275, Lodi, OH 44254.

Bullet Mold, Winchester, 32–165 caliber **45.00**

Bulletin, Biggs Fur Company Bargain Bulletin, 1933, 8 pgs, fold out, shows traps, guns, fur buying prices, chart card **35.00**

Clay Birds, Winchester, complete in orig box, marked "Pat May 29, 1917"   **100.00**

License, celluloid, Tennessee, 1933–34, 1¾" d **45.00**

Moose Call, Adirondack, birchbark, copper rivets **38.00**

Musket, flintlock, model 1816, type II,
marked "Spring/field—1824" **600.00**
Powder Can
Austin Powder Co, green can, tan
paper label, ½ lb **75.00**
Ditmar's Powder Co, New Sporting
Powder, paper label, 1 lb **90.00**
Eureka Powder Works, Imperial Gun
Powder, orange label, 1 lb **30.00**
Hercules Powder Co, Black Sporting
Powder, orange and black label,
1 lb **45.00**
Robin Hood Powder Co, green,
Robin Hood in red on red and
white label, 1 lb **165.00**
Powder Flask, Wheelock, carved
scenes. **1,050.00**
Powder Horn
5⅜" l, Queen Anne style, tapered
screw cap, flat butt plug **115.00**
7½" l, incised compass design highlighted with buckshot, old patina,
no plug, worn, age cracks, 7½" l **115.00**
7⅞" l, brass trim and screw tip, butt
plug missing **950.00**
9" l, turned domed butt plug, turned
tip, York County, PA **250.00**
10½" l, relief carved animal with
horse head and lion body, inscription with partial pitch inlay "Un
requerdo," cracks and wear,
10½" l **55.00**
Powder Keg
American Powder Mills, black, green
and black label, 25 lbs **60.00**
E I du Pont de Nemours Powder Co,
green, dog on black and white la-
bel, 1 lb **55.00**
Hazard Powder Co, Duck Shooting
Gun Powder, red, 6 lbs **75.00**
King Powder Co, Quick Shot, red,
paper label, 6 lbs **50.00**
Presentation Cup, silver
3½" h
Cylindrical body engraved "Presented by Savannah Rifle Club
to E. H. Rogers, Being one of the
prizes won from the Macon
Club in 1842," marked at base
"O.T.H. Dibble" in rect cartouche, (Oscar T. H. Dibble, Savannah, GA,) minor dent, 5 troy
oz **650.00**
Octagonal body engraved "Pre-
sented to E. H. Rogers by the
Savannah Volunteer Guards for
the best shot 22nd Feby 1844,"
and "C. W. & H." in rect cartouche, (Thomas T. Wilmot,
Charleston, SC,) dents, 4 troy oz **1,000.00**
4" h, octagonal body engraved "This
Goblet was Presented to the

Guards by 1st Lieut. W. Bruen as
a Prize to be shot for Jan 8th 1845,"
and "Presented by the Savannah
Volunteer Guards to private E. H.
Rugers the best shot on 8th Jany
1845," marked "N. J. Bogert" in
rect cartouche on base (Nicholas
J. Bogert, w 1801–1830, New York
City,) minor dents, 6 troy oz **1,050.00**
Rifle
Colt Coltsman Standard, 30–06, bolt
action, repeating, 5- shot box
magazine, 22" blued barrel, ramp
front sight, checkered walnut one-
piece pistol grip stock and tapered
forearm, swivels, late 1950s **270.00**
Harrington & Richardson Pioneer
765, 22 caliber, long rifle, bolt
action, single shot, 24" blued barrel, open rear and hooded bead
front sights, wood Monte Carlo
one-piece semi-grip stock and
forearm, c1950 . . . . **45.00**
Iver Johnson Model X, 22 caliber,
bolt action, single shot, 22" blued
barrel, open rear and blade front
sights, wood one-piece pistol grip
stock and forearm, c1930 . . . . . . **70.00**
Kentucky Long Rifle
48½" l, walnut half stock, percussion lock marked "Henry
Parker Warrented," heavy octagonal barrel initialed "R.B.,"
brass and white metal inlays,
33" l barrel **935.00**
56" l, curly maple full stock, per-
cussion lock sgd "H. E. Leman,
Lancaster, PA," barrel sgd
". . . Marker," 41" l barrel **550.00**
56" l, curly maple full stock, decorative brass patch box, oval silver medallion with engraved
eagle, possibly York County,
PA, flint lock converted to percussion lock, 40½" l barrel . . . **1,325.00**

**Rifle, percussion, half-stock, fancy grade
with brass and silver inlays in tiger maple
stock, c1830, 34⅛ " l, $990.00. Photo-
graph courtesy of C G Sloan & Co, Inc.**

56" l, curly maple full stock, percussion lock, brass patch box, stock has damage and age cracks, 40¼" l barrel **525.00**

Long Gun, New England, Kentucky type, flintlock, half stock, 40¾" octagonal barrel stamped "A. Pratt-Concord-MSS.", lockplate engraved "C. Baker" **415.00**

Marlin Model 422 Varmint King, 222 caliber, bolt action, repeating, 3-shot detachable clip magazine, 24" barrel, peep sight rear and hooded ramp front sights, checkered Monte Carlo pistol grip stock and forearm, c1958. . . . .   **280.00**

Remington Model 141 Gamemaster, 30 caliber, slide action, hammerless, takedown model, 5-shot tubular magazine, 24" barrel, ramp front and adjustable rear sights, checkered walnut pistol grip stock, checkered semi-beavertail slide handle, c1940. . . . .   **265.00**

Sporting, percussion, tiger maple full stock, lockplate marked "Taylor," octagonal barrel, some damage   **600.00**

Winchester, Model 56, 22 caliber, bolt action, repeating, 22" blued barrel, plain walnut one-piece semi-pistol grip stock, c1925 . . . .   **180.00**

Rifle Bag, Kentucky, 9 × 7", leather, tarred fabric cov, homemade 6½" l knife in leather covered wooden scabbard attached to leather carrying strap, bag contains old flints and lead balls **175.00**

Shot Flask and Bag, leather, worn **40.00**

Shotgun

Browning Double Automatic Standard, 12 gauge, semi-automatic, hammerless, 2 shot, 28" full choke barrel, blued, checkered walnut pistol grip stock and forearm, late 1950s **290.00**

Harrington & Richardson Huntsman 351, 16 gauge, bolt action, repeating, 2-shot tubular magazine, 26" adjustable choke barrel, blued, plain Monte Carlo semi-pistol grip stock and forearm, recoil pad, c1955 . . . .   **70.00**

Ithaca Hammerless Double Field Grade, 20 gauge, box lock, top lever, break-open, double barrel, blued, checkered walnut pistol grip stock and short tapered forearm, c1930 . . . .   **400.00**

Iver Johnson Super Trap, 12 gauge, box lock, top lever, break-open, hammerless, 32" full choke double barrel, blued, checkered wal-

nut pistol grip stock and forearm, recoil pad, standard grade, c1940   **410.00**

Marlin Model 410, 410 gauge, lever action, exposed hammer, 5-shot tubular magazine, 26" barrel, 2½" chamber, blued, walnut pistol grip stock and beavertail forearm, c1930 . . . .   **325.00**

Mossberg Model 83D, 410 gauge, bolt action, repeating, 2-shot top loading magazine, 23" barrel, blued, hardwood Monte Carlo semi-pistol grip one-piece stock and forearm, 1940s **65.00**

Parker Bros, Meriden, CT, double barrel, top lever, twist barrel, March 23, 1875 patent date, serial #91812 . . . .   **415.00**

Remington Model 11 Sportsman, 16 gauge, semi-automatic, concealed hammer side ejection, repeating, 2-shot magazine, bottom load, blued barrel, wood semi-pistol grip stock, c1940 . . . .   **250.00**

Richland Model 711 Long Range Waterfowl, 10 gauge, box lock, top lever, break-open, hammerless, double trigger, 32" full choke barrel, blued, checkered walnut pistol grip stock and tapered forearm, early 1960s **220.00**

Savage Model 220, 28 gauge, top lever, break-open, single shot, hammerless, automatic ejector, 30" full choke barrel, blued, plain wood pistol grip stock and forearm, c1935 . . . .   **65.00**

Stevens Model 250, 12 gauge, top lever, break-open, exposed hammer, double trigger, 30" double barrel, blued, checkered walnut pistol grip stock and forearm, c1905 . . . .   **165.00**

Western Long Range, 20 gauge, box lock, top lever, break-open, hammerless, double trigger, double barrel, blued, plain walnut pistol grip stock and forearm, c1930 . . .   **225.00**

Winchester Model 20, 410 gauge, top lever, break-open, box lock, exposed hammer, single shot, 26" full choke barrel, blued, checkered wood pistol grip stock and lipped forearm, early 1920s **190.00**

Skeet Trap, Remington Arms Expert, cast iron, portable, single throw . . .   **85.00**

Target Ball

Amber, molded, raised sunburst on overall net pattern, ½" band around middle marked "BOGARDUS GLASS BALL PATd APRIL '10 1877," chips at neck, 2¾" d **200.00**

Cobalt Blue, bands with squares pat-
tern, smooth base, rough sheared
lip, 1870–1880, 2½″ d **100.00**
Lavender, man shooting rifle illus on
raised basketweave design, 2″ d   **120.00**
Target Bird, cast iron, 3⅞″ l **10.00**
Traps
Bear, Newhouse, hand-forged teeth,
early **900.00**
Coyote and Fox, Verbail **100.00**
Kodiak Bear, Herter's #6, chain and
swivel **425.00**
Muskrat, Funsten Brothers, floating .   **500.00**
Partridge, Davenport **110.00**
Wolf, Newhouse #4½, chain and
swivel **160.00**
Trophy, mounted
Antelope Stag Head, 12″ w antlers   **40.00**
Black Bear Head, mouth open **200.00**
Black Bear Rug, head and claws . . .   **350.00**
Caribou Stag Head, full antlers, 56″
w antlers **225.00**
Deer Stag Head, four point antlers,
14″ w antlers. **40.00**
Fox, red, standing, mounted on split
log **145.00**
Gray Squirrel, stuffed, mounted on
bark, climbing, head looking to
one side, 12″ l. **38.00**
Moose Head **900.00**

MUSICAL INSTRUMENTS

History: Music played an important role in rural
life. A parlor organ and/or piano was found in most
well-to-do homes. Family singing as a form of
social interaction was common. In addition, farmers and housewives sang aloud, often to themselves, to pass the time of day.

Within the agrarian community, love of music
enhanced social contact. Many individuals sang
in church and secular choirs. "Barber Shop" harmony was practiced informally.

Most individuals were proficient on a musical
instrument. Community bands flourished. Most
rural town parks had a band stand. Many fraternal
associations, fire companies, and veteran organizations had their own bands to provide marching
music for members during community and regional parades.

Brass instruments such as trumpet, trombone,
and tuba were among the most popular. Many communities had an all-brass band, albeit most had a
few percussion players for marching purposes.

Live music was required for hoe-downs and
community dances. The Country fiddler enjoyed
a prominent position. He was often joined on
stage by a bass, guitar, and banjo player.

The more traditional musical instruments were
often supplemented by a host of folk and improvised instruments, many of which were hand-

made. The best known of the folk instruments is
the dulcimer. Improvised instruments range from
the washboard to the boom-bas, a virtual one
person band.

The most valuable antique instruments are
those associated with the classical music period
of 1650 to 1900, e.g., flutes, oboes, and violins.
Few of these are found in the countryside. Most
Country instruments, e.g., trumpets and guitars,
have more value on the "used" market than they
do as antiques.

Reference: *The Official Price Guide To Music
Collectibles, Sixth Edition,* House of Collectibles,
1986, out-of-print.

Collectors' Clubs: American Musical Instrument
Society, 414 East Clark St, Vermillion, SD 57069;
Fretted Instrument Guild of America, 2344 South
Oakley Avenue, Chicago, IL 60608.

Periodical: *Concertina & Squeezebox,* PO Box
6706, Ithaca, NY 14851.

Museums: Yale University Collection of Musical
Instruments, New Haven, CT; Smithsonian Mu-
seum, Division of Musical History, Washington,
DC; The Musical Museum, Deansboro, NY; The
Museum of the American Piano, New York, NY;
The Shrine to Music Museum, Vermillion, SD.

Reproduction Craftspersons: William J Cooey,
248 Van Horn Rd, Milton, FL 32570; Carl &
Kathleen Gotzmer, June Apple Dulcimers, Rte 1,
Box 709P, Accokeek, MD 20607; John C Hockett,
Maiden Creek Dulcimers, 8 Gerstung Rd, Park
Forest, IL 60466; Ken Ratcliff, Ratcliff String Instru-
ments, 107 N Wilson Ave, Morehead, KY 40351;
John & Ann Rawdon, Dulcimers by JR, Rte 1, CR
21, Newcomerstown, OH 43832.

Banjo
Edgemere, nickel shell, wood lines,
17 nickel plated hexagon brackets,
raised frets, imitation mahogany
finish on birch neck, c1900 . . . . .   **325.00**
Unknown American Maker
Calfskin head, 10″ d, nickel band
on maple shell, imitation cherry
finish on neck, six screw brack-
ets, c1900 . . . .   **225.00**
Homemade, skin stretched over
barrel stave, hardwood neck,
strings missing, skin broken,
c1870 . . . .   **150.00**
Bass Drum, bentwood, hide heads,
rope lacing, leather trim, orig red and
black graining, gold stenciled eagle,
stars and "E. Pluribus Unum," int.
label "G. D. Westlands, Rapids, O,"
worn and repaired rope, one head
torn, 24″ d, 19″ h **1,250.00**
Boom-Bas, one-man band, cymbals,
bells, wood block, and tambourine
attached to pogo stick type pole . . .   **250.00**

Harmonica, M Hohner Echo-Luxe, black, ivory, and orange Art Deco design, 1933 Century of Progress souvenir, 6⅝ " l, orig red and blue emb box, $75.00.

Bugle, brass, Civil War 400.00
Dulcimer, 35½" l, violin shaped, heart
  shaped cutouts, whittled string keys,
  worn dark patina. 350.00
Glockenspiel, carrying strap and case   65.00
Harmonica, Rol-Monica Player, bake-
  lite, 1900s. 165.00
Horn, 14" l, toleware 20.00
Ocarina, 9" l, wood, painted black,
  gold trim. 35.00
Piccolo, ebony, nickel plated fittings,
  end cap missing, fitted case, 12¾" l   40.00
Tambourine, handpainted, birds and
  bee on branch. 70.00
Violin Case, wood, painted and deco-
  rated, American eagle and shield
  flanked by inscriptions "BG" and
  "Musician," red ground, second half
  19th C, 30½" l 465.00
Victor Talking Machine, oak horn. . . . 2,100.00
Washboard, metal, wood frame, thin
  chain with wooden stick at end attached to one side, Appalachia,
  c1890. . . . .   95.00

Victor Talking Machine, oak case and horn, $2,090.00. Photograph courtesy of Skinner, Inc.

Zither, 10 × 12½", J Schilt Solothurn,
  rosewood **50.00**

TOYS, DOLLS, AND GAMES

History: Toys, dolls, and games were a favorite pastime in rural America. Games that involved all members of the family were popular. Many of the toys found in the agrarian household were hand-made.

The first manufactured toys in America were imported from Europe. The first toys manufactured in America were made of cast iron, appearing shortly after the Civil War. Leading 19th century manufacturers include Hubley, Dent, Kenton, and Schoenhut. In the first decades of the 20th century, Arcade, Buddy L, Marx, and Tootsie Toy joined the earlier firms.

The importation of toys never ceased. German toys dominated until World War I. After World War II, Japanese imports flooded the market. To-day, many "American" toys are actually manufactured abroad.

During the 14th through the 18th centuries doll making was centered in Europe, mainly Germany and France. The French dolls produced in the era represented adults and were dressed in the latest couturier designs. They were not children's toys.

During the mid-19th century, child and baby dolls made in wax, cloth, bisque, and porcelain were introduced. Facial features were hand painted; wigs were made of mohair and human hair. They were dressed in baby or children's fashions.

Doll making in the United States began to flourish in the 1900s with names like Effanbee, Madame Alexander, Ideal, and others.

The first American board games have been traced back to the 1820s. Mass production of board games did not begin until after the Civil War. Firms such as Milton Bradley, McLoughlin Brothers, and Selchow and Righter were active in the 1860s. Parker Brothers began in 1883. Milton Bradley acquired McLoughlin Brothers in 1920.

Every toy, doll, and game is collectible. The key is condition and working order if mechanical.

References: There are a wealth of books devoted to the subject of toys, dolls, and games. A basic reference is Harry L. Rinker's *A Collector's Guide to Toys, Games, and Puzzles* (Wallace-Homestead, 1991). The following references are merely starting points. Their bibliographies will point you in additional directions.

Toys: Richard Friz, *The Official Identification and Price Guide to Collectible Toys, Fifth Edition,* House of Collectibles, 1991; David Longest, *Toys: Antique & Collectible,* Collector Books, 1990, 1992 value update; Richard O'Brien, *Collecting Toys: A Collectors Identification and Value Guide, Sixth Edition,* Books Americana, 1993.

Dolls: Jan Foulke, *11th Blue Book Dolls and Values*, Hobby House Press, Inc., *1993; Susan Ann Garrison, The Raggedy Ann and Andy Family Album,* Schiffer Publishing, 1989; Patricia Hall, *Johnny Gruelle: Creator of Raggedy Ann and Andy,* Pelican Publishing, 1993; R. Lane Herron, *Herron's Price Guide to Dolls,* Wallace-Homestead, 1990.

Games: Lee Dennis, *Warman's Antique American Games, 1840-1940, Current Market Values,* Wallace-Homestead, 1991; Bruce Whitehill, *Games: American Games and Their Makers, 1822–1992, with Values,* Wallace-Homestead, 1992.

Periodicals: *Antiques & Collectables,* 1000 Pioneer Way, PO Drawer 1565, El Cajon, CA 92002; *Antique Toy World,* PO Box 34509, Chicago, IL 60634; *Canadian Toy Mania,* PO Box 489, Rocanville, Saskatchewan S0A 3L0 Canada; *Cloth Doll Magazine,* PO Box 1089, Mt Shasta, CA 96067; *Collectible Toys & Values,* Attic Books, 15 Danbury Rd, Ridgefield, CT 06877; *Doll Castle News,* PO Box 247, Washington, NJ 07882; *Doll Life,* 243 Newton-Sparta Rd, Newton, NJ 07860; *Doll Reader,* 6405 Flank Dr, Harrisburg, PA 17112; *Dolls: The Collector's Magazine,* 170 Fifth Ave, 12th Floor, New York, NY 10010; *National Doll & Teddy Bear Collector,* PO Box 4032, Portland, OR 97208–4032; *Rags,* PO Box 823, Atlanta, GA 30301; *Toy Farmer,* HC 2, Box 5, LaMoure, ND 58458; *Toy Shop,* 700 East State St, Iola, WI 54990; *Toy Tractor Times,* PO Box 156, Osage, IA 50461–0156.

Collectors' Clubs: American Game Collectors Association, 49 Brooks Ave, Lewiston, ME 04240; Antique Engine, Tractor, & Toy Club, Inc., 5731 Paradise Rd, Slatington, PA 18080; Farm Toy Collectors Club, PO Box 38, Boxholm, IA 50040; National Organization of Miniaturists & Dollers, 1300 Schroder, Normal, IL 61721; United Federation of Doll Clubs, PO Box 14146, Parkville, MO 64152.

Museums: Enchanted World Doll Museum, Mitchell, SD; Mary Merritt Doll Museum, Douglasville, PA; Smithsonian Institution, Washington, DC; Museum of the City of New York, NY; Margaret Woodbury Strong Museum, Rochester, NY; Victorian Doll Museum, North Chili, NY; Washington Dolls' House & Toy Museum, Washington, DC; Yesteryears Museum, Sandwich, MA.

Reproduction Craftspersons: *Dolls*—Suzanne Berg, 1264 Estate Dr, West Chester, PA 19380; Sylvia June Brown, Hess Mill Rd, RD 2, Box 229 D, Landenberg, PA; Pat Broyles, Rte 1, Box 200, Grottoes, VA 24441; Jacquelyn Trone Butera, Colonial Yard, 500 S Park Ave, Audubon, PA 19403; Beth Cameron, 1000 Washington Ave, Oakmont, PA 15139; Nancy Castendyk, The Penny Wooden Doll, 16 Hall Rd, Sturbridge, MA 01566; Nancy Coblentz, Timber Wool, 10040 Longs Mill Rd,

Rocky Ridge, MD 21778; Maggie deYoung, Poppets, RR 1, PO Box 36, Beaverville, IL 60912; Debbie Jarrett, PO Box 189, Pipersville, PA 18947; Jill R Lawrence, Dutch Hill Rd, RD 2, Union City, PA 16438; Jocelyn Mostrom, Corn Husk Crafts, 16311 Black Rock Rd, Darnestown, MD 20874; Lillian Prillaman Folk Art, Rte 1, Box 148, Kearneysville, WV 25430; Lynne Robuccio, The Linen Bonnet, 29 Lantern Ln, Leominster, Ma 01453; Diana Dale Simpkins, PO Box 143, Kemblesville, PA 19347; Judie Tasch Original Dolls, 3208 Clearview, Austin, TX 78703; *Doll House Furnishings*—Gary Sites, Doll Furniture by Jennifer's Dad, 2 Woodview Ln, Oxford, PA 19363.

Gameboards—K Kautz & Sons, RR 1, Box 156B, Hartland, CT 05048; Robin Lankford, Folk Hearts, 15005 Howe Rd, Portland, MI 48875; Barbara Strickland, 728 Hawthorne, El Cajon, CA 92020; C H Southwell, PO Box 484-B, Suttons Bay, MI 49682; Scott M Switzer, PO Box 729, Frankfort, MI 49635–0729; Randy & Pam Tate, Knot in Vane, 805 N 11th St, DeKalb, IL 60115; Mary Thompson, Games People Played, PO Box 182, Cora, WY 28925; Barbara Wagaman, Ridge Hollow Folk Art, 14 Ridge Dr, Lititz, PA 17543.

General—Faith Allenby & Robert Kauffman, Allenby/Kauffman Wood Designs, RR 2, Box 325, Snake Meadow Rd, S Killingly, CT 06239; Nancy Elizabeth Cook, 272 Diamond Hill Rd, Berwick, ME 03901; Nicolas D Cortes, Nicolas Cortes Gallery & Studio, 405 W 44th St, New York, NY 10036; Eleanor Meadowcroft, 25 Flint St, Salem, MA 01970; Lillian Prillaman, Lillian Prillaman Folk Art, Rte 1, Box 148, Kearneysville, WV 25430; Ken and Bobbie Ralphs, Our Family Toys, PO Box 262, Hatfield, PA 19440; Donna H Pierce, 522 Meadowpark La, Media, PA 19063; Randal A Smith Fine Toys & Fancy Goods, 207 Main St, Gilboa, OH 45847; Jay Trace, 1133 Manor Rd, Coatesville, PA 19320, Meg Whitney, 676 St Charles Ave, Warminster, PA 18974. *Kaleidoscopes*—Anita Troisi, 286 N Hanover St, Pottstown, PA 19464; *Noah's Ark*—Ted Nichols, Noah's Ark, PO Box 1050, Salisbury, MD 21802–1050; *Stuffed Animals*—Carri Landfield, Happily Ever After, 127 W Marquita St, San Clemente, CA 92672; *Teddy Bears*—Ginger Duemler, Designs by Ginger, Box 61, Hilltown, PA 18927; S R Flinn, RD 2, Box 1021, Smyrna, DE 19977.

Reproduction Manufacturers: *Dolls*—Alta's Heirlooms, Raspberry Hill, Rte 1, Box 349, Englewood, TN 37329; Anastasia's Collectibles, 6114 134th St W, Apple Valley, MN 55124; C J's Bailiwick, 6124 Walker Avenue, Lincoln, NE 68507; Cabin Fever, 5770 S Meridian, Laingsburg, MI 48848; Country Ritz, 1217 Moro, PO Box 875, Manhattan, KS 66502; Country Workshop Marketing, 827 Glenside Ave, Wyncote, PA 19095; Days Gone By, 6811 Gleaner Rd, Freeland, MI 48623; Dollspart Supply Co, 46–50 54th Ave, Maspeth, NY 11378; Faith Mountain Country

Fare, Main St, Box 199, Sperryville, VA 22740; Fernswood Strawwork, Box 26, RD 2, New London, OH 44851; Fitz and Frends, 1463 Rainbow Drive, NE, Lancaster, OH 43130; Joyce's Doll House Parts, 20188 Willamson, Clinton Twp, MI 48043–7498; Lin Mac Dolls of Papier-Mâché, 183 Glasgow St, Clyde, NY 14433; Miss Fannie Turgeon's, 119 South Lake, PO Box 211, Mora, MN 55051; Pesta's Country Charm, 300 Standard Ave, Mingo Junction, OH 43938; Pieces of Olde, PO Box 65130, Baltimore, MD 21209; Ricyn: Country Collectables, PO Box 577, Twisp, WA 98856; *Doll Houses*—Dee's Delights, Inc, 3150 State Line Rd, North Bend, OH 45052; Little Lincoln's, 5373 W Houghton Lake Fr, Houghton Lake, MI 48629; *Doll House Furnishings*—Heritage in Miniature, Box 115, Earlville, PA 19519; Meadow Craft, PO Box 100, Rose Hill, NC 28458; Ohio Painted Furniture, Rte 4, Box 200, Athens, OH 45701; Pine Cone Primitives, PO Box 682, Troutman, NC 28166; The Storybook Collection of Miniatures, Inc, PO Box 13770, Richmond, VA 23225; *Doll Supplies*—Dollspart Supply Co, Inc, 5–15 49th Ave, Long Island City, NY 11101; Mini-Magic, 3675 Reed Rd, Columbus, OH 43220; Pattern Plus, 21 Mountain View Avenue, New Milford, CT 06776.

Gameboards—J J Decoy Co, PO Box 60, Fairfield, ME 04937; Kountry Kids, 1446 Snyder Rd, Kingston, OH 45644; The Prairie Stenciler, 7215 Nobel Court, Shawnee, KS 66218; *Teddy Bears*—Bear-in-Mind, 20 Beharrel St, Concord, MA 01742; Bullfrog Hollow, Keeny Rd, Lyme, CT 06371.

General—Cherry Tree Toys, Inc, PO Box 369–115, Belmont, OH 43718; Country Corner Collectibles, PO Box 422, Pitman, NJ 08071; Fearrington's Wooden Toys, PO Box 333, 1371 Lewisville-Vienna Rd, Pfafftown, NC 27040; Good Things, PO Box 2452, Chino, CA 91708; Heritage Toys & Collectibles, Rte 16, Sebec Corners, PO Box 43, Sebec, ME 04481; J P Bartholomew Co, 170 Pearson Lane, McCall, ID 83639; Knot in Vane, 805 N 11th St, DeKalb, IL 60115; Lace Wood 'N tin Tyme, 6496 Summerton, Shepherd, MI 48883; Mill Pond Designs, PO Box 290, East Longmeadow, MA 01028; The Countryside, PO Box 722, Forsyth, MO 65653; Southern Manner, Inc, 106 North Trade St, PO Box 1706, Matthews, NC 28106; Woodbee's, RR #1, Poseyville, IN 47633; *Tavern Puzzles*—Tucker-Jones House, Inc, PO Box 231, E Setauket, NY 11733; *Teddy Bears*—Imriebears, 1929 Lamont St, Wausau, WI 54401; Stuf'd Stuff, 415 W Oliver St, Owosso, MI 48867–2251.

Balancing Toy, man wearing top hat, wood, carved, turned body and limbs, painted eyes, suspended from wire swing, two turned columns, turned ball counterweight, turned disc base, 7½" l, 19th C **600.00**

Bank, still, cast iron
  Beehive, gold, 2½" h **140.00**
  Mammy, polychrome paint, 6" h. .. **150.00**
  Turkey, brown japanning and red, 3½" h **125.00**
BB Gun, Daisy No. 25 .... **30.00**
Bird feeding baby in nest, wood, animated, black, white, and red paint, natural patina, damage to end of rods **125.00**
Blocks
  Animals, set of four, dressed as soldiers, paper litho over cardboard, oblong, c1890 .... **65.00**
  Hills Spelling Blocks, set of twenty, orig box, multicolored chromolithographs on sliding lid, 9½" l **135.00**
  Illustrated Cubes, Albany Embossing Co, Albany, NY, set of twelve, wood, painted and embossed, cube shaped, two emb painted letters, two painted illustrations, one printed letter, and one printed number each block, litho paper label on oblong cardboard box, boy at fence watching child pass in goat-pulled wagon illus, 1920–30, 1 1/16" cubed block, 4⅝ × 3½" box **35.00**
  Picture and Alphabets, set of twelve, paper litho on wood, oblong, c1890 .... **175.00**
  Read and Learn, R Bliss Mfg Co, Pawtucket, RI, set of twenty-four, paper litho on wood, cylindrical, alphabet letters, simple verses, and children illus, c1889, 4" h, 1⅞" d **185.00**
Boat
  Battleship, wood, green and black paint, 36½" l **225.00**
  Canoe, wood, carved, old dark red paint, 9¾" l **65.00**
  Paddle Wheeler, Dent, "Priscilla," cast iron, painted, 10⅜" l **225.00**
Building, warehouse, litho paper on wood, four stories, elevator, inside view of business activities, "Smith, Jones, & Green," c1890, 12" w, 4" d, 20" h **650.00**
Clamp Toy, alligator, pine, carved, hand painted, stylized crosshatched figure, movable jaw and tail, mounted on wood clamp, jaw and tail move when string is pulled, 19th C, 6¾" l, 4½" h **275.00**
Croquet Set, Jacques, London, made for Abercrombie & Fitch Co, NY, wood **325.00**
Cup and Ball, wood, varnished and stained finish, turned stick with wide shallow cup one end, short dowel other end, cord tied in middle connected to solid wooden ball, two

holes in ball, c1910, 6 ⅝" l, 2¾" d
ball. **20.00**
Dancers, black figures
　Couple, seated man playing bell,
　lady dancer, clockwork, mecha-
　nism in wooden base, 1870s, 8⅝"
　l, 9" h **1,325.00**
Black Jig Dancer, American, early
　20th C
　Bell boy, wood, articulated, old red,
　black, blue, and white paint, bro-
　ken rod, early 20th C, 9½" h. . . .   **85.00**
　Man, carved and painted wooden
　head and joined body, celluloid
　hands, wear and small losses,
　11" h.   **325.00**
Doll
　Amish, white cotton and navy wool
　body, green cotton dress, early
　20th C, 13¼" l **140.00**
　Black, cotton body and stuffing, four
　seam rounded head, no hair, pen-
　ciled facial features, blue and
　white dress, white bonnet and
　apron, separately stitched fingers,
　stub feet, late 1800s, 18" l. **300.00**
　Character Doll, Indian, painted
　bisque, orig mohair wig, brown
　glass stationary eyes, closed
　mouth, pierced ears, jointed com-
　position body, imp mark "244 O,"
　damaged foot, 12" h **385.00**
　Cloth, oil painted head and shoul-
　ders, painted flat features, simple
　body and limbs, 17" h. **275.00**
　Lady, papier mâché shoulder head,
　kid body, wooden limbs, period
　costume, some paint chipping on
　head, 1840s, 12" h **325.00**
　Maggie Bessie, three part head, oil
　painted features, cloth body and
　legs, kid arms, damage and re-
　pairs, 19th C, 24" h **465.00**
　Missionary Rag, Beecher, needle
　sculpted stockinet body, jointed
　knees, hips, and shoulders, sparse
　wool yarn hair, needle sculpted
　and painted facial features, blue
　eyes, closed mouth, white baby
　dress and bonnet, stitched fingers
　and toes, c1900, 23" h **2,500.00**
　Moravian Rag, cotton body, jointed
　hips, knees, and shoulders, no
　hair, hand drawn and painted fa-
　cial features, lace ruffle sewn
　around face, blue and white ging-
　ham dress and bonnet, white
　apron, stitched fingers, free stand-
　ing thumbs, stub feet, early 1900s   **900.00**
　M S Davis Co, leather, painted hair
　and features, laced-up body, 1903
　Gussie Decker patent, 12" h **110.00**

Doll, wood, mortise and tenon joints,
pressed and painted features, carved hair,
pewter hands and feet, Cooperative Mfg
Co, Springfield, VT, c1873, 15" h, $850.00.

　Presbyterian Rag, unbleached cotton
　body, cotton stuffing, jointed
　shoulders and hips, flat head, oil
　painted facial features on flat face,
　ankle-length dress and matching
　prairie bonnet, white under-
　clothes, long black stockings and
　black leather shoes on stub feet,
　stitched fingers, separate thumbs,
　late 1800s, 17" l **950.00**
　Raggedy Ann, Gruelle, unbleached
　cotton, cotton stuffing, brown
　wool yarn hair, hand painted fa-
　cial features, shoe button eyes,
　blue dress, white apron, wooden
　heart hidden in chest, 1915, 15" h   **450.00**
Wood
　7¼" h, articulated, carved detail,
　old polychrome repaint **100.00**
　11½" h, articulated, cast white
　metal feet and hands **165.00**
Doll Accessories
　Bed, turned walnut, tester frame, mi-
　nor imperfections, c1830, 24" w,
　29" h.   **2,200.00**
　Blanket Chest, walnut, poplar secon-
　dary wood, dovetailed case,
　molded edge of lid and till, inlaid
　diamond escutcheon, bracket feet,
　old soft finish, 13" l **615.00**
　Bureau, grain painted, stepped back
　top with two small drawers, base
　with two long drawers, sides
　carved with concentric circles,
　wooden knobs, New England,
　c1830, 8" l, 6" d, 9½" h, some
　wear **650.00**
　Carriage
　Mesh, late 1800s **175.00**
　Painted wood body and wheels,
　convertible fabric top, 19th C,
　36" l **195.00**

Doll House, log cabin, two stories, removable shingled roof, white picket fence enclosing front yard, 30″ w, 32″ h, $110.00. Photograph courtesy of James D Julia, Inc.

Chair, ladder back, painted, 13⅞″ h   **85.00**
Kitchen Range, "Little Eva," cast iron, working model on three legs, two griddles, 14″ l, 10¼″ d, 9¼″ h   **300.00**
Doll House
  Bliss, 3 story, four rooms, paper litho on wood, metal, c1910, 25 × 20″ **1,800.00**
  Converse, Red Robin Farm, double barn doors, six stalls, cupola on roof, nine orig animals, 1912, 19½ × 17″ **425.00**
  Handmade, wood, two rooms, includes three corn cob dolls, furniture, curtains, rugs, bedding, and accessories, 19th C, 26½″ l, 12½″ d, 10⅞″ h **250.00**
  Schoenhut, painted wood, fiberboard, and cardboard, two story cottage, front porch, six lithographed paper rooms, two hallways, electrified chandelier, chimney, lift-off roof, name plate, 1920, 23″ w, 22⅞″ d, 27½″ h **1,050.00**
  Tudor style, three story, thatched roofs, pierced glazed windows, includes furniture, c1920, 46 × 69 × 30″ **1,320.00**
  Victorian style, litho paper on cardboard, one room, three sided, hinged, wood furniture, marked "Made in Germany," c1880 . . . . **250.00**
  Whippany, wood, three story, nine rooms, pierced glazed windows, hinged front door, stairs, lattice work, orig wallpaper, carpets, and lace curtains, includes furniture and accessories, electric lights and doorbell, NJ, 1901, 45 × 48 × 16″ **8,250.00**
Doll House Furnishings
  Dining Room Suite, Curtis, cast iron, white lacquer finish, two high

Miniature, wringer washer, cast iron, wooden rollers, painted light blue, Kilgore, 1½″ d, 2½″ h, $45.00.

    backed benches, matching 4¾″ l table openwork legs, 1936 . . . . . . **50.00**
  Dresser, light mahogany, two drawers, mirror, one inch scale **35.00**
  Ice Cream Parlor Set, 3½″ circular table, twisted metal legs, four matching chairs, heart shaped backs, four blue lemonade glasses, matching blown pitcher, 10 pcs **100.00**
  Living Room Suite, Arcade, cast iron, sofa and chair, deep pink, maroon trim, removable cushion **165.00**
  Piano, Renwal, matching bench . . . **30.00**
  Refrigerator, Arcade, cast iron, white lacquer, gray trim, 5 ¾″ h, marked "Leonard" **35.00**
  Secretary Desk, Biedermeier, one inch scale, late 19th C **150.00**
  Wall Box, grain painted, sides carved with concentric circles, American, minor age cracks, 19th C, 2½″ h **250.00**
  Wringer Washer, Sally Ann, cast iron, working rubber wringers, c1920 . . . . **48.00**
Dominoes, twenty-eight, ebony and ivory, mahogany box, 6½″ l **90.00**
Figures, wooden silhouettes, lithographic printed surfaces of ponies, hounds, and children in hunting attire on horseback, detachable wooden stands labeled "Wheildon," set of 13 . . . . **300.00**
Fire Truck, hook and ladder, carved and painted wood, metal fittings, rubber tires, minor imperfections, 1930, 31″ l **880.00**
Gameboard
  14½ × 14¾″, painted, checkers, worn black and natural, gallery border, two gallery sides are old replacements **250.00**
  16 × 16″, painted, two sided, one side with red, black, and green checker board, other side with multicolored parcheesi pattern, some wear **550.00**

Gameboard, reverse painted faux marble playing squares within a stenciled border and molded painted frame, early 20th C, 18¼" sq, $440.00. Photograph courtesy of Skinner, Inc.

16 × 24½", checkers, pine, bright yellow paint, black, white, and red board, oak edge strips, wire nails 155.00

18" sq, Chinese checkers, painted wood, America, 19th C, imperfections 450.00

18¼" sq, checkers, reverse painted faux marble playing squares, stenciled border, molded painted frame, early 20th C 450.00

18¾ × 19", poplar, checkers, black, yellow, green, and blue, decorative striping, red ground, old repaint over earlier gray paint, small holes 385.00

Hay Wagon, wooden, painted, orig worn light blue paint, red striping, 19" l plus tree handle 95.00

Hoop Toy, flat painted equestrian figure inside rolling hoop, 1870s, 4½" d 600.00

Ice Skates, wrought iron, primitive, made to attach to shoes, high curved toe, rust pitted, some edge damage, pr 200.00

Jack-in-the-Box, wood and fabric, carved, painted, exaggerated stylized facial features, relief carved, red and black on white ground, turned wooden dunce cap, painted cloth bag body, spring mounted, gray pine box, hinged lid, hook closure, 19th C, 12" h 275.00

Jumping Jack, wood, carved, monkey on stick, front legs attached to slide, 21" l 420.00

Jump Toy, black boxers, wood, painted, black turned wood heads,

Jump Toy, cowboy, carved wood, jointed, painted black, 19th C, 10" h, estimated price $4,000.00–6,000.00. Photograph courtesy of James D Julia, Inc.

red and yellow bodies, cardboard legs and arms, both fighters suspended from wire attached to central stick, figures bob and jab when stick is twirled, late 19th C, 11" h 450.00

Kaleidoscope, turned walnut, C C Bush, Providence, RI, 1870s, 13¾" h   935.00

Kitchen Playset, painted tin, stove, pots and pans, and outside water pump, worn paint, some parts missing, 14" l, 4⅛" d, 8½" h. 95.00

Marble Toy, wood, carved, painted red, series of descending ramps above stylized and articulated figure of man which catches marble at end of track, shaped wood base, late 19th C, 30½" h, 27" w 4,675.00

Noah's Ark, carved and painted wood, Germany

10" l ark, animals, late 19th C, imperfections 990.00

17⅞" l ark, 27 animals, Noah, and wife, cloth hinges on ark 650.00

Noah's Ark, painted wood, twenty-seven animals, Noah, and wife, Germany, slight damage, cloth hinges need repair, ark is 17⅞" l, 7½" h, $660.00. Photograph courtesy of Skinner, Inc.

Play Set, Judy's Farm, #100, Judy Toys, Minneapolis, MN, wood, four family members, car, tractor, truck, and animals, cardboard fencing and barn, instructions, 14¼ × 10¼ × 1½" box, $15.00.

Nodder, kitten, primitive, pine, carved, painted black, seated articulated figure, bobs head and tail when weighted string is pulled, late 19th C, 6" l, 3½" h 350.00
Piano, Bliss, upright, litho paper on painted wood, 10½" h, 14¼" l 110.00
Pull Toy
　Cow, composition, brown and white, wood base, 12" l 300.00
　Geese, wood platform, three papier mâché geese, orig polychrome, cast iron wheels, 10¼" l 825.00
　Grasshopper, animated, old dark patina, 10" l 150.00
　Horse
　　27" l, 26½" h, brown hair cloth, straw stuffing, glass eyes, partial harness, horsehair tail, painted wood base, pewter spoked wheels, replaced mane and wheels, worn paint 385.00

Pull Toy, horse, plaster over wood, painted dapple gray, leather saddle, wheeled platform, 26" l, 27" h, $291.50. Photograph courtesy of James D Julia, Inc.

5¾" l, 7¾" h, black mohair, steel eyes, leatherette tack, wooden platform with metal wheels, some fiber loss 135.00
Horse and Cart, wood, cast iron wheels, animated tin legs on horse, orig red and silver paint, 13½" l 55.00
Horse and Wagon, driver, early tin, very worn red, black, and yellow paint, light rust, 14½" l 425.00
Oxen Team, alligatored brown and blue paint, 11" l 660.00
Railroad Hand Car, pine, carved, painted, four men, silhouette figures, litho paper on wool costumes, red four wheel hand car, long wood handle, men pump up and down when cart is pulled, late 19th/early 20th C, 31" l, 12½" h 1,650.00
Sheep, wood, wool, and papier mâché, painted, tin wheels, blue collar, 7¼" h 360.00
Puppet Theater, folding wood and cloth stage, painted wood and cloth puppets include Punch, Judy, two clowns, soldier, judge, Chinaman, donkey, bald-headed man, baby, policeman, black man, bearded man, and alligator, puppets have some fiber loss and figures need work, 61" h stage. 935.00
Push Toy
　Bicycle, tandem, wire, fabric clad cyclers, painted faces, back rider plays metal shoe polish lid drum when toy is pushed, 20th C, 13" l, 30" h 700.00
　Clown on Unicycle, wood, articulated, black, white, and brown stain, old patina, 23¼" l 385.00
　Horse and Cart, Ives, cast iron, walking horse, two wheeled cart, leg wires missing, 10⅜" l 550.00
　Horse Team, two white flannel covered horses with metal eyes, leatherette tack, and mohair manes and tails, wooden platforms with metal wheels, some fiber loss and damage, 12⅜" l, 12½" h 775.00
　Mule Cart, pine, carved, painted, brown mule, leather and metal harness, green and red cart, metal banded wheels, black man driver, molded doll's head face, cloth clothed body, leather hat, late 19th C, 9½" h 1,325.00
Wheelbarrow, Paris Manufacturing Co, South Paris, ME, PMC logo and black stenciled squirrel dec

Push Toy, tin, two articulated horses on wire frame, one black, one brown, sgd "J. B. Whitaker," missing tails, 13" l, 14½" h, $2,750.00. Photograph courtesy of James D Julia, Inc.

either side panel, red striping, red wheel, natural varnished finish, 39" l 350.00

Puzzle, adv
  Armour, paper over cardboard, circus tent shape, crowds viewing animal exhibitions, 20 × 28" 190.00
  Hood's Sarsaparilla and Pills, A Wedding in Catland, cardboard, color, feline wedding party leaving church illus, orig box, 17 × 12"   150.00
  Sherwin-Williams Paints, cardboard, two sided, house exterior illus one side, US map other side, 11¼ × 16" 75.00
  White Sewing Machines, paper covered wood, two sided, interior Victorian home one side, US map other side, 11 × 16" 130.00

Rattle, sterling silver, figural teddy bear, bells, mother-of-pearl handle, 4" l   85.00

See-Saw, Albert H Dean, Bridgeport, CT, wood and tin, carved, painted, seated boy and girl figures, painted tin, cloth bodies, yellow wooden see-saw, red, yellow, and black tin and wood base houses windup mechanism, c1873, 10" h, 19" l . . .   9,350.00

Slide Toy
  Fighting Gamecocks, pine, carved, fighting pen flanked by two stylized men holding game cocks, each man straddles sliding wood rods, cocks trade pecks when slide and ratchet mechanism is pulled, late 19th/early 20th C, 17" l, 7" h 650.00
  Man, wood, carved, painted, stylized figure, bearded, wearing top hat and dark suit, carved facial features, peg doweled into torso

slides on wrought iron stand, late 19th C, 8" h 450.00

Squeak Toy
  Blue Bird, felt composition, painted, red breast, turned thimble shaped wood stand on circular straw trimmed bellows base, 19th C, 4½" h 275.00
  Cat, mother and two kittens, felt composition, molded, painted, gray, black, and orange, bellows base, late 19th C, 4½" h 495.00
  Dog, composition, molded, painted, yellow body, white markings, black face, wearing boater hat, seated on bellows base, late 19th C, 5¼" h 1,200.00
  Duck, nesting, composition, painted, blue, white, orange, and red, flapping wings, bellows base, wings flap when base is squeezed, late 19th C, 6½" h 325.00
  Elephant, composition, painted, white body, red and blue trimmed saddle blanket, bellows base, late 19th C, 3½" h 275.00
  Goat, composition, molded, painted, white, black markings, leaping, late 19th C, 5" h 165.00
  Highlander on Donkey, composition and fabric, painted, young boy, stuffed fabric body, lace collared plaid jacket, astride small gray donkey, bellows base, late 19th C, 6¾" h 275.00
  Parrot, composition, molded, painted green, perched on rockwork, bellows base, late 19th C, 5½" h 135.00
  Peacock, composition and feather, painted, blue, green, orange, and black, standing, real tail feather, bellows base, late 19th C 450.00
  Rooster, composition, painted, white, blue, red, and black, iridescent bronze highlights, metal spring legs, bellows base, late 19th C, 6" h 165.00
  Stork, composition, molded, painted yellow, orange beak, black markings, spring legs, bellows base, late 19th C, 6" h 250.00

Stereo Viewer, Triumph model, Universal View Co, Philadelphia, PA, with 35 stereo cards including Teddy Roosevelt's inaugural address, Yellowstone views, and St Louis World's Fair 80.00

Stuffed Animal
  Bear, standing on all fours, gray frosted mohair, jointed head, glass

eyes, embroidered features, fur and fiber loss, stuffing loss, late 19th C, 12″ l, 7½″ h **165.00**

Bucky Beaver, Steiff, studio model, mohair, ear button, glass eyes, felt mouth with wooden teeth, felt tail, mid 20th C, 28″ h **775.00**

Cow, Steiff, mohair, rust and white, glass eyes, felt hoofs, voice box, steel frame, rubber tired wheels, some fiber loss, horns missing, 1950s, 21¼″ l **385.00**

Dog
Cocker Spaniel, sitting, Steiff, movable head, ear button, glass eyes, 1920–30, 6″ h **125.00**

Flannel, beige, glass eyes, white hair, 11″ h **30.00**

St Bernard, on wheels, Steiff, mohair, rust and cream colored, glass eyes, missing ears and one glass eye, bark not functioning, fiber loss, late 1940s, 20½″ l   **325.00**

Wire Haired Fox Terrier, Steiff
Sitting, glass eyes, buttons on ear and collar, some fiber loss, 4¼″ h **225.00**

Standing, movable head, glass eyes, ear button, c1925, 6¾″ h **150.00**

Elephant, printed chintz, red balloon man, 5½″ h **30.00**

Goat, recumbent, Steiff, ear button, partial tag, glass eyes, 5″ l **75.00**

Horse, on wheels, Steiff, shoe button eyes, red saddle blanket, leather saddle, stamped "Steiff," metal wheels, fiber loss, ear button missing, c1913, 9½″ l, 9″ h **375.00**

Monkey, rag, printed, 13½″ h **50.00**

Polar Bear, Steiff, jointed legs **550.00**

Sheep, grazing, Steiff, mohair, ear button, glass eyes, felt and synthetic wool fleece, mid 20th C, 38″ l, 29″ h **825.00**

Teddy Bear
8½″ h, Steiff, blonde mohair, fully jointed, black steel eyes, embroidered snout, wearing overalls and knitted slippers, fiber loss, c1906 . . . .   **525.00**

10½″ h, Germany, golden mohair, dressed, fully jointed, shoe button eyes, embroidered features, felt pads, wearing green and tan suit, straw boater, sitting in wicker armchair, extensive fur and fiber loss, early 20th C . . .   **550.00**

14″ h, Steiff, blonde mohair, fully jointed, shoe button eyes, black

Teddy Bear, gold short mohair, straw stuffing, growler, folded ears, shoe button eyes, embroidered nose and mouth, swivel neck, humped back, jointed arms and legs, 20″ h, $500.00.

embroidered nose, mouth, and claws, blank ear button, excelsior stuffing, some fur loss, small moth damage on felt pads, c1906 . . . .   **1,650.00**

15″ h, Germany, tan mohair, fully jointed, shoe button eyes, embroidered features, felt pads, fur and fiber loss, early 20th C. . . .   **825.00**

16½″ h, Germany, yellow mohair, fully jointed, shoe button eyes, embroidered features, excelsior stuffing, fur and fiber loss, replaced pads, c1906 . . . .   **550.00**

17″ h, England, yellow mohair, fully jointed, glass eyes, embroidered features, felt pads, excelsior stuffing, some fur and fiber loss **250.00**

18″ h, American, yellow mohair, fully jointed, shoe button eyes, embroidered features, woven pads, excelsior stuffing, extensive fur and some fiber loss, c1910 . . . .   **275.00**

18″ h, Steiff, bronze mohair, fully jointed, ear button, shoe button eyes, embroidered features, felt pads, excelsior stuffing, fur and fiber loss, c1906. . . . .   **1,875.00**

18″ h, Steiff, yellow mohair, fully jointed, ear button, glass eyes, embroidered snout, excelsior stuffing, fiber loss, repaired paw, c1910 . . . .   **990.00**

19″ h, American, yellow mohair, fully jointed, black embroidered nose and claws, excelsior and kapok stuffing, some fur loss, seam repairs, replaced eyes and pads, 1920s **165.00**

19¾" h, England, blonde mohair, fully jointed, shoe button eyes, embroidered snout, felt pads, excelsior stuffing, some fiber loss, c1907 . . . . **325.00**

20" h, American, yellow mohair, fully jointed, excelsior stuffing, eyes and felt replaced, fur and fiber loss, 1920s **220.00**

21" h, Germany, golden mohair, fully jointed, shoe button eyes, embroidered features, felt pads, excelsior stuffing, fur and fiber loss, needs stuffing, c1906 . . . . **2,100.00**

23" h, Steiff, blonde curly mohair, fully jointed, center seam, shoe button eyes, ear button, beige nose, claws, and mouth, excelsior stuffing, some hair loss, fabric damage under muzzle and on wrist and ankle, growler not functioning, c1905 . . . . **2,200.00**

24" h, Ideal, blonde plush mohair, fully jointed, accentuated hump, shoe button eyes, rust broadcloth and embroidered nose, embroidered claws, excelsior stuffing, early 20th C . . . **1,210.00**

24" h, Steiff, light yellow mohair, "Mr Bear," fully jointed, shoe button eyes, black nose, mouth, and claws, excelsior stuffing, includes story of his life, fur and fabric loss, replaced pads, ear button missing, c1910 . . . . **715.00**

Tiger Cat, Steiff, mohair, fully jointed, glass eyes, embroidered nose and mouth, ear button, slight fiber loss, early 20th C, 10" l **175.00**

Train

11¾" l, engine, steel, welded, homemade, old black paint, white trim **225.00**

25½" l, steam locomotive, model, metal, old black repaint, incomplete cow catcher **425.00**

Wheelbarrow, wood, tin, and steel, worn orig brown paint and silver stenciled running horse design, 31" l   **385.00**

LIGHTING

Country life cannot stop because the day is cloudy or the electric power fails; daily chores still need to be done. Rural America required cheap, dependable lighting.

The key concerns were utility and durability. Form did follow function—simple design, easy to service; less joints and edges, least likely to snag; and plain surface, less maintenance. Lighting devices, especially those used in barns and field, were expected to withstand rough treatment and last for years. The interchangeability of parts was essential. Repairs often had to be made on the spot.

Until the arrival of electricity, the kerosene lamp was king. Lamps burn fuel and generate heat. Heat attacks surfaces. This is why tin, which was painted and repainted to preserve it, and glass were favored. Fuel oil lamps also generate soot. To work effectively, they have to be cleaned regularly, a chore generally assigned to the children.

Decorative lighting was confined to the household with the best examples located in the dining room and parlor. Among the forms with the widest variety of pattern and color are miniature lamps and fluid lamps. They are important decorative accents in any Country setting.

The arrival of electricity changed life in rural America. Most initial electrical lighting and many appliances were purchased via mail order or at the general store. The arrival of a specialized electrical store in a rural community often was ten to fifteen years behind the arrival of electricity.

Because members of the agrarian community are "savers" by nature, rural basements, attics, sheds, and barns are major sources for early electrical lighting. There is strong tendency to put an old lamp or appliance in storage just in case the new one breaks.

The current Country craze focuses heavily on the kerosene lamp era. However, change is in the wind. There is a growing interest in the rural farmstead of the 1920s through the 1950s. When this period becomes fashionable, electric lighting will play a major role in any decorating scheme.

LAMPS AND LIGHTING

History: An agrarian life means rising at first light and going to bed when the sun sets. While this is the ideal, many a farmer and small town merchant rose before the sun came up and went to bed long after it set. Lamps and lighting were cherished and well-cared-for possessions.

It was not until the late 1930s and, in some areas, the early 1950s that rural electrification was accomplished. As a result, the kerosene oil lamp survived in the countryside long after it disappeared from urban America.

The kerosene oil lamp is an important decorative element in any Country decor. Variety was achieved through a wealth of glass patterns and colors as well as ornately decorated shades. The best, i.e., most decorative, lamps graced the parlor and dining room. Large lamps used in the kitchen and upstairs tended to be plain and highly utilitarian. On the other hand, miniature lamps were highly decorative, often adding a splash of color to a room.

Lighting devices have evolved from simple stone age oil lamps to the popular electrified models of today. Aimé Argand patented the first oil lamp in 1784. Around 1850 kerosene became a popular lamp burning fluid, replacing whale oil and other fluids.

References: J. W. Courter, *Aladdin, The Magic Name in Lamps,* Wallace-Homestead, 1980; J. W. Courter, *Aladdin Collectors Manual & Price Guide #14,* published by author, 1992; Robert De Falco, Carole Goldman Hibel, John Hibel, Larry Freeman, *New Light on Old Lamps,* American Life Foundation, 1984; Nadja Maril, *American Lighting: 1840–1940,* Schiffer Publishing, 1989; Jo Ann Thomas, *Early Twentieth Century Lighting Fixtures,* Collector Books, 1980; Catherine M. V. Thuro, *Oil Lamps,* Wallace-Homestead, 1976; Catherine M. V. Thuro, *Oil Lamps II,* Thorncliffe House, 1983; Catherine M. V. Thuro, *Oil Lamps: The Keroscene Era in North America,* Wallace-Homestead, 1976, 1992 value update.

Collectors' Clubs: Aladdin Knights of the Mystic Light, Route 1, Simpson, IL 62985; Historical Lighting Society of Canada, 9013 Oxbow Road, North East, PA 16428; The Incandescent Lamp Collectors Association, 717 Washington Place, Baltimore, MD 21201; Rushlight Club, Suite 196, 1657 The Fairway, Jenkintown, PA 19046.

Museums: Pairpoint Lamp Museum, River Edge, NJ; Sandwich Glass Museum, Sandwich, MA; Winchester Center Kerosene Lamp Museum, Winchester Center, CT.

Reproduction Craftspersons: Charles Baker Period Reproductions, 6890 N 700 E, Hope, IN 47246; David L Claggett, Artistry in Tin, PO Box 41, Weston, VT 05161; Karen Claggett, Tinsmith, RD #3, Box 330A, Quarryville, PA 17566; Copper House, RR1 Box 4, Epsom, NH 03234; Jim W Darnell, Mill Creek Forge and Blacksmith Shop, Box 494, Rte 2, Seagrove, NC 27341; Jim DeCurtins, Tin Peddler, 203 E Main St, Troy, OH 45373; Charles Euston, Woodbury Blacksmith & Forge Co, PO Box 268, Woodbury, CT 06798; James W Faust, 488 Porters Mill Rd, Pottstown, PA 19464; Dawson Gillaspy, Tinsmith, Covered Bridge Rd, RD 2, Box 312, Oley, PA 19547; Richard L Haddick, Tinsmith, RD 2, Box 27A, Wyoming, DE 19934; Tim Halligan, TH Copper, 1904 W Spruce, Duncan, OK 73533; James A Hoffman, Hoffman's Forge, 2272 Youngstown Lockport Rd, RD1, Ransomville, NY 14131; Robert and Anita Horwood, Horwood's Country House, 4037 Gotfredson Rd, Plymouth, MI 48170; Thomas and Catherine Latane, Po Box 62, Pepin, WI 54759; Ronald Potts, Blacksmith, Chriswill Forge, 2255 Manchester Rd, N Lawrence, OH 44666; Mark Rocheford, Thomas Savriol, Lighting by Hammerworks, 75 Webster St, Worcester, MA 01603; Stephen Smithers, 1057 Hawley Rd, Ashfield, MA 01330; Barry Steierwald, Eagle Lantern, Rte 100, Eagle, PA 19480; Michael P Terragna, The Coppersmith, PO Box 755, Sturbridge, MA 01566; The Tin Man, Gerald Fellers, 2025 Seneca Dr, Troy, OH 45373; Nick Vincent, Nathan's Forge, 3476 Uniontown Rd, Uniontown, MD 21158; Stephen and Carolyn Waligurski, Hurley Patentee Lighting, RD 7, Box 98A, Kingston, NY 12401.

Reproduction Manufacturers: 18th Century Tinware, 1323 Twin Rd, West Alexandria, OH 45381; 19th Century Merchantile, Barbara Amster, No. 2 N Main St, South Yarmouth, MA 02664; American Period Lighting, 3004 Columbia Ave, Lancaster, PA 17603; The Antique Hardware Store, 43 Bridge St, Frenchtown, NJ 08825; The Barn, PO Box 25, Market St, Lehman, PA 18627; Basye-Bomberger/Fabian House, PO Box 86, W Bowie, MD 20715; Briere Design, 229 North Race St, Statesville, NC 28677; Bullfrog Hollow, Keeny Rd, Lyme, CT 06371; Country Lighting and Accessories, PO Box 1279, New London, NH 03257; Country Store of Geneva, Inc, 28 James St, Geneva, IL 60134; Cumberland General Store, Rte 3, Crossville, TN 38555; Frombruche, 132 N Main St, Spring Valley, NY 10977; Independence Forge, Rt 1, Whitakers, NC 27891; Jori Handcast Pewter, 12681 Metro Parkway, Fort Myers, FL 33912; KML Enterprises, RR 1, Box 234L, Berne, IN 46711; Lt Moses Willard, Inc, 1156 State Route 50, Milford, OH 45150; Matthews Emporium, 157 N Trade St, PO Box 1038, Matthews, NC 28106; Mel-Nor, 303 Gulf Bank, Houston, TX 77037; Olde Mill House Shoppe, 105 Strasburg Pike, Lancaster, PA 17602; Period Lighting Fixtures, 1 West Main St, Chester, CT 06412; The Renovator's Supply, 7577 Renovator's Old Mill, Millers Falls, MA 01349; Sandi's, PO Box 170, Lake George, NY 12845;

Sturbridge Yankee Workshop, Blueberry Rd, Westbrook, ME 04092; The Tinhorn, 1852 Forest Lane, Crown Point, IN 46307; Victorian Lightcrafters Ltd, PO Box 350, Slate Hill, NY 10973.

Alcohol, brass, marked "Made in United States of America" on bottom, 3½" h **12.00**

Baker's, tin, rect, two burners, tin shade, wire hanger, hanger, 7" l, 9½" h **180.00**

Banner Electric Lamp, nickel plated brass, triangular punched design around base, kerosene burner, name on flame spreader, c1880, 11½" h **135.00**

Banquet, Rochester Lamp Co, New Rochester Banquet Lamp, brass and brass plated, acid cut Fleur-de-lis pattern on frosted globe, c1890, 28" h to top of shade **495.00**

Betty Lamp
Sheet Iron, with pick and hanger, worn black paint, 3¾" h plus hanger **225.00**
Wrought Iron
3½" h plus hanger, bird cutout finial on font cov, twisted hanger, no pick **350.00**
4½" h plus mismatched twisted hanger **115.00**

Bracket
Buckeye Glass Co, Optic Rib pattern on sapphire blue patent dated font with threaded exterior, Swirled Optic pattern on matching shade, orig black and gold finish on iron bracket and mount, J F Miller patent, c1880, 15" h **685.00**
Unknown Maker, shells and stars design on clear glass font, crudely cast brass bracket, 1870–80, 3⅜" h **55.00**

Bradley & Hubbard
Lemon shaped font, deep saucer base, ring handle, japanned and gilt finish, alcohol burner, c1900, 4¼" h **225.00**
Vase lamp, nickel plated brass and iron, floral decorated opaque white shade, very ornate emb dec and handles, ftd, sgd three places, five patent dates, c1890, 15" h to top of shade **300.00**

Candler, E Miller & Co, tin, marked burner, 1890-1900, 6¾" h **40.00**

Candle Stand, wrought iron
1 Socket, primitive, tripod base, adjustable octagonal pan with candle socket, hanger finial, corner spouts, one foot old replacement, 20½" h **385.00**

Camphor Lamp, pewter, brass caps, 8⅜" h, $190.00.

2 Sockets, adjustable candle arm, 33" h **30.00**

Chamber
Pewter, turned stem, circular dish base, strap handle, marked "S. Rusts Patent New York," 19th C, 8⅝" h, pr **525.00**
Tin, conical font, single spout burner, hinged chimney, mica glazing, worn blue japanning, 4" h   **105.00**

Chandelier
Cast Iron, Bradley & Hubbard, openwork frame, 12-arm, clear glass fonts and crimped chimneys, brass burners, marked with May 26, 1868 patent date in openwork section at top row of arms and inside ceiling fitting, "January 31 1871" patent date marked inside bottom of four fonts, "January 31. 1871" patent date marked inside three fonts, and five fonts marked in⅛" raised letters "Pat'd Jan. 31. 1871," c1870, 58" h, 40" d **1,210.00**
Tin, punched design, six candle sockets on S-shaped arms, PA, c1850 . . . .   **550.00**
Wood and Tin, four candle sockets on S shaped arms, cut nail construction, PA, c1850 . . . .   **500.00**

Double Crusie, wrought iron
6¼" h, chicken finial, hanger **330.00**
7" h plus twisted handle **100.00**

Double Torch, cast iron, "PZL" in high relief both sides, remains of orig wicks inside, 19th C, 7⅜" h **120.00**

Factory, "Bradley's Security Factory Lamp" in raised letters on font bottom and on brass plate inside tin holder, yellow dec on black ground, c1870, 3⅜" h **100.00**

Grease, 4½" h plus three twisted links, wrought iron, hanging, four spout   **55.00**

Hand Lamp, cranberry glass, clear applied handle, No. 1 burner, 4⅛" h, $187.00. Photograph courtesy of James D Julia, Inc.

HandLamp
Brass
  E Miller & Co, "The Miller Lamp," center draft, ornate Spelter handle, punched design around base, opaque white shade, marked "The Miller Lamp/Made in/U.S.A." on shoulder, c1890, 11 ½" h to top of shade 495.00
  Unknown Maker, sloping shoulder, strap handle, 1875–1900, 4¾" h 110.00
Glass
  Boston & Sandwich Glass Co, clear, Lyre pattern, applied handle, 1840–60, 3¾" h 130.00
  Bryce Walker & Co, clear, Diamond Sunburst pattern, applied handle, replacement collar, c1870, 3½" h 35.00
  Central Glass Co, clear, Wheat in Shield pattern, applied handle, c1870, 5⅜" h 190.00
  Sandwich Glass Co, clear, Waffle pattern, applied handle, c1850, 4½" h 465.00
  Union Glass Co, clear Lomax font, patterned font, ftd, c1870, 5⅝" h 175.00
Glass and Tin, F O Dewey, Dillaway patent clear glass font made at Sandwich, brass plate on tin base marked "F.O. Dewey & Sons/Makers, Boston.", strap handle, repainted black, c1870, 3⅝" h 28.00
Tin
  Dietz & Co, marked "Dietz Bestov Lamp" on shoulder, attached bracket for wall mount, brass side filler cap, old chimney marked "Rock Flint," c1890, 9½" h 245.00

J R Rochester, center draft, patented, marked "The J.R. Rochester/Hotel Lamp/Pat. Sep. 14. 1886," 1889 and 1890 patent dates marked on flame spreader on brass burner, punched design around ftd base, tall tubular chimney, c1890 . . . .   120.00
Unknown Maker, squatty, saucer base, strap handle, orig green paint, c1860, 5½" d, 2" h 15.00
Hanging, fluid
  Bradley & Hubbard, embossed brass font, company's mark stamped on shoulder and filler cap, opaque white shade, c1890, 52" h, 13⅝" d shade 600.00
  Unknown Maker, cast iron, 2-arm, "January 31, 1871" patent date marked inside each font holder, clear bracket lamps, etched flowers and butterflies dec on frosted shades, black and gold finish, c1870, 32" h, 26" w to edge of shades 825.00
Hitchcock, brass, marked "Improved Hitchcock Lamp," sidewinder motor stamped with patent dates ranging from Nov 30, 1880 to Feb 28, 1899, 11⅞" h 165.00
Jeweler's, amber glass font, tin egg cup shape base, alcohol burner, two patent dates on shoulder, 1880–90, 3¼" h 20.00
Kitchen, Union Glass Co, clear Lomax font, 1870 patent date on underside, 6⅜" h 65.00
Lacemaker's, globular blown font, fluted clear stem, scalloped diamond point base, 9¾" h 750.00
Lard, tole, cylindrical font, saucer pan, worn black and gold repaint, 6¾" h   75.00

Pan Lamp, hanging type, wrought iron, 16¾" h, $475.00.

Lecturer's, bell in base, orig black paint and gold striping, pricket for candle, 10" h **250.00**

Library, brass, patented, cut and frosted glass font, brass shoulder and drip trough, brass frame and font holder, brass crown on wide conical shaped opaque white shade, brass hanger with chain, c1880, 25" h, 13⅝" d shade **600.00**

Loom Light, wrought iron, hanging, ratchet and candle socket, early 19th C, 21" l **355.00**

Marriage, Ripley, opaque blue and clambroth glass, marked "D.C. Ripley & Co Patent Pending," orig match holder lid, brass and marble base, brass collar, 11" h **1,210.00**

Navigation, reflector, geared wick raisers, late 19th C, 6¾" h **35.00**

Oil, glass

Adams & Co, clear, Plain Band pattern, c1880, 9½" h **25.00**

Angle Lamp Co, wall mount, opaque white shade on clear globular shade, orig black and copper finish on emb font, maker's name and patents marked on clear shade and lamp, c1890, 8" h **325.00**

Atterbury & Co, clear, c1870

Atterbury Filley pattern, 3⅜" h   **30.00**

Atterbury Heritage pattern, 9" h   **65.00**

Atterbury Scroll pattern, Tulip pattern base, 9½" h **55.00**

Grecian pattern, paneled milk glass base, patent date on inside of base, 7½" h **175.00**

Boston & Sandwich Glass Co, clear, Sandwich Grapevine pattern, c1860, 9¾" h **250.00**

Parlor Lamp, hanging, cranberry hobnail shade and font shell, drop-in font, ornate red brass frame, crystal prisms, 40" h, $1,045.00. Photograph courtesy of James D Julia, Inc.

Central Glass Co, clear, Plain Band pattern, amethyst tint, c1870, 9" h   **55.00**

Consolidated Glass Co, opaque light green lamp and shade, Prince Edward pattern, c1890, 18" h to top of shade **900.00**

Dalzell, Gilmore & Leighton, clear, Queen Heart pattern, hand painted flowers with green leaves and brown stems on frosted heart shaped panels, c1900, 9" h **100.00**

Dietz Brothers & Co, NY, clear blown font, brass stem and base, sgd on stem, heraldic eagle over name, c1860, 9" h. **875.00**

George Duncan & Sons, clear, Ribbed Band pattern, c1880, 10" h. **145.00**

Hobbs

Dyott's Patent Stand Lamp, clear, c1870, 8¼" h **65.00**

Snowdon pattern, clear font, cobalt blue base, c1880, 8¼" h. . **190.00**

King Glass Co, clear, Double Arch pattern, circular base, 1880–90, 8" h. **80.00**

LaBelle Glass Co, clear, Corn pattern, c1870, 8⅜" h **250.00**

New England Glass Co

Canary Yellow, Bull's-eye and Ellipse pattern font, pewter collar and whale oil burner, 8¼" h   **550.00**

Clear, Loop pattern font, heavy pressed base, pewter collar and whale oil burner, 9¾" h. **90.00**

Cobalt Blue, Loop pattern font, hexagonal base, pewter collar and whale oil burner, pr, 9¾" h **1,700.00**

Sapphire Blue

Loop pattern font, whale oil burner, pr, 10" h **900.00**

3-Printie Block pattern, whale oil burner, 7⅜" h **1,200.00**

Richards & Hartley, medium yellow, Three Panel pattern, c1880, 7¾" h   **250.00**

Riverside Glass Co, emerald green font, clear stem and base, Riverside Panel pattern, brass patent dated collar, c1880, 8" h. **160.00**

Sandwich Glass Co, clear, Heart and Thumbprint pattern, 1840–60, 8¼" h **190.00**

Unknown Maker

Amethyst

6¼" h, brass saucer base, ring handle, acorn burner, patent date, c1870 . . . . **45.00**

11" h, 4-Printie Block pattern. . **600.00**

Canary Yellow, Bull's-eye and Ellipse pattern font, monumental base, pewter collar and whale oil burner, 10⅛" h **650.00**

Clear
6¼" h, blown shield-shaped font, square waterfall base, whale oil burner, pr **400.00**
7½" h, free blown pear shaped font, crossed base, tin and cork whale oil burner. **190.00**
7⅝" h, partially fluted font, brass standard, marble base   **90.00**
8¼" h, free blown teardrop-shaped font, circular lacy base, whale oil burner and wick, pr **450.00**
9⅝" h, pressed heart, sawtooth, and bull's-eye pattern font, hexagonal base, brass collar   **125.00**
9¾" h, Gothic Arch font, hexagonal base, missing collar   **75.00**
10" h, Lutz-type, threaded, pear-shaped font, fine opaque white spiral threads on clear ground, translucent blue base, double brass camphene burner, pewter caps   **150.00**
Cobalt Blue, Bigler pattern, square base, whale oil burner, pr, 10⅛" h **4,250.00**
Deep Amethyst, Loop pattern, whale oil burner, 8⅛" h. **1,300.00**
Emerald Green font, cobalt blue globe, applied handle, c1880, 6¼" h **165.00**
Medium Purple-blue, 3-Printie Block pattern, unrecorded base, whale oil burner, 7¾" h. **750.00**
Opaque Pink, onion-shaped font, translucent white base, 7½" h .   **250.00**
US Glass Co, clear, King's Crown pattern, c1890, 10" h **90.00**
Petticoat
Japanned Tin, candlestick peg, whale oil burner, 1850–60, 4⅛" h   **35.00**
Tin, brass whale oil burner, handle, repainted flat black, 5 ½" h **35.00**
Pittsburgh Lamp Co, nickel plated brass, cast iron foot, marked "The Pittsburgh," emb scrolled "S" designs around font, spiral design around foot, c1890, 10½" h to top of prongs   **55.00**
Railway Car
Adams & Westlake, hanging, double, cast bronze and brass, maker name marked on fonts, orig white enamel metal shades, c1890, 30" w, 32" h **1,320.00**
Williams & Page Co, Boston, MA, brass, bracket lamp, glass font, cast brass bracket, 1870–80, 7" h **135.00**
Rauschenbergs Formaldehyde Deodorizer, tin, hand lamp, used with deodorizer burner, May 1, 1900 patent date on brass label, 3¾" h **12.00**

Royal Center Draft Lamp, brass, stamped pattern on shoulder, punched design around base, patent dates on flame spreader, opaque white shade, c1890, 15" h to top of shade **135.00**
Rush Light, wrought iron, candle socket counter balance, twisted detail, ring base, 12¼" h. **325.00**
Safety, hand lamp
E Miller & Co, tin, c1890, 5½" h . . .   **45.00**
Perkins & House, brass, custom made burner, early chimney, c1860 . . . .   **385.00**
Unknown Maker
Brass, strap handle, late 19th C, 4½" h **65.00**
Sheet Metal, side filler, patent dated cap, traces of old red paint, resoldered handle, 4⅞" h   **5.00**
Ship's, gimbaled, brass, standing or wall mount, glass font, lead weighted base, c1860, 6¾" h. **75.00**
Spout Lamp, brass, funnel shaped base, removable font, minor battering, polished, 11" h. **75.00**
Student
Bridgeport Brass Co, nickel plated brass, opaque white shade, clear chimney, c1880, 14¾" h to top of shade. **360.00**
Unknown Maker, mercury, brass, font higher than reservoir, fuel level maintained by hydrostatic pressure, reservoir floats on mercury, burner marked "Waterbury," opaque white Vienna shade, c1880, 22" h **495.00**

Student Lamps, left: Manhattan Student Lamp, nickel-plated brass, replaced green-painted white milk glass shade, 7" d, 25" h, $275.00; right: brass, kerosene fuel tank sgd "Kleeman," pink cased ribbed shade, 7" d, 19¾" h, $660.00. Photograph courtesy of James D Julia, Inc.

Whale Oil Lamp, tole, saucer base, stenciled yellow letters "Sam'l Davis' Patented May 6th, 1856," blue ground, 7" h, $250.00.

Taper Jack, silver plated, urn finial, snuffer cap on chain, marked "Exeter," red taper, worn silver, 5½" h	275.00
Victor Wall Lamp, brass, silvered glass reflector, c1890, 10" h	300.00
Whale Oil	
Pewter, baluster stem, Israel Trask, Beverly, MA, 1807–56, 8" h	125.00
Tole, conical font, hinged snuffers, saucer pan, brass and tin burner, worn blue japanning, 3¾" h, pr	240.00

LANTERNS

History: A lantern is an enclosed, portable light source, hand carried or attached to a bracket or pole to illuminate an area. Many lanterns can be used both indoors and outdoors and have a protected flame. Fuels used in early lanterns included candles, kerosene, whale oil, coal oil, and later gasoline, natural gas, and batteries.

Lanterns designed for use on the farm often had special safety features such as a filling cap lock or special base to prevent tipping. When collecting farm lanterns, do not overlook vehicle lanterns and the small hand-held lanterns used to walk to the barn or necessary house.

Reference: Anthony Hobson, *Lanterns That Lit Our World,* published by author, 1991.

Reproduction Craftspersons: Charles Baker Period Reproductions, 6890 N 700 E, Hope, IN 47246; John Kopas, Copper Antiquities, PO Box 153, Cummaquid, MA 02637; Mark Rocheford, Thomas Savriol, Lighting by Hammerworks, 75 Webster St, Worcester, MA 01603; Barry Steierwald, Eagle Lantern, Rte 100, Eagle, PA 19480; Stephen and Carolyn Waligurski, Hurley Patentee Lighting, RD 7, Box 98A, Kingston, NY 12401.

Reproduction Manufacturers: American Period Lighting, The Saltbox, 3004 Columbia Ave, Lan-

caster, PA 17603; Country Accents, RD 2, Box 293, Stockton, NJ 08559; KML Enterprises, RR 1, Box 234L, Berne, IN 46711; Lamb and Lanterns, 902 N Walnut St, Dover, OH 44622; Lt Moses Willard, Inc, 1156 State Rte 50, Milford, OH 45150; Olde Mill House Shoppe, 105 Strasburg Pike, Lancaster, PA 17602; Period Lighting Fixtures, 1 West Main St, Chester, CT 06412.

Barn	
13" h plus wire handle, pine case, mortised construction, chamfered detail on corner posts, hinged door, old dark bluish paint, old glass, three panes damaged, age crack in top of tin heat shield . . .	400.00
Bicycle	
E Miller & Co, 7¾" h, nickel plated brass, Majestic model, carbide fueled, clear lens and reflector, faceted red and green side lights, c1900	160.00
Hawthorne Mfg Co, 6" h, nickel plated, marked "Hawthorne Mfg Co, Old Sol Pat USA"	50.00
Buggy, E T Wright & Co, 9" h, black paint, late 19th C	80.00
Campaign, two spouts, tin, replaced bamboo handle, wire wrap, wire cradle, 48" l.	30.00
Candle, tin	
6" h, cylindrical, pierced conical vent top, horn glazing	235.00
11¼" h plus ring, round, conical top with hanging ring, six glass sides, hinged door, old black paint	225.00
11½" h plus ring	
Round, pyramidal top with large ring handle and star and ray punching, glass sides with wire guards, minor damage	115.00

Candle Lantern, copper and tin, bail handle, 19th C, 11¾" h, $25.00. Photograph courtesy of James D Julia, Inc.

Square, tapered, dark red-cobalt
glass panes all four sides,
painted black, soldered repairs,
one pane cracked **115.00**
13" h, rect, domed top with oval
handle, glass panes front and
two sides, hinged door, old black
paint **135.00**
18" h, hexagonal, turned finials,
good detail, old worn silver, red,
and gold repaint, fastened on pole,
78" h overall **140.00**
21½" h, hexagonal, old black and
gold repaint, finial incomplete,
wooden pole, 63" h overall **110.00**
Clarke's Astronomical Lantern, 12" l,
tole, black and gold paint, two candle sockets, frosted glass, thirteen
cards punched with constellations,
labeled "Clarke's Astronomical Lantern, Manufactured by D. C. Heaty &
Co, Boston," unused condition, orig
wooden box **385.00**
Darkroom, 8¾" h, tin, triangular, ruby
glass panels, outside filler cap, brass
label "The Challenge," 1850–1900   **40.00**
Dashboard, Kemp Mfg Co, 15" h,
spring clips, reflector, red paint, sgd
brass label, c1900 . . . .   **150.00**
Fireman's
Eclipse, green over clear globe,
marked "American La France Fire
Engine Company" **1,000.00**
Ham's, brass and nickel, wire slide,
water shield, distributed by Boston
Woven Hose Co **265.00**
Hurricane, Hurricane Lantern Co,
8⅞" h, brass, chain hanger, sgd,
1860–70 . . . .   **465.00**

**Photographic Common Sense Lantern, tin,
Simplex kerosene burner, stenciled label,
E Miller & Co, Meriden, CT, c1880,
$150.00.**

**Watchman's Lantern, tin, bull's eye lens,
folding handle, whale oil burner, c1850,
6" h, $65.00.**

Kerosene, 12½" h, tin, clear glass
globe, brass trim, kerosene burner,
bail handle **125.00**
Marine, brass
8⅛" h, Fresnel shade, bail handle,
late 19th C **35.00**
10½" h, Wilcox, Crittendon & Co, Inc,
Middletown, CT, wire chimney
guards, bail handle, late 19th C   **220.00**
Miner's
8" h, iron, chicken finial, wick pick.   **250.00**
9½" h, galvanized frame, wire
hanger, late 19th C **25.00**
New England Glass Co, 13½" h, clear
blown glass, worn brown japanning,
pierced star and diamond vent holes,
removable font with whale oil
burner, minor damage to base, ring
handle. **200.00**
Pocket, 5¾" h, folding, wire bail han-
dle, ruby glass panel, black and gold
litho illus of man seated on train,
wearing top hat, lantern clipped to
jacket pocket, reading newspaper,
c1870 . . . .   **225.00**
Railroad
Adlake Reliable, 5⅜" h, single horizontal wire guard, bellbottom
frame, clear globe and frame
marked "KCSRY," May 9, 1922
patent date **160.00**
Armspear Mfg Co, NY, 10" h, trouble
lantern, red globe marked "B & O
RR, Armspear Mfg. Co. New York
1925," two detonators attached to
frame, weighted iron base, bail
handle. **100.00**
Dietz & Co, 11" h, inspector's lan-
tern, New York Central System
logo on globe, "Ideal Inspector
Lamp" imp on back and
"B.R.&P.Ry" on front label, traces
of silver paint on reflector, hanging
ring, wire bail handle, late 19th C   **70.00**

Keystone Lantern Co, The Casey, single horizontal wire guard, twist wick raiser, 5⅜" h amber globe, frame marked "NYP&N R CO," Dec 30, 1902 patent date 850.00

N L Piper Railway Supply Corp, 13" h, tin, S Sargent label, brass top, glass globe, 1861 and 1866 patent dates   150.00

Revere Type, 13" h plus ring handle, punched tin, cylindrical, conical top, old worn green paint, some rust . . .   175.00

Skater's

6½" h, brass, clear globe 45.00

7" h

Brass, "Little Bobs" molded in shade, c1870. . . . .   110.00

Tin, clear glass globe, wire bale handle, light rust 70.00

Tin, 11½" h, square tapered, deep reddish cobalt glass in four sides, damage, soldered repairs, black paint   115.00

MINIATURE AND FAIRY LAMPS

History: Kerosene and candles were a popular lighting source in many rural areas until the 1930s. The trip down the hall or to the outdoor facility at night required a quick, easy to use appliance. Miniature lamps and fairy lamps answered this need.

Like kerosene lamps, there were plain and fancy examples. Plain examples were used on a daily basis. Fancy examples were reserved for the guest bedroom and hallways when friends or relatives spent the night. Occasionally, fancy examples could be found in the master bedroom.

Miniature oil and kerosene lamps, often called "night lamps," are diminutive replicas of larger lamps. Simple and utilitarian in design, miniature lamps found a place in the parlor (as "courting" lamps), hallway, children's rooms, and sickrooms.

Miniature lamps are found in many glass types from amberina to satin glass and measure 2½ to 12 inches in height. The principal parts are the base, collar, burner, chimney, and shade. In 1877 both L. J. Atwood and L. H. Olmsted patented burners for miniature lamps. Their burners made the lamps into a popular household accessory.

Fairy lamps, originating in England in the 1840s, are candle burning night lamps. They were used in nurseries, hallways, and dim corners of the home.

Two leading candle manufacturers, the Price Candle Company and the Samuel Clarke Company, promoted fairy lamps as a means to sell candles. Both contracted with other manufacturers of glass, porcelain, and metal to produce the needed shades and cups. For example, Clarke used Worcester Royal Porcelain Company, Stuart

& Sons, and Red House Glass Works in England, plus firms in France and Germany. Clarke's trademark was a small fairy with a wand surrounded by the words "Clarke Fairy Pyramid, Trade Mark."

Fittings were produced in a wide variety of styles. Shades ranged from pressed to cut glass, from Burmese to Nailsea. Cups are found in glass, porcelain, brass, nickel, and silver plate.

American firms selling fairy lamps included Diamond Candle Company of Brooklyn, Blue Cross Safety Candle Company, and Hobbs, Brockunier & Company of Wheeling, West Virginia.

Fairy lamps are found in two pieces (cup and shade) and three pieces (cup with matching shade and saucer). Married pieces—pieces that were not a set originally—are common.

References: Ann Gilbert McDonald, *Evolution of the Night Lamp*, Wallace-Homestead, 1979, out-of-print; Frank R. & Ruth E. Smith, *Miniature Lamps*, Schiffer Publishing, 1981, 6th printing; Ruth E. Smith, *Miniature Lamps-II*, Schiffer Publishing, 1982; John F. Solverson, *Those Fascinating Little Lamps*, Antique Publications, 1988; John F. Solverson (comp.), "*Those Fascinating Little Lamps*"/*Miniature Lamps Value Guide* (includes prices for Smith numbers), Antique Publications, 1988.

Collectors' Club: Miniature Lamp Collectors, 38619 Wakefield Ct, Northville, MI 48167.

Reproduction Alert: Reproductions abound. Further, study these lamps carefully. Married pieces are common.

FAIRY

Bisque, figural, kitten head, gray, blue collar, green eyes 485.00

Glass

Amber, 3" d, 3⅝" h, pyramid, white opal swirl glass shade, clear base marked "Clarke" 100.00

Burmese, 4½" h, clear pressed base marked "S. Clarke's, Patent, Trademark, Fairy" 325.00

Nailsea type

4½" h, opaque white loopings on blue shade, clear base marked "Clarke Cricklite". 375.00

4¾" h, opaque white loopings on citron shade, clear base marked "Clarke Cricklite". 175.00

Overshot, 3¾" h, green, pyramid, clear base marked "Clarke" 110.00

Peachblow, 6⅜" h, blue, white, brown, and green enamel dec on shade and base, white int., base marked "Clarke Cricklite" 410.00

Satin, 5½" h, rainbow, swirled, crimped top, clear base marked "S. Clarke" 450.00

Fairy Lamp, yellow, emb floral dec, 3 pcs, $65.00.

Miniature Lamp, blue glass, Bull's Eye pattern, stemmed, $90.00.

Spatter, 4" d, 14" h, gold, white, and pink, Swirl pattern shade, white int., clear peg type base marked "Clarke," brass candlestick **425.00**

Vaseline, 2⅞" d, 3½" h, ribbed dome, pressed green base marked "Clarke" **165.00**

Lithophane, 4" h, white lithophane newel post shade, clear base marked "Clarke Cricklite" **450.00**

Porcelain, three faced, owl, cat, and dog **150.00**

Pottery, 3¼" w, 4¾" h, cottage, orange roof, pierced windows and doors, green saucer base, England **110.00**

MINIATURE

Brass

Bradley & Hubbard, 12" h to top of shade, nickel plated, marked "The B & H" on lamp and flame spreader, punched design around base, cased green shade, c1890 **325.00**

Bridgeport Brass Co, 7½" h to top of chimney, nickel plated, bracket lamp, maker's name and address and "All Night" marked on shoulder, late 19th C **55.00**

Lampe-Pigeon, 9" h, clear chimney, foreign burner **35.00**

Glass

Amethyst, 6¼" h, emb gold dec, acorn burner, worn paint **125.00**

Blue

6¾" h, Twinkle, acorn burner, upper shade roughness **165.00**

13" h, emb diamond pattern, nickel plated iron foot, nickel plated foreign burner and collar **400.00**

Clear

2½" h, hand lamp, blown three-mold body made from stopper

mold, applied handle, tin "Patent" burner **300.00**

4½" h, Glow Night Lamp Co, Inc, Boston, swirled pattern on clear font, melon ribbed opaque white shade, c1890 . . . . **110.00**

5½" h, The Handy Night Lamp, tin burner and reflector, c1890 . . . **28.00**

6¾" h, milk glass beehive shade, sgd "Pride of America Time & Light Grand Val's Perfect Time Indicating Lamp" **160.00**

Cranberry

7¼" h, lily of the valley dec on shade and base **1,075.00**

8¼" h, Beaded Swirl pattern, hornet burner, two small shade chips **125.00**

Green, 7¾" h, swirl design, foreign burner **200.00**

Milk Glass

Blue

7⅞" h, owl, emb, nutmeg burner **2,650.00**

8½" h, Defender, nutmeg burner **185.00**

Miniature Lamp, cranberry font, opalescent chimney, silver plated base, Smith I, #18, 5¾" h, $525.00.

White
  5¾" h, emb Greek Key dec,
    acorn burner **60.00**
  7¼" h, eggshell finish, enam-
    eled orange and brown floral
    dec, acorn burner, worn paint   **125.00**
  7⅝" h, owl, painted gray, black,
    and orange, acorn burner. . . **1,100.00**
  7¾" h, Artichoke pattern, pink
    and green painted dec, nut-
    meg burner **150.00**
  8" h, emb beaded swirls and
    flowers, yellow, orange, and
    green painted dec, hornet
    burner, multiple fish scale
    flakes, worn paint **125.00**
  8½" h, fired-on pink, blue, and
    yellow on emb dec, nutmeg
    burner, minor chip on shade   **145.00**
  8¾" h, Chrysanthemum pattern,
    pink and yellow painted dec,
    gold   highlights,   hornet
    burner, two fish scale flakes
    on fitter edge **275.00**
  9" h, yellow, blue, and maroon
    pansy dec, nutmeg burner   **150.00**
  9½" h, Santa Claus, red coat,
    black boots, nutmeg burner   **1,800.00**
  10½" h, emb floral dec font,
    black steel foot, brass cigar
    lighters   and   tubes,   blue
    thumbprint   chimney,   pet
    ratchet burner **325.00**
  10¾" h, paneled and emb, mul-
    ticolored   pansy   dec,   gold
    highlights, hornet burner and
    ring, excellent shade, partial
    repaint **250.00**
Opalescent, 7¼" h, Spanish Lace,
  blue, nutmeg burner, flake on
  shade ext. **900.00**
Satin Glass
  Blue
    7" h, cased, melon ribbed base,
      pansy ball shade, nutmeg
      burner **525.00**
    11"   h,   Diamond   Quilted,
      mother-of-pearl, peg type
      font, brass stem and foot, for-
      eign burner **2,200.00**
  Green
    8" h, Raindrop pattern, mother-
      of-pearl, acorn burner, int.
      burst bubble. **700.00**
    8¼" h, Drape pattern, nutmeg
      burner, three chips at top of
      shade. **135.00**
  Pink
    7½" h, cased, Brady's Night
      Lamp, nutmeg burner, two
      fish scale flakes at shade
      top. **325.00**

8½" h, cased, emb design, hornet burner, tiny fish scale
  flake on top of shade **400.00**
8¾"   h,   Diamond   Quilted,
  mother-of-pearl,   applied
  frosted feet, foreign burner,
  minor flakes **1,250.00**
Red
  8¼" h, emb design, nutmeg
    burner, tiny fish scale shade
    chip **300.00**
  8¾" h, emb design, nutmeg
    burner, two minor fish scale
    flakes at top of shade **100.00**
Spatter Glass, 8" h, red and white,
  emb swirled ribs, clear applied
  feet, nutmeg burner. **1,600.00**
Yellow Cased, 8½" h, fired-on gold
  floral dec, nutmeg burner **900.00**

SHADES AND ACCESSORIES

History: Lamp shades were made to diffuse the
harsh light produced by early gas lighting fixtures.
This was achieved by a variety of methods—using
an opaque glass such as milk glass, frosting the
glass, painting the glass, or developing a mold
pattern that scattered the light. In addition to being
functional, lamp shades often were highly decorative.

During the "golden age" of American art glass
in the last quarter of the 19th century and the first
quarter of the 20th century, many manufacturers
including Durand, Quezal, Steuben, Tiffany, and
others made shades for lamps and gas fixtures.
Most shades are not marked. Examples did work
their way into the countryside.

The popularity of these "high style" designs
quickly led to the manufacturer of inexpensive
copies. These copycats also are collectible. Lamp
and gas shades can provide an important color
highlight in a Country setting.

The most highly prized shades are those in
stained glass. Beware of signed "Tiffany" examples. Over the years unscrupulous individuals
have added Tiffany markings to many lesser quality shades.

Some of the most overlooked collectibles are
electric lamp shades. The agrarian housewife was
often a skilled handcrafter, especially in sewing.
Many added a personal touch to their home by
designing and making their own lamp shades.
Shades were made to match draperies or furniture
upholstery. The variety was endless. Often the
frilliest examples were reserved for the guest bedroom.

Should you decide to take up lamp shade collecting, do not overlook the mass-produced
shades. Many featured ornately printed designs
and pattern on translucent material ranging from
stiff paper to celluloid.

References: Larry Freeman, *New Lights on Old Lamps*, American Life Foundation, 1984; Jo Ann Thomas, *Early Twentieth Century Lighting Fixtures*, Collector Books, 1980, out-of-print.

Reproduction Craftperson: Larry Edelman, Applecore Creations, PO Box 29696, Columbus, OH 43229; Faith Kovach, 201 W Alyea St, PO Box 522, Hebron, IN 46341; Claudia A Minick, Light Up My Life Antiques, RD 4, Box 307, Blairsville, PA 15717–8942.

Reproduction Manufacturers: Anastasia's Collectibles, 6114 134th St W, Apple Valley, MN 55124; Carole Foy's Ruffled Curtains and Accessories, 331 E Durham Rd, Cary, NC 27511; Country Accents, RD 2, Box 293, Stockton, NJ 08559; Country Heart Homespun Collection, Inc, 1212 Westover Hills Blvd, Box 13358, Richmond, VA 23225; Country Lighting and Accessories, PO Box 1279, New London, NH 03257; Designs in Copper, 7541 Emery Rd, Portland, MI 48875; House of Vermillion/Heirloom Quality, PO Box 18642, Kearns, UT 84118; Lamplighter Antiques, 615 Silver Bluff Rd, Aiken, SC 29801; Lt Moses Willard, Inc, 1156 State Rte 50, Milford, OH 45150; Mak-A-Shade, 1340 W Strasburg Rd, West Chester, PA 19382; Mole Hill Pottery, 5011 Anderson Pike, Signal Mountain, TN 37377; Dorothy Primo, Lampshades of Antique, PO Box 2, West Main, OR 97501; Rowe Pottery Works, Inc, 404 England St, Cambridge, WI 53523; Victorian Lightcrafters, Ltd, PO Box 350, Slate Hill, NY 10973; Woodbee's, RR 1, Poseyville, IN 47633.

Carnival Lamp Shade, Soda Gold, 2" fitter, $25.00.

Chimney, clear glass	
Beaded rim	**8.00**
Cut floral dec on frosted bands, fluted rim, c1900, 4¾" d, 6" h	**45.00**
Plain	**6.00**
Lamp Filler, brass, gooseneck spout, strap side handle, polished, 4⅞" h	**70.00**
Lamp Hook, holds hanging lamp, cast iron, mounted on board, c1875, set of nine	**450.00**
Lamp Mantle, Welsbach Junior J Mantle, orig box, early 20th C	**50.00**
Lantern Globe, pale amber glass, fluted, 19th C, 4½" d, 5 ¾" h	**10.00**
Lighting Stand	
7" h, cherry and poplar, turned pedestal, round base, refinished	**40.00**
8" h, pine and poplar, turned pedestal, age crack in square base, old dark patina	**300.00**
8¼" h, poplar, turned, tapers to round base	**165.00**
Oil Container, Ohio Lantern Co, clear blown glass jar, metal container, wire mesh guard marked "Made by Ohio Lantern Co. Tiffen" on one side, 1889 patent dates on other side, 12½" h	**135.00**

Shade	
Caramel Slag, curved glass segments, orange shade crescents and rect border, tag imp "Handel," assembled single socket fitting with chain, 5" h	**880.00**
Clear	
Acid etched floral design, onion shaped, late 19th C, 7¼" d, 4½" h	**60.00**
Pressed pattern imitates cut glass, scalloped sawtooth rim, c1880, 7½" d, 4" fitter, pr	**55.00**
Clear and Frosted	
Acid etched hummingbirds and leaves, c1870, 8" d, pr	**150.00**
Engraved flowers, onion shaped, late 19th C, 7" d, 4½" h	**45.00**
Frosted, chimney shaped, turned-down rim, cut floral design, 1850–1900, 4½" d, 6" h	**90.00**
Gold, Fostoria, green leaves and vines, white luster ground, 5" h	**125.00**
Green, globe, late 19th C, 3¾" d, 2¾" h	**50.00**
Leaded, hanging dome	
25" d, 8½" h, green slag segments, broad border of flying ducks	**660.00**
24" d, 14" h, crown cap, wide border of pink rose blossoms, red cherries	**440.00**
Opalescent	
Block shaped, 10" w, 5¾" h	**50.00**
Swirl pattern, angle lamp shade, c1890, 8½" h	**150.00**
Ruby Red, globe, late 19th C, 3¼" d, 1¾" fitter	**45.00**
White	
Dome, 7¾" d, 6" h	**55.00**
Flat, fluted, late 19th C, 9½" d, 2" h	**10.00**
Onion shaped, 7¼" d, 4¾" h	**32.00**
Shallow dome, late 19th C, 9¾" d, 3½" h	**12.00**
Sloping sides, late 19th C, 7⅝" d, 3¼" h	**25.00**

METALS

In a life filled with uncertainties, the agrarian community welcomed items associated with strength and permanence. Objects made of metal fit the bill. As a result, metal implements and household appliances were among the most treasured possessions.

Wrestled from the earth, metals symbolize man's ability to conquer and tame nature. Raw elements were transformed into useful products. Much of the success of working with metals during the 18th and 19th centuries was achieved through trial and error, a concept that stressed mankind's innovative nature.

The presence of an individual who could work metal was critical to a rural community's survival. In most cases, this task fell to the blacksmith who knew his own craft and dabbled in some of the other metal trades as well. The blacksmith worked at an anvil. His most important roles were the manufacture of tools and hardware along with keeping farm machinery operational.

The role of shoeing horses in agrarian America fell to the farrier. The farrier obtained his horseshoes from the blacksmith. Few farmers had the time or wished to incur the expense of bringing their horses to the village smith. The farrier with his portable forge was a welcome visitor. Because he traveled a wide circuit, he was also a major source of "outside" news.

As a community grew, additional metal workers arrived. Some brought a combination of skills. The rural silversmith manufactured flatware and an occasional hollow piece. Often he acted as a jobber for a silversmith from a larger town or a silver plate manufacturer. A rural silversmith earned the bulk of his income as a jeweler and repairer of clocks, guns, and watches.

Tinsmiths tended to concentrate solely on their craft. Their products, ranging from dinner plates to coffeepots, were easily transportable and durable. Holes and cracks that did appear could be easily repaired. More difficult metal repairs were done by the tinker, who ran a mobile sales and repair service specializing in brass, copper, and tin.

By the mid-19th century industrial production reached the point where most of the metal product needs of the rural community were not manufactured locally. The repair function far outweighed the production function of the local craftsman. The repair business was a viable one. Metal products were expected to last for generations provided they were well cared for and kept in good repair.

As times changed, so did the rural metal craftsperson. The blacksmith became the auto mechanic. Many silversmiths opened a jewelry store. Others, such as the tinsmith, entered the mercantile community. The farrier shifted his portable forge from the back of a wagon to a pickup truck.

Most of the metal products that are encountered in a Country setting are utilitarian in nature and found in a patinated finish. There was enough to do without having to spend time keeping an item polished. Of course, there were a few pieces that were "kept for nice," but these were brought out only on special occasions.

Most metal products in a Country setting are displayed out of context. Few individuals want to recreate a "shop" within their home environment. Shop settings along with individuals who have revived the old techniques are frequently found at farm museums.

The crafts revival of the 1970s and 1980s witnessed a rebirth of many of the metal crafts. Blacksmiths and tinsmiths abound. Their products often are exact duplicates of their historic counterparts. Most are unmarked. In time, the only way to distinguish them from period piece will be to analyze the metal content.

Museum: National Ornamental Metal Museum, Memphis, TN.

BRASS

History: Brass is a durable, malleable, and ductile metal alloy consisting mainly of copper and zinc. It achieved its greatest popularity for utilitarian and decorative art items in the 18th and 19th centuries.

When collecting brass, check to make certain that the object is not brass plated. This can be done with a magnet. A magnet will not stick to brass. If a magnet sticks to a "brass" item, it is plated.

References: Mary Frank Gaston, *Antique Brass and Copper,* Collector Books, 1992; Peter, Nancy, and Herbert Schiffer, *The Brass Book,* Schiffer Publishing, 1978.

Reproduction Alert: Many modern reproductions of earlier brass forms are being made, especially in the areas of buckets, fireplace equipment, and kettles.

Reproduction Craftspersons: *General*—Michael Bonne, Coppersmith, RR 1, Box 177R, Carthage, IN 46115; James Chamberlain, Colony Brass, PO Box 266, Williamsburg, VA 23187; Christopher E Dunham, Brassfounder, PO Box 423, Worthington, MA 01098; Stephen Smithers, 1057 Hawley Rd, Ashfield, MA 01330; *Hardware*—Steve Kayne, Kayne & Son Custom Forged Hardware, 76 Daniel Ridge Rd, Candler, NC 28715.

Reproduction Manufacturers: *General*—KML Enterprises, RR 1, Box 234L, Berne, IN 46711; Lemee's Fireplace Equipment, 815 Bedford St, Bridgewater, MA 02324; Olde Mill House Shoppe, 105 Strasburg Pike, Lancaster, PA 17602; Virginia Metalcrafters, 1010 East Main St, Waynesboro, VA 22980; *Hardware*—The Antique Hardware Store, 43 Bridge St, Frenchtown, NJ 08825; Bathroom Machineries, 495 Main St, PO Box 1020, Murphys, CA 95247; Bedlam Brass, 137 Rte 4 Westbound, Paramus, NJ 07652.

Balance Scale, 23¾" h, rect mahogany bevel edged base, inscribed "To weigh one pound"	120.00
Bank, 3" h, cylindrical, tooled band, traces of gilding	60.00
Bed Warmer	
43" l, tooled lid with flowers and peacock, turned wood handle	350.00
44" l, floral design, pierced, turned wood handle, old dark finish	200.00
44½" l, engraved rooster, turned cherry handle	450.00
45½" l, stylized bird and leaves dec lid, red and ochre grain painted ring-turned birch handle, late 18th C	1,200.00
Candlestick	
5" h, baluster stem, drum base, brazed edge repair on base	250.00
5⅝" h, octagonal base	250.00

Brass Bed Warmer, incised floral dec, turned wood handle, 10½" d, 41" l, $225.00.

6" h, wide scalloped plate shaped base	550.00
6½" h, brass base with coiled adjustable iron spiral stem, 18th C	100.00
6¾" h, Queen Anne, wide flaring lip, baluster stems, square base with inverted corners, pr	550.00
6¾" h, sq base, paw feet	250.00
6⅞" h, Victorian, pushups, pr	55.00
7" h, Victorian, pushups, beehive and diamond quilted detail, pr.	75.00
7⅛" h, push-up, slender turned shaft, round base, England, c1800, pr	300.00

Brass Candlestick, beehive standard, 10¾" h, 19th C, price for pr, $187.00. Photograph courtesy of Freeman Fine Arts.

Brass Pot, riveted handles, 12" d, $180.00.

8" h, turned stem, sq base with four
feet **210.00**
8" h, Victorian, pushup
Baluster stem, square base, pr . . .   **85.00**
Beehive and diamond quilted de-
tail. **60.00**
9½" h, mismatched top, sq base, four
short feet **110.00**
10" h, Victorian, pushups, beehive
and diamond quilted detail, price
for set of four. **245.00**
11¾" h, Victorian, diamond detail,
pushups missing, price for pair   **155.00**
Chamberstick, threaded stem, loose
drip pan, long handle, 4" h, 9½" l   **55.00**
Dipper, flat shape, wrought iron handle
with hanger dec, 19th C, 22⅜" l . . .   **75.00**
Door Knocker
Architectural, engraved "J. Frey.
1805," 7¾" h **80.00**
Horse Head, 5½" h. **130.00**
Flagpole Finial, 7" w, spreadwinged
eagle. **25.00**
Kettle, spun brass, iron bail handle
American Spun Brass Kettle, marked,
some damage, 17½" d **110.00**

**Brass School Bell, turned wood handle,
4⅝ " d, 8" h, $50.00.**

Hayden's Patent label, some dam-
age, old repair, 11" d. **50.00**
Kettle Stand, 8 × 9 × 10" h, reticulated
top, wrought iron base **115.00**
Ladle, wrought iron handle, 19½" l   **140.00**
Pail, spun brass, "American Brass Kettle" label, wrought iron bale handle,
22½" d, 15" h. **140.00**
Plate, 5½" d, hammered. **5.00**
School Bell, No. 7, turned wood handle   **40.00**
Skimmer, copper rivets, well formed
wrought iron handle, heart shaped
hanger, late 18th-early 19th C,
26¼" l **125.00**
Stencil, 13½" sq, rooster design,
marked "HA&Co 56 Boston". **200.00**
Trolley Car Bell. **125.00**
Trivet, 4¾ × 6¼", rect, pierced top, cast
legs. **45.00**
Warming Pan, turned wood handle   **175.00**
Wick Trimmer Scissors, tray, 9¾" l . . .   **140.00**

COPPER

History: Copper objects, such as kettles, tea kettles, warming pans, measures, etc., played an
important part in the 19th century household.
Outdoors, the apple butter kettle and still were the
two principal copper items. Copper culinary objects were lined with a thin protective coating of
tin to prevent poisoning. They were relined as
needed.

Great emphasis is placed by collectors on
signed pieces, especially those by American
craftsmen. Since copper objects were made
abroad as well, it is hard to identify unsigned
examples.

References: Mary Frank Gaston, *Antique Brass
and Copper,* Collector Books, 1992; Henry J.
Kauffman, *Early American Copper, Tin, and Brass,*
Medill McBride Co., 1950.

Reproduction Alert: Reproductions, especially
those made thirty years ago and longer, are extremely difficult to distinguish from their historical
counterparts without electrospectography analysis.

Reproduction Craftspersons: *General*—Michael
Bonne, Copper Smith, RR 1, Box 177R, Carthage,
IN 46115; Tim Halligan, T. H. Copper, 1904 W
Spruce, Duncan, OK 73533; John Kopas, Copper
Antiquities, PO Box 153, Cummaquid, MA
02637; Peter Renzetti, 301 Brinton's Bridge Rd,
West Chester, PA 19382; Kurt P Strehl, Orpheus
Coppersmith, 52 Clematis Rd, Agawam, MA
01001; Michael P Terragna, The Coppersmith, PO
Box 755, Sturbridge, MA 01566; Galen Walters,
Walters Unique Metals, 140 Sandy Hill Rd, Den-
ver, PA 17517; *Hardware*—Steve Kayne, Kayne &
Son Custom Forged Hardware, 76 Daniel Ridge
Rd, Candler, NC 28715.

Reproduction Manufacturers: The Calico Corner, 513 E Bowman St, South Bend, IN 46613; Cape Cod Cupola Co, Inc, 78 State Rd, Rte 6, N Dartmouth, MA 02747; Designs in Copper, 7641 Emery Rd, Portland, MI 48875; KML Enterprises, RR 1, Box 234L, Berne, IN 46711; Rustique Designs, Rte 4, Box 295, Parsons, KS 67357.

Bedwarmer, copper pan, tooled brass lid, turned wooden handle with old brown graining, basket of flowers design on lid, 43½" l	325.00
Candlesticks, pr, brass handle, 19th C, 5½" h	45.00
Coal Scuttle, 22" l	100.00
Coffeepot, fits in stove top opening, Continental, 19th C, 18" h	300.00
Dipper	
10¾" l, wrought iron handle	70.00
20¾" l, wrought iron handle	45.00
23½" l, wrought iron handle	45.00
33½" l, brass handle	125.00
Food Mold	
Fruit Basket, 20th C, 10" l	90.00
Turk's Head, decorative detail, dovetailed seams, dents, 10" d	125.00
Funnel, 5" d	20.00
Hot Water Bottle, marked "WAFAX," 8½" h	65.00
Kettle, oval, wrought iron handle, 19th C, 16" l, 19½" h	190.00
Ladle, wrought iron handle, 17¾" l	135.00
Measure, set of three	
Dry, NY excise marks, c1869, 9" d × 4¼" h, 11½" d × 5½" h, and 14" d × 6⅞" h	875.00
Liquid, graduated sizes, dents, 3⅝" h	105.00
Milk Pail, iron bail handle, England, 19th C.	200.00
Mug, wrought iron handle, 18th C, 7½" h	55.00
Pitcher, dovetailed, 12" h	110.00
Pot, cov, applied rim handles with tulip ends, dovetailed bottom	295.00

Copper Coffee Server, iron stand, 16½" h, $325.00.

Roaster, diamond shaped, England, 19th C, 27" l, 20" w	360.00
Sauce Pan, dovetailed seams	
Wrought iron handle, tinned int., 5" d, 11½" l	55.00
Wrought copper handle, some edge damage, 5½" d, 7¼" h to handle	75.00
Scoop, turned wooden handle, lip split, old soldered reinforcement, 14½" l	75.00
Skimmer, wrought iron handle, 18½" l	100.00
Still, sour mash whiskey, three piece, boiler, extended spout, coiled condenser	200.00
Tea Kettle	
10" h, eagle mark, minor denting	350.00
10½" h, dovetailed, gooseneck spout, brass trim, acorn finial, well-shaped stationary handle, maker's mark of intertwined initials "W.C. & S."	95.00
10¾" h, marked "I Roberts Phila"	575.00
11¼" h, marked "J Geddes/Baltimore," minor denting	850.00
11½" h, marked "J Bollinger"	500.00
12¼" h, marked "W Heyser, 6, Chambersburg," minor denting	275.00
Watering Can, long spout, "Joseph Breck & Sons, Boston" label	145.00

IRONWARE

History: Iron, a metallic element that occurs abundantly in combined forms, has been known for centuries. Items made from iron range from the utilitarian to the decorative. Early hand-forged ironwares are of considerable interest to Country collectors.

The malleability of iron appealed to farmers. It could be shaped by hand into a wealth of useful products. It weathered well when properly cared for; when broken, it was easily repaired.

References: Frank T. Barnes, *Hooks, Rings & Other Things: An Illustrated Index of New England Iron, 1660–1860*, The Christopher Publishing House, 1988; *Griswold Cast Iron: A Price Guide*, L–W Book Sales, 1993; Kathryn McNerney, *Antique Iron*, Collector Books, 1984, 1993 value update; George C. Neumann, *Early American Antique Country Furnishings: Northeastern America, 1650–1800's*, L–W Book Sales, 1984, 1993 reprint; Herbert, Peter, and Nancy Schiffer, *Antique Iron*, Schiffer Publishing, 1979.

Reproduction Craftpersons: *General*—Michael Bonne, RR 1, Box 177R, Carthage, IN 46115; Kevin P Clancy, 2819 Old Liberty Rd, Eldersburg, MD 21784; Michael Dutcher, 415 W Market St, West Chester, PA 19380; Ian Eddy, Blacksmith, RFD 1, Box 975, Putney, VT 05346; Charles W. Euston, Woodbury Blacksmith & Forge Co, PO

Box 268, Woodbury, CT 06798; James W Faust, 488 Porters Mill Rd, Pottstown, PA 19464; Louie Frantz, Ye Old Workshoppe, 420 E Market St, Hallam, PA 17406; Ernest Frederick, 340 Fairview Dr, Kutztown, PA 19530; James A Hoffman, Hoffman's Forge, 2272 Youngstown Lockport Rd #1, Ransomville, NY 14131; Charles Keller, Forge and Anvil, PO Box 51, Newman, IL 61942; Thomas M Latane, T & C Latane, PO Box 62, Pepin, WI 54749; Greg Leavitt, 476 Valleybrook Rd, Wawa, PA 19063; Thomas Loose, Blacksmith, Rte 2, Box 2410, Leesport, PA 19533; Jonathan Marshall, The J Marshall Co, 1310 Westview, E Lansing, MI 48823; David Mathews, Stone County Ironworks, Rte 73, Box 427, Mountain View, AR 72560; C Leigh Morrell, West Village Forge, PO Box 2114, Marlboro Rd, W Brattleboro, VT 05301; Ronald Potts, Blacksmith, Chriswill Forge, 2255 Manchester Rd, North Lawrence, OH 44666; Peter Renzetti, 301 Brinton's Bridge Rd, West Chester, PA 19382; Darold Rinedollar, Blacksmith, PO Box 365, Clarksville, MO 63336; DJ Stasiak, Blacksmith 5421 Beaver Dam Rd, West Bend, WI 53095; Nick Vincent, Nathan's Forge, PO Box 72, Uniontown, MD 21157; *Hardware*—Jerry W Darnell, Mill Creek Forge and Blacksmith Shop, Box 494–B, Rte 2, Seagrove, NC 17341; Charles Euston, Woodbury Blacksmith & Forge Co, PO Box 268, Woodbury, CT 06798; Steve Kayne, Kayne & Son Custom Forged Hardware, 76 Daniel Ridge Rd, Candler, NC 28715; Elmer L Roush, Jr, Roush Forged Metals, Rte 2, Box 13, Cleveland, VA 24225.

Reproduction Manufacturers: *General*—Bullfrog Hollow, Keeny Rd, Lyme, CT 06371; Lancaster Collection, PO Box 6074, Lancaster, PA 17603; Lemee's Fireplace Equipment, 815 Bedford St, Bridgewater, MA 02324; Matthews Emporium, 157 N Trade St, PO Box 1038, Matthews, NC 28106; Town and Country, Main St, East Conway, NH 04037; The Vine and Cupboard, PO Box 309, George Wright Rd, Woolwich, ME 04579; *Hardware*—American Country House, PO Box 317, Davison, MI 48423; The Antique Hardware Store, 43 Bridge St, Frenchtown, NJ 08825; Antiques Americana, Box 19, North Abington, MA 02382; Old Smithy Shop, Box 336, Milford, NH 03055; South Bound Millworks, PO Box 349, Sandwich, MA 02563; Williamsburg Blacksmiths, Inc, Goshen Rd, Williamsburg, MA 01096.

Andirons, pr	
Cast, potted flower finials, old gold paint, 12" h	85.00
Wrought, gooseneck finials, penny feet, pitted, 12" h	85.00
Apple Butter Kettle, cast, iron bail handle, ftd	125.00
Architectural Ornament, cast	
Eagle, old paint, 8½" h	50.00
Eagle on Sphere, gold repaint, 14" h	225.00
Bathtub, cast, claw and ball feet	65.00
Bean Pot, cast, thimble finial, three stubby feet, emb "Blue Valley Co. Kansas City, Mo.," 1920s	100.00
Bell, cast, yoke	
Church, large clapper, emb "C.S. Bell & Co., Hillsboro, O.," c1900, 24" d	975.00
Farm, painted black	85.00
Plantation	375.00
Betty Lamp, floor type, wrought, 45" h	250.00
Bookends, cast, pr	
Basket of flowers, worn polychrome paint, 5¼" h	60.00
Indian Chief, painted, late 19th C, 6" h, pr	110.00
Oval, farmhouse, trees, and bridge over stream, painted	110.00
Saddled horse, grazing, painted, pr	25.00
Boot Jack, cast	
Beetle, painted black, 9¼" l	35.00
Open Heartand Circle, scalloped sides, 13" l	220.00
Pheasants, two birds, 19" l	225.00
V-shaped, ornate	45.00
Boot Scraper	
Cat, cast, walking with tail extended, 17¾" l	300.00
Double scroll ram's horn finials, wrought, weathered white stone base, 15" h	385.00
Lyre shape, cast, diamond shape base, old green paint, 12" w, 8½" h	150.00
Ram's Horn, wrought, 13" w	275.00
Rooster, pecking, traces of polychrome paint, 19th C, 14" l, 9" h	1,500.00
Bottle Opener, cast	
Advertising, Bishop & Babcock, nickel finish, cork screw, 6⅝" h	95.00
Cockatoo on Perch, polychrome dec, 5½" h	60.00
Candleholder, miner's, Sticking Tommy, wrought, 7½" l	70.00
Candlestand, floor type, wrought, Delaware, OH, 62½" h	310.00
Candlestick	
Adjustable, turned wood base	
Thin spiral stem, 7¾" h	75.00
Wide spiral stem, 7⅛" h	165.00

Iron Boot Jack, cast, filigree base, wrench sockets at end, John Van Buren, 13¼" l, $50.00.

Hog Scraper
  6" h, pushup and lip hanger, old
    pitted surface, illegible name on
    pushup **115.00**
  7" h, pushup, lip hanger missing   **65.00**
  7¼" h, lip hanger, pushup marked
    "Shaw," pitted **125.00**
  7⅜" h, pushup, lip hanger, brass
    trim on base, pr **185.00**
Chandelier, wrought, grape leaf
  molded frame, three scrolling arms
  holding glass chimney shades, center
  dished shade with geometric leaf de-
  sign, Muller Freres, 42" h **1,500.00**
Cotton Scale Weight, 4 lbs **35.00**
Door Knocker, cast
  Amish Man, movable eyes **25.00**
  Fruit Cluster **25.00**
  Hand, worn black repaint, 7" l **95.00**
  Rooster **65.00**
  Spider, hanging from web, bee
    caught in web, 3½" l **95.00**
Doorstop, cast
  Basket of Flowers
    9½" h, worn polychrome repaint   **55.00**
    9¾" h, marked "John Wright,"
      polychrome paint **65.00**
  Boston Terrier, full bodied, black
    and white polychrome paint,
    9¾" h **45.00**
  Boxer, full figure, facing forward,
    brown, tan markings, 8½" h **165.00**
  Campbell Kids with Dog, worn poly-
    chrome paint, 8½" h **160.00**
  Cat
    7¾" h, sitting, white, ribbon col-
      lar, worn polychrome paint . . .   **190.00**
    9" h, sitting, Hubley, white re-
      paint, rust **85.00**
    10¾" h, lying down, Hubley,
      white repaint, rust **80.00**
  Colonial Woman, Hubley, 8" h **115.00**

**Iron Door Stop, bird, cast, painted green,
7" h, $25.00.**

Cottage
  5¾" h, 8⅝" w, blue roof, flowers,
    fenced garden, marked "Eastern
    Specialty Mfg Co. 14" **135.00**
  6½" h, three-dimensional garden,
    tan roof, 3 red chimneys, 2 pc
    casting, Ann Hathaway **250.00**
Duck, white, green bush and grass,
  7½" h **225.00**
Dutch Boy, hands in pockets, blonde
  hair, blue hat and jumpsuit, red
  collar and belt, brown shoes,
  11" h **375.00**
Fisherman, standing at wheel, hand
  blocking sun from eyes, wearing
  rain gear, 6¼" h **140.00**
Frog, yellow and green, 3" h **50.00**
German Shepherd, full bodied, orig
  paint **95.00**
Girl, white hat, flowing cape, hold-
  ing orange jack-o-lantern with cutout eyes, nose, and mouth,
  13¾" h **650.00**
Goldenrods, natural color, sgd
  "Hubley 268," 7⅛" h **150.00**
Horse and Jockey, jumping fence,
  sgd "Eastern Spec Co #790,"
  7⅞" h **185.00**
House, woman walking up front
  steps, grapevines, sgd "Eastern
  Spec Co," 6" h **175.00**
Jonquils, yellow, red and orange
  cups, sgd "Hubley 453," 7" h . . .   **150.00**
Lighthouse, three-dimensional
  buildings and lighthouse, High-
  land, 7¾" h **275.00**
Mammy, blue dress, white apron,
  red and white polka dot kerchief,
  sgd "copyright Hubley" inside,
  12" h **300.00**
Parrot, perched on ring, two sided,
  heavy gold base, sgd "B & H,"
  13¾" h **210.00**
Pekingese, full figure, life-like size
  and color, brown, sgd "Hubley,"
  9" h **500.00**
Pheasant, brown, bright markings,
  green grass, sgd "Fred Everett" on
  front, sgd "Hubley" on back,
  8½" l **200.00**
Quail, pair of brown, tan, and yellow
  birds, green, white, and yellow
  grass, sgd "Fred Everett" on front,
  sgd "Hubley 459" on back, 7¼" h   **225.00**
Pointer, full bodied, worn orig paint,
  15½" l **95.00**
Rabbit, old worn white repaint,
  10¾" h **110.00**
Rooster, full bodied, black, red
  comb, yellow beak and feet, 12" h   **350.00**
Squirrel, holding nut, old worn layers
  of paint, 8⅜" h **140.00**

Three Fish, fantailed, orig paint, sgd
"Hubley 464," 9¾" h 135.00
Three Kittens in Basket, marked "M.
Rosenstein, Lancaster, PA,"
c1932, 7" h. 325.00
Tulips, polychrome paint, 13" h . . . 450.00
Wire Haired Fox Terrier, facing side-
ways, tan, brown markings, 8" h 90.00
Zinnias, multicolored, blue and
black vase, detailed casting,
marked "B & H," 11⅝" h 175.00
Ember Carrier, wrought, sliding lid,
31" l. 235.00
Fencing, 19th C, 47" l, 41" h 440.00
Figure
Cat, cast, oval base, worn silver repaint, 4¾" l. 75.00
Pigeon, cast, full bodied, simple detail, claws clutching threaded cylindrical rod base, traces of old
white paint 350.00
Fireback, cast, armorial design, 28" h 110.00
Fireplace Grate, cast, arched crest, relief crown, shield, lion, and unicorn
dec, England, 18th C, 25 × 21½" 325.00
Fireside Trivet, wrought, twisted detail,
18" l. 50.00
Foot Warmer, sheet iron, pierced both
sides, double heart dec on top, brass
turnip feet, handle, and maker's label, W O Dryer, Poughkeepsie, NY,
dated 1864, 11" l, 8" w, 9" h 600.00
Garden Stake, wrought, symmetrical
sunburst, scrolled lyre shapes, and
urns on center stake, 30" h 250.00
Griddle, cast, ribbed handle with heart
hanger, three feet, 12 ½" d, 10½" l
handle 95.00
Gypsy Kettle, cast, wire bale handle,
9" d 35.00
Hat Rack, cast, painted, flower basket
form, late 19th C, 33" w, 40½" h 800.00
Hinges, wrought
10" h, "H–L," price for pair. 45.00
20" l, strap, rect plate pintles, price
for set of six. 90.00
23" l, strap, horseshoe shaped pin-
tels, price for pair 150.00
Hitching Post Finial, horse head, cast,
10" h 110.00
Hog Scalding Kettle, bulging bottom,
ear handles for cradle, 27" d, 17" h 450.00
Hook, wrought, spike ends, scroll finials, set of four. 90.00
Lard Kettle, sloping sides, iron bail
handle, ftd, wrought stand, late
18th C 550.00
Lock, wrought, scrolled detail, old
paint, 10" l 85.00
Maple Sugar Mold, cast, eight fruit
and vegetable sections, fluted han-
dles. 165.00

Maple Sugar Spigot. 10.00
Match Holder, cast, fist shape, cross on
wrist, lighting device, 5½" h 150.00
Meat Hooks and Rack, wrought, four
hooks, three prongs each, hanging bar with eye and ring hanger,
12" l 150.00
Miniature
Sadiron and Trivet, swan shaped,
2¾" h 65.00
Tea Kettle, cast, gooseneck spout,
wire bail handle, tin lid, black
paint, 3⅝" h 155.00
Mortar and Pestle, cast, urn shaped,
pedestal base, late 1800s, 4" h 75.00
Paperweight, cast, frog, worn black
paint, 5" l 45.00
Plate Holder, wrought, triangular tier,
seven graduated shelves, 59" h 250.00
Receipt Spike, cast, ornate back, wire
spike, painted green, wall mount 25.00
Rushlight Holder, wrought, turned
wood base, 9½" h. 220.00
Sadiron, emb "Enterprise Mfg. Co.,
Phila. U.S.A., Star, Patd. October 1,
'87," fluted handle 45.00
Shelf Brackets, cast, ornate, 6½" h, pr 20.00
Shoe Last, cobbler's, cast, 1850–90 . . 18.00
Shooting Gallery Targets
Rooster, black finish, 4½" h 25.00
Star, 4¼" l. 35.00
Shutter Dogs, cast, girl's head, "Brevete
SGDG" anchor mark, 8⅝" l ex-
tended length, set of four. 140.00
Skewer Holder, wrought, 3⅜" h 25.00
Snowbirds, cast, eagles, 5¼" h, pr . . . 130.00
Spider Pan, cast, 3¾" d, 4" h 85.00
Spill Holder, wrought, circular stepped
wood base, 11¼" h. 150.00
Spittoon, granite lined, 9¾" d, 10" h 25.00
Stove
Burnside No. 20A, Enterprise, pot-
belly, name emb on door, 48" h 395.00
Peoria, parlor, round, emb stylized
leaf and swirl designs, name on
side. 500.00
Station Agent, Union Stove Work,
NY, name emb on circular top rim,
25½" d, 56½" h 375.00
Stove Lid Lifter, Jewel, emb name,
openwork handle, c1890 . . . . 15.00
Stove Plate, cast, emb wild turkey and
trees design, 5" d 35.00
Tape Dispenser, cast, Victorian, or-
nate 125.00
Tea Kettle, cast, gooseneck spout
4½" h, wire bail handle, brass lid
knob 495.00
7¾" h, wrought iron bail handle. . . 135.00
8" h, wrought iron bail handle 115.00
Toaster, 14" w, wrought, twisted iron
and wood handle 60.00

Iron Trivet, oval, marked "Double Point 'IWANTU' Comfort Iron, Strause Gas Iron Co. Phila. PA. U.S.A.," 7⅜ " l, 4⅛ " w, $45.00.

Trivet, wrought

Heart shaped, pitted, 9¾" l	300.00
Heel shaped, turned curly maple handle with simple chip carved dec, scrolled feet bent and one replaced, 11¼" l	25.00
Utensil Rack, wrought, scrolled crest, five hooks, 16"	
Utensils, wrought, simple tooling on handles, price for five piece set	305.00
Washboiler, cast, oval, two handle bars, four short legs	35.00
Water Pump, force, Mast Foos & Company, Springfield, OH, emb name, cutout crisscross pattern on base, bucket bail spur on spout	85.00
Weight, cast, tassel shaped, 8½" h . . .	35.00

PEWTER

History: Pewter is a metal alloy, consisting mostly of tin with small amounts of lead, copper, antimony, and bismuth added to improve malleability and hardness. The metal can be cast, formed around a mold, spun, easily cut, and soldered to form a wide variety of utilitarian articles.

Pewter ware was known to the ancient Chinese, Egyptians, and Romans. English pewter fulfilled most of the needs of the American colonies for nearly 150 years before the American Revolution. The Revolution ended the embargo on raw tin and allowed the small American pewter industry to flourish. This period lasted until the Civil War.

Pewter fits more easily into the early American decorative motif than it does in a Country decor. Wooden and tin utensils were far more common in the countryside than was pewter. However, since Country decorators like the patinated look of unpolished pewter, it is included in this book.

The listing concentrates on the American and English pewter forms most often encountered by the collector.

Reference: Donald L. Fennimore, *The Knopf Collectors' Guides to American Antiques, Silver & Pewter,* Alfred A. Knopf, 1984.

Collectors' Club: Pewter Collector's Club of America, 29 Chesterfield Road, Scarsdale, NY 10583.

Reproduction Craftpersons: S Barrie Cliff, Pewter Crafters of Cape Cod, 927 Main St, Yarmouthport, MA 02675; Fred Danforth, Danforth Pewterers, 52 Seymour St, Middlebury, VT 05753; Christopher E Dunham, PO Box 423, Worthington, MA 01098; Raymond and Jonathan Gibson, Gibson Pewter, 18 E Washington Rd, Hillsborough Centre, NH 03244; Richard & Louise Graver, 504 W Lafayette St, West Chester, PA 19380; Stuart & Karen Helble, K & S Pewter, Rte 4, Box 591, Leesburg, VA 22075; Lydia Withington Holmes, Pewterer, Barton Hill, Stow, MA 01755; David & Sharon Jones, Three Feathers Pewter, Box 232, Shreve, OH 44676; William Melchior, 410 Swedesford Rd, North Wales, PA 19454; Don Miller, Spring Valley, Box 11, Charles Town, WV 25414; Donald W Reid, Plymouth Pewter Works, PO Box 1696, Plymouth, MA 02360; Peter Renzetti, 301 Brinton's Bridge Rd, West Chester, PA 19382; Jay Thomas Stauffer, Stauffer's Pewter Shop, 707 W Brubaker Valley Rd, Lititz, PA 17543; Barbara L Strode, The Pewter Spoon, 1033 Tony Circle, St Cloud, FL 34772; David & Becky Weber, Village Pewter, 320 W Washington St, Medina, OH 44256; James W Wilson, Jori Handcast Pewter, 12681 Metro Pkwy, Ft Myers, FL 33912.

Reproduction Manufacturers: Homespun Crafts, Box 77, Grover, NC 28073; Ingrid's Handcraft Crossroads, 8 Randall Rd, Rochester, MA 02770; Lancaster Collection, PO Box 6074, Lancaster, PA 17603.

Basin

Austin, Nathaniel, Charlestown, MA, faint eagle touchmark, 8" d, 2" h	135.00
Belcher, Joseph, faint touchmark, pitting and scratches, 8" d	650.00
Boardman, Thomas Danforth, faint eagle touchmark, 8" d	210.00
Danforth, Samuel, Hartford, CT, very faint touchmark, 6⅝" d, c1800	400.00
Ellis, Samuel, London, 9⅛" d, 18th C	200.00
Hamlin, Samuel, partial touchmark, 5¾" d, 2" h	250.00
Jones, Gershom, Providence, RI, c1800, 8" d	95.00
Lee, Richard, Springfield, VT, 5¾" d, 1795–1815	300.00
Mabberley, Stephen, England, old repair in bottom, 9" l, c1670	75.00
Stafford, Spencer, Albany, NY, 7¾" d, c1820	300.00
Unmarked	
6" d, 2" h	105.00
8" d, 2" h, split in rim	50.00
Beaker, J B Woodbury, Beverly, MA and Philadelphia, PA, good touchmark, handle, 3" h, 1830–38	400.00

Pewter Candle Mold, 32-tube, pine frame, 21 × 7½ × 16", $1,250.00.

Bedpan, Thomas Danforth Boardman, Hartford, CT, triple touchmarks, 10½" l, c1820 . . . . 400.00

Bowl, unmarked
  American, ftd, 6" d 250.00
  English, ftd, 5⅛" d, 3⅝" h 55.00

Candle Mold, twelve tube, pine frame, 16 × 16 × 16¼" h 825.00

Candlestick
  American, unmarked, pr
    8" h, pushup 325.00
    9¾" h 450.00
  Crowned rose touch, early style, 7" h 275.00
  Dunham, Rufus, Westbrook, ME, straight line touchmark, 6" h, c1840, pr 900.00
  Endicott & Sumner, New York City, NY, 8⅜" h, 1846–51 . . . . 350.00
  Flagg & Homan, 7⅝" h, pr 420.00
  Gleason, Roswell, Dorchester, MA, 6½" h, c1840 . . . . 250.00
  Hopper, Henry, NY, straight line touchmark, 10" h 275.00
  Ostrander & Norris, New York City, saucer base, resoldered, 4" h, 1848–50 . . . . 150.00
  Smith & Co, Boston, MA, curved line touchmark, 6⅛" h, mid 19th C 150.00
  Wildes, Thomas, Philadelphia, PA and New York City, NY, straight line touchmark, complete with bobeche, 10" h, 1829–40 . . . . . . 200.00

Castor Set
  Smith, Eben, Beverly, MA, four clear bottles, 1813–56 . . . . 375.00
  Trask, Israel, Beverly, MA, five clear Sandwich Glass Gothic Arch pattern bottles, three with orig pewter tops, 9½" h, 1807–56 . . . . 250.00

Chalice, unmarked, dark patina, 6⅜" h 105.00

Chamberstick, Meriden Britannia Co., saucer base, gadroon molding, 4¼" h, 1850 . . . . 225.00

Charger
  Austin, Nathaniel, MA, c1800, 13½" d 650.00
  Badger, Thomas, Boston, MA, eagle touchmark, 13⅜" d 650.00

Cloudsley, Nehemigh, England, multiple reed rim, 18¼" d, c1690 600.00

Continental, angel touch mark, scalloped rim, minor wear, 12 ½" d 110.00

Danforth, Samuel, Hartford, CT, faint touchmark, wear and pitting, 13¼" d 225.00

Eadem, Semper, Boston, MA, 12⅛" d 600.00

Ellis, Samuel, scratches and pitting, 15" d 250.00

Hamlin, Samuel, Providence, RI, c1800, 13½" d 650.00

Jones, Gershom, Providence, RI, 14½" d, late 18th C 725.00

King, Richard, London, England, 16½" d 375.00

Langworthy, Lawrence, Devonshire, England and Newport, RI, 15" d 400.00

Leapidge, Thomas, London, 15" d, 1673–1725 . . . . 200.00

Leigh, Charles White, London, England, 14¾" d 300.00

Melville, David, Newport, RI, dents, 1804–10, 14" d 300.00

Chocolate Pot, William Calder, Providence, RI, "Calder" touch, wood handle, 11" h 360.00

Coffee Pot
  Broadhead, R & Co, Sheffield, England, 6½" h, minor repair 55.00
  Calder, William, Providence, RI, lighthouse, 11" h, c1839 . . . . 650.00
  Danforth, Josiah, Middletown, CT, dome lid, 11" h, early 19th C . . . 1,100.00
  Dixon, James & Sons, England, octagonal, wooden handle, 10½" h 175.00
  Dunham, Rufus, Westbrook, ME, gooseneck spout, ftd, mid 19th C, dents, 12" h 275.00
  Gleason, Roswell, Dorchester, MA
    10" h, wood handle and finial . . . 325.00
    11" h, wooden finial wafer with glued repair, repair to bottom edge 225.00

Pewter Coffeepot, cov, gooseneck spout, Whitlock, Troy, NY, 11" h, $325.00.

Griswold, Ashbill, Meriden, CT, pyramid shaped, 10½" h	**350.00**
Homan & Co, Cincinnati, OH, cast foliage finial, engraved floral design, marked "H Homan," 10¼" h	**235.00**
Lewis, Isaac C, Meriden CT, 11½" h, 19th C	**175.00**
Porter, Freeman, Westbrook, ME, pear shape, marked "F Porter No. 2/Westbrook," 10¾" h, c1840	**250.00**
Richardson, George, Boston & Cranston, RI, "G Richardson, Warranted" touchmark, 11" h, 1818–45	**525.00**
Smith & Co, Boston, MA, pedestal foot, wood handle, 10" h	**265.00**
Trask, Israel, Beverly, MA, lighthouse shape, bright cut engraved band, 11" h, c1830	**350.00**
Unmarked	
10" h, cylindrical, flared base	**325.00**
11½" h, shaped wooden handle, dents and soldered repair on bottom	**125.00**
Communion Bowl, Hiram Yale & Co, Yalesville, CT, ftd, 10¼" d, 5¾" h, 1824–35	**600.00**
Communion Flagon, Eben Smith, Beverly, MA, lighthouse shape, straight line touchmark, 10½" h, 1814–56	**425.00**
Communion Plate, Thomas Boardman, Hartford, CT, eagle touchmark, 13⅛" d, 1805–50	**550.00**
Creamer	
American, unmarked, cast ear handle, 5⅝" h	**175.00**
Joseph, Henry, London, three small feet, marked "HJ," 1740–85	**2,500.00**
Cup, American, unmarked, ebonized handle, hinged lid, 5" h	**100.00**
Deep Dish	
Danforth, Samuel, Hartford, CT, c1800, 12¼" d	**225.00**
Derby, Thomas S, Middletown, CT, Derby's General Jackson touchmark, 13¼" d, c1840	**600.00**
Hamlin, Samuel, Hartford, CT, late 18th C	**600.00**

Creamer: 3⅛ " h; sugar: 3" h; oval tray: 10¼ × 6¼"; Hallmark Pewter, $35.00.

Melville, David, Newport, RI, late 18th C, 14" d	**250.00**
Desk Set, rect, two hinged lids, divided compartments hold ink well and pull-out sander, hollow feet, 6¼" l	**190.00**
Egg Cup, American, unmarked	**50.00**
Flagon	
Continental	
Fleur de Lis touch mark, thumb piece, lid engraved "A R G 1811," 12½" h	**200.00**
German eagle touch mark, thumb piece, lid engraved "GOP 1842," 10" h	**200.00**
Boardman & Hart, NY, domed lid, shaped thumb piece and handle, tapering sides, stepped circular base, Laughlin touch mark, 12½" h, c1835	**1,325.00**
English, unmarked, 10¾" h, dated 1718	**160.00**
Smith & Fletman, Albany, touchmark, 12" h	**350.00**
Food Mold, English, cylindrical	
6" h, int. flutes and fruit design top	**72.00**
6½" h, int. flutes and fruit design top	**85.00**
Funnel, American, unmarked, ring hanger, 4⅜" d, 6⅜" l	**125.00**
Gimbal Lamp, brass and pewter burner, pedestal base, bail handle, 8" h	**175.00**
Inkwell, American, unmarked, five quills, 6⅞" d	**150.00**
Jar, 9" h, octagonal, screw cap, ring handle, engraved tulip, initials and "1839," some battering	**85.00**
Jardiniere, James Putnam, Malden, MA, three paw feet stand horizontally from the bottom, 7¾" d, c1840, pr	**350.00**
Ladle	
Danforth, Josiah, Middletown, CT, 13¼" l	**600.00**
Yates, John, Birmingham, England, minor pitting on bowl int., 13½" l, c1835	**80.00**
Lamp	
American, unmarked, brass and pewter burner, snuffer caps missing, 4" h	**200.00**
Dunham, Rufus, Portland, ME, shale oil burner, R Dunham touch, 5⅝" h	**325.00**
Porter, Allen, Westbrook, ME, brass and tin whale oil burner, "A. Porter" touch, 8⅜" h	**715.00**
Measure	
Townsend & Compton, England, T & C touchmark, quart, tankard size, 6" h	**115.00**
Unmarked, attributed to Thomas Danforth III, tankard shape, 6" h	**325.00**
Yates, James, England, quart, bellied, 6⅛" h	**85.00**

Pewter Lamp, double font, Morey and Smith, Boston, 6" h, $300.00.

Muffineer, 7½" h	200.00

Mug
Hamlin, Samuel, quart, Hartford, Middletown, CT, and Providence, RI, dent at base, 1767–1801, 5⅞" h **605.00**
Unmarked, tankard, tulip shape, 3¾" h **55.00**
Whitmore, Jacob, Middletown, CT, quart, fair touchmark, 1758–90 **1,750.00**

Pitcher
American, unmarked, hinged lid, cast ear handle, some battering, 6¼" h **200.00**
Dunham, Rufus, Westbrook, ME, two quart size, cider type, 6½" h, c1845 . . . . **350.00**
Gleason, Roswell, Dorchester, MA, cov, 12" h, c1840 . . . . **650.00**
Homan & Co, Cincinnati, OH, hinged lid, resoldered finial, touchmark, 12" h **110.00**

Plate
Austin, Nathaniel, Charlestown, MA, eagle touch mark, 8" d **100.00**
Badger, Thomas, Boston, MA, 7¾" d, stamped initials on rim **300.00**
Barns, Blakeslee, Philadelphia, PA, eagle touch mark, 7⅞" d **300.00**
Billings, William, Providence, RI, touchmark, pitting, 8¼" d **45.00**
Boardman, Thomas Danforth, Hartford, CT
Eagle in oval touch, 9⅜" d **440.00**
Lion touch with "Boardman," scratches, 8⅞" d **250.00**
Calder, William, Providence, RI, 8⅜" d, eagle touchmark, c1840 **375.00**
Danforth, Josiah, Middletown, CT, rampant lion touchmark, 7⅝" d **275.00**
Danforth, Samuel, Hartford, CT, eagle touchmark, soldered repair near center, 7⅞" d **95.00**
Danforth, Thomas I, lion touchmark, 8" d **350.00**

English, unidentified hallmarks, 8¼" d, 18th C **150.00**
Griswold, Ashbill, Meriden, CT, eagle touchmark, 7⅞" d **1330.00**
Jones, Gershom, Providence, RI, single reed, 8⅜" d, 1774–1808 . . . . **550.00**
Kilbourn, Samuel, Baltimore, MD, eagle touchmark, 7¾" d **155.00**
Lightner, George, Baltimore, MD, "G Lightner, Baltimore" touchmark, 7⅞" d **225.00**
Love touch, Philadelphia, PA, 8½" d **325.00**
Porter, James, Baltimore, MD, faint eagle touchmark, pitting, 8" d . . . **35.00**
Platter, English, "Made in London," engraved monogram and griffin, 14" l **245.00**

Porringer
Boardman, Thomas Danforth and Sherman Boardman, Hartford, CT, keyhole type crown handle, triangular bracket, 5" d, 1810–30 . . . . **325.00**
Green, Samuel, Boston, MA, cast crown handle, 5½" d **550.00**
Hamlin, Samuel Jr, Providence, RI, touch mark on flower handle, 5¼", 1801–56 . . . . **500.00**
New England unmarked, cast crown handle, 5" d **175.00**

Salt
Boyd, Parks, Philadelphia, PA, beaded rim and base, ftd, 1795–1819 . . . . **950.00**
Unmarked, cast design on foot, 2" h **45.00**
Salt Spoon, marked "TW," 4⅛" l **15.00**
Sauce Ladle, Yates, England, 7" l **35.00**
Soup Plate, Boardman & Hart, NY, eagle touchmark, marked "Boardman Warranted," 9⅜" d **250.00**
Spoon, William Bradford, New York City, NY, round bowl, 6⅝" l, 1719–85 . . . . **1,600.00**

Sugar Bowl
Hiram Yale & Co, Yalesville, CT, 5½" h, 1824–35 . . . . **50.00**
Richardson, George, Boston, MA and Cranston, RI, 1818–45 . . . . . **3,000.00**
Unmarked, attributed to Boyd Parks, Philadelphia, PA, beaded lid, rim, and foot, 1795–1819 . . . . **7,500.00**
Syrup, American, unmarked, miniature lighthouse coffeepot shape, lid resoldered to hinge, 5½" h **225.00**

Tall Pot
Richardson, G, Warranted, old soldered lid hinge repair, 10½" h . . **300.00**
Sellew & Co, Cincinnati, OH, 11½" h **325.00**

Tankard
American, dome lid, heart in thumb tab, touch mark on bottom, 1 quart **400.00**
IH, London, touchmark, hinged lid, resoldered hinge, 8" h **150.00**

Teapot
   American, unmarked, wood handle,
     minor damage to hinge, some re-
     soldering, 6⅝" h **140.00**
   Boardman, Thomas D and Samuel,
     Hartford, CT, cast acorn finial,
     copper bottom marked "TD & SB,"
     8⅜" h **100.00**
   Dixon, James & Sons, England, oc-
     tagonal, wooden handle and fin-
     ial, 8" h **160.00**
   Gleason, Roswell, 1822–71, Dor-
     chester, MA, marked at base, im-
     perfections, 8¼" h **285.00**
   Grenfell, griffin touchmark, individ-
     ual size, pear shaped, old soldered
     repair, replaced wooden handle,
     5½" h **200.00**
   Putnam, James, Walden, MA,
     marked "Putnam," 7⅝" h **300.00**
   Simpson, Samuel, Yalesville, CT,
     wood handle, bulbous shape, "S.
     Simpson" touch, 7¾" h **325.00**
   Wilcox, R C, cylindrical, C shaped
     wooden handle, marked "R. C.
     Wilcox & Co," dents, split in bot-
     tom seam, tip of spout battered,
     8¾" h **105.00**
Tobacco Box, Thomas Stanford, cast
   eagle feet, engraved label with scroll
   work "Thomas Stanford, Gospel Hill,
   1838," wear, finial and one foot sol-
   dered, 4⅜" h **115.00**

SILVER AND SILVERPLATE

History: Sterling silver never enjoyed great popularity in the agrarian community. If a farmer or
small town merchant hoarded anything, the preferred metal was gold. When a touch of class was
needed, elaborately decorated silverplate was
more than adequate.

Most pieces of silver and silverplate appeared
only on special occasions. The rural housewife
simply did not have the time or help to keep them
polished. The best pieces were displayed on the
dining room buffet when company came and then
stored inside for the balance of the time.

The natural beauty of silver lends itself to the
designs of artists and craftsmen, often pricing it out
of reach for most members of the Country community. Pure silver is too soft to be fashioned into
strong, durable, and serviceable utensils. Alloys of
copper, nickel, and other metals are added to give
silver its required degree of hardness.

Plated silver production by an electrolytic
method is credited to G. R. and H. Ekington,
England, in 1838. In electroplating silver, the article is completely shaped and formed from a base
metal, then coated with a thin layer of silver. In
the late 19th century, the base metal was Britan-

nia, an alloy of tin, copper, and antimony. Other
bases are copper and brass. Today the base metal
is nickel silver.

In 1847 the electroplating process was introduced in America by Rogers Bros., Hartford, Connecticut. By 1855, a number of firms were using
the method to mass produce silver plated items.
The quality of plating is important. Extensive use
or polishing can cause the base metal to show
through. Silverplate has enjoyed a revival due to
the Victorian decorating craze of the late 1980s.

References: Frederick Bradbury, *Bradbury's Book
of Hallmarks,* J. W. Northend, Ltd, 1987; Mary-
anne Dolan, *1830's–1990's American Sterling Sil-
ver Flatware: A Collector's Identification and
Value Guide,* Books Americana, 1993; Rachael
Feild, *Macdonald Guide To Buying Antique Silver
and Sheffield Plate,* Macdonald & Co., 1988;
Donald L. Fennimore, *Silver & Pewter,* Alfred A.
Knopf *Knopf Collector's Guides To American An-
tiques,* 1984; Tere Hagan, *Silverplated Flatware:
An Identification and Value Guide, Revised Fourth
Edition,* Collector Books, 1990; *Jewelers' Circular
Keystone Sterling Flatware Pattern Index, 2nd Edi-
tion,* Chilton Company, 1989; Dorothy T. Rain-
water, *Encyclopedia of American Silver
Manufacturers, 3rd Edition,* Schiffer Publishing,
1986; Dorothy T. and H. Ivan Rainwater, *Ameri-
can Silverplate,* Schiffer Publishing, 1988; Jeri
Schwartz, *The Official Identification And Price
Guide To Silver and Silver-Plate, Sixth Edition,*
House of Collectibles, 1989; Peter Waldon, *The
Price Guide To Antique Silver, Second Edition,*
Antique Collectors' Club, 1982 (price revision list
1988); Seymour B. Wyler, *The Book Of Old Silver,
English, American, Foreign,* Crown Publishers,
1937 (available in reprint).

Periodicals: *Silver,* PO Box 1243, Whittier, CA
90609; *The Silver Update,* 3366 Oak West Dr,
Ellicott City, MD 21043; *The Sterling Silver Hol-
loware Update,* 3366 Oak West Dr, Ellicott City,
MD 21043.

Museums: Wadsworth Atheneum, Hartford, CT;
Yale University Art Gallery, New Haven, CT; Bos-
ton Museum of Fine Arts, Boston, MA; The Bayou
Bend Collection, Houston, TX.

Reproduction Craftpersons: Stephen Smithers,
1057 Hawley Rd, Ashfield, MA 01330.

COIN SILVER, AMERICAN

Bowl, S Kirk & Son, 19th C, 9" d, round,
   repousse, monogram, 11 troy oz . . .   **200.00**
Caudle Cup, Jeremiah Dummer, Bos-
   ton, 1645–1718, engraved "NsM" at
   base, marked "I.D." in heart car-
   touche, 6 troy oz **2,100.00**
Chamberstick, Jacobi and Jenkins, 5½"
   d, repousse, marked "A. Jacobi," 5
   troy oz **385.00**

Coffeepot, William Hollingshead, Philadelphia, PA, 1760–85, 12½" h, inverted pyriamid shape, domed, hinged lid, gadrooned finial and molding, carved wood handle with foliate scrolled terminals, cast S-scrolled spout with ruffled cartouche, domed and molded circular foot, engraved foliate script initials "LP" within rococo cartouche, marked three times on base, 33 oz, 10 dwt **52,800.00**

Creamer and Sugar, Ephraim Brasher, NY, 1744–1810, bright cut dec, 5½" creamer, 4¾" ftd bowl, repair, imperfections **1,540.00**

Ewer, John Kitts & Co, 14⅜" h, Neoclassical, cast floral handle **990.00**

Julep Cup, Duhme & Co, 3½" h **165.00**

Platter, Jacobi and Jenkins, 14" l, oval rim, monogram, 20 troy oz **330.00**

Pepper Box, John Cooney, Boston, MA, 1700–20, 2½" h, cylindrical, low domed pierced lid, double molded rim, double scrolled and beaded handle, bottom engraved with contemporary initials, marked on side and base, repair to handle joints, 2 oz, 10 dwt **9,350.00**

Porringer
Hanners, George, Boston, MA, c1720, 4¾" d, marked twice, small dent **2,640.00**

Wilson, Robert and William, Philadelphia, PA, 1¼" h, c1825–46, marked "R & W Wilson" on reverse of handle, lion rampart mark on side, 6 troy oz **385.00**

Punch Strainer, Daniel Parker, Boston, MA, 1755–75, 10⅜" l, circular bowl,

Silver Porringer, George Hanners, Boston, MA, marked twice, small dent, c1720, 4¾" d, $2,640.00. Photograph courtesy of Skinner, Inc.

Coin Silver, spoons, J M Mitksch, Bethlehem, PA, monogram, set of six, $250.00.

decorative piercing, molded rim flanked by two open handles with stylized leafage and terminals, engraved on back, marked on back of handle, 4 oz, 10 dwt **6,600.00**

Salt, Robert and William Wilson, Philadelphia, PA, 3" h, c1935, chased floral swag, oak leaf handle, price for pair, 7½ troy oz **440.00**

Serving Spoon, Robert and William William, Philadelphia, early 19th C, shell pattern, some wear, 14 troy oz, price for set of six **275.00**

Spectacles, John Owen Jr, Philadelphia, PA, 1804–31, 4⅝" w, oval lens frame, hinged and sliding temple pieces, marked on one arm, 1 oz . . . **550.00**

Spoons, J Sargent, Hartford, CT, c1795, coffin end, price for set of six teaspoons, six tablespoons, minor wear and dents, 12 troy oz **660.00**

Sugar Basket, A E Warner, 19th C, repousse, 4½" h, 10 troy oz **330.00**

Tea and Coffee Service, Joseph Lownes, Philadelphia, c1820, two teapots, 10½" h coffeepot, creamer, cov sugar, waste bowl, each marked at base, 128 troy oz **3,520.00**

Tea Service, S Kirk & Son, 19th C, 15" h hot water kettle on stand, teapot, hot milk pitcher, creamer, sugar, and waste bowl, repousse, engraved crest, later burner, 136 troy oz **6,100.00**

Water Pitcher, H B Stanwood, Boston, MA, mid 19th C, 13" h, chased grapevine and foliage, 44 troy oz **1,430.00**

SILVER, AMERICAN, MOSTLY STERLING

Bowl
Redlich, shaped circular rim, chased roses, monogram, 14 troy oz **500.00**

Reed & Barton, 11" d, Francis I pattern, 42 troy oz, price for pair . . . **990.00**

Starr, Theodore B, 11" d, shaped circular rim with chased and pierced carnations dec, 20 troy oz **660.00**

Tiffany, 12" l, oval, egg and dart molded rim, c1875, 24 troy oz **525.00**

Cake Plate, Tiffany, 10¾" d, etched neoclassical design, monogram, 21 troy oz **770.00**

Candlesticks, pr, Shreve Crump and Low, 7" h, Queen Anne style, 22 troy oz **550.00**

Center Bowl
Tiffany, 12" d, 3" h, everted rim, chased C-scrolls, brass insert, 41 troy oz **1,155.00**
Wood & Hughes, 13" l, c1890, leaf form, fruiting grape vines applied at rim, inscription, 34 troy oz . . . **4,500.00**

Coffee Service, Gorham, coffeepot, hot water kettle on stand, creamer, and sugar, half reeded Regency style, 73 troy oz **990.00**

Compote
Smith, Frank, 10¼" d, pierced and shaped rim, chased leaf and scroll dec, monogram, 22 troy oz **825.00**
Tiffany, low, applied reticulated chyrsanthemum rim, surface scratches, 35 troy oz, price for pair **1,980.00**

Demitasse Service, Tiffany, 1907–38, coffeepot, creamer, sugar, tray, twelve cups and saucers with Lenox porcelain liners, 101 troy oz **4,400.00**

Dresser Set, Wallace, c1917, Carthage pattern, c1917, three brushes, comb, hand mirror, jar, and tray, hammered and linear design, monogram, imp marks, dents, price for seven piece set **275.00**

Flatware Service
Gorham, Versailles pattern, dinner, luncheon, dessert, salad, and seafood forks, teaspoons, demitasse spoons, tablespoons, luncheon knives, butter knives, large serving spoons, carving set, fifteen assorted serving pieces, some monogrammed, 118 pieces, 163 troy oz **4,400.00**
Tiffany, King William pattern, luncheon forks, salad forks, butter knives, luncheon knives, teaspoons, tablespoons, and sugar tongs, price for 32 pieces, approx 38 troy oz weighable. **525.00**

Fork, Tiffany, 7" l, shaped handle, daisies in relief, monogram verso, set of eight, 13½ troy oz **550.00**

Hot Water Kettle on Stand
Gale, William and Son, NY, 1852, 16¾" h, baluster form, twisted wire trim, monogram, burner may be replaced, 59 troy oz **935.00**
Towle, 13" h, 40 troy oz **415.00**
Wallace, c1917, 14" h, pear form, scrolled legs, 43 troy oz **525.00**

Mug, Whiting Mfg Co, 1892, 4⅛" h, cylindrical sides deeply repousse,

chased with putti and scrolling acanthus, acanthus terminals on handles, base inscribed, 8 oz **1,320.00**

Porringer, Edward E Oakes, Boston, MA, c1920, 4½" d, 2" h, hammered bowl, raised rim, curvilinear handle, applied oak leaves, imp marks, 9 troy oz **935.00**

Punch Ladle, Tiffany, 13" l, Wave Edge pattern, monogram, 9 troy oz **440.00**

Salad Set, fork and spoon, Gorham, 10" l, Imperial Chrysanthemum pattern, monogram, 8 troy oz **360.00**

Sauce Boat, Gorham, 1873, 4½" h, baluster form, acanthus leaf borders, 13 troy oz **275.00**

Serving Spoon, Shiebler, chyrsanthemum and cornucopia design, monogram, 5 troy oz **360.00**

Spoon, Wood & Hughes, NY, miniature, late 19th C, retailed by Mills, 2½" l, marked at back of handle, price for pair **225.00**

Tea and Coffee Service
Durgin, retailed by J E Caldwell Co, tea and coffee pots, creamer, cov sugar, waste bowl, engraved Colonial Revival style, ivory finials, monogram, some dents, 87 troy oz **1,430.00**
Gorham, c1926, tea and coffee pots, creamer, cov sugar, waste bowl, flattened baluster form, engraved inscription and initial, 80 troy oz . **1,100.00**
International, tea and coffee pots, creamer, cov sugar, waste bowl, Colonial style, chased floral and scroll dec, 90 troy oz **1,100.00**
Lownes, Joseph, Philadelphia, c1820, two teapots, 10½" h coffeepot, creamer, cov sugar, waste bowl, each marked at base, 128 troy oz **3,520.00**
Starr, Theodore B, hot water kettle on stand, tea and coffee pots, creamer, sugar, and waste bowl, globular, scalloped gadroon rim and paw feet, monogram, minor dents, 126 troy oz **1,980.00**

Teaspoon, Wallace, c1917, Carthage pattern, c1917, hammered and linear design, set of twelve in orig case, imp marks, approx 7 troy oz **275.00**

Toast Server, Shiebler, chyrsanthemum and cornucopia design, monogrammed, 5 troy oz **385.00**

Tray
Gorham, 25" l, oval, molded rim, 83 troy oz **1,210.00**
Leinonen, Karl F, Boston, MA, Arts and Crafts era, 12¼" d round, hammered finish, banded rim, imp marks, 26 troy oz **500.00**

Stone, Arthur J, Gardner, MA, 12½"
sq, rounded corners, 35 troy oz   **825.00**

Vase
Gorham, 15" h, early 20th C, trumpet
shape, applied and engraved
prunus dec, hammer textured
ground, 14 troy oz **360.00**
Tiffany
3" h, 1891–1902, melon form,
etched violet design, mono-
gram, 6 troy oz **615.00**
12" h, tapering cylindrial form,
etched linear rim dec, base
dents, price for pair, 48 troy oz   **1,760.00**
Vegetable Dish, cov, Tiffany, 9½" d
round, molded domed cov, 35 troy
oz. **880.00**
Water Pitcher
Gorham, 10" h, c1870, Greek Revival design, inscriptions, 26 troy
oz **825.00**
Tiffany, c1865, 9" h, band of neo-
classical designs, 22 troy oz **935.00**

SILVER, CONTINENTAL

Bowl
Denmark, Georg Jensen, 7" h, leaf
and seed openwork base, Model
19A, 23 troy oz **2,200.00**
Netherlands, 13" l, shaped oval, fo-
liate and geometric reticulated
piercing, 14 troy oz **440.00**
Eggcup Set, France, 19th C, engraved
egg form container, two pedestal
bases, 950 fine, 3 troy oz, price for
three pc set **200.00**
Flatware Set
Germany, Menner, early 20th C, dinner forks, luncheon forks, salad
forks, dessert forks, teaspoons, ta-

English Silver, inkstand, Joseph Craddock
and William Reid, London, heavily
gadrooned border, twin pen channels,
three square collars with basketweave design, faceted crystal jars, pierced silver
caps, c1813–14, 27½ troy oz, 10½" w,
$1,760.00. Photograph courtesy of Wil-
liam Doyle Galleries.

blespoons, soup spoons, egg
spoons, demitasse spoons, dinner
knives, luncheon knives, dessert
knives, butter knives, ladles, carving set, serving forks, serving
spoons, stirrers, other serving
pieces, monogram, 244 pieces,
approx 284 troy oz weighable sil-
ver. **2,200.00**
Inkstand, Austria, 19th C, 7" l, shaped
rect, inkpot, pounce pot, and central
raised dish, engraved foliate and
lapis finials, silver gilt, 10 troy oz   **660.00**
Salad Set, fork and spoon, Denmark,
Georg Jensen, Acorn pattern, approx
5 troy oz **525.00**
Salt, France, c1880, 2½" h, everted rim
on bowl supported by cast openwork
grapevine and mistletoe, marked
"Veyrat" in lozenge, 950 fine, 14 troy
oz, pr **690.00**
Snuff Box, France, oval, chased design,
maker's mark "AD" on lozenge, 3
troy oz **200.00**
Tankard, Germany, Altenberg, mid
19th C, 9¼" h, engraved design,
pierced apron, marked "AFB," 20
troy oz **525.00**
Tea and Coffee Service
Germany, H Mau & G Rutger, tea
and coffee pots, creamer, waste
bowl, cov jar, and tray, fluted pear
form, 152 troy oz **1,870.00**
Netherlands, 1896, hot water kettle
on stand, tea and coffee pots,
creamer, milk jug, sugar, waste
bowl, two vases, repousse tavern
scenes, dents, stand loose, marked
AV/34, 110 troy oz **2,750.00**

English Silver, salver, William Peaston,
London, pie crust and shell border, engraved lion crest within floral and acanthus leaf design, scroll feet, 1747, 30 troy
oz, 12" d, $1,430.00. Photograph courtesy
of Leslie Hindman Auctioneers.

Vegetable Dish, cov, France, 19th C, round, foliate scrolled legs and handles, 8" h, 38 troy oz. 880.00

Water Pitcher, France, M Fray, mid 19th C, 12½" h, fluted baluster, chased leafy rococo scrolls, scroll handle with female figures, minor dents, 36 troy oz. 1,980.00

SILVER, ENGLISH

Bowl, C S/H, London, 1901–02, Victorian, shaped oval, repousse flowers, gilt int., 12 troy oz 440.00

Candlesticks

Cafe, J, London, George II, 1751–52, 8¼" h, knopped stem, square shell and scroll base, engraved crest, price for set of four, 66 troy oz   4,290.00

Hutton, W & Son, London, 1899–1900, Victorian, 5½" h, stop fluted, stepped base, weighted, slight dents, price for pair 615.00

Castor, cov, Boardman, Glossop & Co, Ltd, London, 1904, Edward VII, 8¼" h, vase shaped, pierced partly domed lid with baluster finial, rising circular base, three angular handles, two applied leaves. 350.00

Coffeepot, attributed to C Wright, London

George II, 13" h, baluster form, later chased gadroons, engraved armorial, 40 troy oz. 2,100.00

George III, 11" h, baluster form, later chased flowers, engraved armorial, repaired, 39 troy oz 1,430.00

Cup, cov, J Robins, London, 1799–1800, George III, 14" h, half reeded urn form body, two handles, acorn finial, engraved arms, 54 troy oz. . .   1,430.00

Hot Water Kettle on Stand

Attributed to B Brewood, London, 1755–56, George III, inverted pear form, engraved crest, filigree base, burner inset missing, 39 troy oz   1,650.00

Stoddart, T, Newcastle, 1746–47, George II, globular form, later chased swags, 63 troy oz. 1,210.00

Mug, W Rudkins, London, 1809–10, Regency, 5" h, baluster form, later rococo chasing, 11 troy oz 475.00

Salver, G Hindmarsh, London, 1732–33, George II, 16" d, scrolled border, scrolled feet, engraved armorial, 56 troy oz 2,530.00

Sauce Tureen, cov, Joseph Angell, London, 1835, George IV, 9" l, molded oval, applied rocaille and foliate scroll rim, foliate ring handle with cast tied anchor finial, stylized leaf

Plated, spooner, ruby insert, c1875, 6½" 2, 6¼" h, $85.00.

calyx and beaded border, two foliate capped upcurved loop handles, four lion's paw feet with acanthus joints, 35 oz 1,210.00

Spoon, Smith & Fearn, London, 11⅜" l, sauce strainer in bowl, 1795, engraved animal and monogram on handle. 375.00

Stuffing Spoon, W Welch, Exeter hallmarks, 12" l, 1825–26, monogrammed handle. 140.00

Sugar Castor, JA/JS, London, 1884–85, Georgian style, 9" h, maker's mark in quatrefoil, 9 troy oz. 200.00

Taperstick, M Cooper I, London, 1813–14, Queen Anne, 5" h, knobbed stem, octagonal base, later chased, 4 troy oz 275.00

Teapot, Jas Young, London, 1784–85, George III, 5" h, oval cylindrical form, engraved design and arms, 14 troy oz 660.00

Tea Set

Comyns, W, London, c1903, Edward VII, teapot, creamer, sugar, and two demitasse cups and saucers, silver mounted on Staffordshire Pottery.   500.00

Hennell, R & S, London, 1802–03, George III, teapot and stand, creamer and sugar, globular, engraved design and crest, 37 troy oz   825.00

Plated, sugar basket, Reed & Barton, red liner, c1868, 4¼" w, 4" h, $90.00.

Plated, syrup, Samson, Hall, Miller & Co, floral relief and incising, monogram, 7½" h, $85.00.

Waiter, R Hennell I, London, 1784–85, George III, 6" l, oval, pierced rim, engraved crest, 5 troy oz **275.00**

SILVER, ENGLISH, SHEFFIELD

Cake Basket, c1820, 14⅞" l, flower dec gadrooned rim, sides with chased scrolls and berried foliage, interlaced ribbonwork handle, satyr masks terminals, four paw feet **725.00**

Coffee Urn, c1780, two handles, beaded rim, engraved crest and initial, bud finial, pedestal foot, four ball supports **600.00**

Dish, cov, J Dixon & Sons, c1840, 14⅜" l, rect, acanthus scrolled rims, shells and flower sprays at intervals, lid engraved with contemporary arms and Continental coronet, detachable foliate finials, two handled warming base, price for pair **950.00**

Hot Water Urn, 18th C, George III, 18" h, vasiform, two handles, minor dents and rosing **360.00**

Jug, 1807, 15½" h, baluster form, repousse clover thistle and rose dec, thistle finial, marked "Danels" **2,200.00**

Muffineer, 1839, pierced dome lid, circular ftd base, custom case, 5 troy oz   **60.00**

Sauce Tureen, cov, c1820, 8¼" l, oval bombe form, gadrooned rims with flowerheads and leaves, acanthus handles, four paw feet with spreading acanthus, leafy scroll ring finial topped with shell, lid with dense bed of leaves and flowerheads, price for pair **1,100.00**

Tea Set, 19th C, Regency style, 6" h teapot, creamer, and sugar, marked "TM" **220.00**

SILVER, PLATED

Biscuit Box, 8½" l, book form, hinged cov, engraved scrolling foliage within matting, applied tied gilt rib-

Sterling, napkin ring, hallmarked "SSMC," monogrammed, 1⅝ " d, $35.00.

bon, molded spine engrave "Biscuits," engraved hinged latch, gilt pages, int. with hinged and pierced gilt grille, four bun feet **600.00**

Bowl, Derby Silver Company, 9" h, foliate repousse, surmounted by figure of squirrel on oak branch **330.00**

Claret Jug, 19th C, Victorian, 11½" h, minor nicks **300.00**

Cruet Set, 19th C, Victorian, 10¾" h, cut glass bottles, minor nicks **350.00**

Flatware Service, luncheon set, twelve knives, eleven forks, two crumbers, serving knife and fork, engraved blades, ivory handles **125.00**

Inkstand, c1810, 9" l, rect, two rect reeded bottle frames, cut glass bottles, cylindrical chamberstick holder, two pen trays, dentilated borders, wood stand with drawer, plated ball handle, four ball feet **825.00**

TINWARE

History: Beginning in the 1700s many utilitarian household objects were made of tin. Tin is non-toxic, rust resistant, and fairly durable. It can be used for storing food and was often plated to iron to provide strength. Because it was cheap, tinware and tin plated wares were within the price range of most people.

Almost every small town and hamlet had its own tinsmith, tinner, or whitesmith. Tinsmiths used patterns to cut out the pieces, hammered and shaped them, and soldered the parts. If a piece was to be used with heat, a copper bottom was added because of the low melting point of tin. The Industrial Revolution brought about machine made, mass produced tinware pieces. The hand-made era ended by the late 19th century.

In addition to utilitarian tinware, the Country look also focuses on decorated tinware. Decorating sheet iron, tin, and tin-coated sheet iron dates back to the mid-18th century. The Welsh called the practice pontipool, the French To'le Peinte. In America the center for tin-decorated wares was Berlin, Connecticut.

Several styles of decorating techniques were used—painting, japanning, and stenciling. Designs were created by both professionals and itinerants. English and Oriental motifs strongly influenced both form and design.

There were two revival periods of handcrafted painted tin—1920–1940 and 1950 to the early 1960s. The easiest way to identify later painted pieces is by their brighter color tone and their design.

Pennsylvania tinsmiths are noted for their punch work on unpainted tin. Forms include foot warmers, spice boxes, lanterns, and pie safe panels.

Reproduction Craftspersons: Charles Baker Period Reproductions, 6890 N 700 E, Hope, IN 47246; D James Barnette, The Tinner, PO Box 353, Spencer, NC 28159; David Claggett, Artistry in Tin, PO Box 41, Weston, VT 05161; Karen Claggett, Tinsmith, RD 3, Box 330A, Quarryville, PA 17566; Dale the Tinker, PO Box 21, St Albans, WV 25177; Jim DeCurtins, Tin Peddler, 203 E Main St, Troy, OH 45373; Dawson Gillaspy, Tinsmith, Covered Bridge Rd, RD 2, Box 312, Oley, PA 19547; Robert and Anita Horwood, Horwood's Country House, 4037 Gotfredson Rd, Plymouth, MI 48170; Philip B Kelly, Colonial Tinware, 2389 New Holland Pike, Lancaster, PA 17601; Charles Messner, Colonial Lighting and Tinware Reproductions, 316 Franklin St, Denver, PA 17517; Diana M Mihaltse, Whimsies & Folk Art on Tin, 24 Overidge Lane, Wilton, CT 06897; David & Marlene Moszak, Americana Today, 321 Wyndale Rd, Rochester, NY 14617; Peter Renzetti, 301 Brinton's Bridge Rd, West Chester, PA 19382; Reda Sypherd, RD 2, Phoenixville, PA 19460; The Tin Man by Gerald Fellers, 2025 Seneca Dr, Troy, OH 45373.

Reproduction Manufacturers: Applecore Creations, PO Box 29696, Columbus, OH 43229; Basye-Bomberger/Fabian House, PO Box 86, W Bowie, MD 20715; Bullfrog Hollow, Keeny Rd, Lyme, CT 06371; Clark Manufacturing Co, 1611 Southwind Dr, Raymore, MO 64083; Conewago Junction, 805 Oxford Rd, New Oxford, PA 17350; Country Accents, RD 2, Box 293, Stockton, NJ 08559; KML Enterprises, RR 1, Box 234L, Berne, IN 46711; Lamb and Lanterns, 902 N Walnut St, Dover, OH 44622; Lt Moses Willard, Inc, 1156 State Rte 50, Milford, OH 45150; Matthews Emporium, 157 N Trade St, PO Box 1038, Matthews, NC 28106; McClanahan Country, 217 Rockwell Rd, Wilmington, NC 18405; Olde Mill House Shoppe, 105 Strasburg Pike, Lancaster, PA 17602; The Tinhorn, 9610 W 190th, Lowell, IN 46356; The Vine and Cupboard, PO Box 309, George Wright Rd, Woolwich, ME 04579.

ABC Plate, emb
   4¼" d, two kittens playing with basket of wool **75.00**

7¾" d, Who Killed Cock Robin? . . .   **120.00**
8" d, Mary Had A Little Lamb, light rust **110.00**
Bed Warmer, 42½" l, brass trim, turned wooden handle, old black paint . . .   **85.00**
Betty Lamp, 11" h, matching stand, hanger, and wick pick, both stamped "J.D.," (J. Deer), stand with crimped rusted top edge, damage, soldered repair **250.00**
Box, 4½" d, drum shape, lid on each end, worn black paint **12.00**
Candle Mold
  3 Tube, 10¼" h, ear handle **140.00**
  6 Tube
    10¾" h, ear handle **145.00**
    11" h **85.00**
  8 Tube
    9¾" h, ear handle, curved base   **150.00**
    10" l, wood rack, early 1800s . . .   **495.00**
    12 tube, 10½" h, handle **75.00**
Candle Sconce, pr
  9¼" h, simple crimped crest **210.00**
  10¾" h, simple star flower tooling   **130.00**
  11¼" h, tombstone shaped, punched dec around edge **75.00**
  13" h, oval fluted sunburst reflectors, S-curve arms, crimped drip pans **1,000.00**
  14" h, oval, crimped edge reflectors   **700.00**
Candlestick, hog scraper
  6½" h, plume-like pushup knob . . .   **80.00**
  7¼" h, pushup and lip hanger. **110.00**
Coffee Maker
  9¾" h, removable drip top, black wooden handle, pewter finial . . .   **75.00**
  13¾" h, two pc, drip top, brass spigot, cast leaf and ring handles, pitted. **85.00**
Coffeepot
  10½" h, parrot beak spout, cutout heart shaped air hole, stamped "J Brinkhouse". **450.00**

Tin Candlemold, 16-tube, pie plate top and base, strap handle, $375.00.

11¼" h, pewter handle, spout, and lid, some rust, battered finial 72.00

11½" h, double spout, emb brass label "Maxim's patent coffee pot . . .," rust damaged, holes in one spout 60.00

Collander, 4¼" h, heart shape, circle feet 130.00

Cookie Cutter, 7½" l, horse 85.00

Dipper, 14" l, turned wood handle. . .   50.00

Double Boiler. 60.00

Food Cover, 12 × 15", dome top, oval, platter, reticulated base, light rust 30.00

Food Mold, 7¼" l, oval, fruit 50.00

Footwarmer, punched panels
9 × 7½ × 5¾", rect
Butternut frame, turned posts, punched dec 225.00
Walnut frame, mortised, punched hearts and circles, turned corner posts, old finish, wear 225.00
9" sq, turned wood frame and handle.   165.00

Grater, 13½" l, punched design, pine back, cutout handle, old finish 140.00

Hair Comb, 9" h, anniversary, 19th C   358.00

Lantern
14½" h, Paul Revere type, candle, punched design, ring handle 150.00
28" h, triangular, glass panels, old red repaint 200.00

Memorial Sign, 18½" h, shield shape, emb detail, worn black paint, "Daniel Taylor Jr. O.B. Dec. 9th 1825 AE 55 years" 110.00

Parade Torch
38" l, barrel shaped font, three burners, tin handle, some damage . . .   50.00
44" l, jack-o-lantern, orange and black paint, wood rod, 44" w . . .   775.00

Pitcher, 11" h, punched and tooled sunburst designs, scrolled ear handle   145.00

Lunch Bucket, tin cup lid, bail handle, 9¾ × 6¾ × 9", $50.00.

Teapot
5¾" h, oval, punched tulip and intersecting wavy line border design, ribbed handle, hinged lid with three ring finial, 5¾" h 225.00
8" h, pewter finial 100.00

Utility Tray, 9" l, knife box shape, center handle, double slant tip lids each with three int. compartments. 80.00

TOLEWARE

Bowl, 12¾" l, 7¾" w, 3⅝" h, oval, dark brown japanning, red, yellow, and white floral dec, minor wear 350.00

Box, very worn black paint, gold striping and flowers, removable int. tray, engraved brass label in lid "H. W. Butterworth, Phila, 1850," cast pewter feet, brass bail handle, minor damage, hinges loose 115.00

Bread Tray
12¾" l, dark brown japanning, brown crystalized center, yellow, green, black, olive, and red stylized floral dec 190.00
13" l, worn dark japanning, floral dec   75.00
14" l, orig green paint, fruit, flowers, and foliage dec, yellow striping, polychrome stenciled bronze powder dec 55.00

Bucket, 20" h, helmet shaped, worn old black paint, gilt Chinoiserie dec, European, battered and damaged   300.00

Candle Box, 9" l, worn red ground, traces of floral dec, black striping, hinged lid 75.00

Canister
8" h, 8" d, cylindrical, hinged lid, ghost images of tole dec 40.00
8¼" h, worn black paint, red, green, and yellow floral dec, cap resoldered 115.00

Coffeepot
8½" h, orig worn black ground, red, yellow, blue, and black floral dec   225.00
10½" h, orig dark brown japanning, yellow, two shades of red, white, and green floral dec, minor wear   3,100.00

Creamer
4" h, orig dark brown japanning, green and red foliage, white band   165.00
4⅛" h, worn dark brown japanning, red, green, and yellow floral dec   450.00

Cup, orig red paint 65.00

Cuspidor, 8¼" d, smoked white ground, red stripes, gold stenciled dec, worn gold rim bands 75.00

Desk Set, 8" l, old worn black paint, brass bail handle, paw feet, three part int. with ink bottle, sander, one wire repaired hinge 95.00

Tole, document box, domed lid, coral, red, yellow, and white floral and swag dec, black ground, int. lined with early floral dec wallpaper, Sturbridge, MA, c1820, 12″ l, 5″ h, $4,500.00. Photograph courtesy of James D Julia, Inc.

Document Box, dome top

    3″ l, miniature, brown japanning, white band, yellow striping, yellow, red, and green dec **330.00**

    4¼″ h, worn brown japanning, white band, yellow, red, and green dec, incomplete hasp **55.00**

    6¾″ l, worn brown japanning, white band, yellow, red, and green dec, ring handle missing, incomplete hasp **75.00**

    7″ l, dark brown and black japanning, red, green, yellow, black, and white floral dec, minor wear, lid seam loose **200.00**

    8″ l, dark brown japanning, white band, yellow commas, green, red, and black floral dec. **300.00**

    9″ l, worn brown japanning, polychrome and gold stenciled floral dec, some battering **125.00**

    10″ l, brown japanning, white band, red and yellow swags, red, black, and green floral dec, some wear, good colors **415.00**

Flour Sifter, red ground, floral dec . . .   **135.00**

Food Warmer, 8¼″ h, cylindrical, orig brown japanning, stenciled floral dec, font and whale oil burner, two pans, minor wear **275.00**

Foot Warmer, 7½ × 6½″, rect, worn brown japanning, gold stenciled lyre, wooden base and top **95.00**

Lamp

    5½″ h, petticoat, three spout whale oil burner, dark brown japanning. **70.00**

    6½″ h, double wick slots on font, saucer base, traces of black **30.00**

Lunchbox, domed top, black ground, white band around center with leaf and berry dec, feather and flower dec, bail handle, early 20th C. **50.00**

Match Holder, 7⅜″ h, traces of orig black paint, red and yellow dec . . .   **60.00**

Mug, 4¾″ h, japanning with polychrome floral and fruit dec **600.00**

Snuff Box

    2″ l, mustard yellow ground, red, black, green, and white floral dec   **190.00**

    2½″ l, book shape, polychrome paint   **45.00**

Spice Box

    6½″ d, round, seven canisters, brown japanning, stenciling and striping **40.00**

    6¾″ d, round, brown japanning, gold striping, seven blue-green japanned canisters with gold stenciled labels **90.00**

    8″ d, round, brown japanning, yellow and red striping, brass bail handle, orig seven canisters with stenciled labels **145.00**

    9¼″ l, rect, six canisters, dark brown japanning, silver stenciled labels, nutmeg grater in lid **100.00**

    9½″ l, rect, six canisters, black and brown japanning, stenciled labels   **30.00**

Sugar Bowl, 3½″ h, worn red paint, brown and yellow comma-type foliage, foot slightly battered **165.00**

Syrup, 5½″ h, dark blue japanning, red comma-type foliage on lid and handle, gold stenciled "Molasses". **45.00**

Tea Caddy

    2⅞″ h, miniature, orig black paint, stenciled gold label **50.00**

    4¼″ h, dark brown japanning, red, yellow, white, and green stylized floral dec. **110.00**

    4½″ h, oval, worn black japanning, yellow and red floral dec, red ground lid with black comma dec   **165.00**

    5¾″ h, dark brown japanning, red, green, and yellow floral dec **165.00**

    8¼″ l, dark ground, worn stenciled bronze powder dec, int. lift out tray fits over two lidded compartments, orig emb brass handle, minor damage **200.00**

Wall Sconces, Deer Isle, ME, 19th C, 14⅞″ h, price for pair, $1,760.00. Photograph courtesy of Skinner, Inc.

Tea Canister, 7" h, orig dark brown japanning, yellow and orange-red dec, worn **115.00**

Teapot, 2⅝" h, miniature, red repaint with floral dec beneath **45.00**

Tobacco Box, 4½" l, 2¾" w, cov with worn painting of young girl with flowers, int. lid with view of nude young lady trimming her toe-nails **225.00**

Tray

12¼" l, 9⅜" w, dark green-blue japanning, gilt floral rim, center with detailed painting of village with stream, boat, and people, minor edge battering **450.00**

14⅜" l, 10⅞" w, black japanning, gilt floral rim, well detailed painting of farmers meeting on country road **375.00**

15½" l, center dec depicts "The Landing of the Fathers, Plymouth, Dec 22, 1620," late 19th C **110.00**

26¾" l, 19¾" w, scenic dec, two men and young woman hidden in trees scene. **200.00**

PAPER EPHEMERA

Maurice Rickards, author of *Collecting Paper Ephemera*, suggests that ephemera are the "minor transient documents of everyday life," material destined for the wastebasket that never quite makes it. This definition is more fitting than traditional dictionary definitions that stress length of time, e.g., "lasting a very short time." A driver's license, which is used for a year or longer, is as much a piece of ephemera as is a ticket to a sporting event or music concert. The transient nature of the object is the key.

Collecting ephemera has a long and distinguished history. Among the English pioneers were John Seldon (1584–1654), Samuel Pepys (1633–1703), and John Bagford (1650–1716). Large American collections can be found at historical societies, libraries, and museums, e.g., Wadsworth Antheneum, Hartford, CT, and Museum of the City of New York, across the country.

When used by collectors, "ephemera" usually means paper objects, e.g., billheads and letterheads, book plates, documents, labels, stocks and bonds, tickets, valentines, etc. However, more and more ephemera collectors are recognizing the transient nature of some three-dimensional material, e.g., advertising tins and pinback buttons. Today's specialized paper shows include dealers selling both two- and three-dimensional material.

References: Anne F. Clapp, *Curatorial Care of Works of Art on Paper*, Nick Lyons Books, 1987; Joseph Raymond LeFontaine, *Turning Paper To Gold*, Betterway Publications, 1988; John Lewis, *Printed Ephemera*, Antique Collectors' Club, 1990; Norman E. Martinus and Harry L. Rinker, *Warman's Paper*, Wallace-Homestead, 1994; Maurice Rickards, *Collecting Paper Ephemera*, Abbeville Press, 1988; Demaris C. Smith, *Preserving Your Paper Collectibles*, Betterway Publications, 1989.

Periodicals: *The Check Collector*, PO Box 577, Garrett Park, MD 20896; *PAC (Paper & Advertising Collector)*, PO Box 500, Mt. Joy, PA 17552; *PCM (Paper Collector's Marketplace)*, PO Box 127, Scandinavia, WI 54977.

Collectors' Club: Ephemera Society of America, Inc., PO Box 37, Schoharie, NY 12157.

ALMANACS, BIBLES AND OTHER BOOKS

History: The agrarian community enjoyed a relatively high reading level due in part to their desire to read almanacs and the Bible, as well as other books. Every rural farmstead had a minimum of one bookcase filled with books. The family Bible was given a prominent place in the parlor or sitting room. Children's books were a means of education as well as enjoyment.

Practical books ranging from accounting to home medicine were prevalent, the latter serving as a reference in cases of emergency. Picture books also were found. The agrarian community did a great deal of traveling with their imaginations.

Most books were ordered through the mail. Literature sets were popular since many publishers sold them on a one-book-a-month basis.

Eighteenth and early 19th century almanacs contain astronomical data, weather forecasts, and agricultural information carefully calculated to the area of publication. They are a combination of things reasoned and things mystic—showing the dualistic nature of early rural America.

As important documents of early printing in the United States, their value increases when they contain woodcuts such as the astrological man, ships, exotic animals (elephants, tigers, etc.), and genre scenes. The Pennsylvania almanacs were among the first to label Washington as "Father" of this country and hence, are eagerly sought by collectors.

By the mid-19th century, almanacs became a compendia of useful information—stage coach routes, court schedules, business listings, humorous stories and jokes, health information, and feature articles. Their emphasis became strongly rural-agricultural. Businesses also began to issue almanacs to help advertise and promote their products.

The Bible, in its many early editions, versions, languages, and translations, is the most popular and widely published book in the world. Recently Bible collecting has gained wider appreciation with a corresponding increase in prices.

King James version English Bibles printed after 1800 are common, not eagerly sought, and command modest prices. Fine leather bindings and handsome illustrations add to value. Check for ownership information, family records, and other ephemera concealed within the pages of a Bible. These items may be worth more than the Bible itself.

References: *American Book Prices Current, Volume 99, 1993,* Bancroft-Parkman, 1993; *Huxford's Old Book Value Guide, Fifth Edition,* Collector Books, 1993; Nancy Wright, *Books, Identification and Price Guide,* Avon Books, 1993.

Barbara Bader, *American Picture Books From Noah's Ark To The Beast Within,* Macmillan, 1976; E. Lee Baumgarten, *Price List for Children's and Illustrated Books for the Years 1880–1950, Sorted by Artist,* published by author, 1993; E. Lee Baumgarten, *Price List for Children's and Illustrated Books for the Years 1880–1950, Sorted by Author,* published by author, 1993; Margery Fisher, *Who's Who In Children's Books: A Treasury of the Familiar Characters of Childhood,* Holt, Rinehart and Winston, 1975; Virginia Haviland, *Children's Literature, A Guide To Reference Sources,* Library of Congress, 1966, first supplement 1972, second supplement 1977, third supplement 1982; Bettina Hurlimann, *Three Centuries Of Children's Books In Europe,* tr. and ed. by Brian W. Alderson, World, 1968; Cornelia L. Meigs, ed., *A Critical History of Chil-*

dren's Literature, Second Edition, Macmillan, 1969.

Periodicals: *Book Source Monthly,* 2007 Syosset Dr, PO Box 567, Cazenovia, NY 13035; *Martha's KidLit Newsletter,* PO Box 1488, Ames, IA 50010.

Collectors' Clubs: Antiquarian Booksellers Association of America, 50 Rockefeller Plaza, New York, NY 10020; National Book Collectors Society, Suite 349, 65 High Ridge Road, Stamford, CT 06095.

Museum: American Bible Society, New York, NY.

Reproduction Craftspersons: *Handmade Paper—* JoAnne Schiavone, Schiavone Books, 60 Itaska Place, Oceanport, NJ 07757.

Reproduction Manufacturers: *Children's—*Serenity Herbs, Box 42, Monterey Stage, Great Marrington, MA 01230; *General—*Amazon Vinegar & Pickling Works Drygoods, 2218 East 11th St, Davenport, IA 52803; Antiquity Reprints, PO Box 370, Rockville Centre, NY 11571.

Almanacs

1796, Poor Will's Almanack for . . . 1796, Philadelphia, printed and sold by Joseph Crukshank, woodcut of the astrological man, 40 pgs	**40.00**
1822, Poor Richard's Almanac . . . New York, David Young, printed by S Marks for Daniel D Smith, 36 pgs	**25.00**
1877, Clarks ABC Almanac, 32 pgs, black and yellow	**20.00**
1880, Ayers Almanac, yellow cov, printed color	**6.00**
1882–83, Greens Diary Almanac, color, 32 pgs	**15.00**
1883, New Favorite Cooking Receipts of the Shakers and Illustrated Almanac for 1883, black and white, 6 × 7¾"	**40.00**

Poor Richard Almanac, **Wilmer Atkinson Co, Philadelphia, 48 pages, 1916, $15.00.**

1884, The Michigan State Almanac Diary and Gazeteer, Wells, Richardson & Co, Burlington, VT, color **25.00**

1892, Shaker Almanac, testimonials and adv, blue and gray, 32 pgs . . **75.00**

1893, Hazeltine's Pocket Book Almanac, color **8.00**

1894, The Ladies Birthday Almanac for 1894, Wine of Cardui, Thedfords Black Drought, color **15.00**

1895, Wright's Pictorial Family Almanac, 24 pgs, yellow and black **8.00**

1902, Dr Morse's Indian Root Pills Almanac, color **8.00**

1905, Marshall's Almanac, 48 pgs, color illus **6.00**

1913, Flying Dutchman Almanac and Farmer's Catalog, Moline Plow Co, 32 pgs, yellow and black **25.00**

Bibles

1805, Reading PA, *Biblia, Das Ist: Die Ganze Gottliche Heilige Schrift . . . Erste Auflage,* Gottlob Jungmann, 1,235 pgs, 8 × 10", contemporary polished calf binding **125.00**

1846, New York, *The Illuminated Bible,* morocco gilt, two engraved titles, 1,600 plates, 8 × 10" **250.00**

1850, Philadelphia, PA, *Bible,* woodcut illus, English medical recipe (Pow-Wow) broadside on rear paste down, Petre family record **35.00**

1854, Philadelphia, PA, *Holy Bible: Comprehensive Bible . . .,* gilt emb leather cov **35.00**

1866, *23rd Psalm,* Hurd Houghton, NY, 7 chromolithographs, gilt binding **45.00**

Children's Books

Alcott, L. M., *Little Women,* A. B. Stephens illus, Little, Brown pub, 1914, 15 black and white plates, 617 pgs **45.00**

Bambi's Children, Whitman Better Little Books #1497, 1943 . . . . . . **35.00**

Barringer, M., *Martin the Goose Boy,* Petershams illus, Doubleday pub, 1932, 1st ed, black cloth covers, 8 color plates, dj **60.00**

Brown, E., *Manni The Donkey In The Forest World,* Walt Disney Studios illus, Disney Little Golden Book #D75, c1959. . . . . **5.00**

Burgess, T., *Farmer Brown's Boy becomes Curious,* N. Jordan illus, Whitman pub, 1929, illustrated boards, color illus, 24 pgs **40.00**

David Copperfield, Whitman Big Little Book #1148, 1934 . . . . **85.00**

Buffalo Bill's Boyhood, **Elmer Sherwood, Whitman Publishing Co, Racine, WI, illus by Neil O'Keefe, 122 pages, color cov, undated, 4⅝ × 6⅞", $20.00.**

Dickens, Charles, *Mr. Pickwick's Christmas,* G. A. Williams illus, Baker/Taylor pub, 1st ed, 6 color plates, 149 pgs **60.00**

Farjeon, E., *Old Nurse's Stocking Basket,* E. H. Whydale illus, Stokes pub, 1931, 1st American illus ed, 154 pgs **35.00**

Gene Autry, Cowboy Detective, Whitman Better Little Books #1494, 1940 . . . . **40.00**

Gilbert, W. S., *Pinafore Picture Book,* A. B. Woodward illus, G. Bell pub, 1908, 1st ed, 16 color plates **75.00**

Hough, E., *Singing Mouse Stories,* W. Bradley illus, Forest/Stream pub, 1895, 1st ed, 182 pgs **100.00**

Just Kids, Whitman Big Little Book #1401, 1937 . . . . **45.00**

Kipling, R., *Just So Stories . . .,* R. Kipling illus, MacMillan pub, 1902, 1st ed, red cloth covers, 22 black and white plates, 249 pgs **225.00**

Lee, E. D., *Ever Living Fairy Tales,* E. D. Lee illus, NY, 1924, green cloth covers, 18 color plates. **50.00**

Lenski, L., *Alphabet People,* L. Lenski illus, Harper pub, 1928, 1st ed, blue cloth covers, 104 pgs **45.00**

Lockwood, H., *The Golden Book of Birds,* Feodor Rojankovsky illus, Little Golden Book #13, c1943, dj **20.00**

McEvoy, J. P., *Bam Bam Clock,* J Gruelle illus, Volland pub, 1st ed, illus boards, color illus, 38 pgs **70.00**

Moffat, A., *Our Old Nursery Rhymes,* H. W. LeMair illus, Augener pub, 1911, 1st ed, color illus, 63 pgs. **150.00**

The Little Red Hen, Saalfield Publishing, No. 857, 28 pages, color illus, includes 10-page "Little Black Sambo" story, 1932, 8½ × 11¼", $95.00.

Mother Goose, K. Greenaway illus, McLoughlin pub, 1882, illus boards, color illus, 48 pgs 150.00

Nast, E. R., *Our Puppy,* Feodor Rojankovsky illus, Little Golden Book #56, c1948. . . . . 10.00

Nicholson, Wm., *Square Book of Animals,* W. Nicholson illus, Russell pub, 1900, 1st American ed, 12 color plates, illus boards. 300.00

Polly and Her Pals on the Farm, Saalfield Little Big Books #1060, 1934 32.00

Pool, M. L., *Red-Bridge Neighborhood,* C. Carleton illus, Harper pub, 1898, 1st ed, 13 black and white plates, 369 pgs. 30.00

Pyle, K., *Tales of Two Bunnies,* K. Pyle illus, Dutton pub, 1913, 1st ed, red cloth covers, black and white illus 45.00

Rollins, P. A., *Jinglebob,* N. C. Wyeth illus, Scribner pub, 1st ed, 7 color plates, 263 pgs 125.00

Shute, H. A., *Farming It,* R. Birch illus, Houghton pub, 1909, 1st ed, 16 black and white plates 35.00

Three Little Kittens, K. Wiese illus, MacMillan pub, 1928, 1st ed, illus boards, 40 pgs. 30.00

Uncle Ray's Story of the United States, Whitman Big Little Book #722, 1934 . . . . 60.00

Werner, J., *Animal Friends,* Garth Williams illus, Little Golden Book #167, c1953 . . . . 5.00

White, E. O., *When Molly Was Six,* K. Pyle illus, Houghton pub, 1894, 1st ed, cloth covers, 3 black and white plates, 133 pgs 45.00

Yonge, C., *The Little Duke,* B. Stevens illus, Duffield pub, 1923, 1st ed, 4 color plates 35.00

Non-Fiction Works

Anderson, R. C., *The Rigging of Ships in the Days of the Spritsail Topmast, 1600–1720,* Salem, 1927, cloth covers. 45.00

Arms, Dorothy Noyes, *Fishing Memories,* William J. Schaldach illus, New York, 1938, cloth covers, dj 45.00

Bewick, Thomas, *A General History of quadrupeds. The Figures Engraved on Wood By . . .,* Newcastle Upon Tyne, 1824, 8th ed, 526 pgs, re-backed using orig leather covers 85.00

Bigelow, Horatio, *Flying Feathers, A Yankee's Hunting Experiences in the South,* Richmond, 1937 . . . . . 45.00

Choules, John Overton, *The Cruise of the Steam Yacht North Star: A Narrative of the Excursion of Mr. Vanderbilt's Party to England, Russia, Denmark, France, Spain, Italy, Malta, Turkey, Madeira, etc.,* Boston, 1854, cloth covers 75.00

Davison, Gideon M, *Fashionable Tour in 1825. An Excursion to the Springs, Niagara, Quebec and Boston,* Saratoga Springs, 1825, 2nd ed, leather-backed marbled boards, 169 pgs 40.00

Eaton, Elon Howard, *Birds of New York,* Albany, 1910 and 1914, 2 vols, 1st ed, green cloth covers, color plates 145.00

Everitt, Simon W., *Tales of Wild Turkey Hunting,* William C. Hazelton, Chicago, 1928, cloth covers 300.00

Gibson, William H., *The Complete American Trapper; or The Tricks of Trapping and Trap Making,* New York, 1876, wood engraved frontispiece, divisional titles, plates, and text illus, cloth covers 150.00

Gilmor, Colonel Harry, *Four Years in the Sadddle,* New York, 1866, 1st ed, engraved frontispiece, blue cloth covers, 291 pgs. 225.00

House, Homer D., *Wild Flowers of New York,* Albany, 1923, 2nd printing, 2 vols, green cloth covers, color plates 110.00

Hubert, Philip G., *Liberty and a Living. The Record of an Attempt to secure Bread and Butter, Sunshine and Content, by Gardening, Fishing, and Hunting,* New York, 1889, frontispiece, cloth covers 75.00

The Birds of America, from Drawings Made in the United States and Their Territories, after John James Audubon, 7 volume set, 1841 Bowen edition, $15,000.00. Photograph courtesy of Butterfield & Butterfield.

Hurd, D Hamilton, comp, *History of New London County, Connecticut, with Biographical Sketches,* Philadelphia, 1882, gild dec leather-backed covers, 678 pgs **70.00**
Illustrated Atlas of Massachusetts, 1894 .... **45.00**
Kippis, Andrew, *A Narrative of the Voyages Round the World performed by Captain James Cook,* NY, c1870 .... **55.00**
Marshall, John, *Life of George Washington,* Philadelphia, 1804–07, 1st ed, 5 vols, gilt spines, red leather spine labels, some foxing **165.00**
Merrill, Samuel, *The Moose Book: Facts and Stories from Northern Forests,* New York, 1916, plates reproducing photos and paintings by Carl Rungius and others, cloth covers, dj **145.00**
Neihardt, John G., *The Song of the Indian Wars,* Allen True illus, NY, 1925, 1st ed, publisher's slipcase, cloth covers, author sgd, limited to 500 numbered copies **45.00**
Oliphant, J Orin, ed, *On the Arkansas Route to California in 1849. The Journal of Robert B Green of Lewisburg, Pennsylvania,* Bucknell U Press, 1955, 1st ed, glassine wrapper **100.00**
Perlam, *The American Farmer's Pictorial Cyclopedia of Live Stock,* Perlam et al., St Louis, 1890, black and white engravings, eight animal chromolithographs, 7 × 10" **60.00**

Pollard, Edward A., *The Lost Cause; A New Southern History of the War of the Confederates,* NY, 1867, 6 plates, cloth covers, faded spine, 752 pgs **925.00**
Roosevelt, Theodore, *Outdoor Pastimes of an American Hunter,* New York, 1905, 1st ed, pictorial cloth covers **55.00**
Scudder, Horace E., *American Commonwealths,* Boston, 1888, 12 vols representing 11 states, cloth covers, frontispiece maps, ex-library ed................... **250.00**
Seton, Ernest Thompson, *Lives of Game Animals,* Garden City, 1925, illus, 4 vol, cloth covers, publishers 2-pc boxes, limited first ed, unsgd **415.00**
Sewell, William, *A History of the Rise, Increase and Progress of the Christian People called Quakers intermixed with Several Remarkable Occurences. To Which is Prefixed a Brief Memoir of the Author Compiled From Various Sources,* Baker & Crane, NY, 1844, 1st ed, 2 vols bound as one, 422 pgs and 465 pgs **1,350.00**
The Fishermen's Own Book, Procter Brothers, 1882, list of men and vessels lost from the Port of Gloucester, MA, from 1874 to Apr 1, 1882, illus.............. **85.00**
Walsh, John Henry, *The Dog in Health and Disease . . . by Stonehenge . . . Third Edition,* London, 1879, illus, cloth covers **100.00**
Wheeler, Colonel Homer W., *Buffalo Days. Forty Years in the Old West: The Personal Narrative of a Cattleman, Indian Fighter and Army Officer,* Indianapolis, 1925, 1st ed, 18 plates, cloth covers ... **150.00**

BAND BOXES

History: Storage was a major problem in 19th and early 20th century rural America. Because most homes had limited closet space, storage space was utilized in attics, basements, and sheds. Many bedrooms contained a trunk as well as a chest of drawers. Supplemental storage was provided by boxes, one version of which was the band box.

The name "band box" came from the utilitarian, lightweight pasteboard boxes used in England to store men's neckbands and lacebands. During their period of greatest popularity in America, 1820 to 1850, large band boxes were used to store hats and clothing while smaller boxes held gloves, handkerchiefs, powder, ribbons, and sewing materials.

Most band boxes were covered with highly decorative wallpaper. Floral, marble, and geometric designs were commonplace. The most desirable boxes are those covered with paper picturing an historical theme, e.g., the Erie Canal or a balloon ascent.

Individuals, such as Hannah Davis of East Jaffrey, New Hampshire, made a living as band box makers. A maker's label can double the value of a box. Band boxes also were sold as sets. A matching set commands a premium price.

Although the band box relates more to the early American rather than the Country look, Country collectors and decorators have found that they add a splash of color to several room decors. Before investing in a contemporary example, check the prices and availability of some of the more commonly found 19th century paper patterns. In many cases the historic examples will be cheaper and have a great deal more character.

Reproduction Craftspersons: Lindsay E Frost, Band Boxes, Box A, Campbell St, Avella, PA 15312; Virginia Kent, 340 S Russell St, York, PA 17402; Terry D Koher, Old Northwest Freedom Press, PO Box 218, Z Hill Rd, New Matamoras, OH 45767; Richard & Bess Leaf, Box 223, Rte 5, Jenkins Chapel Rd, Shelbyville, TN 37160; Elizabeth Mondress, 1045 Spring View Dr, Southampton, PA 18966; Eileen Sherrard, 2404 Lagonda Ave, Springfield, OH 45503; Caroline Wissinger, 721 Elm Rd, Bradford Woods, PA 15015; Michelle Worthing, Nancy Yeiser, The Band Box, 2173 Woodlawn Circle, Stow, OH 44224.

Reproduction Manufacturers: *General*—Bandboxes, Box AH, Avalla, PA 15312; Checkerberry Hill, 253 Westridge Ave, Daly City, CA 94015; *Kit*—Band Boxes by Irene, 480 Beechnut Dr, Blue Bell, PA 19422.

Bird and Flower design wallpaper, repairs and losses, 19th C, 19" l **110.00**
Brick house with farm yard, trees in background, road in foreground, printed wallpaper, red and brown on blue ground, imperfections, c1830, 11" h **880.00**
Buildings and Trees
    Black, blue, brown, tan, and white, cardboard, 16" l **500.00**
    Blue, brown, green, and white, bentwood, 19" l **400.00**
Clayton's Ascent pattern wallpaper, hot air balloon over trees and houses, pink, bittersweet, yellow, and white, c1835, 16½" l, 11" h **500.00**
Drapery Swag with Three Roses and Vase design wallpaper, imperfections, c1830, 10½" h **500.00**

Band Box, Brick House and Farmyard pattern wallpaper, red and brown, blue ground, c1830, 11" h, $880.00. Photograph courtesy of Skinner, Inc.

Floral and Fruit design, printed wallpaper over bentwood, flowers, bowls of fruit, and foliage, white, brown, black, and faded red, blue ground, int. lined with 1835 newspaper, printed label "Warranted Nailed Band-Boxes Made by Hannah Davis, Jaffrey N.H.," some wear, edge damage, damaged lid banding, 20" l . . .   **685.00**
Floral design wallpaper
    Brown and green, off white ground, bentwood, 13¾" l **175.00**
    White and yellow, faded blue ground, cardboard, 18" l **200.00**
    Red and gold, light blue ground, cardboard, newspaper lined, 5" l   **325.00**
Floral design with seascape and pastoral vignettes wallpaper, attributed to Hannah Davis, Jaffrey, NH, minor imperfections, c1850, 14" h **325.00**
Foliage design wallpaper, box, green, red, and brown, off white ground, cardboard, lined with 1839 Hagerstown newspaper, 7¾" l **275.00**
Geometric Floral design wallpaper, purple, orange, olive green, black, and yellow, cream colored ground, bentwood, 19¾" l **800.00**
Harbor Scene, eagle and foliage scrolls, green, gray, black, and white, cardboard, 17¼" l **275.00**
Heraea Games pattern wallpaper, c1830
    Block printed, losses, 14" l, 10¾" h   **360.00**
    Horses and chariots, landscape background, 19½" l, 13½" h **350.00**
"Les Trois Jours" pattern wallpaper, commemorates July 27–29, 1830 restoration of Louis Philippe to French throne, c1830, 19¾" l, 15" h   **375.00**
Peacocks and Flowers pattern wallpaper, pink, green, and white, light blue ground, newspaper lined, c1834, 12" l, 6⅝" h **550.00**

Quadriga Filled with Flowers pattern
  wallpaper, couple pulling chariot
  loaded with flowers, c1830, 19" l,
  12" h **550.00**
Squirrel design wallpaper, hand
  blocked, blue, tan, and white, 19th
  C, 15" l, 12" h **325.00**
Swag and Tassel pattern wallpaper, int.
  lined with 1833 and 1834 *Patriot
  Marine Journal,* 19½" l, 12" h **600.00**
The Three Days pattern wallpaper, re-
  pairs and losses, c1830, 17" l **110.00**
Walking Beam Sidewheeler pattern
  wallpaper, repairs and losses, 19th C,
  17½" l **135.00**
Waterfalls with Deer and Trees pattern
  wallpaper, brown, green, and pale
  blue, white ground, cardboard,
  15½" l **85.00**

CERTIFICATES

History: Carefully stored in a trunk or bureau
drawer were the documents that chronicled the
life of a member of the agrarian community: birth
certificate, baptismal certificate, diploma, marriage certificate, professional appointments, and
rewards of merit. Few were framed to hang on the
wall. The major exception was an appointment
document.

These certificates record the evolution of American printing. The wood block certificates of the
early 19th century were replaced by lithographed
examples in the 1870s and 1880s. The presentation was often elaborate.

In addition, many of these certificates are
very colorful and decorative. This is the feature
that attracts the Country collector. Today these
certificates are no longer hidden. They are framed
and prominently displayed as major accent
pieces.

Reproduction Craftspersons: Sally Green Bunce,
4826 Mays Ave, Reading, PA 19606; Meryl Grif-
fiths, 1101 Gypsy Hill Rd, Lancaster, PA 17602;
Joan Kopchik, 1335 Stephen Way, Southampton,
Pa 18966; Michael S Kreibel, 1756 Breneman Rd,
Manheim, PA 17545.

Reproduction Manufacturers: The Evergreen
Press, Inc, 3380 Vincent Rd, Pleasant Hill, CA
94523; Harwell Graphics, PO Box 8, Napoleon,
IN 47034; Precious Memories, PO Box 313, Cali-
fon, NJ 07830.

Baptismal
  1873, Currier & Ives, 14 × 10" **15.00**
  1925, Aldine May Sittler, PA,
    printed, pink flowers, white dove,
    cream to blue-green ground,
    Abingdon Press, New York and
    Cincinnati, No. 60, 11½ × 16"   **8.00**

**Birth Certificate, Northampton County,
PA, Trexler & Hartzell Printers, Allentown, PA, 1874, 14 × 17", $50.00.**

Bond
  1905, Consolidated Railway Com-
    pany, $10,000, horse-drawn trol-
    ley vignette, brown printing,
    unissued **25.00**
  1929, City of Fort Wayne, Paul Baer
    Field Aviation, $1,000, early plane
    vignette, brown border, coupons,
    issued **45.00**
  1947, Southern Bell Telephone &
    Telegraph, $1,000, vignettes of ru-
    ral landscapes and telephone,
    coupons, issued. **15.00**
Confirmation
  1877, Samuel W Gerhab, PA, black
    etching, gold printing, red and
    gold Bible verses, framed, 8 × 11"   **12.00**
  1926, Miriam Margaret Schroy, PA,
    white violets and roses, ribbons,
    dove, and church in shades of
    pink, purple, blue, and green,
    ground shades from blue-green to

**Geburts and Taufschein (Birth and Bap-
tism), printed, enhanced by watercolor,
Adarras County, PA, 1803, 12½ × 14½",
$350.00. Photograph courtesy of Skinner,
Inc.**

cream color, Abingdon Press, New York and Cincinnati, No. 80, framed, 11½ × 16" **8.00**

Cradle Roll, 1912, Providence Litho, eight children around end of cradle, 10½ × 13½" **18.00**

Customs, 1804, Benjamin Lincoln, Boston, emb seal, 5 × 9½" **55.00**

Deed, 1856, Pike County, IL, receipt, emb seals **18.00**

Honorable Discharge, Vicksburg Muster-Out Roll, Aug 1, 1863, Lt Joseph Treadway, 23rd Wisconsin Volunteers, sgd by officers **30.00**

Inspection Certificate, bark *Carolina* of NY, inspection for hidden slaves, sgd by Inspector Gibson, 4½ × 7" **75.00**

Land Grant, 1815, parchment, Tuscarawas County, OH, sgd "James Madison" with seal, faded ink, damage at fold lines, old grained frame, 17" w, 13" h **350.00**

Marriage, 1898, E A Strohl and Matilda C Hahn, PA, six vignettes of different stages of married life, Bible verses, multicolored, Ernst Kaufmann, NY, No. 105, 12¾ × 17" **15.00**

Membership

1882, Members Exchange of St Louis Certificate of Membership, engraved, exchange and three buildings, 11½ × 9½" **10.00**

1898

Association of Descendants of Edward Foulke, Martha Kinsey, commemorates 200th anniversary of landing of Edward and Eleanor Foulke, multicolored emb coat of arms, framed, 8¼ × 7" **8.00**

Trinity Reformed Church, Sarah Ann Fried, PA, hymn verse, decorative border, gold and red lettering, Daniel Miller pub, Reading, PA, 8½ × 11½" **5.00**

1899, American Flag House & Betsy Ross Memorial Association, numbered and sgd, 11 × 14" **25.00**

1900s, Merchants Exchange of St Louis Certificate of Membership, waterfront vignette, 11½ × 10"   **5.00**

1908, Francis Scott Key Memorial Association, Charles H Weigerber, 14½ × 11½" **25.00**

1926, Stockman Protective Association, OK, farm scene vignette . . .   **6.00**

1937, Oak Park Republican Committeemen's Organization, IL, Office of Secretary of State, engraved, 8½ × 14" **25.00**

Reading Circle, 1896, Indiana Young People's, organized by the State

Flag Certificate, American Flag House and Betsy Ross Memorial Association, C H Weisgerber Printing, framed, 1917, $38.00.

Teachers' Association, ornate, 5¾ × 3¼" **10.00**

Occupational, 1905, Teacher's Elementary School Certificate, Perry County, OH, sunrise over mountain vignette, 9¼ × 13" **15.00**

Reward of Merit

1871, Card of Approbation, 50 token of merit, Swiss landscape litho on back **5.00**

1872, Testimonial of Approbation, black and white, 8½ × 10 ¼" . . .   **12.00**

1876, Toledo Public Schools Grade One Card of Worth, blue and red   **8.00**

1879, Card of Honor, Diligency-One Hundred tokens of Merit, multicolored chromolithograph **15.00**

Stock

1870, Chicago Cotton Manufacturing Co, brown center, factory vignette, ornate design, unissued   **10.00**

1873, Santa Clara Valley Mill & Lumber Co, CA, lumber mill vignette, unissued **15.00**

1883, Providence, Boston Railroad Co, boats, factories, and train vignette **25.00**

1900, Fairview Golden Boulder Mining Co, NV, brown, gold nugget vignette, unissued **12.00**

1903, Ishpeming Livery Co, Ltd, MI, horse vignette, unissued **6.00**

1911, North Butte Mining co, miners working in mine vignette **7.00**

Treasury, dated Jan 1, 1780, Revolutionary War, MA, payable to John Bradford **400.00**

MAPS

History: Most agrarian libraries contained copies of world and county atlases. They provided a means of keeping in touch with the world and one's local community. County atlases from the

19th century often contained the names of individual property owners. When county directories arrived upon the scene in the mid-20th century, county atlases disappeared.

Maps provide one of the best ways to study the growth of a country or region. From the 16th to the early 20th century, maps were both informative and decorative. Engravers provided ornamental detailing which often took the form of bird's eye views, city maps, and ornate calligraphy and scrolling. Many maps were hand colored to enhance their beauty.

Maps generally were published in plate books. Many of the maps available today result from these books being cut apart with sheets sold separately.

In the last quarter of the 19th century, representatives from firms in Philadelphia, Chicago, and elsewhere traveled the United States preparing county atlases, often with a sheet for each township and a sheet for each major city or town. Although mass produced, they are eagerly sought by collectors. Individual sheets sell for $25 to $75. The atlases themselves can usually be purchased in the $200 to $400 range. Individual sheets should be viewed solely as decorative and not as investment material.

Collectors' Clubs: The Association of Map Memorabilia, 8 Amherst Road, Pelham, MA 01002; The Chicago Map Society, 60 West Walton St, Chicago, IL 60610.

Periodical: *Antique Map & Print Quarterly,* PO Box 290–681, Wethersfield, CT 06129–0681.

Atlas
    Beers, F. W., *Atlas of Staten Island, Richmond County, New York,* New York, 1874, 35 litho maps, most double page and color, folio   **165.00**
    Cary, John, *Cary's New Universal Atlas,* London, 1811, 55 engraved double page maps, hand colored in outline, 19th C cloth, folio . . . **4,400.00**
    Cornell, S. S., *Cornell's Grammar-School Geography,* New York, 1864, hand colored maps, tall 8vo   **120.00**
    Harper's School Geography, New York, 1894, color, small 4to **50.00**
    Manhattan Land Book, New York, 1934, 188 color street plans, some with overlays updating from an earlier edition, cloth covers, oblong 4to **190.00**
    Morse, Jedidiah and Sidney, *A New Universal Atlas,* New Haven, 1822, 20 hand colored engraved maps, contemporary 1/4 morocco covers, small 4to **450.00**
    New Historical Atlas of Rockland County, New York, New York, 1876, 21 litho maps, some double

page and linen backed, missing title and preliminaries, folio. **120.00**
    Raleigh, Sir Walter, *The History of the World,* London, 1614, engraved double page maps, contemporary calf, rebacked, missing letterpress title, thick large folio   **525.00**
    Smith, Charles, *New English Atlas,* London, 1808, 2nd ed, 46 double page maps, hand colored, contemporary 1/2 calf, folio **2,850.00**
    The Times Atlas, London, 1895, 117 double page color maps, 1/2 morocco, small folio **165.00**
Map
  America
    1719, "A New Map of the English Empire in America," John Senex, London, engraved, hand colored in outline, wide margins, double page, slight scattered browning, 505 × 595 mm **1,875.00**
    c1730, "America Septentrionalis—America Meridionalis," Peter Schenk, Amsterdam, shows California as an island, engraved, hand colored in outline, double page, top margin trimmed to plate mark, 500 × 565 mm. **1,000.00**
  Eastern United States
    1819, "The United States drawn by Sally B L Ingell, aged 10 yrs, Saunton, August 23, 1819, Private School," eastern states from Maine to Georgia, west to Louisiana territory, hand drawn, pen and ink and watercolor on paper, matted and framed, 34¼ × 28¼" **750.00**

Florida and the Caribbean, Indiarum Occidentalium Tractus Littoralis Cum Insulis, F De Wit, hand-colored engraving, Dutch, 17th C, 19⅛ × 22⅛ ", $825.00. Photograph courtesy of Leslie Hindman Auctioneers.

1844, "Mitchell's National Map American Republic," color, 28 eastern states, Indian Territories with tribal claims, 32 cities detailed, population charts, 41 × 49" **135.00**

Georgia, "A New And Accurate Map Of The Province Of Georgia In North America," J. Hinton, London, 1779, engraved, published in *The Universal Magazine,* 12¾ × 10¾".................... **300.00**

Illinois, "Railroad Map of Illinois," Rand McNally, Chicago, 1891, color, folding, folds into orig 12mo letterpress wrappers.......... **100.00**

Iowa, "Sketch of the Public Surveys in Iowa," McClelland, Washington, c1846, shows area between the Mississippi and Missouri Rivers, folding, engraved, wide margins, 480 × 605 mm **50.00**

New Hampshire, "An Accurate Map of New Hampshire in New England," c1795, folding, engraved, hand colored in outline, margins trimmed within plate mark, 335 × 295 mm **190.00**

New Haven, CT, "A Plan of the Town of New Haven", Nathaniel Currier, NY, litho city map, 560 × 400 mm sheet size **385.00**

New York
  1851, "The Empire State," Ensign, Thayer & Co, NY, engraved, hand colored in outline, expertly closed tears, 555 × 745 mm **325.00**
  1901–02, "New York State, Railroad, Post Office, Township, and County," lists 71 railroad lines with mileage between junctions, terminals, 71 steamship lines, details major cities of New York, Jersey City, and Hoboken, 42 × 48" **125.00**

North Carolina, "Map of the State of North Carolina," G. W. and C. B. Colton, NY, 1866, two folding hand colored litho maps, each pictures 1/2 of state, orig 8vo cloth folder, each measures 850 × 760 mm **525.00**

Ohio, "Map of Ohio," John Kilborne, Columbus, 1822, engraved, hand colored, framed, 31 × 32" **650.00**

South America, Thomas Kitchin, London, 1794, engraved, hand colored in outline, double page, wide margins, very browned, 450 × 540 mm **85.00**

South Atlantic States, "A Map of the Seat of War in the Southern Part of Virginia, North Carolina, and Northern Part of South Carolina," Thomas Kitchin, London, 1781, engraved, linen backed, ample margins, 285 × 355 mm........ **250.00**

Texas
  c1840, "Texas in 1836," NY, engraved, hand colored, extracted from a Harper's Bros atlas, matted, 215 × 240 mm **120.00**
  c1852, "Map Of The State Of Texas From The Latest Authorities," J. H. Young, Thomas Cowperthwait pub, Philadelphia, Galveston City and Northern Texas inset, multicolored, 17 × 14"...................... **150.00**

Virginia, "Americae pars Nunc Virginia," John White, 1590, first separate map of Virginia, engraved, hand colored, ample margins, double page, extensive repairs and restoration in 3 margins on verso, several tears in image neatly closed, 325 × 430 mm **2,425.00**

PHOTOGRAPHS AND PHOTOGRAPH ALBUMS

History: Next to the Bible, the most important book a rural family owned was the nucleated family photo album. Filled primarily with individual head and shoulder photographs, it provided a visual chronicle of the family's ancestry.

The chief problem is that most photographs are unidentified. The individual who received them knew who they were. This information was passed orally from generation to generation. Most was lost by the third and fourth generation.

The principal photographs are Cartes de Visite and Cabinet Cards. It is also common to find memorial cards and mass-produced photographs of important military and historical figures. Pictures that show a person in a working environment, identifiable building or street scene, or a special holiday, e.g., Christmas, are eagerly sought. Most studio shots have little value.

Many of the albums were ornately decorated in velvet and applied ormolu. Some covers contained celluloid pictures, ranging in theme from a beautiful young woman to the battleship *Maine.* The Victorian decorating craze drew attention to these albums in the late 1980s. Prices have risen significantly over the last several years.

Cartes de Visite, or calling card, photographs were patented in France in 1854, flourished from 1857 to 1910, and survived into the 1920s. The most common Carte de Visite was a $2\frac{1}{4} \times 3\frac{3}{4}"$ head and shoulder portrait printed on albumen paper and mounted on a $2\frac{1}{2} \times 4"$ card. Multi-lens cameras were used by the photographer to produce four to eight exposures on a single glass negative plate. A contact print was made from this which would yield four to eight identical photographs on one piece of photographic paper. The photographs would be cut apart and mounted on cards. These cards were put in albums or simply handed out when visiting, similar to today's business cards.

In 1866 the Cabinet Card was introduced in England and shortly thereafter in the United States. It was produced similarly to Cartes de Visite, but could have utilized several styles of photographic processes. A Cabinet Card measured $4 \times 5"$ and was mounted on a $4\frac{1}{2} \times 6\frac{1}{2}"$ card. Portraits in cabinet size were more appealing because of the larger facial detail and the fact that images could be retouched. By the 1880s the Cabinet Card was as popular as the Cartes de Visite and by the 1890s was produced almost exclusively. Cabinet Cards flourished until shortly after the turn of the century.

Tintypes, another photographic form, are also utilized in a Country decor. Sometimes called ferrotypes, they are positive photographs made on a thin iron plate having a darkened surface.

References: Stuart Bennett, *How To Buy Photographs*, Salem House, 1987; William C. Darrah, *Cartes de Visite in Nineteenth Century Photography*, William C. Darrah, 1981; B. E. C. Howarth-Loomes, *Victorian Photography: An Introduction for Collectors and Connoisseurs*, St. Martin's Press, 1974; O. Henry Mace, *Collector's Guide To Early Photographs*, Wallace-Homestead, 1990; Lou W. McCulloch, *Card Photographs, A Guide To Their History and Value*, Schiffer Publishing, 1981; Floyd and Marion Rinhart, *American Miniature Case Art*, A. S. Barnes and Co., 1969; John Waldsmith, *Stereoviews: An Illustrated History and Price Guide*, Wallace-Homestead, 1991.

Collectors' Clubs: American Photographical Historical Society, 1150 Avenue of the Americas, New York, NY 10036; Photographic Historical Society of New England, Inc., PO Box 189, Boston, MA 02165; Western Photographic Collectors Association, PO Box 4294, Whittier, CA 90607.

Periodicals: *Photograph Collector*, 163 Amsterdam Ave, #201, New York, NY 10023.

Museums: International Museum of Photography, George Eastman House, Rochester, NY; Smithsonian Institution, Washington, D.C.; University of Texas at Austin, Austin, TX.

Reproduction Alert: Excellent reproductions of Lincoln as well as other Civil War era figures on Cartes de Visite and Cabinet Cards have been made.

Note: Prices listed are for cards in excellent condition. Cards with soiling, staining, tears, or copy photographs are worth about half the prices listed. The categories on the list are for the most common or collectible types; other collecting categories do exist.

Reproduction Manufacturers: *Albums*—The Roos Collection, PO Box 20668, New York, NY 10025.

Album, red velvet cov front and back, emb scroll design trim on front cov, emb brass clasp, gold-edged heavy cardboard pgs, $10\frac{1}{2} \times 14\frac{1}{2}"$	**55.00**
Cabinet Card, black and white	
Boy, sitting on tricycle, Kansas	**15.00**
Fireman, Chicago, $4\frac{1}{4} \times 6\frac{1}{2}"$	**12.00**
Girl, standing with bicycle	**12.00**
Tom Thumb and Wife, other unidentified man	**20.00**
Two Women, holding violins, Springfield, NY	**8.00**
Woman, seated, looking at her reflection in mirror, EW Lyon, Maple Rapids, MI.	**10.00**
Cartes De Visite	
All Mine, child surrounded by toys, black and white.	**15.00**
Beating Grandpa, grandfather playing game with grandson, printed, hand colored, 1860s	**8.00**
Christmas Tree, boy and girl carrying tree, printed, hand colored, 1860s	**12.00**
His Only Pair, grandmother mending grandson's pants, printed, hand colored, 1860s	**5.00**
Kittens at Peace, three kittens, black and white	**6.00**
Red Riding Hood, in woods, printed, hand colored, 1860s	**15.00**
Sinking the Alabama, boy urinating on boat, printed, black and white	**20.00**
The Little Barber, girl and cat, printed, hand colored, 1860s ...	**10.00**

Album, emb cardboard covers, gold script "Photographs," dark blue, 24 pages, c1935, $11 \times 8\frac{1}{2}"$, $18.00.

Untitled

    Civil War Soldier, seated, black
and white **10.00**

    Post Mortem, deceased child in
mother's arms, black and white   **20.00**

    Young Dressmaker, three girls hold-
ing dolls, black and white **12.00**

Photograph, black and white

    Baseball Player, Kalkaska, MI, 6 × 9″   **10.00**

    Boat, *Maid of the Mist,* Niagara Falls,
close-up, 5 ½ × 6″. **15.00**

    Barryton Fair, entitled "The Fair at
Barryton Mich., Oct. 11th 1909,"
Lyong photo, horses and buggies,
9 × 12″ **40.00**

    Charles Lindbergh, standing in front
of Spirit of St Louis, close-up, 8 ×
10″ **20.00**

    Christmas Tree, decorated branches,
on table, gifts on table and floor,
child sitting in rocker, 10 × 12″   **25.00**

    Civil War theme, inscribed "Nine-
teenth Regiment, Iowa Vol. Inf. as
they appeared on the 24th day of
July at New Orleans, La. after an
imprisonment of 10 months in the
State of Louisiana and Texas" . . .   **600.00**

    Fabric Store, interior, photographer
Welsh, Cadillac, MI, 10 x 12″ . . .   **20.00**

    Family Reunion, large family posed
on lawn before large house, 8 ×
10″ **12.00**

    Horse and Buggy, decorated for pa-
rade, close-up, 10 × 12″ **10.00**

    Lumber Camp, marked "Redy's
Camp #2," 8 × 10″ **25.00**

    Lumberjacks, standing on mountain
of cut logs, winter view, 7 × 9″   **12.00**

    Memorial, "The Maine as she Lay in
Havana Harbor," statistics on
back, 5 × 7″. **10.00**

    Minstrels, nine men, six with black
faces, 8 × 9¾″. **20.00**

    President and Mrs Harding, pr **8.00**

**Daguerrotype Case, wood, raised bee hive
and farm tools within foliate border on lid,
velvet lining, 3¼ × 3¾″, $45.00.**

**Snapshot, black and white, baby in buggy,
1900s, 5 × 3¼″, $8.00.**

    Railroad, marked "Railroad men at
new Camp B. Oct., 21st 1909," 27
men posed outside building, 8 ×
10″ **12.00**

    Road Crew, horse-drawn road grad-
ers, 7 × 9″ **10.00**

    School Children, standing in front of
school, oak leaves cover bare feet,
8 × 9½″. **15.00**

    Ship, Great Lakes ship *D.C. Kerr,*
glued to cardboard, 4 × 6″. **8.00**

    Steamboat, "The *Quincy* on Missis-
sippi River," close-up, 5½ × 6½″   **15.00**

    Street Car, conductors standing out-
side, 5½ × 6½″ **10.00**

    Theater Players, man and woman,
Keene, NH, 5¾ × 7¾″. **10.00**

    US 4th Cavalry, men, wagon, horses,
and tents, 11 × 13″ **25.00**

Tintype, black and white

    Boy, wearing Confederate uniform   **80.00**

    Civil War Soldier, seated, holding
sword, dressed in uniform, in case,
1860s **150.00**

    Girl, doll in doll bed, 2¾ × 3¼″ . . .   **10.00**

    Outdoor View, house and people,
3½ × 5″. **6.00**

    Post Mortem, child, doll under arm,
in case, 1860s **60.00**

    Two Black Women **20.00**

    Woman, Civil War, wearing fancy
dress with stars on blouse, holding
striped shield, 5 × 7″ **85.00**

POST CARDS

History: America went post card crazy in the first
decades of the 20th century. Sending post cards
to friends and relatives became a national pastime.
"Postal" exchanges involving sending packs of
unused cards were commonplace.

    Special albums were developed to store and
display post cards. These quickly found their way
onto library shelves and parlor tables. A typical

album held between one and two hundred cards. In the past, collectors and dealers stripped the cards from these albums and discarded them. Now they are beginning to realize that there is value in the albums themselves as well as the insight that can be achieved from studying the post card groupings.

The golden age of post cards dates from 1898 to 1918. While there are cards printed earlier, they are collected for their postal history. Post cards prior to 1898 are called "pioneer" cards.

European publishers, especially in England and Germany, produced the vast majority of cards during the golden age. The major post card publishers are Raphael Tuck (England), Paul Finkenrath of Berlin (PFB-German), and Whitney, Detroit Publishing Co., and John Winsch (United States). However, many American publishers had their stock produced in Europe, hence, "Made in Bavaria" imprints.

Styles changed rapidly, and manufacturers responded to every need. The linen post card which gained popularity in the 1940s was quickly replaced by the chrome cards of the post-1950 period.

The more common the holiday, the larger the city, or the more popular the tourist attraction, the easier it will be to find post cards about these subjects because of the millions of cards that still remain in these categories. The smaller runs of "real" photo post cards are the most desirable of the scenic cards. Photographic cards of families and individuals, unless they show occupations, unusual toys, dolls, or teddy bears, have little value.

Stamps and cancellation marks rarely affect the value of a card. When in doubt, consult a philatelic guide.

Post cards fall into two main categories: view cards and topics. View cards are easiest to sell in their local geographic region. European view cards, while very interesting, are difficult to sell in America.

It must be stressed that age alone does not determine price. A birthday post card from 1918 may sell for only ten cents, while a political campaign card from the 1950s may bring ten dollars. Every collectible is governed by supply and demand.

References: Many of the best books are out-of-print. However, they are available through libraries. Ask your library to utilize the inter-library loan system.

Diane Allmen, *The Official Price Guide Postcards*, House of Collectibles, 1990; J. L. Mashburn, *The Postcard Price Guide: A Comprehensive Listing*, WorldComm, 1992; Frederic and Mary Megson, *American Advertising Postcards—Set and Series: 1890–1920*, published by authors, 1985; Dorothy B. Ryan, *Picture Postcards In The United States, 1893–1918*, Clarkson N. Potter,

1982, paperback edition; Jack H. Smith, *Postcard Companion: The Collector's Reference*, Wallace-Homestead Book Company, 1989; Jane Wood, *The Collector's Guide To Post Cards*, L–W Promotions, 1984, 1993 value update.

Periodicals: *Barr's Postcard News*, 70 S. 6th Street, Lansing, IA 52151; *Postcard Collector*, Joe Jones Publishing, PO Box 337, Iola, WI 54945; *The Postcard Dealer*, PO Box 1765, Manassas, VA 22110.

Special Note: An up-to-date listing of books about and featuring post cards can be obtained from Gotham Book Mart & Gallery, Inc., 41 West 47th Street, New York, NY 10036.

Collectors' Clubs: *Barr's Postcard News* and the *Postcard Collector* publish lists of over fifty regional clubs in the United States and Canada. Two national groups are: Deltiologists of America (PO Box 8, Norwood, PA 19074) and International Postcard Association (PO Box 66, 1217 F.S.K. Highway, Keymar, MD 21757).

Reproduction Manufacturers: The Evergreen Press, Inc, 3380 Vincent Rd, Pleasant Hill, CA 94523.

Advertising

Argand Base Burning Stove, Perry & Co, Albany, NY, woman and little girl by parlor stove, July 18, 1874 text on back	75.00
Dinger & Conard Co, Leading Rose Growers of America, West Grove, PA, undivided back, 1901–07	8.00
Jack Dempsey's Restaurant, printed, black and white, white border	10.00
La Moreaux Nursery Co, seed catalog, printed, color, divided back, 1913	9.00
Lasha Bitters, view of lower New York from airship, printed, color, divided back, copyright 1911	10.00
Lexington Hotel, comic illus, George McManus, printed, color, white border	15.00
Lindsay Gas Lights and Gas Mantels, the Lindsay Girl, printed, color, divided back, 1907–15	8.00
Voights Milling Co Flour, uncut, printed, color, includes advertising sheet	10.00

Artist Signed

Boileau, Philip, Mis Pat, R & N series, #283, divided back, 1907–15	6.00
Clapsaddle, Ellen	
Halloween, mechanical, black child in white robe, pumpkin in arm moves, #1236, emb, divided back, 1907–15	150.00
St Patrick's Day, #1249, emb, divided back, 1907–15	8.00

Post Card Album, olive green emb cardboard covers, slotted heavy paper pages, 18 pages, 7½ × 13 ½", $15.00.

Fidler, Alice Luella, Utah State Girl, printed, color, divided back, 1907–15 . . . .   12.00

Gassaway, Katherine, "What are little boys . . .," printed, color, undivided back, 1901–07. . . . .   10.00

Gibson, Charles Dana, "In Days to Come the Churches will be Fuller," #103, pictorial comedy, printed, black and white, divided back, 1907–15 . . . .   8.00

Greiner, M, Christmas Bear under mistletoe, #791, emb, divided back, 1907–15 . . . .   8.00

Kirchner, Raphael
  Girl, looking at butterfly on flower, Tuck Continental series 4025, printed, color, gilt trim, white border, undivided back, 1901–07 . . . .   50.00
  Woman with insects, printed, color, gilt trim, undivided back, 1901–07 . . . .   45.00

Leach, B K, San Francisco fire, comic, printed, color, undivided back, copyright 1906 . . . .   10.00

McClure, "On the Golf Links," rabbits playing golf, printed, black and white, undivided back, 1901–07 . . . .   6.00

O'Neill, Rose, Santa being lowered by Kewpies, Gibson #86180, printed, color, divided back, 1907–15 . . . .   45.00

Outcault, R F
  "A Quiet Day in Town," #1, comic souvenir, printed, color, undivided back, P C Co, 1901–07   10.00
  Tige and Bees, "Don't Be Surprised," printed, color, undi-

vided back, J Ottmann Lithograph, 1901–07 . . . .   8.00

Price, Mary Evans, (M.E.P.), "Christmas Wishes," two stockings, baby on pillow, series 875–C, emb, divided back, 1907–15 . . . .   8.00

Twelvetrees, Charles, black girl, series 658, printed, color, divided back, 1907–15 . . . .   10.00

Geographic
  Davenport, IA, "Night View Municipal Stadium," linen, printed, color   15.00
  Hot Springs, disaster, "Central Ave. looking South from Goddard Hotel after the fire, Sept. 6, 1913," black and white, divided back, 1907–15 . . . .   12.00
  New York World's Fair, "The Royal Visitors, King George & Queen Elizabeth," Miller Art Co, linen   6.00
  Tonapab, NV, The Bottle House, house made out of bottles, E Mitchell, Publisher, printed, black and white, divided back, 1907–15   10.00
  Virginia City, MN, bird's-eye view, Stern Publisher, printed, black and white, divided back, 1907–15 . . .   6.00

Holiday
  Christmas
    Santa
      Maroon Suit, walking in snow, emb, divided back 15.00
      Red Suit, in car, emb, divided back, Winsch, 1913 . . . .   30.00
      Tree, child and toys, photographic, divided back, 1915. . .   20.00
  Halloween
    "A Joyful Halloween," three witches riding brooms, man in the moon, emb, divided back, Whitney 15.00
    "May Halloween bring you a joy like this," boy and girl and jack-o-lanterns, series #188, emb, divided back, Tuck, 1907–15 . . . .   8.00

Advertising Post Card, Case Threshing Machine Co, color photo, divided back, c1915, 5½ × 3½", $25.00.

"The Halloween Spirit," cat and witch riding broom and bat in front of full moon, series 80, emb, divided back, 1909 . . . . .   **10.00**

Thanksgiving, Indian couple with turkey, emb, dark green border, divided back, Winsch, 1907–15   **20.00**

Valentine's Day, valentine

Japanese Girl, with cupid, emb, divided back, Winsch, 1910   **20.00**

Mushroom, large, one in install- ment set, #353, emb, divided back, 1907–15 . . . .   **15.00**

Novelty

Copper Harbor, MI, copper, moose, poem, divided back, 3 × 5¼", 1924 . . . .   **8.00**

Empire State Building, card opens, building rises from city, printed, color, white border, Sherwin Baas & Co, 1931 . . . .   **12.00**

Farmer, leather, printed, color, undi- vided back, 1901–07 . . . .   **6.00**

Magic Moving Pictures, pull tab, man kisses woman, printed, black and white, divided back, G Felsen- thal & Co, Chicago, patented Aug 1906 . . . .   **15.00**

Your Fortune Teller, Oracle, Charles Gerlach, emb, divided back, 1910   **8.00**

Photographic, black and white

Colonel W F Cody and his group of Sioux Indians, divided back, trimmed on two ends, 1907–15   **50.00**

Harvesting Tobacco, Weston, MO, tobacco drying in field, undivided back, 1901–07 . . . .   **6.00**

Indians, attacking white men, staged, divided back, 1907–15 . . . .   **8.00**

Masqueraders, five people costumed for Halloween, one with black face, one woman dressed as man, divided back, 1907–15 . . . .   **5.00**

Performing Bears, standing on hind legs, Main St, divided back, 1907– 15 . . . .   **35.00**

Pool Hall, interior, cigars, tables, di- vided back, 1907–15 . . . .   **25.00**

Surfing, Hawaii, divided back, 1907–15 . . . .   **8.00**

Political

Abraham Lincoln, "Log Cabins to the White House," 1905, printed, black and white, undivided back   **8.00**

Republican National Convention, Chicago, June 7, 1916, no women, black and white, divided back **15.00**

Taft and Bryant, presidential elec- tion, "May the Best Man Win," Taft and Bryant in boxing ring, Uncle Sam referee, World Leaders be-

Photographic Post Card, early aviation, black and white, divided back, c1908, 5½ × 3½", $40.00.

hind in stands, printed, color, di- vided back, artist sgd, 1908 . . . . .   **65.00**

Woodrow Wilson, addressing Con- gress, Max Stein, sepia, divided back, 1907–15 . . . .   **12.00**

Transportation

Airplane, "Lincoln Beachy, The World's Greatest Aviator, Souve- nir of Oakland-San Francisco Aviation Meet, Feb 17 to 25, 1912," aeroplane station and avia- tion field, cancellation on back, black and white, divided back . . .   **40.00**

Automobile, auto dealer card, 1936 Hudson Super Straight Eight, printed, color, white border **10.00**

Great Lake Ship, *Clarence A Black,* black and white, white border . . .   **10.00**

Paddle Wheeler, *Mt Washington* on Lake Winnepesucker, NH, black and white, divided back, 1907–15   **12.00**

Motor Car, "San Diego & La Jolla Motor Car, San Diego, CA," printed, color, divided back. **6.00**

Motorcycle, attached sidecar, black and white, divided back **12.00**

Railroad Depot, Boyne City, Gaylord & Alpena Depot, Boyne City, MI, printed, black and white, divided back, 1907–15 . . . .   **10.00**

Sight-Seeing Car, "Seeing Sandusky, OH," printed, color, divided back, 1907–15 . . . .   **12.00**

PRINTS

History: Every room in a Country home had sev- eral wall decorations, the vast majority of which were prints. Several themes dominated—historic, panoramic, nostalgic, patriotic, and religious. In almost every instance, color was the key—the more colorful, the better.

Prints were inexpensive, meaning that they could be changed every few years. Instead of throwing them out, they went into storage. Most prints were framed. In today's market, check the frame. It could be more valuable than the print.

Prints serve many purposes. They can be reproductions of an artist's paintings, drawings, or designs, original art forms, or developed for mass appeal as opposed to aesthetic statement. Much of the production of Currier & Ives fits this last category. Currier & Ives concentrated on genre, urban, patriotic, and nostalgic scenes.

References: Frederic A. Conningham and Colin Simkin, *Currier & Ives Prints, Revised Edition,* Crown Publishers, Inc., 1970; Victor J. W. Christie, *Bessie Pease Gutmann: Her Life and Works,* Wallace-Homestead, 1990; William P. Carl and William T. Currier, *Currier's Price Guide to American and European Prints at Auction, Second Edition,* Currier Publications, 1991; Peter Falk, *Print Price Index 93: 1991–1992 Auction Season,* Sound View Press, 1992; Denis C. Jackson, *The Price & Identification Guide to J. C. Leyendecker & F. X. Leyendecker,* published by author, 1983; Denis C. Jackson, *The Price and Identification Guide to Maxfield Parrish, Eighth Edition,* published by author, 1992; M. June Keagy and Joan M. Rhoden (eds.), *More Wonderful Yard-Long Prints,* published by authors, 1992; William Keagy, et al., *Those Wonderful Yard-Long Prints and More,* published by authors, 1989; Robert Kipp and Robert Weiland, *Currier's Price Guide to Currier & Ives Prints, Second Edition,* Currier Publications, 1991; Stephanie Lane, *Maxfield Parrish: A Price Guide,* L–W Book Sales, 1993; Craig McClain, *Currier & Ives: An Illustrated Value Guide,* Wallace-Homestead, 1987; Rita C. Mortenson, *R. Atkinson Fox: His Life and Work,* Revised, L–W Book Sales, 1991; Rita C. Mortenson, *R. Atkinson Fox, Book Two* L–W Book Sales, 1992; Richard J. Perry, *The Maxfield Parrish Identification and Price Guide,* Starbound Publishing, 1993; Ruth M. Pollard, *The Official Price Guide To Collector Prints, 7th Edition,* House Of Collectibles, 1986; Susan Theran and Katheryn Acerbo (eds.), *Leonard's Annual Price Index of Prints, Posters & Photographs,* Auction Index, Inc., 1993.

Periodicals: *The Illustrator Collector's News,* PO Box 1958, Sequim, WA 98382; *The Print Collector's Newsletter,* 119 East 79th St, New York, NY 10021.

Collectors' Clubs: American Antique Graphics Society, 5185 Windfall Rd, Medina, OH 44256; American Historical Print Collectors Society, PO Box 201, Fairfield, CT 06430; Prang-Mark Society, PO Box 306, Watkins Glen, NY 14891.

Reproduction Alert: Reproductions are a problem, especially Currier & Ives prints. Check the dimensions before buying a print.

Reproduction Craftspersons: Rose Brein Finkel, 11 Salem Way, Malvern, Pa 19355.

Reproduction Manufacturers: Adirondack Store and Gallery, 109 Saranac Ave, Lake Placid, NY 12946; The Americana Collection, 29 W 38th St, New York, NY 10018; Basye-Bomberger/Fabian House, PO Box 86, W Bowie, MD 20715; Cate Mandigo Editions, PO Box 221, Hadley, NY 12835; Country Artworks, PO Box 1043, Orem, UT 84057; Country Lady, PO Box 68, 201 E Main St, Larwill, IN 46764; The Fay Gallery, PO Box 749, 2155 Teton Village Rd, Wilson, WY 83014; Mt Nebo Gallery, RR, Box 243B, Grandma Moses Rd, Eagle Bridge, NY 12057; Southern Scribe, 515 E Taylor, Griffin, GA 30223.

Bachelder, John Badger, publisher, Henry Bryan Hall Jr engraver, Gettysburg, engraving on paper, identified within the matrix, sheet size 18½ × 37¼", framed **325.00**

Bartlett, William Henry, View from Mt Holyoke, hand colored lithograph, 8" w, 6" h **65.00**

Baumann, Gustave, Big Timber Upper Pecos, color woodblock on laid paper, sgd "Gustave Baumann" in pencil with hand in heart chop lower right, titled in pencil lower left, numbered "15 of 100" in pencil lower center, identified on labels on back, 9¾ × 11¼", framed. **1,100.00**

Bradford, L H and Company lithographers, To the Firemen and Citizens of Troy N.Y. . . Presented by Union Fire Company No. Three of Providence, R.I. . . 1854, chromolithograph with hand coloring on paper, identified within the matrix, staining and scattered foxing, sheet size 19¼ × 14½", period frame **325.00**

Currier and Ives, Publishers, 1857–1907

American Homestead Summer, minor stains in margins, repaired tear in top margin, c1868, 15¾" h, 19½" w, matted and framed **225.00**

The Celebrated Boston Team Mill Boy and Blondine . . ., chromolithograph on paper, fully identified in inscription lower margin, staining, losses, stray pencil marks, 1882, sheet size 24½ × 36⅝ ," framed. **325.00**

The Great Ocean Yacht Race between the Henrietta, Fleetwing and Vesta . . ., Charles Parsons lithographer, printed color, additional hand coloring, heavy paperboard, fully identified in inscriptions in lower margin, label from the Old Print Shop, NY, on back, sheet size 23⅛ × 32¾", framed. **2,200.00**

Built by the Amoskeag Manufacturing Company, chromolithograph, Charles H Crosby & Co, Boston, 1819–96, 24 × 31⅞", matted, $4,675.00. Photograph courtesy of Skinner, Inc.

The Ivy Bridge, pen and ink presentation inscription in border, stains, 17" w, 12¾" h, framed **75.00**

The Miniature Ship Red, White and Blue, hand colored lithograph on paper, fully identified in inscriptions in lower margin, toning, minor wrinkles, sheet size 12 × 16", framed **150.00**

The US Sloop of War, Kearage Seven Guns, sinking the Pirate Alabama Eight Guns, hand colored lithograph heightened by gum arabic on paper, fully identified in inscriptions in lower margin, 1864, sheet size 13½ × 17¼", matted, unframed **225.00**

Currier, Nathaniel, Publisher
American Country Life/May Morning, Frances Flora (Fanny) Palmer lithographer, printed color on paper, additional hand coloring,

Golden-Spangled Polish, color litho bookplate, Harrison Weir, Leighton Bros Litho, 1873, image size 5¾ × 7½", $35.00.

Mexican Marmot-Squirrel, No. 25, Plate CXXIV, fully identified in inscriptions on the stone, litho with hand coloring on paper, 25⅞ × 19¼" sheet size, framed, $220.00. Photograph courtesy of Skinner, Inc.

fully identified in lower margin, 1855, sheet size 20¼ × 26¾", period frame **650.00**

Clipper Ship Nightingale, Charles Parsons lithographer, hand colored lithograph on paper, fully identified in inscription in lower margin, label from Old Print Shop, NY, on reverse, 1854, sheet size 18¾ × 25", framed **3,025.00**

The Sinking of the Cumberland (sic) by the Iron Clad Merrimac off Newport News, VA, March 8th 1862, hand colored lithograph, fully identified in inscription in lower margin, sheet size 12 × 15½", framed **440.00**

Endicott & Co
New York Clipper Ship Challenge . . ., lithograph, printed color, additional hand coloring, fully identified in inscription beneath image, label from Old Print Ship, NY on reverse, 1852, sheet size 23½ × 32½", framed **3,300.00**

View of Newburyport, Massachusetts, after John Badger Bachelder, hand colored lithograph, gum arabic, heavy paper, identified in inscription on reverse, sheet size 22¾ × 29½", framed **400.00**

Gearhart, Frances Hammel, Incoming Fog, color woodblock on Japan paper, sgd "Frances H. Gearhart" in pencil lower right, titled in pencil lower left, minor creasing, tape to edges, 10 × 11", matted and framed   **1,430.00**

Mayer and Stetfield lithographers, Built by the Amoskeag Manufacturing Co, Manchester, NH., printed lithograph on paper, black and tan, identified within the matrix, staining, foxing, minute abrasions, sheet size 19½ × 27½", period frame. **465.00**

Unknown Artist

Birdseye View, Centennial Buildings, Phila 1876, chromolithograph, 30¼" w, 24" h, shadowbox frame with gilded liner **50.00**

G Washington, lithograph, black and white, 7⅝" w, 9½" h, eglomise glass and gilt frame **38.00**

Landscape, Bethlehem, Pennsylvania, handcolored engraving, stains, small tears and repairs in margins, 24" w, 18¼" h, framed   **110.00**

Red Peony, Pratt, chromolithograph, 9⅞ × 12⅞", matted and framed . . .   **100.00**

SHEET MUSIC

History: The parlor piano played a major role in the social life of the Country homestead. Family members could often play one or more musical instruments. Families kept abreast of the latest tunes through the purchase of sheet music. Catalogs were the principal source of supply.

Sheet music often was exchanged among friends, thus accounting for the large number of sheets found with an individual's name added in pencil or ink on the cover. Music sheets frequently were bound in volumes. A young bride took her volumes with her when establishing a new home. Based upon the quantity and variety of sheet music found at Country auctions, rural Americans were musically literate.

Sheet music, especially piano scores, dates to the early 19th century. Early music sheets contain some of the finest examples of American lithography.

Sheet music covers chronicle the social and political trends of any historical period. The golden age of the illustrated cover dates from 1885. Leading artists such as James Montgomery Flagg used their talents in the sheet music industry. The cover frequently sold the song.

Once radio and talking pictures became popular, sheet music covers featured the stars. A song sheet might be issued in as many as six different cover versions depending on who was featured. When piano playing lost popularity in the 1950s, the market for sheet music declined. Further, song sheets failed to maintain their high quality of design. There is little collector interest in sheet music issued after 1960 unless associated with a famous personality or rock group.

Center your collection around a theme—show tunes, songs of World War I, Sousa marches, Black material, songs by a particular lyricist or composer—the list is endless. Beware of dealers who attach a high price to subject theme sheets based upon the concept that the specialized collector will pay anything to get what they want. Learn the value of a sheet to a sheet music collector and buy accordingly.

Be careful about stacking your sheets on top of one another. Cover inks tend to bleed. The most ideal solution is to place acid free paper between each cover and sheet. Unfortunately, people used tape to repair tears in old sheet music. This discolors and detracts from value. Seek professional help in removing tape from rarer sheets.

References: Debbie Dillon, *Collectors Guide To Sheet Music*, L–W Promotions, 1988, 1993 value update; Anna Marie Guiheen and Marie-Reine A. Pafik, *The Sheet Music Reference and Price Guide*, Collector Books, 1992; Norman E. Martinus and Harry L. Rinker, *Warman's Paper*, Wallace-Homestead, 1994. **Note:** It is the authors' opinion that the pricing in the Guiheen and Pafik guide is inaccurate and highly manipulative. The book has been roundly criticized, and rightly so, within the sheet music community.

Collectors' Clubs: National Sheet Music Society, 1597 Fair Park, Los Angeles, CA 90041; New York Sheet Music Society, PO Box 1214, Great Neck, NY 11023; Remember That Song, 5821 North 67th Ave., Suite 103–306, Glendale, AZ 85301; The Sheet Music Exchange, PO Box 69, Quicksburg, VA 22847.

Animal Crackers In My Soup, Shirley Temple, 1935 . . . .   **18.00**

April Showers, Al Jolson **10.00**

As Time Goes By, Humphrey Bogart and Ingrid Bergman cov **12.00**

Babes in Toyland **10.00**

Bible Tells Me So, 1940, Roy Rogers and Dale Evans **4.00**

Bicycle Girl, Lena Hulett, 1896. . . . . .   **45.00**

Boy Scout March, Buck & Lowney, St Louis, MO, full color cov, 1912, 11 × 13" **95.00**

By A Wishing Well, Sonja Henie and Richard Greene, 1938 . . . .   **8.00**

Cape May Mount Vernon Polka, Lee & Walker, 1855, 10 × 13" **90.00**

Chattanooga Choo Choo, 1941. . . . . .   **3.00**

Clicqout Club Fox Trot March, banjo playing eskimos, 1926. . . . .   **5.00**

Comin' on the Six-Fifteen, Roy West & Range Riders, 1945 . . . .   **5.00**

Cycling Maid, National Music Co, Chicago, 1895, 10 × 14" **45.00**

For Me and My Gal, Judy Garland . . .   **8.00**

Gathering Sea Shells From the Seashore, Morgan Litho, Cleveland, 1877, 10 × 13" **65.00**

Glow Worm, Paul Lincke, 1902 . . . . .   **5.00**

Gold Dust Twins Rag, multicolored, framed **250.00**

Gone With The Wind, Irving Berlin, 1937, 9 × 12" **25.00**

Good Ship Lollipop, Shirley Temple   **12.00**

Hand Me Down My Walkin' Cane, Calumet Music, 1935 . . . .   **12.00**

Happy Trails, Roy Rogers **25.00**

In The Baggage-Coach Ahead, Herbert H Taylor, NY, red, white, and blue cov, 1908, 10¾ × 14″, $10.00.

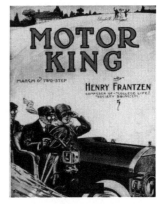

Motor King March & Two-Step, F B Haviland, NY, red and green tone cov, 1910, 10½ × 13½″, $12.00.

Hi-Yo Silver, Lone Ranger, 1938, 9 × 12″   65.00
I Love You California, 1913 . . . .   7.00
I Met Her On The Ferris Wheel, National Music Co, Chicago, 1893, black and white litho of Columbian Expo wheel, 10 × 14″ 75.00
Just A Lonely Hobo, Cole, Autry cov, 1932. . . . .   20.00
Lay Him Low Dirge, dedicated in memory to Gen'l Philip Kearny, 1863, 10 × 13″ 50.00
Lincoln Centennial March, E T Paull, New York, 1909, 11 × 14″ 65.00
Listen To The Mocking Bird, Drumheller, 1908. . . . .   7.50
Little Orphan Annie 15.00
Meet Me In St Louis, Louis, 1904 . . . .   5.00
Moonbeams and Dreams of You, 1907   4.00
Mother O'Mine, 1903, Rudyard Kipling   10.00
Mrs Casey Jones, Newton, 1915. . . . .   30.00
Muzzle the Back Seat Driver & Drive Wherever You May, McDermott, 1928. . . . .   12.00
My Prairie Songbird, 1909, Indian girl cov. 3.00
Oh How I Hate To Get Up In The Morning, Irving Berlin, 1914. . . . . .   7.00
Oh Susanna
  1923, 9 × 12″ 45.00
  1935, Foster 4.00
On the Atchinson, Topeka & Santa Fe, 1945, Judy Garland cov 25.00
Our Flag & Freedom, 1917. . . . .   3.00
Over The Rainbow, whole cast pictured on cov 30.00
Paul Revere's Ride, E T Paull, black and white 30.00
Red River Valley, Gene Autry cov, 1935. . . . .   10.00
Rockaway-Or On Old Long Island's Sea Girt Shore, Geo P Reed, Boston, 1860, 10 × 14″ 65.00

Rosey's Scorcher, George Rosey, 1897, 11 × 14″ 70.00
Saratoga Schottisch, Horace Waters, New York, 1851, 13 × 10″ 85.00
Scorcher, Popular Bicycle Song, Willis Woodward, 1897, 11 × 14″ 95.00
Silver Sleigh Bells, 1906, E T Paull color illus. 30.00
Skating Rink Girl, W Woodward & Co, New York, 1907, 11 × 14″ 45.00
Texas-Where The Mockin Bird Is Singin, Passenger Department, Texas & Pacific Railway, 1898, 11 × 14″   100.00
The Banjo Pickers, Frederic Groton, Carl Fisher Inc, 1929, green illus, white background 20.00
The Baseball, Johann C. Schmid, 1915, published by United States Music Co, blue on yellow 50.00
The Dying Drummer, Thomas Manahan & Mrs Parkhurst, 1864, 10 × 14″   35.00
The Grandpappy Polka, Johnny Giacoma, Gordon Jennings, 1947. . . . .   5.00
The Light of Western Stars, Zeke Williams, 1945. . . . .   5.00
The Little Ford Rambled Right Along, C R Foster, 1914, 11 × 14″ 50.00
The Midnight Fire Alarm, E T Paull, minor wear 25.00
The Trolley Song, Judy Garland, 1944   35.00
That International Rag, Irving Berlin, Uncle Sam cov 10.00
Union Soldier's Battle Song, Oliver Ditson & Co, Boston, 1864, 10 × 13″   35.00
When It's Circus Day Back Home, c1917 . . . .   8.00
White Christmas, Irving Berlin, 1924 .   7.00
When I Dream About the Wabash, Roy Rogers, 1945. . . . .   10.00
You Don't Learn That In School, Nat King Cole, 1947 . . . .   4.00

POTTERY AND PORCELAIN

Rural housewives liked their pottery and porcelain to be decorative, functional, and durable. While the family may own a set of bone china to use on holidays and when special guests visit, their ordinary dinner service was a modestly priced set of American dinnerware.

Use was heavy; breakage inevitable. Replacement pieces had to be readily available. An everyday dinner service lasted between ten and fifteen years before it had to be replaced. When acquiring a new service, the rural housewife wanted the latest pattern.

American dinnerware manufacturers made patterns that appealed strongly to the rural family. Designs were simple and colorful. Bodies and glazes were thick. Fruits and animals often were part of the pattern. Colors were vivid, albeit several patterns stressed pastels and earth tones.

Occasionally sets were assembled through premium offers from a manufacturer, grocery store, or movie theater. The premiums normally provided only place setting pieces. Serving pieces were sold during the premium giveaway period.

Pottery storage vessels were common during the 19th century. Redware had to be glazed on the interior to prevent it from leaking. Pottery baking molds were an important kitchen utensil.

Every rural housewife kept a stash of pottery vases. Flower beds and gardens were a source of pride and accomplishment. Products from Roseville and Weller were highly favored. Occasionally an art pottery piece joined the stash.

Among the pottery in a rural homestead were family heirlooms, objects that belonged to grandparents and great grandparents. Most of these were English in origin since "English" pottery was perceived to be more valuable. English softpaste, especially pieces decorated in gaudy patterns, flow blue, historical Staffordshire, and Staffordshire chimney ornaments are a few of the most commonly found forms.

Finally, do not overlook the souvenir china, ranging in form from plates to vases. This category is still surprisingly affordable. Many pieces sell for under twenty-five dollars despite the fact that they date from the turn of the century.

References: Susan and Al Bagdade, *Warman's English & Continental Pottery & Porcelain, Second Edition*, Wallace-Homestead, 1991; Jack Chipman, *Collector's Encyclopedia of California Pottery,* Collector Books, 1992; Jo Cunningham, *Collector's Encyclopedia of American Dinnerware,* Collector Books, 1982, 1992 value update; Gerald DeBolt, *DeBolt's Dictionary of American Pottery Marks: Whiteware and Porcelain,* Collector Books, 1993; Harvey Duke, *The Official Identification and Price Guide to Pottery and Porcelain, Seventh Edition*, House of Collectibles, 1989; Paul Evans, *Art Pottery of the United States,* Feingold & Lewis Publishing Corp., 1987; Lois Lehner, *Lehner's Encyclopedia of US Marks on Pottery, Porcelain & Clay,* Collector Books, 1988.

Periodicals: *The Daze,* Box 57, Otisville, MI 48463.

ABINGDON POTTERY

History: The Abingdon Sanitary Manufacturing Company, Abingdon, Illinois, was founded in 1908 for the purpose of manufacturing plumbing fixtures. Sometime during 1933–34 Abingdon introduced a line of art pottery ranging from decorative pieces to vases. The company produced over 1,000 shapes and used over 150 colors to decorate their wares. In 1945 the company changed its name to Abingdon Potteries, Inc. Production of the art pottery line continued until 1950 when fire destroyed the art pottery kiln.

After the fire, the company placed its emphasis once again on plumbing fixtures. Eventually, Abingdon Potteries became Briggs Manufacturing Company, a firm noted for its sanitary fixtures.

Collectors' Club: Abingdon Pottery Club, 212 South Fourth, Monmouth, IL 61462.

Bookends, pr
　Cactus, 6" h **60.00**
　Horse Head, black, #441 . . . . **50.00**
　Quill, black and white **125.00**
　Seagull, 6" h **40.00**
Bowl, low, blue, floral decals, 12" d,
　#518. . . . . **25.00**
Candleholders, pr, pink, double, #575   **25.00**
Cookie Jar
　Daisy, 8" h **30.00**
　Granny, white. **225.00**
　Hobby Horse **250.00**
　Jack-O-Lantern **265.00**
　Little Bo Peep **375.00**
　Pineapple, 10½" h **70.00**
　Sunflower. **25.00**
　Windmill **225.00**
Cornucopia, 4½" h, #449. . . . . **25.00**
Drippings Jar, daisy dec, #679 . . . . . . **40.00**
Figure, fish, #444 . . . . **30.00**
Flowerpot
　Cattails, #150 . . . . **30.00**
　Florals, hand dec **45.00**
Geranium Bowl, #543 . . . . **45.00**
Pitcher, ice lip, two quart, #200 . . . . . **35.00**
Planter
　Cactus, Mexican man taking siesta,
　　No. 600 . . . . **75.00**
　Daffodil, No. 668D. **30.00**
　Donkey, blue, No. 669 . . . . **35.00**
String Holder, mouse, 8½" d **80.00**
Vase
　Cactus, #669 . . . . **15.00**
　Classic, blue, No. 115 . . . . **45.00**
　Hourglass, blue, No. 594 . . . . **20.00**
　Tulip, No. 604D **40.00**
Wall Pocket
　Book. **40.00**
　Butterfly, #601 . . . . **65.00**
　Calla Lily, #586D **45.00**
　Cookbook, #676D **45.00**
　Leaf, #724 . . . . **40.00**

pots, which accounted for half the company's sales. The Bauer family sold their interest before the incorporation of the firm in 1922–23. The firm was sold to the Batchelder Tile Co around 1933. The plant closed in 1938 and reopened in 1948. The firm closed for the last time in 1962.

Colored dinnerware was introduced in 1930. A line of art pottery, mainly in Art Deco shapes featuring pastel matte glazes or dark high fired glazes, also was produced. The popularity of this dinnerware pattern kept Bauer alive. New patterns were added in the 1940s, including Monterey and La Linda, but they did not surpass the popularity of the original pattern, Ring.

The wares made in the art line were mostly molded and are usually found with molded marks. Other pieces of Bauer pottery have cobalt blue imprinted marks. Many items were not marked, or were simply stamped "Made In USA."

Gloss Pastel Kitchenware
　Batter Bowl, green, 2 quart **42.00**
　Mixing Bowl, chartreuse, #18 . . . . . **25.00**
　Pitcher, gray, 1 quart. **30.00**
　Teapot, Aladdin, cov
　　Burgundy, 8 cup **65.00**
　　Ivory, 4 cup. **45.00**
La Linda
　Ball Jug, ivory **45.00**
　Carafe, chartreuse, wood handle. . . **20.00**
　Casserole, cov, chartreuse, individ-
　　ual, copper frame, 1½ pint **25.00**
　Chop Plate, blue **32.00**
　Creamer and Sugar, green. **25.00**
　Cup and Saucer, gray **20.00**
　Custard, olive green **10.00**
　Plate
　　6" d, bread and butter
　　　Chartreuse **6.00**
　　　Pink. **5.00**
　　7½" d, salad
　　　Burgundy. **10.00**
　　　Dark Brown. **12.00**
　　9½" d, dinner
　　　Ivory **12.00**
　　　Pink. **15.00**

BAUER POTTERY

BAUER POTTERY LOS ANGELES CAL

History: In 1909 John Andrew Bauer established the Bauer Pottery in Los Angeles, California by relocating workers from the former family owned Paducah Pottery, Paducah, Kentucky. Carloads of machinery were shipped from the Kentucky factory to the new plant.

Production included utilitarian items and an artware line. At one point Bauer was the only California pottery manufacturing red clay flower-

Creamer, La Linda, medium green, imp "Bauer USA" in bottom, 4¾" w, 3" h, $10.00.

Platter, oblong
   10" l, blue **15.00**
   12" l, chartreuse **18.00**
Shaker
   Ivory, small **5.00**
   Turquoise, large **6.00**
Vegetable
   Ivory, oval, 8" l **20.00**
   Pink, round, 9½" d **25.00**
Monterey
   Cake Plate, orange-red, pedestal
     base **100.00**
   Candleholder, yellow **30.00**
   Casserole, cov, metal stand, warmer,
     turquoise. **45.00**
   Cereal Bowl, ivory **15.00**
   Chop Plate, yellow, 13" d **35.00**
   Console Set, Monterey blue, 3 pc   **245.00**
   Cookie Jar, cov, orange-red. **125.00**
   Creamer and Sugar
     Green, individual **40.00**
     Light blue **35.00**
   Cup and Saucer, burgundy **20.00**
   Custard Cup, black **20.00**
   Fruit Bowl, ivory, ftd, 9" d **32.00**
   Gravy Bowl, orange-red **35.00**
   Mustard Jar, cov, ivory **75.00**
   Pitcher, green, 2 quart. **45.00**
   Plate
     6" d, bread and butter
       Turquoise **8.00**
       Yellow. **10.00**
     7½" d, salad
       Light blue **15.00**
       White **15.00**
     9" d, luncheon
       Monterey blue **18.00**
       Turquoise **12.00**
   Platter, orange-red, oval, 12" l **30.00**
   Sauce Boat, turquoise **40.00**
   Saucer, red-brown **8.00**
   Shaker, orange-red **10.00**
   Soup Bowl, burgundy, 7½" d **25.00**
   Stack Set, cov, set of three, orange-
     red, green, and yellow. **100.00**
   Teapot, 6 cup, yellow **60.00**
   Tumbler, ivory, 8 oz **15.00**
   Vase, green, 6" h. **35.00**
   Vegetable Bowl, green, oval, divided   **45.00**
Ring
   Baking Dish, cov, orange-red, 4" d   **25.00**
   Ball Jug, orange-red **75.00**
   Batter Jug, cov, dark blue **95.00**
   Butter Dish, cov, round, dark blue,
     chip inside base rim **60.00**
   Candlestick, ivory **40.00**
   Casserole, turquoise, metal holder,
     7½" d **50.00**
   Cereal Bowl, light blue, 4½" d **20.00**
   Coffee Server, 8 cup, metal handle
     Orange-red **50.00**
     Yellow.   **45.00**

   Custard, white. **1.200**
   Dish, cov, 4" d, dark blue **30.00**
   Eggcup, turquoise **75.00**
   Mixing Bowl
     #12, green. **30.00**
     #18, yellow **32.00**
     #24, dark blue **20.00**
   Pitcher, ivory, ice lip, metal handle,
     2 quart.   **85.00**
   Plate, 10½" d, dinner
     Dark Blue **50.00**
     Orange-Red. **50.00**
     Yellow.   **50.00**
   Platter, 12" l
     Dark blue **40.00**
     Yellow.   **30.00**
   Refrigerator Dish, orange-red base,
     dark blue cov. **50.00**
   Soup Plate, green, 7½" d **25.00**
   Sugar, cov, individual, yellow **27.00**
   Teacup, orange-red **30.00**
   Teapot, black, 2 cup **100.00**
   Tumbler
     Juice, burgundy **40.00**
     Water, yellow, 12 oz **25.00**
   Vase, green, 6" h. **35.00**

BENNINGTON AND BENNINGTON-TYPE POTTERY

History: In 1845 Christopher Webber Fenton joined Julius Norton, his brother-in-law, in the manufacture of stoneware pottery in Bennington, Vermont. Fenton sought to expand the company's products and glazes; Norton wanted to concentrate solely on stoneware. In 1847 Fenton broke away and established his own factory.

   Fenton introduced to America the famous Rockingham glaze, developed in England and named after the Marquis of Rockingham. In 1849 he patented a flint enamel glaze, "Fenton's Enamel," which added flecks, spots, or streaks of color (usually blues, greens, yellows, and oranges) to the brown Rockingham glaze. Forms included candlesticks, coachman bottles, cow creamers, poodles, sugar bowls, and toby pitchers.

   Fenton produced the little known scroddled ware, commonly called lava or agate ware. Scroddled ware is composed of different colored clays, mixed with cream colored clay, molded, turned on a potter's wheel, coated with feldspar and flint, and fired. It was not produced in quantity, as there was little demand for it.

   Fenton also introduced Parian ware to America. Parian was developed in England in 1842 and known as "Statuary ware." Parian is a translucent porcelain which has no glaze and resembles marble. Bennington made the blue and white variety in the form of vases, cologne bottles, and trinkets.

Five different marks were used, with many variations. Only about 20 percent of the pieces carried any mark; some forms were almost always marked, others never. Marks: (a) 1849 mark (4 variations) for flint enamel and Rockingham; (b) E. Fenton's Works, 1845–47, on Parian and occasionally on scroddled ware; (c) U. S. Pottery Co., ribbon mark, 1852–58, on Parian and blue and white porcelain; (d) U. S. Pottery Co., lozenge mark, 1852–58, on Parian; and (e) U. S. Pottery, oval mark, 1853–58, mainly on scroddled ware.

The hound handled pitcher is probably the best known Bennington piece. Hound handled pitchers also were made by some 30 potteries in over 55 different variations. Rockingham glaze was used by over 150 potteries in 11 states, mainly the Mid-West, between 1830 and 1900.

References: Richard Carter Barret, *How To Identify Bennington Pottery*, Stephen Greene Press, 1964; Laura Woodside Watkins, *Early New England Potters And Their Wares*, Harvard University Press, 1950.

Museums: Bennington Museum, W Main St, Bennington, VT 05201; Museum of Ceramics at East Liverpool, 400 E 5th Street, East Liverpool, OH 43920.

Bank, 6½″ h, figural, Rockingham glaze, imp "Anna L Curtis Pittsfield Mass," minor imperfections **275.00**
Book Flask, 5¼″ h, flint enamel, spine imp "Ladies Suffering G," attributed to Lyman Fenton & Co, imperfections, mid 19th C **410.00**
Candlesticks, pr, 7½″ h, Rockingham glaze, attributed to Lyman, Fenton & Co, mid 19th C **425.00**
Coffeepot, 12¾″ h olive and mottled amber glaze, fluted finial, 1849–58   **1,700.00**
Cow Creamer, 5½″ h, Rockingham glaze, imp "N" **300.00**
Curtain Tiebacks, 4¼ and 4½″ d, Rockingham glaze, attributed to Lyman, Fenton & Co, mid 19th C, price for set of four **175.00**
Cuspidor
  8″ d, flint enamel glaze, Lyman Fenton & Co, mid 19th C **200.00**
  10″ d, Rockingham glaze, base marked "Lyman Fenton & Co., Bennington" **225.00**
Figure
  Lion
    7½″ h, Rockingham glaze, attributed to Lyman Fenton & Co, damage, mid 19th C **1,760.00**
    9″ h, 11″ l, mottled flint enamel glaze, marked "Lyman, Fenton & Co, patented 1849, Ben-

nington, VT," imperfections, price for pair **11,000.00**
Poodle, 8″ h, Rockingham glaze, coleslaw dec, attributed to Lyman, Fenton & Co, mid 19th C, minute losses to coleslaw, price for pair **11,000.00**
Flower Pot
  3″ h, redware, molded, imp "Bennington Centennial Aug 16, 1877," small flake **140.00**
  4½″ h, flint enamel glaze, attributed to Lyman, Fenton & Co, mid 19th C, George S McKearin Collection label, star crack **715.00**
Inkwell, Rockingham glaze, attributed to Lyman, Fenton & Co, mid 19th C   **165.00**
Paperweight
  Brick shape, mottled flint enamel glaze, sgd on base "Bennington 1849," repaired handle **165.00**
  Reclining Spaniel, 4½″ l, base marked, imperfections, c1850 . . .   **300.00**
Picture Frames, 8 to 11¾″ h, attributed to Lyman, Fenton & Co, mid 19th C, each with hollow cut silhouette, imperfections, price for set of four. . . .   **385.00**
Pie Plate, 8¼″ d, imp 1849 mark **150.00**
Pipkin
  5½″ d, Rockingham glaze, attributed to Lyman, Fenton & Co, mid 19th C **165.00**
  6¼″ h, cov, Rockingham glaze, molded ribbed body, indistinct Lyman Fenton & Co mark, chips . . .   **990.00**
Pitcher
  7″ h, Rockingham glaze, molded grape dec, marked "Lyman R Fenton East Bennington Vt," c1844–47, repaired. **165.00**
  7¼″ h, flint enamel glaze, attributed to Lyman Fenton & Co, Bennington, VT, small chip on spout, c1850 . . . .   **250.00**

Whiskey Flask, book shape, Departed Spirits/G, flint enamel glaze, 5¾″ h, $625.00.

9" h, Rockingham glaze, hound handle, 19th C, imperfections **200.00**

10½" h, Rockingham glaze, hound handle, 19th C, imperfections . . . **225.00**

12½" h, flint enamel, attributed to Lyman Fenton & Co, mid 19th C, base marked "E" **825.00**

Snuff Jar, 4" h, toby hat, Rockingham glaze, Fenton, 1849 mark **400.00**

Soap Dish, 5¼" l, olive brown and cream flint enamel glaze, green flecks, bottom dated "1849" **125.00**

Teapot, Alternate Rib pattern, flint enamel glaze, pierced pouring spout, period lid **400.00**

Toby Bottle, 10¾" h Rockingham glaze, Lyman Fenton & Co, mid 19th C, marked at base, imperfections **715.00**

Vase

6½" h, flint enamel, hand shape, attributed to Lyman Fenton & Co, mid 19th C **275.00**

9" h, flint enamel, tulip, shape, attributed to Lyman Fenton & Co, mid 19th C **385.00**

Wash Bowl, 14½" d, flint enamel glaze, Alternate Rib pattern, marked "Fenton's Enamel Patented 1849 Lyman, Fenton & Co. Bennington, V.T.", c1855 . . . . **525.00**

BLUE RIDGE WARE

History: Blue Ridge dinnerware was produced by Southern Potteries of Erwin, Tennessee, from the late 1930s until 1956. The company used eight shapes and over 400 different patterns. Reasons for the company's success included cheap labor, easily changed and decorated patterns, and the use of dinnerware as premiums. Many a set of Blue Ridge china was accumulated by going to the theater or using a particular brand of gasoline. Sales of this popular dinnerware were through Sears and Montgomery Ward in the 1950s.

Blue Ridge Pottery is especially appealing to the Country decorator and collectors because of its simple designs. Flowers, roosters, and similar designs grace the patterns. Bright, cheery colors predominate.

Southern Potteries products, including the Blue Ridge patterns, are identified by a variety of marks, ranging from simple script names to elaborate marks featuring rocky landscapes and trees.

References: Winnie Keillor, *Dishes, What Else? Blue Ridge of Course!*, privately printed, 1983; Betty Newbound, *Southern Potteries, Inc. Blue*

Ridge Dinnerware, 3rd Edition, Collector Books, 1989, 1993 value update.

Collectors' Club: Blue Ridge Collectors Club, Rte 3, Box 161, Erwin, TX 37650.

Periodical: *National Blue Ridge Newsletter,* 144 Highland Dr, Blountville, TN 37617.

Beaded Apple

Cup and Saucer. **7.00**

Plate, 10½" d, dinner **6.00**

Blossom Top, Skyline shape, salt and pepper shakers, pr. **28.00**

Carnival, Candlewick shape

Cereal Bowl **8.00**

Creamer and Sugar, cov **20.00**

Cup and Saucer. **7.00**

Plate

6" d, bread and butter **3.00**

9½" d, luncheon **7.50**

Platter, 13" l **15.00**

Salad Bowl, 9" d **15.00**

Soup **10.00**

Vegetable Bowl **12.00**

Cherry Tree Glen

Cereal Bowl, 6¼" d. **6.00**

Creamer **8.00**

Fruit Bowl, 5½" d **5.00**

Plate

6" d, bread and butter **3.00**

7½" sq. **15.00**

9½" d, luncheon **8.00**

Salad Bowl, 9½" d **12.00**

Vegetable Bowl, oval, 9¼" l **15.00**

Chrysanthemum

Cup and Saucer. **9.00**

Plate

6" d, bread and butter **3.00**

7" d, salad **5.00**

9¾" d, dinner **8.00**

Platter, oval, 12" l **10.00**

Soup, flat, 8" d **10.00**

Vegetable Bowl, 9½" d **12.00**

Colonial

Cake Knife. **10.00**

Cake Plate. **12.00**

Cereal Bowl **5.00**

Coaster **8.00**

Cup and Saucer. **5.00**

Demitasse Cup and Saucer **15.00**

Fruit Bowl, 5½" d **4.00**

Gravy Boat **15.00**

Plate

6" d, bread and butter **4.00**

7" d, luncheon. **5.00**

9¼" d, dinner **9.00**

Relish, divided **18.00**

Salt and Pepper Shakers, pr. **15.00**

Vegetable Bowl. **10.00**

Corsage, Astor shape, soup bowl **16.00**

County Fair, Colonial shape, plate, 7" d, salad **15.00**

Crab Apple, Colonial shape
Cereal Bowl	4.00
Creamer, individual	20.00
Cup and Saucer	8.00
Plate	
6" d, bread and butter	5.00
8½" d, luncheon.	8.00
9½" d, dinner	9.00
Platter, oval, 13½" l	8.00
Vegetable Bowl, oval	10.00

French Peasant
Cake Tray, maple leaf shape	85.00
Celery, leafy	100.00
Creamer, pedestal base.	70.00
Ramekin, red base, 5" d	10.00
Salad Bowl	125.00
Salt and Pepper Shakers, pr.	150.00
Vase, handled.	70.00

Garden Lane, Colonial shape, platter, 11¾" l	10.00

Green Briar, Piecrust shape
Cup	5.00
Gravy Boat	24.00
Plate, 9" d, luncheon	5.00

June Bouquet, Colonial shape
Cereal Bowl, tab handle	6.00
Vegetable Bowl, 9½" d.	16.00

Kismet, Skyline shape, teapot	55.00

Mardi Gras
Creamer	3.00
Cup and Saucer	7.50
Fruit Bowl.	4.00
Gravy Boat, underplate.	20.00
Plate	
6½" d, bread and butter	2.00
7" d, salad.	3.00
9½" d, dinner	4.00
Vegetable Bowl, 9" d	8.00

Mountain Crab Apple
Cereal Bowl, 6" d	6.00
Creamer	7.00
Cream Soup, tab handle, 6" d.	9.00
Platter, 15" l	12.00

Mountain Ivy, Candlewick shape
Cup and Saucer	6.00
Plate	
6" d, bread and butter	2.50
10" d, dinner.	10.00
Vegetable Bowl	20.00

Muriel, demitasse cup and saucer. . . .	32.00
Normandie, Skyline shape, cereal bowl	18.00

Pembroke, Colonial shape
Fruit Bowl, 5½" d	3.00
Plate, 9" d, luncheon	5.00

Plantation Ivy
Creamer and Sugar	7.00
Cup and Saucer	5.00
Gravy Boat	15.00
Plate, 6" d, bread and butter	3.00

Poinsettia
Creamer and Sugar	18.00
Cup and Saucer	8.00

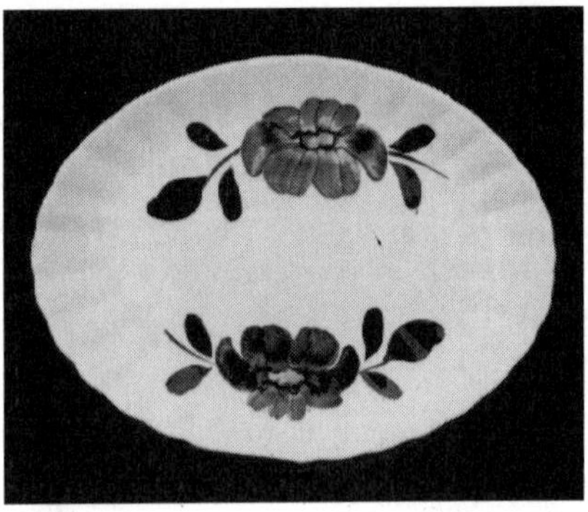

Platter, blue and pink flowers, yellow center, green leaves, 12½" l, $12.00.

Plate	
6¼" d, bread and butter	3.00
9¼" d, dinner	8.00
Tumbler	7.00

Quaker Apple
Cereal Bowl, 6" d	6.00
Dinner Service, service for four. . . .	130.00
Platter, 11" l	15.00
Soup, flat, 8" d	12.00

Red Rooster, Skyline shape
Cup and Saucer	32.00
Plate	
6" d, bread and butter	8.00
9" d, luncheon	25.00
Platter, 11" l	22.00

Rock Rose, Colonial shape, eggcup	18.00

Rustic Plaid, Skyline shape
Casserole, open.	10.00
Creamer and Sugar, cov	7.00
Cup and Saucer	5.00
Dinner Service, service for eight plus salt and pepper shakers, butter, creamer and sugar, gravy, and serving platters, 69 pcs	145.00
Shaker.	8.00

Saratoga, Skyline shape, salt and pepper shakers, pr.	15.00

Stanhome Ivy
Fruit Bowl, 5¼" d	4.00
Cup.	5.00
Dinner Service, service for eight plus serving pcs	150.00
Plate, 6" d, bread and butter	2.50

Sunflower, Colonial shape, plate, 10" d, dinner.	9.00

Sungold #1, Candlewick shape
Creamer and Sugar, cov	30.00
Cup and Saucer	12.00
Fruit Bowl.	4.00
Plate, 10" d, dinner.	10.00
Platter, 14" l	22.00
Salad Bowl, 9½" d	20.00
Soup, flat, 8" d	10.00

Sunny Spray, Skyline shape

Cup and Saucer	3.00
Tumbler	
Juice	7.00
Water	12.00
Wall Sconce	65.00

Waltz Time

Cup and Saucer	10.00
Fruit Bowl, 6" d	8.00
Plate	
7½" sq	15.00
10½" d, dinner	15.00
Platter, 14½" l	25.00
Sugar, cov...................	15.00

Wrinkled Rose, Colonial shape, salad

bowl, 10" d.................	40.00

Yellow Nocturne, Colonial shape

Cereal Bowl, 6" d	5.00
Cup and Saucer	6.00
Demitasse Cup and Saucer	25.00
Dinner Service, service for eight ...	150.00
Fruit Bowl, 5½" d	8.00
Gravy	20.0
Plate	
6" d, bread and butter	3.50
6½" sq	5.00
9¼" d, luncheon	8.00
10" d, dinner...............	9.00
Platter, oval, 11½" l	15.00
Salad Bowl, 9¼" d	17.00
Soup, flat	10.00

CHALKWARE

History: William Hutchinson, an Englishman, invented chalkware in 1848. It was a substance used by sculptors to imitate marble. It was also used to harden plaster of Paris, creating a confusion between the two products.

Chalkware often copied many of the popular Staffordshire items of the 1820 to 1870 period. It was cheap, gayly decorated, and sold by vendors. The Pennsylvania German "folk art" pieces are from this period.

Carnivals, circuses, fairs, and amusement parks awarded chalkware pieces as prizes during the late 19th and early 20th centuries. They were often poorly made and gaudy. Don't confuse them with the earlier pieces. Prices for these chalkware items range from $10 to $50.

Reference: Thomas G. Morris, *Carnival Chalk Prize,* Prize Publishers, 1985.

Reproduction Craftsman: Peg McCormack, Folkwerks, 1760 Elbow Lane, Allentown, PA 18103.

Reproduction Manufacturers: *General*—Basye-Bomberger/Fabian House, PO Box 86, W Bowie, MD 20715; *Santas*—The Painted Pony, 8392 West M-72, Traverse City, MI 49684; Vaillancourt Folk Art, PO Box 582, Millbury, MA 01527.

19TH CENTURY

Bank, dove, orig polychrome paint, damaged and repairs, 11" h.......	100.00
Belsnickle, Santa, polychrome paint, holding feather tree, 10 ½" h.....	150.00
Figure	
Cat	
Reclining, black and white stripe paint, colorful bow, 12" l....	165.00
Seated, polychrome paint, 9½" h	1,250.00
Church, molded, white, decorative pierced pattern, colored glass windows, PA, 9½ × 18"	1,050.00
Dog, seated, painted red, green, and brown, 6" h...............	365.00
Dove, standing on base, pr	750.00
Horse, brown and green polychrome paint, 10⅜" h	900.00
Lamb, reclining, polychrome paint, one ear repaired, 4¼" h.......	150.00
Lovebirds, kissing, polychrome paint, 5" h.................	300.00
Rabbit, seated, yellow and black highlights, 10" h	200.00
Robin, red, black, brown, and gold, old touch-up repairs, 6¾" h.....	535.00
Rooster, yellow, black, and red polychrome paint, worn, 5¼" h	675.00
Squirrel	
6½" h, worn surface, traces of paint	125.00
8" h, solid cast body, old yellow tinted varnish finish, wear and old chips	65.00
Stag, reclining, polychrome, minor paint loss, 16" l, 16" h........	925.00
Woman, elderly features, holding parasol, polychrome paint, 9 ½" h	225.00
Garniture	
Basket of Fruit, pair of lovebirds above, yellow, red, and black, 7¾" h	400.00
Fruit and Foliage, name and "1857" date incised on back, 12½" h ...	2,600.00
Fruit Compote, urn shaped, polychrome paint, 9" h............	850.00

Bank, pear, painted yellow and brown, crazed finish, 4¾" h, $25.00.

Tabby Cat, sleeping, blue collar with red dots, 6" l, $50.00.

Nodder
Cat, worn dark gray patina, black, red, and yellow dec, wear, damage to side of head, 8½" l 200.00
Rabbit, reclining, black and red, neck chip 950.00
Plaque, horse head, polychrome paint, 9½" w, 9" h 100.00
Watch Hutch and Diorama, bust of woman, cloth and paper flowers, mottled brownish yellow paint, bright red, gold, black, and flesh painted bust, reset glass, corner chip on case, paint touch up, 13 ½" h   900.00

CARNIVAL STATUES, 1920s–40s

Buffalo 35.00
Cat, seated, gray and beige, black eyes, 7½" h 45.00
Dog
Boxer, 12" h 25.00
Mother and two pups, seated, completely repainted surface, white, yellow, red, and black, bank, undetermined age, 6½" h 25.00
Spaniel, seated, 6¼" h 15.00
Lady and Dog, full ruffled skirt, floral trim, c1935, 11¼" l 15.00
Little Red Riding Hood, marked "Connie Mamat," 1930s, 14" h. 30.00
Pig, standing, carrying tray, wearing jacket and hat, marked "J Y Jenkins," 1937, 10" h 20.00
Rabbit, holding carrot, white, worn paint, 6⅜" h 50.00

CHILDREN'S FEEDING DISHES

History: Unlike toy dishes meant for play, children's feeding dishes are the items actually used to serve to a child. Their colorful designs of animals, nursery rhymes, and children's activities are meant to appeal to the child and make meal times fun. Many plates have a unit to hold hot water, thus keeping the food warm.

Although glass and porcelain examples from the late 19th and early 20th centuries are most popular, collectors are beginning to seek some of the plastic examples from the 1920s to 40s, especially those with Disney and other character designs on them.

References: Doris Lechler, *Children's Glass Dishes, China and Furniture,* Vol. I (1983, 1991 value update), Vol. II (1986, 1993 value update), Collector Books; Lorraine May Punchard, *Playtime Kitchen Items and Table Accessories,* published by author, 1993; Margaret & Kenn Whitmyer, *Collector's Encyclopedia of Children's Dishes: An Illustrated Value Guide,* Collector Books, 1993.

Collectors' Clubs: Children's Things Collectors Society, *CTCS Newsletter,* PO Box 983, Durant, IA 52747; Toy Dish Collectors, PO Box 351, Camilus, NY 13031.

ABC Plate
Baby Bunting and Little Dog Bunch   55.00
Boy, fishing, Staffordshire, 6" d 35.00
Elephant and two girls, pink transfer, Staffordshire 85.00
Gathering Cotton, blue transfer, craquelure, England, 19th C, 6" d   550.00
Punch and Judy, ironstone, blue transfer, marked "Allertons, England," 7" d. 75.00
Robinson Crusoe, pink transfer, Brownhills Pottery Co, England, 1887–88, 6¼" d 110.00
Shepherd Boy, horn, dog, and goat, 5¼" d 75.00
Stilt Walking, black transfer, polychrome enameling, imp "Meakin," Staffordshire, England, stains and hairline, 5¼" d 95.00
Zebra, transfer, polychrome trim, emb border, Powell & Bishop, 1876–78, 6⅛" d 85.00
Bowl
ABC, multicolored transfer, doctor examining little girl, gold alphabet, scalloped edge, 3½" d 70.00
Dollie Dimples and Sammy, gold rim, Buffalo Pottery 75.00

Britton-Hoffman Co, Little Bo Peep, blue ribbon rim, $45.00.

Buffalo Pottery, transfer, girl petting dog, white ground, gold trim, 6" d, $35.00.

Cereal Set, bowl, mug, and plate
| | |
Bunnykins, Royal Doulton . . . . | **100.00** |
Jack and Jill, Royal Bayreuth, 6" d | **125.00** |

Chamber Pot, garden scene, multicolored transfer, garden scene, gilt trim, Royal Staffordshire Pottery Dickinsen Ltd, England, 8¾" d **60.00**

Creamer
Elephant juggling **35.00**
Rabbit wearing red jacket, green band, Roseville **40.00**
Spatterware, Fort pattern, green, black, and red, blue spatter, 3¼" h **1,450.00**
Tea Leaf, ironstone, lily of the valley blank **195.00**

Cup and Saucer
Children marching, "One Foot Up and One foot Down, That's the Way to London Town," multicolored, Germany **75.00**
Children playing with toys, multicolored, paneled and scrolled body, Bavaria, Germany, U.S. Zone . . . **10.00**
Spatterware, Peafowl pattern, blue, red, and yellow peafowl, rainbow spatter **100.00**

Dinner Service
Floral design, purple transfer, Morley, c1860, 22 pcs **550.00**
Humphrey's Clock, blue transfer, Ridgway, 15 pcs **400.00**
Leaves and Vines, black transfer, pink green, and yellow highlights, pink border, Dimmock, c1860, 26 pcs **550.00**

Dish, Peter Rabbit and Farmer, Beatrix Potter, Wedgwood, 6½" d, 1½" h **32.00**

Feeding Dish
Buddy Tucker with bear **100.00**
Little Bo Peep, Liverpool **60.00**
Little girl with two puppies, marked "Royal Baby Plate, Patd 2–1905". **75.00**
Seated dog, gray band, Roseville, 8" d **65.00**
Two girls dancing with butterflies, sgd "Nippon" **105.00**

Mug
ABC, G for goose, H for horse, black transfer, red and green highlights, 19th C, 2⅜" h **175.00**
Boys with sailboat, fence, brown transfer, c1840, 2½" h **135.00**
Children at play, three scenes, iron-red transfer, printed alphabet, 3" h **125.00**
Faith and Hope, black transfer, pink luster border, 2¼" h **50.00**
Farmer's Arms, God Speed the Plough, marked "B & L, England," 3" h **65.00**
Floral design, black transfer, polychrome enamel highlights, Staffordshire, 3" h **60.00**
Four Children, VWX, "W" is for Whipping, multicolored, Staffordshire **110.00**
Girl and puppy, "Playing With Pompey," black transfer, red, yellow, and green enamel highlights **120.00**
Hickory, Dickory, Dock, transfer, 2½" h **25.00**
Humpty Dumpty on wall, multicolored decal, gold lettering "Humpty Dumpty Sat on a Wall, Humpty Dumpty Had a Great Fall," 2⅝" h **45.00**
The Little Plunderer, multicolored transfer, 2⅜" h **165.00**
The Sisters, blue transfer, barrel shaped, c1860, 4½" h **125.00**
Two children, cat, and dog, brown transfer, 2½" h **35.00**
Two Girls, black transfer, black lettering "A Present for my dear Girl," red border, creamware, 2⅛" h . . . **250.00**

Plate
Blue Willow, 4" d **8.00**
Boy and two dogs, black transfer, polychrome highlights, emb border, purple luster rim, 5⅝" sq . . . **95.00**
Children hanging wash, Germany, 7" d **25.00**
Dr Franklin Maxim, "It Is Hard For An Empty Bag To Stand Free," pawn shop scene, black line border, 6½" d **75.00**

Portland Pottery, cup, brown train scene transfer, yellow handle, 2½" h, $35.00.

Hey Diddle Diddle, brown transfer, Hanley, Great Britain, 4¾″ d	**30.00**
Jesus with scriptures, Staffordshire, c1850, 7″ d	**40.00**
Little Bo Peep, Shenango China . . .	**40.00**
Little May, red transfer, 5½″ d	**35.00**
Old Mother Hubbard and dog at cupboard, brown transfer, polychrome highlights, printed alphabet border, 5½″ d	**145.00**
Punch and Judy, multicolored, Allerton, England, 5½″ d	**30.00**
Sleeping girls and angels, polychrome transfer, 6″ d	**60.00**
Zebra, black transfer, polychrome highlights, raised alphabet border, Powell and Bishop, 6⅛″ d	**95.00**

Platter

Aesop's Fable, "Fox and Sick Lion," brown transfer, Copeland and Garrett, 1833, 15½″ l	**85.00**
Dutch children, multicolored decal, blue line rim, 12″ l	**20.00**

Sugar

Gaudy Staffordshire, black stripe, red, green, and blue floral band, 3¾″ h	**75.00**

Spatterware

Fort pattern, green, black, and red, blue spatter, 4″ h	**625.00**
Peafowl pattern, blue, green, red, and black, blue spatter, paneled, 4⅞″ h	**450.00**
Teapot, spatterware, Fort pattern, green, black, and red, blue spatter, 4⅜″ h	**1,050.00**

Tea Service

Ironstone, floral pattern transfers, teapot, creamer, sugar, six 5″ d plates, six cups, and five saucers	**200.00**
Spatterware, teapot, creamer, cov sugar, waste bowl, six plates, and six cups and saucers, brown bands, white ground, brown stick spatter, England	**485.00**
Star pattern, red transfer, 4¼″ h teapot, sugar, and two cups and saucers, Staffordshire	**170.00**

COORS POTTERY

COORS
ROSEBUD
U. S. A.

History: Coors Pottery was manufactured in Golden, Colorado. Adolph Coors founded both the Coors Porcelain Company and the Coors Brewing Company. By 1914, the war and Prohibition caused the Coors family to concentrate on pottery production. A close alliance with the Herold China and Pottery Company was established. In

1920, the Herold company became part of the Coors Porcelain Company. The demand for good quality American made pottery continued after the war. Coors eagerly tried to fill the need.

Coors produced high gloss, brightly colored dinnerware several years before Fiesta became the rage. Dinnerware lines contained standard table settings as well as casseroles, teapots, coffeepots, waffle sets, and other essentials for the homemakers of the 1930s and 40s. Rosebud is the most widely collected Coors pattern.

Government orders caused the factory to discontinue dinnerware production during World War II. Expansion of other lines caused large quantities of dinnerware to be given to major customers who often used it as premiums. After World War II, a variety of wares, including ovenware, teapots, beer mugs, ashtrays, and vases were made. By the 1980s, all tableware and ovenware lines had been discontinued.

Coors' glazes and colors were industry leaders. Because of this, many companies hired Coors for commemorative pieces. Limited edition items served as employee gifts or giveaways. These are eagerly sought by collectors.

The Coors Porcelain Company continues, but no longer produces the vibrant dinnerware known to Country collectors.

Reference: Robert H. Schneider, *Coors Rosebud Pottery*, Busche-Waugh-Henry Publications, 1984.

Periodical: *Coors Pottery Newsletter,* 3808 Carr Pl N, Seattle, WA 98103.

Mello-Tone

Cereal Bowl, Spring green, 6¼″ d	**10.00**
Cup and Saucer, Azure blue	**15.00**
Gravy, attached underplate, Spring Green	**20.00**
Pitcher, Canary yellow, 2 quart	**25.00**
Plate	
4″ d, Canary yellow	**8.00**
7″ d, Coral pink	**12.00**
Platter, Spring green, oval, 15″ l . . .	**20.00**
Vegetable Bowl, Azure blue, 9″ d	**20.00**

Rosebud

Bean Pot, cov, yellow	**18.00**
Cake Knife, rose, 10″ l	**20.00**
Cake Plate, blue	**30.00**
Casserole, cov	
Blue, French	**50.00**
Green, triple service, medium . . .	**40.00**
Rose	
Straight	**35.00**
Triple service, small	**38.00**
Cereal Bowl, yellow, 6″ d	**10.00**
Cookie Jar, cov, yellow	**35.00**
Cream Soup, blue, 4″ d	**15.00**
Cup and Saucer, green	**8.00**
Custard Cup, blue	**12.00**
Honey Pot, cov, rose	**25.00**

Mixing Bowl, handle, orange 30.00
Pie Baker, yellow 18.00
Plate
  6" d, bread and butter, rose. 8.00
  7" d, salad, yellow. 10.00
  9½" d, dinner
    Blue. 12.00
    Green 15.00
    Yellow. 15.00
Platter
  Ivory 35.00
  Orange 25.00
Pudding
  Orange, large 60.00
  Rose
    Medium. 30.00
    Small. 12.00
Salt and Pepper Shakers, pr, blue 20.00
Soup Plate, 8" d, green 15.00
Teapot, large, rose 50.00
Utility Jar, cov, yellow 35.00
Vase, 8" h, yellow. 20.00

CROOKSVILLE CHINA COMPANY

History: The Crooksville China Company, Crooksville, Ohio, was founded in 1902 for the manufacture of artware such as vases, flowerpots and novelties. Dinnerware soon became its stock in trade. Crooksville made a good grade of semi-porcelain that rivaled more expensive vitrified ware. The factory continued until 1959 and employed over 300 people.

Crooksville China produced several patterns. The decoration of their wares was primarily through the use of decals. These detailed decals are very colorful and durable. Silhouette was one of the most popular patterns. The Silhouette decal is in black on a yellow glaze ground and shows two men sitting at a table with a dog looking up at them, waiting for food. Other patterns feature country-type decorations.

Crooksville answered the need for attractive utilitarian pieces. Earliest production included teapots, waffle sets, jugs, spice jars, and covered baking sets. Dinnerware followed this line of interestingly shaped pieces.

The Crooksville China Company used over fifteen different marks. Some contain pattern names and dates, others were simply the company name.

Autumn
  Casserole, 8" d 15.00
  Coaster, 4" d. 5.00
  Coffeepot 25.00
  Cup and Saucer 6.00
  Pie Baker, 10" d 7.50

Plate
  6" d, bread and butter 1.50
  9¾" d, dinner 4.00
Platter, rect, 11½" l. 5.00
Sugar. 10.00
Vegetable Dish, rect, 9¼" l 9.00
Petit Point House
  Cereal Bowl, 6" d 5.00
  Cup and Saucer. 6.00
  Fruit Bowl, 5" d. 4.00
  Pie Baker. 15.00
  Plate
    6" d, bread and butter 3.00
    9" d, luncheon. 8.00
  Platter, 11" l 12.00
  Soup Bowl, 7¼" d. 4.00
  Teapot. 25.00
  Utility Jar, cov. 45.00
  Vegetable Bowl, 9" d 8.00
Silhouette
  Batter Jug, cov. 45.00
  Casserole, cov. 30.00
  Creamer 12.00
  Cup and Saucer. 10.00
  Juice Pitcher, large 20.00
  Mixing Bowl, Pantry Bak-In. 10.00
  Pie Baker, 10" d 18.00
  Plate
    8" d, salad 8.00
    10" d, dinner 10.00
  Platter, oval, 11½" l 15.00
  Teapot. 20.00
  Tray, handled, 11¾" l 18.00
  Tumbler 15.00
Vegetable Medley
  Casserole, 8" d 18.00
  Coffeepot 30.00
  Creamer 8.00
  Cup and Saucer. 5.00
  Custard Cup 4.00

Silhouette, cake plate: $20.00; pie baker: $18.00.

Plate

6" d, bread and butter	**4.00**
9" d, luncheon	**6.00**
9¾" d, dinner	**8.00**
Platter, rect, 15½" l.	**12.00**
Sugar	**10.00**
Syrup Pitcher	**20.00**
Vegetable Dish, rect, 9¼" l.	**15.00**

DEDHAM POTTERY

History: Alexander W. Robertson established the Chelsea Pottery in Chelsea, Massachusetts, in 1860. In 1872 it was known as the Chelsea Keramic Art Works.

In 1895 the pottery moved to Dedham, and the name was changed to Dedham Pottery. Their principal product was gray crackleware dinnerware with a blue decoration, the rabbit pattern being the most popular. The factory closed in 1943.

The following marks help determine the approximate age of items: (1) Chelsea Keramic Art Works, "Robertson" impressed, 1876–1889; (2) C.P.U.S. impressed in a cloverleaf, 1891–1895; (3) Foreshortened rabbit, 1895–1896; (4) Conventional rabbit with "Dedham Pottery" stamped in blue, 1897; (5) Rabbit mark with "Registered", 1929–1943.

References: Paul Evans, *Art Pottery of the United States,* Feingold & Lewis Publishing Corp, 1987; Lloyd E. Hawes, *The Dedham Pottery And The Earlier Robertson's Chelsea Potteries,* Dedham Historical Society, 1968.

Reproduction Manufacturers: Country Loft, 1506 South Shore Park, Hingham, MA 02043; The Potting Shed, 43 Bradford St, Box 1287, Concord, MA 01742.

Bowl

Azalea pattern, cut edge, "Dedham Pottery, Registered," two imp rabbits, 9¼" d, 2¼" h	**925.00**
Grape pattern, "Dedham Pottery," 7" d, 3¼" h	**225.00**
Rabbit pattern	
5¾" d, cov, blue rabbit stamp . . .	**175.00**
7½" d, flared rim, blue rabbit stamp	**150.00**
8" sq	**300.00**
Candle Holders, pr, Rabbit pattern around base, blue bands around socket and rim, blue "Dedham Pottery, Registered," 1⅜" h	**375.00**

Candle Snuffer, rabbit border, 2" h . . .	**650.00**
Celery Tray, Rabbit pattern, 10" l	**300.00**
Charger, Elephant pattern, stamped and imp marks, early 20th C, 12" d	**1,500.00**
Chop Plate, 12" d	
Lobster pattern, imp marks and stamp, glaze bursts	**875.00**
Rabbit pattern, imp mark twice and stamp	**275.00**
Coaster, single elephant medallion, "Dedham Pottery, Registered, Dedham Tercentenary," 4" d	**1,325.00**
Coffeepot, Rabbit pattern, blue rabbit stamp on bottom, 8" h	**175.00**
Creamer and Sugar, Rabbit pattern, stamped mark, 4¾" h sugar.	**350.00**
Cup and Saucer	
Azalea pattern, blue rabbit stamp	**50.00**
Elephant pattern, stamp registered mark, 6" d saucer	**775.00**
Demitasse Cup and Saucer, Rabbit pattern, blue "Dedham Pottery, Registered" and two imp rabbits on saucer bottom, 2½" h cup	**425.00**
Eggcup, blue rabbit stamp on bottom, 2½" h, set of six	**350.00**
Flower Holder, standing rabbit dec, applied blue facial features, fifteen holes, "Dedham Pottery, Registered," 6¼" h	**1,975.00**
Humidor, two elephants, inscribed "Dedham Pottery/May 1917/#79," 7" h.	**1,980.00**
Mug, Rabbit pattern, incised and stamped marks, 6" h	**325.00**
Pitcher	
Elephant pattern, baby elephant, "Dedham Pottery, Registered," 5" h.	**2,100.00**
Rabbit pattern, rabbit leaping over lower handle, initialed "P," imp and stamp marks, 8⅜" h.	**1,325.00**
Plate	
Azalea pattern, blue rabbit mark, 9¾" d	**45.00**
Butterfly pattern, blue ink mark, one imp rabbit, 8¾" d	**425.00**

Plate, bread and butter, Azalea, 6" d, $75.00.

Cherry pattern, stamped mark, 20th
C, 9¾" d **130.00**
Duck pattern, imp and stamped
marks, 8⅝" d **375.00**
Golden Gate, San Francisco, in-
scribed on reverse to "M Sheperd,"
artist's cipher for Hugh C Robertson, imp mark, enhanced blue
stamp, chip on foot, glaze bursts,
10" d **2,750.00**
Grape pattern, stamped and imp rab-
bit marks, early 20th C, 9 ¾" d   **75.00**
Horse Chestnut pattern, stamped
mark, two imp marks, base chip,
early 20th C, 7½" d **125.00**
Iris pattern, blue rabbit stamp, 6½" d   **45.00**
Lion and Owl pattern, bisque, dark
pattern, imp mark, artist initials of
Hugh C Robertson, c1900, 10" d.   **1,550.00**
Lobster pattern, imp and stamped
marks, foot chip, 8¾" d, price for
set of five. **1,650.00**
Lotus Water Lily pattern, "Dedham
Pottery, Registered," 8¼" d **200.00**
Magnolia pattern, blue rabbit stamp
and one incised rabbit mark,
8⅜" d **25.00**
Moth pattern, imp and stamped
marks, 6¼" d. **375.00**
Poppy pattern, imp mark, stamp and
inscribed cross, 8½" d **495.00**
Snow Tree pattern, slightly raised,
blue rabbit stamp, 6" d **75.00**
Swan pattern, blue rabbit stamp and
two incised rabbits, 6⅛" d. **250.00**
Turkey pattern, stamped and imp
marks, minor imperfections, 20th
C, 8½" d **135.00**
Salt and Pepper Shakers, pr, Rabbit pat-
tern, early 20th C, 2 ¾" h **300.00**
Sugar Bowl, cov, blue rabbit mark,
4¼" h **60.00**
Teapot, Rabbit pattern, blue band
around lid and rim, blue ink "Dedham Pottery, 7" w handle to spout,
6" h **1,875.00**

**Plate, bread and butter, Butterfly, 6⅛ " d,
$165.00.**

Tile, Rabbit pattern, 5½" sq **250.00**
Vase, Chelsea Keramic Art Works
4½" h, bisque, c1880, imp "CKAW"
Eight recesses framed and ac-
cented by incising **275.00**
Rounded shoulder, incised shad-
owing, four sq sides, circular ftd
base **275.00**
6⅝" h, center cylindrical neck sur-
rounded by four smaller necks,
bulbous body, circular foot, mustard glaze, imp mark of Hugh C
Robertson, c1880 . . . .   **825.00**
6¾" h, gray crackle glaze, imp mark,
peppering, c1886 . . . .   **165.00**
9½" h, dragon's blood and olive
green iridescent gloss glaze, imp
"CKAW," crazing, base pulls,
c1888 . . . .   **1,540.00**

DORCHESTER POTTERY

History: Dorchester Pottery was a contemporary
of Dedham Pottery. George Henderson made this
stoneware type pottery in Dorchester, Connecticut. Production began in 1895 and continued
until the 1980s.

One of the most popular lines began in the
1940s. The motif is blue and white and uses a New
Jersey clay base. Complete dinner services were
made. The decoration varied from a painted cobalt blue decoration to a sgraffito decoration,
where pieces are almost totally glazed with cobalt
blue and then have portions scraped away to
reveal the light body below. Both molded and
thrown pieces are known. Traditional New England designs of codfish, pinecones, scrolls, stripes,
lace, blueberries, and even pussy willows are
common. Some special order patterns have a
bayberry green or gold glaze.

Like many other pottery companies, Dorchester
Pottery also made commercial items. Their high-
fired stoneware was excellent for acid proof appli-
cations and was used widely in the medical and
food preparation industries. It is the hand decorated and hand thrown pieces that attract the
attention of the Country decorators and collectors.

Most pieces of Dorchester Pottery are signed by
the decorators and potters. Each bears the pottery
name. A lead stamped mark was used until 1941.

Bowl
Bicentennial, blue plum dec, 8" d   **165.00**
Blueberry pattern, cobalt blue,
marked "CAH," 6" d, set of seven   **315.00**
Clown face, cobalt blue dec, white
ground, 5¾" d **110.00**
Candy Dish, starfish shape, marked
"JM" **75.00**
Casserole, cov, Blueberry pattern,
8½" d **125.00**

Cup, blue dec, stamp mark, 2¾" d, 2" h, $25.00.

Chowder Bowl, cobalt blue whale dec,
  marked "CAH" 100.00
Cup, Blueberry pattern, marked
  "CAH," set of three 65.00
Foot Warmer, brown glaze, attached
  wood back rest, 9½" h 75.00
Mug
  Advertising, Tuft's Dental, 1933–
  1958, ochre and blue striped
  glazes, white ground, 4⅝" h 75.00
  Bicentennial, grapes dec 145.00
Pitcher
  Blueberry pattern, marked "N Ricci,
  CAH" 100.00
  Sgraffito dec, cov, blue glaze, syrup   85.00
Shell Dish, ochre 65.00
Soup Tureen, cov, double handles,
  blue glaze, orig paper labels, 5¾" d,
  set of eight 200.00

EDWIN M. KNOWLES CHINA COMPANY

History: In 1900 Edwin M. Knowles established the Edwin M. Knowles China Company in Chester, West Virginia. Company offices were located in East Liverpool, Ohio. The company made semiporcelain dinnerware, kitchenware, specialties, and toilet wares and was known for its commitment to having the most modern and best equipped plants in the industry.

In 1913 a second plant in Newell, West Virginia, was opened. The company operated its Chester pottery until 1931, at which time the plant was sold to the Harker Pottery Company. Production continued at the Newell pottery. Edwin M. Knowles China Company ceased operations in 1963.

The Edwin M. Knowles Company name resurfaced in the 1970s when the Bradford Exchange acquired rights to the company's name. The Bradford Exchange uses the Knowles name to front some of its collector plate series, e.g., *Gone with the Wind* and *The Wizard of Oz*. The name also has been attached to Rockwell items. Bradford Knowles marked pieces are made by off shore manufacturers, not in the United States at either of the old Knowles locations.

Do not confuse Edwin M. Knowles China Company with Knowles, Taylor, and Knowles, also a manufacturer of fine dinnerware. They are two separate companies. The only Edwin M. Knowles China Company mark that might be confusing is "Knowles" spelled with a large "K".

Knowles dinnerware lines enjoyed modest sales success. No one line dominated. Among the more popular lines with general collectors are: Deanna, a solid color line found occasionally with decals introduced in 1938; Esquire, designed by Russel Wright and manufactured between 1956 and 1962; and Yorktown, a modernistic line introduced in 1936 found in a variety of decal patterns such as Bar Harbor, Golden Wheat, Penthouse, and Water Lily.

Country collectors concentrate on Daisy, Fruits, Poppy, Tulip, Tuliptime, Wheat, and Wildflower decal patterns. The patterns are colorful, light, and airy. Most are commonly found on plain white pieces with little or no border decoration.

When collecting decal pieces, buy only pieces whose decals are complete and still retain their vivid colors. Edwin M. Knowles China Company did make a Utility Ware line that has found some favor with kitchen collectibles collectors. Prices for Utility Ware range between half and two-thirds of the prices for similar pieces in the dinnerware patterns.

References: Jo Cunningham, *The Collector's Encyclopedia of American Dinnerware*, Collector Books, 1982, 1992 value update; Harvey Duke, *The Official Identification and Price Guide to Pottery and Porcelain, Seventh Edition*, House of Collectibles, 1989; Lois Lehner, *Lehner's Encyclopedia of U. S. Marks on Pottery, Porcelain & Clay*, Collector Books, 1988.

Deanna
  Coffeepot, cov, red and blue stripes   40.00
  Creamer and Sugar, cov, light blue   25.00
  Cup and Saucer, yellow 10.00
  Eggcup, double, turquoise 12.00
  Plate
    6" d, bread and butter, yellow . . .   4.00
    8" d, salad, orange-red 6.00
    10" d, dinner, dark blue 10.00
  Platter, green, 12" d 15.00
  Vegetable Bowl, orange-red, 8" d   18.00
Esquire
  Bowl
    5½" d, fruit, Snowflower 8.00
    6¼" d, cereal, Queen Anne's Lace   10.00
  Cup and Saucer, Snowflower 18.00
  Plate
    6¼" d, bread and butter, Botanica   6.00
    8¼" d, salad, Seeds 9.00
    10¾" d, dinner, Grass 12.00
  Platter, oval
    13" l, Queen Anne's Lace 20.00
    16" l, Solar 30.00

Yorktown, chop plate, maroon, 11¾" d, $12.00.

Teapot, Botanica.	**95.00**
Vegetable Bowl, divided, Seeds . . .	**65.00**

Yorktown

Bowl, cereal, green, 6" d.	**6.00**
Casserole, yellow	**35.00**
Chop Plate, burgundy, 10¾" d	**15.00**
Cup and Saucer, orange-red	**8.00**
Custard Cup, green	**6.00**
Gravy Boat, pink.	**18.00**
Plate	
6" d, bread and butter, yellow. . .	**5.00**
8" d, salad, cadet blue.	**10.00**
10" d, dinner, orange-red	**12.00**
Platter, russet, 12" d	**20.00**
Teapot, orange-red	**50.00**

FIESTA WARE

History: The Homer Laughlin China Company introduced Fiesta dinnerware in January, 1936, at the Pottery and Glass Show in Pittsburgh, Pennsylvania. Fredrick Rhead designed the pattern; Arthur Kraft and Bill Bensford molded it. Dr. A. V. Blenininiger and H. W. Thiemecke developed the glazes. A vigorous marketing campaign took place between 1939 and 1943.

The original five colors were red, dark blue, light green (with a trace of blue), brilliant yellow, and ivory. In 1938 turquoise was added; red was removed in 1943 because of the war effort and did not reappear until 1959. In 1951 light green, dark blue, and ivory were retired and forest green, rose, chartreuse, and gray were added to the line. Other color changes took place in the late 1950s, including the addition of a medium green.

Fiesta ware was redesigned in 1969 and discontinued in 1972–73. In 1986 Fiesta was reintroduced by Homer Laughlin China Company. The new china body shrinks more than the old semi-vitreous and ironstone pieces, thus making the new pieces slightly smaller than the earlier pieces. The modern colors also differ in tone. The cobalt blue is darker than the old blue. Other modern colors are black, white, apricot, and rose.

Fiesta is one of the most widely recognized dinnerware patterns. During its heyday it was probably the most popular dinnerware made in America. Original production began with fifty-four items. Several specialized pieces and sets were made in the 1940s as sales stimulators. These limited production items, such as handled chop plates, covered refrigerator jars, and French casseroles are highly prized today. Millions of pieces of Fiesta ware were manufactured during its forty years of production.

The molds used originally had the name molded into the base of the piece. The new 1986 line is made from original molds but also carries a stamped mark making them easily recognizable.

There is some concern today over the red glaze. Uranium oxide was used as a base for this bright glaze. During World War II this glaze was suspended and the popular color did not reappear until May of 1959. Production of this uranium oxide glaze continued until 1972. Some radiation can be detected on the red glazed pieces and these should not be used. Care should be taken when storing and displaying them as well.

References: Linda D. Farmer, *The Farmer's Wife Fiesta Inventory and Price Guide,* published by author, 1984; Sharon and Bob Huxford, *The Collectors Encyclopedia of Fiesta, Seventh Edition,* Collector Books, 1992.

Periodical: *Fiesta Collector's Quarterly,* 19238 Dorchester Circle, Strongsville, OH 44136.

Ashtray	
Green	**25.00**
Red.	**35.00**
Yellow	**25.00**
Bowl	
4¾" d	
Dark green.	**20.00**
Light green.	**15.00**
5½" d, fruit	
Cobalt blue	**20.00**
Light green.	**15.00**
Red.	**20.00**
Yellow.	**18.00**
6" d, dessert	
Chartreuse.	**50.00**
Gray	**50.00**
Light green.	**22.00**
Rose	**50.00**
Turquoise	**50.00**
8½" d	
Cobalt blue	**30.00**
Green	**20.00**
Bud Vase, ivory.	**50.00**
Cake Plate, yellow, Kitchen Kraft	**30.00**

Candlesticks, pr
   Ivory, bulbous........................ **45.00**
   Pink, tripod........................... **85.00**
   Turquoise, bulbous.................... **60.00**
   Yellow, tripod........................ **415.00**
Carafe
   Cobalt blue........................... **225.00**
   Red.................................. **225.00**
   Yellow............................... **115.00**
Casserole, cov, 8½" d, Kitchen Kraft
   Cobalt blue........................... **125.00**
   Light green........................... **40.00**
   Turquoise............................ **90.00**
   Yellow............................... **200.00**
Chop Plate, 13" d
   Chartreuse........................... **75.00**
   Cobalt blue........................... **50.00**
   Gray................................. **30.00**
   Light green........................... **20.00**
   Turquoise............................ **20.00**
   Yellow............................... **35.00**
Coffeepot, cov
   Ivory................................ **90.00**
   Red.................................. **180.00**
   Turquoise............................ **135.00**
   Yellow............................... **135.00**
Compote, 12" d
   Cobalt blue........................... **135.00**
   Turquoise............................ **110.00**
Creamer
   Cobalt blue
      Side handle..................... **25.00**
      Stick handle.................... **30.00**
   Ivory, side handle.................... **15.00**
   Red, stick handle.................... **16.00**
   Turquoise, side handle.............. **15.00**
Cream Soup
   Cobalt blue, cov..................... **35.00**
   Red.................................. **40.00**
   Turquoise............................ **35.00**
   Yellow............................... **30.00**
Cup
   Chartreuse........................... **18.00**
   Cobalt blue........................... **20.00**
   Dark green........................... **18.00**
   Gray................................. **24.00**

Pitcher, juice, ice lip, yellow, 5⅞" h, $32.00.

   Turquoise............................ **18.00**
   Yellow............................... **18.00**
Deep Plate
   Dark green........................... **30.00**
   Gray................................. **35.00**
   Light green........................... **24.00**
   Red.................................. **27.00**
   Rose................................. **30.00**
   Turquoise............................ **22.00**
   Yellow............................... **22.00**
Demitasse Cup and Saucer, cobalt
   blue................................. **50.00**
Demitasse Pot, red..................... **275.00**
Eggcup
   Cobalt blue........................... **35.00**
   Light green........................... **30.00**
   Yellow............................... **30.00**
Fork, light green, Kitchen Kraft....... **65.00**
Gravy Boat
   Cobalt blue........................... **50.00**
   Green................................ **20.00**
   Light blue............................ **35.00**
   Red.................................. **50.00**
Jar, cov, red, Kitchen Kraft........... **315.00**
Jug
   Cobalt blue, two pint................. **75.00**
   Green, cov, Kitchen Kraft............ **170.00**
   Ivory, 3 pint......................... **50.00**
Juicer, cobalt blue..................... **25.00**
Marmalade
   Green................................ **150.00**
   Turquoise............................ **160.00**
Mixing Bowl
   #1
      Red.......................... **90.00**
      Turquoise.................... **95.00**
   #2
      Cobalt blue.................. **70.00**
      Turquoise.................... **60.00**
   #3, ivory............................ **65.00**
   #4
      Red.......................... **80.00**
      Turquoise.................... **60.00**
   #5, cobalt blue...................... **85.00**
   #6, turquoise........................ **80.00**
   #7, green............................ **150.00**
   Nested Set, #1 turquoise, #2 red, #3
     cobalt blue, #4 yellow, #5 tur-
     quoise, #6 red, #7 turquoise, price
     for set............................ **550.00**
Mug
   Cobalt blue........................... **60.00**
   Forest green.......................... **40.00**
   Rose................................. **40.00**
Mug, Tom and Jerry
   Chartreuse........................... **65.00**
   Forest green.......................... **60.00**
   Ivory................................ **30.00**
Mustard, cov
   Light green........................... **50.00**
   Red.................................. **145.00**

Nappy
  8½" d
    Gray **40.00**
    Red **32.00**
    Rose **45.00**
  9½" d, cobalt blue **60.00**
Onion Soup, cov, ivory **450.00**
Pie Baker, green, Kitchen Kraft **35.00**
Pitcher, red, disc. **145.00**
Plate
  6" d
    Cobalt blue **5.00**
    Ivory **6.00**
    Red **4.50**
    Rose **9.00**
    Turquoise **5.00**
  7" d
    Gray **10.00**
    Rose **10.00**
    Turquoise **6.00**
    Yellow. **7.00**
  9" d
    Chartreuse. **10.00**
    Cobalt blue **18.00**
    Dark green **10.00**
    Gray **19.00**
    Ivory **18.00**
    Light green **10.00**
    Red **12.50**
    Rose **18.00**
    Turquoise **10.00**
    Yellow. **10.00**
  10" d
    Light green **20.00**
    Red **25.00**
  10½" d, grill, cobalt blue **40.00**
  12" d, grill
    Ivory **32.00**
    Yellow. **30.00**
  13" d, grill, cobalt blue **25.00**
Platter
  12" l, oval
    Chartreuse. **35.00**
    Forest green. **28.00**
    Medium green. **45.00**
    Turquoise **15.00**
  15" d
    Cobalt blue **40.00**
    Red **55.00**
    Turquoise **25.00**
Refrigerator Dish, cov, round, Kitchen
  Kraft
    Cobalt blue. **75.00**
    Green **25.00**
Relish Tray, light blue **20.00**
Salad Bowl
  Ivory, ftd **150.00**
  Red, individual **60.00**
Salt and Pepper Shakers, pr
  Dark green **40.00**
  Red, Kitchen Kraft. **75.00**

Vase, turquoise, 6¼" h, $35.00.

Sauce Boat
  Chartreuse. **55.00**
  Gray **80.00**
Saucer
  Chartreuse. **4.00**
  Cobalt blue **4.00**
  Ivory **3.00**
  Red **4.00**
  Turquoise **2.00**
  Yellow **3.00**
Spoon, cobalt blue, Kitchen Kraft **65.00**
Sugar, cov, cobalt blue **25.00**
Syrup, ivory **195.00**
Teacup and Saucer
  Chartreuse. **35.00**
  Light green **20.00**
  Medium green. **45.00**
  Yellow **20.00**
Teapot
  Red, large, pinpoint flake on rim . . .   **100.00**
  Yellow **90.00**
Tidbit Tray, 3 tiered, medium green   **175.00**
Tray, figure 8, cobalt blue **55.00**
Tumbler
  Cobalt blue, water. **40.00**
  Cobalt blue, juice **30.00**
  Green, juice **15.00**
  Rose, juice **35.00**
  Red, water. **55.00**
Vase
  8" h
    Green **295.00**
    Ivory **250.00**
    Turquoise **300.00**
  10" h, cobalt blue **500.00**

FLOW BLUE

History: Flow blue, or flowing blue, is the name
applied to a cobalt blue and white china, whose
color, when fired in a kiln, produced a flowing or
smudged effect. The blue varies in color from dark
cobalt to a grayish or steel blue. The flow varies
from very slight to a heavy blur where the pattern
cannot be easily recognized. The blue color does
not permeate through the china.

Flow blue was first produced around 1835 in the Staffordshire district of England by a large number of potters including Alcock, Davenport, J. Wedgwood, Grindley, New Wharf, and Johnson Brothers. Most early flow blue, 1830s to 1870s, was ironstone. The late patterns, 1880s to 1910s, and modern patterns, after 1910, were usually a more delicate semi-porcelain variety. Approximately 95% of the flow blue was made in England, with the remaining 5% made in Germany, Holland, France, Belgium, and the United States. American manufacturers included Mercer, Warwick, and Wheeling Pottery companies.

References: Mary F. Gaston, *The Collector's Encyclopedia Of Flow Blue China,* Collector Books, 1983, 1993 value update; Jeffrey Snyder, *Flow Blue: A Collector's Guide To Pattern, History and Values,* Schiffer Publishing, 1992; Petra Williams, *Flow Blue China—An Aid To Identification, Revised Edition,* Fountain House East, 1981; Petra Williams, *Flow Blue China II, Revised Edition,* Fountain House East, 1981; Petra Williams, *Flow Blue China and Mulberry Ware-Similarity and Value Guide, Revised Edition,* Fountain House East, 1993.

Collectors' Club: Flow Blue International Collectors' Club, PO Box 205, Rockford, IL 61105.

Museum: Hershey Museum of American Life, 170 West Hershey Park Drive, Hershey, PA 17033.

Berry Bowl
Pelew, E Challinor, c1840	**100.00**
Whampoa, Mellor & Venables, c1840	**80.00**

Bone Dish
Agra, F Winkle & Co, c1891	**40.00**
Touraine, Stanley Pottery Co, c1898	**85.00**

Butter Dish, cov, Kyber, W Adams & Co, c1891 . . . . **475.00**

Butter Pat, Touraine, Stanley Pottery Co, c1898 . . . . **60.00**

Chamber Pot, Glenwood, Johnson Bros, c1900, $8^1/_2 \times 5^1/_4$" **170.00**

Chocolate Cup and Saucer, Kyber, W Adams & Co, c1891 . . . . **135.00**

Coffeepot, Temple, Wood & Brownfield, c1845 . . . . **795.00**

Creamer
Hindustan, Wood & Brownfield, c1845	**275.00**
Manilla, Podmore Walker, c1845 . .	**550.00**
Non Pareil, Burgess & Leigh, c1891	**350.00**
Seville, New Wharf Pottery, 1891 . .	**210.00**
Temple, Wood & Brownfield, c1845	**550.00**

Cup and Saucer
Kyber, W Adams & Co, c1891	**120.00**
Rhoda Gardens, Hackwood, 1850, handleless	**165.00**
Scinde, J & G Alcock, c1840	**145.00**
Verona, Wood & Son, 1891	**95.00**

Gravy Boat, Marie, W H Grindley & Co, $8^1/_2$" l, $65.00.

Cup Plate, Amoy, Davenport, 1844	**110.00**
Demitasse Cup and Saucer, Lorne, WH Grindley, 1900	**75.00**
Dessert Bowl, Chen-Si, John Meir, c1835, 5" d	**135.00**

Gravy Boat
Dainty, John Maddock & Son, 1896	**145.00**
Holland, Johnson Bros, c1891, attached undertray	**150.00**
Mongolia, Johnson Bros, c1900, double spouts, attached underplate	**165.00**
Scinde, J & G Alcock, c1840	**575.00**

Honey Dish, Manilla, Podmore Walker, c1845 . . . . **135.00**

Milk Pitcher
La Belle, WH Grindley, c1893	**450.00**
Tonquin, Joseph Heath, 1850, $10^1/_2$" h	**1,100.00**

Pitcher
Coburg, John Edwards, c1860, 8" h	**795.00**
Flora, Davenport, 1850	**435.00**
Formosa, Thomas, John & Joseph Mayer, c1850, 7" h	**695.00**
Non Pareil, Burgess & Leigh, c1891	
6" h	**275.00**
8" h	**325.00**
Shell, Wood & Challinor, 1840	**465.00**
Temple, Wood & Brownfield, c1845, 9" h	**850.00**

Plate
Amoy, Davenport, 1844, $7^1/_4$" d . . .	**100.00**
Bamboo, Thomas Dimmock, c1845, $10^1/_4$" d	**135.00**
Carlton, Samuel Alcock, 1850, $7^1/_4$" d	**85.00**
Cashmere, Francis, Morley, c1850, $9^1/_2$" d	**250.00**
Coburg, John Edwards, c1860, $10^1/_4$" d	**150.00**
Corinthian Flute, Cauldon, 1905 . . .	**72.00**
Fairy Villas, W Adams & Co, c1891, 9" d	**90.00**
Hong Kong, Charles Meigh, c1845	
7" d	**95.00**
$10^3/_8$" d	**175.00**
Lakewood, Wood & Sons, c1900, $9^1/_2$" d	**75.00**
Lorne, WH Grindley, 1900, 10" d	**90.00**

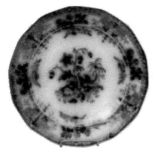

Plate, marked "Shell, E. C.," 9½" d, $75.00.

Waste Bowl, Waldorf, New Wharf Pottery, 6" d, 3¾" h, $55.00.

Manilla, Podmore Walker, c1845	
9" d.	125.00
9⅞" d	135.00
Pelew, E Challinor, c1840.	105.00
Sabroan, unknown maker, c1845,	
10¾" d	175.00
Scinde, J & G Alcock, c1840.	155.00
Waldorf, New Wharf Pottery, c1892,	
9" d.	75.00
Wild Rose, George Jones, c1910,	
10½" d	85.00
Platter	
Argyle, WH Grindley, 1896	
17¼ × 12".	395.00
19 × 13¼".	545.00
Bamboo, Thomas Dimmock, c1845,	
16¾ × 13⅞".	595.00
Beauties of China, Mellor, Venables	
& Co, 1845, 10" l	295.00
Chapoo, John Wedgwood, c1850,	
16" l	400.00
Chen-Si, John Meir, c1835, 16 ×	
12¼".	775.00
Gainsborough, Ridgway, c1905,	
scalloped, 16 × 12".	235.00
Hong Kong, Charles Meigh, c1845,	
16" l	350.00
Indian Jar, Jacob & Thomas Furnival,	
1843, 12"	215.00
Lorne, WH Grindley, 1900	
12" l	165.00
16" l	335.00
18" l	395.00
Lucerne, New Wharf Pottery, 1891,	
19" l	435.00
Manilla, Podmore Walker, c1845	
16" l	795.00
18" l	895.00
Oregon, T J & J Mayer, c1845, 13⅜" l	375.00
Potato Bowl, Oregon, T J & J Mayer,	
c1845.	735.00
Razor Box, cov, Leaf and Swag, brush	
stroke type, unknown maker	850.00
Relish Dish	
Coburg, John Edwards, c1860.	220.00
Tonquin, Heath, c1850.	270.00

Sauce Dish, Non Pareil, Burgess &	
Leigh, c1891, 5¼" d	40.00
Saucer, Tokio, Johnson Bros, c1891,	
6" d.	25.00
Sauce Tureen, Manilla, Podmore	
Walker, c1845, three pc	1,595.00
Soup Plate	
Amoy, Davenport, 1844, 9" d	110.00
Cashmere, Francis, Morley,	
c1850,10½" d	260.00
Kyber, W Adams & Co, c1891	120.00
Touraine, Stanley Pottery Co, c1898	95.00
Soup Tureen	
Clarence, WH Grindley, 1900.	495.00
Messina, Alfred Meakin, 1891,	
matching ladle.	1,600.00
Willow, Ashworth Bros, 1862, two	
pc	775.00
Sugar, cov	
Amoy, Davenport, 1844, slight rim	
wear	495.00
Manilla, Podmore Walker, c1845	850.00
Non Pareil, Burgess & Leigh, c1891	265.00
Teapot	
Arabesque, G Kent	895.00
Rhine, Thomas Dimmock, c1844	650.00
Undertray, Manilla, Podmore Walker,	
c1845, 7" l	275.00
Vegetable Bowl, cov	
Cashmere, Francis, Morley, c1850,	
8⅝ × 6⅝"	775.00
Landscape, WT Copeland & Sons,	
c1891	225.00
Manilla, Podmore Walker, c1845,	
10⅞" l	795.00
Wash Bowl, Doreen, WH Grindley,	
1891, octagonal	400.00
Wash Bowl and Pitcher, Whampoa,	
Mellor & Venables, c1840.	2,250.00
Waste Bowl	
Cashmere, Francis, Morley, c1850,	875.00
Touraine, Stanley Pottery Co, c1898	250.00

FRANCISCAN WARE

History: Franciscan Ware was manufactured by Gladding, McBean and Company, located in Glendale and Los Angeles, California. Charles

Gladding, Peter McBean and George Chambers organized the firm in 1875. Early products included sewer pipes and architectural items.

Production of dinnerware and art pottery began in 1934. The dinnerware was marketed under the trademark Franciscan and first appeared in plain shapes and bright colors. Soon, skillfully molded underglaze patterns were developed. Patterns like Desert Rose, Ivy, Autumn, and Apple are eagerly sought by Country collectors. Numerous setting and service pieces allow collectors to assemble large collections. More pieces are seen at flea markets and antique shows.

Franciscan Ware has been marked with over eighty different marks. Many contain the pattern name, patent numbers or dates.

Reference: Delleen Enge, *Franciscan Ware*, Collector Books, 1981, out-of-print.

Apple

Ashtray, 9" l	30.00
Butter Dish	36.00
Casserole	
Individual	35.00
Large, cov	75.00
Cereal Bowl, 6"	12.00
Cigarette Box	85.00
Coffeepot, cov	125.00
Cookie Jar	190.00
Creamer	22.00
Eggcup	30.00
Fruit Bowl, 5"	10.00
Jam Jar	75.00
Mug, short	15.00
Plate, 6" d, bread and butter	6.00
Platter	
14" l	35.00
Turkey	250.00
Ramekin, cov, handled	35.00
Relish Dish, three part	75.00
Salt and Pepper Shakers, pr, tall	55.00
Soup, flat	30.00
Sugar	25.00
Syrup	75.00
Tumbler, 10 oz	25.00
Vegetable Bowl, 8½" d	36.00
Water Pitcher	95.00
Autumn, starter set	55.00

California Poppy

Plate	
8" d, salad	18.00
10" d, dinner	30.00
Salt and Pepper Shakers, pr	20.00
Sauce Boat	38.00

Coronado Swirl

Carafe, cov, light green	55.00
Casserole, cov, pink	65.00
Celery Dish, yellow	15.00
Chop Plate, yellow	25.00
Coffeepot, after dinner, turquoise	95.00
Cream Soup, coral	22.00
Creamer, gray	24.00

Cup and Sauce, after dinner	
Coral	25.00
Ivory	25.00
Maroon	25.00
Turquoise	25.00
Yellow	25.00
Gravy, attached underplate, yellow	22.00
Plate	
6" d, bread and butter, turquoise	3.00
7½" d, salad, coral	5.00
10½" d, dinner, turquoise	8.00
Teacup, maroon	9.00
Vegetable, oval, yellow	25.00

Desert Rose

Ashtray	
Individual	15.00
Large	65.00
Buffet	65.00
Casserole	75.00
Cereal Bowl, ftd	30.00
Chop Plate, 12" d	45.00
Cigarette Box	125.00
Coffeepot	95.00
Compote	65.00
Eggcup	30.00
Jam Jar	75.00
Mug, 7 oz	20.00
Plate	
6½" d, bread and butter	6.00
8" d, salad	11.00
9½" d, luncheon	12.00
10½" d, dinner	15.00
Platter, 14" l	15.00
Relish, divided 11"	75.00
Salt and Pepper Shakers, pr	
Rosebud	15.00
Tall	55.00
Saucer, jumbo	10.00
Syrup	85.00
Teapot	85.00
Tumbler, juice	30.00
Vase, bud	195.00
Vegetable Bowl, divided	48.00
Water Pitcher	125.00

Duet

Ashtray, individual	12.00
Butter Dish, cov	25.00
Chop Plate, 13"	18.00
Creamer and Sugar, cov	18.00
Cup and Saucer	7.00
Gravy, underplate	15.00
Plate	
6" d, bread and butter	5.00
7¼" d, salad	9.00
10" d, dinner	12.00
Platter, 15"	20.00
Salt and Pepper Shakers, pr	15.00
Starter Set	55.00

El Patio

Coffee Server, cov	50.00
Cream Soup, saucer	30.00
Cup and Saucer, after dinner	25.00

Mug	10.00
Tea Set, individual	45.00
Tumbler, 4" h	20.00
Water Pitcher	50.00
Ivy	
Ashtray, individual	40.00
Butter Dish, cov, ¼ lb.	30.00
Cereal Bowl, 7½" d	25.00
Chop Plate, 14" d	85.00
Cup and Saucer, jumbo	65.00
Fruit Bowl, 5" d	8.00
Gravy, underplate	30.00
Pitcher, water	125.00
Plate	
6" d, bread and butter	6.00
10½" d, dinner	16.00
Platter	
13" l, oval	45.00
Turkey	225.00
Soup bowl, flat	30.00
Vegetable Bowl, 8¼" l	40.00
Starburst	
Ashtray	
Individual	20.00
Large	65.00
Bowl	
9" d	20.00
11" d	25.00
Casserole, small	35.00
Cup and Saucer	6.00
Fruit Bowl	10.00
Gravy	15.00
Milk Pitcher	75.00
Plate	
6" d, bread and butter	7.00
8" d, salad	9.00
10½" d, dinner	12.00
Soup Bowl 7¼" d	20.00
Starter Set	55.00
Teapot	195.00
TV Tray	75.00
Vegetable Bowl, divided	20.00
Water Pitcher	95.00

GAUDY WARES

History: Gaudy Ware is the name used by many collectors and dealers to describe a particular type of pottery. This white bodied ware usually sports stylized floral, luster, and enamel under-the-glaze decorations. Gaudy Ware is made up of three basic types—Gaudy Dutch, Gaudy Ironstone, and Gaudy Welsh.

Gaudy Dutch is an opaque, soft-paste ware made between 1790 and 1825 in England's Staffordshire district. Most pieces are unmarked although marks of various potters, including the impressed marks of Riley and Wood, have been found.

Pieces were first hand decorated in an underglaze blue, then fired, and finally they received additional decoration over the glaze. This over glaze decoration is extensively worn on many of today's examples. Gaudy Dutch found a ready market within the Pennsylvania German community because of its intense color and inexpensive price. It had little appeal in England.

Gaudy Ironstone was made in England around 1850. Most pieces are impressed "Ironstone" and bear a registry mark. Ironstone is an opaque, heavy-bodied earthenware which contains large proportions of flint and slag. Gaudy Ironstone is decorated in patterns and colors similar to Gaudy Welsh.

Gaudy Welsh is a translucent porcelain that was originally made in the Swansea area of England from 1830 to 1845. Although the designs resemble Gaudy Dutch, the body texture and weight differ. One distinguishing factor is the gold luster on top of the glaze.

All of the Gaudy Wares are welcome additions in a Country setting. Their brightly colored decorations add an interesting dash to cupboards and shelves. The patterns are fun to identify. Variety can be achieved through shapes and sizes.

References: Eleanor and Edward Fox, *Gaudy Dutch*, published by author, 1970, out-of-print; John A. Shuman, III, *The Collector's Encyclopedia of Gaudy Dutch & Welsh*, Collector Books, 1990, 1991 value update; Howard Y. Williams, *Gaudy Welsh China*, Wallace-Homestead, out-of-print.

Reproduction Alert: Gaudy Dutch cup plates, bearing the impressed mark "CYBRIS," have been reproduced and are collectible in their own right. The Henry Ford Museum has issued pieces in the Single Rose pattern, although they are porcelain rather than soft-paste.

GAUDY DUTCH

Bowl, Grape, luster trim, 6½" d	375.00
Coffeepot, Sunflower, 9½" h	1,650.00
Creamer	
Butterfly, 3½" h	650.00
Dove, 4⅞" h	450.00
Cup and Saucer, handleless	
Carnation	350.00
Single Rose, minor wear, small flake on cup table ring	325.00
Urn, small rim chip on saucer	250.00
Deep Dish	
Butterfly, 9⅞" d	1,000.00
Single Rose, 7⅜" d	350.00
War Bonnet, 9½" d	825.00
Jug, Double Rose, mask spout with light beard, 6¼" h	550.00
Pitcher	
Double Rose, 8¼" h	1,425.00
Grape, 8" h	2,450.00
Plate	
Carnation, 9¾" d	575.00
Double Rose, 10" d	725.00

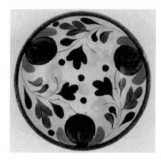

Gaudy Dutch, cup bowl, cobalt blue, green, brown, and yellow dec, incised mark "Clews Warranted Staffordshire" around crown on bottom, 6" d, 1¼" h, $350.00.

Grape, rim hairline, minor enamel
  flakes, 8¼" d 400.00
Oyster, 6½" d 450.00
Primrose, 4¾" d 415.00
Single Rose, 8½" d 225.00
Straw Flower, 5½" d 375.00
Sunflower, 6½" d 750.00
Urn, 5¼" d 375.00
Zinnia, 6⅜" d 550.00
Platter
  Butterfly, oval, 14" l 1,800.00
  Double Rose, 15" l 3,625.00
Soup Plate
  Carnation, 8⅜" d 425.00
  War Bonnet, red, yellow, green, and
    black, underglaze blue, 8⅛" d   725.00
Sugar Bowl, cov
  Double Rose, stains, small flakes on
    sawtooth lip, lid with chipped int.
    flange, 5¼" h 550.00
  Dove, 5¼" h 625.00
  Oyster, very worn, enamel flakes,
    hairlines, chips, 5⅝" h 375.00
Tea Bowl and Saucer
  Leaf 775.00
  Oyster 425.00
  Single Rose 250.00
Teapot, cov
  Carnation, 6½" h 650.00
  Double Rose, rect, 6¼" h 1,980.00
  Grape, old yellowed repairs, 6¼" h   550.00
Waste Bowl, Single Rose, dark stains,
  enamel flakes on rim, 5 ½" d 225.00

GAUDY IRONSTONE

Coffeepot, cov, Strawberry, 10" h 575.00
Creamer
  Floral, molded, polychrome enamel,
    blue underglaze 125.00
  Morning Glory, paneled, foliage
    handle, 6½" h 150.00

Cup and Saucer, handleless
  Floral, red, blue, black, and two
    shades of green, imp mark 65.00
  Morning Glory and Berries, under-
    glaze blue, red, green, and yellow
    enamel, hairline in cup, chips on
    table ring 95.00
Demitasse Cup and Saucer, handleless,
  floral, red and blue, green rim 65.00
Jug, Tulips, yellow, red, white, and
  blue, light blue pebble ground, luster
  trim and rim, 7½" h 300.00
Pitcher
  Floral, molded design, blue and lus-
    ter highlights, 7⅞" h 165.00
  Rose, blue, red, and green enamels,
    blue underglaze, minor edge
    flakes, 8" h 225.00
Plate
  Blackberry, twelve sided, 1850s,
    9¼" d 165.00
  Floral, underglaze blue and luster,
    imp "Ironstone," wear
    8¾" d 125.00
    9½" d 175.00
  Morning Glory, underglaze blue, red
    and two shades of green enamel-
    ing, chip on table ring, 8⅝" d . . .   100.00
  Pansies and Vines, blue, yellow,
    green, red, and black, scalloped
    edge, 8" d 85.00
  Rose, red, blue, green, and black,
    9½" d 90.00
  Strawberry, underglaze blue, poly-
    chrome enamel and luster, wear
    and chip on table ring, 8½" d . . .   150.00
  Sunflower, yellow, green, and black,
    6¾" d 60.00
  Tulips and Berries, underglaze blue,
    red, green, and black enamel,
    stains, 8¾" d 150.00
  Urn and Flowers, minor enamel
    flakes, 9⅜" d 165.00
  Vintage, underglaze blue, red and
    green enameling and luster, 9" d   115.00
Platter
  Adam's Rose, red, green, and black,
    imp "Adams," 19½" l 300.00
  Strawberry, 15⅛" l 525.00

Gaudy Ironstone, cup and saucer, handleless, 5¾" d saucer, $75.00.

Serving Dish, cov, Urn and Flowers, minor wear, 9½" d, 7¾" h **775.00**

Soup Plate, floral, red, black, and teal green, 9¼" d **50.00**

Sugar Bowl, cov
Morning Glory, paneled, underglaze, foliage handles, 8" h **150.00**
Urn and Flowers, stains, damage, finial glued, 7⅜" h **165.00**

Teapot, floral, luster trim, fruit finial, marked "Walley" and English registry mark, 9½" h **235.00**

Waste Bowl, floral, red, purple, black, and two shades of green, 6⅝" d, 3⅜" h **65.00**

GAUDY WELSH

Bowl
Columbine, polychrome enamel, blue underglaze, ftd, 10" d **400.00**
Flower Basket, 10½" d **185.00**
Oyster, 6" d **80.00**
Tulip, 6¼" d **45.00**

Cake Plate, Tulip, molded handles, 10" d **100.00**

Compote, Aberystwyth, blue, burnt orange, green, and luster, ftd, 8⅛" d **375.00**

Creamer, polychrome enamel, luster trim
Lotus, 4¾" h **125.00**
Oyster, 4½" h **100.00**

Cup, Wagon Wheel **60.00**

Cup and Saucer
Drape **75.00**
Honeysuckle **100.00**
Lotus, underglaze blue, polychrome enamel **110.00**

Eggcup, Tulip, c1840, 2½" h **145.00**

Loving Cup, 4" h **250.00**

Mug
Flower Basket, 4" h **85.00**
Grape, c1840, 2" h **145.00**
Oyster, 4⅛" h **225.00**

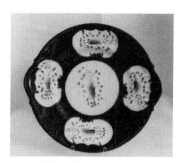

Gaudy Welsh, cake plate, Feather, 10" w handle to handle, $50.00.

Pitcher
Anglesey, 4¼" h **90.00**
Hanging Basket, small crack, c1825, 7½" h **225.00**
Wagon Wheel, 8½" h **175.00**

Plate, underglaze blue, polychrome enamel, luster trim
Lotus, 9" d, price for pair. **190.00**
Oyster, wear, 8½" d **100.00**

Soup Plate, Strawberry, 9" d **115.00**

Sugar, cov
Daisy and Chain **200.00**
Flower Basket, lion's head handles, luster trim **150.00**

Teapot, underglaze blue, polychrome enamel, luster trim
Peach, crow's foot, 6" h **325.00**
Vine, stains, chips, and short hairlines, 9¼" h **225.00**

Tea Set, Tulip pattern, 41 piece set consists of teapot, creamer, covered sugar, waste bowl, two cake plates, twelve cups, saucers, and plates, 19th C **1,050.00**

HALL CHINA COMPANY

History: Robert Hall founded the Hall China Company in 1903 in East Liverpool, Ohio. He died in 1904 and was succeeded by his son, Robert Taggart Hall. After years of experimentation, Robert T. Hall developed a leadless glaze in 1911, opening the way for production of glazed household products.

The Hall China Company made many types of kitchenware, refrigerator sets, and dinnerware in a wide variety of patterns. Some patterns were exclusive, such as Heather Rose for Sears.

One of the most popular patterns was Autumn Leaf, an exclusive premium designed in 1933 for the Jewel Tea Company by Arden Richards. Still a Jewel Tea property, Autumn Leaf has not been listed in catalogs since 1978 but is produced on a replacement basis with the date stamped on the back.

References: Harvey Duke, *Hall: Price Guide Update,* ELO Books, 1992; Harvey Duke, *Superior Quality Hall China,* ELO Books, 1977; Harvey Duke, *Hall 2,* ELO Books, 1985; Harvey Duke, *The Official Price Guide To Pottery And Porcelain,* Collector Books, 1989; Margaret and Kenn Whitmyer, *The Collector's Encyclopedia of Hall China,* Collector Books, 1989; 1992 value update.

Collectors' Club: National Autumn Leaf Collector's Society, 7346 Shamrock Dr, Indianapolis, IN 46217.

Periodical: *The Hall China Encore,* 317 N. Pleasant St., #C1C, Oberlin, OH 44074.

Autumn Leaf
Berry Bowl, 5½" d	4.00
Creamer, ruffled-D	7.00
Cup and Saucer	8.00
Custard	5.50
French Baker	8.00
Gravy Boat	20.00
Plate	
7¼" d, salad	5.00
9" d, dinner	6.00
Platter, 13½" l	14.00
Stack Set	75.00
Sugar, cov, ruffled-D	10.00

Blue Blossom
Bean Pot, #5	195.00
Creamer and Sugar, cov, Morning	145.00
Jug, loop handle	195.00
Leftover	
Loop Handle	165.00
Zephyr	195.00

Blue Bouquet
Casserole	35.00
Coffeepot	
Connie	125.00
Five Band	80.00
Creamer and Sugar, cov, Boston	45.00
Cup	13.00
Salt and Pepper Shakers, pr, handled	35.00
Serving Bowl, oval	35.00
Soup, flat	25.00

Blue Garden
Batter Bowl, Sundial	165.00
Bean Pot, #5	195.00
Creamer and Sugar, cov, Morning	145.00
Leftover, loop handle	165.00

Blue Willow
Casserole, cov	
5½" l	55.00
7½" l, low	65.00
Cereal Bowl, 6" d, 2⅛" h	25.00

Rice Bowl, shallow	25.00
Teacup	20.00
Teapot, Boston, 4 cup	150.00

Cameo Rose
Gravy	24.00
Soup, flat	14.00
Vegetable Bowl, cov	35.00

Carrot (a.k.a. Carrot and Beet)
Baker, oval, 12½" l	85.00
Ball Jug, #4	125.00
Casserole, Thick Rim, 8¾" l	95.00
Cookie Jar, Zeisel	150.00
Salt and Pepper Shakers, pr, handled	65.00
Teapot, Windshield	195.00

Clover
Casserole, small	55.00
Jug, Five Band, 2 pt	65.00
Shakers, flour, pepper, and sugar, price for 3 pcs	95.00
Teapot, Windshield	195.00

Crocus
Bean Pot, one handle	175.00
Casserole, cov	48.00
Mixing Bowl, large	42.00
Platter, 13" l	35.00
Soup Tureen, cov	175.00
Vegetable Bowl, round	35.00

Chinese Red
Ball Jug	35.00
Batter Bowl, Five Band	75.00
Bean Pot, #5	150.00
Butter, Zephyr	185.00
Casserole, Sundial, #1	55.00
Coffeepot, #691, 4 pcs, all china	175.00
Cookie Jar, Sundial	225.00
Drip Jar, open, #1188	35.00
Jug, cov, Radiance, #3	75.00
Pretzel Jar, cov, hairline crack in bottom	95.00
Water Bottle, Zephyr, missing stopper	70.00

Floral Lattice (a.k.a. Flowerpot)
Batter Bowl, Five Band	45.00
Casserole, #99, oval, handled, 9" l	45.00

Crocus, D-style, tidbit tray, platinum trim, 11½" h, $40.00.

Autumn Leaf, ball jug, 8½" h, $125.00.

Onion Soup, cov, individual	**65.00**
Salt Shaker, canister style	**55.00**
Syrup, Five Band	**45.00**
Meadow Flower	
Ball Jug, #3	**125.00**
Canister, Radiance, flour	**150.00**
Custard, Thick Rim	**20.00**
Jug, Five Band, 2 pt	**75.00**
Salt and Pepper Shakers, pr, handled	**35.00**
Teapot, Streamline	**350.00**
No. 488	
Drip Jar, cov	**60.00**
Jug, Radiance, #5, no cov	**50.00**
Pepper Shaker, Novelty	**30.00**
Refrigerator Jar, cov, square	**60.00**
Teapot, Radiance	**225.00**
Orange Poppy	
Bean Pot	**60.00**
Cake Plate	**15.00**
Drip Jar, cov	**15.00**
French Baker	**14.00**
Platter, 13″ l	**15.00**
Salad Bowl	**11.00**
Salt and Pepper Shakers, pr, handled	**30.00**
Vegetable Bowl, round	**20.00**
Pastel Morning Glory (a.k.a. Pink Morning Glory)	
Ball Jug	**85.00**
Bean Pot, handled	**150.00**
Berry Bowl, 5½″ d	**8.50**
Cake Plate	**55.00**
Casserole, cov, Radiance	**35.00**
Cereal Bowl, 6″ d	**20.00**
Coffeepot, Terrace	**95.00**
Creamer and Sugar, cov, D-style . . .	**55.00**
Cup and Saucer	**15.00**
Gravy Boat	**35.00**
Mixing Bowl, Radiance, #2	**55.00**
Plate	
6″ d, bread and butter	**6.00**
7″ d, salad	**14.00**
9″ d, dinner	**15.00**
Platter, 11½″ l	**30.00**
Pretzel Jar, cov	**150.00**
Soup, flat	**20.00**
Red Dot (a.k.a. Eggshell Polka Dot)	
Baker, individual, handled	**30.00**
Bean Pot, #2, one handle	**125.00**
Jug, cov, #5	**85.00**
Onion Soup, cov	**35.00**
Pitcher, Baron	**95.00**
Punch Set, ftd punch bowl and 12 cups	**350.00**
Teapot, Rutherford	**195.00**
Red Poppy	
Cereal Bowl, 6″ d	**16.50**
Coffeepot, Daniel, metal dripper . . .	**35.00**
Cup and Saucer	**13.50**
Jug, Radiance, #5	**35.00**
Plate, 10″ d, dinner	**13.50**

Soup, flat	**20.00**
Stack Set	**65.00**
Serenade (a.k.a. Eureka Serenade)	
Berry Bowl, 5½″ d	**5.50**
Casserole, cov	**30.00**
Coffeepot, 4 pc, all china	**125.00**
Creamer and Sugar, cov	**29.00**
Cup and Saucer	**13.50**
Plate, 9″ d, dinner	**13.50**
Platter, 13½″ l	**20.00**
Salad Bowl, 9″ d	**20.00**
Teapot, Boston	**110.00**
Silhouette (a.k.a. Taverne)	
Drip Jar, cov	**80.00**
Leftover, 7″ sq	**80.00**
Mug	**30.00**
Pie Baker, 9″ d	**50.00**
Teapot, New York	**245.00**
Wildfire	
Bowl, straight sided, 5″ d	**18.00**
Cereal Bowl, 6″ d	**14.00**
Creamer and Sugar, Pert	**95.00**
Gravy Boat	**30.00**
Jug, Pert, 5″ h	**85.00**
Plate	
7″ d, salad	**11.00**
9″ d, dinner	**13.00**
Platter, oval, 13½″ l	**28.50**
Salad Bowl, 9″ d	**22.50**
Salt and Pepper Shakers, pr, Teardrop	**35.00**
Teapot, Aladdin, oval infuser	**95.00**
Tidbit Tray, 3 tiers	**45.00**
Wild Poppy (a.k.a. Poppy and Wheat)	
Bean Pot, #5, one handle	**175.00**
Canister Set, cov, set of four	**600.00**
Coffeepot, Washington, 12 cup	**350.00**
Cookie Jar, cov, Five Band	**225.00**
Creamer and Sugar, New York	**110.00**
Jug, cov, Radiance, #6	**95.00**
Leftover, sq	**125.00**
Stack Set, Radiance	**165.00**
Teapot, Manhattan, 2 cup	**325.00**
Tea Tile, 6″ sq	**85.00**
Teapots	
Aladdin, yellow	**45.00**
Basket, emerald, platinum dec	**175.00**
Hollywood, red, 8 cup	**200.00**
Hook Cover, Chinese red	**135.00**
Los Angeles, cobalt blue	**35.00**
McCormick, maroon, 6 cup	**35.00**
Medallion Crocus (a.k.a. Colonial) .	**95.00**
Melody, Chinese red	**175.00**
New York, Crocus	**90.00**
Parade, canary yellow	**28.00**
Philadelphia, pink, 5 cup	**35.00**
Streamline, canary yellow	**95.00**
Surfside, emerald green, gold dec . .	**125.00**
Thorley, Brilliant Series, Windcrest, #1524, lemon yellow ground, gold dec	**125.00**
Windshield, maroon	**35.00**

HARKER POTTERY

History: The Harker Company began in 1840 when Benjamin Harker, an English slater turned farmer in East Liverpool, Ohio, built a kiln and began making yellow ware products from clay deposits on his land. The business was managed by members of the Harker family until the Civil War when David Boyce, a brother-in-law, took over. Although a Harker resumed management after the war, members of the Boyce family assumed key roles within the firm; David G. Boyce, a grandson of David, served as president.

In 1879 the first whiteware products were introduced. A disastrous flood in 1884 caused severe financial problems which the company overcame. In 1931 the company moved to Chester, West Virginia, to escape the flooding problems. In 1945 Harker introduced Cameoware made by the engobe process. The engobe or layered effect was achieved by placing a copper mask over the bisque and sand blasting to leave the design imprint. The white rose pattern on blue ground was marketed as "White Rose Carv-Kraft" in Montgomery Ward stores.

The Harker Company used a large variety of backstamps and names. Hotoven cookingware featured a scroll, draped over pots, with a kiln design at top. Columbia Chinaware had a circular stamp with the Statue of Liberty.

Harker made a Rockingham ware line in the 1960s. The hound handled pitcher and mugs were included. The Jeannette Glass Company purchased the Harker Company and the plant was closed in March, 1972. Ohio Stoneware, Inc., utilized the plant building until it was destroyed by fire in 1975.

In 1965 Harker China had the capacity to produce 25 million pieces of dinnerware each year and many patterns also were kept in production for decades. Hence, there is a great deal of Harker material available at garage sales and flea markets.

Between 1935 and 1955 the Harker Company organized Columbia Chinaware, a sales organization used to market Harker products in small towns across the country. The line included enamel ware, glass, and aluminum products. One pattern of Columbia Chinaware was "Autumn Leaf," eagerly sought by Autumn Leaf collectors.

There are dozens of Harker patterns involving flowers, foliage, and fruit that will work well in any Country decorating scheme. Some patterns are relatively simple, others quite elaborate. When selecting a pattern to collect, make certain that the pattern contains a large number of forms so that an elegant, full table can be set.

Also consider focusing on Harker patterns by famous designers. Among these are Russel Wright's White Clover and George Bauer's Cameoware. Many patterns will be found with different color grounds. Other patterns were designed to have mass appeal. Colonial Lady was popular at "dish nites" at the movies or other businesses.

Shapes and forms did change through the decades. An interesting collection might focus on one object, e.g., a sugar or creamer, collected in a variety of patterns from different historical periods. Watch for unusual pieces. Harker produced rolling pins in many patterns including Amy, Fruit Basket, and Petit Point Rose. The Countryside pattern features a rolling pin, scoop and cake server.

References: Neva W. Colbert, *The Collector's Guide To Harker Pottery, U.S.A.: Identification and Values,* Collector Books, 1993; Jo Cunningham, *The Collector's Encyclopedia Of American Dinnerware,* Collector Books, 1982, 1992 value update.

Cameoware
Bowl, pink, 7" d	**10.00**
Cake Server.	**12.00**
Casserole, cov.	**15.00**
Child's Feeding Dish.	**30.00**
Cup and Saucer	**9.00**
Pie Baker	**10.00**
Pitcher, cov.	**15.00**
Plate	
7" d, salad.	**6.00**
10" d, dinner.	**10.00**
Sugar, cov.	**7.50**
Colonial Lady	
Cake Plate.	**22.00**
Cereal Bowl	**10.00**
Creamer and Sugar	**20.00**
Cup and Saucer	**12.00**
Dessert Bowl.	**7.00**
Pie Baker and Server.	**35.00**
Plate	
6¼" d, bread and butter	**4.00**
7" d, salad.	**6.00**
Salt and Pepper Shakers, pr, small	**16.00**
Soup Bowl	**18.00**
Vegetable Bowl.	**22.00**
Deco-Dahlia	
Baker, cov, individual, set of four on	
rotating rack	**50.00**
Cake Lifter	**28.00**

Berry Dish, floral decal center, gray rim, $2.50.

Jug, 6" h	**18.00**
Pie Baker, 9" d	**17.00**
Rolling Pin	**85.00**
Utility Plate, 12" d	**15.00**

Mallow
Bowl

5" d.	**15.00**
10" d.	**30.00**
Jug, cov.	**25.00**
Plate, 8" d, luncheon	**10.00**
Spoon, hairline crack	**10.00**

Pansy

Ashtray	**30.00**
Cereal Bowl	**10.00**
Cup.	**10.00**
Pie Baker	**30.00**
Plate, 9¾" d, dinner	**10.00**
Platter.	**30.00**
Salt Shaker	**15.00**

Red Apple

Custard	**6.00**
Mixing Bowl, 10" d.	**30.00**
Pie Server	**20.00**
Spoon.	**25.00**
Utility Plate.	**20.00**
Vegetable Bowl, 9" d	**28.00**

Rolling Pin

Amy	**85.00**
Basket of fruits and flowers	**75.00**
Cameoware, pink	**110.00**
Countryside	**115.00**
Fruit Basket.	**85.00**
Petit Point Rose.	**100.00**

Vine

Casserole, cov.	**15.00**
Cereal Bowl	**3.00**
Creamer	**5.00**
Cup and Saucer	**4.00**
Fruit Bowl.	**2.00**

Plate

7¼" d, salad	**3.00**
10" d, dinner.	**4.00**
Platter, 11¼" l.	**10.00**
Sugar, cov.	**7.00**
Vegetable Bowl.	**8.00**

HOMER LAUGHLIN CHINA COMPANY

History: Homer Laughlin and his brother, Shakespeare, built two pottery kilns in East Liverpool, Ohio, in 1871. Shakespeare withdrew in 1879, leaving Homer to operate the business alone. Laughlin became one of the first firms to produce American-made whiteware. In 1896, William Wills and a Pittsburgh group led by Marcus Aaron bought the Laughlin firm.

Expansion followed. Two new plants were built in Laughlin Station, Ohio. In 1906, the first plant (#4) was built in Newall, West Virginia. In 1923

plant #6 was built at Newall and featured a continuous tunnel kiln. Similar kilns were added at the other plants. Other advances included spray glazing and mechanical jiggering.

In the 1930 to 1960 period several new dinnerware lines were added, including the Wells Art Glaze line. Ovenserve and Kitchen Kraft were the cooking ware lines. The colored glaze lines of Fiesta, Harlequin, and Rhythm captured major market shares. In 1959 a translucent table china line was introduced. Today, the annual manufacturing capacity is over 45 million pieces.

The original trademark from 1871 to 1890 merely identified the products as "Laughlin Brothers." The next trademark featured the American eagle astride the prostrate British lion. The third marking featured a monogram of "HLC" which has appeared, with slight variations, on all dinnerware since about 1900. The 1900 trademark contained a number which identified the month, year and plant at which the product was made. Letter codes were used in later periods.

So much attention has been placed on Fiesta that other interesting patterns have not achieved the popularity which they deserve. Prices still are moderate. Some of the patterns from the 1930 to 1940 period have contemporary designs that are highly artistic.

There are dozens of Homer Laughlin patterns that would fit comfortably in any Country decorating scheme. Collectors are advised first to select a shape they like, e.g., Virginia Rose or Yellowstone octagonal, and then the decal pattern. Virginia Rose is a shape, not a pattern name. Several different decals can be found, with delicate pink flowers the most common.

References: Jo Cunningham, *The Collector's Encyclopedia of American Dinnerware*, Collector Books, 1982, 1992 value update; Joanne Jasper, *The Collector's Encyclopedia of Homer Laughlin China: Reference & Value Guide*, Collector Books, 1993.

Reproduction Alert. Harlequin and Fiesta lines were reissued in 1978 and marked accordingly.

Dogwood

Bowl, 5¾" d	**3.00**
Creamer and Sugar	**10.00**
Plate, 9" d, luncheon.	**5.00**
Platter, 11¾" l.	**9.00**
Soup	**6.00**
Vegetable, oval	**9.00**

Harlequin
Ball Jug, 22 oz

Gray	**54.00**
Maroon	**60.00**
Rose	**40.00**

Bowl, 5½" d

Maroon	**10.00**
Medium green	**16.00**
Red	**7.50**

Butter, cov
Maroon **95.00**
Yellow **95.00**
Candle Holders, pr
Maroon **185.00**
Turquoise **75.00**
Casserole, cov
Maroon **135.00**
Medium green **135.00**
Cereal Bowl
Turquoise **7.00**
Yellow **7.00**
Creamer
Maroon, individual **22.00**
Medium green, large **40.00**
Turquoise, individual **10.00**
Yellow, individual **10.00**
Cream Soup
Mauve blue **21.00**
Turquoise **15.00**
Cup and Saucer
Gray **9.50**
Yellow **5.00**
Demitasse Cup and Saucer
Turquoise **40.00**
Yellow **35.00**
Eggcup
Gray
Double **28.00**
Individual **31.00**
Maroon, individual **25.00**
Mauve blue, individual **20.00**
Medium green, double **18.00**
Spruce green, individual **30.00**
Turquoise
Double **14.00**
Individual **20.00**
Gravy
Maroon **12.00**
Yellow **10.00**
Nappy
Mauve blue **30.00**
Yellow **30.00**
Nut Dish, three part, Mauve blue   **6.60**

Eggshell Theme, dinner plate, emb fruit and vine border, floral decal center, #C48N5, 10″ d, $6.00.

Pitcher, water
Maroon **68.00**
Medium green **70.00**
Plate
6″ d, bread and butter
Gray **4.00**
Maroon **6.00**
7″ d, salad
Chartreuse **6.50**
Gray **6.50**
Maroon **9.00**
Medium green **12.00**
Rose **9.00**
9¼″ d, luncheon, Rose **6.00**
10″ d, dinner, Gray **25.00**
Salad Bowl, individual
Chartreuse **20.00**
Yellow **20.00**
Soup, flat, Rose **14.00**
Teacup
Mauve blue **16.00**
Medium green **16.00**
Teapot, Medium green **60.00**
Jubilee
Coffee Server, Shell pink **35.00**
Mayonnaise, underplate, Shell pink   **70.00**
Plate, dinner
Cream beige **5.00**
Mist gray **5.00**
Saucer
Celadon green **3.00**
Shell pink **3.00**
Rhythm
Bowl, 5″ d, Maroon **4.00**
Plate
7″ d
Gray **3.00**
Maroon **3.00**
9″ d, Chartreuse **6.00**
Platter, 11½″ l, Forest green **13.00**
Saucer, Gray **3.00**
Soup Bowl, 8″ d
Chartreuse **8.00**
Forest green **8.00**
Harlequin yellow **8.00**
Riviera
Casserole, Mauve blue **60.00**
Creamer and Sugar, cov, Light green **14.00**
Cream Soup, Yellow **30.00**
Cup
Light green **7.50**
Mauve blue **7.50**
Deep Plate, Yellow **15.00**
Nappy
Red **18.00**
Yellow **18.00**
Plate, 7″ d, Dark blue **20.00**
Platter, 11½″ l, Yellow **18.50**
Salt Shaker, Red **8.00**
Sugar, cov, Mauve blue **10.00**

Virginia Rose, pickle dish, oblong, silver trim, #K49N8, 9⅜ " l, $12.00.

Virginia Rose
Butter Dish	40.00
Cake Plate	15.00
Cereal Bowl, 6" d	3.00
Cup and Saucer	3.50
Eggcup	12.00
Fruit Bowl, 5½" d	4.50
Plate	
6" d, bread and butter	2.50
9" d, dinner	8.00
Salt and Pepper Shakers, pr	12.00
Soup	7.00
Vegetable, cov	45.00

HULL POTTERY

History: In 1905 Addis E. Hull purchased the Acme Pottery Company, Crooksville, Ohio. In 1917 the A. E. Hull Pottery Company began making a line of art pottery, novelties, stoneware, and kitchenware, later introducing the famous Little Red Riding Hood line. Most items had a matte finish with shades of pink and blue or brown predominating.

After a disastrous flood and fire in 1950, J. Brandon Hull reopened the factory in 1952 as the Hull Pottery Company. Newer, more modern styles, most with a glossy finish, were introduced. The company currently produces pieces, e.g. the Regal and Floraline lines, for sale to florists.

Hull pottery molds and patterns are easily identified. Pre- 1950 vases are marked "Hull USA" or "Hull Art USA" on the bottom. Many also retain their paper labels. Post-1950 pieces are marked "Hull" in large script or "HULL" in block letters.

Each pattern has a distinctive number, e.g., Wildflower with a "W" and number, Waterlily with an "L" and number, Poppy with "600" numbers, and Orchid with "300" numbers. Early stoneware pieces have an "H."

References: Barbara Loveless Gick-Burke, *Collector's Guide To Hull Pottery: The Dinnerware Lines: Identification and Values,* Collector Books, 1993; Brenda Roberts, *Roberts Ultimate Encyclo-*pedia of Hull Pottery, Walsworth Publishing, 1992; Brenda Roberts, *The Collectors Encyclopedia Of Hull Pottery,* Collector Books, 1980, 1993 value update; Brenda Roberts, *The Companion Guide to Roberts' Ultimate Encyclopedia of Hull Pottery,* Walsworth Publishing, 1992; Joan Hull, *Hull: The Heavenly Pottery, Revised Third Edition,* published by author, 1993; Mark E. Supnick, *Collecting Hull Pottery's "Little Red Riding Hood": A Pictorial Reference and Price Guide,* L–W Book Sales, 1989, 1992 value update.

Periodicals: *Hull Pottery Newsletter,* 11023 Tunnel Hill NE, New Lexington, OH 43764; *The Hull Pottery News,* 466 Foreston Place, St Louis, MO 63119.

Basket	
Blossom Flite, T–4–8½"	85.00
Bow Knot, B–25–6½"	250.00
Ebbtide, E–11–16½"	200.00
Tokay/Tuscany, 15–12"	100.00
Tulip, 102–33–6"	225.00
Candleholders, pr, Magnolia, H–24	75.00
Candy Dish, Butterfly, B–6–5½"	40.00
Console Bowl	
Jack-in-the-Pulpit, 590–33–13"	150.00
Magnolia, H–23	75.00
Cornucopia	
Bow Knot, B–5–6½"	150.00
Rosella, R–13–8½"	60.00
Tokay/Tuscany, 1–6½"	30.00
Woodland, W–10–11"	45.00
Double Cornucopia, Magnolia, 6–12"	100.00
Flower Arranger, gray colt	35.00
Flower Bowl, Capri, round, C–47–5¼" × 8"	40.00
Hanging Basket, Woodland, W–17–7½"	150.00
Jardiniere	
Tulip, 117–30–5"	85.00
Waterlily, L–24–8½"	200.00
Lamp Vase, Open Rose, 139–10½"	400.00
Pitcher	
Bow Knot, B–1–5½"	175.00
Iris, 401–8"	150.00
Poppy, 610–13"	650.00
Serenade, S–2–6"	35.00
Tropicana, 56–13½"	550.00
Waterlily, L–3–5½"	50.00
Wildflower, W–19–13½"	450.00
Woodland, W–3–5½"	40.00
Planter	
Capri, twin swan, C–81	75.00
Figural	
Deer, 62, 12"	55.00
Madonna, 24	35.00
Unicorn, 98, 10"	45.00
Parchment & Pine, scroll, S–5–10½"	85.00
Poppy, 602–6½"	150.00

**Planter, twin geese, large, #95, 1951, 7¼"
h, $35.00.**

Salt and Pepper Shakers, pr, Sunglow, 54	**25.00**
Tea Set	
Blossom Flite, T–14, 15, and 16	**125.00**
Open Rose, 110, 111, 112	**450.00**
Vase	
Blossom Flite, T–7–10½"	**60.00**
Bow Knot, B–10–10¼"	**350.00**
Butterfly, B–9–9"	**45.00**
Continental	
C–53–8½"	**40.00**
C–54–12½"	**60.00**
Dogwood	
503–8½"	**95.00**
510–10½"	**200.00**
517–4¾"	**50.00**
Ebbtide, twin fish, E–2–7"	**65.00**
Iris	
407–7"	**95.00**
414–10½"	**300.00**
Jack-in-the-Pulpit	
501–33–6"	**65.00**
510–33–8"	**100.00**
Magnolia	
1–8½"	**85.00**
13–4¾"	**45.00**
17–12½", winged	**225.00**
Open Rose	
102–8½"	**95.00**
120–6¼"	**60.00**
Parchment & Pine, S–4–10"	**95.00**
Rosella, R–2–5"	**30.00**
Serenade, S–11–10½"	**75.00**
Sunglow, 91, 6½"	**35.00**
Tokay/Tuscany, 8–10	**85.00**
Tulip, 100–33–6½"	**90.00**
Waterlily, L–11–9½"	**100.00**
Wildflower	
W–9–8½"	**75.00**
W–15–10½", fan shaped	**95.00**
Woodland	
W–4–6½"	**50.00**
W–8–7½"	**40.00**
Wall Pocket	
Sunglow, pitcher, 81	**45.00**
Woodland, shell, W–13–7½"	**75.00**

IRONSTONE, WHITE PATTERNED

History: White patterned ironstone is a heavy earthenware, first patented in 1813 by Charles Mason, Staffordshire, England, using the name "Patent Ironstone China." Other English potters soon began copying this opaque, feldspathic, white china.

White ironstone dishes first became available in the American market in the early 1840s. The first patterns had simple Gothic lines similar to the shapes used in transfer wares. Pattern shapes, such as New York, Union, and Atlantic, were designed to appeal to the American housewife. Embossed designs, inspired by the American western prairie, included wheat, corn, oats, and poppy motifs. Eventually over 200 shapes and patterns, with variations of finials and handles, were made.

White patterned ironstone is identified by shape names and pattern names. Many potters named only the shape in their catalogs. Pattern names usually refer to the decoration motif.

There is something elegant about these all white ironstone pieces. Country collectors and decorators alike eagerly seek this ware. Large, crisp, white tureens look quite at home in the country setting.

References: Jean Wetherbee, *A Look At White Ironstone*, Wallace-Homestead, 1980; Jean Wetherbee, *A Second Look At White Ironstone*, Wallace-Homestead, 1985.

Reproduction Manufacturers: Homespun Crafts, Box 77, Grover, NC 28073.

Bowl, cov, Leaf Fan, Alcock, 7⅞" d	**100.00**
Butter, cov, Athens, Podmore Walker, 1856	**80.00**
Cake Plate	
Brocade, handled, Mason, 9" w	**125.00**
Cable and Ring, reticulated handles, Anthony Shaw and Son, 12" w	**15.00**
Chamber Pot	
Corn and Oats, Wedgwood, 1863	**125.00**
Wheat and Blackberry, Meakin	**40.00**
Coffeepot, cov	
Washington shape, John Meir	**125.00**
Wheat and Blackberry, Clementson Bros.	**100.00**
Compote	
Gothic, ten sided, handled, I Meir and Son, c1850, 7½" h	**95.00**
Pearly Sydenham, ftd, Meakin	**175.00**
Creamer	
Basketweave, rect, Anthony Stone and Son	**30.00**
Fig, Davenport	**60.00**
Wheat and Clover, Turner and Tomkinson	**60.00**

Coffeepot, Wheat and Clover, melon ribbed sides, 10½″ h, $125.00.

Wheat in the Meadow, Powell and
Bishop, 1870. . . . . 40.00
Cup and Saucer
Grape and Medallion, Challinor . . . 35.00
Oak Leaf, handleless, Parkhurst,
1863 . . . . 50.00
President, handleless, Edwards 45.00
Cup Plate, Prairie, J Clementson, 1862,
4¾″ d 18.00
Ewer
Corn and Oats, Wedgwood, 12¾″ h 150.00
Scalloped Decagon, Wedgwood . . . 140.00
Food Mold, oval, geometric design, 6″ l 575.00
Gravy Boat
Bordered Fuchsia, Anthony Shaw 40.00
Wheat and Blackberry, Meakin 25.00
Vintage, Challinor. 30.00
Nappy
Mocho, T and R Boote, 5″ d 8.00
Prairie Flowers, Livesley Powell . . . 15.00
Pitcher
Berlin Swirl, Mayer and Elliot 115.00
Ceres, Elsmore and Forster, 10¾″ h 125.00
Japan, Mason, c1815 . . . . 275.00
Sydenham, T and R Boote, 7⅞″ h 185.00
Plate
Bell Flower, J and J Edwards, 1860s,
9¾″ d 15.00
Corn, Davenport, 10½″ d 20.00
Gothic, Adams, 9½″ d 18.00
Prairie Flowers, Powell and Bishop,
8½″ d 18.00
Scalloped Decagon, Davenport,
1852, 9¼″ d 4.00
Wheat and Clover, Turner and
Tomkinson, 7″ d 15.00
Platter
Columbia, octagonal, 20″ l 125.00
Lily of the Valley, Alfred Meakin,
14½″ l. 40.00
Rolling Star, octagonal, J Edwards . . 50.00
Wheat, Meakin, 20¾″ l 50.00
Punch Bowl
Adriatic, scalloped edge 335.00
Berry Cluster, J Furnival 125.00

Relish
Ceres, Elsmore and Forster, 1860 40.00
Wheat, 1860s, 8¼″ l. 20.00
Sauce Dish, cov, ladle, Baltic, T Hulme,
4″ l 85.00
Sauce Tureen
Fluted Pearl, underplate, J Wedg-
wood. 100.00
Ribbed Bud, cov, oval, underplate,
ladle, 1860s. 225.00
Wheat and Blackberry, Clementson
Bros. 60.00
Soap Dish, cov, insert, Bordered Hya-
cinth, W Baker and Co, 1860s,
4¼″ h 150.00
Soup Plate
Paneled Grape, JF, 8⅞″ d 18.00
Wheat and Clover, Turner and
Tomkinson, 9″ d 25.00
Soup Tureen
Hyacinth, oval, ladle. 225.00
Lily of the Valley, Shaw. 225.00
Sugar
Ceres, Elsmore and Forster 70.00
Fuchsia, Meakin 40.00
Paneled, T J and J Mayer 45.00
Syrup Pitcher, Paneled Columbia,
1850s, 5″ h 60.00
Teapot
Forget-Me-Not, Wood, Rathbone
and Co, 8⅞″ h. 80.00
Ivy, William Adams, 10″ h 75.00
Niagara, Walley 110.00
Trent, T and R Boote 90.00
Toothbrush Holder
Bell Flower, Burgess 45.00
Cable and Ring, Cockson and Sed-
don 40.00
Hyacinth, cov, Wedgwood 60.00
Wheat and Clover, underplate,
Turner and Tomkinson. 50.00
Tray, Moss Rose, handled, gold trim,
Wedgwood, 9″ w 15.00
Vegetable Dish
Blackberry, cov, unmarked 45.00
Cable and Ring, Savoy shape, cov, T
and R Boote. 50.00
Hebe, John Alcock, 1853, 9⅜ ″ l. . . 40.00
Memnon, John Meir and Son, 11¼″ l 115.00
Prairie Flowers, cov, Livesley and
Powell. 85.00
Tiny Oak and Acorn, J W Parkhurst,
11¾″ l. 110.00
Waste Bowl, Columbia, unmarked,
4⅛ × 6⅜″ 75.00

MAJOLICA

History: Majolica, an opaque, tin-glazed pottery, has been produced by many countries for centuries. It originally took its name from the Spanish

Island of Majorca, where figuline (a potter's clay) is found. Today majolica denotes a type of pottery which was made during the last half of the 19th century in Europe and America.

Majolica designs frequently depict elements in nature: leaves, flowers, birds, and fish. Human figures were rare. Designs were painted on the soft clay body using vitreous colors, then fired under a clear lead glaze to impart the characteristically rich brilliant colors.

English majolica manufacturers who marked their works include Wedgwood, George Jones, Holdcraft, and Minton. Most of their pieces can be identified through the English Registry mark and/or the potter-designer's mark. Sarreguemines in France and Villeroy and Boch in Baden, Germany, produced majolica that compared favorably with the finer English majolica. Most Continental pieces had an incised number on the base.

Although 600 plus American potteries produced majolica between 1850 and 1900, only a handful chose to identify their wares. Among these manufacturers were George Morely, Edwin Bennett, the Chesapeake Pottery Company, the New Milford-Wannoppee Pottery Company, and the firm of Griffen, Smith, and Hill. The others hoped their unmarked pieces would be taken for English examples.

References: Nicholas M. Dawes, *Majolica,* Crown Publishers, 1990; Marilyn G. Karmason with Joan B. Stacke, *Majolica: A Complete History And Illustrated Survey,* Abrams, 1989; Mariann Katz-Marks, *The Collector's Encyclopedia of Majolica,* Collector Books, 1992; M. Charles Rebert, *American Majolica 1850–1900,* Wallace-Homestead, 1981; Mike Schneider, *Majolica,* Schiffer Publishing, 1990.

Collectors' Clubs: *Majolica Collectors Association,* PO Box 332, Wolcotville, IN 46795; *Majolica International Society,* 1275 First Ave, Suite 103, New York, NY 10021.

Reproduction Craftsperson: Marlene Humberd, 2314 Guthrie Ave, NW, Cleveland, TN 37311.

Bowl, Bird and Fan, ftd, Wedgwood, c1870, 10" d, 5" h, price for pair	850.00
Bread Plate	
Oak Leaf with Acorns, 12¼" l	115.00
Yellow Wheat, green ground, brown rim, cobalt blue center, emb "Eat thy bread with joy and thankfulness," 13" l	150.00
Cake Stand	
Bird and Fan, Wedgwood, c1870, 9" d, 3" h	225.00
Fruit, Wedgwood, c1870, 9" d, 5" h	250.00
Compote, Daisy, light pink int., Griffin Smith & Hill, imp GSH monogram, 9" d, 5¼" h	375.00

Dish, Etruscan Begonia Leaf Tray, dark green center, burgundy border, 8" l, $60.00.

Cup and Saucer, cauliflower shape, blue ground, imp "Wedgwood"	110.00
Dish	
Begonia Leaf, Griffin, Smith & Hill, imp GSH monogram, 7" l	185.00
Yellow Butterfly, olive green trim, 3¼" d	90.00
Ewer, Heron, standing among reeds and lily pads, fish in beak, multicolored, dated 1876, Minton, 21¾" h	2,340.00
Pitcher	
Fish, figural, 7" h	155.00
Flower and leaf pattern, English, dated 1859, 9½" h	475.00
Frog, figural, mauve spots on green back, yellow belly and feet, mauve twist handle, green lily pad base, 6½" h	150.00
Planter, tree trunk, figural, central well surrounded by three smaller wells, molded leaves, central bird's nest flanked by two bird figures, imp mark on base, Taft, Keene, NH, late 19th C, 10" h	300.00
Plate	
Bird and Fan, blue fans, Wedgwood, c1870, 8" d	150.00
Blackberry, Wedgwood, c1870, 8" d	100.00

Pitcher, Fruit, Clifton sgd, 10" h, $135.00.

Fruit, Wedgwood, c1870, 7″ d **80.00**
Grape Leaf, Wedgwood, c1870
  6″ d..................... **90.00**
  9″ d..................... **135.00**
Platter, Wild Rose and Rope, aqua
  ground, cobalt blue center, 11″ l... **115.00**
Serving Plate, Strawberry, center well,
  Wedgwood, c1870, 7″ d........ **100.00**

McCOY POTTERY ꟿcꟼoy

Mixing Bowls, nesting, Nelson McCoy Sanitary Stoneware Co, shield in circle mark, 1926, left: yellow, #4, 11½″ d, $24.00; right: green, marked "4", 9⅝″ d, $18.00.

History: The J. W. McCoy Pottery Co. was established in Roseville, Ohio, in September, 1899. The early McCoy Co. produced both stoneware and some art pottery lines, including Rosewood. In October, 1911, three potteries merged to create the Brush-McCoy Pottery Co. This company continued to produce the original McCoy lines and added several new art lines. Many early pieces are not marked.

In 1910, Nelson McCoy and his father, J. W. McCoy, founded the Nelson McCoy Sanitary Stoneware Co. In 1925, the McCoy family sold their interest in the Brush-McCoy Pottery Co. and concentrated on expanding and improving the Nelson McCoy Co. The new company produced stoneware, earthenware specialities, and artware. Most pottery marked McCoy was made by the Nelson McCoy Co.

McCoy Pottery is best known for its cookie jars, kitchenwares, tablewares, and florist pieces. Bright colors and country motifs abound. Several types of glazes were used. The highly glazed utilitarian wares are valued as they stand the test of time and hard use. One of the most widely recognized McCoy pieces is a small brown glazed mustard jar which was made for the Heinz Company.

Over twenty different marks have been identified.

References: Sharon and Bob Huxford, *The Collectors Encyclopedia of McCoy Pottery,* Collector Books, 1980, 1993 value update; Harold Nichols, *McCoy Cookie Jars: From The First To The Last, Second Edition,* Nichols Publishing, 1991; Martha and Steve Sanford, *The Guide To Brush-McCoy Pottery,* published by authors, 1992.

Periodical: *Our McCoy Matters,* PO Box 14255, Parkeville, MO 64152.

Ball Jug, yellow, unmarked, 1950s ... **20.00**
Basket
  Basketweave design, green and white ext., white int., marked "McCoy USA," 1956.......... **25.00**
  Oak Leaves and Acorns, marked "McCoy USA," 1952.......... **30.00**
Bird Feeder, hanging, brown, 1975 .. **12.00**

Bookends, pr
  Horses, jumping, marked "Nu-Art" **20.00**
  Lily, marked "McCoy Made in USA," 1948..................... **50.00**
Console Bowl
  Leaf, brown, 1960s............ **10.00**
  Tulips, blue, 8¾″ d............ **8.00**
Cookie Jar
  Apple, red.................. **40.00**
  Cat, pink basketweave base....... **45.00**
  Log Cabin................... **45.00**
  Mother Goose................ **100.00**
  Nabisco.................... **125.00**
  Picnic Basket................. **35.00**
  Potbelly Stove, white........... **30.00**
Flowerpot, paneled, slightly flared at top, pink, saucer, marked "McCoy USA," 1959.................. **6.00**
Grease Jar, cabbage head, 1954 ..... **35.00**
Hanging Basket
  Early American, marked "McCoy USA," 1967................ **15.00**
  Ivy Leaves, emb design, green, 1950 **18.00**
Jardiniere, pine cone, 7½″ w, 6½″ h **20.00**
Pitcher, vegetable design **35.00**
Pitcher and Bowl Set, white, blue trim, 1967..................... **15.00**
Planter
  Duck, holding umbrella **75.00**
  Fish, pink, green fins and tail, marked "McCoy USA," 1955.......... **40.00**
  Hunting Dog, Sidney Cope design **75.00**

Vase, chrysanthemums, hand painted, incised mark and paper label, late 1940s, 8¼″ h, $28.00.

Rooster, gray, marked "McCoy
USA," 1951. . . . .   **18.00**
Sprinkling Can, white, rose decal   **8.00**
Wishing Well **8.00**
Vase
Blossomtime, two handled, marked
"McCoy," 1946. . . . .   **20.00**
Fawn and Cornucopia, brown,
marked "McCoy USA," 1954 . . .   **25.00**
Ginger Jar, cobalt blue, marked "NM
USA," 1940. . . . .   **10.00**
Magnolia, marked "McCoy USA,"
1953.   **30.00**
Sunflower, 1954. . . . .   **30.00**
Uncle Sam, green **25.00**
Wall Pocket
Apple, 1953 . . . .   **35.00**
Flower, rustic glaze, 1946. . . . . . .   **12.00**
Mailbox, blue, marked "McCoy
USA," 1951. . . . .   **45.00**

METLOX POTTERY

History: In 1921 T. C. Prouty and Willis, his son, founded Proutyline Products, a company designed to develop Prouty's various inventions. In 1922 Prouty built a tile plant in Hermosa Beach, California to manufacture decorative and standard wall and floor tiles.

Metlox (a contraction of metallic oxide) was established in 1927. Prouty built a modern all-steel factory in Manhattan Beach to manufacture outdoor ceramic signs. The Great Depression had a strong impact on the sign business. When T. C. Prouty died in 1931, Willis reorganized the company and began to produce a line of solid color dinnerware similar to that produced by Bauer. In 1934 the line was fully developed and sold under the Poppytrail trademark. The poppy is the official state flower for California. Fifteen different colors were produced over an eight year period.

Other dinnerware lines produced in the 1930s include Mission Bell, sold exclusively by Sears & Roebuck; Pintoria, based on an English Staffordshire line; and Yorkshire, patterned after Gladding-McBean's Coronado line. Most of these lines did not survive World War II.

In the late 1930s Metlox employed the services of Carl Romanelli, a designer whose work appeared as figurines, miniatures, and Zodiac vases. A line called Modern Masterpieces featured bookends, busts, figural vases, figures, and wallpockets.

During World War II Metlox devoted its manufacturing efforts to the production of machine parts and parts for the B–25 bombers. When the war ended, Metlox returned its attention to the production of dinnerware.

In 1947, Evan K. Shaw, whose American Pottery in Los Angeles had been destroyed by fire, purchased Metlox. Dinnerware production with hand painted patterns accelerated. The California Ivy pat-

tern was introduced in 1946, California Provincial and Homestead Provincial in 1950, Red Rooster in 1955, California Strawberry in 1961, Sculptured Grape in 1963, and Della Robbia in 1965. Bob Allen and Mel Shaw, art directors, introduced a number of new shapes and lines in the 1950s, including Aztec, California Contempora, California Free Form, California Mobile, and Navajo.

When Vernon Kilns ceased operation in 1958 Metlox bought the trade name and select dinnerware molds. A separate Vernon Ware branch was established. Under the direction of Doug Bothwell the line soon rivaled the Poppytrail patterns.

Artware continued to flourish in the 1950s and 60s. Harrison McIntosh was among the key designers. Two popular lines were American Royal Horses and Nostalgia, scale model antique carriages. Between 1946 and 1956 Metlox made a series of ceramic cartoon characters under license from Walt Disney.

A line of planters designed by Helen Slater and Poppets, doll-like stoneware flower holders, were marketed in the 1960s and '70s. Recent production includes novelty cookie jars and Colorstax, a revival solid color dinnerware pattern.

Management remained in the Shaw family. Evan K. was joined by his two children, Ken and Melinda. Kenneth Avery, Melinda's husband, eventually became plant manager. When Evan K. died in 1980, Kenneth Avery became president. In 1988 Melinda Avery became the guiding force. The company ceased operations in 1989.

The choices of patterns and backstamps is overwhelming. Collectors should concentrate on one specific line and pattern. Among the most popular Poppytrail patterns are California Ivy, Homestead Provincial, and Red Rooster.

The recent cookie jar craze has attracted a number of collectors to Metlox's cookie jar line. Most examples sell within a narrow range. A full selection of cookie jars is listed on pages 135–138 of the Kitchen Collectibles section.

References: Jack Chipman, *Collector's Encyclopedia of California Pottery*, Collector Books, 1992; Harvey Duke, *The Official Identification and Price Guide to Pottery and Porcelain, Seventh Edition*, House of Collectibles, 1989; Lois Lehner, *Lehner's Encyclopedia of U. S. Marks on Pottery, Porcelain & Clay*, Collector Books, 1988.

Aztec
Creamer **18.00**
Fruit Bowl. **10.00**
Gravy Boat **40.00**
Platter, 13" l **32.00**
Soup, dark int. **8.00**
Sugar, cov. **35.00**
California Ivy
Bowl, 9" d. **25.00**
Chop Plate, 15" d **25.00**
Coaster **10.00**

Creamer and Sugar, cov	15.00
Cup and Saucer	5.00
Demitasse Cup and Saucer	18.00
Fruit Bowl, 5¼" d	6.50
Gravy, underplate	25.00
Pitcher, ice lip	35.00
Plate, 6" d, bread and butter	3.00
Salt and Pepper Shakers, pr	12.00

California Provincial

Bread Tray	40.00
Chop Plate, 12" d	18.00
Coaster	12.00
Creamer	6.00
Cup and Saucer	8.00
Fruit Bowl, 6" d	6.00
Gravy	15.00
Mug, large	25.00

Plate

6" d, bread and butter	4.00
8" d, salad	8.00
10" d, dinner	10.00
Platter, 13½" l	25.00
Salt and Pepper Shakers, pr	15.00
Saucer	1.00
Soup, flat, 8½" d	7.00
Vegetable Bowl, 10" d	20.00

Homestead Provincial

Bread Tray	25.00
Casserole, cov, 10" d	25.00
Cereal Bowl, handle	10.00
Chop Plate, 12" d	12.00
Coffeepot	30.00
Creamer and Sugar, cov	25.00
Cup and Saucer	8.00
Gravy	20.00
Jewelry Box	45.00
Match Holder	30.00
Mug	20.00
Plate, 10" d, dinner	8.00
Platter, 13½" l	20.00
Salad Bowl, 11" d	22.00
Salt and Pepper Shakers, pr	15.00
Sprinkling Can	25.00
Teapot	28.00

Vegetable Dish

8½" l, two part, stick handle	22.00
13" l, three part, handled	22.00
Wall Pocket	42.00

Navajo

Bowl, 13" d	45.00
Butter Dish	30.00
Creamer and Sugar, cov	30.00
Gravy, underplate	30.00
Plate, 12" d, chop	30.00
Platter, 11¾" l	30.00
Teapot	50.00

Provincial Fruit

Bowl

5" d, tab handled	4.00
6" d	4.00
7" d, deep	8.00
10" d	18.00

Butter Dish	25.00
Coffeepot	45.00
Creamer	7.00
Cup and Saucer	8.00
Gravy, handled	12.00
Pepper Shaker	4.00

Plate

6½" d, bread and butter	4.00
7¾" d, salad	8.00
10½" d, dinner	9.00
Platter, 13½" l	18.00
Relish, rect, divided, handled	12.00
Salt and Pepper Shakers, pr	7.00
Soup, 8½" d	8.00
Vegetable Bowl, 10" d	18.00

Red Rooster

Butter, cov	30.00
Canister, flour	40.00
Cereal Bowl, 7" d	12.00
Chop Plate, 12" d	13.00
Coffeepot, cov	40.00
Cup	8.00
Oil and Vinegar Cruets	22.00
Pitcher, 6" h	40.00

Plate

7½" d, salad	6.00
10" d, dinner	10.00
Platter, 13½" l	20.00
Salt and Pepper Shakers, pr, handled	12.00
Sugar, open	12.00
Vegetable Bowl, 10" d	15.00

Strawberry

Bowl

7" d	12.00
9" d	15.00
Creamer	15.00
Cup and Saucer	15.00

Plate

8" d, salad	10.00
10" d, dinner	15.00
Sugar, cov	18.00

Vineyard

Cereal Bowl, 7½" d	5.00
Cup and Saucer	7.00

Plate

6¼" d, bread and butter	4.00
7½" d, salad	6.00
10½" d, dinner	7.00

MOCHA WARE

History: Mocha decoration is usually found on utilitarian creamware and stoneware pieces and is produced through a simple chemical action. A color pigment of brown, blue, green, or black is made acidic by an infusion of tobacco or hops. When the acidic colorant is applied in blobs to an alkaline ground, it reacts by spreading in feathery, seaweed-like designs. This type of decoration usually is supplemented with bands of light colored slip.

Types of decoration vary greatly, from those done in a combination of motifs, such as "Cat's Eye" and "Earthworm," to a plain pink mug decorated with green ribbed bands. Most forms of mocha are hollow, e.g., mugs, jugs, bowls, and shakers.

English potters made the vast majority of the pieces. Marked pieces are extremely rare. Collectors group the ware into three chronological periods: 1780–1820, 1820–1840, and 1840–1880.

Country collectors treasure mocha ware. Warm colors and interesting designs lend themselves well to Country collections.

Bowl
  4¼" d
    Cup shape, blue seaweed dec on white band, hairline **215.00**
    Mug shape, gray band with orange stripes and white, brown, and blue dots, tooled, green glaze, leaf handle **300.00**
  5⅛" d, 3⅛" h, white, brown, and blue cat's eye dec on orange band, black stripes **200.00**
  8¼" d, 4" h, tooled rim, pale blue and black earthworm dec on orange-tan band, black and green stripes **600.00**
Castor, 4½" h, cat's eye dec **425.00**
Chamber Pot, cov, 9" d, 8" h, tan, olive, chocolate brown, and white cat's eye and leaf dec on emb green band, emb leaf handle **500.00**
Creamer, 3½" h, emb green band, brown and pale blue stripes, emb spout and leaf handle **175.00**
Cup and Saucer, handleless, black and white checkerboard band around rim, white fluted band around base, medium blue ground, matching saucer **125.00**
Flower Pot
  4¼" h, blue, white, brown, and ochre earthworm design, blue bands, ochre and brown stripes, tooled blue lip, no saucers, price for pair **3,190.00**

Bowl, brown, cream, and orange earthworm dec on tan ground, raised green border, c1790–1820, 6¼" d, $600.00.

7¼" h, flared lip, black seaweed dec and stripes, pale salmon pink ground, detachable saucer, imp "Creil," wear and chips **600.00**
Jar, 7" d, 5½" h, blue seaweed dec, dark brown stripes, white band, hairlines, replaced wooden lid **100.00**
Jug, 8¼" h, one gallon, chocolate brown seaweed dec, gray band, blue bands top and bottom **350.00**
Mug
  3⅛" h, blue earthworm dec on pale blue band, brown stripes, white ground, leaf handle, hairline and flake on base **300.00**
  3½" h, blue seaweed dec on white band, blue stripes, leaf handle . . . **410.00**
  3¾" h, blue and black seaweed dec on white band, blue and black stripes, leaf handle, hairline **165.00**
  4⅝" h, brown and white geometric bands, blue and brown stripes, white ground, leaf handle **150.00**
  4⅞" h
    Tan, white, and brown earthworm dec, chocolate brown bands, blue ground, emb band and leaf handle, wear, rim badly chipped **165.00**
    White, tan, and brown striped fanlike designs, pale orange ground, white leaf handle, wear and chips **2,200.00**
  5" h, black seaweed dec on teal band, blue band around rim, black stripes, white ground **185.00**
  5⅝" h
    Black and white checkerboard band around top, tan stripes, gray-green ground, leaf handle, wear, chips, hairline **165.00**
    Gray band with black and blue dots, black stripes, emb blue band **410.00**
  5⅞" h, brown and blue foliage design on white ground, blue bands, chocolate brown, blue, and white stripes, emb rim band and leaf handle, wear, rim chips, hairline **225.00**
  6" h, tan, green, and chocolate brown stripes on emb bands, leaf handle **225.00**
Mustard Pot, cov, 3⅝" h, orange, chocolate brown, and white stripes, emb green band and leaf handle, chips and repair **465.00**
Pepper Pot, 3½" h, pale blue, brown, and yellow scroddled design, white ground **525.00**
Pitcher
  4¾" h, pint, black seaweed dec on teal band, blue band at rim, black stripes, white ground **190.00**

Pitcher, dark brown seaweed dec on rust band, cream handle and spout, 6¾" h, $800.00.

6¾" h, tan, blue, and black earthworm design and stripes, two tone
blue band, white ground, emb
bands and leaf handle, small
chips, hairline in spout, poorly re-
paired chip on lip 385.00
7" h
    Black stripes and leaves, light
    green and blue bands, leaf han-
    dle.   110.00
    Brown cat's eye dec, light grayish
    blue band, brown stripes, leaf
    handle. 215.00
7½" h, white and chocolate brown
    stripes, blue bands, yellow ground   450.00
7⅝" h, blue and black earthworm
    dec on white band, blue, white,
    and black stripes, chips and hair-
    lines 325.00
7¾" h
    Blue, orange, black, and emb
    green stripes, white ground, leaf
    handle, broken and glued,
    stains and chips 190.00
    Brown earthworm dec, blue and
    white bands, emb green stripes   325.00
8" h, baluster shape, twig, wave, and
    cat's eye dec, incised green bands
    enclosing central butternut,
    brown, and white bands, molded
    foliate spout and handle, imper-
    fections 2,750.00
Salt
    2¼" d, earthworm dec, blue and
    brown bands, ochre ground, rim
    flake 140.00
    3" d, brown seaweed dec, white
    band, ftd 225.00
Shaker
    4¼" h, tan cat's eyes on choco-
    late brown band, slate blue, tan,
    olive gray, and chocolate brown
    stripes, white ground, damage and
    repair 325.00
    5⅛" h, blue, white, tan, and choco-
    late brown earthworm design and
    stripes, chips and old repairs 225.00

Spill Holder, 4⅜" h, machine tooled,
    chocolate brown stripes, green
    glaze, short hairline, small chips,
    glued flake 160.00
Sugar Bowl, 2⅜" h, miniature, brown,
    tan, and white marbleizing, stains,
    small edge chips, short hairline 425.00
Tea Caddy, cov, 4⅞" h, black, tan, and
    blue geometric design 525.00
Teapot
    4½" h, marbleized brown, sienna,
    and white, green Leeds type rim,
    minor nicks on cov and base 2,000.00
    5½" h, globular body, black and
    white checkerboard band around
    shoulder, medium blue ground,
    acorn finial 200.00
Waste Bowl, 5½" d, 2⅞" h, brown and
    white cat's eye dec on pale orange
    band, light blue stripes, hairline . . .   100.00

MORTON POTTERIES

History: Pottery was produced in Morton, Illinois,
for 99 years. In 1877 six Rapp brothers, who
emigrated from Germany, established the first pottery, Morton Pottery Works. Over the years sons,
cousins, and nephews became involved in the
production of pottery. Other Morton pottery operations were spin-offs from the original. When it
was taken over in 1915 by second generation
Rapps, Morton Pottery Works became the Morton
Earthenware Company. Work at that pottery was
terminated by World War I.

The Cliftwood Art Potteries, Inc., operated from
1920 to 1940. One of the original founders of the
Morton Pottery Works and his four sons organized
it. They sold out in 1940, and the operation continued for four more years as the Midwest Potteries, Inc. A disastrous fire brought an end to that
operation in March 1944. These two potteries
produced figurines, lamps, novelties, and vases.

In 1922 the Morton Pottery Company, which
had the longest existence of all the Morton's potteries, was organized by the same brothers who
had operated the Morton Earthenware Company.
The Morton Pottery Company specialized in beer
steins, kitchenwares, and novelty items for chain
stores and gift shops. They also produced some of
the Vincent Price National Treasures reproductions for Sears Roebuck and Company in the
mid-1960s. The Morton Pottery closed in 1976,
thus ending the 99 years of pottery production in
Morton.

By 1947 the brothers who had operated the
Cliftwood Art Potteries, Inc., came back into the
pottery business. They established the short-lived
American Art Potteries, which made flower bowls,
lamps, planters, some unusual flower frogs, and
vases. Their wares were marketed by florists and
gift shops. Production at American Art Potteries

was halted in 1961. Of all the wares of the Morton potteries, those of the American Art Potteries are the most elusive.

The potteries of Morton, Illinois, used local clay until 1940. The clay fired out to a golden ecru color which is quite easy to recognize. After 1940 southern and eastern clays were shipped to Morton. These clays fired out white. Thus, later period wares are sharply distinguished from the earlier ones.

Few pieces were marked by the potteries. Incised and raised marks for the Morton Pottery Works, the Cliftwood Art Potteries, Inc., and the Morton Pottery Company do surface at times. The Cliftwood, Midwest, Morton Pottery Company, and American Art Pottery all used paper labels in limited amounts. Some of these have survived, and collectors do find them.

Glazes from the early period, 1877–1920, usually were Rockingham types, both mottled and solid. Yellow ware also was standard during the early period. Occasionally a dark cobalt blue was produced, but this color is rare. Colorful drip glazes and solid colors came into use after 1920.

Reference: Doris and Burdell Hall, *Morton's Potteries: 99 Years,* published by author, 1982.

Museums: Illinois State Museum, Springfield, IL; Morton Public Library (permanent exhibit), Morton, IL.

Baker, brown Rockingham glaze, Morton Pottery Works, 5½" d	**35.00**
Candlesticks, pr, square base, chocolate drip glaze, Cliftwood Art Potteries, 11" h	**50.00**
Figure	
Boxer, sitting, Morton Pottery Co	**65.00**
Cat, reclining, cobalt blue glaze, Cliftwood Art Potteries, 4 ½" l. . .	**25.00**
Chickens, 7" h hen, 8" h rooster, white, gold highlights, Midwest Potteries	**35.00**
Cocker Spaniel, standing, Morton Pottery Co.	**45.00**
Dalmatian, sitting, Morton Pottery Co.	**45.00**
Goose, white, yellow highlights, Midwest Potteries, 5¾" h	**8.00**

Stallion, rearing, gold, Midwest Potteries, 10¾" h	**25.00**
Flower Bowl, round, brown, yellow drip glaze, 2 pcs, Midwest Potteries, 10" d, 5½" h	**16.00**
Jar, stoneware, 2 gallon, Albany slip glaze, marked on side, Morton Pottery Works	**65.00**
Lamp Base, owl on log, yellow, Cliftwood Art Potteries, 7½" h	**35.00**
Milk Jug, adv, Woodland Glaze, yellow ware, brown and green spatter, Morton Pottery Co, 4½" h	**80.00**
Mixing Bowl, yellow ware, wide white band and narrow blue stripes, Morton Pottery Works, 12½" d	**45.00**
Pie Bird, Morton Pottery Co	
Bird, white body, multicolored wings and back, 5" h	**18.00**
Duck, white, pink wings and base, 5" h	**24.00**
Pie Plate, Morton Pottery Works	
9" d, brown Rockingham glaze	**100.00**
11" d, yellow ware	**80.00**
Planter	
Cowboy and Cactus, natural colors, Morton Pottery Co, 7" h	**12.00**
Cowboy Boot, blue, pink spray glaze, American Art Potteries, 6" h	**12.00**
Mother Earth Line, Morton Pottery Co, natural colors	
Apple	**3.00**
Pineapple	**5.00**
Quail, natural color spray glaze, American Art Potteries, 9½" h. . .	**24.00**
Rabbit, male, wearing top hat and blue vest, egg planter, Morton Pottery Co, 9½" h.	**12.00**
Squirrel on Log, gray spray glaze, American Art Potteries, 7" h	**15.00**
Salt and Pepper Shakers, pr, Woodland Glaze, yellow ware, brown and green spatter, Morton Pottery Co, 5" h.	**110.00**
Spittoon, scalloped design, brown Rockingham glaze, Morton Pottery Works	**55.00**
Teapot, 1 cup, acorn shape, brown Rockingham glaze, Morton Pottery Works, 4½" h	**30.00**

Mug, yellow ware, blue slip stripes, Morton Pottery Works, $12.00.

Piebirds, left: duck, white, blue wings, pink base, 5" h, $24.00; right: bird, multicolored wings and back, 5" h, $18.00.

Vase

Bulbous, bud, long neck, multicolored, Morton Pottery Co, 6" h . . .   **6.00**

Cornucopia, shell base, blue, Morton Pottery Co, 8½" h **15.00**

Wall Pocket

Teapot, white, red apple dec, red finial, Morton Pottery Co, 6½" h   **12.00**

Tree Stump, applied woodpecker figure, brown spray glaze, American Art Potteries, 5" h **15.00**

PAUL REVERE POTTERY

History: Paul Revere Pottery, Boston, Massachusetts, was an outgrowth of a club known as "The Saturday Evening Girls." The S.E.G. was a group of young female immigrants who met on Saturday nights for reading and crafts such as ceramics.

Regular production began in 1908. The name Paul Revere was adopted because the pottery was located near the Old North Church. In 1915 the firm moved to Brighton, Massachusetts. Known as the "Bowl Shop," the pottery grew steadily. In spite of popular acceptance and technical advancements, the pottery required continual subsidies. It finally closed in January, 1942.

Items produced range from plain and decorated vases to tablewares to illustrated tiles. Many decorated wares were incised and glazed either in an Art Nouveau matte finish or an occasional high glaze.

In addition to the impressed mark, paper "Bowl Shop" labels were used prior to 1915. Pieces also can be found dated with P.R.P. or S.E.G. painted on the base.

References: Paul Evans, *Art Pottery of the United States, Second Edition,* Feingold & Lewis Publishing Corp, 1987; Ralph and Terry Kovel, *The Kovels' Collector's Guide to American Art Pottery,* Crown Publishers, Inc., 1974.

Collectors' Club: American Art Pottery Association, 125 E. Rose Ave, St Louis, MO 63119.

Creamer, sgraffito, white wild rose border, blue and gray ground, black matte outlines, white int., sgd "FR/255–6–09/SEG," 2⅞" h **350.00**

Jar, cov, purple moths border, blue and green stylized band, white ground, sgd by Sara Galner and Ida Goldstein, 1911, 5" d, 4 ½" h. **1,550.00**

Jardiniere, flared, repeating yellow, green, and blue tulip border, matte black outlines, yellow ground, sgd on back "11–26 PRP," X in circle artist cipher **350.00**

Luncheon Set, blue and green repeating tree and sky border, black outlines, cream ground, sgd and numbered, five cups, luncheon plates, and dessert plates, price for fifteen piece set   **1,650.00**

Mug

Incised tree filled landscape, solitary nightingale over inscription "In the forest must always be a nightingale and in the soul a faith so faithful that it comes back even after it has been slain," green, brown, blue, cream, and yellow glazes, dec by Sara Galner, incised artist's initials and marks, c1915, 4" h **1,425.00**

Strolling Rabbit design, inscribed "John Fisk/Zueblin" below rim, matte brown and blue, cream ground, blue band, inscribed "Xmas/1914/S.E.G.," hairline, 3" h   **385.00**

Pitcher

Incised and dec stylized yellow tulips, brown leaves, black outlines, yellow ground, white horizontal ring below spout, sgd "SEG/AM," spout loss, hairline, 7¾" h **650.00**

White singing chickens, wide white and yellow border, black matte outlines, white and yellow int., sgd "SEG/JT/MD/9–19," 1919 . . . . . .   **275.00**

Planter, shallow, stylized brown and tan tree clusters border, white and yellow landscape, black matte outlines, yellow ground, sgd "SEG/FL/1–23" **1,875.00**

Plate

Quarter moon, star filled sky, lakeside cottage, tall trees, flowering daffodils, black matte outlines, dark and light shades of blue, green, brown, and yellow, sgd "SEG/SG/11–15, 1915 . . . .   **11,000.00**

Pitcher, yellow-brown ground, rabbit medallion, "David, His Jug," applied loop handle, 4½" h, $225.00.

Running pigs border, Helen Os-
bourne Storrow monogram incised at center, bands of brown,
yellow, and green, dec by Lily
Shapiro and Rose Bikini, artists'
ciphers, numbered, and marked
"SEG," 3½" d, price for pair **3,200.00**

Teapot, cov, repeating yellow crocus
border, black matte outlines, white
ground, tiny glaze chip on spout, sgd
"196–EG/SEG," 1912 . . . .   **200.00**

Tile, central cottage by lake scene,
green, brown, white, and orange,
black outlines, light blue ground, sgd
and numbered, 5¾" d. **425.00**

Vase

Band of flying ducks over blue water,
horizon of green land, yellow and
blue sky, black outlines, light blue
ground, inscribed marks, remnants of paper label, rim pepper-
ing, 8⅜" h. **1,325.00**

Matte yellow, green, and brown stylized floral band, black outlines,
matte white-yellow band at shoulder and rim, matte yellow glaze
body, inscribed marks, two hair-
lines at rim, 9⅛" h **525.00**

Stylized trees, black outlines, gray-
green glaze, flaring cylindrical
shape, 7¼" h, sgd "SEG" **450.00**

PENNSBURY POTTERY

History: Henry and Lee Below established
Pennsbury Pottery in 1950, named for its close
proximity to William Penn's estate "Pennsbury,"
three miles west of Morrisville, Pennsylvania.
Henry, a ceramic engineer and mold maker, and
Lee, a designer and modeler, had previously
worked for Stangl Pottery in Trenton, New Jersey.

Many of Pennsbury's forms, motifs, and manufacturing techniques have Stangl roots. A line of
birds similar to those produced by Stangl were
among the earliest Pennsbury products. The
carved design technique is also Stangl in origin.

Pennsbury products are easily identified by their
brown wash background. The company also made
pieces featuring other background colors: do not
make the mistake of assuming that a piece is not
Pennsbury because it does not have a brown wash.

Pennsbury motifs are heavily nostalgia, farm,
and Pennsylvania German related. Among the
most popular lines were Amish, Black Rooster,
Delft Toleware, Eagle, Family, Folkart, Gay
Ninety, Harvest, Hex, Quartet, Red Barn, Red
Rooster, Slick-Chick, and Christmas plates (1960-
70). The pottery made a large number of commemorative, novelty, and special order pieces.

In the late 1950s the company had 16 employees, mostly local housewives and young girls. In
1963 employees numbered 46, the company's
peak. By the late 1960s, the company had just over
20 employees. Cheap foreign imports cut deeply
into the pottery's profits.

Marks differ from piece to piece depending on
the person who signed the piece or the artist who
sculptured the mold. The identity for some initials
has still not been determined.

Henry Below died on December 21, 1959,
leaving the pottery in trust for his wife and three
children with instructions that it be sold upon the
death of his wife. Lee Below died on December
12, 1968. In October 1970 the Pennsbury Pottery
filed for bankruptcy. The contents of the company
were auctioned on December 18, 1970. On May
18, 1971, a fire destroyed the pottery and support
buildings.

Since the pieces were hand carved, aesthetic
quality differs from piece to piece. Look for pieces
with a strong design sense and a high quality of
execution. Buy only clearly marked pieces. Look
for decorator and designer initials that can be
easily identified.

Pennsbury collectors are concentrated in the
Middle Atlantic states. Many of the company's
commemorative and novelty pieces relate to local
businesses and events, thus commanding their
highest prices within this region.

Reference: Lucile Henzke, *Pennsbury Pottery*,
Schiffer Publishing, 1990.

Ashtray

Amish People **15.00**
Don't Be So Doppish, 5" l **20.00**
Doylestown Trust **15.00**
Outen the Light **15.00**
Such Schmoltzers **15.00**
What Giffs? **15.00**

Beer and Pretzel Set, Sweet Adeline, 9
pcs **120.00**

Beer Mug, Amish **18.00**
Bread Tray, Wheat pattern **25.00**
Cake Stand, Amish **75.00**
Candleholders, pr, Rooster **110.00**
Coaster, Shultz **15.00**
Cookie Jar, Rooster **75.00**

Creamer, 2" h

Amish Woman's Head **13.00**
Red Rooster **15.00**

Cup and Saucer

Black Rooster **12.00**
Red Rooster **15.00**

Desk Accessory, bucket, National Ex-
change Club **18.00**

Mug

Eagle **20.00**
Sweet Adeline, 4½" h **25.00**

Pie Plate, apple tree **85.00**

Pitcher

Amish Man, miniature, 2" h **12.00**
Amish Woman, 5" h **45.00**
Red Rooster, 4" h **27.00**

Plaque, Central R.R. of New Jersey, 1870, "Star," 7⅞" l, $30.00.

Plaque
    Lafayette, B & O Railroad **45.00**
    NEA Centennial **24.00**
Plate
    Black Rooster, 10" d, dinner **13.00**
    Hex Sign
        8" d, luncheon **18.00**
        10" d, dinner. **20.00**
    Mother's Day
        1972 . . . .   **9.00**
        1975 . . . .   **9.00**
    Red Rooster, 10" d, dinner **18.00**
    Yuletide, 1970, first edition. **9.00**
Pretzel Bowl, eagle, 8 × 11" **50.00**
Salt and Pepper Shakers, pr, Amish
    heads **55.00**
Snack Tray and Cup, red rooster. **20.00**
Tile, 4" square, Outen the Light **25.00**
Vegetable Dish, red rooster, divided. .   **30.00**

PURINTON POTTERY

Purinton
SLIP WARE

History: Bernard Purinton founded Purinton Pottery in 1936 in Wellsville, Ohio. In 1941 the pottery relocated to Shippenville, Pennsylvania. The plant ceased operations around 1959. William H. Blair and Dorothy Purinton were the chief designers.

Purinton Pottery did not use decals as did many of its competitors. All slipware was cast. Greenware was hand painted by locally trained decorators who then dipped the decorated pieces into glaze. This demanded a specially formulated body and a more expensive manufacturing process. Hand painting also allowed for some of the variations in technique and colors found on Purinton ware today.

Reference: Pat Dole, *Purinton Pottery, Book I* (1985) and *Book II* (1990), Denton Publishing.

Periodical: *Purinton Pastimes,* 20401 Ivybridge Court, Gaithersburg, MD 20879.

Apple
    Bowl, 12" d **20.00**
    Butter Dish, cov,¼ lb **50.00**

Canister Set, cov, flour, sugar, coffee,
    and tea **90.00**
Casserole, cov, oval **24.00**
Cereal Bow **7.50**
Chop Plate, 12" d **20.00**
Coffeepot, cov. **25.00**
Creamer and Sugar, cov **30.00**
Cup and Saucer. **15.00**
Drip Jar, cov **20.00**
Honey Pot. **15.00**
Kent Jug, pint **15.00**
Plate
    8" d, salad **9.00**
    9" d, luncheon. **14.00**
Platter, 12" l **22.00**
Range Shaker **10.00**
Salad Bowl, ftd, 11" d **30.00**
Salt and Pepper Shakers, pr, small,
    jug. **15.00**
Teapot, 2 cup **20.00**
Vegetable Bowl, 8½" d **18.00**
Water Set, pitcher and six tumblers   **85.00**
Fruit
    Coffeepot **25.00**
    Creamer and Sugar, cov **18.00**
    Pitcher, water **30.00**
    Plate, 9¾" d, dinner **12.00**
    Range Salt and Pepper Shakers, pr   **15.00**
    Relish Dish, three part, handled . . .   **15.00**
    Teapot, 2 cup **25.00**
Pennsylvania Dutch
    Bread Tray. **35.00**
    Butter Dish, cov,¼ lb **35.00**
    Canister Set, cov, flour, sugar, coffee,
        and tea **175.00**
    Casserole, 9" d **40.00**
    Cereal Bowl **12.00**
    Chop Plate, 12" d **28.00**
    Cookie Jar, cov **50.00**
    Creamer and Sugar, cov
        Individual **25.00**
        Large **36.00**
    Plate
        8½" d, luncheon **12.00**
        9¾" d, dinner **18.00**
    Platter, 12" l **30.00**
    Relish Dish, 6" l **10.00**
    Salad Bowl, ftd, 11" d **40.00**
    Spaghetti Bowl, rect, 14½" l **75.00**
    Teapot, 2 cup **28.00**
    Vegetable Bowl, divided **32.00**
    Vinegar and Oil Jugs, pr **45.00**

REDWARE

History: The availability of clay, the same used to make bricks and roof tiles, accounted for the great production of red earthenware pottery in the American colonies. Redware pieces are mainly utilitarian—bowls, crocks, jugs, etc.

Lead glazed redware retained its reddish color,

but a variety of colored glazes were obtained by the addition of metals to the basic glaze. Streaks and mottled splotches in redware items resulted from impurities in the clay and/or uneven firing temperatures.

"Slipware" is a term used to describe redwares decorated by the application of slip, a semiliquid paste made of clay. Slipwares were made in England, Germany, and elsewhere in Europe for decades before becoming popular in the Pennsylvania German region and colonial America.

"Sgraffito" is a term used to describe redware that has a unique decoration. The entire surface is covered with a thick yellow glaze and the design is scratched into it, removing thin lines to create stylized decorations. Other colors may be added as highlights. Sgraffito ware is time consuming to produce and the glaze often flaked. Pieces in good condition command high prices. Sgraffito ware makes an excellent display piece and new reproductions should not be overlooked.

Reference: Kevin McConnell, *Redware: America's Folk Art Pottery,* Schiffer Publishing, 1988.

Reproduction Craftspersons: *Figures*—James J Nyeste, RD 1, Green Valley Rd, Seven Valleys, PA 17360; *General*—Lester Breininger, Breininger Pottery, 476 S Church St, Robesonia, PA 19551; Susan Campbell, 32 S Merion Ave, Bryn Mawr, PA 19010; Carolyn Nygren Curran, CNC Pottery, 8 Pershing Rd, Glens Falls, NY 12804; David & Mary Farrell, Westmoore Pottery, Rte 2, Box 494, Seagrove, NC 27341; C Ned Foltz, The Foltz Pottery, 225 N Peartown Rd, Reinholds, PA 17569; Ron Geering, 1284 State Rd, Plymouth, MA 02360; Gris Pottery, 111 W Main St, Dundee, IL 60118; Richard L Hamelin, The Pied Potter Hamelin, PO Box 1082, Warren, MA 01083; Debra and Joel Huntley, Wisconsin Pottery, W3199 Hwy 16, Columbus, WI 53925; Scott R Jones, 1005 Oak Ln, New Cumberland, PA 17070; The Long Family Potters, Old Eagle Studios, 237 Bridge St, Phoenixville, PA 19460; Nancy Martindale, Handworks, 215 Countryman Lane, Spring City, TN 37381; Becky Mummert, 30 Fish and Game Rd, East Berlin, PA 17316; Stephen Nutt, Yankee Redware Pottery, 25 Ellicott Place, Staten Island, NY 10301; Greg Shooner, Greg Shooner American Redware, 1772 Jeffery Rd, Oregonia, OH 45054; Jeff White, Hephaestus Pottery Studio, 2012 Penn St, Lebanon, PA 17042; Gerald Yoder and William Logan, Oley Valley Redware, RD 5, Box 5–095, Fleetwood, PA 19522.

Reproduction Manufacturers: Basye-Bomberger/Fabian House, PO Box 86, W Bowie, MD 20715; Country Lighting and Accessories, PO Box 1279, New London, NH 03257; Country Loft, 1506 South Shore Park, Hingham, MA 02043; Faith Mountain Country Fare, Main St, Box 199, Sperryville, VA 22740; Gooseberry Patch, PO Box 634, Delaware, OH 43015; Turtlecreek Potters,

3600 Shawhan Rd, Morrow, OH 45152; The Vinery, 103 Alta Vista, Waterloo, IA 40703.

Apple Butter Jar, 6¾" h, applied strap handle, spout, incised band around top, minor hairline	**90.00**
Bank	
Apple, 3¼" h, red and yellow paint	**140.00**
Beehive, 6½" h, peg finial, clear lead glaze, slight greenish tint	**210.00**
Face, 3" h, painted, back inscribed "Josephine Chute Age 1," late 19th/early 20th C	**225.00**
Basket, 5¼" h, marbleized brown and white slip, crimped rim, rope twist handle	**8,250.00**
Bean Pot, 5⅝" h, dark brown glazed int., two rim chips	**225.00**
Bottle, 5¾" h, pinched sides and tooling, green glaze, brown flecks, green striping, incised label "Made by I S Stahl, 11–1–1939"	**55.00**
Bowl	
5½" d, yellow slip, worn int.	**75.00**
6½" d, cream colored slip dec, brown spots, flakes	**80.00**
10" d	
Brown sponged glaze	**95.00**
Slip dec, brown, white, and green	**140.00**
12½" d, 2½" h, sgraffito, eagle, flowers, and "1827," late 19th/early 20th C	**425.00**
Bucket, 20" h, pierced cylindrical body, strap handle	**85.00**
Bust, 13" h, young boy, brown glaze, late 19th C	**55.00**
Cake Mold, 7½" d, incised, PA, 19th C	**140.00**
Charger, 14½" d, yellow slip dec, cogled rim	**285.00**
Colander, 9¾" d, 7" h, clear glaze, brown flecks, orangish brown glaze, rim handles, three applied feet	**300.00**
Creamer, 3¾" h, pinpoint flakes	**50.00**
Crock, 9" h, clear glaze, brown splotches, applied handles	**175.00**
Cup, oversized	
3¼" h, 5¼" d, dark greenish brown glaze	**85.00**

Crock, Strasburg, VA, green slip, emb label, $150.00.

3½" h, 5¼" d, strap handle, brown
splotches, edge wear, chips **110.00**
Cup and Saucer, brown glaze, black
highlights, set of seven **115.00**
Cuspidor
  3¾" d, 2" h, lady's, applied tooled
  floral dec, bottom incised label
  partially obscured by firing crack
  and kiln shelf adhesion, "A. L. S.
  Manufactured, St. Jobs, Ohio" . . . **45.00**
  5½" d, reddish brown glaze, mottled
  dark brown, handle **75.00**
Dish
  8" d, white, green and brown slip
  dec, rope handles, imp "J Bell &
  Son, Strasburg, VA" **2,300.00**
  11½" d, round, concentric circles
  slip dec, notched rim, chips, 19th
  C **1,050.00**
  11½" l, oblong, deep green glaze,
  orange spots, wear **275.00**
Figure
  Poodle, 4" l, 4½" h, glazed **250.00**
  Squirrel, 7½" h, early 20th C **165.00**
Flask, 8" h, brown splotches, clear
  glaze, orange ground, New England **275.00**
Flower Pot, 8¾" h, brown sponged
  glaze, tooled and finger crimped rim,
  mismatched saucer **225.00**
Food Mold, Turk's head
  6" d, amber glaze **55.00**
  6¼" d, 1½" h, fluted, scalloped rim,
  greenish glaze, amber spots,
  brown splotches, small edge flakes **95.00**
  7¼" d, 2¾" h, fluted, scalloped rim,
  clear glaze, brown edge sponging
  with rich orange color, filed letter
  "M" on rim, small flakes, minor
  edge wear **100.00**
  7½" d
    Green glaze, amber spots **85.00**
    Reddish glaze, brown flakes,
    daubs of white slip and dark
    brown, small chips **65.00**
  8½" d, amber glaze, molded leaf
  design **30.00**
Grotesque Jug, 10" h, green ash glaze,
  incised "Chute Hewell" **325.00**

**Food Mold, Turk's head, Midwest, late,
10" d, $45.00.**

Herb Pot, 4¼" h, glazed, brown splotch
  dec, ochre ground, imperfections,
  19th C **525.00**
Ink Well, 3½" d, 3½" h, incised chain
  design, clear lead glaze, ruffled edge,
  applied pheasant handle cov, head
  of pheasant glued **350.00**
Jar
  5⅜" h, ovoid, dark brown glaze,
  glaze flakes **25.00**
  5½" h, ovoid
    Black, brown, and amber mottle
    glaze **60.00**
    Dark reddish glaze, brown
    splotches, small chips **55.00**
  5¾" h, shiny glaze, dark amber and
  brown splotches, ribbed strap han-
  dle **50.00**
  6" h, cov, ovoid, dark orange glaze
  with brown splotches, strap han-
  dle, old chips **50.00**
  6½" h, cov, ovoid, greenish yellow
  slip glaze with brown flecks, green
  and reddish brown floral design,
  old chips, badly chipped lid **2,000.00**
  6¾" h, cov, ovoid, clear glaze with
  brown sponging, rim spout, strap
  handle, bottom imp "1½," minor
  chips **200.00**
  8" h, greenish orange glaze, Galena,
  edge chips **100.00**
  8¾" h, ovoid, dark brown mottled
  glaze **30.00**
  9¼" h, cov, dark brown glaze **80.00**
  9½" h, glazed, manganese
  splotches, 19th C **525.00**
  10" h, tooled bands, imp stamp de-
  signs and vining border on lip,
  tooled lid with incised label "S. J.
  Jewitt, Monmouth, —18, 1838,"
  tooled inscription around base "S.
  J. Jewitt," glaze varies slightly,
  wear and edge chips **1,300.00**
  10¼" h, green alkaline glaze, flakes,
  19th C **165.00**
Jug, ovoid
  5½" h, green speckled glaze, hair-
  lines **105.00**
  7" h, strap handle, brown splotches,
  wear and chips **95.00**
  8" h, manganese splotches, rim and
  base chips, 19th C **135.00**
  9½" h, greenish amber glaze, orange
  spots **200.00**
Loaf Pan, 16¼" l, coggled edge,
  fine line yellow slip dec, flakes and
  chip **1,250.00**
Milk Pan
  8" d, rim spout **145.00**
  10½" d, 3¾" h, amber glaze, brown
  flecks, dark brown daubs, hairline
  and wear **60.00**

Milk Pitcher, 4⅝" h, clear glaze, running brown splotches, imp tooled dec bands, edge wear, small flakes ... **75.00**

Muffin Pan, 12" l, 15½" w, green glaze ... **30.00**

Mug, 3¼" h, brown speckled glaze, all surfaces glazed, handmade, undetermined age. **25.00**

Pie Plate

7½" d, coggled rim, yellow slip "X" dec, crazing and rim chips **150.00**

7⅞" d, dark brown fleck glaze **75.00**

8" d, folded rim, white slip, green and brown plaid design. **575.00**

8¼" d, coggled rim

Clear orange glaze **30.00**

Yellow slip spots and green dec **110.00**

8⅝" d, three line yellow slip dec, coggled rim, small rim chips **225.00**

9" d, coggled rim, three line yellow slip dec, old edge chips. **475.00**

9¼" d, coggled rim, three line yellow slip dec

Center wavy line, four sprigs, minor wear, old flakes, crazing **375.00**

Three wavy lines, wear, chips, and hairlines **150.00**

9½" d, coggled rim, four line yellow slip dec. **225.00**

9⅝" d, coggled rim, random three line yellow slip dec, small chips **385.00**

9¾" d, coggled rim, three line yellow slip dec. **475.00**

10¼" d, coggled rim. **385.00**

10¾" h, coggled rim, three line yellow slip dec, wear and small chips **250.00**

Pitcher

6⅛" h, mottled dark brown metallic glaze. **55.00**

6¼" h, green glaze, orange spots and brown flecks, chips and wear . . . **75.00**

6¾" h, white slip with marbleized red, green, and brown, some edge ware, glaze flakes **45.00**

7¼" h

Green glazed int., ovoid **25.00**

White slip, green and brown **310.00**

7¾" h, ovoid, strap handle, light green slip, brown splotches, small chips. **250.00**

8" h, dark brown glaze, molded stylized floral detail, cherub heads, imp "Nathaniel Sellers, Upper Hanover, PA" **200.00**

8¼" h, greenish amber glaze, ribbed strap handle **225.00**

Plate

6¼" d, coggled rim, dark brown glaze. **140.00**

7¾" d, yellow slip, green wavy line on rim, brown polka dots **195.00**

8¼" d, white slip, brown combed dec **385.00**

10½" d, dark amber glaze, incised distlefink, flowers, German inscription, and name. **200.00**

11" d, slip dec, stylized double figure 8's and three line dec, notched rim, chips, 19th C **875.00**

Pot, cov, 5" h, dark brown glaze, brown splotches, pouring spout, strap handle, mismatched lid, chips **75.00**

Preserving Jar

4⅝" h, glazed, mottled green and brown dec, attributed to southern U.S., 19th C **935.00**

7" h, ovoid, yellow glaze, minor glaze flakes on lip **45.00**

Salt, 3" d, 2" h, ftd, greenish brown mottled glaze **50.00**

Toddy Plate, 5⅝" d, yellow slip dec, green wavy line rim **500.00**

Vase, 3⅝" h, sgraffito, birds and flowers, tri-color, bulbous base, marked "DDR, June 5, 1828, PA" **1,500.00**

RED WING POTTERY

History: The Red Wing pottery category covers several potteries from Red Wing, Minnesota. In 1868 David Hallem started Red Wing Stoneware Co., the first pottery with stoneware as its primary product and with a red wing stamped under the glaze as its mark. The Minnesota Stoneware Co. started in 1883. The North Star Stoneware Co., 1892-1896, used a raised star and the words Red Wing as its mark.

The Red Wing Stoneware Co. and the Minnesota Stoneware Co. merged in 1892. The new company, the Red Wing Union Stoneware Company, made stoneware until 1920 when it introduced a pottery line which it continued until the 1940s. In 1936 the name was changed to Red Wing Potteries, Inc. During the 1930s it introduced several popular lines of hand painted pattern dinnerware distributed through department stores, Sears Roebuck and Co., and gift stamp centers. Dinnerware production declined in the 1950s, being replaced with hotel and restaurant china in the early 1960s. The plant closed in 1967.

Red Wing stoneware is the most commonly pictured Red Wing in Country magazines. While it is true that the utilitarian and advertising stoneware pieces played a major role in the small towns and rural communities of the Midwest, so also did Red Wing dinnerware patterns, a fact often overlooked. Red Wing's Bob White pattern, designed by Charles Murphy, is touted by some as the most popular dinnerware pattern of the 1950s. Those desiring a solid color ware that was a bit more traditional than modern designs such as Fiesta often chose Red Wing's Village Green or Village Brown pattern. Each was available in thirty-six different forms.

References: Stanley Bougie and David Newkirk, *Price Guide & Supplement for Red Wing Dinnerware (1990–1991 Edition)*, published by authors, 1990; Dan and Gail DePasquale and Larry Peterson, *Red Wing Collectibles*, Collector Books, 1983, 1992 value update; David A. Newkirk, *A Guide To Red Wing Markings*, Monticello Printing, 1979; Dolores Simon, *Red Wing Pottery With Rumrill*, Collector Books, 1980; Gary and Bonnie Tefft, *Red Wing Potters and Their Wares, Second Edition*, Locust Enterprises, 1987; Lyndon C. Viel, *The Clay Giants, The Stoneware of Red Wing, Goodhue County, Minnesota*, Book 2 (1980), Book 3 (1987), Wallace-Homestead.

Collectors' Club: Red Wing Collectors Society, Route 3, Box 146, Monticello, MN 55362.

Basket, white	**20.00**
Bean Pot, cov, stoneware, adv	**65.00**
Bookends, pr, fan and scroll, green. . .	**15.00**
Bowl	
Spongeware, 7¼" d	**85.00**
Stoneware, blue dec, Greek Key border, marked "Luhman & Sanders, Pottsville, Iowa," 8" d	**75.00**
Butter Crock, stoneware, gray stripe	**175.00**
Console Set, 12" d bowl, deep green, three holes on rim hold 2" h white baby birds on branch, mother and father birds sit inside bowl, six pcs, orig label	**65.00**
Cookie Jar	
Chef	**60.00**
Rooster, green.	**35.00**
Cornucopia, burgundy, leaf dec	**15.00**
Crock, stoneware, cobalt blue quill work design with leaves and "20," 22½" h	**165.00**
Dinnerware	
Bob White	
Bread Tray.	**75.00**
Butter Dish	**65.00**
Casserole, 2 quart	**25.00**
Cereal Bowl, 6½" d.	**12.00**
Creamer and Sugar, cov	**40.00**
Cup and Saucer.	**18.00**
Fruit Bowl, 5½" d	**8.00**
Hors d'oeuvre Bird	**45.00**
Lazy Susan	**85.00**
Pitcher.	**35.00**
Plate, 6" d, bread and butter	**4.00**
Platter, 13" l	**15.00**
Salt and Pepper Shakers, pr	**25.00**
Vegetable Bowl, divided	**20.00**
Country Garden	
Gravy	**22.00**
Nappy.	**16.00**
Plate	
8" d, salad	**10.00**
10½" d, dinner	**15.00**
Sauce Dish	**10.00**
Vegetable, divided	**20.00**

Pot, applied loop handles, imp label "Red Wing Provincial Ware," brown glazed int., matte tan ext., 5" d, 4" h, $25.00.

Driftwood	
Cup and Saucer	**6.00**
Gravy Boat, blue	**18.00**
Nappy, 6½" d	**15.00**
Plate, 8" d, salad	**8.00**
Iris	
Bowl, 5½" d	**8.00**
Casserole, cov, skillet shaped . . .	**25.00**
Creamer.	**5.00**
Relish, three part, 12" l	**15.00**
Jar, stoneware, Kansas Druggist adv	**100.00**
Planter	
Canoe, ivory ext., brown int.	**28.00**
Puppy, aqua	**18.00**
Square, white ext., green int., projecting rectangles.	**8.00**
Teapot, yellow rooster, gold trim	**65.00**
Vase	
Aqua with brown sprinkles ext., ivory int., V designs, 10½" h	**12.00**
Chartreuse, stylized leaves on vertical strips, handled, 8" h	**10.00**
Yellow ext., aqua int., horizontal rib, ring handles, 7" h	**8.00**

ROCKINGHAM BROWN-GLAZED WARE

History: Rockingham ware can be divided into two categories. The first consists of the fine china and porcelain pieces made between 1826 and 1842 by the Rockingham Company of Swinton, Yorkshire, England, and its predecessor firms: Swinton, Bingley, Don, Leeds, and Brameld.

The second category of Rockingham ware includes pieces produced in the famous Rockingham brown glaze, that became an intense and vivid purple-brown when fired. It had a dark, mottled tortoise shell appearance. The glaze was copied by many English and American potteries. American manufacturers who used Rockingham glaze include D. & J. Henderson of Jersey City, New Jersey, United States Pottery in Bennington, Vermont, potteries in East Liverpool, Ohio, and several potteries in Indiana and Illinois.

Rockingham glazed pieces are eagerly sought by Country collectors and decorators. The warm brown glazes blend with earth tones and similar color palettes. Rockingham ware is also found in unusual forms, such as foot warmers, bedpans, and spittoons.

Bank	
Opossum, 5⅝″ h	**250.00**
Pig, 2¾″ h, Rockingham glaze	**40.00**
Bedpan, 17″ l	**10.00**
Bottle, shoe shape	
Donut shape, 8¾″ h, molded ivy and foliage	**55.00**
Shoe shape	
5¾″ h, old gold paint on sole	**65.00**
6″ h, emb "Ann Reid 1859"	**250.00**
Bowl	
8½″ d, 3¼″ h	**65.00**
10½″ d, 2¾″ h, shallow	**85.00**
11¼″ d, molded flutes, hairline, small chips	**25.00**
11½″ d, 3″ h, emb leaf design ext., imp "Fire Proof, J.E. Jeffords & Co., Phila."	**175.00**
11¾″ d, 3¼″ h, shallow	**85.00**
12¾″ d, monogram mark "SVPNT"	**60.00**
13″ d, 3⅞″ h	**30.00**
Colander, 3 ftd	**195.00**
Creamer, 2⅝″ h	**45.00**
Crock, cov, 6½″ d, 5″ h, emb peacocks	**65.00**
Dish, 9″ sq, emb rim	**45.00**
Figure	
Cat, 11″ h, sitting, chipped ears, reglued to base	**95.00**
Dog, 9¾″ h, green and brown running glaze	**325.00**
Flask	
7¼″ h, emb morning glory, eagle, and flag	**100.00**
11″ l, pistol shape, repaired	**75.00**
Flower Pot, 10¼″ h, emb acanthus leaves, underplate	**45.00**
Food Mold, Turk's head, 10½″ d, 4″ h, straight tapered sides, blue flecks in glaze	**145.00**
Jug, 8″ h, man's head, two-tone green and brown glaze	**35.00**
Muffin Tray, 14¾″ h, 19th C	**110.00**
Mug, 3½″ h, cuspidor shape	**185.00**
Mustache Cup, 4¼″ h, toby	**115.00**
Pie Plate, 9½″ d, 19th C, price for set of four	**110.00**
Pitcher	
3⅛″ h, miniature, hound handle, pinpoint edge flakes	**280.00**
4⅜″ h, squatty, C scroll handle	**72.00**
7⅞″ h, minor edge chips	**55.00**
8½″ h, molded peacock	**75.00**
11″ h, emb hunting scenes and vintage design, hound handle, William Bromley, Zanesville, eagle mark	**1,700.00**
11¼″ h, shoulder rings, strap handle	**125.00**

Spittoon, emb bows and flower petal design on top and around sides, 9¾″ d, 4½″ h, $80.00.

Plate, 10½″ d	**100.00**
Platter, 15″ l, oval	**170.00**
Preserving Jar	
5½″ h, keg shaped	**20.00**
6¼″ h	**95.00**
Salt box, 6″ d, emb peacocks, crest, hanging hole	**45.00**
Soap Dish	
4⅞″ l, oval	**50.00**
5½″ d, round, rim chip	**25.00**
5½″ l, 4¼″ w, oval, wear, glaze flakes	**18.00**
Spittoon	
6½″ d, 3¾″ h, molded portrait medallion	**35.00**
7½″ d, molded shells, surface flake	**35.00**
Sugar Bowl, cov, 5⅞″ h	**275.00**
Teapot, cov	
6″ h, marked "Rebekah at the Well"	**65.00**
7¾″ h, emb ribs and acanthus leaves	**120.00**
8″ h, molded leaf designs	**40.00**
Vegetable Dish, 11″ d, 19th C, price for pair	**110.00**
Washboard, 12¾″ w, 25½″ h, pine frame, Rockingham scrubber insert	**525.00**

ROSEVILLE POTTERY

Roseville U.S.A.

History: In the late 1880s a group of investors purchased the J. B. Owens Pottery in Roseville, Ohio, and made utilitarian stoneware items. In 1892 the firm was incorporated and joined by George F. Young who became general manager. Four generations of Youngs controlled Roseville until the early 1950s.

A series of acquisitions began: Midland Pottery of Roseville in 1898, Clark Stoneware Plant in Zanesville (formerly used by Peters and Reed), and Muskingum Stoneware (Mosaic Tile Company) in Zanesville. In 1898 the offices moved from Roseville to Zanesville.

In 1900 Roseville introduced its art pottery—Rozane. Rozane became a trade name to cover a large series of lines. The art lines were made in limited amounts after 1919.

The success of Roseville depended on its commercial lines, first developed by John J. Herald and Frederick Rhead in the first decades of the 1900s. In 1918 Frank Ferrell became art director and developed over 80 lines of pottery. The economic depression of the 1930s brought more lines, including Pine Cone.

In the 1940s a series of high gloss glazes were tried to revive certain lines. In 1952 Raymor dinnerware was produced. None of these changes brought economic success. In November 1954 Roseville was bought by the Mosaic Tile Company.

Country collectors are fond of Roseville Pottery. Large collections of interesting patterns, shapes, and colors may be easily acquired. Baskets, urns, and vases readily lend themselves to country settings as accent pieces. Because most Roseville pieces are marked, identification is easy and accurate.

References: John W. Humphries, *A Price Guide To Roseville Pottery By The Numbers,* published by author, 1993; Sharon and Bob Huxford, *The Collectors Encyclopedia Of Roseville Pottery,* Collector Books, 1976, 1993 value update; Sharon and Bob Huxford, *The Collectors Encyclopedia Of Roseville Pottery, Second Series,* Collector Books, 1980, 1993 value update.

Collectors' Clubs: American Art Pottery Association, 125 E Rose Ave, St Louis, MO 63119; Roseville's of the Past Pottery Club, PO Box 681117, Orlando, FL 32868.

Ashtray
Pine Cone, blue, 4" w	120.00
Snowberry, pink	45.00
Zephyr Lily, blue	70.00

Basket
Bittersweet, green, 810–10	175.00
Columbine, blue, 376–10	175.00
Freesia, blue, 391–8	95.00
Imperial I	80.00
Peony, pink, 378–10	135.00
Snowberry, blue	145.00
White Rose, pink, 363–10	115.00

Bookends, pr, Pine Cone, blue	150.00

Bowl
Baneda, pink	180.00
Carnelian I, pedestal, blue	55.00
Clematis, blue, 12" d	145.00
Columbine, blue, 402	75.00
Fuschia, green, 847–8	95.00
Pine Cone, blue, 179–9	150.00
Sunflower, 4" d	180.00
White Rose, handles, 389, 6" d	75.00

Candleholders, pr
Carnelian II	125.00
Fuschia, green, 1133–5	165.00
Rosecraft, blue, 8" h	80.00
Zephyr Lily, green, 1163–4½	75.00

Candy Dish, Zephyr Lily, handled, sienna tan, #473-6, 1946, 6" d, 2½" h, $45.00.

Console Bowl
Apple Blossom, blue, 331–12	85.00
Fuschia, green, 353–14	150.00
Gardenia, gray, 627–8	90.00
Teasel, beige, 345–12	55.00
White Rose, blue, 393–12	95.00
Zephyr Lily	
Blue, 478–12	95.00
Green, 475–10	85.00

Console Set, Thorn Apple, brown, 13" w bowl, pair of 5½" h double bud vases	185.00

Cornucopia
Columbine, 7" h	65.00
Cosmos, blue, 136–6	75.00
Foxglove, blue, 166–6	45.00
Snowberry, 6" h	45.00

Double Cornucopia, White Rose, blue, 145–8	85.00

Ewer
Bleeding Heart, blue, 972–10	175.00
Foxglove, blue, 5–10	155.00
Freesia, blue, 15" h	350.00
Gardenia, tan, 618, 15" h	225.00
Magnolia, brown, 15–15	245.00

Flowerpot, saucer, Bushberry, 5" h	175.00
Flower Frog, Peony, green	30.00

Hanging Basket
Apple Blossom, green	135.00
Bushberry, pink	150.00
Donatello	125.00
Fuschia, brown	195.00
Iris, blue, 10" d	95.00
Ixia, yellow	185.00
Jonquil	320.00
White Rose, blue	145.00
Zephyr Lily, green	125.00

Jardiniere
Clematis, 667–4	60.00
Columbine, blue, 655–4	65.00
Foxglove, 659–3	65.00
Fuschia, brown, 645–4	85.00
Moss, pink	80.00
Pine Cone, 632–5	110.00
Rozane	310.00
Sunflower	85.00
Water Lily, pink, pedestal	700.00

Planter
Apple Blossom, hanging	110.00
Magnolia, green, 183–6	50.00

Vase, White Rose, pink, 7" h, $60.00.

Peony, 387, 8" l	**85.00**
Water Lily, brown, hanging	**160.00**
Umbrella Stand, Chloron line, matte green glaze, raised floral dec, octagonal, c1907, 23¼" h	**275.00**
Urn	
Cherry Blossom, brown, 7" h	**185.00**
Foxglove, 161–6	**80.00**
Magnolia, blue, 446–6	**100.00**
Vase	
Apple Blossom, 388–10	**95.00**
Baneda, pink, 4½" h	**160.00**
Blackberry, beehive, 5½" h	**235.00**
Bushberry, brown, 156–8	**90.00**
Carnelian II, red, 5" h	**95.00**
Cherry Blossom, pink, 1/95/3/2, 7" hp	**225.00**
Clematis, brown, 128–8	**50.00**
Cosmos, tan, 135–8	**120.00**
Foxglove, green and pink, 53–14	**275.00**
Fuschia, brown, 900–9	**185.00**
Futura, 427–8	**300.00**
Jonquil, 4" h	**75.00**
Laurel, yellow, 1/99/2/4, 6" h	**90.00**
Magnolia, green, 98–15	**225.00**
Mayfair, 10" h	**65.00**
Monticello, brown, 1/91/1/1, 4" h	**130.00**
Peony, bud, handles, 173, 7¼" h	**75.00**
Pine Cone, blue, 711–10	**425.00**
Primrose, brown, 767–8	**80.00**
Rozane, light, artist L. Mitchell, Rozane Royal seal, 8½" h	**385.00**
Savona, green, 12" h	**150.00**
Sunflower, bulbous, curved handles, 5" h	**145.00**
Teasel, beige, 888–12	**55.00**
Tourmaline	**45.00**
Tuscany	
6" h, handles	**75.00**
8" h, gray	**85.00**
White Rose, blue, 147–8	**75.00**
Wincraft, green, 287–12	**90.00**
Zephyr Lily	
131–7, green	**40.00**
201, bud, 7" h	**80.00**
Wall Pocket	
Clematis, brown	**95.00**
Freesia, blue	**125.00**

Mostique, 10½" l	**145.00**
Peony, yellow	**130.00**
Tuscany, orig label	**110.00**
Window Box	
Freesia, brown	**75.00**
Gardenia, green, 669–19	**115.00**

ROYAL CHINA COMPANY

History The Royal China Company, located in Sebring, Ohio, utilized remodeled facilities that originally housed the Oliver China Company and later the E. H. Sebring Company. Royal China began operations in 1934.

The company produced an enormous number of dinnerware patterns. The backs of pieces usually contain the names of the shape, line, and decoration. In addition to many variations of company backstamps, Royal China also produced objects with private backstamps. All records of these markings were lost in a fire in 1970.

The company's Currier and Ives pattern, designed by Gordon Parker, was introduced in 1949–50. Early marks were date coded. Other early 1950s patterns include Colonial Homestead and Old Curiosity Shop.

In 1964 Royal China purchased the French-Saxon China Company, Sebring, which it operated as a wholly owned subsidiary. On December 31, 1969, Royal China was acquired by the Jeannette Corporation. When fire struck the Royal China Sebring plant in 1970, Royal moved its operations to the French-Saxon plant.

The company changed hands several times, being owned briefly by the Coca-Cola Company, the J. Corporation from Boston, and Nordic Capitol of New York, New York. Production continued until August 1986 when operations ceased.

Country collectors concentrate on specific patterns. Among the most favored are Bluebell (1940s), Currier and Ives (1949–50), Colonial Homestead (ca. 1951–52), Old Curiosity Shop (early 1950s), Regal (1937), Royalty (1936), blue and pink willow ware (1940s), and Windsor (1930–?).

Royal China patterns were widely distributed. Colonial Homestead was sold by Sears Roebuck and Co. through the 1960s, so pieces are relatively common and prices moderate.

Because of the ease of accessibility, only purchase pieces in fine to excellent condition. Do not buy pieces whose surface is marked or marred in any way.

References: Jo Cunningham, *The Collector's Encyclopedia of American Dinnerware*, Collector Books, 1982, 1992 value update; Harvey Duke, *The Official Identification And Price Guide To Pottery And Porcelain, Seventh Edition*, House of Collectibles, 1989; and Lois Lehner, *Lehner's Encyclopedia of U. S. Marks on Pottery, Porcelain & Clay*, Collector Books, 1988.

Colonial Homestead
Cake Plate, handled, 10" d	**12.00**
Casserole, cov.	**30.00**
Cereal Bowl, 6¼" d	**5.00**
Chop Plate, 12" d	**12.00**
Creamer and Sugar, cov	**12.00**
Cup and Saucer	**4.00**
Fruit Bowl, 5½" d	**3.00**
Gravy, underplate.	**18.00**
Plate	
6" d, bread and butter	**1.50**
7" d, salad.	**2.50**
10" d, dinner.	**3.50**
Salt and Pepper Shakers, pr.	**10.00**
Soup, flat	**6.00**
Teapot, cov.	**35.00**
Vegetable Bowl	
9" d.	**8.00**
10" d.	**10.00**

Currier & Ives
Ashtray.	**7.50**
Cake Plate, handled, 10" d	**12.00**
Casserole, cov.	**50.00**
Cereal Bowl, 6" d	**9.00**
Chop Plate, 12" d	**15.00**
Creamer and Sugar, cov	**10.00**
Cup and Saucer	**3.50**
Fruit Bowl, 5½" d	**3.00**
Gravy Boat	**10.00**
Pie Baker	**12.00**
Plate	
6" d, bread and butter	**2.00**
10¼" d, dinner	**4.00**
Platter, oval.	**15.00**
Salt and Pepper Shakers, pr.	**12.00**
Soup, flat	**6.00**
Vegetable, open	
9" d.	**10.00**
10" d.	**18.00**

Memory Lane
Creamer and Sugar, open	**12.00**
Cup and Saucer	**3.00**
Fruit Bowl.	**4.00**
Plate	
6" d, bread and butter	**4.00**
10" d, dinner.	**7.00**
Soup, flat	**5.00**

Old Curiosity Shop
Cake Plate, handled, 10" d	**15.00**

Currier & Ives, cup and saucer, blue and white, $3.50.

Casserole, cov.	**45.00**
Creamer and Sugar, cov	**10.00**
Cup and Saucer.	**5.00**
Fruit Bowl, 5½" d	**3.50**
Gravy	**10.00**
Plate	
6" d, bread and butter	**2.00**
10" d, dinner.	**4.00**
Salt and Pepper Shakers, pr.	**10.00**
Soup, flat, 8½" d	**6.00**
Teapot.	**50.00**
Vegetable Bowl, open	
9" d.	**12.00**
10" d.	**16.00**

SHAWNEE POTTERY

History: In 1937 Malcolm A. and Roy W. Schweiker, brothers, acquired the 650,000 square foot plant in Zanesville, Ohio, that formerly housed the American Encaustic Tiling Company. Addis E. Hull, Jr., ceramic engineer and president/general manager of the A. E. Hull Pottery Company, was hired as president. Louise Bauer, the in-house designer, developed a company logo consisting of an arrowhead inside of which was a profile of a Shawnee Indian head.

Shawnee Pottery produced its first wares in August 1937. Dinnerware production was targeted toward companies such as S. S. Kresge, McCrory Stores Corporation, Sears Roebuck and Company, and F. W. Woolworth. In 1938 Rum Rill Pottery Company moved its production of art pottery from its Red Wing, Minnesota, location to Shawnee.

Between 1942 and July of 1946 over 90 percent of Shawnee's production came from war contracts. Realizing that the war would soon end, Shawnee hired Robert Heckman, a designer, in 1945. Heckman was responsible for the Corn King line, Pennsylvania Dutch line, and numerous figurine, planter, and vase designs.

Like many potteries, Shawnee experienced major financial difficulties following World War II. The wholesale market was simply not lucrative enough. During this period Shawnee sold vast quantities of pieces to small sales outlets. Many of these individuals added decals and gold paint to Shawnee factory stock.

Financial difficulties continued. 1953 witnessed record losses.

When John F. Bonistall became president in 1954, he eliminated hand painted decoration in favor of spray painted motifs. He also shifted emphasis from the dinnerware to decorative items. The Corn Queen line replaced the King Corn line. The company survived until 1961.

Shawnee can be marked "Shawnee," "Shawnee U.S.A." "USA —," "Kenwood," or with character names, e.g., "Pat. Smiley," "Pat. Winnie," etc. Many pieces are unmarked.

Many Shawnee pieces came in several color variations. Some pieces also contained both painted and decal decorations. The available literature will indicate some, but not all, of these variations. Because of limited collector interest, Shawnee dinnerware lines such as Cameo, Cheria (Petit Point), Diora, and Touche (Liana) remain modestly priced.

References: Jim and Bev Mangus, *Shawnee Pottery: An Identification and Value Guide,* Collector Books, 1994; Mark Supnick, *Collecting Shawnee Pottery: A Pictorial Reference And Price Guide,* L–W Book Sales, 1989, 1992 value update; Duane and Janice Vanderbilt, *The Collector's Guide To Shawnee Pottery,* Collector Books, 1992.

Collectors' Club: Shawnee Pottery Collectors Club, PO Box 713, New Smyrna Beach, FL 32170.

Bank, Smiley Pig, dark brown base	350.00
Coffeepot, large emb flower, #54	100.00
Cookie Jar	
Basket of Fruit	85.00
Dutch Boy, gold trim	250.00
Owl, gold trim	275.00
Puss 'N Boots	125.00
Smiley Pig, tulips	185.00
Creamer, tulips	30.00
Dinnerware	
Corn King	
Bowl	
#92, 6" d	30.00
#94, 6¾" d	32.00
#95, 9" d	35.00
Butter Dish, cov, #72	65.00
Casserole, cov	
#73	55.00
#74, 11"	48.00
Cookie Jar, #66	145.00
Creamer and Sugar, cov	48.00
Cup and Saucer	38.00
Mixing Bowl, nested set of three	85.00
Pitcher, #71	60.00
Plate, #93, 7½" d	28.00
Platter, 12" l	45.00
Salt and Pepper Shakers, pr	
Range	22.00
Small	15.00

Corn King, pitcher, 4¾" h, $20.00.

Teapot	
#65	135.00
#75	55.00
Corn Queen	
Bowl, #5	25.00
Mug	30.00
Plate, #69	15.00
White Corn	
Salt and Pepper Shakers, pr, range	30.00
Sugar, cov	30.00
Teapot, cov	60.00
Figure	
Dog, gold trim	75.00
Rabbit	30.00
Pitcher	
Bo Peep, blue bonnet	75.00
Chanticleer Rooster	60.00
Grist Mill, #35	10.00
Little Boy Blue, #46	50.00
Planter	
Butterfly	15.00
Conestoga Wagon, green, 6 × 9½"	20.00
Fawn, yellow, #624	25.00
Grist Mill, #169	18.00
Salt and Pepper Shakers, pr	
Dutch Boy and Girl, small	25.00
Fruit, small	25.00
Puss 'N Boots	15.00
Chanticleer Rooster, range	45.00
Spoon Rest, flower, green and yellow	18.00
Sugar Jar, cov, fruit basket	25.00
Teapot, cov, Granny Anne	60.00
Vase	
Cornucopia, #865	15.00
Leaf	24.00
Swan, bud, gold trim	12.00
Wall Pocket	
Bo Peep, #586	20.00
Telephone, #529	18.00

SPATTERWARE

History: Spatterware is made of common earthenware, although occasionally creamware was used. The earliest English examples were made about 1780; peak production took place from 1810 to 1840. Marked pieces are rare. Firms known to have made spatterware are Adams, Barlow, and Harvey and Cotton.

The amount of spatter decoration varies from piece to piece. Some objects simply have decorated borders. These often are decorated with a brush, requiring several hundred touches per square inch to achieve the spatter effect. Other pieces have the entire surface covered with spatter. Aesthetics of the final product is a key to value.

Collectors today focus on the patterns, such as Cannon, Castle, Fort, Peafowl, Rainbow, Rose, Thistle, and Schoolhouse. On flat ware the decoration is in the center. On hollow pieces it occurs on both sides.

Color of spatter is another price key. Blue and red are most common. Green, purple, and brown are in a middle group. Black and yellow are scarce.

Like any soft paste, spatterware was easily broken or chipped. Prices are for pieces in very good to mint condition.

References: Kevin McConnell, *Spongeware and Spatterware,* Schiffer Publishing, 1990; Carl and Ada Robacker, *Spatterware and Sponge,* A. S. Barnes & Co., 1978.

Reproduction Manufacturers: The Vine and Cupboard, PO Box 309, George Wright Rd, Woolwich, ME 04579.

Bowl, 7¾" d, 4½" h, stick spatter, marked "Villeroy & Boch," wear... **100.00**
Cow Creamer, 5" h, black and orange, green base **450.00**
Creamer
  2¾" h, Peafowl, blue, red, black, and yellow ochre, green spatter **155.00**
  4" h, Rose, red, black, and green dec, brown and black spatter **250.00**
  5⅜" h, Rose and Cornflower, paneled, red, blue, green, and black dec, red and blue spatter, stains and hairlines **150.00**
Cup and Saucer, handleless
  Flower, blue, black, and red, brown spatter **465.00**
  Peafowl, miniature, blue, red, black, and yellow ochre, green spatter **275.00**
  Plaid, blue, red, and green spatter **525.00**
  Rainbow, red, blue, and green spatter, imp "Adams"............. **525.00**
  Rose, red, green, and black, purple spatter, pinpoint flake on saucer table ring................... **250.00**
  School House, red, green, and brown dec, red spatter......... **175.00**
  Stick Spatter, miniature, blue spatter, red striping, imp "Tunstall," stains..................... **70.00**

Shallow Bowl, blue, green, and red peafowl center, blue spatter rim, incised "Y" in circle mark, 5" d, $275.00.

Thistle, red and green, yellow spatter **650.00**
Tick-Tack-Toe, red and green, set of six **725.00**
Inkwell, 4½" l, stick spatter, shoe shaped, red, black, and green spatter, edge chip, small hole **55.00**
Pepper Pot, 4¾" h, pierced domed cov, Peafowl, blue, ochre, rose, and black, yellow spatter, marked "Staffordshire," c1840 .... **1,200.00**
Pitcher
  5⅞" h, stick spatter, red, blue, and green spatter **465.00**
  7½" h, Rainbow, red, blue, green, yellow, and black **575.00**
  7⅝" h, Flower, white reserves with green, pink, yellow, and black flower and black border on front and back, blue spatter, stains and wear **325.00**
Pitcher and Bowl Set
  11" h pitcher, 13½" d bowl, Peafowl, red, green, blue, and black, imp "Adams" **625.00**
  12" h pitcher, 13¾" d bowl, Adam's Rose, red, green, and black, blue spatter, hairlines, small chips.... **875.00**
Plate
  7½" d, Rose, red, green, and black, blue spatter, Adams........... **325.00**
  7¾" d
    Rainbow, criss-cross center, red and blue **215.00**
    Snowflake, red, blue, and green, stick spatter, chip on underside of lip **100.00**
  8¼" d
    Peafowl, blue, yellow, green, and black, red spatter **250.00**
    Star, red, green, and yellow, blue spatter **605.00**
  8⅜" d
    Castle, green spatter........... **250.00**
    Gaudy polychrome floral dec, blue and green spatter **350.00**
    Bull's Eye center, black and purple, rainbow spatter **275.00**
  8½" d, Star, red, blue, and green, red spatter **275.00**
  8¾" d, Dahlia, blue, green, and black, yellow spatter **1,015.00**
  8⅞" d, stick spatter, red, green, and black...................... **55.00**
  9¼" d, Bull's Eye, red spatter, set of six **595.00**
  9⅜" d, Bull's Eye, red and blue spatter **110.00**
  9⅝" d
    Bull's Eye, red and green spatter **450.00**
    Rainbow, red, blue, and green spatter, scalloped rim........ **465.00**

Sugar Bowl, cov, Holly Leaf, purple and green spatter, light blue bands, 7½" h, $175.00.

10" d, Gaudy polychrome floral dec, red stick spatter, marked "Scotch Ivory" 190.00
10⅛" d, stick spatter, red and blue   125.00
10½" d, Rainbow, red, blue, and green spatter, scalloped rim 200.00
Platter
10⅞" l, Holly Berry, purple spatter   180.00
17½" l, Rainbow, red, blue, and green spatter, white center, imp "Adams" 365.00
Saucer, Peafowl, purple, green, red, and black, green spatter, stains 175.00
Soup Plate, 10½" d, Tulip, red, blue, green, and black, purple spatter, imp "Barber & Till, Opaque China" 225.00
Sugar, cov
3¾" h, Peafowl, blue, red, black, and yellow ochre, green spatter 225.00
4⅜" h, Rainbow, red and blue spatter, stains, wear, some damage, glued break in lid 150.00
4¼" h, Peafowl, purple, red, green, and black 145.00
4½" h, Peafowl, purple, green, red, and black, green spatter 135.00
4¾" h, Peafowl, red, orange, green, and black, blue spatter, applied ring handles, chips and hairlines, mismatched glued lid 125.00
5" h
Rainbow, red and blue spatter. . .   115.00
Red and blue drape design, blue spatter 330.00
Teapot
4¼" h, Peafowl, miniature, blue, red, black, and yellow ochre, green spatter. 375.00
5½" h, Rainbow, red and green spatter. 250.00
5¾" h, Rooster, red, blue, yellow, and black, blue spatter 275.00
6¼" h, Rose, red and green spatter   275.00

8¼" h, Acorn and Oak Leaf, green, black, teal, and yellow ochre, red spatter.   550.00
9" h, Holly Berry, red, green, and black, blue spatter 275.00
Toddy Plate, 5¼" d, Bull's Eye, blue spatter. 85.00
Waste Bowl, 6½" d, blue eagle and shield transfer, blue spatter, hairline on base 125.00

SPONGEWARE

History: Spongeware is a specific type of decoration, not a type of pottery or glaze.

Spongeware decoration is found on many types of pottery bodies—ironstone, redware, stoneware, yellow ware, etc. It was made in both England and the United States. Marked pieces indicate a starting date of 1815, with manufacturing extending to the 1880s.

Decoration is varied. In some pieces the sponging is minimal with the white underglaze dominant. Other pieces appear to be sponged solidly on both sides. Pieces from 1840–1860 have sponging which appears in either a circular movement or a streaked horizontal technique.

Examples are found in blue and white, the most common colors. Other prevalent colors are browns, greens, ochres, and greenish-blue. The greenish-blue results from blue sponging which has been overglazed in a pale yellow. A red overglaze produces a black or navy color.

Other colors are blue and red (found on English creamware and American earthenware of the 1880s), gray, grayish-green, red, dark green on stark white, dark green on mellow yellow, and purple.

References: Kevin McConnell, *Spongeware and Spatterware,* Schiffer Publishing, 1990; Earl F. and Ada Robacker, *Spatterware and Sponge,* A. S. Barnes & Co., 1978.

Reproduction Craftsman: Carolyn Nygren Curran, CNC Pottery, 8 Pershing Rd, Glens Falls, NY 12804.

Reproduction Manufacturers: Wesson Trading Co, PO Box 669984, Marietta, GA 30066.

Bank
Eagle, teal sponge dec, Roseville, 1900–10 . . . .   225.00
Pig, brown and blue sponge dec . . .   65.00
Bean Pot, blue sponge dec 450.00
Bowl
6" d, stoneware, blue sponge dec, white ground. 150.00
7" d, tan and blue sponge dec, light gray ground. 65.00
7" w, oval, ironstone, blue sponge int., 1850–60. . . . .   195.00

Cup and Saucer, handleless, purple dec, unmarked, 6" d saucer, 3⅞" d × 2 ¾" h cup, $125.00.

Jug, applied strap handle, $135.00.

10" d, paneled, red sponge dec, Cobb, WI adv	295.00
12¼" d, mixing, molded design, blue sponge dec, white ground	125.00
Bread Plate, open handles, blue sponge dec, 10" l	100.00
Chamber Pot, salesman's sample, blue sponge dec	95.00
Cookie Jar, sponge dec band, barrel shaped, Red Wing	125.00
Creamer	
4" h, waisted, green sponge dec	65.00
4¼" h, figural cat, polychrome sponging	30.00
Cup and Saucer, blue sponge dec, c1840	130.00
Cup Plate, blue sponge dec, white ground, 3⅛" d	60.00
Food Mold, Turk's head, brown and green sponge dec, imp "Upton M Bell, Waynesboro, PA," 5¾" d	325.00
Ink Pot, stoneware, blue sponge dec	65.00
Jardiniere, blue sponge dec, gold flecked green rim, white ground, 11" d	100.00
Jug, flared top, blue sponged bands, cream ground, applied handle, 7¼" h	125.00
Mug	
4" h, blue sponge dec	160.00
4¼" h, brown sponge dec, yellow ground	75.00
Nappy, rect, blue sponged int., white ground, 8½" l	175.00
Pie Baker, brown and green sponge dec, cream ground, 9" d	50.00
Pitcher	
4½" h, brown and green sponge dec, yellow ground	65.00
8¼" h, blue and white dec, blue stripes	225.00
8⅞" h, blue and white, chip on base	300.00
10" h, beige and blue sponge dec, white ground, edge chips and hairlines	125.00
Pitcher and Bowl, blue and olive green sponged dec, blue bands, white ground	325.00

Plate, emb scalloped edge, blue sponge dec, white ground, 10 ¼" d	175.00
Platter, blue sponge dec, white ground, Trenton, NJ, c1865, 12" l, 8" w	215.00
Salt and Pepper Shakers, pr, green and amber sponge dec, white ground	85.00
Spittoon	
7½" d, blue sponge dec and bands, white ground	90.00
10" d, 4" h, blue and white, brass top, 1880–1900	110.00
Syrup Jug, green and rust sponge dec	395.00
Teapot, olive green and white dec, 7¼" h	300.00
Toddy Plate, blue sponge dec, white ground, marked "Burford Bros"	45.00
Water Cooler, stoneware, drip catcher, cobalt sponge dec	395.00

STAFFORDSHIRE

History: The Staffordshire district of England is the center of the English pottery industry. There were 80 different potteries operating there in 1786; the number increased to 179 by 1802. The district includes Burslem, Cobridge, Eturia, Fenton, Foley, Hanley, Lane Delph, Lane End, Longport, Shelton, Stoke, and Tunstall. Among the many famous potters were Adams, Davenport, Spode, Stevenson, Wedgwood, and Wood.

In Staffordshire historical pottery the view depicted is the most critical element. American collectors pay much less for non-American views. Dark blue pieces are favored; light-colored views continue to remain undervalued. Among the forms, soup tureens have shown the highest price increases.

A wide variety of ornamental pottery items originated in England's Staffordshire district, beginning in the 17th century and extending to the present. The height of production was from 1820 to 1890.

These naive pieces are considered folk art by many collectors. Most items were not made carefully; some were even made and decorated by children.

The types of objects varied, e.g., animals, cottages, and figurines (chimney ornaments). The key to price is age and condition. Generally, the older the piece, the higher the price.

References: David and Linda Arman, *Historical Staffordshire: An Illustrated Check List,* published by author, 1974, out-of-print; David and Linda Arman, *First Supplement, Historical Staffordshire: An Illustrated Check List,* published by author, 1977, out-of-print; Ada Walker Camehl, *The Blue China Book,* Tudor Publishing Co., 1946, (Dover, reprint); A. W. Coysh and R. K. Henrywood, *The Dictionary Of Blue And White Printed Pottery, 1780–1880,* Antique Collectors' Club, 1982; Pat Halfpenny, *English Earthenware Figures, 1740–1840,* Antique Collectors' Club; P. D. Gordon Pugh, *Staffordshire Portrait Figures Of The Victorian Era,* Antique Collectors' Club; Charles Kenyon Kies, *Collecting Victorian Staffordshire Pottery Figures,* Antique Publications, 1989; Ellouise Larsen, *American Historical Views On Staffordshire China, 3rd Edition,* Dover Publications, 1975; Dennis G. Rice, *English Porcelain Animals Of The 19th Century,* Antique Collectors' Club; 1989.

Museum: Hershey Museum of American Life, 170 West Hershey Park Drive, Hershey, PA 17033.

Cup Plate
   3½" d, America and Independence, dark blue transfer, Clews **275.00**
   9¼" d, Gilpins Mills, dark blue transfer, Wood **410.00**
Cup and Saucer, handleless, dark blue floral transfer, Adams, small flakes **160.00**
Deep Dish, 9¾" d, Doctor Syntax Mistakes a Gentleman House for an Inn, blue transfer, Clews, rim chip, mid 19th C **135.00**
Dinner Service, partial, nine cups, eleven saucers, eight 7½" d plates, William Penn's Treaty, brown transfer, Thomas Green, Fenton, England, mid 19th C, chips and minor hairlines **550.00**
Figure
   Cat, 9" h, seated, 19th C, pr **450.00**
   Dog
      3" l, pearlware, green, brown, and blue enamel **265.00**
      5½" h, sitting, red and white, polychrome **180.00**
   Hen on Nest, polychrome enamel dec
      3¾" l **135.00**
      5¼" l **225.00**
   Lamb, white sanded coat with polychrome enamel dec, oblong base **195.00**
   Man, 5¼" h, holding whip, polychrome enamel dec **100.00**

Spaniels, pr, rust on white, black muzzles, gold collars, unmarked, 8" h, $185.00.

Rooster, 3¼" h, pearlware, polychrome enamel dec **250.00**
Mug
   1½" h, yellow glaze, ABC, early 19th C **400.00**
   2" h, yellow glaze, early 19th C
      A New Carriage for Anne **425.00**
      A Nightingale for Eliza **400.00**
      A Rocking Horse for John **550.00**
      A Trifle for Richard **425.00**
   2⅛" h, transfer dec, Lovejoy the first Martyr to American Liberty, imperfections **375.00**
Pitcher
   6¾" h, Denton Park, Yorkshire, Riley, medium blue transfer, wear, chips, stains **250.00**
   10½" h, Good Samaritan, red transfer, Clews **410.00**
Plate
   7⅞" d, Picturesque Views, West Point, Hudson River, black transfer, chip on table ring and back edge of rim **75.00**
   8" d, Gunton Norfolk, blue transfer, mid 19th C, set of three **250.00**
   8½" d
      Boston State House, medium blue transfer, unmarked **165.00**
      Nahant Hotel Near Boston, medium dark blue transfer, small edge flake **225.00**
      Texan campaign scene, purple transfer, stains **200.00**

Pitcher, English Scenery, brown transfer, yellow, green, and blue accents, Enoch Wood, 4½" h, $45.00.

8⅞" d, Landing of General Lafayette, medium dark blue transfer, Clews, wear and internal hairline **85.00**

9" d

Battle Monument, Baltimore, red transfer, minor glaze flakes on rim **110.00**

Clyde Scenery, purple transfer, minor stains................ **35.00**

9⅛" d, The Baltimore & Ohio Railroad, dark blue transfer, Enoch Wood & Sons, minor wear, scratches.................. **650.00**

9¾" d

Beauties of America, City Hall, New York, floral border, blue transfer, marked at base, J & W Ridgway, second quarter 19th C **110.00**

Exchange Baltimore, medium dark blue transfer, stains and old chip on back edge of rim........ **350.00**

9½" d, General W H Harrison, Hero of the Thames 1813, black transfer, Philadelphia importers mark on back.................. **2,365.00**

10" d

Commodore MacDonnough's Victory, blue transfer, imperfections **150.00**

Harvard College, oak and acorn border, blue transfer, marked at base, scratches, Ralph Stevenson and Williams, 19th C **325.00**

Landing of Lafayette, dark blue transfer, Clews............ **355.00**

Mitchell & Freeman's China & Glass Warehouse, Chatham Street, Boston, dark blue transfer, Adams... **775.00**

10¼" d

Cadmus, dark blue transfer, Enoch Wood & Sons, minor wear.... **450.00**

City Hall, New York, purple transfer, minor stains and glaze edge flakes.................... **110.00**

City of Albany State of New York, shell border, blue transfer, marked at base, flake to underside of rim, Enoch Wood & Sons, Burslem, England, second quarter 19th C............ **450.00**

English Cathedral, dark blue transfer, Clews **85.00**

Quadrupeds series, dark blue transfer **125.00**

The Baltimore & Ohio Railroad, shell border, blue transfer, marked at base, minor glaze wear, Enoch Wood & Sons, second quarter 19th C **650.00**

Union Line, shell border, blue transfer, marked at base, minor glaze, wear, Enoch Wood & Sons, second quarter 19th C **450.00**

10½" d, America and Independence, dark blue transfer, Clews **300.00**

10¾" d, Winter View of Pittsfield, Mass, dark blue transfer, Clews, old staple repairs **120.00**

Platter

11" l, Fountain Scenery, red transfer, Adams.................... **125.00**

14¾" l, America and Independence, dark blue transfer, Clews **825.00**

17" l, India Temple, blue transfer, J & W Ridgway, first quarter 19th C **250.00**

18" l, Tomb of the Emperor Shah Jehan Oriental Scenery, blue transfer, J Hall & Sons **660.00**

18½" l, British Scenery, floral border, blue transfer, England, mid 19th C.................... **412.00**

18¾" l

London Views, George's Chapel, Regent Street, grape border, blue transfer, marked at base, some imperfections, Enoch Wood & Sons, second quarter 19th C **770.00**

Windsor Castle Berkshire, floral border, blue transfer, marked at base, minor imperfections, William Adams, second quarter 19th C **715.00**

19" l, Upper Ferry Bridge over the River Schuylkill, medium dark blue transfer............... **300.00**

20¾" l, English Gothic style building, tree, and well, medium blue transfer, edge wear, large chip on back edge, one foot missing..... **165.00**

Sauce Tureen, cov, underplate, classical ruins, black transfer, chips, matching ladle broken in three pieces, 6⅝" h **85.00**

Soup Plate

8⅜" d, View of Liverpool, dark blue transfer **275.00**

9⅞" d, Fair Mount near Philadelphia, dark blue transfer............ **275.00**

Soup, Allegheny Scenery, pink transfer, 10⅝ " d, $35.00.

10" d, fisherman with wife and child, medium blue transfer **85.00**

10¼" d, cows in pasture, grapevine border, blue transfer, William Adams, second quarter 19th C, minor imperfections, price for set of five **825.00**

10⅝" d, Indian Temples, purple transfer, minor stains, edge wear, glaze flakes **50.00**

Soup Tureen, 14½" l, Belleville on the Passaic River, eagle at base, cov with different view, blue transfer, Enoch Wood & Sons, imperfections **4,675.00**

Sugar Bowl, cov, dark blue floral transfer, Adams, damage, old repair, 5¾" h **75.00**

Tea Service, winter sleigh ride, blue transfer, Enoch Wood & Sons, second quarter 19th C, 7¾" h teapot, price for eleven piece set **825.00**

Tea Set, child's, Forest, light blue tree transfer, covered teapot, creamer, covered sugar bowl, footed waste bowl, two 5" d plates, four cups and saucer, teapot finial glued, price for 14 pc set **300.00**

Vegetable Dish

12" l, cov, light blue Canton transfer, small chips and hairlines in lid **150.00**

12¾" l, open, Yale College & State House, New Haven, black transfer, minor edge flakes **300.00**

Waste Bowl

3" d, 3½" h, birds and flowers, medium blue transfer, wear, pinpoint flakes **115.00**

6¼" d, 3½" h, American eagle and shield, dark blue transfer **875.00**

STANGL
POTTERY

History: The Stangl Pottery, located in Trenton and Flemington, New Jersey, was founded in 1930 by J. M. Stangl, formerly of Fulper Pottery. In 1978 it was purchased by the Pfaltzgraff Company. The Flemington factory currently serves as a Pfaltzgraff factory outlet. One of the original kilns remains intact to exemplify the hard work and high temperatures involved in the production of pottery.

Stangl Pottery produced several lines of highly collectible dinnerware and decorative accessories, including the famed Stangl birds. The red bodied dinnerware was produced in distinctive shapes and patterns. Shapes were designated by numbers. Pattern names include: Country Garden, Fruit, Tulip, Thistle, and Wild Rose. Special Christmas, advertising and commemorative wares were also produced.

Bright colors and bold simplistic patterns have made Stangl Pottery a favorite with Country collectors. Stangl's factory sold seconds from its factory store long before outlet malls became popular. Large sets of Stangl dinnerware currently command high prices at auctions, flea markets, and even antique shops.

Stangl's ceramic birds were produced from 1940 until 1972. The birds were produced at Stangl's Trenton plant, then shipped to the Flemington plant for hand painting.

During World War II the demand for these birds and Stangl pottery was so great that 40 to 60 decorators could not keep up with the demand. Orders were contracted out to private homes. These pieces were then returned for firing and finishing. Colors used to decorate these birds varied according to the artist.

As many as ten different trademarks were used. Dinnerware was marked and often signed by the decorator. Most birds are numbered; many are artist signed. However, signatures are useful for dating purposes only and add little to values.

Several birds were reissued between 1972 and 1977. These reissues are dated on the bottom and worth approximately one half the value of the older birds.

References: Harvey Duke, *Stangl Pottery,* Wallace-Homestead, 1993; Joan Dworkin and Martha Horman, *A Guide To Stangl Pottery Birds,* Willow Pond Books, Inc., 1973; Norma Rehl, *The Collectors Handbook of Stangl Pottery,* Democrat Press, 1982.

Ashtray

Antique Gold, 9" sq **10.00**

Apple Tree, 5" d **15.00**

Flower, 5" d **12.00**

Sportsman, oval, 10⅝" l

Pheasant **35.00**

Quail. **48.00**

Wood Duck **45.00**

Basket, Terra Rose, 11" w **75.00**

Bird Figures

#3581, Chickadees **175.00**

#3596, Cardinal, gray **62.00**

#3598, Kentucky Warbler **40.00**

#3628, Fieffers Hummingbird **115.00**

#3635, Goldfinches **175.00**

#3716, Blue Jay with leaf **450.00**

#3814, Black Throated Warbler . . . **85.00**

#3848, Gold Crowned Kinglet **110.00**

#34020, Orioles, small chip on beak **80.00**

#34060D, Double Kingfishers **150.00**

#37510, Red Headed Woodpecker **300.00**

Cigarette Box, cov, rect, 7¼ × 3⅜"

Heart **35.00**

Hummingbird **40.00**

Food Molds, set of four, two with grape clusters, two with peach, brown ground, 4⅝ " l, 3½" w, 2" h, price for set, $35.00.

Bleeding Heart, plate, 8¼" d, $6.00.

Coaster
Apple Tree	**6.00**
Country Garden	**10.00**

Dinnerware
Antique Gold
Bowl, 8" d.	**25.00**
Pitcher, 14½" h	**35.00**
Server, center handle.	**15.00**

Apple Delight
Cake Stand	**20.00**
Casserole, 6" d	**15.00**
Cereal Bowl	**12.00**
Gravy, underplate	**35.00**
Plate	
8" d, salad	**10.00**
10" d, dinner	**15.00**
Relish Tray	**22.00**
Salad Bowl, 10" d	**35.00**
Snack Plate, 8¼" d	**3.50**

Bella Rosa
Butter Dish, cov, ¼ lb	**35.00**
Casserole, individual, stick handle	**15.00**
Cup and Saucer.	**12.00**
Fruit Bowl, 5½" d	**10.00**
Pitcher, ½ pint	**20.00**
Plate, 6" d, bread and butter	**5.00**
Server, center handle.	**10.00**

Colonial
Ball Jug, ice lip, Colonial blue. . .	**35.00**
Bean Pot, individual, Persian yellow	**18.00**
Casserole, Tangerine, 8" d.	**35.00**
Chop Plate, Silver green, 12½" d	**12.00**
Eggcup, Colonial blue	**8.00**

Bluebird, #3276, blue and yellow, 5" h, $80.00.

Plate
8" d, salad, Silver green	**8.00**
10" d, dinner, Persian yellow	**12.00**
Relish Dish, two parts, Colonial blue, 7" l	**20.00**
Teapot, individual, Tangerine . . .	**30.00**
Vegetable Bowl, oval, Tangerine, 10" l.	**16.00**

Country Garden
Creamer and Sugar	**25.00**
Cup and Saucer.	**15.00**
Gravy Boat, underplate	**32.00**
Pickle Dish	**20.00**
Pitcher, 2 quart	**45.00**
Soup Bowl, lug handle.	**15.00**

Fruits
Bean Pot, handled	**60.00**
Chop Plate, 14½" d	**40.00**
Coffeepot, 4 cup	**60.00**
Dinner Service, 40 pcs.	**425.00**
Mixing Bowl, 7" d	**25.00**
Plate, 10" d, dinner	**18.00**
Relish Dish	**25.00**
Salad Bowl, 12" d	**50.00**
Sherbet	**25.00**
Teapot, individual	**18.00**

Garden Flower
Casserole, Balloon Flower, 6" d	**22.00**
Chop Plate, Tiger Lily, 12½" d. . .	**40.00**
Creamer, individual, Rose	**12.00**
Cup and Saucer, Rose cup, Leaves saucer	**15.00**
Fruit Bowl, Calendula, 5½" d . . .	**12.00**
Pitcher, 2 quart, Sunflower	**40.00**
Plate	
8" d, salad, Bleeding Heart. . . .	**12.00**
9" d, luncheon, Tiger Lily.	**12.00**
Teapot, Sunflower	**45.00**

Golden Harvest
Cup	**5.00**
Mug, 2 cup	**25.00**
Plate	
8" d, salad	**5.00**
10" d, dinner	**7.50**
Salt and Pepper Shakers, pr	**24.00**
Vegetable Bowl, divided	**35.00**

Magnolia

Butter Dish	**35.00**
Condiment Tray	**22.00**
Creamer and Sugar	**20.00**
Cup and Saucer.	**10.00**
Pitcher, 1 quart	**30.00**
Salt and Pepper Shakers, pr.	**12.00**
Planter, Platina, swan, 6¾" h	**20.00**

Vase

Terra Rose, No. 3442, 6" h	**20.00**
Tropical Ware, No. 2027, 8" h	**100.00**
Wall Pocket, Cosmos, green matte, 1937.	**40.00**

TAYLOR, SMITH, AND TAYLOR

History: C. A. Smith and Colonel John N. Taylor founded Taylor, Smith, and Taylor in Chester, West Virginia, in 1899. In 1903 the firm reorganized and the Taylor interests were purchased by the Smith family. The firm remained in the family's control until it was purchased by Anchor Hocking in 1973. The tableware division closed in 1981.

Taylor, Smith, and Taylor started production with a nine-kiln pottery. Local clays were used initially. Later only southern clays were used. Both earthenware and fine china bodies were produced. Several underglaze print patterns, e.g. Dogwood and Spring Bouquet were made. These prints, made from the copper engravings of ceramic artist J. Palin Thorley, were designed exclusively for the company.

Taylor, Smith, and Taylor also made Lu Ray, produced from the 1930s through the early 1950s. Available in Windsor Blue, Persian Cream, Sharon Pink, Surf Green, and Chatham Gray, their coordinating colors encourage collectors to mix and match sets.

Competition for a portion of the dinnerware market of the 1930s through the 1950s was intense. LuRay was designed to compete with Russel Wright's American Modern. Vistosa was Taylor, Smith, and Taylor's answer to Homer Laughlin's Fiesta.

Taylor, Smith, and Taylor used several different backstamps and marks. Many contain the company name as well as the pattern and shape names.

Autumn Harvest

Butter, cov	**20.00**
Casserole, cov	**18.00**
Cup and Saucer	**6.00**
Plate, 6" d, bread and butter	**4.00**

Platter

11" l	**12.00**
13½" l.	**18.00**
Salt and Pepper Shakers, pr.	**10.00**

Lu-Ray

Casserole, cov, Sharon pink	**45.00**
Chop Plate, 14" d	
Persian cream	**28.00**
Surf green	**20.00**
Windsor blue	**28.00**
Cup and Saucer, Chatham gray	**20.00**
Demitasse Cup, Persian cream	**16.50**
Demitasse Cup and Saucer	
Sharon pink.	**20.00**
Windsor blue	**20.00**
Demitasse Sugar, cov, Windsor blue	**20.00**
Eggcup	
Persian cream	**14.00**
Sharon pink.	**18.00**
Windsor blue	**18.00**
Gravy, Persian cream	**18.00**
Mixing Bowl, 8¾" d, Surf green . . .	**70.00**
Pitcher, ftd	
Sharon pink.	**60.00**
Windsor blue	**50.00**
Plate	
6½" d, bread and butter, Sharon pink.	**4.00**
8" d, salad	
Chatham gray	**20.00**
Sharon pink.	**14.00**
Surf green	**15.00**
Windsor blue.	**12.00**
9" d, luncheon	
Chatham gray	**15.00**
Sharon pink.	**7.00**
10" d, dinner	
Persian cream	**12.00**
Windsor blue.	**12.00**
Platter	
12" l, Surf green	**10.00**
13" l, Chatham gray	**30.00**
Relish, four part	
Persian cream	**80.00**
Surf green	**85.00**

Golden Button, Ever Yours shape, dinner plate, 10¼" d, $3.00.

Salad Bowl

    Persian cream **40.00**

    Surf green **40.00**

    Windsor blue **55.00**

Salt and Pepper Shakers, pr, Michi-

    gan decal **12.00**

Sauce Boat, Windsor blue. **12.00**

Soup

    Flat

        Chatham gray **30.00**

        Persian cream **15.00**

        Surf green **15.00**

        Windsor blue. **12.00**

    Tab Handles

        Sharon pink. **18.00**

        Surf green **18.00**

        Windsor blue. **18.00**

Starter Set, Surf green, 29 pcs **55.00**

Teapot

    Persian cream, curved. **60.00**

    Sharon pink. **50.00**

Tray, center handle, Chatham gray **80.00**

Tumbler

    Juice

        Persian cream **37.00**

        Sharon pink. **35.00**

        Windsor blue. **32.00**

    Water, Chatham gray **45.00**

Vase, bud, Surf green **150.00**

Vegetable Dish, oval, 10" l

    Chatham gray **30.00**

    Persian cream **10.00**

    Windsor blue **12.00**

Petit Point Bouquet

    Cake Plate, 11" d, tab handled **10.00**

    Mixing Bowl, 9" d. **15.00**

    Plate, dinner. **6.00**

    Platter, 12½" d, tab handled **12.00**

Vistosa

    Bowl, 8" d

        Cobalt blue **65.00**

        Mango red. **65.00**

    Chop Plate, 11" d

        Deep yellow **20.00**

        Mango red. **15.00**

    Creamer, Light green. **10.00**

    Cup and Saucer, Light green **18.00**

    Gravy Boat, Cobalt blue **150.00**

    Jug, Mango red **50.00**

    Pitcher, Deep yellow **40.00**

    Plate

        6" d, bread and butter, Light

           green. **5.00**

        7" d, salad, Cobalt blue. **10.00**

        9" d, luncheon, Deep yellow. . . . **12.00**

    Salt and Pepper Shakers, pr, Cobalt

        blue. **20.00**

    Soup, flat

        Deep yellow **20.00**

        Mango red. **20.00**

    Sugar, cov, Light green **20.00**

    Teacup, Cobalt blue **8.00**

UNIVERSAL POTTERY

History: In 1934 The Oxford Pottery Company created Universal Potteries of Cambridge, Ohio. It purchased the Atlas-Globe plant properties. The Atlas-Globe operation was a merger of the Atlas China Company (formerly Crescent China Co. in 1921, Tritt in 1912, and Bradshaw in 1902) and the Globe China Company.

Even after the purchase, Universal retained the Oxford ware, made in Oxford, Ohio, as part of their dinnerware line. Another Oxford plant was used to manufacture tiles. The plant at Niles, Ohio, was dismantled.

The most popular lines of Universal were "Ballerina" and "Ballerina Mist." The company developed a detergent-resistant decal known as permacel, a key element in keeping a pattern bright. Production continued until 1960, when all plants were closed.

Not all Universal pottery carried the Universal name as part of the backstamp. Wares marked "Harmony House," "Sweet William/Sears Roebuck and Co.," and "Wheelock, Peoria" are part of the Universal production. Wheelock was a department store in Peoria, Illinois, that controlled the Cattail pattern on the Old Holland shape.

Like many pottery companies, Universal had many shapes or styles of blanks, the most popular being Camwood, Old Holland, and Laurella. The same decal might be found on several different shapes. Decals with an appeal to the Country collector include Hollyhocks, Iris, Largo, Rambler Rose, and Red Poppy. Universal's booster Woodvine line, often used as a premium by grocery stores to stimulate business, is readily available and attractive to a collector willing to blend Country and modern themes.

The Cattail pattern had many accessory pieces. The 1940 and 1941 Sears catalogs listed an oval wastebasket, breakfast set, kitchen scale, linens, and bread box. Calico Fruits is another pattern with accessory pieces.

The Calico Fruits decal has not held up well over time. Collectors often have to settle for less than perfect pieces.

Bittersweet

    Drip Jar, cov **20.00**

    Mixing Bowl **30.00**

    Platter. **30.00**

    Salad Bowl **32.00**

    Stack Set **35.00**

Calico Fruits

    Batter Jug **25.00**

    Cookie Jar, cov **30.00**

    Creamer **6.00**

    Cup and Saucer. **8.00**

    Custard **6.00**

    Plate, 10" d, dinner **8.00**

    Salt and Pepper Shakers, pr **15.00**

Cattails

Batter Jug, metal lid	**80.00**
Bowl	
6" d, tab handle	**10.00**
7½" d, cov	**18.00**
8½" d	**12.00**
Bread Box, double compartment	**25.00**
Butter Dish, cov	**35.00**
Casserole, cov, 8¼" d.	**15.00**
Creamer and Sugar, cov	**24.00**
Cup and Saucer	**9.00**
Fruit Bowl, 5" d	**4.00**
Gravy Boat	**20.00**
Milk Pitcher, 1 quart.	**20.00**
Pie Baker	**20.00**
Plate	
6" d, bread and butter	**3.00**
7" d, salad.	**6.00**
9½" d, luncheon.	**8.00**
10" d, dinner.	**12.00**
Platter, oval, 11½" l	**15.00**
Salad Bowl, 9¾" d	**20.00**
Salad Set, fork and spoon	**28.00**
Soup, flat, 7¾" d	**10.00**
Syrup, metal lid	**65.00**
Teapot	**30.00**
Vegetable Bowl, oval, 10" l	**18.00**

VERNON KILNS

History: During the Great Depression, many small potteries flourished in southern California. One of these, Poxon China, was founded in Vernon, California, in 1912. Faye G. Bennison purchased this pottery in 1931 and renamed it Vernon Kilns. It also was known as Vernon Potteries, Ltd. Under Bennison's direction, the company became a leader in the pottery industry.

The high quality and versatility of its wares made it very popular. Besides a varied dinnerware line, Vernon Kilns also produced Walt Disney figurines, as well as advertising, political, and fraternal items. One popular line was historical and commemorative plates, which included several series featuring scenes from England, California missions, and the West.

Vernon Kilns survived the Depression, fires, earthquakes, and wars. However, it could not compete with the influx of imports. In January, 1958, the factory was closed. Metlox Potteries of Manhattan Beach, California, bought the trade name and molds along with the remaining stock.

Like many pottery companies, Vernon Kilns developed a number of dinnerware lines and then offered them in a wide variety of decal and hand painted decorations. Decorative motifs varied from extremely traditional, e.g., Romantic Staffordshire style transfer patterns on a line of traditional English forms, to post-World War II modern.

Country collectors might consider the San Fernando shape line with the R.F.D. pattern (featuring a rooster weathervane) or one of the four hand-tinted patterns: 1860, Hibiscus, Vernon Rose, and Desert Bloom.

Vernon Kilns used 48 different marks during its period of operation.

Reference: Maxine Nelson, *Versatile Vernon Kilns, An Illustrated Value Guide, Book II,* Collector Books, 1983, out-of-print.

Periodical: *Vernon View,* PO Box 945, Scottsdale, AZ 85252.

Early California

Carafe, brown.	**25.00**
Cup and Saucer, turquoise	**5.00**
Demitasse Creamer, dark blue	**20.00**
Demitasse Cup and Saucer, orange	**25.00**
Eggcup, turquoise	**10.00**
Platter, orange, 12" l	**18.00**
Salt and Pepper Shakers, pr, yellow	**18.00**
Vegetable Bowl, orange, 8½" d. . . .	**10.00**

Gingham

Carafe.	**28.00**
Casserole, handled	**25.00**
Chop Plate	**10.00**
Cup and Saucer	**6.00**
Eggcup	**18.00**
Pitcher, ice lip, 11½" h.	**45.00**
Plate	
6" d, bread and butter	**3.00**
10½" d, dinner	**6.00**
Range Salt and Pepper Shakers, pr	**35.00**
Salad Bowl, 9" d	**16.00**
Soup Bowl, 8½" d.	**12.00**
Syrup Pitcher	**55.00**
Teapot, cov.	**20.00**

Homespun

Butter Dish	**35.00**
Coaster, 3⅞" d	**8.00**
Creamer and Sugar, cov	**15.00**
Cup and Saucer	**5.00**
Fruit Bowl, 5½" d	**4.00**
Gravy	**10.00**
Mixing Bowl, 8" d.	**16.00**
Pitcher, 8½" h.	**18.00**
Plate	
6" d, bread and butter	**4.00**
7" d, salad.	**5.00**
9½" d, luncheon	**7.00**
10" d, dinner.	**9.00**
Salt and Pepper Shakers, pr.	**8.00**
Sauce Boat, 6½" l	**10.00**
Soup, lug handle.	**7.00**
Vegetable Bowl, divided	**12.00**

Modern California

Bowl	
6" d, Orchid, handled	**12.00**
9" d, Azure blue	**35.00**

Cup and Saucer

Orchid	....	**15.00**
Pistachio green	....	**12.00**
Straw yellow	....	**13.00**
Fruit Bowl, 5½" d, Azure blue	....	**8.00**
Mug, Azure blue	....	**32.00**

Plate

6¼" d, bread and butter		
Azure blue	....	**6.00**
Pistachio green	....	**6.00**
9¾" d, dinner		
Azure blue	....	**12.00**
Orchid	....	**12.00**
Vegetable Bowl, oval, 9½" l, Azure blue	....	**20.00**

Organdie

Bowl, 7¼" d	....	**5.00**
Butter Dish	....	**35.00**
Casserole, cov, individual	....	**15.00**
Chop Plate, 12" d	....	**12.00**
Creamer and Sugar, cov	....	**10.00**
Cup and Saucer	....	**7.00**
Eggcup	....	**25.00**
Gravy	....	**20.00**
Mixing Bowls, nesting, set of five		**125.00**

Plate

6" d, bread and butter	....	**2.00**
7" d, salad	....	**3.50**
9½" d, luncheon	....	**6.00**
10½" d, dinner	....	**10.00**

Platter, oval

12¾" l	....	**8.00**
14" l	....	**10.00**
Salad Bowl, 9" d	....	**15.00**

Soup

Flat	....	**7.00**
Lug Handle	....	**18.00**
Teapot, cov	....	**45.00**
Tidbit Tray, 2 tiers	....	**24.00**

WATT POTTERY

History: Watt Pottery, founded in 1922 in Crooksville, Ohio, was well known for its stoneware. The pottery occupied the site of the former Globe Stoneware Company (1901–1919) and the Zane W. Burley Pottery (1919–1922). Local Crooksville clay was used. Kitchenware production began in 1935; the plant was destroyed by fire in 1965 and never rebuilt.

It is the color tones and patterns of Watt Pottery that appeal to Country collectors and decorators. The background consists of earth tones in off-white and light tan. It is similar in feel to many patterns from Pennsbury, Pfaltzgraff, and Purinton as well as the English Torquay pieces.

Most Watt Pottery features an underglaze decoration. The Red Apple pattern was introduced in 1950, the Cherry pattern in 1955, and the Star Flower in 1956. Other popular patterns include

Pennsylvania Dutch Tulip and Rooster. Examples with advertising are highly collectible.

Reference: Sue and Dave Morris, *Watt Pottery: An Identification and Value Guide,* Collector Books, 1993.

Collectors' Club: Watt Pottery Collectors, USA, PO Box 26067, Fairview Park, OH 44126.

Periodical: *Watt's News,* PO Box 708, Mason City, IA 50401.

Reproduction Alert: A Japanese copy of a large spaghetti bowl marked simply "U.S.A." is known. The Watt example bears a "Peedeeco" and "U.S.A." mark.

Apple

Bowl

#6, adv, ribbed	....	**60.00**
#7, adv	....	**40.00**
#8	....	**50.00**
#63	....	**55.00**
#66	....	**85.00**
Canister, cov, #72	....	**250.00**
Casserole, cov, #67	....	**120.00**
Cereal Bowl, #52	....	**25.00**
Cookie Jar, #503	....	**365.00**
Creamer, #62	....	**75.00**
Grease Jar, #1	....	**250.00**

Mixing Bowl, ribbed

#5	....	**55.00**
#6	....	**65.00**
#9	....	**125.00**
Pie Plate	....	**65.00**

Pitcher

#15, adv	....	**80.00**
#16	....	**100.00**
#62	....	**65.00**
Salad Bowl, #73	....	**60.00**
Spaghetti Bowl, #39	....	**150.00**
Vegetable Bowl, cov	....	**50.00**

Bleeding Heart

Bean Pot	....	**125.00**
Bowl, #7	....	**30.00**
Creamer	....	**70.00**
Pitcher, #15	....	**50.00**

Open Apple, mixing bowl, #7, 7" d, 3⅞" h, $100.00.

Cherry
Berry Bowl, #4 . . . .   25.00
Cereal Bowl
#23 . . . .   35.00
#52 . . . .   25.00
Cookie Jar, cov, #21 . . . .   160.00
Mixing Bowl
#6 . . . .   35.00
#8 . . . .   45.00
Pitcher
#15 . . . .   55.00
#17 . . . .   125.00
Platter, #31 . . . .   145.00
Salt Shaker 50.00
Spaghetti Bowl, #39 . . . .   50.00
Open Apple, mixing bowls, nesting set
of four
#5 . . . .   85.00
#6 . . . .   85.00
#7 . . . .   100.00
#8 . . . .   125.00
Rooster
Baking Dish, rect 1,000.00
Bowl
#5, cov 135.00
#58 . . . .   90.00
#67, cov 125.00
#73 . . . .   75.00
Casserole, individual, #18 . . . .   225.00
Creamer, #62 . . . .   95.00
Ice Bucket 125.00
Pitcher, adv 50.00
Sugar, cov, #98 . . . .   150.00
Vegetable Bowl, adv 50.00
Starflower
Bean Pot, handled, #76 . . . .   90.00
Bowl, #55 . . . .   60.00
Casserole, cov, #65 . . . .   100.00
Grease Jar, #47 . . . .   175.00
Ice Bucket 185.00
Mixing Bowls, nesting set of four, #4,
#5, #6, and #7 . . . .   175.00
Mug, #501 . . . .   85.00
Pitcher
#15 . . . .   40.00
#16 . . . .   85.00
Salt and Pepper Shakers, pr
Barrel shaped 150.00
Hourglass shaped 175.00
Platter, #31 . . . .   140.00
Spaghetti Bowl, #39 . . . .   95.00
Tear Drop
Bean Pot, cov, #76 . . . .   95.00
Bowl, #66 . . . .   45.00
Casserole, cov, square 275.00
Cheese Crock, #80 . . . .   275.00
Creamer, #62 . . . .   75.00
Mixing Bowl, ribbed, #7 . . . .   40.00
Pitcher, #16 . . . .   75.0
Salt and Pepper Shakers, pr, barrel
shaped 150.00

WELLER POTTERY

History: In 1872 Samuel A. Weller opened a small factory in Fultonham, Ohio, to produce utilitarian stoneware, e.g. milk pans and sewer tile. In 1882 he moved his facilities to Zanesville. In 1890 Weller built a new plant in the Putnam section of Zanesville along the tracks of the Cincinnati and Miskingum Railway. Additions followed in 1892 and 1894.

In 1894 Weller entered into an agreement with William A. Long to purchase the Lonhuda Faience Company, which had developed an art pottery line under the guidance of Laura A. Fry, formerly of Rookwood. Long left the company in 1895 and this line was renamed Louwelsa. Charles Babcock Upjohn became the new art director. He, along with Jacques Sicard, Frederick Hurten Rhead, and Gazo Fudji, developed Weller's art pottery lines.

At the end of World War I, many high prestige lines were discontinued and Weller concentrated on commercial wares. Rudolph Lorber joined the staff and designed the Roma, Forest, and Knifewood lines. In 1920 Weller acquired Zanesville Art Pottery and claimed to be the largest pottery in the country.

Art pottery enjoyed a revival in the 1920s and 30s with the introduction of the Hudson, Coppertone, and Graystone Garden lines. However, the Great Depression forced the closing of the Putnam and Marietta Street plants in Zanesville. Following World War II, cheap Japanese imports took over Weller's market. In 1947 Essex Wire Company of Detroit bought the controlling stock. Early in 1948 operations ceased.

References: Sharon and Bob Huxford, *The Collectors Encyclopedia Of Weller Pottery*, Collector Books, 1979, 1992 value updated; Ann Gilbert McDonald, *All About Weller: A History And Collectors Guide To Weller Pottery, Zanesville, OH,* Antique Publications, 1989.

Collectors' Club: American Art Pottery Association, 125 E Rose Ave, St. Louis, MO 63119.

Basket
Forest, hanging, 10" d 225.00
Wild Rose, peach, 6" d 35.00
Bowl
Bouquet, cov, #8 . . . .   70.00
Louwelsa, brown glaze, gold floral
dec, artist sgd, 7¼" d, 3" h 95.00
Pumila, flower form, pink, green
leaves, 3½" d 35.00

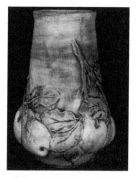

Vase, Baldin, incised "Weller," 11" h, $125.00.

Candleholder
Paragon, 2" h 95.00
Sydonia, double, green 20.00
Compote, Bonito, 4" h 60.00
Console Bowl
Hobart, boy with goose flower frog,
9" d, 3" h 135.00
Softone, 10" d, 3" h 15.00
Wild Rose, 7½" d 30.00
Console Set, Blossom, bowl and two
candlesticks 75.00
Cornucopia
Softone, light blue, 10" d 25.00
Wild Rose 30.00
Ewer, Floretta, 12½" h 250.00
Mug, Eocean, mushrooms, 5¾" h 145.00
Pitcher, Zona, cobalt blue, apple dec   70.00
Planter
Pastel, P–5, 8" l, 4" h 28.00
Softone, oval, ftd, blue, 8" l. 35.00
Woodcraft, log, 11" l, 5" h 50.00
Stein, Louwelsa, long stemmed flowers,
11½" h 250.00
Teapot
Forest 250.00
Utility Ware
Pineapple, 6½" h 125.00
Pumpkin, 6" h. 85.00

Vase, Louwelsa, pillow, artist sgd "M. Mitchell," stamped mark, 7⅛ " h, $495.00.

Vase
Baldin, 8½" h 95.00
Bonito, handled, 6" h 80.00
Bouquet, double, green, 4" h 10.00
Darsie, aqua, 7" h 40.00
Eocean, raspberries, 8½" h 200.00
Fleron, 6½" h 65.00
Floretta, flask, B33, 8" h 100.00
Hudson, sgd "Timberlake," 7" h . . .   700.00
Ivoris, double, 9½" h 25.00
Knifewood, 7" h 175.00
LeMar, 9" h. 265.00
Louwelsa
7" h, pansies, circle seal 95.00
10½" h, blue, floral 750.00
Malvern, burgundy and yellow,
13½" h 125.00
Patricia, goose neck handles, 8½"h   100.00
Roma, triple bud, 7½" h 75.00
Wall Pocket
Squirrel 130.00
Wild Rose 75.00
Woodland, azaleas 135.00

YELLOW WARE

History: Yellow ware is a heavy earthenware of differing weight and strength. Yellow ware varies in color from a rich pumpkin to lighter shades which are more tan than yellow. Although plates, nappies, and custard cups are found, kitchen bowls and other cooking utensils are most prevalent.

The first American yellow ware was produced at Bennington, Vermont. English yellow ware has additional ingredients which make its body much harder. Derbyshire and Sharp's were foremost among the English manufacturers.

Yellow ware has long been a favorite of Country collectors. Large bowls, unusual molds, and other household items are cornerstone collection pieces and desirable decorative accents.

References: John Gallo, *Nineteenth and Twentieth Century Yellow Ware,* Heritage Press, 1985; Joan Leibowitz, *Yellow Ware: The Transitional Ceramic,* Schiffer Publishing, 1985; Lisa S. McAllister and John L. Michael, *Collecting Yellow Ware,* Collector Books, 1993.

Basin, 12" d, c1870 . . . .   85.00
Bowl
8¾" l, oval, brown sponge dec 25.00
9¾" d, brown and blue sponge dec,
Red Wing Saffron Ware 30.00
Butter Tub, dark blue stripes, ribbed
bottom, 7¼" d. 100.00
Chamber Pot, miniature, white band,
brown stripes, blue seaweed dec,
1¾" h 195.00
Colander, yellow bands, white int. . . .   175.00

Creamer, green and brown sponge dec,
4½" h **75.00**
Creamer and Sugar, molded floral de-
sign, classical figures, 3 ⅛" h
creamer, 4⅝" h sugar **300.00**
Crock, brown bands, 5½" h **30.00**
Figure
Cat, sitting, oval base, brown and
blue-green running glaze **2,000.00**
Lion, 6½" l, brown glaze **75.00**
Food Mold
Corn, ovoid, fluted sides, 5½" l . . .   **90.00**
Pinwheel **100.00**
Rabbit, 8" l **125.00**
Turk's Head, brown sponge dec, 9" d   **110.00**
Foot Warmer, wedge shaped, cork plug   **100.00**
Jar, brown slip dec, 8¾" h **525.00**
Ladle, 7½" l **25.00**
Meat Tenderizer, wood handle. **295.00**
Medallion, oval, white molded bust of
Washington, 6¼" h. **250.00**
Milk Pan, 11½" d **60.00**
Mixing Bowl
6¼" d, 3½" h, molded bark pattern
and rim **25.00**
15½" d, 6½" h, brown stripes. **75.00**
22½" d, molded rim, blue band . . .   **75.00**
Nested set of three, molded rim,
brown and green spatter dec, 7" to
9½" d **165.00**
Mug
3¼" h, brown polka dot dec **675.00**
3⅞" h, white band with brown
stripes **115.00**

Mixing Bowls, nesting set of six, continuous molded design, girl watering flowers outside window, price for set, $350.00.

Pie Plate, 9½" d **155.00**
Pitcher
5½" h, slip dec, minor flakes, 19th C   **135.00**
5⅝" h, molded ribs, green and
brown dripping glaze, chip on
spout **25.00**
6¼" h, molded shoulder and neck,
blue spotted glaze **40.00**
8" h, medium blue bands, white
stripes, strap handle, small flakes
on spout **385.00**
Pitcher and Bowl, black, tan, and blue
stripes, T G Green & Co, England   **225.00**
Rolling Pin, wood handles **175.00**
Spittoon, green, blue, and tan sponge
dec, 7½" d, 5" h **60.00**
Vegetable Dish, octagonal, Bennett &
Brothers, Liverpool, OH, 12⅜" l,
9⅜" w, 2" h **475.00**
Washboard.   **595.00**

SHAKER

When looking for an elegant, but handcrafted look, Country collectors and decorators turn to Shaker. The look has a natural and utilitarian emphasis; warm earth tones dominate.

Because the Shakers were self–sufficient, they developed products for all aspects of daily living. Individuals who are only familiar with Shaker furniture are missing much of the picture. The Shaker way of life is understood only in its totality.

The Shakers, so named because of a dance used in worship, are one of the oldest communal religious organizations in the United States, founded by Mother Ann Lee, who emigrated from England and established the first Shaker community near Albany, New York, in 1784. The Shakers reached their peak in 1850 with 6,000 members.

Shakers lived celibate and self–sufficient lives. Their philosophy stressed cleanliness, order, simplicity, and economy. Highly inventive and motivated, the Shakers created many utilitarian household forms and objects. Their furniture reflected a striving for quality and purity in design.

In the early 19th century, the Shakers produced many items for commercial purposes. Chair making and the packaged herb and seed business thrived. In every endeavor and enterprise, the members followed Mother Ann's advice: "Put your hands to work and give your heart to God."

References: Charles R. Muller and Timothy D. Rieman, *The Shaker Chair,* The Canal Press, 1984; Don and Carol Raycraft, *Shaker, A Collector's Source Book II,* Wallace–Homestead,

1985; Timothy D. Rieman and Jean M. Burks, *The Complete Book of Shaker Furniture,* Harry N. Abrams, 1993; June Sprigg and David Larkin, *Shaker Life, Work, and Art,* Stewart, Tabori & Chang, 1987.

Periodicals: *The Shaker Messenger,* PO Box 1645, Holland, MI 49422.

Museums: Hancock Shaker Village, Pittsfield, MA; Shaker Historical Museum, Shaker Heights, OH; Shaker Village of Pleasant Hill, Harrodsburg, KY; The Shaker Museum and Library, Old Chatham, NY.

Reproduction Craftspersons: *Baskets*—Darryl & Karen Arawjo, PO Box 477, Bushkill, PA 18324; John E McGuire, Baskets & Bears, 398 S Main St, Geneva, NY 14456; Gary A O'Brien, Meadow Farm, Ruggles Hill Rd, Hardwick, MA 01037; Martha Wetherbee, Martha Wetherbee Basket Shop, HCR 69, Basket St, Sanbornton, NH 03269; Stephen Zeh, Basketmaker, PO Box 381, Temple, ME 04984; *Boxes*—Donald Butler, 402 Lombard St, Philadelphia, PA 19147; Charles Harvey, Simple Gifts, 201C N Broadway, Berea, KY 40403; *Furniture*—Dan Backenstose, Jr, Spring House Classics, PO Box 541, Schaefferstown, PA 17088; Gene Cosloy, Great Meadows Joinery, PO Box 392, Wayland, MA 01778; Lenore Howe & Brian Braskie, North Woods Chair Shop, 237 Old Tilton Rd, Canterbury, NH 03224; Ian Ingersoll Cabinetmakers, Main St, W Cornwall, CT 06796; Paul & Bonnie Rung, Llewellyn House, 2198 Mont Alto Rd, Chambersburg, PA 17201; Gregory Vasileff Reproductions, 740 North St, Greenwich, CT 06831.

Reproduction Manufacturers: *General*—C H Southwell, PO Box 484, Suttons Bay, MI 49682; Country Loft, 1506 South Shore Park, Hingham, MA 02043; The Country Stippler, Rte 2, Box 1540, Pine Mountain, GA 31822; David T Smith & Co, 3600 Shawhan Rd, Morrow, OH 45152; Faith Mountain Country Fare, Main St, Box 199, Sperryville, VA 22740; Five Trails Antiques and Country Accents, 116 E Water St, Circleville, OH 43113; Hammermark Associates, 10 Jericho Turnpike, Floral Park, NY 11001; J T Nicholas & Son, 704 N Michigan Ave, Howell, MI 48843; McClanahan Country, 217 Rockwell Rd, Wilmington, NC 28405; Mulberry Magic, PO Box 62, Ruckersville, VA 22968; Olde Virginea Floorcloth and Trading Co, PO Box 3305, Portsmouth, VA 23707; Our Home, Articles of Wood, 666 Perry St, Vermilion, OH 44089; Shaker Accents, PO Box 425, 4 Martin Ave, Lee, MA 01238; Shaker Carpenter Shop, 8267 Oswego Rd, Liverpool, NY 13090; Shaker Shops West, Five Inverness Way, Inverness, CA 94937; Spring House Classics, PO Box 541, Schaefferstown, PA 17088; Traditions, RD 4, Box 191, Hudson, NY 12534.

Basket
- 4" l, sewing, heart shaped, woven splint and raffia, faded painted floral dec on lid **100.00**
- 4½" sq, finely woven poplar splint, worn green satin lining and ext. ribbons, stamped label "Sabbath Day Lake Shakers," accessories included **175.00**
- 6" d, round, swing handle **775.00**
- 24" sq, gathering, black ash, sgd "Seed Shop, N.F." and "N.F.L.S." **600.00**

Blanket, wool, handwoven, initialed "LMF 68," Canterbury, NH, slight moth damage **450.00**

Blanket Chest
- 33¼" w, 16¼" d, 24¾" h, child's, orig red stain, single drawer, Canterbury, NH, minor repairs, minor repairs, early 19th C **8,250.00**
- 39¼" w, 19¼" d, pine, painted, two graduated thumb molded drawers, old red wash, orig wood pulls, replaced lock, Canterbury, NH, c1820 . . . . **1,200.00**

Bonnet Mold, poplar, woven, white glaze ext., paper label "8" **135.00**

Bottle, Shaker Digestive Cordial **150.00**

Bowl, 9" d, turned, mustard wash, Harvard, MA, late 19th C **8,250.00**

Box, cov
- 3⅜" l, oval, varnished, base with pencil inscription "Bl . . ." **650.00**
- 4⅝" l, oval, yellow varnish, finger construction, inside lid pencil inscription "M. Catherine Allen, North Family 1882," four small wooden bobbins **4,100.00**
- 4¾" l, oval, varnished, minor imperfections **450.00**

Blanket Chest, Cantebury, NH, pine, lift top, int. with two lift top tills, single long drawer, bootjack ends, handmade metal escutcheon plate, orig red painted finish, c1840, 35″ w, 17″ d, 25¾″ h, $1,595.00. Photograph courtesy of James D Julia, Inc.

5½″ l, oval, painted ochre, base carved with initials "E.R." **3,575.00**

5⅞″ l, oval, branded initials "N R," worn orig blue and gray paint . . . **450.00**

6⅜″ l, oval, bird on lid, old green repaint **375.00**

6½″ l, oval, painted red, lid inscribed "1852 K. E. Myers" **5,225.00**

7¼″ l, oval, varnished, lid with pencil inscription "Anna White from Elder Richard 1857," minor imperfections **875.00**

8¾″ l, oval, varnished, base with paper inscription "S.B." **725.00**

8¾″ l, 3¼″ h, oval, four finger construction, New England, late 19th C. **250.00**

12⅞″ l, 6¼″ d, 6½″ h, rect, red stain, traces of orig chromium yellow, hinged lid, molded lip, iron escutcheon, New England, late 19th C **625.00**

13½″ l, oval, varnished, paper labels, one typed "handles of knives for cutting straw," imperfections **775.00**

13½″ l, 5½″ d, 8″ h, document, pine, dovetailed, Copley–Lyman Family, Enfield, NH **300.00**

14½″ l, oval, painted ochre, paper label inscribed "bee's wax," minor imperfections **5,500.00**

Brush, 10½″ l, horsehair bristles, turned maple handle, painted black, stamped "44," 19th C **195.00**

Bucket, yellow wash, carved "A.D.56" and pressed "D.H." in bottom **550.00**

Candlestand, cherry, round top
14⅜″ d, 24½″ h, turned tapered column, arched tripod base, snake feet, mahoganized surface with red–brown stain, New Lebanon, NY, 1800–50 . . . . **9,900.00**

18″ d, 25¼″ h, chamfered cherry cleat held with inset screws, turned column, shaped iron plate, tripod base, tapered spider legs, attributed to Samuel Turner, Church Family, New Lebanon, NY, c1837 . . . . **55,000.00**

Carrier, oval, handle
9″ l
Painted red, imperfections **3,400.00**
Varnished, inscribed "52," imperfections **1,425.00**
11″ l, painted red
Imperfections **4,675.00**
Minor imperfections, rich patina **7,150.00**
12¾″ l, varnished, imperfections. . . **500.00**

Chair
Arm, Mount Lebanon, NY, 1880–1920, No. 6. . . . . **875.00**
Ladder Back
40½″ h, maple, old refinish, minor imperfections, early 19th C . . . **425.00**
40¾″ h, maple and birch, tilting, slat back, refinished, early 19th C **550.00**
41″ h, tiger maple, tilting, slat back, old finish, minor imperfections, early 19th C **4,675.00**
41½″ h, 17½″ h seat, cherry and tiger maple, turned finials, three slightly arched slats, rush seat, old finish, Harvard Community, 1840–50 . . . . **875.00**

Chest of Drawers
36″ w, 19¼″ d, 74″ h, pine, old finish, eight slightly graduated drawers, New Hampshire community, minor imperfections, early 19th C. **4,400.00**

Chest of Drawers, New Lebanon, sgd "Made by Daniel J. Hawkins," tiger maple, five long drawers, shaped bracket feet, wood pulls, dated 1831 or 1851, 37¼″ w, 19″ d, 51½″ h, $7,700.00. Photograph courtesy of James D Julia, Inc.

43½" w, 23" d, 55" h, walnut, varnish finish, five slightly graduated drawers, minor imperfections, attributed to Union Village, OH, minor imperfections, mid 19th C. . . . 9,350.00

Cobbler's Bench, 54½" l, painted blue, Canterbury, NH 4,125.00

Cupboard

38⅜" w, 18½" d, 56¼" h, pine, old green paint, pair of raised panel doors, six dovetailed small drawers below, int. with thirty pigeonholes and two shelves, turned wood knobs, inside of one door branded "C.W. Durrell," damaged back boards, repairs to feet, edge damage 4,125.00

39½" w, 19" d, 96½" h, walnut, single door over four drawers, attributed to Daniel Baird, Union Village, OH, c1832 . . . . .11,000.00

43½" w, 78" h, pine, old refinish, molded cornice, two glazed doors over two panels, three graduated drawers, shaped scalloped apron, signed in pencil on underside of second drawer "Made by Levi Swain 1845," minor imperfections 2,850.00

52½" w, 20" d, 84" h, pine, old varnish finish, two doors over two banks of five graduated drawers, minor imperfections, mid 19th C. 6,050.00

Dipper, 5½" d, painted ochre, imperfections 225.00

Drying Rack, 30" w, 36½" h, cherry, three bars, trestle feet, refinished, New England, mid 19th C 300.00

Dust Pan and Scoop, tin, rust, soldered repair 40.00

Kerchief, woven, colored cotton and wool, plain and twill weave, windowpane, and check, changeable and border stripe pattern, cross-stitched initials, wear, various sizes, New England, late 19th/early 20th C, price for set of four 525.00

Ladder, 12" w, 109" l, painted, labeled "L.A. Shepard Canterbury, NH". . . . 1,650.00

Mailbox, 20 × 24 × 11", pine, hinged lid, natural finish, Enfield. 500.00

Pail, painted

4" h, green, New England, 19th C 775.00

6" h, ochre, cov, imperfections 1,550.00

Pot, 6" h, tin, two strap handles, pouring spout 75.00

Rocker

Armchair, Mount Lebanon, NY, 1880–1920

No. 0, 23½" h, child's, armchair, refinished, Mt Lebanon, NY, c1870, 9¼" h seat 1,050.00

No. 6. . . . . 875.00

No. 7. . . . . 825.00

Armless

33½" h, Canterbury, refinished 325.00

39½" h, maple, orig red stain, slat back, Enfield, early 19th C, minor imperfections 3,575.00

40½" h, maple, old natural finish, early 19th C 450.00

Sauce Pan, cov, 8½" w, 6" d, 8½" l handle, tin, oval, traces of red paint, crack in soldered handle joint 85.00

Seed Box, cov, 22" l, "Shakers' Choice Vegetable Seeds," pine and poplar, six section int., Mount Lebanon, NY 1,200.00

Sewing Desk, Enfield, NH, birch, maple, and pine, paneled and framed construction, six drawers and door in top gallery, pullout work slide in front, base with three drawers in front and three drawers in side, turned legs, traces of old red finish, 32" w, 26" d, 39" h, $15,400.00. Photograph courtesy of James D Julia, Inc.

Rocker, Mt Lebanon, NY, web-back, new olive and blue taping, 20th C, 34" h, $225.00. Photograph courtesy of Skinner, Inc.

Sewing Box

3⅝" l, 2¼" w, 2½" h, pine and poplar, oval, light brown wool covered pincushion, red and black tape border, copper tacks and points, three finger construction, chrome yellow finish, c1830 .... **8,800.00**

5" h, lower drawer has sewing implements, imperfections **325.00**

Stand

17" d, 27" h, cherry, old shellac finish, round top, underside signed in pencil "Made by Thomas Hammond–Annie W (illegible name) 1883," Harvard, MA, 1883 ..... **5,500.00**

19¼" d, 24½" h, birch and maple, old refinish, round top, underside of top inscribed in chalk "E.D. 24," in pencil "ED 31," early 19th C **2,300.00**

Steps, sewing, 13¾" w, 13¼" d, 17¼" h, pine, orig chrome yellow paint, mid 19th C **2,100.00**

Storage Box, 27" w, 14½" d, 13" h, pine, orig yellow stain, sgd "Dorothy Cochran" in pencil, labeled "Dorothy J. Cochran born Jan 5, 1844, admitted May 1, 1857, died Dec 29, 1912, first eldress for 14 yrs from Aug 1898 to Dec 29, 1912," late 19th C **275.00**

Table

26" w, 18" d, 26" h, cherry and birch, old shellac finish, minor imperfections, attributed to Canterbury, NH, early 19th C **1,650.00**

27½" w, 17¼" d, 24½" h, birch, old shellac, inscribed underside of top in pencil, attributed to Canterbury, NH, early 19th C **9,350.00**

30" w, 18½" d, 26" h, maple and birch, old refinish, single drawer, minor imperfections, attributed to Canterbury, NH, early 19th C ... **2,425.00**

36" w, 24" d, 28½" h, cherry, old finish, drawer, underside of drawer inscribed in chalk "Shaker," minor imperfections, at-

Stove, iron, attributed to New Lebanon community, 19th C, 31" l, 11" d, 18¾" h, $550.00. Photograph courtesy of Skinner, Inc.

tributed to Canterbury, NH, early 19th C **1,650.00**

36¼" w, 25" d, 29¼" h, cherry and pine, work, attributed to New York State, rect top, single drawer, mid 19th C **3,850.00**

Tool Box, 24⅝" w, 13¾" d, 13" h, walnut and bird's eye maple, fitted int. tray, minor paint spatter, c1850 **1,200.00**

Tray, 11⅛" l, oval, painted deep salmon, imperfections **625.00**

Tub, painted mustard, interlocking stave construction **350.00**

Wash Bench, 62" l, pine, mortised legs, gray paint **400.00**

Washstand, 45¾" w, 16" d, 38" h, pine, painted, orig chrome yellow wash, c1850 .... **6,050.00**

Wood Box

34⅝" w, 18½" d, 30⅞" h, pine and poplar, orig red stain, single drawer, minor imperfections **1,100.00**

37½" w, 21" d, 31" h, pine, old red stain, single drawer, minor imperfections, mid 19th C **625.00**

Work Box, 29½" w, 11½" d, 17" h, pine, orig ext. red stain, yellow painted fitted int., minor imperfections, early 19th C. **1,550.00**

STONEWARE

While slip- and sgraffito-decorated redware dominate the early American look, the pottery of choice for the Country collector and decorator is stoneware.

Made from dense kaolin clay and commonly salt–glazed, stonewares were hand–thrown and high–fired to produce a simple, bold vitreous pottery. Stoneware crocks, jugs, and jars were produced for storage and utility purposes. This use dictated shape and design—solid, thick–walled forms with heavy rims, necks, and handles with little or no embellishment. When decorated, the designs were simple: brushed cobalt oxide, incised, slip trailed, stamped, or tooled.

Stoneware has been made for centuries. Initially, early American settlers imported stoneware items but soon began producing their own. Two major North American traditions emerged based only on the location or type of clay. North Jersey and parts of New York comprise the first area; the second was eastern Pennsylvania spreading westward and into Maryland, Virginia, and West Virginia. These two distinct locations, style of decoration, and shape are discernible factors in classifying and dating early stoneware.

By the late 18th century, stoneware was manufactured in all sections of the country. During the 19th century, this vigorous industry flourished until glass "fruit jars" appeared and the widespread use of refrigeration. By 1910, commercial production of salt–glazed stoneware came to an end.

References:: Dan and Gail DePasquale and Larry Peterson, *Red Wing Stoneware,* Collector Books, 1983, 1992 value update; Georgeanna H. Greer, *American Stoneware: The Art and Craft of Utilitarian Potters,* Schiffer Publishing, Ltd., Don and Carol Raycraft, *Country Stoneware And Pottery,* Collector Books, 1985, 1992 value update; Don and Carol Raycraft, *Collector's Guide To Country Stoneware & Pottery, 2nd Series,* Collector Books, 1990, 1993 value update; George Sullivan, *The Official Price Guide To American Stoneware,* House of Collectibles, 1993.

Museums: Museum of Ceramics at East Liverpool, East Liverpool, OH; The Bennington Museum, Bennington, VT.

Reproduction Craftspersons: Bastine Pottery, RR 3, Box 111, Noblesville, IN 46060; Heather & Jack Beauchamp, Salt O' Thee Earth Pottery, 71456 Bates Rd, Guernsey, OH 43741; Gerald T Beaumont, Beaumont Pottery, 293 Beech Ridge Rd, York, ME 03909; Al & Barbara Blumberg, Bon Aqua Pottery, Rte 1, Box 396–10, Bon Aqua, TN 37025; Wendy Cotton, RR 1, Box 528, Avondale, PA 19311; Robert and Bruce Diebboll, Pines End Pottery, 58031 Mount Rd, Washington, MI 48094; David Eldreth, Eldreth Pottery, 902 Hart Rd, Oxford, PA 19363; David & Mary Farrell, Potters, Westmoore Pottery, Rte 2, Box 494, Seagrove, NC 27341; Tim Galligan & Kathy Kellagher, Cooksburg Pottery, Star Rte, Box 155, Marienville, PA 16239; Lee Gilbert, The Studio in Swarthmore, 14 Park Ave, Swarthmore, PA 19081; Joel & Debra Huntley, Wisconsin Pottery, Inc, W3199 Hwy 16, Columbus, WI 53925; Jean Lehman, 103 Dickinson Ave, Lancaster, PA 17603; David C Meixner, Buffalo Pottery Co, Rte 6, Box 108, Menomonie, WI 54751; Linda Milliner, 49 Bluestone Dr, Chadds Ford, PA 19317; Becky Mummert, 30 Fish and Game Rd, East Berlin, PA 17316; Rowe Pottery Works, Inc, 404 England St, Cambridge, WI 53523; Sandra McKenzie Schmitt, 12770 Kain Rd, Glen Allen, VA 23060; Yvonne Snead, Plantation Days Dinnerware by Yvonne, 327 Magnolia St, Raeford, NC 28376; Stebner Studios, 3933 Smith–Kramer St, Hartville, OH 44632; Sid & Eileen Vernon, Vernon Pottery, 1537 Quail Pt Rd, Virginia Beach, VA 23454; Jonathan and Jan Wright and Rick Fitzsimmons, Crocker & Springer Stoneware, PO Box 212, Elsah, IL 62028.

Reproduction Manufacturers: Adirondack Store and Gallery, 109 Saranac Ave, Lake Placid, NY 12946; Anastasia's Collectibles, 6114 134th St W, Apple Valley, MN 55124; The Barn, PO Box 25, Market St, Lehman, PA 18627; Bastine Pottery, RR 3, Box 111, Noblesville, IN 46060; Basye–Bomberger/Fabian House, PO Box 86, W Bowie, MD 20715; Bathroom Machineries, 495 Main St, PO Box 1020, Murphys, CA 95247; Bearly Country, 11 East Pine St, Selinsgrove, PA 17870; Beaumont Bros Stoneware, Inc, 410 Keystone, Crooksville, OH 43731; Chinaberry General Store, 1846 Winfield Dunn Highway, Sevierville, TN 38762; Clay City Pottery, Inc, Box 305, RR 2, Clay City, IN 47841; Conner Prairie Crafts, 13400 Allisonville Rd, Noblesville, IN 46060; Country Loft, 1506 South Shore Park, Hingham, MA 02043; Crazy Crow Trading Post, PO Box 314B, Denison, TX 75020; Cumberland General Store, Rte 3, Crossville, TN 38555; Eldreth Pottery, 4351 Forge Rd, Nottingham, PA 19362; Faith Mountain Country Fare, Main St, Box 199, Sperryville, VA 22740; Georgia Folk Pottery, 2579 W Fontainebleau Court, Doraville, GA 30360; Gooseberry Patch, PO Box 634, Delaware, OH 43015; Lamb and Lanterns, 902 N Walnut St, Dover, OH 44622; Log Cabin Shop, Box 275, Lodi, OH 44254; Mole Hill Pottery, 5011 Anderson Pike, Signal Mountain, TN 37377; Monroe Salt Works, Stovepipe Alley, Monroe, ME 04951; Party House Pottery, 633 Maple St, Carrollton, IL 62016; Pure and Simple, PO Box 535, 117 W Hempstead, Nashville, AR 71852; Rockdale Union Stoneware, PO Box 231, 1858 Artisan Rd, Edgerton, WI 53534-0231; Rowe Pottery Works, Inc, 404 England St, Cambridge, WI 53523; Salmon Falls Stoneware, The Engine House on Oak St, PO Box 452, Dover, NH 03820–0452; Southern Manner, Inc, 106 North Trade St, PO Box 1706, Matthews, NC 28106; Stebner Pottery, 3933 Smith–Kramer St, Hartville, OH 44632; Three Rivers Pottery Productions, Inc, PO Box 462, 139 S Third St, Coshocton, OH 43812.

Apple Butter Crock, 2 quart, F H Cowden, Harrisburg, strap handle, imp label	55.00
Baking Dish, dark color, 9" d	12.00
Bank, jug shaped	
4" h, blue band around shoulder	125.00
6⅜" h, brown Albany slip	175.00
Batter Pail, 1 gallon	
Cowden & Wilcox, Harrisburg, PA, brushed cobalt blue feathery leaf dec, wire bail with turned wood handle, tightly glued cracks, chips on spout	500.00
E & L P Norton, Bennington, VT, imp label, cobalt blue "4", wire bail with turned wood handle, tin cap on spout, minor chips	165.00
F H Cowden, Harrisburg, imp label, brushed cobalt blue five–bloom flower dec front and back, blue at handles, wire bail with wood handle, orig tin lids on spout and top, minor chips	1,475.00
John Burger, Rochester, brushed floral dec, sgd 9½" h	310.00
Unknown Maker, imp "4," dark brown Albany slip dec, wire handle, 9¼" h	90.00
Bean Pot, cov	
Unknown Maker, molded dec and figures, emb "Boston Baked Beans," int. crazing, 6⅜" h	185.00
Whites, Utica, coggle wheel dec around neck, handle with thumbhold, raised "Boston Baked Beans" label, cobalt blue at handle, label, and all around, chip on lid	200.00
Bedpan, Albany, brown glaze	35.00
Bottle	
6" h, J Whittemore, brown Albany slip	40.00
1 Quart	
T McGovern, Lemon Beer, solid cobalt blue from lip to shoulder	125.00
Unknown Maker	
Cobalt blue band, beer, minor chip on bottom	30.00

Cobalt blue lip and "C"	150.00
Cobalt blue script "Post," glob top, repaired	40.00
Brandy Pig, 1½" gallon, cobalt blue scalloped, feather, and leaf bands around	1,200.00
Butter Crock	
1 Quart, unknown maker, incised name "F. L. Burber"	30.00
1 Gallon	
Old Sleepy Eye, cobalt blue rim band and molded Indian design	575.00
P Herman, cov, handles, cobalt blue feathery leaf and floral dec all around lid and crock, inner rim chip on lid	325.00
Unknown Maker, lug handles, incised lines top and bottom, cobalt blue leafy dec around, tight glued cracks on side	150.00
1½ Gallon	
Hamilton & Pershing, Johnstown, PA, lug handles, cobalt blue feather dec around	500.00
PA, cobalt blue floral dec, chips, mismatched lid, 13" d	225.00
Unknown Maker, cov, cobalt blue dec	
Brushed floral dec, imp "1½," hairline in base and minor chip on inside of lid flange, 12" d	425.00
Quillwork label "6 Butter 1870" and flourish dec, applied handles, 13¾" d	375.00
Cake Crock	
2 Gallon	
A Conrad, New Geneva, PA, cobalt blue stenciled label and "2", brushed accents	300.00
Cowden & Wilcox, Harrisburg, PA, lug handles, imp label, strong cobalt blue leaf dec and "2", blue at label, small stone ping on side	650.00
T F Reppert, Greensboro, PA, handles, cobalt blue stenciled label, freehand "2" and sheaf design	425.00

Cake Crock, 2 gal, unmarked, handled, cobalt blue floral dec around, tight crack on side and across bottom, $250.00. Photograph courtesy of Arthur Auctioneering.

4 Gallon

Attributed to P Herman, handles, cobalt blue floral dec around, cinnamon colored, minor rim chips 450.00

NY Stoneware Co, Ft Edward, NY, handles, imp label, cobalt blue quillwork flower, tight glued crack on side, minor chips, some glaze flaking 125.00

Cheese Crock, 1 quart, cobalt blue stenciled adv label "Vanity Fair, Wm. S. Kimball & Co., Rochester, NY" . . 50.00

Chicken Fountain, 1 gallon

A L Hyssong, Bloomsburg, attached underplate, brushed cobalt blue flower 450.00

Unknown Maker, tan colored, no underplate. 25.00

Churn

5½" h, miniature, gray salt glaze, craquelle finish 50.00

3 Gallon, unknown maker, ovoid, imp "3," brushed cobalt blue dec, applied shoulder handles, 15¼" h 325.00

4 Gallon

E Norton & Co, Bennington, VT, imp label, cobalt blue slip stylized floral dec, chips, flaking, 17½" h 165.00

New Geneva, tan clay, tooling, two–tone amber and brown slip with stenciled design, wear and chips, 18¾" h 150.00

Unknown Maker, ovoid, red clay body, gray salt glaze, brushed cobalt blue floral dec and "4," 16½" h 85.00

6 Gallon, red clay, orangish green glaze, incised "6," 19¾" h 85.00

Cooler

2 Quart, marked "A. A. Co. Patent Applied For," barrel shaped, blue bands, minor chip on end 185.00

3 Gallon

S S Reilly, 400 & 409 Canal St, New York, barrel shaped, imp

Churn, 6 gal, Whites, Utica, cobalt blue large fantail bird in floral and fern dec, blue at imp label, crack through dec, $1,045.00. Photograph courtesy of Arthur Auctioneering.

label, blue bands, tight crack on side 65.00

Unknown Maker, cov, barrel shaped, cobalt blue bands on lid and crock, cobalt blue "3" in crown 125.00

10 Gallon, unknown maker, ovoid, applied shoulder handles, high neck, wheel turned ridges, remains of applied decorative detail on shoulder between handles, cobalt blue quill work flourishes, old chips and firing cracks, 21½" h 350.00

16 Gallon

Alderman and Scott, Belpre, OH, ovoid, stenciled cobalt blue label and "16" in wreath, double ear handles, applied tooled ornaments around bung hole, hairlines and repair, 23½" h. . . 825.00

Unknown Maker, cobalt blue slip simple flower and flourish, imp

Cooler, 3 gal, handled, cobalt blue rings and vining floral dec, blistered surface, $350.00. Photograph courtesy of Arthur Auctioneering.

screw head design at double ear handles and bung hole, chips, hairline on one handle, 26½" h   **200.00**

Cooler Jug

3 Gallon, unknown maker, brushed cobalt blue floral bouquet......   **500.00**

4 Gallon, W H Farrar, Geddes, NY, imp label, cobalt blue "4" and tornado–like designs, spigot hole at base, spout chip............   **325.00**

Crock

3½" h, miniature, brushed cobalt blue flower and "ABB"........   **70.00**

2 Quart, unknown maker, semi–ovoid, imp adv label "D. P. Hobart, Agent, Williamsport, PA," minor rim chip.............   **65.00**

1 Gallon

A L Hyssong, Bloomsburg, semi–ovoid, cinnamon colored, rim chip, tightly glued crack.....   **70.00**

Cowden & Wilcox, Harrisburg, PA, semi–ovoid, imp label, brushed cobalt blue flower...   **325.00**

D P Shenfelder, PA, semi–ovoid, incised lines around shoulder, cobalt blue brushed feather dec around, very tight crack at top edge, spider line in bottom...   **90.00**

Evan R Jones, Pittston, PA, semi–ovoid, imp label, incised line around shoulder, cobalt blue brushwork lollipop flower, cobalt blue at label, cracks, some glaze flaking on back.......   **80.00**

H B Pfaltzgraff, York, PA, semi–ovoid, flanged lip, brushed cobalt blue flower, rim chip....   **300.00**

I Seymour & Co, Troy, semi–ovoid, handles, imp label, blue at label and handles, minor rim chips..................   **50.00**

Ithaca, NY, semi–ovoid, handles, incised line below lip, imp label, brushed cobalt blue flower, blue at label, crack in back...   **75.00**

Crock, 1 gal, Whites, Utica, handled, cobalt blue fantail roadrunner, $550.00. Photograph courtesy of Arthur Auctioneering.

John Burger, Rochester, handles, imp label, cobalt blue flower, tight crack on side.........   **385.00**

Sipe & Sons, W'msport, PA, handles, imp label, brushed cobalt blue single spike flower dec, tight crack back bottom, minor rim chips................   **110.00**

T D Metcalf, Sunbury, PA, semi–ovoid, imp label, simple cobalt blue leafy dec, rim chip, age marks...................   **225.00**

Unknown Maker, semi–ovoid, brushed cobalt blue feather and leaf dec around...........   **450.00**

Whites, Utica, handles, cobalt blue slip "1863," rim chip on back...................   **125.00**

1½ Gallon

Evan R Jones, Pittston, PA, semi–ovoid, handles, flanged rim, handles, imp label and "1½", brushed cobalt blue flower, blue at label, minor rim chip   **275.00**

G Apley & Co, Ithaca, NY, sides taper to base, handles, imp label, brushed cobalt blue double bloom flower, blue at label, large chip bottom edge......   **60.00**

John B Claire & Co, Main St, Poughkeepsie, NY, imp label, cobalt blue stylized flower dec, flakes, 10½" h............   **325.00**

Sugar Valley, PA, semi–ovoid, imp label, cobalt blue floral dec, minor spider line at bottom.....   **650.00**

Unknown Maker

Cobalt blue brushed leaf design, hairline, 7¼" h..........   **90.00**

Semi–ovoid, urn shaped, handles, incised lines around shoulder, cobalt blue feathery leaf dec around, small rim chip, seealed crack on side   **185.00**

2 Gallon

A O Whittemore, Havana, NY, handles, imp label, cobalt blue bird on branch, cracks on back   **135.00**

Burger & Co, Rochester, NY, imp label, ornate cobalt blue fan shaped flower with two serrated leaves, blue "2" in flower center, blue at label...........   **250.00**

Cross Bros, Sterling, PA, imp label, brushed cobalt blue slip flower, applied handles, minor bubbling and flaking to dec, 9½" h   **150.00**

E S Fox, Athens, semi–ovoid, handles, incised line around shoulder, imp label, cobalt blue "2", date "1833", and at label and handles, minor rim chips.....   **150.00**

Crock, 2 gal, Lyons, handled, cobalt blue floral dec, tightly glued crack through dec, $300.00. Photograph courtesy of Arthur Auctioneering.

Crock, 3 gal, Whites, Utica, semi–ovoid, handled, cobalt blue floral dec, imp label, repaired crack, $225.00. Photograph courtesy of Arthur Auctioneering.

I Seymour, Troy, semi–ovoid, handles, incised lines around shoulder, imp label, cobalt blue feather dec, blue at label, minor chips top and bottom edges . . .   **65.00**

J M Mott & Co, Ithaca, NY, semi–ovoid, handles, imp label and "2", brushed cobalt blue double bloom flower with leafy stems, minor spider line on side **140.00**

Lyons, handles, incised lines around top, imp label, two cobalt blue "2"s, strong cobalt blue brushed leafy design, blue at label and handles, inner rim chip, chip on bottom edge. . . .   **185.00**

N Clark Jr, Athens, NY, semi–ovoid, handles, blue at handles and imp label and "2", brushed cobalt blue double flower, minor rim chips **110.00**

N White & Co, Binghamton, semi–ovoid, handles, incised line around shoulder, imp label, cobalt blue at label, "2", and large poppy, very tight crack on side   **150.00**

Unknown Maker, cov, cobalt blue brushed dec, 12" d, 7½" h. . . .   **475.00**

3 Gallon

Charlestown, imp label, cobalt blue grapevine dec, 9¾" h. . . .   **325.00**

C Hart, Sherburne, semi–ovoid, handles, imp label and "3", brushed cobalt blue plow flower dec, blue at label, spider lines in back, minor rim chips   **135.00**

E B Hissong, Cassville, PA, semi–ovoid, handles, flared rim, ring around neck, cobalt blue floral branch, minor rim chip **1,975.00**

Evan R Jones, Pittston, PA, handles, imp label and "3", brushed cobalt blue horizontal flower, tight spider lines on side **165.00**

F B Norton & Co, Worcester, MA, handles, imp label, cobalt blue bird in tree dec, chip on bottom edge **550.00**

Fulper Bros, Flemington, NJ, handles, imp label, incised line at handles, strong cobalt blue stylized three leaf design, rim chips, repaired **165.00**

Hubbell & Chesebro, Geddes, NY, handles, imp label and "3", cobalt blue stylized branch with flower and leaves, rim chip . . .   **100.00**

J H Dipple, Lewistown, PA, handles, imp label, brushed cobalt blue feathery design, rim chip, crack on back **275.00**

J Swank & Co, Johnstown, PA, semi–ovoid, handles, imp label, cobalt blue feathery dec around, cinnamon tan color. . .   **350.00**

Sipe & Sons, Williamsport, PA, semi–ovoid, handles, flanged lip, imp label, cobalt blue grape cluster, rim chips **375.00**

T Harrington, Lyons, handles, imp label, cobalt blue "3" and tulip, blue at handles, crack at left of flower, inner rim chip **100.00**

Thomas & Bros, Huntingdon, PA, handles, imp label and "3", brushed cobalt blue flower. . . .   **625.00**

Unknown Maker

Brushed cobalt blue stylized flower and "3," 11¼" h **95.00**

Incised bands, cobalt blue floral dec, 14" h **275.00**

4 Gallon

Brady & Ryan, Ellenville, NY, handles, imp label, cobalt blue bird on branch **450.00**

Cowden & Wilcox, Harrisburg, PA, semi–ovoid, handles, imp label and "4", incised lines around shoulder, brushed cobalt blue floral bouquet, blue at label, tight spider line on side   **650.00**

Johnson & Knapp, Olean, NY, blue and imp label and "4", brushed cobalt blue double daisy, tight crack at top back   **190.00**

Millburn, B C, semi–ovoid, imp label under handle, applied handles, incised band at neck, cobalt blue leafy floral bouquet dec, 14" h **425.00**

Morgan, David, NY, front and back dec with imp and cobalt blue floral dec, early 19th C, 12" h **1,100.00**

N W White & Son, Utica, NY, handles, imp label, cobalt blue compote and flowers dec **450.00**

NY Stoneware Co, Ft Edward, NY, handles, imp label, cobalt blue bird on branch dec, repair on side, glued crack, glaze flaking around bottom. **90.00**

Ottman Bros, Fort Edwards, NY, imp label and "4," cobalt blue slip bird on branch dec, crack in back, 11¼" h **200.00**

R S Rand, Portland, ME, handles, imp label and "4", cobalt blue grape cluster, tight crack in back, one handle replaced . . .   **150.00**

Unknown Maker

Cobalt blue fancy fantailed bird on branch dec above spigot .   **350.00**

Semi–ovoid, urn shaped, tab handles, incised lines around neck and shoulder, brushed cobalt blue tulips around shoulder. **300.00**

Whites, Utica, semi–ovoid, handles, incised lines around shoulder, strong cobalt blue paddletail bird on branch dec, rim chips, cracked **125.00**

5 Gallon

Cowden & Wilcox, Harrisburg, PA, semi–ovoid, imp label and "5", brushed cobalt blue feathery fan shaped flower dec, blue at handles, rim chip, tightly glued crack on side **325.00**

Evan R Jones, Pittston, PA, handles, imp label and "5," cobalt blue bird on stump, blue at label, tight crack bottom back edge   **525.00**

Riedinger & Caire, Poughkeepsie, NY, handles, cobalt blue fancy bird on stump dec, glaze flaking, handles replaced **150.00**

W H Farrar & Co, Geddes, NY, semi–ovoid, handles, incised band around shoulder, cobalt blue slip three bloom stylized flower bouquet, minor rim chips   **415.00**

6 Gallon

J H Dipple, Lewistown, handles, imp label, cobalt blue daisy and leaves, tight crack bottom back   **575.00**

Crock, 5 gal, unknown maker, cobalt blue stenciled "5" and eagle holding banner dec, tight line crack on back side, $250.00. Photograph courtesy of Arthur Auctioneering.

Unknown Maker, cobalt blue brushed vintage dec and "6," 13" h **75.00**

20 Gallon, William Lintons Pottery and Sales Room, Corner of Lexington and Pine Streets, Baltimore, MD, lug handles, imp label both front and back, brushed cobalt blue dandelions around, gray with tan speckles, sales room showpiece, tightly glued crack on side, 24" h **3,075.00**

Crock Lid

Cobalt blue floral band around rim, 9" d, 7" inner rim **40.00**

Unglazed, 12½" d, 10½" inner rim, minor chip **40.00**

Cup, child's, incised checkerboard design around, cobalt blue squares, minor chip bottom edge **60.00**

Dish, coggle wheel dec edge, minor chip, 8" d **45.00**

Figure

Lion, standing, salt glaze, 6 × 7½"   **75.00**

Pig, Macomb Pottery Co, one leg glued. **300.00**

Flowerpot, 1 gallon, Wm Everson, incised script label, marked "Patented April 27, 1875," brown and gray. . .   **45.00**

Flower Vase, semi–ovoid, ruffled rim, circular openings around shoulder, cobalt blue at rim and around each opening **100.00**

Food Mold, Turk's head, rim chips . . .   **35.00**

Foot Warmer, no dec, cork stopper. . .   **25.00**

Grotesque Jug, Burlon Craig, Lincoln County, NC, imp mark at base, c1980, 16½" h **325.00**

Inkwell

N Boors, Vanport, PA, incised "Union," cobalt blue stars dec, sgd, early 20th C, 1½" h **875.00**

Unknown Maker, round, dark color, tight spider crack on side, 4" d **50.00**

Jar

3" h, miniature, cobalt blue slip dec, marked "A B B" **125.00**

1 Quart, unknown maker, incised lines, cobalt blue brushed leafy dec, minor chips top and bottom. **40.00**

2 Quart

A P Donaghho, Parkersburg, WV, cobalt blue stenciled label, 8½" h **95.00**

New York, incised lines at shoulder, cobalt blue tadpole–like design, dark **75.00**

Shenfelder, incised rings around neck, brushed cobalt blue flower **225.00**

Sipe Nichols & Co, Williamsport, PA, ovoid, imp label, cobalt blue brushed dec, surface flakes, 8" h. **275.00**

Unknown Maker

Albany slip, incised "Norwich" **30.00**

Brushed cobalt blue tulip, ovoid, tan salt glaze, 7½" h . **225.00**

Script cobalt blue date "1851" front and back **300.00**

Slip cobalt blue spiky flower dec, incised lines around shoulder, rim chips **225.00**

1 Gallon

Cowden & Wilcox, Harrisburg, PA, lug handles, incised line around shoulders, imp label, cobalt blue bluebell–like flower, minor rim chips **195.00**

Hamilton & Pershing, Johnstown, PA, semi–ovoid, raised ring around neck, brushed cobalt blue feathery dec around shoulder. **250.00**

James Hamilton & Co, Greensboro, PA, cobalt blue stenciled label and rose **165.00**

N Clark & Co, Lyons, ovoid, handles, incised lines around shoulder, cobalt blue slip "1" and leaf, minor rim chips **200.00**

Nichols & Co, Williamsport, PA, flared rim, incised lines around shoulder, imp label, cobalt blue floral dec, minor rim chip, discolored spot on side **65.00**

P Herman, cobalt blue feathered dec around, very tight crack at bottom edge **90.00**

Unknown Maker, semi–ovoid, handles, incised line above handles, brushed cobalt blue leafy branches around **185.00**

Whites, Utica, handles, imp label, cobalt blue bird looking back, perched on twig. **225.00**

1½ Gallon

Hamilton & Jones, Greensboro, PA, ovoid, stenciled cobalt blue label, 9¼" h **110.00**

C Boynton & Co, Troy, ovoid imp label, brushed cobalt blue design, blue trim on applied handles and at label, small chips, 10¾" h **250.00**

W Flesher, imp label, brushed cobalt blue flourish on each side, stains, 11¼" h **200.00**

2 Gallon

Clark & Fox, Athens, ovoid, lug handles, incised lines around neck and shoulder, imp label, cobalt blue slip date "1834," cobalt blue at label and handles, minor chips on handles, some tight spider lines. **300.00**

Cortland, NY, cov, handles, imp label and "2," brushed cobalt blue double tulip, blue at label, crack in dec **145.00**

Cowden & Wilcox, ovoid, imp label, brushed cobalt blue floral dec, 10" h **450.00**

John Burger, Rochester, handles, imp label, cobalt blue leafy dec, small discolored spots **225.00**

Lyons, lug handles, imp label

Brushed cobalt blue flower flanked by two "2s," four feathery leaves at corners, cov, lid stamped "2," minor chip on lid **725.00**

Slip dec, two cobalt blue slip "2s" and double bloom flower, minor rim chip **165.00**

N Clark & Co, Lyons, ovoid, handles, imp label, brushed cobalt blue flower, blue at label **165.00**

N White & Co, Binghamton, handles, imp label and "2," cobalt blue feathery bird on branch dec, tight crack in back, minor chips **325.00**

P H Smith, cobalt blue splotch at label **65.00**

Unknown Maker, ovoid, open loop handles, incised dec around, cobalt blue leafy dec, minor rim chip, tight spider line cracks on side **425.00**

Western PA, semi–ovoid, incised lines, cobalt blue band around shoulder, "2," and feathery leaf design, tight spider line on side **190.00**

3 Gallon

J F Ack & Bro, Mooresburg, PA, handles, incised lines around neck, imp label and "3," simple brushed cobalt blue leafy design, minor chips on one handle, stone ping on side, tight crack at top edge 350.00

Norton & Fenton, Bennington, VT, ovoid, imp circular label, cobalt blue brushed floral dec, 12¾" h   385.00

Unknown Maker, brushed cobalt blue floral dec

Ovoid, applied handles, minor chips, 12½" h 350.00

Pebble finish, lime stains, 12¾" h 175.00

W R F Weimer & Bro, Snydertown, PA, handles, imp label, cobalt blue dec, professionally repaired 475.00

4 Gallon

I M Mead, Portage Co, OH, ovoid, cov, imp label, cobalt blue floral design, applied shoulder handles, hairlines and shallow chips, chip and hairline on lid, 15½" h 275.00

White & Wood, Binghamton, NY, imp label, cobalt blue quill work bird on branch, hairlines, 13¾" h 425.00

6 Gallon, D Albright, imp label, ovoid, mottled grayish–tan glaze, tan spots, tooled lines, applied handles, 17" h 175.00

8 Gallon, Hamilton, Greensboro, PA, ovoid, imp label, applied shoulder handles, good brushed cobalt blue floral dec, badly cracked, 18½" h 850.00

Jug

1 Pint, unknown maker, brown top, gray bottom, ink stamped label in rect "Pure Old Rye Whiskey, Salzman & Spiegelman, Brooklyn, NY"   20.00

1 Quart, unknown maker, ovoid, cobalt blue blobs around neck 65.00

2 Quart

A P Donaghho, Parkersburg, WV, cobalt blue stenciled label, strong blue at handle 75.00

Connell & Son, Newport, imp label, cobalt blue script "Vinegar," spout chip, crack on side   35.00

Hamilton & Jones, Greensboro, PA, stenciled cobalt blue label, minor chips on bottom 130.00

J J O'Connor, cobalt blue script label and patches, minor spout chip 90.00

Sipe & Sons, Williamsport, PA, imp label, brown, spout chip   35.00

Unknown Maker, cobalt blue freehand adv label "J. M. Connelly," speckled gray 150.00

Jug, 1 gal, Whites, Utica, cobalt blue pine tree dec, $220.00. Photograph courtesy of Arthur Auctioneering.

1 Gallon

Bartmann Kruge, tan glaze, 8½" h   500.00

Brewer & Halm, Havana, NY, semi–ovoid, imp label, cobalt blue flower, blue at label, small repair one side 65.00

Clark & Co, Rochester, ovoid, imp label, cobalt blue leafy dec . . .   125.00

Cowden & Wilcox, Harrisburg, PA, imp label, brushed cobalt blue flower, blue at label, replaced handle 135.00

James Ryan, Pittston, PA, imp label, cobalt blue stenciled adv label "Drink '67' Rye, P. J. Conwway, Pittston, PA," rim chip 30.00

J Fisher & Co, Lyons, NY, cobalt blue freehand adv label "M. Callaghan & Co., 250 Seneca St., Buffalo, NY" 75.00

J Hayes & Co, Manchester, NH, imp label with cobalt blue highlights, minor lip flakes, 9½" h   175.00

Mask Head Jug, Meaders Pottery, Georgia, green glaze, painted eyes, 20th C, 11" h, $550.00. Photograph courtesy of Freeman Fine Arts.

Moyer, Harrisburg, imp label, brushed cobalt blue feathery dec, blue at label and handle ... **475.00**

N A White & Son, Utica, imp label, cobalt blue slip tree design ... **175.00**

North Bay, cobalt blue eagle on slip trail branch dec ... **350.00**

Penn Yan, imp label, brushed cobalt blue feather dec, strong blue at handle ... **190.00**

Shenfelder, unmarked, brushed cobalt blue feathery flower dec, blue at handle ... **250.00**

Unknown Maker, adv
Cobalt blue at imp label "A. Bullins Groceries, Provisions, Crockery & Co., Chicopee, Mass.," minor rim chip ... **75.00**
Cobalt blue from shoulder up, coggle wheel bands, imp label "Johnston, Warner & Co. Grocers' Wine and Spirit Merchants, 1017 Market St., Philadelphia," cobalt blue at label and bands ... **550.00**

W Roberts, Binghamton, NY, imp label, cobalt blue dec
Bird on branch, looking back, dark color, crack in back ... **125.00**
Slip trailed flower, blue at label, replaced handle ... **75.00**

1½ Gallon

J & E Norton, Bennington, imp label, cobalt blue slip stylized floral dec, strap handle, minor wear, small chips, 10½" h ... **350.00**

Unknown Maker, ovoid, imp "Gin," 12¼" h ... **175.00**

2 Gallon

Bartmann Kruge, tan glaze, 13" h **250.00**
Boston, MA
Impressed label, ovoid, two tone brown and gray salt glaze, tooled lines, ribbed strap handle, 14½" h ... **700.00**
Ovoid, incised bands at neck, cobalt blue fish and foliage dec, some chips and abrasions, 15" h ... **1,550.00**

Clark & Fox, Athens, ovoid, imp label, cobalt blue feather dec and at handle ... **275.00**

Cowden & Wilcox, Harrisburg, semi–ovoid, imp label, brushed cobalt blue dec
Fan shaped leaf, blue at handle **300.00**
Flower, spout chip ... **165.00**

F H Cowden, Harrisburg, imp label, cobalt blue stenciled flower dec, blue at handle ... **110.00**

Fort Edward, NY, imp label, cobalt blue brushwork rose design, fitted as lamp, 14½" h ... **190.00**

Harrington & Burger, Rochester, semi–ovoid, imp label, strong cobalt blue flower ... **250.00**

I M Mead, & Co, ovoid, imp label with cobalt blue highlight, 13" h ... **160.00**

James Ryan, Pittston, PA, imp label, cobalt blue script adv label "S J Freeman, Pittston, Pa," minor chip on bottom ... **165.00**

J Burger Jr, Rochester, NY, cobalt blue slip dec, polka dot flower and "2," minor spout chips ... **300.00**

J J Lawlow, Albany, NY, imp label, large cobalt blue stylized flower **190.00**

J Mantell, Penn Yan, imp label, brushed cobalt blue dec
Double bloom flower, handle replaced ... **65.00**
Triple bloom flower, blue at label ... **325.00**

John Burger, Rochester, imp label, cobalt blue "2" and quillwork flower, spout chip, glazed flake repair on back ... **325.00**

Moyer, Harrisburg, semi–ovoid, simple cobalt blue feather dec, blue at handle, small spider line on side ... **325.00**

N A White & Son, Utica, NY, imp label, brushed cobalt blue flower, strap handle, short hairline crack in base, 14" h ... **300.00**

N Clark & Co, Lyons, ovoid, imp "2" and label, cobalt blue floral dec, chips on bottom ... **185.00**

NY Stoneware Co, Ft Edwards, NY, imp label and "2," cobalt blue script and printed adv label "M. A. Ingalls, Liquor Dealer, Little Falls" ... **125.00**

Thomas D Chollar, Cortland, ovoid, imp label, cobalt blue "2" and feathery leaf, blue at label and handle ... **275.00**

Unknown Maker, ovoid
Brushed cobalt blue floral design, 13½" h ... **125.00**
Gray salt glaze, amber highlights, brown brushed tulip and "2," surface wear, pitting, chips, 13¼" h ... **185.00**

W Roberts, Binghamton, NY, imp label, cobalt blue polka dot roadrunner and foliage dec, blue at label, minor spout chip **575.00**

3 Gallon

Bergan & Foy, imp label, cobalt blue quillwork bird on branch, 15" h ... **1,075.00**

Clark & Fox, Athens, ovoid, imp label, brushed cobalt blue double bloom flower, blue at label and handle, discolored all around. 250.00

Cowden & Wilcox, Harrisburg, PA Bird on stump dec, imp label and "3," cobalt blue design, blue at label. 3,750.00

Sunflower dec, semi–ovoid, imp label, brushed cobalt blue sunflower in wreath, blue at handle, tight crack near spout 525.00

H & G Nash, Utica, ovoid, imp label, simple cobalt blue flower and "3," dent on side in making   225.00

Ithaca, NY, cobalt blue leafy dec   125.00

J & E Norton, Bennington, VT, imp label, strong cobalt blue quill-work floral dec, blue at label, glaze flake repair on back, stone ping in dec 250.00

John Young & Co, Harrisburg, PA, imp label, cobalt blue quill-work, stylized two blossom flower, 19th C, 17" h 925.00

Moore Nichols & Co, Williamsport, PA, semi–ovoid, imp label and "3," cobalt blue floral dec 550.00

M & T Miller, Newport, PA, entire jug covered with elaborate cobalt blue flowers and leaves design, tight crack through dec   2,525.00

Perry, S S & Co, West Troy, imp label, brushed cobalt blue flower, ribbed strap handle, 15½" h 250.00

S T Brewer, Havana, imp label and "3", brushed cobalt blue triple bloom flower, blue at label, tight crack at top, some repair on bottom edge 110.00

T & J Ducey Manufacturers, Petersburg, VA, imp label, cobalt blue dec, imperfections, mid 19th C, 14" h 1,325.00

Unknown Maker, ovoid

Cobalt blue slip design, 16" h   225.00

Incised long tailed bird, cobalt blue highlights, gray–tan salt glaze, chip on lip, ribbed handle, 14" h. 900.00

W E Welding, Brantford, ovoid, imp label, cobalt blue brushed floral design, 16¼" h. 375.00

W Roberts, Binghamton, NY, imp label and "3," cobalt blue slip double bloom flower with spiky leaves and polka dot dec, chip on bottom edge, dark color . . .   185.00

4 Gallon

Nichols & Boynton, Burlington, VT, imp label, cobalt blue quill-work stylized floral design, large chip on lip, hairline in handle, flake on base, 17¼" h 125.00

Whites, Utica, NY, imp label and "4," ornate cobalt blue dec, two peafowl perched in tree, bodies are crossed and both are looking back at the other, minor chip on spout, glaze fry on dec 550.00

5 Gallon

I M Mead, Mogadore, OH, ovoid, imp label, brushed cobalt blue floral decoration and "5," double ear handles, professionally restored, 18½" h 375.00

Penn Yan, ovoid, imp label, two polka dot birds, cobalt blue quillwork "5," minor wear, short hairlines, 18½" h 2,600.00

10 Gallon

NY Stoneware Co, Fort Edwards NY, ovoid, imp label, cobalt blue dec of bird with banner dated "1876" in beak, flakes, 19½" h 1,550.00

W Lunn, ovoid, brushed cobalt blue labels "10" and "1882" on one side, "W. Lunn" on reverse, double ear handles, lip and one handle glued, 19½" h 190.00

Milk Pan, 1 gallon, pouring spout, cobalt blue running dec around, some rim chips.   175.00

Mixing Bowl, 1 gallon, Thomas D Chollar, Homer, lug handles, imp label, minor chips 75.00

Molasses Jug, 1 gallon, I Seymour, Troy, ovoid, cobalt blue brushed feather, blue at label, spout chip 625.00

Mug

Old Sleepy Eye, cobalt blue handle and Indian design, bottom marked "W. S. Co., Monmouth, Ill.", tight age line at top edge, small chip bottom edge 190.00

Milk Pan, 1 gal, Pennsylvania, handled, pour lip, cobalt blue floral and leaf dec around, bottom chip, $410.00. Photograph courtesy of Arthur Auctioneering.

Whites Pottery, NY, Pan American Expo souvenir, cobalt blue bands and highlights, logo front, tavern scene back, crack at top edge . . . **125.00**

Pie Plate, 11″ d, white clay, coggled rim, amber glaze **125.00**

Pitcher
1 Pint
Old Sleepy Eye, bottom marked "W. S. Co., Monmouth, Ill.", age lines at top edge, 4″ h **125.00**
Unknown Maker
Paneled, brown Albany slip, molded figures, 6″ h **25.00**
Raised ring around rim and shoulder, brushed cobalt blue leaf design, 6½″ h **425.00**

1 Quart
F & E Norton, Bennington, VT, ovoid, imp label, cobalt blue quillwork bird on branch dec, extensive professional repair, 12½″ h **175.00**
Lyons, ovoid, imp label, brushed cobalt blue leaf design, rim hairline at handle, 10″ h **375.00**
Unknown Maker, brushed cobalt blue dec
Feather design all around, minor inner rim chip, minor bottom chips, 7″ h **1,100.00**
Floral dec, spout chip, 10½″ h **650.00**

2 Quart
Attributed to Whites Pottery, molded and cobalt blue dec crane design, tight age line at spout **125.00**
Unknown Maker
Cobalt blue dec, wavy line around neck, brushed floral design around shoulder, ribbed strap handle, 14½″ h **1,750.00**
Hourglass shaped, Albany slip covered **25.00**

Pitcher, 1 gal, F H Cowden, Harrisburg, PA, imp label, cobalt blue stenciled dec, professionally repaired rim chip, $990.00. Photograph courtesy of Arthur Auctioneering.

Raised bands at neck and shoulder, brushed cobalt blue triple flower dec around, rim chips, blue at missing handle **300.00**
Whites, Utica, squatty, imp label, emb hunting scene, cobalt blue highlights and at label **325.00**

1 Gallon
Attributed to Williamsport maker, brushed cobalt blue leafy dec, blue at handle **375.00**
Lyons, imp label, cobalt blue double tulip, blue at handle, professional rim chip repair **350.00**
PA, attributed to Remmey, cobalt blue leafy flower dec, minor outer rim chip **725.00**

Preserving Jar
1 Pint, Jas Hamilton & Co, Greensboro, PA, cobalt blue stenciled label, freehand dec, minor rim chips **150.00**
1 Quart
A P Donaghho, Parkersburg, WV, incised lines around shoulder, cobalt blue stenciled label **100.00**
Excelsior Works, Isaac Hewitt, Jr., Rices Landing, PA, incised lines around neck, cobalt blue stenciled label, wax seal, minor inner rim chips **450.00**
Hartford City Salt Co, Dealers in Salt & General Merchandise, Hartford City, WV, cobalt blue stenciled label, chips and hairlines, 6¾″ h **275.00**
Lock Haven, PA, imp label, brown **100.00**
2 Quart
A Conrad, New Geneva, PA, cobalt blue stenciled label, 8½″ h **225.00**
Hamilton & Jones, Greensboro, PA, cobalt blue stenciled label, wax seal **150.00**
New Geneva Pottery, cobalt blue wavy lines, stenciled label, small flake on lip, 9½″ h **275.00**
Unknown Maker
Barrel shaped, narrow mouth, molded blue highlighted bands, chip on base, 8″ h . . . **275.00**
Cobalt blue brushed and stenciled design, small flake on base, 8″ h **175.00**
1 Gallon
Unknown Maker, cobalt blue dec
Brushed shoulder design, 10″ h **125.00**
Stenciled and freehand label "S & L Vickers, Dealers in Dry Goods & Groceries & C. Loydsville, O" **475.00**
Wilkinson & Fleming, Shinnston, WV, cobalt blue stenciled label with rose, 10″ h **275.00**

1½ Gallon, unknown maker, cobalt blue brushed floral design, imp "1½" ext. lime deposits, 11" h. . .   **45.00**

Rolling Pin, cobalt blue flowers and adv label "Compliments of D. C. Struthers, Phillipsburg, NJ," replaced wood handle **300.00**

Salt Crock, Old Sleepy Eye, molded Indian design, cobalt blue band and highlights **725.00**

Spittoon, waisted, coggle wheel dec, blue bands **100.00**

Tenderizer, round stoneware mallet with pyramid shaped knobs all around, turned wood handle, dated 1877 . . . .   **110.00**

Vase, Old Sleepy Eye, cylindrical, raised Indian design and rings at top and bottom, cobalt blue Indian and rings **275.00**

Water Bottle, stamped "Dorchest Pottery Wks., Boston, Mass". **12.00**

Wine Jug, 1 gallon, unmarked, ovoid, porcelain stopper on wire bail. **20.00**

TEXTILES

Thrift was a way of life in agrarian America. Few had money to waste. Textiles were purchased that would wear well. When something did "wear out," it was recycled. Patchwork quilts and hooked rugs are the final resting place for many a shirt and dress. Feed bags wound up as dresses and shirts when times were lean.

Textiles are cloth or fabric items, especially anything woven or knitted. Those that survive usually represent the best since these were the objects that were used carefully and stored by the housewife.

Textiles helped brighten life in rural America. Red and blue are dominant colors with block, circle, and star pattern motifs the most common. Colorful window curtains were changed seasonally. The same held true for bedspreads. A party dress or shirt was a welcome respite from the pastel colors of daily work clothes.

Textiles are collected for many reasons—to study fabrics, understand the elegance of an historical period, and for decorative and modern use. The renewed interest in clothing has sparked a revived interest in textiles of all forms.

References: Suzy Anderson, *Collector's Guide to Quilts,* Wallace–Homestead Book Co, 1991; Alda Horner, *The Official Guide to Linens, Lace, and Other Fabrics,* House of Collectibles, 1991; Florence Montgomery, *Textiles in America: 1650–1870,* W. W. Norton & Co, 1984; Betty Ring, ed, *Needlework: An Historical Survey,* revised edition, The Main Street Press, 1984; Carlton Safford and Robert Bishop, *America's Quilts and Coverlets,* reprint, Bonanza Books, 1985.

Collectors' Club: Costume Society of America, 55 Edgewater Dr, PO Box 73, Earleville, MD 21919.

Museums: Cooper–Hewitt Museum, New York, NY; Ipswich Historical Society, Ipswich, MA; The Textile Museum, Washington, DC; Museum of American Textile History, North Andover, MA.

CLOTHING AND ACCESSORIES

History: Farm clothing can be divided into two groups—workday and Sunday. Within each group, clothing is further divided into manufactured and homemade. The agrarian housewife was usually an expert seamstress.

Most collectors of vintage clothing and accessories have focused on high style items. Only in the last few years have some collectors begun to focus on clothing used in rural America. While Country decorators have used clothing as decorative highlights within room settings for years, emphasis has fallen largely on accessories such as aprons and infant wear.

"Vintage clothing" is a broad term used to describe clothing manufactured from the late Victorian era (1880s) to the end of the psychedelic era (1970s). While purists would prefer a cutoff date of 1940, clothing from World War II, the fifties, and sixties is also highly collectible. In reality, vintage clothing is defined by what is available and current collecting trends.

A few clues to dating clothing are: (1) do not depend on style alone; (2) check labels; (3) learn which fabrics and print patterns were popular in each historical period; and, (4) examine decorative elements.

Clothing is collected and studied as a reference source to learn about fashion, construction and types of materials used. Collecting vintage clothing appears to have reached a plateau. Although there are still dedicated collectors, the category is no longer attracting a rash of new collectors annually.

The hot part of the clothing market in the 1990s is accessories. Clothing collectors acquire everything from hats and shoes to handbags and jewelry to accessorize their garments. However, because many clothing accessories are collectibles in their own right (compacts, hatpins, purses, etc.), collectors of clothing often find themselves competing with these specialized collectors.

Country auctions are usually rich in clothing accessories. Hand–me–down was a way of life. However, many items in the hand–me–down pile never made it to their next owner, winding up in long–time storage instead.

References: Maryanne Dolan, *Vintage Clothing, 1880–1960, Second Edition,* Books Americana, 1988; Ellen Gehret, *Rural Pennsylvania Clothing,* Liberty Cap Books, 1976; Tina Irick–Nauer, *The First Price Guide to Antique and Vintage Clothes,* E. P. Dutton, 1983; Terry McCormick, *The Consumer's Guide To Vintage Clothing,* Dembner Books, 1987; Diane McGee, *A Passion For Fashion,* Simmons–Boardman Books, Inc, 1987; Merideth Wright, *Everyday Dress of Rural America: 1783–1800,* Dover Publications, 1992.

Periodicals: *Lady's Gallery,* PO Box 1761, Independence, MO 64055; *Lill's Vintage Clothing Newsletter,* 19 Jamestown Dr, Cincinnati, OH 45241; *Vintage Clothing Newsletter,* PO Box 1422, Corvallis, OR 97339; *Vintage Fashion Sourcebook,* 904 N 65th St, Springfield, OR 97478–7021; *Vintage Gazette,* 194 Amity St, Amherst, MA 01002.

Collectors' Club: The Costume Society of America, 55 Edgewater Dr, PO Box 73, Earleville, MD 21919.

Museums: Levi Strauss & Co Museum, San Francisco, CA; Metropolitan Museum of Art, New York, NY; the Costume and Textile Department of the Los Angeles County Museum of Art, Los Angeles, CA; Philadelphia Museum of Art, Philadelphia, PA.

Reproduction Craftspersons: Barbara Lawn, Tomorrow's Heirlooms, Main Line–Berwyn, C–303, Berwyn, PA 19312; Sherry D Pees, Pees Poor

Ridge Farms, 10357 St, Route 81, Dola, OH 45835; Kathi Reynolds, Creative Clothes, 330 N Church St, Thurmont, MD 21788–1640; Mike and Pat Stevens, PO Box 2, Myersville, MD 21773; Time Warp Custom and Vintage Attire, 179 Jay St, Schenectady, NY 12305.

Reproduction Manufacturers: *Aprons*—Olde Virginea Floorcloth and Trading Co, PO Box 3305, Portsmouth, VA 23707; *General*—Amazon Vinegar & Pickling Works Drygoods, 2218 East 11th St, Davenport, IA 52803; The Calico Corner, 513 E Bowman St, South Bend, IN 46613; Campbell's, RD 1, Box 1444, Herndon, PA 17830; Country Heart Homespun Collection, Inc, 1212 Westover Hills Blvd, Box 13358, Richmond, VA 23225; The Cover Up Handweaving Studio, Rte 1, Box 216, Rabun Gap, GA 30568; Cumberland General Store, Rte 3, Crossville, TN 38555; Lamb and Lanterns, 902 N Walnut St, Dover, OH 44622; Log Cabin Shop, Box 275, Lodi, OH 44254; Pesta's Country Charm, 300 Standard Ave, Mingo Junction, OH 43938; *Patterns*—Amazon Vinegar & Pickling Works Drygoods, 2218 East 11th St, Davenport, IA 52803; Campbell's, RD 1, Box 1444, Herndon, PA 17830; Crazy Crow Trading Post, PO Box 314B, Denison, TX 75020; Old World Sewing Pattern Co, Rte 2, Box 103, Cold Spring, MN 56320; Past Patterns, 2017 Eastern, Grand Rapids, MI 49507; *Restoration*—Mountain Shadow Studio, PO Box 619, Nederland, CO 80466.

Apron

Cotton, hand sewn, patchwork design, waist length, ties	**25.00**
Gingham, cross stitch trim, 1950s	**40.00**
Baby Bonnet, cotton, tatted, ribbon rosettes	**15.00**
Baby Booties, wool, cream colored, red braid trim, c1850	**85.00**
Baby Coat, cotton, gathered yoke and capelet, embroidery, flannel lining	**25.00**
Baby Dress, cotton, tucked, eyelet trimmed yoke, sleeves, skirt, 3½" open work, scalloped hem, 38" l . . .	**20.00**
Baby Shoes, leather, high top, 1930s	**20.00**
Bag, drawstring, cotton homespun	
8½" sq, white silk facing, wool and silk floral green, brown, and beige embroidery, fragile, stains and damage	**125.00**
9" h, 10½" w, pen and ink drawn floral dec, poem, "Mary Littlefield 1816" on one side, landscape on rev, fragile, wear, stains, small tears	**225.00**
Bloomers, wool, cream colored	**25.00**
Blouse, cotton, white, crocheted accents on large collar, fitted at waist	**35.00**
Christening Gown, cutwork embroidery bodice, tuck pleats around ruffled skirt	**65.00**

Baby's Jacket, cotton, hand made, c1900, $35.00.

Dress

    Calico, blue, 2 pc, matching bonnet,
      c1900 . . . . **165.00**

    Gingham, child's, blue and white,
      hand and machine sewn, white
      embroidery trim, 25" h **50.00**

    Homespun Linen, child's, blue, yel-
      low, and white plaid, drawstring
      neck, high waist, long set–in
      sleeves, c1830, minor discolora-
      tion **300.00**

    Muslin, embroidered stripes, long
      sleeves, tucking edges, c1820 . . . **135.00**

    Wool, Amish, dark green, c1830   **45.00**

Gloves, man's, clipped buffalo and
    leather, medium **50.00**

Lap Robe, wool, embroidered, leather
    binding **50.00**

Nightgown, cotton, white, leg O' mut-
    ton sleeves, high collar, handmade
    eyelet lace trim **285.00**

Nightshirt, man's, cotton, white, long   **25.00**

Petticoat

    Cotton, white, crocheted insert, wide
      crocheted hem **45.00**

    Muslin, white, deep laced edge
      flounce, 24" waist **18.00**

Shawl

    Lace, black, flowers, scalloped hem,
      112" w, 54" l **36.00**

    Wool, green, beige, and olive green
      plaid, fringed **25.00**

**Fan, mourning, cockade, glazed black fab-
ric, emb paper over wood sticks, wire clip,
8½" d open size, $50.00.**

Shirt, man's, homespun linen, natural
    color, button closure **50.00**

Shoes

    Child's, high button, leather **25.00**

    Lady's, brown leather, high button
      top **40.00**

Skirt

    Felt, gray, velvet embroidered bor-
      der, c1880 . . . . **40.00**

    Muslin, white, full length, deep
      tucks, ruffled flounce, hand em-
      broidered **40.00**

    Overshot, slate blue, walking, adjust-
      able 24" waist **30.00**

Skirt and Top, homespun, black lace
    bodice and cuffs, high neck **125.00**

Slip, cotton

    Full, white, rows of tucks and lace
      inserts, crocheted top and flowers **25.00**

    Half, string waist, lace bottom **35.00**

COVERLETS

History: A loom in every Country home is a myth.
Most coverlets were woven by a semi–professional (a farmer who supplemented his income by
weaving in the winter months) or a professional
weaver.

A coverlet is made by weaving yarns together
on a loom. A quilt, made by sewing together layers
of fabric, is an entirely different textile.

The earliest coverlets are overshot. The double
weave dates from 1725 to 1825. Single weave,
double face coverlets (winter/summer) were
popular in the first quarter of the 19th century.

The Jacquard loom arrived upon the scene in
the early 1820s. It allowed the manufacture of
wide, single piece coverlets. However, the pieced
coverlet tradition continued well into mid–century.

Natural dyes in soft hues made from animal,
mineral, and plant matter were used prior to 1820.
Mineral dyes made between 1820 and 1860 are
harsher in color. Synthetic dyes, which retain a
bright, permanent color, were in use by the early
1860s.

By the 1860s, commercially made blankets replaced coverlets and quilts as the principal bed-
covering. While quilt making survived, coverlet
production ceased.

References: Harold and Dorothy Burnham, *'Keep
Me Warm One Night': Early Handweaving in
Eastern Canada*, Toronto Press, 1972; John W.
Heisey, *A Checklist of American Coverlet Weav-
ers*, The Colonial Williamsburg Foundation, 1978;
Carleton Safford and Robert Bishop, *America's
Quilts and Coverlets*, Bonanza Books, 1985.

Reproduction Craftspersons: *General*—Betsy
Bourdon, Traditional Handweaving, Scribner Hill,
Wolcott, VT 05680; Ieva Ersts, Rosemary Hill

Farm, PO Box 196, Church Hill, MD 21623; J Francis & Co, Box 990, Rte 228, Mars, PA 16046; Kathy & Bob Harman, Old Abingdon Weavers, PO Box 786, Abingdon, VA 24210; Anita Heist, Handweaver, 800 Cedar Springs Rd, Athens, TN 37303; Jeanne M Henderson, Woven Concepts, 825 Hanover St, New Oxford PA, 17350; Maggie Kennedy, Ozark Weaving Studio, PO Box 286, Cane Hill, AR 72717; William A Leinbach, The Itinerant Weaver, 356 Royers Rd, Myerstown, PA 17067; Dotty Lewis, 9 Indian Hill Rd, Conestoga, PA 17516; Karen Monson–Thompson, The Summer/Winter Studio, 2608 E 6th St, Superior, WI 54880; Donna Nedeeisky, Handweaver, The Coverlet Co, PO Box 02–616, Portland, OR 97202; Jacki Schell, Jacki's Hand-woven Originals, RD 4, Box 352, Lewistown, PA 17044; Mary Worley, Traditional Textiles, RD 2, Box 3120, Middlebury, VT 05735; *Jacquard*—Gabrielle & Robert Black, Jr, Black's Handweav-ing Shop, 497 Main St, W Barnstable, MA 02668; David and Carole Kline, Family Heir–Loom Weavers, RD 3, Box 59E, Red Lion, PA 17356; *Overshot*—Susan Eikenberry, 611 N Van Buren St, Batavia, IL 60510; Julia A Lindsey, Lindsey Wool-seys of Ohio, 275 N Main St, Germantown, OH 45327.

Reproduction Manufacturers: *General*—Good-win Weavers, PO Box 408, West Cornish Rd, Blowing Rock, NC 28605; Homespun Crafts, Box 77, Grover, NC 28073; The Manual Woodwork-ers and Weavers, Inc, Highway 74, Gerton, NC 28735; Winters Textile Mill, 9110 Winters Rd, PO Box 614, Winters, CA 95694; *Restoration*—Mountain Shadow Studio, PO Box 619, Neder-land, CO 80466.

Bedspread, candlewick
   70 × 80", floral design, matching
   pillow sham, small holes and re-
   pairs **75.00**
   100 × 76", floral medallion center
   enclosed by geometric devices,
   stylized floral swag border, cotton,
   natural white, initialed "SSF12,"
   old mends, imperfections, c1830   **60.00**
Blanket, woven
   Linen, 98 × 88", broken twill check
   pattern, squash and cream colors,
   some fiber loss **150.00**
   Wool
      62 × 80", one piece, blue and
      natural white, hand sewn hems,
      small holes **115.00**
      67 × 80", indigo, ochre, and
      brown plaid **100.00**
      70 × 80", two piece, madder and
      teal, twill, PA, minor imperfec-
      tions **185.00**
      72 × 90", two piece, madder and
      blue plaid twill **525.00**

      74 × 86", two piece, madder and
      indigo check twill, some fringe
      loss **225.00**
      75 × 68", madder and natural twill **190.00**
      76 × 76", two piece, madder, gray,
      and red, twill, PA, minor imper-
      fections **215.00**
      78 × 82", two piece, bright green,
      indigo, and rose madder plaid
      twill, full fringe on three sides,
      PA **250.00**
      80 × 81", two piece, madder,
      green, natural white, and taupe,
      novelty design **80.00**
      82 × 68", indigo, madder, and
      natural broken point twill,
      goose eye pattern, initials
      "SMB" **225.00**
      86 × 72", two piece, two shades of
      indigo point twill, goose–eye
      and table pattern fringe on three
      sides **525.00**
Wool and Linen, 70 × 86", home-
   spun, three piece, madder and
   black wool, natural linen **225.00**
Comforter, 66 × 76", pieced and knot-
   ted, four square basket patches, reds,
   pinks, goldenrod, and orange **95.00**
Jacquard
   64 × 80", two piece, single weave,
   flowers and stars with bird and
   house borders, corners labeled
   "Somerset, Ohio 1845, L. Hesse,
   Weaver," tomato red, navy blue,
   natural white, and teal, overall and
   edge wear, fringe loss, light stains **250.00**
   64 × 86", two piece, single weave,
   vintage type pattern, medium
   blue, salmon, and natural white,
   wear and some damage **80.00**
   66 × 70", two piece, single weave,
   flowers, vintage, corners labeled
   "Samuel Meily, Mansfield, Richland, Ohio 1844," blue, teal, red,
   and natural white, very worn,
   holes, no fringe **150.00**
   66 × 79", two piece, single weave,
   floral, eagle corners, labeled
   "Knox County, Ohio 1847," red,
   teal, blue, and natural white, incomplete fringe, halves not sewn **425.00**
   66 × 85", two piece, single weave,
   four rose medallions, tree and
   eagle borders, corner labeled
   "Leanette Gould, Lodi, 1833,"
   navy blue and natural white,
   worn, incomplete fringe **225.00**
   66 × 86", single weave, two piece,
   four rose medallions, bird and
   double headed eagle borders, corners labeled "Gabriel Rausher
   1847," blue and natural white . . . **500.00**

Jacquard, blue and white, woven by Samuel Melly, 72 × 85", $375.00.

66 × 90", single weave, one piece, stars and flowers, bird borders, corners dated 1857, blue and natural white. 575.00

67 × 77", two piece, double weave, snowflakes, pine tree border, navy blue and natural white, some wear   125.00

68 × 90", two piece, single weave, roses and stars, medium blue and natural white, minor overall wear   225.00

70 × 74", two piece, single weave, floral, eagle border, corner labels "Samuel Meily, Mansfield, Richland, Ohio 1844," navy blue, red, faded green, and natural white, worn, stains, two halves unsewn, torn edge. 165.00

70 × 82", single weave, one piece, star center, eagle corners, blue and natural white. 325.00

70 × 84", two piece, double weave
Bold floral design, Greek key border, corners dated 1848, navy blue and natural white, minor wear 500.00

Star and flower with bird and rose borders, corners labeled "G. Stich, Newark, Ohio 1839," navy blue, tomato red, and natural white, worn, very worn fringe, small holes and stains   325.00

70 × 88", two piece, double weave, floral with birds, corners labeled "Maria Hill AD 1846," navy blue, blue, and natural white, fringe on one end, some overall and edge wear, small holes 500.00

71 × 71", two piece, single weave, four large medallions, steam ship borders, labeled "B. Lichty, Bristol, Wayne Co, Ohio 1845," medium blue and natural white,

wear, rebound, seam resewn, minor fringe damage and repair. . . .   575.00

71 × 77", one piece, single weave, floral design with zigzags, red and natural white, some wear 125.00

71 × 79", two piece, single weave, flowers, bird border, labeled "Zur Ruhe 1853," navy blue and deep tomato red, gold color, very poor condition, holes, and tears, no fringe. 135.00

73 × 90", two piece, single weave, floral with vining borders and corners, "Coverlet, Wm. H. VanGordon, Weaver, Covington, Miami Co, Ohio 1849," medium blue and natural white, overall and top edge wear, some moth damage   450.00

74 × 82", two piece
Double weave, snowflake and pine tree, navy blue and natural white, wear and stains 175.00

Single weave, foliage medallions, rose borders, corners labeled "Made by Jacob Saylor, Saltcrick Townsp. Pickaway Co. Ohio 1854," blue, red, olive, and natural white, minor end wear 450.00

74 × 100", two piece, double weave, Christian and Heathen, pots of flowers and fruit, peacocks, blue and natural white, small holes and repairs 325.00

75 × 82", one piece, double weave, star center, birds, deer, and capitol buildings borders, red, navy blue, brown, olive green, and natural white, minor stains 450.00

75 × 86", two piece, single weave, stars and flowers, bird border, corner labeled "John Redick, Troy Township, Richland, Ohio 1852," blue, green, deep pink, and natural white, very worn, moth damage, edge wear, no fringe 225.00

75 × 98", one piece, single weave, floral, Oriental buildings in borders, black, pale yellow, salmon, and natural white, wear, salmon wool very worn, some fringe damage 85.00

76 × 80", two piece, single weave, four rose medallions, basket of flowers in borders, corners dated "1858," navy blue, olive, red, and natural white, some wear, stains, minor fringe loss 55.00

76 × 82", two piece, single weave, star and flower medallions, vintage border and corner labels: "W. in Mt. Vernon Knox County, Ohio

by Jacob and Michael Ardner 1852," rust red and natural white, edge wear, small holes, incomplete fringe **475.00**

76 × 88", two piece, double weave, floral designs, pots of flowers in border, edges labeled "United We Stand Divided We Fall, 1841," navy blue and natural white, wear, repair, and minor stains. **350.00**

76 × 90", two piece, single weave, floral, double vintage border, navy blue and natural white, worn and holes **200.00**

76 × 96", two piece, single weave, stars and flowers with bird and urn, corners labeled "G. Foore, 1843," navy blue and natural white, worn, fringe loss **220.00**

76 × 98", two piece, single weave, small stars, double tree border, navy blue and natural white, very minor stains. **470.00**

77 × 81", one piece, single weave, central floral medallion, capitol buildings border, red, green, and natural white, overall and edge wear **165.00**

78 × 84", two piece, double weave, turkeys and peacocks in trees, vintage border, navy blue and natural white, wear, small holes, stains, top edge very worn **110.00**

78 × 88", two piece, single weave, four rose medallions, double head eagle borders, corner labeled "Peter Lorenz 1841," deep blue/black and natural white, overall wear, stains, and fringe loss **475.00**

78 × 90", two piece, single weave, floral with turkey in tree corners, "Manufactured by Henry Oberly, Womelsdorf, Penn," tomato red and natural white, some overall wear, fringe removed, ends rebound **550.00**

78 × 96", Masonic, floral medallions center, eagle, building, pillars, stars, and Masonic symbol border, corner block inscribed "Agriculture & Manufacturers are the foundation of our independence, July 4, 1827," ends inscribed "GNRL LaFayette" and "McGuernsey". . . **725.00**

79 × 90", one piece, double weave, floral, block border, teal, red, and natural white, wear, small holes **165.00**

80 × 88", two piece, double weave, four rose medallions and stars, corners labeled "Mary Ann Dyeart 1841," navy blue and natural white, wear and holes **400.00**

80 × 89", very dark blue, tomato red, and natural white, bold geometric floral design, corners labeled "1848," ends machine sewn, one end turned **525.00**

81 × 82", two piece, double weave, birds and flowers, corners labeled "Bird of Paradise," navy blue and natural white, very worn, holes, and repairs. **275.00**

81 × 92", two piece, double weave, floral medallions, navy blue and tomato red, wear, edge damage, and small holes **450.00**

82 × 82", two piece, double weave

Bold floral medallions, floral borders, corners with cupola and dated 1852, navy blue and natural white **190.00**

Bold geometric floral, navy blue and natural white, overall and edge wear, no fringe **225.00**

Urns of fruit and flowers, birds, and peacocks feeding young, buildings border, corners with "Manufacd by Jay A Vanvleck, Gallipolis, O," navy blue and natural white **500.00**

84 × 90", one piece, single weave, large center floral medallion, bird and floral border, maroon and natural white, warp end red wool fringe, minor stains **325.00**

84 × 96", two piece, double weave, seaweed and shell design, navy blue and natural white, overall wear, stains, small holes, no fringe **350.00**

85 × 71", one piece, single weave, bold floral design, olive, dark green, and tomato red **325.00**

86 × 92", two piece, double weave, floral with compotes of fruit borders and eagles in corners with "E. Pluribus Unum" and "Mary A. Martin, Jefferson Co. N.Y. 1847," navy blue, black, and natural white, no fringe **1,700.00**

86 × 95", two piece, double weave, floral medallions, bird borders and corners, corner labeled "J.B.M.Z. Fancy Coverlet Woven by G. Heilbronn, Lancaster, O. 1853," red, green, and blue, overall and edge wear **440.00**

87 × 80", birds and floral medallions central panel, two piece, scattered losses and discoloration. **475.00**

87 × 87", two piece, single weave, four rose medallions, bird and star border, corners labeled "Andre Kump, Hanover 1839, J. Bachman," red, navy blue, and natural

white, light stains, minor moth damage.................... **350.00**

Overshot

58 × 62", two piece, navy blue and natural white, overall and edge wear, no fringe **110.00**

59 × 84", two piece, navy blue and natural white, fringe on one end, hanging support added to other **200.00**

60 × 88", three piece, maroon, natural white, and salmon, tied fringe on ends, some wear and damage **90.00**

62 × 94", two piece, Frenchman's Fancy variation, navy blue, salmon, and natural white, no fringe, some wear **135.00**

64 × 92", two piece, navy blue, salmon and natural white, overall wear, no fringe **55.00**

65 × 80", two piece, stars and flowers, navy blue, red, olive, and natural white, worn, fringe **90.00**

66 × 93", two piece, bowties and diamonds, red, blue, teal, and natural white, minor wear...... **225.00**

66 × 96", two piece, navy blue, tomato red, and natural white, worn, no fringe **150.00**

68 × 82", two piece, Pine Tree, medium blue, chocolate brown, and natural white, no fringe, edge wear **150.00**

68 × 90", two piece, faded olive gold, red, and natural white, wear, damage, and woven fringe, incomplete.................. **55.00**

70 × 89", two piece, stars, trees, flowers, and stick soldiers, navy blue, salmon red, gold, and natural white, wear, edge damage, missing fringe.................. **325.00**

70 × 96", two piece, stars and flowers, red, navy blue, and natural white, sewn on fringe, wear, repair, and some color bleeding... **250.00**

74 × 88", two piece

Optical pattern, navy blue and natural white, wear, moth damage, and stains............. **90.00**

Snowflake and pine tree pattern, deep navy blue and natural white, some edge wear, holes and stains **250.00**

Star, diamond, and stripe design, red, navy blue, gold, olive, and natural white, some edge wear, small holes and stains **250.00**

74 × 90", two piece, Chariot Wheel pattern, cotton and wool, blue and natural white................ **110.00**

74 × 100", two piece, olive, red, and natural white, edges turned and whip bound, no fringe......... **175.00**

76 × 94", two piece, blue and natural white..................... **100.00**

79 × 80", one piece, starlike design, red, navy blue, gold, and natural white, minor fringe wear....... **150.00**

80 × 85", two piece, stars and flowers, red, navy blue, olive, and natural white, overall, edge, and fringe wear, repairs **125.00**

80 × 90", two piece, Goose Eye and Check pattern, red and teal wool yarns, some discoloration at ends **80.00**

80 × 96", two piece

Blue and natural white **150.00**

Gold, olive, and natural white, minor wear **200.00**

Navy blue and natural white, single weave, summer/winter, good fringe, minor wear....... **450.00**

81 × 88", two piece, twill weave, olive green, tomato red, and natural white, minor wear, even fading, some edge wear, fringe on ends **150.00**

85 × 95", two piece, single weave, tan and natural white optical pattern, woven fringe on three sides **275.00**

86 × 92", two piece, geometric pattern, linen and wool, bittersweet colored wool, natural linen **275.00**

FEED AND GRAIN BAGS

History: The first cotton grain bags appeared in the early 1800s and were used as an alternative to the barrel. They were handmade and not widely used.

The invention of the sewing machine and machines expressly designed to manufacture flour sacks opened the door to the daily use of textile bags in areas such as the packaging of feed, grains, sugar, and fertilizer. Feed bags reached their peak of popularity from the 1930s through the 1950s.

The original sizes of bags corresponded to barrel measurements. One barrel of flour weighed 96 lbs, a half barrel weighed 48 lbs, and so forth down to ⅛ barrel at 12 lbs. In 1943 the War Production Board standardized weights at 100, 50, 25, 10, 5, and 2 lb sizes.

The first manufactured bags were solid colors, usually white. Labels were either printed directly on the bag or paper labels were sewn or pasted to the front. Bags printed with floral or striped designs or doll and clothing patterns were introduced during the late 1920s and early 1930s. The rural housewife made clothing, dish towels, quilts, and toys from them.

References: Anna Lue Cook, *Textile Bags,* Books Americana, 1990.

Reproduction Manufacturers: Country Heart Homespun Collection, Inc, 1212 Westover Hills Blvd, Box 13358, Richmond, VA 23225; Creative Signs, 5640 S 92nd St, Hales Corners, WI 53130; Lamb and Lanterns, 902 N Walnut St, Dover, OH 44622.

Airlight All Purpose Flour, H C Cole Milling Co, Chester, IL, 10 lbs, Werthan Bag Co, Nashville, TN, striped floral print, 18 × 10½"..... **14.00**

Ascension Self Rising Flour, Pinckneyville Milling Co, Pinckneyville, IL, 12 lbs, Bemis Brother Bag Co, woman holding staff, mountains in background, white, 17½ × 11"........ **28.00**

Aunt Jemima, Quaker Oats Co, 100 lbs, Aunt Jemima illus, white, 37 × 23". **60.00**

Bannock Chief Flour, Peavey Flour Co, MO, 25 lbs, Hutchinson Bag Corp, narrow stripes on white, 26½ × 12½" **18.00**

Bell's Brand Seeds, American Seed Co, Fort Worth, TX, Fulton Bags, Dallas, TX, bell in wreath illus, white, 24 × 14"....................... **18.00**

Birchmont Flour, St Cloud Milling Co, St Cloud, MN, 98 lbs, Fulton Bag Co, building illus front, eagle over "Fulton seamless A junior size" in circle on back, white, 36 × 20"........ **75.00**

Blackhawk Wheat Bran, International Milling Co, Minneapolis, MN, 100 lbs, blackhawk illus, white, 38 × 23" **42.00**

Blair's Certified Flour, Blair Milling Co, Atchison KS, 98 lbs, script "Certified" on sunburst front, pig doll pattern back, white, 34 × 16".......... **30.00**

Buffalo Alfalfa Seed, 60 lbs, buffalo illus, white, 28 × 14 ½" **20.00**

Bull Brand Dairy Rations, Maritime Milling Co, Inc, Buffalo, NY, 100 lbs, center bull illus, "BB" printed overall in rows, 38 × 25" **40.00**

Chippewa Medium Salt, Ohio Salt Co, Wadsworth, OH, 50 lbs, Indian head illus, white, 28 × 14½"......... **40.00**

Clover Hill Hybrid Seed Corn, Clover Hill Hybrid Seed Corn Co, Audubon, IA, 56 lbs, Hutchinson Bag Corp, Hutchinson, KS, four ears of corn illus, white, 32 × 17".......... **12.00**

Colonial Pure Cane Sugar, Colonial Sugars Co, New Orleans, LA, 100 lbs, two narrow bands vertical red and blue stripes on white, 34 × 18" **30.00**

Dekalb Seed Corn, Dekalb Agricultural Assoc, Inc, Dekalb, IL, 56 lbs, Bemis Bros Bag Co, winged ear of corn over banner "More Farmers Plant Dekalb Than Any Other Brand" illus, white, 30 × 18" **25.00**

Deltapine 15 Cotton Seed, Delta & Pine Land Co, Scot, MS, 100 lbs, Fulton Bags, New Orleans, LA, pine tree illus, white, 28 × 23"........... **22.00**

Double Diamond Feed, Daily Mills, Inc, Olean, NY, 100 lbs, large floral print, 38 × 23"............... **48.00**

Eclipse Hog Supplement, Eclipse Feed Mills, Inc, Highland, IL, 100 lbs, Werthan Bag Corp, Nashville, TN, solar eclipse illus, white, 39 × 20 **15.00**

Happy Dog Food, Happy Mills, Memphis, TN, 25 lbs, Bemis Bros Bag Co, dog head illus, white, 25 × 13".... **15.00**

Heard's Best Flour, Raymond Heard Inc, Ruston, LA, 24 lbs, Percy Kent Bag Co, shield illus front, printed quilt block patterns back, white, 24 × 12½" **42.00**

Jockey Oats, M J Pritchard, Inc, Minneapolis, MN, 96 lbs, horse and jockey illus, white, 38 × 21" **28.00**

Merit Poultry Feed, Clark–Burkle and Co, Memphis, TN, 100 lbs, rooster, hen, and chick illus, white, 33 × 17½". **40.00**

Plowman Seed, W L Crawford Seed Co, Mayfield, KY, 1 bushel, Werthan Bag Co, Nashville, TN, farmer plowing field illus, white, 29 × 16"........ **32.00**

Purina Flock Chow, Purina Co, 100 lbs, checkerboard print, 38 × 22"...... **15.00**

Quaker Oats Poultry Feed, Quaker Oats Co, Chicago, IL, 100 lbs, chicken and clock illus, white, 38 × 18" **35.00**

Quaker Pure Cane Sugar, Pennsylvania Sugar Co, Philadelphia, PA, 10 lbs, woman wearing bonnet illus, white, copyright 1930, 16 x 9" **20.00**

Quaker Pure Cane Sugar, Pennsylvania Sugar Co, Philadelphia, PA, 5 lbs, Quaker woman in keystone, red and blue printing, white, 7¼ × 12", $18.00.

Silver Springs Salt, Worcester Salt Company, Silver Springs, NY, 100 lbs, black lettering, white, 18 × 33", $25.00.

Red Head White Corn Meal, Shreveport Grain and Elevator Co, Shreveport, LA, 25 lbs, Central Bag Co, Kansas City, MO, woodpecker and ear of corn illus, white, 26 × 13". . .   30.00

Revere Granulated Cane Sugar, Revere Sugar Refinery, Boston, MA, 10 lbs, Paul Revere illus, white, 16 × 9". . .   25.00

Sea Island Sugar, Western Sugar Refinery, San Francisco, CA, doll pattern back, white, copyright 1936, 16 × 10½" 42.00

HOMESPUN, LINENS AND DOILIES

History: Homespun is a loosely hand–woven fabric, usually of handspun linen or wool yarns. Flax was an important secondary crop on many agrarian farmsteads of the 18th and first half of the 19th century. During this period, the rural housewife often spun her own linen thread. However, once spun, the housewife took the thread to a semi–professional or professional weaver to have it woven into cloth.

The mass–production of inexpensive cloth by the 1840s and '50s meant that the rural housewife could store the spinning wheel up in the attic for good. Time devoted to spinning was rechanneled into sewing and handcrafting decorative textile pieces.

In Pennsylvania a unique textile form known as the show towel developed. These long, narrow towels of white homespun linen were gaudily decorated with colorful embroidery and drawn–thread panels. They were generally worked by adolescent girls for pastime and pleasure. They hung on the door between the sitting room and kitchen in the Pennsylvania German household.

The golden age of the show towel was between 1820 and 1850.

The literature explosion, especially in the first quarter of the 20th century, included a number of magazines devoted to sewing and needlework. The rural housewife was an eager subscriber. Among the most popular handcrafted needlework was crocheting.

Most fine crochet work was done during the period between 1850 and 1950, almost exclusively by women. Crochet is done by hand using a crochet hook and varying sizes of cotton thread. Occasionally linen or wool threads are used. The thread came in a variety of colors. The most widely used were white, cream, and ecru. Among the most popular patterns are fillet work, pineapple, and Irish.

The Country wife believed in the adage of "waste not, want not." Textiles used for one purpose were recycled for something else. The rural housewife was decades ahead of her time.

References: Maryanne Dolan, *Old Lace & Linens Including Crochet: An Identification and Value Guide,* Books Americana, 1989; Ellen J. Gehret, *This is the Way I Pass My Time: A Book about Pennsylvania German Decorated Hand Towels,* The Pennsylvania German Society, 1985.; Frances Johnson, *Collecting Antique Linens, Lace, & Needlework: Identification, Restoration, and Prices,* Wallace–Homestead, 1991.

Collectors' Club: International Old Lacers, Inc., PO Box 481223, Denver, CO 80248.

Periodical: *The Lace Collector,* PO Box 222, Plainwell, MI 49080.

Museum: The Lace Museum, Mountain View, CA.

Reproduction Craftspersons: Gabrielle & Robert Black, Jr, Black's Handweaving Shop, 497 Main St, W Barnstable, MA 02668; Nancy Borden, PO Box 4381, Portsmouth, NH 03801; Betsy Bourdon, Weaver, Scribner Hill, Wolcott, VT 05680; Elsie Carter, Carter Canopies, PO Box 808, Troutman, NC 28166; Andrea Cesari, Handweaver, PO Box 123, Nobleboro, ME 04555; Connie Sue Davenport, 1293 Goshentown Rd, Hendersonville, TN 37075; Helen Deuel, 2020 Kensington, Ocean Springs, MS 39564; Christine H Dexter, 1414 Carlton Dr, Lancaster, PA 17601; Janice L Ebert, Traditional Handweaver, 4375 S Kessler–Frederick Rd, West Milton, OH 45383; Ieva Ersts, Rosemary Hill Farm, PO Box 196, Church Hill, MD 21623; Lynn Garringer, Rte 2, Box 253, Lewisburg, WV 24901; Kathy & Bob Harman, Old Abingdon Weavers, PO Box 786, Abingdon, VA 24210; Jeanne M Henderson, Woven Concepts, 10 Chestnut Rd, Newburg, PA 17240; Maggie Kennedy, Ozark Weaving Studio, PO Box 286, Cane Hill, AR 72717; Beckie R Kiever, Cross Eyed Sheep, 3054 Canandaigua Rd, Macedon, NY 14502; David & Carole Kline, Family Heir–Loom Weavers, RD 3, Box 59E, Red Lion, PA 17356;

Thomas E Knisely, Handweaver, 1785 York Rd, Dover, PA 17315; Sandra H Lambiotte, Crabapple Woolens & Textiles, 3864 Dawley Rd, Virginia Beach, VA 23456; Ellen Leone, Plain and Fancy, RD 2, Box 450, Bristol, VT 05443; Julia A Lindsey, Lindsey Woolseys of Ohio, 275 N Main St, Germantown, OH 45327; Judy Robinson's Country Textiles, 3350 Chickencoop Hill Rd, Lancaster, OH 43130; Jacki Schell, Jacki's Handwoven Originals, RD 4, Box 352, Lewistown, PA 17044.

Reproduction Manufacturers: American Country House, PO Box 317, Davison, MI 48423; Basye–Bomberger/Fabian House, PO Box 86, W Bowie, MD 20715; Bullfrog Hollow, Keeny Rd, Lyme, CT 06371; Carole Foy's Ruffled Curtains and Accessories, 331 E Durham Rd, Cary, NC 27511; Carter Canopies, PO Box 808, Troutman, NC 28166; Checkerberry Hill, 253 Westridge Ave, Daly City, CA 94015; Country Curtains, Stockbridge, MA 01262; Country Heart Homespun Collection, Inc, 1212 Westover Hills Blvd, Box 13358, Richmond, VA 23225; The Cover Up Handweaving Studio, Rte 1, Box 216, Rabun Gap, GA 30568; Cumberland Weavers, 51 Cleversburg Rd, Shippensburg, PA 17257; Custom Crochet House Granny Square Inc, 336 Woodcrest, Sulphur Springs, TX 75482; Das Federbett, 961 Gapter Rd, Boulder, CO; Dianthus, PO Box 870, 130 Camelot Dr, Plymouth, MA 02360; Donna's Custom Hand–Made Canopies, Rte 1, Box 456, Banner Elk, NC 28604; Especially Lace, 120½ Fifth St, West Des Moines, IA 50265; The Examplarery, PO Box 2554, Dearborn, MI 48123; Five Trails Antiques and Country Accents, 116 E Water St, Circleville, OH 43113; The Flower Patch & Herbal Co, Inc, RD 2, Box 21, Mifflintown, PA 17059; Goodwin Guild Weavers, Blowing Rock Crafts, Inc, Box H–314, Blowing Rock, NC 28604; Gooseberry Patch, PO Box 634, Delaware, OH 43015; Great Coverups, 484 New Park Ave, W Hartford, CT 06110; Homespun Crafts, Box 77, Grover, NC 28073; House of Vermillion/Heirloom Quality, PO Box 18642, Kearns, UT 84118; Ingrid's Handcraft Crossroads, 8 Randall Rd, Rochester, MA 02770; Kentucky Hills Industries, Box 186, Pine Knot, KY 42635 Lace Wood 'N Tin Tyme, 6496 Summerton, Shepherd, MI 48883; Legendary Folk Art, 342 East St, Pittsford, NY 14534; Olde Mill House Shoppe, 105 Strasburg Pike, Lancaster, PA 17602; Pesta's Country Charm, 300 Standard Ave, Mingo Junction, OH 43938; South Bound Millworks, PO Box 349, Sandwich, MA 02563; Southern Manner, Inc, 106 North Trade St, PO Box 1706, Matthews, NC 28106; Sturbridge Lace Co, 559 Main St, Sturbridge, MA 01518; Traditions, RD 4, Box 191, Hudson, NY 12534; The Sugar Street Weavers, PO Box 5125, Hendersonville, NC 28793; The Vine and Cupboard, PO Box 309, George Wright Rd, Woolwich, ME 04579; *Restoration*—Mountain Shadow Studio, PO Box 619, Nederland, CO 80466.

Antimacassar, 12 × 15″, filet crochet, cream colored, reclining cat design, scrollwork around border, three pc set **35.00**
Bed Tick, homespun, blue, red, green–blue, and cream plaid, New England or PA, 19th C, 75 × 58″ **250.00**
Bread Tray Cover, 12½″ l, filet crochet, white, "Staff of Life," c1925 . . . .   **5.00**
Clothespin Apron, 16 × 18″, feed bag, floral print, rounded bottom edge   **10.00**
Clothespin Bag
  10 × 11½″, homespun, worn around waist, brown, blue, and natural white ticking stripe, hand sewn, worn tape tie **95.00**
  35 × 15″, bushel size feed bag **8.00**
Dish Towel, 38 × 18″, white textile bag, embroidered designs and day of week on each towel, set of seven   **25.00**
Doily
  8″ d, white cotton center, crocheted edging **5.00**
  18″ d, crocheted twine cotton thread, pineapple pattern **12.00**
  24 × 24″, quatrefoil shape, formed filet crochet with roses, white, late 19th C **35.00**
Hand Towel, homespun, embroidered initials, 13″ l **19.00**
Laundry Bag, 28 × 22″, cotton, printed textile bag **10.00**
Mattress Cover, homespun
  52 × 68″, blue and white plaid, white backing **150.00**
  60 × 104″, blue and white, one seam, white homespun backing, minor wear and age stains **115.00**
Napkin, 18 × 19½″, homespun, blue and white, hand sewn hem **55.00**
Pillow Case
  17 × 28″, white 25 lb flour bag, pr   **15.00**
  19½ × 33″, pieced, red and white, pr   **55.00**
  21 × 32″, homespun, blue and white   **40.00**
  21 × 35″, white muslin, 3″ crocheted and tatted edging, unused, pr **22.00**

Dish Towel, embroidered, stamped design of boy chef with hatchet and utensils, peeking at duck and chicken, 17 × 25″, $4.00.

Doily, white cotton center, crocheted floral border, 13" d, $10.00.

Doily, crocheted, white cotton thread, eight-sided star shape with three-dimensional stuffed swans at each point, 21½" w, 4" h swans, $25.00.

30 × 30", woven, red, blue, and white plaid, machine sewn, button closure	65.00
Pot Holder, 8" sq, white textile bag, embroidered, face on flower surrounded by leaves	4.00
Sheet	
54 × 40", crib size, cotton textile bags, white . . . ., ...	10.00
64 × 92", homespun, two pc, hand sewn seam and hem, ink corner signatures	40.00
68 × 92½", homespun, embroidered initials	65.00
76 × 100", homespun linen, two pc, hand hemmed, Ephrata, PA	45.00
77 × 78", cotton homespun, two piece, center seam, hand sewn hem	65.00
80 × 90", homespun, two pc, hand sewn hems and seams, red embroidered initials	65.00
Sheet Set, sheet and pillow case, homespun linen, embroidered, strawberry motif, sgd "Ann Eliza Chubb No. 3," red and blue, initialed pillow case	35.00
Show Towel	
10 × 10", homespun, cross stitch and cut work, tied fringe, gray and several shades of brown embroidery floss, fringe, framed	475.00
13½ × 51", homespun, linen and cotton cutwork, floral embroidery, sgd "C.L.," minor stains	100.00
15 × 60", linen, pink embroidered stars, flowerheads, birds, reindeer, dogs, potted flowering shrubs, zigzag crochet panel, fringed bottom, sgd "Anna Marie Nies, 1816" . . .	350.00
17 × 54", homespun, simple floral embroidery	75.00
18½ × 51", white, pink embroidered stars, pots of flowers, and two chairs, sgd "Lea Sartham 1834," fringed bottom	195.00
Tablecloth	
Drawnwork, white	30.00
Embroidered, Scotty dogs, red and white, 1937, 50 × 70"	50.00

Homespun	
33 × 52", blue and white plaid check, minor stains, small holes	85.00
38 × 71", white on white	35.00
39 × 55", linen, gold and white check, unhemmed	125.00
40 × 60", blue and white check, machine woven, hand sewn hem one end, unhemmed other end	55.00
54 × 76", two piece, gold and white plaid, hand sewn hem one edge, basted selvage other	125.00
58 × 72", two piece, cotton and linen, white, woven diamond design, center seam	25.00
60 × 74", two piece, white on white design, red embroidered initials and date "1862," hand sewn seam	25.00
60 × 76", two piece, blue and white plaid, off center seam, hand sewn hem	165.00
76 × 116", linen, cutwork and filet lace inserts, twelve matching napkins	310.00
Table Runner, homespun linen, natural, brown pinstripe, two pc, hand sewn seam, hand hemmed, embroidered initials, stains, 66 × 85"	45.00
Ticking	
Cotton	
Blue and white plaid, New England, 19th C	100.00
Light blue, red, green, and cream plaid, PA, 19th C	125.00
Linen	
Blue and cream, plain weave, PA, 19th C	90.00
Butternut and cream check, partial initials, New England, 19th C	120.00
Towel, homespun	
11½ × 32", natural linen, natural and white embroidery	20.00
13½ × 40", natural linen, coarsely woven, hand sewn hem	20.00

14 × 39", linen, red embroidered
    initials, hand hemmed **7.50**
14½ × 44½", blue and white, hang-
    ing loops, hand hemmed **60.00**
15 × 39", woven diamond pattern,
    red embroidered initials, hand
    hemmed, hanging tabs **30.00**
16 × 46", brown embroidered in-
    itials, hand sewn hem, tab hanger   **15.00**
16½ × 51", woven overshot bands,
    red embroidered initials "B.M."   **25.00**
17 × 26", brown and white check,
    three sides hand hemmed, wear,
    small holes and thin spots **65.00**
17 × 52", red initials and date "1851"
    on white, tab hanger **30.00**
18 × 56", white on white design, tab
    hanger.   **12.00**

NEEDLEWORK AND SAMPLERS

History: Finding time to do needlework in rural America was a luxury. It was an art form that was centered along the eastern seaboard, primarily in urban areas. Needlework is found in many forms: clothing, embroidered pictures, fire screens, pocketbooks, samplers, and seat coverings.

Country collectors and decorators have romanticized needlework. They have formulated an idyllic image of a woman sitting in front of a blazing fireplace at the end of day, happily doing needlework as a means of relaxation. If this were true, tens of thousands more examples would have survived. Executing a needlework picture was time consuming and required great skill. Few were trained and capable of doing it.

English needlework has flooded the American market. The following clues will help you distinguish American examples from their English counterparts. Identify the maker and check vital statistic records in the region of the needlework's origins. Do not rely on town names. Many English and American town names are identical. By 1750 American needlework was more naturalistic in style and often contained a greater variety of stitches than its English counterpart. British samplers are usually more balanced and possess brighter colors because of better dyes. By 1800 Americans favored the pictorial approach to the more formal, horizontal band style. When doubt exists, assume the piece is English.

Samplers, a needlework form, served many purposes. For a young child they were a practice exercise and permanent reminder of stitches and patterns. For a young woman they demonstrated her skills in a "gentle" art and preserved key elements of family genealogy. For the mature woman they were a useful occupation and functioned as gifts or remembrances, e.g., mourning pieces.

Schools for young ladies of the early 19th century prided themselves on the needlework skills they taught. The Westtown School in Chester County, Pennsylvania, and the Young Ladies Seminary in Bethlehem, Pennsylvania, are two examples. These schools changed their teaching as styles changed. Berlin work was introduced by the mid-19th century.

Examples of samplers date back to the 1700s. The earliest ones were long and narrow, usually done only with the alphabet and numerals. Later examples were square. At the end of the 19th century, the shape tended to be rectangular.

The same motifs were used throughout the country. The name is a key element in determining the region. Samplers are assumed to be on linen unless otherwise indicated.

References: Tandy and Charles Hersh, *Samplers of the Pennsylvania Germans*, The Pennsylvania German Society, 1991; Glee Krueger, *A Gallery of American Samplers: The Theodore H. Kapnek Collection*, Bonanza Books, 1984 edition; Betty Ring, *American Needlework Treasures; Samplers and Silk Embroideries From The Collection of Betty Ring*, E. P. Dutton, 1987; Anne Sebba, *Samplers: Five Centuries of a Gentle Craft*, Thames and Hudson, 1979.

Collectors' Club: Stumpwork Society, PO Box 122, Bogota, NJ 07603.

Reproduction Craftspersons: *Samplers*—Liz Chronister & Kathleen Brock, Country Baskets and Collectables, RD 2, Dillsburg, PA 17019; Virginia Colby, Samplers by Virginia Colby, 205 Richmond Ave, Amityville, NY 11701; Elizabeth Creeden, The Sampler, 12 N Park Ave, Plymouth, MA 02360; Susan R Diefenderfer, 12 Esther Circle, Sinking Spring, PA 19608; Jean Hipp, Kitnit Needlecrafts, 20 Valley Rd, Neffsville, PA 17601; Kathleen Hoffman, Ramsgate Limited, 1269 Harbor Cut, Okemos, MI 48864; Terry W Rose, 8510 N Knoxville, Suite 205, Peoria, IL 61615; Alyce Schroth, Sampler Recreations, 3598 Buttonwood Dr, Doylestown, PA 18901; Elizabeth Thompson, 414 Storck Rd, Hartwood, VA 22406.

Reproduction Manufacturers: *Kits, Patterns, and Supplies*—Dawn Bradford, Sheepish Design, 15120 Huntersville Concord Rd, Huntersville, NC 20878; The Examplarery, PO Box 2554, Dearborn, MI 48123; Folk Art Emporium, 3591 Forest Haven Ln, Chesapeake, VA 23321; Ginny's Stitchins, 106 Braddock Rd, Williamsburg, VA 23185; Mill Pond Designs, PO Box 390, East Longmeadow, MA 01028; Mini–Magic, 3675 Reed Rd, Columbus, OH 43220; Darlene O'Steen, Needles Prayse, 7330 Chapel Hill Rd, Suite 109, Raleigh, NC 27607; Ramsgate Limited, PO Box 143, Okemos, MI 48864; Lydia Reed, Wyndham Needleworks, Box 65, 233 Old Colony Road, Eastford CT 06242; Schoolroom Samplers, Box 227, 3 Brookhollow Drive, Gladstone, NJ

07934; Nancy Sturgis, Threads Thru Time, 450 Bedford Court, Naperville, IL 60540; T & N Designs, Inc, 901 Brookshire Dr, Evansville, IN 47715; *Restoration*—Mountain Shadow Studio, PO Box 619, Nederland, CO 80466; *Samplers*—The Americana Collection, 29 W 38th St, New York, NY 10018; Pure and Simple, PO Box 535, 117 W Hempstead, Nashville, AR 71852; Ramsgate Limited, PO Box 143, Okemos, MI 48864.

Birth Record, 15 × 16½" homespun, blue and white, alphabets and inscription "Clara Goodale of Deering was born March 16th, year 1806," framed **1,325.00**

Family Record
1828, 17¾ × 17½", MA, silk threads, black names, dates, and inscription within arch, green, yellow, and cream floral border, sgd "Wrought by Mary E. Adams aged 10 yrs.".................. **1,210.00**
1835, silk threads, shades of blue, green, gold, cream, and black, Daniel and Deborah Moulton Family, ME, dated "June 9, 1835," list of twelve children's births enclosed by stylized meandering floral border, framed **775.00**

Memorial
c1800, 8 × 9⅜", silk picture, classical figure mourns before monument dedicated to George Washington, backboard labeled "John Gibbs, Portsmouth," framed **1,100.00**
1805, West Springfield, MA, silk ground, silk threads and paint, printed inscription "sacred to

Family Record, Mary E. Adams, Massachussetts, c1825, silk threads, green, yellow, black, and cream, 17½ × 17¾", $1,210.00. Photograph courtesy of Skinner, Inc.

memory of Abigail E. Stearns, died Nov. 2, 1798, aged 11 weeks," woman standing, one arm on monument, other around willow tree, splits, fiber loss to inscription **475.00**
1807, 20½ × 20¾", Roxbury, MA, silk ground, silk threads and paint, monument inscribed "Sacred to the memory of Mrs. Rebecca Sumner, obit November 13th 1805, age 40, this monument is inscribed by her affectionate daughter Marta Sumner," urn inscribed "Marta Sumner obit Ap 30th 1807, age 22, cut off in her bloom," woman seated by monument, large willow tree in background, framed **1,100.00**
1809, 20½ × 24½", Hartford, CT, silk ground, paint, chenille, and silk threads, gold, green, and umber gold, angel walking across fallen tree used as narrow bridge, old man and rocky landscape, eglomise mat inscribed "L. A. Merrick but scarce his speech began when the strange partner seem'd no longer Man," framed, paper label on back inscribed with provenance **600.00**
c1810, 11¼ × 11¼", silk ground, polychrome silk threads and sequins, central memorial vignette with figure of mourning gentleman, undulating rose vine border, framed..................... **165.00**
1815, 23½ × 29½", silk ground, silk, chenille, and paint, monument inscribed "in memory of Catherine Pruyn who died Feb. 17th 1788, aged 50 years, in memory of Sarah Lansing who died April 23, 1788, aged 44 years, 5 mo and 9 days," orig frame, good color, splits **250.00**
1821, 26¼ × 28½", Frances E Owen, Leicester/Worcester, MA, silk ground, silk and chenille threads, painted details, green, blue–green, gold, yellow, and cream, calligraphic inscription on monument "Sacred to the memory of Charles More, obit. September 11, 1798, aged 37 years, also the memories of Lydia More, obit. November 2, 1821, aged 75 years," eglomise and inscribed mat, framed...... **3,850.00**
Hooked Yarn Panel, 19 × 17", sailboat **60.00**
Needlepoint Panel
30 × 26¾", wool on canvas, girl and two dogs in flowering garden, "Catharine Galbraith Busby, Aged 11," soft colors, stained canvas, rosewood frame with gilt liner... **435.00**

Needlepoint Picture, Sarah S. L. Padelford, the Balch School, Providence, RI, 1786, satin weave silk ground, blue, green, red, pink, gold, and cream silk threads, framed, paper label affixed to back with dates and provenance, $1,320.00. Photograph courtesy of Skinner, Inc.

33¾ × 27¼", child and dog, faded reds, white, blue, and browns, olive ground, damage and taped repair **45.00**
Needlework Picture, early 19th C, 13¾ × 15¾", silk ground, silk threads, paint, and velvet, yellow, green, blue, and bittersweet, "Shepherdess," attributed to school of Abby Wright, South Hadley, MA, inscribed, reverse painted mat, framed **4,950.00**
Sampler
    1788, 14½ × 18½", cotton homespun, silk stitches, soft colors, inner floral wreath encircling verse, stylized trees, buildings, birds, and vining border, "Elisa Chapman 9 years old work'd May 1788," gilt frame.   **475.00**
    1793, 9½ × 13½", linen homespun, silk threads, gold, green, and gray, alphabets, numerals, crows, trees, birds, and inscription "Mary Steel in the 6th year of her age 1793," framed. **1,100.00**
    1796
        7½ × 11½", linen ground, silk threads, pink, green, and cream, rows of alphabets, zig-zag border, trees, figures, and "Elizabeth Stone was born in Danvers Janury (sic) 30th worked this in the 10th year of her age 1796" **3,100.00**
        12½ × 13¾", MA, silk threads, green, pink, cream, umber, blue, and black, "Polly Wilde Sampler Wrought in Salem,

June 1796," and further inscribed "Massachusetts State Salem . . .," rows of alphabets, middle section of two floral urns, center lion, lower section of two seated facing ladies, trees, birds, florals, and animals, two inner borders of pyramid shaped devices, framed **8,800.00**
    1797, 12 × 15¼", linen ground, silk threads, blue, green, yellow, and beige, rows of alphabets and inscription "Sally Whitneys Sampler Worked in the eleventh year of her age AD 1797" above tree and flowers, geometric borders. **1,750.00**
    1798, 7 × 10", MA, silk threads, pink, green, yellow, and burnt umber, "Lydia Ashleys sampler, aged eleven years, worked September 1798," some color loss, framed   **1,045.00**
    1799, 14½ × 17½" MA, linen–woolsey ground, pink, blue, and cream, green ground, rows of alphabets, flowering border, floral urns, "Wrought by Elizabeth Somerby aged 8 years, 1799," repairs **3,300.00**
    1802, 13¼ × 15½", linen homespun, silk and wool threads, red, pink, shades of green, blue, white, and gold, alphabet, rows of trees, flowers, strawberries, birds, and "June Potter, Dec The 7th 1802, aged 8 years," some wear, stains, small holes **450.00**
    1808, 15½ × 16", linen ground, silk threads, shades of cream, central panel enclosed by floral and cor-

Sampler, Elizabeth Scott Fulton, 1799, silk threads, shades of green, yellow, brown, red, and cream, linen ground, 12¾ × 17¾", estimated price $1,200.00–1,500.00. Photograph courtesy of Skinner, Inc.

nucopia border, inscribed "Lois Newhall aged 12 years Lynn 2nd day September 1808," framed . . . **600.00**

1810, 6½ × 10¼", linen ground, silk threads, green, gold, red, and blue, "MP" (for Mary Perry), unframed . **325.00**

1812, 12¾ × 18", linen homespun, silk threads, green, blue, gold, black, and white, vining border, verse, pots of flowers, conical tree, "Ann Wild, Aged nine years, Decr. 1812," dark stains, bleeding of black floss, framed **300.00**

1817
12½ × 14", linen ground, green silk thread, bands of alphabet and verse over inscription, "Louisa Perkins at Miss Williams School, Boston, June 18th, 1817," some discoloration, bleeding, unframed **450.00**

12¾ × 17", linen homespun, intricate silk stitches, brown, gold, green, white, black, and light blue, vining border, verse, cottage, barn, farm, people, and wild animals, "Mary Ann Jewell finished this work, April 24th, 1817 at Mrs. Venthams Boarding School, Winton, Aged — Years," framed **1,595.00**

1820
16¼ × 17¼", linen ground, blue, green, and yellow, alphabet and verse, floral and vine border, "Worked by Olive Handley, aged 11 years, 1820," discoloration, fading, framed **1,100.00**

17½ × 17¾", New England, linen ground, silk threads, blue, green, pink, yellow, coral, cream, and black, "Abigail E. Read," paper label on reverse inscribed "Daughter of George and Abigail, sister of Elisa T. Read. Abigail E. Read born August 2, 1814, died January 28, 1881," framed **5,500.00**

18 × 21½", Anna Meck, linen homespun, silk stitches, red, blue, sage, and black, alphabets, stylized flowers, animals, and people, poplar frame **325.00**

1823
9¼ × 11⅜", linen homespun, silk threads, beige, olive, blue, and black, alphabets, trees, dogs, teapots, "Eunice Ewing 1823," faded colors, framed **300.00**

11 × 18¼", dark homespun linen, silk stitches, alphabets, geometric designs, stylized animals,

trees, flowers, and inscription "Ann Thomas her work in the 13th year of her age 1823," framed **1,000.00**

15 × 15½", linen homespun, silk threads, pink, olive, ivory, gray, green, and gold, flowering border, verse, birds, angels, flowers, and "Catharine Foster, Aged 12, 1823," some moth damage, orig molded black frame **700.00**

1825
21¼ × 28", homespun linen, alphabets, stylized pots of strawberry like flowers, "Catherine Kellar worked this in the twelve year of her age 1825," matted, gilt frame **245.00**

23½ × 27½", Chester County, PA, natural linen and green gauze ground, silk threads, blue, green, yellow, cream, and peach, quilted silk ribbon trim, corner rosettes, framed, minor fiber loss **8,800.00**

1826, 14¼ × 11", linen homespun, silk threads, shades of blue, beige, green, black, and white, alphabets, stylized trees, flowers, birds, animals, verse, and "Mary Spencer worked this sampler in Anno Do Mini 1826, aged 8 years," minor stains, fading, minor floss loss, framed **1,200.00**

1827, 17 × 23½", dark linen homespun, silk stitches, green, pink, white, and blue, alphabets, verse, baskets of flowers, strawberry border, "Sarah Hunts sampler Age 15 years, Waterford, May the 31, 1827," unframed **1,100.00**

1828
11½ × 13½", homespun, silk and linen threads, green, tan, yellow, white, black, and beige, vining floral border, rows of alphabets, stylized flowers and birds with verse, "Mary Ann Smith aged 7 Y 7 M, Sept. 2nd 1828," stains and some fading, matted and framed **500.00**

22¾ × 23¼", Elizabeth Lyndall, homespun, flowering vine border, butterflies, birds, flowers, and verse "Gratitude," stains, faded colors, possibly Quaker, framed **900.00**

1830, 15 × 24", Margaret Jane Morice, Sackville, NJ, linen, alphabets, numerals, verse, flowers, insects, birds, and beasts **495.00**

1834, multicolored silk stitches, alphabets, numbers, house, trees, vining border, and inscription "Jane D Baillie, Miss McCallum's School, Oban, in the year 1834," framed. **1,150.00**

1835, 16 × 21½", linen homespun, silk threads, shades of red, pink, orange, green, light blue, brown, and black, flowering border, baskets of flowers, animals, crowns, verse, and "Thomasin Lenn, aged 10 years 1835," wear, stains, damage to one border, modern frame **225.00**

1836, 13½ × 13½", homespun, silk stitches, brown, green, and gold, alphabets, flowers, building, birds, acorn border, verse, and inscription "Emma Webber Aged Twelve 1836," framed. **750.00**

1837, 17¾ × 19¼", linen homespun, silk threads, side by side design with rows of alphabets and numerals on left half, right side with memorial to Sidney J Gregory, verse, stylized people, trees, and church scene of Sidney ascending to heaven, "Wealthy A. Gregory, Aged 12 years, 1837," attributed to Pembrook, MA, minor stains, framed. **1,250.00**

1838, 17¾ × 16⅝", silk threads, shades of blue, green, yellow, and bittersweet, rows of alphabets, verse, and inscription "Wrought by Mary H. Parker Aged 11 Waltham Dec. 22, 1838," floral border, minor fading, framed. . . . **1,325.00**

1839, 10¾ × 17", linen homespun, silk threads, red, shades of green, and white, alphabets, verse, trees, flowers, animals, and inscription "Cecilia Patersons work 1839" **495.00**

1842

10½ × 15¼", natural linen homespun, silk stitches, blue, green, red, black, and pink, alphabets, birds, heart, and vining border, "Emma Ann Gould, age 8 years 1842," stapled to cardboard, unframed. **610.00**

15¼ × 18¼", MA, silk threads, pink, green, blue, yellow, brown, and black, "Wrought by Charlotte Chapin in the 12th year of her age 1842," foxing to ground, some discoloration . . . **1,540.00**

1845, 12⅝ × 17¼", dark linen homespun, silk threads, shades of green, brown, gold, and blue, vining strawberry border, stylized Adam and Eve, church, windmill,

Sampler, Lillie S. A. Beddall, dated 1862, cross-stitched, homespun linen, 20½ × 16", $500.00.

angels, flowers, animals, trees, and "Ellen Sullivan, her work age 11 years, 1845," small holes, brown marker used to highlight some designs, modern frame **700.00**

1853, 16¼ × 16¼", homespun linen, silk threads, small precise stitches, rows of alphabets, numbers, flowers, deer, and wreath with date, stains, small holes, puckered linen, pine frame **475.00**

1860, 15 × 17½", homespun, silk stitches, green, brown, gold, and red, baskets of flowers, floral bouquets, and vining floral border, "Harriet Adams, March 13, 1860," beveled bird's eye veneer frame . **475.00**

1876, 15¾ × 16¾", linen ground, wool stitches, vining border, alphabets, flowers, verse, and "Mary Margret Callishaw '76," matted, framed. **275.00**

Undated

6⅛ × 7⅝", linen homespun, multicolored silk threads, rows of alphabets and numbers, some fading, reds and blues bright, some missing floss, framed. . . . **215.00**

9⅜ × 13¼", attributed to Hollowell, ME, natural linen homespun, silk threads, shades of brown, green, blue, red, yellow, and white, vining strawberry border, rows of alphabets and numerals, vase of flowers, butterfly and bird, variety of embroidery stitches, framed **1,350.00**

11 × 13", linen homespun, silk and wool threads, rows of alphabets above single row of stylized flowers. **250.00**

11¼ × 25", linen homespun, blue, green, and lavender, two stylized floral banners, matted and framed **75.00**

Sampler, Ann Young, Waldoboro, ME, linen ground, silk threads, blue, green, yellow, beige, and black silk threads, framed, 16½ × 21¾", $1,540.00. Photograph courtesy of Skinner, Inc.

12¼ × 15⅞", linen homespun, wool stitching, alphabets, numerals, house, animals, flowers, and "Ann Frith, aged 9 years," linen slightly puckered, minor wear, small holes, some stitches missing, beveled walnut frame   **825.00**

14¼ × 14¾", Elizabeth Smith, wool homespun, silk threads, shades of brown, green, gold, and white, small precise stitches, vining floral border, stylized birds, trees, flowers, spotted dog, windmill, verse and name, small hole in upper right, modern frame **1,000.00**

18⅝ × 20", linen homespun, silk threads, blue–green, beige, and white, rows of alphabets in several different stitches, beige stitched "Lucy P. Sewall, Age 9 years", satin stitch floral border, minor stains, attributed to ME, modern frame **700.00**

QUILTS

History: In the agrarian household a quilt combined beauty with function. Most were not showpieces; they were meant to be used. Quilts varied in weight. It was customary to change quilts with the season.

The quilting bee, a group of women working together to quilt a pieced top to its backing, was an important form of social interaction. Almost every rural farmstead, especially in the nineteenth century, had a quilting frame set up in a room corner. When another woman came to call, it was common for them to spend some time talking over the quilting frame.

Quilts have been passed down as family heirlooms for many generations. Each is an individual expression. The same pattern may have hundreds of variations in both color and design.

The advent of the sewing machine increased, not decreased the number of quilts being made. Quilts are still being sewn today.

The key considerations for price are age, condition, aesthetic beauty, and design. Prices are now at a level position. The exceptions are the very finest examples which continue to bring record prices.

References: Suzy Anderson, *Collector's Guide to Quilts*, Wallace–Homestead, 1991; American Quilter's Society, *Gallery of American Quilts, 1849–1988*, Collector Books, 1988; Cuesta Benberry, *Always There: The African–American Presence in American Quilts*, The Kentucky Quilt Project, 1992; Barbara Brackman, *Clues in the Calico: A Guide To Identifying and Dating Antique Quilts*, EPM Publications, 1989; Barbara Brackman, *Encyclopedia of Pieced Patterns*, Prairie Flower Publications, 1984; Liz Greenbacker and Kathleen Barach, *Quilts: Identification and Price Guide*, Avon Books, 1992; Schnuppe von Gwinner, *The History of the Patchwork Quilt*, Schiffer Publishing, 1988; Carter Houck, *The Quilt Encyclopecia Illustrated*, Harry N. Abrams and The Museum of American Folk Art, 1991; William C. Ketchum, Jr., *The Knopf Collectors' Guides to American Antiques: Quilts*, Alfred A. Knopf, 1982; Jean Ray Laury and California Heritage Quilt Project, *Ho For California: Pioneer Women and Their Quilts*, E. P. Dutton, 1990; Lisa Turner Oshins, *Quilt Collections: A Directory For The United States And Canada*, Acropolis Books, Ltd., 1987; Rachel and Kenneth Pellman, *The World of Amish Quilts*, Good Books, 1984; Carleton L Safford and Robert Bishop, *America's Quilts and Coverlets*, Bonanza Books, 1985.

Collectors' Clubs: The American Quilter's Society, PO Box 3290, Paducah, KY 42002; The National Quilting Association, Inc., PO Box 393, Ellicott City, MD 21043.

Periodicals: *Quilter's Newsletter Magazine*, Box 394, Wheat Ridge, CO 80033; *Vintage Quilt Newsletter*, PO Box 744, Great Bend, TX 67530.

Reproduction Craftspersons: June Blackburn, 4148 S Norfolk Ave, Tulsa, OK 74105; Arlinka Blair, 2301 N Grant Ave, Wilmington, DE 19803; Jane Blair, 504 Dogwood Ln, Conshohocken, PA 19428; Sherri Dunbar, 105 Hewett Rd, Wyncote, PA 19095; Molly Fish, The Garden Patch, 1228 N W Dixon St, Corvallis, OR 97330; Jo Morton, Prairie Hands, 1801 Central Ave, Nebraska City, NE 68410; R C Pirrone, 107 E Chestnut St, West Chester, PA 19380.

Reproduction Manufacturers: *Amish*—Amish Country Collection, RD 5, Sunset Valley Rd, New Castle, PA 16105; Pure and Simple, PO Box 535, 117 W Hempstead, Nashville, AR 71852; *Baby*—The Roos Collection, PO Box 20668, New York, NY 10025; *General*—Apple Tree Quilts, Box 335–E, Berlin, OH 44610; Basye–Bomberger/Fabian House, PO Box 86, W Bowie, MD 20715; Calico Expressions, 1350 Dorset St, South Burlington, VT 05403; Cooper Hill Quiltworks, PO Box 345, Johnson, VT 05656; Country Loft, 1506 South Shore Park, Hingham, MA 02043; Donna's Custom Hand–Made Canopies, Rte 1, Box 456, Banner Elk, NC 28604; Faith Mountain Country Fare, Main St, Box 199, Sperryville, VA 22740; Gooseberry Patch, PO Box 634, Delaware, OH 43015; Great Expectations Quilts, 155 Town & Country Village, Houston, TX 77024; Hands All Around, Inc, 971 Lexington Ave, New York, NY 10021; Hearthside Quilts, Box 429, Rte 7, Shelburne, VT 05482; Judy's of Cape Cod, PO Box 677, Osterville, MA 02655; Kate Adams Designs, PO Box 3025, Kennebunkport, ME 04046; Patricia du Pont, Country Folk Inc, 18 Rocky Point Rd, Rowayton, CT 06853; Quilted Selections, Rte 1, Box 137, Luthersville, GA 30251; The Quiltery, Box 337, RD 4, Boyertown, PA 19512; Quilts Unlimited, 124 W Washington, PO Box 1210, Lewisburg, WV 24901; Strunk, Box 77, Main St, Virginville, PA 19564; *Kit*—Cotton Exchange, 105 Silverwood Ln, Cary, NC 27511; Folk Art Emporium, 3591 Forest Haven Ln, Chesapeake, VA 23321; Hearthside Quilts, Box 429, Rte 7, Shelburne, VT 05482; Judy's of Cape Cod, PO Box 677, Osterville, MA 02655; *Restoration*—Mountain Shadow Studio, PO Box 619, Nederland, CO 80466; *Quilt Stencils*—Olde Mill House Shoppe, 105 Strasburg Pike, Lancaster, PA 17602.

Album, 76 × 76″, appliqued, sixteen different stylized designs including flowers, eagle, heart, hands, wreaths, and arrows, embroidered highlights, red, green, and yellow calico, white ground, minor stains **875.00**
American Shield, 75 × 84″, pieced, stars and stripe border, c1885 . . . . . **1,100.00**
Amish
  Crosses and Losses, 79 × 90″, pieced, white and lavender, blue–green ground, Mary Ann Miller, Holmes County, OH, c1935 . . . . **425.00**
  Four Point Star, 75 × 88″, pieced, gray, red, and orange, colors faded, some overall and edge wear **225.00**
  Geometric design, 64½ × 75½″, pieced, black and burgundy red, c1925 . . . . **750.00**
  Monkey Wrench, 106 × 119″, pieced, green, medium blue, and maroon, machine sewn binding,

Album Quilt Top, pieced and appliqued, green, red, and blue patches, white ground, sixteen square panels of flowers and foliage, swag and bow border, 19th C, 98 × 98″, $1,540.00. Photograph courtesy of Butterfield & Butterfield.

  rest hand sewn, minor small stains, Indiana, c1975 . . . . **225.00**
Stripes, 85 × 87″, pieced, bright color stripes, three quilting patterns, red and yellow calico bar back **1,300.00**
Baskets, 82 × 82″, pieced, 25 baskets, single stripe border, orange, white ground, machine sewn binding **100.00**
Calimanco, 84 × 90″, glazed worsted fabric, pink center, navy blue borders, geometric and floral quilted pattern, gold linsey woolsey backing with gold and blue stripes, cutouts for bed posts, very worn, damage and repairs **925.00**
Carolina Lily, 71 × 71″, pieced, red and blue, white ground, hand sewn design, machine sewn appliqued stems, wear and stains **200.00**
Centennial Exposition, 86 × 82″, tied, printed cotton, repeating scenic vignettes, some fiber loss, patches, and discoloration **495.00**
Checkerboard, 30 × 32″, pieced, red and black print, hand pieced, machine quilted, worn, small holes . . . **45.00**
Chintz, 88 × 92″, brown floral print with red, blue, green, and yellow patches, brown ground, stains, wear, small holes and tears **425.00**
Crazy, pieced and embroidered
  60 × 72″, painted and printed silk, satin, and velvet, some with Kate Greenaway type designs, sgd and dated "E.Y. 1883," some discoloration to painted patches **450.00**

66 × 54", satin and velvet, c1880 **425.00**
68 × 68, silk, satin, and velvet, embroidered flowers, peacocks, fans, and "Lizzie M. Bradley 1884"... **1,425.00**
Crosses, 72 × 85", pieced, stylized crosses, green, red, and navy blue calico, white and black print ground **225.00**
Drunkard's Path, 84 × 96", pieced, blue, brown, and mustard, machine pieced, hand quilted, one corner marked "Rocky Road to Doublin (sic) 1971"...................... **165.00**
Eight Point Star
  29½ × 30", pieced, five red and white stars, white ground, red and white borders, machine sewn, crib size, worn.................. **80.00**
  86 × 100", pieced and appliqued, swags with buds border, blue and white print, white ground, feather quilted circles, minor wear...... **1,500.00**
Flag, 72½ × 83", pieced, pattern, red, white, blue, brown, and green, c1910...................... **850.00**
Floral
  36½ × 38½", appliqued, center stylized floral medallion, red and green calico, yellow center, feather quilting, crib size....... **700.00**
  44 × 69", appliqued, fifteen red and green stylized flowers, red swag border, white ground, youth size **800.00**
  66 × 90", appliqued, four white diamonds in red square with stylized floral design centers, green, red, and yellow, blue and white edge stripes, visible quilting pattern... **110.00**
  67 × 76", appliqued, nine stylized floral medallions, stripe border, teal green, red, and goldenrod, white ground, quilted designs have an almost trapunto appearance, stains, very minor color loss in some yellows............ **450.00**
  72 × 84", appliqued, bold stylized flowers, red, teal blue, goldenrod, and pink calico, machine sewn appliques, hand quilting, made by Margaret Holloway, central MO, c1870, small stains and repair... **1,100.00**
  76 × 98", appliqued, twelve stylized floral medallions, leafy vining border, red, yellow, and green calico, green calico border, white ground, stains..................... **500.00**
  77 × 80", pieced and appliqued, nine stylized flowers, three stripe border, red and white, slightly faded..................... **175.00**
  79 × 81", appliqued, green, red, and goldenrod stylized flowers, white ground.................. **775.00**

84 × 84", appliqued, four large scalloped edged flowers, border fans, beige, goldenrod, and red, white ground, goldenrod binding, stains, some fading............... **650.00**
84 × 101", appliqued, red and green calico stylized floral medallions, white ground, scalloped edges, 20th C.................... **450.00**
86 × 88", appliqued, four large flowers, border swags with buds, red and green, goldenrod flower centers, worn and faded......... **300.00**
86 × 102", appliqued, nine floral medallions, vining floral border, floral print green, red, yellow, and maroon, pink calico, solid red, white ground, stains, 86 × 102" **2,975.00**
92 × 92", appliqued, twenty-five stylized stemmed flowers, stylized vintage border with vine and grape bunches, red, green, and goldenrod solids and pink calico flowers, blue and red border, well quilted, stains, wear, reds have small holes **375.00**
95 × 100", pieced, seventy-two stylized flowers in rows, red and teal–blue print, red leaf borders, white ground, beautifully quilted, stains **650.00**
Flower Baskets, 82 × 82", appliqued and pieced, green and pink calico, goldenrod flower centers, pink calico borders, overall wear, light stains **425.00**
Four Patch, 67 × 76", pieced, diagonal rows of blue and beige calico squares, white ground, very worn **85.00**

Hawaiian, appliqued, cotton, red and white, radiating stylized scrolling foliate tree-form motif, alternating red and white applied border, stamped "St Elmo," late 19th/early 20th C, 78¾ × 77½", estimated price $2,000.00–5,000.00. Photograph courtesy of Butterfield & Butterfield.

Four Patch and Block, 88 × 96", pieced, center design of printed patches arranged in four patch and block pattern, border with polychrome chintz patches arranged in palm trees and birds pattern, mid 19th C **400.00**

Friendship, 69 × 81", pieced, wool and other fabrics, circular designs, embroidery and names of makers, dated 1916, made at Crown Hill Mennonite Church, Orrville, OH, minor wear and small stains **325.00**

Irish Chain
75 × 76", pieced, three stripe border, beige, tan, red, goldenrod, and white, made by Myra Ellis, Crystal Springs, MS, 1894, small repairs **300.00**
78 × 79", pieced, flying geese border, red and white, worn, stained, holes and fading to red patches **175.00**
82 × 85", pieced and appliqued, printed cotton red, mustard, and green patches, leaf medallion pattern enclosed by swag and tassel border, conforming diamond and parallel line quilting **475.00**

Linsey Woolsey, 86 × 101", salmon red one side, gold other side, quilted floral pattern with meandering foliage design, wear, fading, old repairs, corners cutout for bed posts **275.00**

Log Cabin
Center Medallion, 70 × 71", pieced, four patch, brightly colored prints and solids, some wear **275.00**
Sunshine and Shadow, 76 × 89", pieced, multicolored prints and solid red, purchased in Osage City, KS, machine sewn binding, overall wear **375.00**

Lone Star
70 × 77", appliqued and pieced, star surrounded by sunburst circles, solid green, red and green calico, wear, stains **175.00**
76 × 74", pieced, brightly colored solids, pale blue calico ground, red binding, green calico backing, stains **1,100.00**
78 × 88", pieced, red, navy, and teal blue patches, goldenrod ground, pencil quilt pattern intact, made by Mary Green Knietzing, Louisville, KY, 1922, machine sewn binding **625.00**
90 × 90", pieced, multicolored patches, white ground **190.00**

Mennonite, Lancaster County, PA
Grid pattern, 83 × 84", pieced, multicolored prints and pink calico, green calico border, white sawtooth binding. **600.00**

Weathervane pattern, 78 × 82", pieced, pale green and blue print and red and white polka dot patches, white ground, solid green border stripe, blue and white check backing, wreath and geometric quilting, attributed to Mrs Clarence Hooley **1,200.00**

Miniature Nine Patch, 78 × 98", pieced, multicolored prints, yellow sawtooth border, overall wear, stains. **95.00**

Monkey Wrench, 68 × 84", pieced, multicolored, tan sateen border stripes **400.00**

Optical Triangles, 68 × 75", pieced, red and white, star quilting, c1875 . . . . **425.00**

Philadelphia Pavement, 74 × 77", pieced, multicolored prints, calico, and white, from Chesapeake Bay area, machine sewn binding, some stains and minor wear **375.00**

Pine Tree, 92 × 110", four patch, pieced, green calico, white ground **725.00**

Pinwheel, 45 × 52", nine patch, pieced, white and green, red ground, wear, stains, colors faded **55.00**

Pinwheel Stars, 70 × 82", pieced, sawtooth border, green calico, yellow, green, and brown, white ground, pronounced diagonal bands of feather quilted trapunto work, color fading, stains, wear **275.00**

Pinwheels With Star Centers, 80 × 83", appliqued, plume pinwheels, red and khaki stars and grid, white ground, Eureka, MO origin, stains **625.00**

Plume and Star pattern, 82 × 84" appliqued, cotton, red and blue solid patches, white ground, swag border, conforming, diamond, and parallel line quilting, 19th C **650.00**

Poinsettia, 84 × 86", appliqued, potted poinsettias, multi–floral border, solid red and green, yellow calico, white ground, old paper label reads "Made in 1844," stains and minor wear, some color loss **1,400.00**

Potted Flowers, 84 × 88", appliqued, stylized design, sixteen diamonds each with potted flower, orange and blue–green, pale yellow ground, scalloped edge, minor wear and fading **450.00**

Puss in the Corner, 86 × 95", pieced, multicolored prints and calico, beige gingham print ground, red floral stripe print backing, PA **375.00**

Rose, 82 × 83" appliqued and reverse appliqued, nine patch patterns, center rose, lollipop stylized flower motifs, green swag border, c1865 . . . . . **3,250.00**

Snow Crystal, 79 × 79", pieced, triangular and hexagonal patches, multicolored prints, yellow ground, Elta Hargie, Kansas City, KS **400.00**

Snow Flakes, 72 × 86", pieced, blue, white ground, overall wear and staining **190.00**

Spools, 73 × 83", pieced, multicolored prints, made by Maud Severson, Lincoln, NE, c1890, small stains **165.00**

Star

70 × 70", pieced 16 eight-point stars in white diamonds alternating with printed diamonds, striped borders, blue print, white, red and pink calico, solid goldenrod, attributed to Sarah Williamson, Salina, KS, small tear in backing   **500.00**

72 × 72", pieced, 45 eight-point stars in ten alternating rows of five and four stars each, sawtooth border, pink calico, white ground, embroidered initials in corner **450.00**

80 × 81", pieced, goldenrod print, white ground, machine sewn binding **250.00**

86 × 100", pieced, eight point stars, swag border, blue and white print, feather quilted circles, minor overall wear **1,050.00**

90 × 96", pieced, nine large eight point stars with sawtooth edges, green red, and pink calico, green calico vining border, white ground, green binding with red piping, made near Crittendon, KY, stains, some color fading **1,700.00**

Star pattern, pieced, pink, red, yellow, and ivory printed and solid colored cotton patches, shell and conforming quilting, late 19th C, 71 × 69", $412.50. Photograph courtesy of Skinner, Inc.

92 × 93", pieced, center small eight-point star within concentric star rings, striped border with nine patch pinwheel design corner blocks, red calicoes, solid greens, and white star design, red and goldenrod stripes, multicolored print and navy blue calico corner blocks, overall wear, some fading, small spots of color loss **275.00**

Star of Bethlehem

76 × 65", pieced, solid red, blue, green, mustard, and lavender patches, conforming feather, leaf, and diamond quilting, c1940 . . .   **525.00**

77 × 90", pieced, goldenrod and orange, white ground **200.00**

Stars and Squares, 41 × 60", pieced, red, white, and blue, quilted hearts, c1910, crib size **150.00**

Stevengraph Memorial to Abraham Lincoln, silk and velvet patches, lithographed pictures, embroidery and needlework **325.00**

Thousand Pyramid Medallion, 75 × 75", pieced, multicolored prints, solid pink and white, pencil pattern intact, made by Martha Ann Ford Ashby, (1829–1912), Parkville, MO   **450.00**

Tulips

40 × 42", pieced and appliqued, crib size, solid and printed cotton patches, red, green, and cream, parallel line quilting, imperfections **165.00**

80 × 80", pieced and appliqued, sixteen bunches of three tulips each, two shades of pink and medium green, green border, pink binding **475.00**

96 × 98", appliqued, stylized design of three bloom flowers, four center flowers surrounded by identical border flowers, solid red and green, yellow calico, white ground, green piped binding, stains, minor spots of color loss   **1,000.00**

Tulips and Oak Leaves, 80 × 80", appliqued, stylized design, two shades of green and red, slightly puckered   **450.00**

Tumbling Blocks, 70 × 78", black and dark solid colors, some wear, stains, small holes **190.00**

Turkey Tracks

68 × 84", pieced and appliqued, red and pale green, attributed to Amanda Baker, Sevier County, TN, machine sewn border stripes   **325.00**

78 × 92", pieced, multicolored prints, faded **175.00**

Twenty–Five Patch Squares, 67 × 80", pieced, fifteen diamond shaped blocks, striped border, multicolored calico, gray print ground, pink calico border, some stains **135.00**

Victorian, 67 × 77", richly patterned squares, embroidered motifs, novelty stitched border, inscribed "To JHS from SJM, September 14, 1889"   **1,500.00**

Vining Flowers, 84 × 84", appliqued, nine stylized flowers attached to two full length vines, swag and bud border, green, pink, red, and yellow calico, embroidered corner date "Jan. 18th, 1851," stains, wear, some reds have small holes, some color loss to greens **1,750.00**

Zig–Zag, 86 × 98", pieced worsted, olive and pink patches, feather and parallel line quilting, solid butternut backing, discoloration, 19th C **925.00**

QUILT TOPS

Rose Medallions, 78 × 86", appliqued, vining bud border, red and green solids, and pink calico **165.00**

Tulips, 60 × 60", appliqued, thirteen stylized tulips, red, goldenrod, and teal–blue, white ground, matching pillow cover, some blues faded. . . .   **55.00**

RUGS

History: Although American mass–produced rugs were available as early as 1830, many agrarian families made do with handmade examples during much of the 19th century. Yarn–sewn rugs, constructed with two–ply yarn on a homespun linen backing or a two grain sack, were popular between 1800 and 1840. Popular patterns were patriotic, nautical, animal, floral, and geometric motifs.

The importation of burlap to America in the 1850s opened the door for the hooked rug. The hooked rug tradition began in New England, and quickly spread throughout the country. The rug was made by pulling narrow stripes of fabric up through holes in the burlap. Most of the early designs were free–form. By 1900 preprinted patterns were available from Diamond Dye Co. and Montgomery Ward Co.

Rug hooking enjoyed a revival in the 1920s and 1930s when the early American decorating craze dominated. In the 1970s the folk art community discovered hooked rugs and turned them into an art form. Design motif and artwork were stressed. Many collectors and dealers failed to realize that factory production of hooked rugs was well established by the 1930s. Examples that can be easily confused with handworked pieces have been found marked "MADE IN OCCUPIED JAPAN."

Three other types of rugs also appeared in the rural homestead—woven, braided, and penny. Woven rugs, also called rag rugs, were done on simple wooden hand looms. Braided rugs became popular in the 1830s and have continued ever since. Penny rugs date from the 1880 to 1915 period.

Prosperous members of the agrarian community liked to demonstrate their wealth and good taste by placing an oriental rug in their parlor and/or dining room. Hall runners were another favorite way of introducing oriental rugs to a rural home.

Oriental rugs first appeared in the west in the 16th century. The rugs originated in the regions of Central Asia, Iran (Persia), Caucasus, and Anatolia. Early rugs can be classified into basic categories: Iranian, Caucasian, Turkoman, Turkish, and Chinese. Later, India, Pakistan, and Iraq produced rugs in the oriental style.

The pattern name is derived from the tribe which produced the rug, e.g., Iran is the source for Hamadan, Herez, Sarouk, Tabriz, and others.

When evaluating an oriental rug, age, design, color, weave, knots per square inch, and condition determine the final value; silk rugs and prayer rugs bring higher prices.

Native American Indian rugs are also commonly found in Country settings. Many examples of these colorful woven rugs have been brought back east by visiting tourists. Others were purchased and used as accent rugs to brighten country homes. Today these rugs can be identified by tribes or region and may command high prices.

References: Murray Eiland, *Oriental Rugs: A New Comprehensive Guide,* Little, Brown and Company, 1981; H L James, *Rugs And Posts,* Schiffer Publishing, 1988; Linda Kline, *Beginner's Guide To Oriental Rugs,* Ross Books, 1980; Ivan C. Neff and Carol V. Maggs, *Dictionary of Oriental Rugs,* Van Nostrand Reinhold Company, 1979; Marian Rodee, *Weaving Of The Southwest,* Schiffer Publishing 1987; Helene Von Rosenstiel, *American Rugs and Carpets: From the Seventeenth Century to Modern Times,* William Morrow and Company, 1978; Jessie A. Turbayne, *Hooked Rugs: History and the Continuing Tradition,* Schiffer Publishing, 1991; Jessie A. Turbayne, *The Hooker's Art: Evolving Designs in Hooked Rugs,* Schiffer Publishing, 1993; Joyce C. Ware, *The Official Price Guide to Oriental Rugs,* House of Collectibles, 1992.

Periodical: *Oriental Rug Review,* PO Box 709, Meredith, NH 03253.

Reproduction Craftspersons: *Braided*—Janice Jurta, Country Braid House, RFD 2, Box 29, Clark Rd, Tilton, NH 03276; Pat Nolan, The Rug House, 1437 Herschel Ave, Cincinnati, OH 45208; *General*—Jane D Connors, 4953 North Ardmore, Whitefish Bay, WI 53217; Elizabeth Black Designs, PO Box 28, Bentonville, VA 22610; Judy Robinson's Country Textiles, 3350 Chicken Coop

Rd, Lancaster, OH 43130; Julia A Lindsey, Lindsey Woolseys of Ohio, 275 N Main St, Germantown, OH 45327; Judy Robinson's Country Textiles, 3350 Chickencoop Hill Rd, Lancaster, OH 43130; *Hooked*—Chris Bock–Howell, Highfields Sheep & Wool Farm, Box 327, Remsen, NY 13438; Betsy Bourdon, Weaver, Scribner Hill, Wolcott, VT 05680; Janet Carja Brandt, Carijarts II, 2136 Silver Lane Dr, Indianapolis, IN 46203; Ramona Cann, Cottage Rugs, 460 Shiloh Dr, Dayton, OH 45415; Fay's Garret, 2633 Chestnut Valley Dr, Lancaster, PA 17601; Pat Hornafius, 113 Meadowbrook Ln, Elizabethtown, Pa 17022; Sue Jones, 2221 Bonhaven, Lexington, KY 40515; Polly A Minick, 3111 Dale View Dr, Ann Arbor, MI 48015; Suzanne C & Cleland E Shelby, Aged Ram, PO Box 201, Essex, VT 05451; Peggy Teich, 7846 N Sherman Blvd, Milwaukee, WI 53209; *Penny*—Barbara Bond, American Rugs, RR1 Box 137A, Nebraska City, NE 68410; Jo Morton, Prairie Hands, 1801 Central Ave, Nebraska City, NE 68410; *Rag*—Betsy Bourdon, Traditional Handweaving, Scribner Hill, Wolcott, VT 05680; Rebecca Francis, Weaver, Box 307, Dillsburg, PA 17019; Beckie R Kiever, Cross Eyed Sheep, 3054 Canandaigua Rd, Macedon, NY 14502; Martha Richard, The Weaver's Corner, 1406 E Spring St, New Albany, IN 47150.

Reproduction Manufacturers: *Braided*—Braid–Aid, 466 Washington St, Rte 53, Pembroke, MA 02359; Chinaberry General Store, 1846 Winfield Dunn Highway, Sevierville, TN 38762; Jugtown Mountain Rugs, 791 Tower Rd, Enola, PA 17025; Olde Mill House Shoppe, 105 Strasburg Pike, Lancaster, PA 17602; The Rug Factory Store, PO Box 249, 560 Mineral Spring Ave, Pawtucket, RI 02860; *General*—Country Loft, 1506 South Shore Park, Hingham, MA 02043; David C Kline, Family Heir–Loom Weavers, RD 3, Box 59E, Red Lion, PA 17356; The Cover Up Handweaving Studio, Rte 1, Box 216, Rabun Gap, GA 30568; *Hooked*—Hooked on Rugs, 44492 Midway Dr, Novi, MI 48375; *Hooked Rug Kit*—The Hooking Room, 1840 House, 237 Pine Point Rd, Scarborough, ME 04074; National Carpet Co, 1384 Coney Island Ave, Brooklyn, NY 11320; See Holly Hooked Rug Shop, 1906 North Bayview Dr, Kill Devil Hills, NC 27948.

Indian—Crazy Crow Trading Post, PO Box 314B, Denison, TX 75020; *Kit*—Folk Art Emporium, 3591 Forest Haven Ln, Chesapeake, VA 23321; *Oriental*—National Carpet Co, 1384 Coney Island Ave, Brooklyn, NY 11320; *Rag*—Checkerberry Hill, 253 Westridge Ave, Daly City, CA 94015; Country Rugs, Box 99 H, RD 1, Kintnersville, PA 18930; Country Weavers Unlimited, PO Box 1683, London, KY 40743; Faith Mountain Country Fare, Main St, Box 199, Sperryville, VA 22740; Folkheart Rag Rugs, 18 Main St, Bristol, VT 05443; Heritage Rugs, PO Box 404, Street Rd, Lahaska, PA 18931; Jugtown Mountain Rugs, 791

Tower Rd, Enola, PA 17025; Kentucky Hills Industries, Box 186, Pine Knot, KY 42635; Lancaster Collection, PO Box 6074, Lancaster, PA 17603; Mulberry Magic, PO Box 62, Ruckersville, VA 22968; The Sugar Street Weavers, PO Box 5125, Hendersonville, NC 28793; Weavers Corner Inc, 11664 Boston Rd, Boston, KY 40107; *Stenciled*—Adirondack Store and Gallery, 109 Saranac Ave, Lake Placid, NY 12946; The Barn, PO Box 25, Market St, Lehman, PA 18627; Legendary Folk Art, 342 East St, Pittsford, NY 14534; The Vine and Cupboard, PO Box 309, George Wright Rd, Woolwich, ME 04579.

Hooked

15 × 15½", multicolored ring design	80.00
18 × 28", stylized evergreen tree, gold and orange, blue, gray, and green geometric ground.......	60.00
18½ × 32", trout, shades of purple, blue, cream, green, brown, beige, and red, late 19th C, minor fading, some wear.................	475.00
21 × 37", squirrel and scrolls, brown, gray, green, maroon, and black, scalloped black felt border, minor damage and fading	150.00
23 × 43", geometric design, multicolored	150.00
24 × 44", blue and purple leopard crouched on branch, red tropical fruit, and green leaves, gray ground	175.00
25 × 34", floral design, semicircular, brown, orange, faded green, pink, and white, dark blue and purple ground, brown scalloped border....................	70.00
25 × 36", Oriental rug pattern, red, blue, and green, late 19th C	225.00
26 × 70", tumbling block pattern, browns, blue, and gray	225.00

Hooked, wool, shades of green, brown, red, blue, pink, yellow, and black, fringed, made by Elizabeth Atwood Childs, New Hampshire, mid 19th C, 74½ × 42", $4,950.00. Photograph courtesy of Skinner, Inc.

27 × 40", Canadian geese flying above evergreens, orig label "Grenfell Labrador Industries," early 20th C **375.00**

28 × 52", three masted ship, rose border, polychrome yarns, 20th C, repairs.................... **500.00**

29 × 41", bird looking back, red, blue, yellow, green, white, beige, and gray, hearts and vining foliage border, mounted on stretcher ... **650.00**

30 × 58", geometric pattern, polychrome cotton and wool, late 19th/early 20th C **175.00**

30½ × 51", two standing deer, polychrome yarns, dated 1934...... **175.00**

34 × 45", three masted ship, *Blue Nose*, polychrome yarn, burlap ground, some wear and soiling **250.00**

39 × 46", white cat, pink, blue, and green leafy floral border, variegated gray ground, American, 19th C.................... **3,850.00**

44½ × 78", brick pattern, braided circles border, late 19th C..... **925.00**

45 × 72", Oriental rug pattern, blue, green, and rust yarn, cream ground, 20th C **825.00**

46 × 88", floral design, rows of medallions with polychrome roses on variegated beige ground, old repairs, some wear, late 19th C ... **350.00**

46½ × 78", Oriental rug pattern, green, yellow, blue, cream, raspberry, and burgundy, prayer rug type, c1978................ **525.00**

48 × 20", running horse, polychrome fabrics, burlap ground, America, 19th C, old repairs, discoloration, fiber loss **525.00**

144 × 176", floral, polychrome yarn on burlap ground, worked by Caroline Cleaves Saunders, Clinton, MA, mid 20th C, minor imperfections **2,100.00**

Navaho

27 × 49", Ganado area, black triangular geometric design, tan ground, red border, warp breaks, holes, selvage damage, some color bleeding, c1920 .... **135.00**

29 × 50", hand spun and carded wool, step terrace diamond design, white, orange, gray, black, and red **110.00**

30 × 58", Two Gray Hills weaving, Spirit Line break, hand carded wool, black, gray, tan, and natural colors, 1960s............... **325.00**

34 × 62", Toadlena area, natural browns and tan, holes, wear, selvage damage, stains, 1930s..... **250.00**

Navajo, wool, possibly Crystal area, shades of natural black, gray, brown, white, and aniline red, two central diamond motifs terminating in angular hooks and four red crosses, c1930, 66 × 106", $1,650.00. Photograph courtesy of W E Channing & Co, Inc.

38 × 65", serrated diamonds, gray, black, white, and red, 1920s **350.00**

39 × 54", Klagetoh, sunrise design, double dye red, dark brown, and nautral hand carded wool **225.00**

39 × 68", Klagetoh, central diamond design, red, black, gray, brown, and natural white, West Reservation border design **275.00**

40 × 57", Chinle, serrated bands and three center motifs, red, grayish–brown, white, and black, 1920s **650.00**

40 × 74", upright and inverted triangle columns, white, gray, black, and red, 1920s **225.00**

46 × 70", cross design, red, brown, orange, gray, black, and natural **175.00**

47" × 65", CN cotton type, hand carded red, dark brown, arbrush gray and natural wool, no wear, sheen, c1900............... **1,320.00**

47 × 71", Crystal area, predominantly rabbit brush, hand carded wool, soft natural native dyes, stains...................... **225.00**

52 × 74½", serrated diamond, red, brown, natural, black, and beige **385.00**

55 × 75", transitional period, analine dye carded, red, orange, dark brown, gray, faded purple, and natural colors, long staple wool with remnants of corner fringe, color bleeding to white areas.... **385.00**

56" × 95", finely woven Crystal area, hand carded soft orange–red, dark brown, tan, and white wool, c1915, sheen, small holes 660.00

58" × 83", early diamond design, heavy weight hand carded red, dark and mixed brown, and natural wool, slight red bled, c1910 . . . .   500.00

Penny

25¾ × 61", table type, wool appliques, red, yellow, orange, green, blue, and brown, late 19th/early 20th C 825.00

28 × 46", wool, rect, concentric diamonds, olive, gray, and maroon, red outer corners with floral embroidery, worn, holes and repairs 185.00

35 × 66", appliqued wool circles, dark red, blue, gray, and black, white cotton ground, black velvet binding 110.00

Oriental

2' 6" × 12' 8", runner, Mahal, west Persia, early 20th C, red, blue, ivory, and dark blue–green diamond medallion, olive border, moth damage 770.00

3' 8" × 5' 8", Kuba, northeast Caucasus, last quarter 19th C, four ivory, red, and light blue Lesghi stars, midnight blue field, blue border, even wear, moth damage, repaired crease 440.00

Oriental, Qashqai Kelim, Southwest Persia, late 19th C, two diamond medallions in blue, gold, brown, and light green on a light red field, stepped reciprocal border, 122 × 60", $1,870.00. Photograph courtesy of Skinner, Inc.

Oriental, Senneh Kelim, Northwest Persia, late 19th C, serrated midnight blue medallion with matching spandrels on an ivory field, gold border, small repairs, 80 × 52", $3,575.00. Photograph courtesy of Skinner, Inc.

4' 5" × 7', Gendje, south central Caucacus, last quarter 19th C, three red, gold, and blue–green medallions, blue field, ivory border, slight moth damage, small hold, small crease 660.00

4' 7" × 6' 9", Khamseh, southwest Persia, late 19th C, three ivory diamond medallions, midnight blue field, gold border, even wear to center, slight moth damage, minor end fraying 990.00

6' 2" × 4', Bidjar, northwest Persia, late 19th C, dark slate blue diamond medallion on red field, sky blue spandrels, red border, slight moth damage, small areas of minor wear, reovercast edges 1,875.00

6' 2" × 4' 9", Senneh, northwest Persia, last quarter 19th C, ivory field with overall design of bouquets of European–style roses, birds, and leaves in blue, rose, red, and dark blue–green, red rosette and vine border, even wear, reovercast edges 3,300.00

6' 2" × 5' 2", Soumak, northeast Caucasus, last quarter 19th C, three navy blue, gold, and blue–green square medallions on the rust–red field, dark brown border, slight moth damage 5,500.00

6' 6" × 4' 4", Kurd, northwest Persia, second half 19th C, staggered red, blue, gold, and blue–green ashik fuls on dark brown field, red border, even wear, brown corrosion, repaired creases 1,975.00

6' 8" × 4' 4", Senneh Kelim, northwest Persia, late 19th C, serrated midnight blue medallion with matching spandrels on ivory field, gold border, small repairs **3,575.00**

7' × 5' 2", Moghan, southeast Caucasus, late 19th/early 20th C, three concentric octagonal medallions in red, blue, gold, and blue–green on ivory field, red border. **2,475.00**

7' 8" × 3' 5", Shirvan long rug, east Caucasus, mid 19th C, three red, ivory, and blue–green medallions on navy blue field, gold serrated leaf border, small areas of wear, brown corrosion, small crude repairs **2,200.00**

7' 9" × 5' 2", Karabagh, south Caucasus, late 19th C, Kasim Usag design on an abrashed red cruciform cartouche on the abrashed sky blue field, within a narrow gold geometric border, slight moth damage, small creases, brown corrosion **4,125.00**

7' 9" × 5' 4", Chajli, southeast Caucasus, late 19th C, three deep red and ivory octagonal medallions share the abrashed medium blue field with small rosettes, stars, and geometric motifs, red octagon and diamond border with calligraphic inscription, good pile, brown corrosion, small crease **4,400.00**

8' × 5' 2", Kazak, southwest Caucasus, second half 19th C, three red, blue, and ivory medallions on blue–green field, ivory border, even wear, small areas of repiling. **2,750.00**

8' 6" × 11' 4", Heriz, northwest Persia, early 20th C, abrashed blue–green rosette medallion, terra cotta red field, ivory spandrels, navy blue border, small area of moth damage **2,530.00**

8' 8" × 5' 7", Timuri main carpet, northeast Persia, mid 19th C **9,900**

8' 8" × 6' 3", Central Asian Suzani, embroidered silk on cotton, second half 19th C, circular blossoms and foliage in red, cochineal, sky blue, and blue–green, ivory field, similar border, good condition, slight stains **2,975.00**

9' × 3' 2", northwest Persia long rug, last quarter 19th C, column of seven hooked stepped polygons in red, gold, ivory, and blue–green, midnight blue field, narrow ivory geometric border, even wear, slight moth damage **935.00**

9' × 4', Chi–Chi long rug, northeast Caucasus, third quarter 19th C, staggered rows of hooked stepped polygons in red, sky blue, aubergine, gold, and light blue–green cover the abrashed navy blue field, within a characteristic dark brown rosette and diagonal bar border, slight moth damage, spots of repiling, reovercast edges **3,850.00**

9' × 4' 9", Kuba, northeast Caucasus, early 20th C, five dark red and blue–green medallions on midnight blue field, ivory border, good pile, small repairs **4,675.00**

9' 6" × 5' 6", Qashqai, southwest Persia, last quarter 19th C, three large ivory and aubergine connected diamond medallions, small motifs, and red spandrels on sky blue field, narrow black rosette and vine border, small areas of slight wear. **3,300.00**

9' 10" × 7' 6", Mohtashem Kashan carpet, west Persia, last quarter 19th C, midnight blue and ivory diamond medallion on red field, ivory spandrels, midnight blue border, even wear, reovercast edges, new fringes added. **9,350.00**

10' 2" × 6' 9", Sarouk carpet, west Persia, late 19th C, red medallion and floral motifs in blue, pale gold, and blue–green on midnight blue field, red spandrels, midnight blue border, small areas of wear, small crude repairs **5,225.00**

10' 3" × 7' 5", Heriz carpet, northwest Persia, early 20th C, overall floral motifs in rose, sky blue, tan–gold, and blue–green on terra cotta red field, midnight blue border, small areas of minor wear. . . **5,500.00**

11' × 4' 3", Luri long rug, southwest Persia, early 20th C, three columns of stylized flowering plants with serrated leaves in dark red, medium blue, gold, and blue–green, navy blue field, dark red spandrels, dark red crab border. **3,300.00**

12' × 9' 4", Isphahan carpet, central Persia, 17th C, red diamond lattice of blossoming gold and blue–green plants on navy blue field, red border, heavily restored **6,050.00**

12' 2" × 8' 10", Kashan carpet, west Persia, early 20th C, circular array of summer blossoms in blue, rose, tan–gold, and deep blue–green on burgundy field with palmettes and curved serrateed leaves, midnight blue palmette and ara-

besque vine border, very good
condition **5,500.00**
12' 6" × 8' 9", Bidjar carpet, north-
west Persia, early 20th C, rose,
midnight blue, and blue–green
diamond medallion on deep red
field, camel spandrels, midnight
blue border, small area of slight
wear **11,000.00**
12' 8" × 10', Kashan carpet, central
Persia, second quarter 20th C,
large cochineal and sky blue medallion with ivory silk highlights
on navy blue field, with palmettes
and vines in royal blue, rose,
camel, deep gold, and blue–green,
cochineal spandrels, sky blue and
arabesque vine border, small areas
of wear, new fringes added **3,300.00**
13' 4" × 8' 2", Fereghan–Sarouk car-
pet, west Persia, late 19th C, ivory
and blue–green diamond medallion on abrashed rust–red field
with palmettes, cloudbands, and
floral sprays in blue, tan, beige,
and blue–green, midnight blue
palmette and leaf border, even
wear, small repair, new fringes
added **6,600.00**
16' 2" × 13', Meshed carpet, north-
east Persia, early 20th C, palmettes
and floral sprays in sky blue,
cochineal, rose, camel, and light
blue–green on midnight blue field,
red floral border, small areas of
wear, small repair **4,125.00**
16' 4" × 10' 10", Meshed carpet,
northeast Persia, early 20th C,
midnight blue field with four trees
dense with blossoms in blue,
cochineal, rose, soft brown, and
blue–green, within a midnight
blue palmette and flowering vine
border, small areas of wear,
touch–up, slight moth damage **2,750.00**
17' 6" × 12' 8", Lavar Kerman carpet,
southeast Persia, third quarter 19th
C, navy blue, ivory, and tan–gold
medallion on ivory field with blossoming vines, cochineal and navy
blue spandrels, within a cochineal
rosette and leafy vine border, areas
of wear, several small patches . . . **2,475.00**
Rag
25½ × 34½", geometric pattern, olive, red, and maroon earth tones,
checkerboard type design in cor-
ners and center **160.00**
29 × 41", multicolored stripes, rect
blocks, some wear and damage **45.00**
33 × 56½", multicolored stripes,
square blocks, minor wear **250.00**

36 × 186", striped, shades of blue,
gray, and red, blue and white
warp, PA, minor wear **110.00**
Shag, polychrome knitted woolens on
knitted   cotton   ground,   late
19th/early 20th C **140.00**
Shirred, wool fabric, rect, floral bou-
quet center, vining floral border,
shades of blue, red, green, brown,
and cream, 19th C, 29 × 62" **2,750.00**
Table, appliqued and pieced, red, blue,
yellow, cream, and brown wool
patches, initialed and dated "E. B.
1858," England, some discoloration
and loss, 66 × 66" **875.00**

SEWING AND WEAVING IMPLEMENTS

History: A wide variety of sewing items were
found in almost every rural home. Necessity required that rural housewives were skilled in dress
making, sewing, and repairs. Just as the farmer
valued his tools, the rural housewife treasured her
favorite sewing implements.

Many implements served special functions.
Sewing birds, an interesting convenience item,
were used to hold cloth (in the bird's beak) while
sewing. Made of iron or brass, they could be
attached to table or shelf with a screw–type fixture.
Later models featured a pincushion.

Sewing implements were frequently received as
gifts and passed down from generation to generation. Many manufacturers used sewing implements as giveaway premiums, such as advertising
needle threaders and needle holders.

Although large–size weaving was left to professionals, many rural housewives did have small
tape and ribbon looms. Also found along with
sewing implements are tools associated with card-
ing and spinning. Although no longer used, they
tended to be saved for nostalgic reasons.

References: Joyce Clement, *The Official Price
Guide To Sewing Collectibles,* House of Collect-
ibles, 1987, out–of–print; Victor Houart, *Sewing
Accessories: An Illustrated History,* Souvenir Press
(London), 1984; Gay Ann Rogers, *American Silver
Thimbles,* Haggerston Press, 1989; Gay Ann Ro-
gers, *An Illustrated History of Needlework Tools,*
Needlework Unlimited, 1983, 1989 price guide;
Estelle Zalkin, *Zalkin's Handbook Of Thimbles &
Sewing Implements, First Edition,* Warman Pub-
lishing Co., 1988.

Collectors' Club: Thimble Collectors International, 6411 Montego Bay Rd, Louisville, KY
40228.

Periodical: *Thimbletter,* 93 Walnut Hill Road,
Newton Highlands, MA 02161.

Museums: Fabric Hall, Historic Deerfield, Deerfield, MA; Museum of American History, Smithsonian Institution, Washington, D.C.; Shelburne Museum, Shelburne, VT.

Reproduction Manufacturers: *General*—Braid-Aid, 466 Washington St, Rte 53, Pembroke, MA 02359; The Examplarery, PO Box 2554, Dearborn, MI 48123; Hearthside Quilts, Box 429, Rte 7, Shelburne, VT 05482; The Hooking Room, 1840 House, 237 Pine Point Rd, Scarborough, ME 04074; *Old Spools, Bobbins, and Shuttles*—Joel S Perkins & Son–Vt, Inc, PO Box 76, South Strafford, VT 05070; *Spinning Wheels and Supplies*—Log Cabin Shop, Box 275, Lodi, OH 44254; The Coverlet Co, PO Box 02–616, Portland, OR 97202; *Weaving*—The Golden Lamb, 9 Meadow Ln, Lancaster, PA 17601.

Bobbins, lace maker's, wooden, turned, orig box 45.00
Crochet Thread Holder, figural, apple, thread through stem, 4 x 3½" 25.00
Darner, ebony, emb floral handle marked "Sterling" 40.00
Distaff, chip carved designs, 42" l. . . . 85.00
Emery, cat head, black 18.00
Hatchel, flax comb
  11½" l, hardwood, treenware, simple scratch carving dec, cutout handle. 8.00
  16" l, cov, cherry, chestnut, and walnut, chip carved dec, sheet metal trim, steel spikes, old patina 80.00
  23½" l, primitive, hardwood and pine, one fine and one coarse group of iron spikes. 45.00
Loom, pine, mortised and pinned construction, wrought iron fittings, two replaced treadles, 27 x 37½ x 49" h 275.00
Loom Light, wrought iron, hanging, candle arm on adjustable trammel, adjusts from 33" h. 150.00
Needle Case
  Toleware, dark brown japanning, red and yellow stylized foliage dec, 9" l 105.00
  Wood, turned, holds tatting needles, bullet shaped, threaded lid, early 1800s, 2" d, 6½" h 45.00
Niddy–Noddy
  9" l, cherry, turned detail, old dark finish. 195.00
  18½" l, wood, turned, bentwood brace is old replacement 25.00
Pin Cushion
  Dog, stuffed velvet, embroidered features, glass eyes, orange ribbon bow, worn and faded, 5¼" h. . . . 15.00
  Dog on ball, red corduroy dog, tape measure, 4" h 50.00
  Heart, red satin, colored–head pins dec, 6¼" h 45.00

Lamb, cast white metal, gold cloth 50.00
Strawberry, folk art, red and green, large inverted strawberry on pressed glass base, four smaller hanging needle–sharpener strawberries, 8" h. 200.00
Woman, wood head, holding parasol, black dress and shawl, label "Made for Ann Coth Emaldt by Miss Becky Staples, Baltimore 1830," 3¼" h 195.00
Quilting Template, tin, six point starflower, set of five range in size from 5" to 7¼" d 55.00
Quilt Rack, primitive, old blue paint on 33" l oak tapered and chamfered legs, adjustment holes in four pine bars, 95 x 111" largest size, missing fastening wedges. 25.00
Rug Hook, wood, cast iron, and steel, marked "Jewel," block and floral dec, dated 1886 . . . . 105.00
Sewing Bag, ink decorated and inscribed, verse, floral swag, and birds on branches, inscribed "Martha Welsh Jackson to Miss Abigail Whitney Bancroft, 1818," Groton, MA, 9¾" l, 7⅜" w 165.00
Sewing Bird
  4" h, cast and wrought iron, heart shaped thumb screw 150.00
  4¼" h, iron, heart shaped thumb screw 135.00
  4½" h, gilded brass, pin cushions covered in salmon pink corduroy, c1850 . . . . 225.00
  4¾" h, brass, old worn pin cushion, heart shaped thumb screw 160.00
  5" h, brass, two worn pin cushions, table clamp 165.00
  5¼" h, silver plated brass, large and small pin cushions, table clamp 125.00
Sewing Box
  6¾" d, 3" h, round, cov, Shaker, bentwood, swivel handle, orig pale blue silk damask lining, old varnish finish 400.00
  7" h
    Hardwood, Shaker, one drawer, thread compartment, pin cushion finial, old red varnish stain finish 75.00
    Mahogany, old black alligatored varnish, one drawer, pin cushion, pin thread spool holders, turned pedestal, turned feet . . . 95.00
  7¼" l, oval, cov, Shaker, bentwood, three finger construction base, one finger construction lid, copper tacks, bentwood swivel handle, worn silk lining, accessories, natural finish 250.00

10" l, rect, cov, rosewood veneer, inlaid brass and wood floral designs, fitted red satin and gold star–patterned red paper interior. **125.00**

11½" l, cov, Lehneware, pine, red, black, and yellow striping, gilded transfer designs, floral decoupage, and "1875" date on brown ground, turned feet, lift–out fitted interior tray, orig lock and key   **350.00**

12" h, primitive, hardwood and pine, one drawer, tiered thread caddy, wooden pins, traces of old finish   **25.00**

13" l, 4½" h, cov, pine, rect, decorated, grain painted. **80.00**

13½" d, cov, bentwood, natural smoked finish, gold and silver stenciled dec. **100.00**

Shuttle, wood. **60.00**

Spinning Wheel

19¼" l, cast iron, table clamp, hand crank, orig yellow striping on black paint, old welded repair. . .   **85.00**

23½" h, wood, slender turnings, chip carving, damaged **130.00**

30" h, wood, chair frame type, gray weathered finish, old repairs and replacements, new distaff **50.00**

32½" h, wood, two spindles, turned members, old patina, age cracks in wheel **150.00**

35" h, wood, hardwood, two spindles, three turned legs, chip carved detail, stamped "S.B.," old brown finish. **150.00**

39" h, hardwood, chair frame type, old refinish **175.00**

39½" h, hardwoods, turned and chip carved detail, old dark patina . . .   **200.00**

45½" h, wood, chair frame type, hardwood, old brown patina. . . .   **300.00**

32" h, hard and soft woods, 19" d wheel, replaced distaff **325.00**

46" h, vertical, hardwoods, turned details, double bobbins and spinners, old dark finish. **245.00**

Spool Caddy, pine, mortised frame and base, holds four spools or bobbins, decorative cutout designs, replaced wire and two spools, glued crack in base, one spool chipped, 15" w, 11" h   **125.00**

Stretcher Frame, 23½" w, 30" h, mahogany, turned, adjustable, worn finish **275.00**

Swift

17" h, wood, table clamp, needs restringing **55.00**

23½" h, wood, orig yellow varnish finish.   **100.00**

24" h, umbrella type, wood, accordion folding slats, table clamp, orig yellow varnish **125.00**

Silk Spools, wood, silk company name on end, 4½ to 5" h, price each, $5.00.

39½" h, hardwood and pine, four squirrel cages, vertical adjustable post, old patina **45.00**

47" h, hard and soft woods, two squirrel cages, adjustable reel, four legs, old dark patina, 47" h **105.00**

Table Clamp

3½" l, cast bronze. **35.00**

4" l, cast iron, table screw clamp, set of four **100.00**

Tape Loom

14¾" l, oak, spatula shaped, fish tail handle, old patina **155.00**

19" l, 10" w, pine, old patina, dovetailed box, two ratchet spindles, cracked heddle frame **275.00**

19¼" l, poplar, old gray–blue paint   **125.00**

20¾" l, 8" w, paddle shaped, old patina **115.00**

21½" l, 12½" w, hard and soft woods, leather and metal fittings, two heddles. **150.00**

22" l, wood, two heddles, old patina   **250.00**

24¼" l, pine, primitive, old patina, age crack. **50.00**

25½" l, primitive, pine, wrought iron nails, old patina. **40.00**

27¾" h, vertical, hardwood, paddle shaped, ftd base **55.00**

28" l, primitive, paddle shaped, oak, old worn patina. **45.00**

Tape Measure, pig in red shoe, celluloid **35.00**

Tatting Shuttle

Celluloid, adv, Lydia Pinkham, portrait top, adv bottom **100.00**

Sterling Silver, marked "1912" **65.00**

Tape Measure, figural iron, plated brass, agate handle, wind return, 2⅛ " l, 1½" h, $165.00.

Thimble
  Advertising
    Clark's O.N.T., "Our New
      Thread," brass **20.00**
    Domestic Sewing Machine, silver **50.00**
  Scenic Band, silver, early 20th C. . . **25.00**
Thimble Holder, 3" l, ivory, acorn
  shaped, allover sinuous leaf carving **85.00**
  Sterling Silver, ornate **35.00**
Thread Caddy
  9½" h, turned hardwood, ebonized
    trim, flanged base **90.00**
  9⅝" h, mahogany, turned, two tiers,
    flanged base **150.00**
Thread Reel, hardwood, table clamp,
  old patina, small chips on clamp
  threads, 6½" h **185.00**
Yarn Winder
  24" h, reel type, mortised frame, shoe
    feet, pine, worn light green paint,
    cast iron handle, black marker
    number **85.00**
  30" h, 24" d wheel, hard and soft
    woods, old dark patina, turned
    legs, chip carved detail, branded
    label "N. Lindsay, Reading," wear
    and edge damage, gear box hous-
    ing damaged and renailed **100.00**
  31½" h, 26½" d reel, geared count-
    ing mechanism, four turned
    spokes, gray weathered finish, age
    cracks, handle missing from reel **90.00**

  32" h, 26" d reel, hardwood, geared
    counting mechanism, good pat-
    ina **75.00**
  34½" h, 30" d reel, turned hard-
    woods, six spokes, chip carved
    base stamped "A. Love," refin-
    ished **95.00**
  35" h, 27" d reel, horizontal shaft,
    geared counting mechanism, four
    splayed legs, old worn patina, age
    cracks in reel **110.00**
  36" h, 25" d reel, turned detail, box
    base, four splayed legs, geared
    counting mechanism with "click,"
    old red paint **90.00**
  36½" h, 30" d reel, floor standing,
    turned hard and soft woods,
    geared counting mechanism with
    "click," old brown patina. **75.00**
  37" h, primitive, pine, turned post,
    four part interior in dovetailed box
    base, scalloped dividers. **150.00**
  38¾" h, vertical type, hardwood
    frame, pine staves, old natural pat-
    ina, some staves replaced **50.00**
  42" h, 26½" d reel, hardwoods, four
    spokes, four splayed legs, geared
    counter mechanism, wooden
    hand, scored face **100.00**
  45" h, New England, early 19th C,
    painted blue, inset counter, imper-
    fections **275.00**

VEHICLES AND ACCESSORIES

While Country collectors and decorators emphasize the vehicles and accessories from the horse–drawn vehicle era, there is a growing collector interest in steam and gasoline powered equipment. Country collecting is focusing more and more on 20th century rural America. The following is the first listing in a general Country price guide to blend old with new.

The decorating community views vehicles and vehicle accessories primarily as accent pieces. They frequently can be found in department store window displays. Favorite forms include sleighs and surreys. Animal–drawn children's carts are also popular. Since decorators want the vehicles for effect, they are willing to accept defects.

Individuals who collect and restore vehicles for display or use are much more demanding. They want the vehicles in working order with as many original parts as possible. Just as in the automobile field, there is a strong tendency to over restore, i.e., make the vehicle look as though it just left the carriage shop or factory.

The formation of collectors' clubs contributed significantly to the preservation of farm equipment. These clubs, along with specialized periodicals, allowed a network to be established for the exchange of information and parts. You will find them exhibiting at most farm shows and state agricultural fairs.

Within the paper collecting community, farm equipment advertising and catalogs enjoy strong interest. Again, the principal emphasis is on horse–drawn vehicles, albeit the interest in steam and gasoline powered vehicle material is growing.

Periodicals: *Antique Power*, PO Box 838, Yellow Springs, OH 45387; *The Belt Pulley*, PO Box 83, Nokomis, IL 62075; *The Country Wagon Journal*, PO Box 331, West Milford, NJ 07480; *Draft Horse Journal*, PO Box 670, Waverly, IA 50677; *The Driving Digest Magazine*, PO Box 467, Brooklyn, CT 06234; *Driving West*, PO Box 2675, China, CA 91708; *Farm Antique News*, 812 N Third St, Tarkio, MO 64491; *Iron Man Album*, PO Box 328, Lancaster, PA 17603; *Rusty Iron Monthly*, PO Box 342, Sandwich, IL 60548.

Collectors' Clubs: American Driving Society, PO Box 160, Metamora, MI 48455; American Wagon Association, PO Box 436, Ronceverte, WV 24970; Antique Engine, Tractor & Toy Club, 5731 Paradise Rd, Slatington, PA 18080; J. I. Case Collectors' Association, Inc., Rt 2, Box 242, Vinton, OH 45686; Early American Steam Engine & Old Equipment Society, PO Box 652, Red Lion, PA 17356; International Harvester Collectors, RR 2, Box 286, Winamac, IN 46996; The M–M Collectors Club, 409 Sheridan Drive, Eldridge, IA 52748; Midwest Old Settlers & Threshers Association, Rt 1, Threshers Rd, Mt. Pleasant, IA 52641; Rough & Tumble Engineers' Historical Association, Box 9, Kinzers, PA 17535.

Museums: Billings Farm & Museum, Woodstock, NY; Landis Valley Farm Museum, Lancaster, PA; Living History Farms, Urbandale, IA; The Museum at Stony Brook, Stony Brook, NY; National Agricultural Center, Bonner Springs, KS.

Reproduction Manufacturers: *Horse–Drawn Vehicles*—Cumberland General Store, Rte 3, Crossville, TN 38555; J T Nicholas & Son, 704 N Michigan Ave, Howell, MI 48843; Nineteenth Century Mercantile, No. 2 N Main St, South Yarmouthport, MA 02664. *Miniature Vehicle Kits*—Criss–Cross Creations, Box 324, Wayne, NJ 07470; *Sleigh Bells*—Conewago Junction, 805 Oxford Rd, New Oxford, PA 17350.

ACCESSORIES

Coach Lamp, brass, beveled glass panes, eagle finial, converted to electric lamp, 29" h **50.00**
Conestoga Wagon Box, pine, slant top, wrought iron strap hinges and decorative hardware
  17" w, 21" h, traces of old paint ... **300.00**
  18½" w, 17½" h, old blue repaint **1,000.00**
Lap Robe, tiger head, Stroock **100.00**
Seats
  Buggy, child size, 27½" l, wooden plank seat and back, wrought iron frame **375.00**
  Conestoga Wagon, 30½" w, hard and soft woods, cutout ends, chamfered edges, shoe feet, old worn red repaint over black **575.00**
  Sleigh, 33" w, hardwood, bench style **70.00**
Wagon
  22¼" h, double, ladder back, pointed finials, turned, woven splint seat, old finish **650.00**
  32¼" h, 33½" w, double, ladder back, turned front legs, replaced woven splint seats **550.00**
  40" w, pine, bootjack ends, old refinishing **240.00**
Sleigh Bells, 8 feet long, twenty 2½" h numbered brass bells, wide leather strap, orig red paint, geometric dec, 1880 .... **135.00**
Step
  Buggy, cast iron, rect foot plate attached to angled support, ornamental treads, pr **28.00**
  Carriage, cast iron, cut–out plate on U–shaped support, c1870 ...... **25.00**
Tool Box, wagon, 16 feet long, 5¼" w, 8½" h to top of spout, wooden, cast iron oil spout dome and cut–out end panels, marked "Whitely" **145.00**
Trim, from horse–drawn carriage, cast iron, ornamental, cross designs, 19th C **24.00**
Wagon Jack, wood and wrought iron, good iron work with tooled design and "1814, P. Ordver," traces of old red paint, adjustable lift bar, 19½" h **95.00**

HORSE–DRAWN VEHICLES

Brougham
  Demarest & Co, dark blue body, blue suede upholstery, wheels on rubber, orig front wheel brakes, pole, restored **4,100.00**
  Healey & Co, NY, ¾ size, equipped with brakes, wheels on rubber, serial #2590 .... **5,700.00**
  Henry Killam, Broadway, NY, serial #3259, marked on hubcaps..... **1,075.00**

Stage Coach Chest, New England, three drawers, dovetailed, yellow stenciled labels list stage stops, orig red paint, replaced hardware, 19th C, 32¼" w, 15 ¼" d, 39¼" h, $1,650.00. Photograph courtesy of Skinner, Inc.

Buckboard
    J J Haydock Carriage Co, Cincinnati, OH, natural wood body, burgundy wheels and shafts, stick seat, shafts **1,650.00**
    Unknown Maker, stick seat, black body, burgundy running gear and upholstery, brass trim, cargo rack on back, removable back seat, wheels on rubber, shafts **2,800.00**
Buggy
    Concord type, W A Patterson, Flint, MI, folding top, side springs, wheels on rubber, shafts, restored **1,800.00**
    Doctor's
        Unknown Maker, 50" wheels, painted, gold leaf trim, shafts **1,800.00**
        W F Whiton & Co, Bangor, ME, pneumatic tires, shafts **325.00**
    Pony, unknown maker, pony size, wicker sides, fenders, wheels on rubber, shafts, pole, restored **3,000.00**
    Road, A P Stevens, Athens, PA, midnight blue, white stick seat, leather sides, pole, shafts, restored **2,300.00**
    Side Bar, H H Babcock Co, dark green body, white stick seat, gold trim, wire spoke wheels. **900.00**
    Side Spring, Clarence Lowell, New Bedford, MA, black, top, shafts **750.00**
Carriage
    Amish, unknown maker, brakes, lights, shafts. **285.00**
    Child's, C L Stone & Sons, Harford, CT, black, red and green striping, red striped wheels, fold–down top, black tufted upholstery, maker's name stamped under seat **1,000.00**

Buggy, E Hayward & Son, Hacketstown, NY, fold-down top, wood spoke wheels, tufted leather upholstered seat, cast iron step each side, 63" l, 37" w, 82" h, $650.00.

Cart
    Governess
        Van Tassell and Kearney, NY, four wheels, black body, yellow wicker basket, wheels on rubber   **700.00**
        Unknown Maker, pony size, maroon and black body, wicker basket, gray upholstery, wheels on rubber, restored. **2,900.00**
    Horse, Brewster & Co, Broome St, NY, marked on brass wheel caps, small horse size **400.00**
    Pony, D & J Furniture Co. **775.00**
    Road, unknown maker, storage under seat, orig leather harness **200.00**
    Tandem, Columbia Buggy Co, Detroit, MI, black and maroon, ivory wicker sides and back, drivers wedge, wheels on rubber, two sets of shafts, product #976 marked under seat, restored **3,100.00**
    Village, Van Tassell & Kearney, NY, burgundy body, yellow running gear, black upholstery, wood hub, wheels on rubber, Dennet 3– spring suspension, wooden dash and fenders, fulcrum shafts, height adjustment at rear, two rear steps, c1905, restored **1,100.00**
Coach
    Pall Bearer's, Cunningham, maroon and black body, beveled glass windows, wheels on rubber, pole **10,000.00**
    Pony, unknown maker, black and yellow body, black striping, red running gear, brakes, crab end pole, leader bars **15,500.00**
    Road, Brewster & Co, New York, NY, The Outlaw, black and yellow body, yellow striping, wheels on

rubber, brakes, boxes in rear boot,
crab end pole, serial #22800. . . . **49,500.00**
Stage, Abbott & Downing, red body,
yellow gear, leather slung, side
curtains, brakes, pole, serial #339 **11,200.00**
Gig
  Brewster & Co, NY, Stanhope, Brewster green and black, leather dash
  and fenders, wheel wrench, shaft
  stand, serial #24788, marked on
  brass wheel hub **5,000.00**
  Unknown Maker, wicker body and
  dash, woven diamond design on
  sides, c–spring. **2,700.00**
Hansom Cab, unknown maker, black
body, red tufted upholstered interior   **400.00**
Hearse
  C P Kimball & Co, Chicago, IL, black,
  ornately carved wood, lamps,
  shafts, hub wrench, plated
  cross, wheels on rubber, removable sleigh runners, funeral estab-
  lishment name painted both
  sides **5,800.00**
  Unknown Maker, bowed front, full
  fifth wheel cut under, wheels on
  steel, pole **2,400.00**
Jenny Lind, unknown maker, side
springs, stick seat, side curtains. . . .   **850.00**
Phaeton
  American Stanhope, unknown
  maker, folding top, royal blue,
  camel hair cloth upholstery, cut
  under with reach, wheels on rub-
  ber, shafts **3,500.00**
  Doctor's, Ferd F French & Co, Ltd,
  Boston, MA, folding top **1,400.00**
  Drop Front, Brewster & Co, NY, bur-
  gundy and natural wood finish,
  black folding top, wheels on rub-
  ber, shafts, serial #18301 . . . . . . **5,500.00**
  Folding Top, Kimball, Boston, MA,
  wheels on rubber, shafts, old res-
  toration. **2,150.00**
Gentleman's
  Studebaker, black body, carmine
  gear, tuckaway groom's seat,
  cut under with reach, wheels on
  rubber, shafts, restored **7,700.00**
  Unknown Maker, green, yellow
  striping, wicker seat, dash, and
  groom's seat, cut under, wheels
  on rubber, shafts **6,600.00**
Lady's
  J E Guyer, Waverly, NY, parasol
  top, burgundy, black, and
  wicker body, wicker dash, fenders, and groom's seat, wheels on
  rubber, tan Bedford cord upholstery, shafts, shaft stand, pole,
  yoke, serial #3711, tag located
  under toeboard, restored **7,200.00**

J M Quimby, Newark, NJ, parasol
top, Webster green, yellow
striping, wicker seat, groom's
seat, and dash, whipcord cushioned seats, shafts with patent
leather, restored **5,700.00**
T W Lane Carriage Co, Amesbury,
MA, drop front, blue and black,
auto folding top, fenders, shafts,
wrench **2,900.00**
William R Bishop, 36 Warren St,
NY, wicker, natural finish, shafts **1,900.00**
Rockaway
  Coupe, H H Babcock Co, Watertown, NY, black, red, and natural
  body, natural finish wheels,
  wheels on rubber, shafts, whipple
  tree, old restoration **2,500.00**
  Curtain, S E Bailey Co, Lancaster, PA,
  dark green and wine, leather upholstery, cut under with reach,
  pole, shafts, c1910 . . . . **2,600.00**
Runabout
  Columbus Carriage & Harness Co,
  Columbus, OH, spindle seat,
  shafts, bicycle axle **1,225.00**
  John Moore & Co, Warrent St, NY,
  pony size, wheels on rubber, shafts   **540.00**
  Unknown Maker, tulip seat, black
  body, restored black upholstery,
  yellow wheels, wheels on rubber,
  shafts. **900.00**
  Van Tassell & Kearny, 130–132 E
  13th St, NY, pony size, natural
  wood finish, cut under with reach,
  wheels on rubber, shafts and pole **3,600.00**
  Viceroy, unknown maker, natural
  wood finish, stick seat, wire spoke
  pneumatic wheels, two sets of shafts   **300.00**
Wagon
  Amish, Harper, sliding doors, 1920s **2,500.00**
  Bronson
    Clark Coach Co, black and ma-
    roon, ivory striping, maroon up-
    holstery, cut under with reach,
    wheels on rubber, pole, shafts,
    lamps, restored **3,500.00**
    Unknown Maker, natural wood
    finish, cut under with reach,
    driver's wedge seat, wheels on
    rubber, shafts. **2,500.00**
  Calliope, Gus Kelting, Germany,
  pony size, 114" long, 69" wide
  hub to hub, 91" h to top of flare
  board, carved and painted, circle
  gear, tongue pole, body pole for
  six–up hitch, red sunburst wheels **1,600.00**
  Democrat, unknown maker, natural
  wood finish, oak shadow box side
  panels, adjustable seats, five sets of
  springs, new foam rubber cush-
  ions, c1870, restored **2,100.00**

Wagon, buckboard, Studebaker Jr, 83″ l including hitch, 29″ h, estimated price $2,000.00–3,000.00. Photograph courtesy of James D Julia, Inc.

Explosives, unknown maker, parasol top, black body, red running gear, side springs, brakes, wheels on steel, "Explosives" painted on sides **2,300.00**

Express, C Eastman & Sons, West Concord, NH, former fire wagon from South Berwick, ME, brass rails on sides of body, gold striping, pole, shafts **3,500.00**

Farm
 Studebaker, green, red gear, spring seats, brakes, pole **575.00**
 Unknown Maker, high box body, stenciled sideboards, metal wheels, handset brake, cast iron step **225.00**

Hay
 Gruber Wagon Works, 1¾″ axle, 14 foot hay bed, pole, hay rack, serial #1116 running gear **4,500.00**
 Unknown Maker, stake body, rect hardwood bed, iron–rimmed wheels **135.00**

Hitch, unknown maker, red, white wheels, gold trim, full fifth wheel cut under, brakes, brass trim, pole, restored **1,850.00**

Huckster, unknown maker, "W. Steigerwalt, Bowmanstown, PA" painted on sides, brakes, pole, lamps **5,200.00**

Ice, unknown maker, stenciled sideboards **550.00**

Mail, unknown maker, red and blue body, red running gear, shafts, "Rural Delivery Route No. 2, U. S. Mail" and American flag painted on sides, restored **725.00**

Popcorn, Cretors, cut under, advertising painted on sides **2,000.00**

Showman's, Smith & Sons Carriage Co, Barnesville, GA, louvered racks on back hold circus tent, brakes, c1880 . . . . **2,100.00**

Spray Rig, unknown maker, NY, cast iron axles, cast iron and forged spoked wheels, wood plank platform, 1890–1900. . . . . **145.00**

Spring
 Studebaker, six passenger, brakes, pole **1,800.00**
 Unknown Maker, upholstered seats, steel leaf springs, cast iron steps, painted, faded stenciling **450.00**
 Wright Bros, Deckertown, NJ, four passenger, canopy top, Brewster green body, red gear, wheels on rubber, brakes, pole, shafts, c1890, restored **2,700.00**
 Water, Studebaker, yellow, black trim, wheels on steel, brakes, full fifth wheel cut under, meter on top of tank, sprinkler on rear, restored **7,500.00**

Sleigh
 Albany Cutter
  Charles Schlosser, 03 Loch St, Syracuse, NY, black, maroon panels and runners, striping, burgundy upholstery, shafts, restored. **2,100.00**
  C T Nevens, Auburn, ME, striping, artist sgd paint "G. Gisgen, Pntr.," shafts, c1865 . . . . **1,000.00**
  Flandrau & Co, NY, four passenger, black body, red runners, gold striping, decorative plumes attached to dash, shafts **1,400.00**
  H Murray, Niles, MI, burgundy, green, and black, striping, shafts **2,500.00**
  R Millers Son, Kutztown, PA, Brewster green and burgundy body, tufted upholstered seat, shafts with shaft bells **2,000.00**
  Unknown Maker, four passenger, dark green and maroon, brushed striping and scroll work, scene on back, triple striping, maroon mohair upholstery, pole, restored **3,100.00**
  William Winter, Schoharie, NY, carved eagle heads on dash ironwork, orig paint and striping **1,450.00**
 Basket, unknown maker, wicker body **290.00**
 Bob
  J Colyer & Co, Newark NJ, pony size, four passenger, black body, red bob runners **2,100.00**
  Unknown Maker, black, red trim and runners, collapsible driver's seat swings both directions, brakes, pole, 12 volt headlight **750.00**

Box, T C Sawyer, South Amesbury, MA, red and black body, black leatherette upholstery, shafts, restored 400.00

Butcher's, unknown maker, painted "E. L. Whitcomb" on sides, bob runners, canvas sides, orig butcher block and tools 3,400.00

Cabriolet, unknown maker, black body, gold striping, ornate ironwork 1,550.00

Child's
  36" l, wood, metal fittings, cutter style, old red repaint, old damage and repair 190.00
  38" l, primitive, wood and tin, old red repaint, black and yellow striping, upholstered seat, black leatherized fabric. 100.00

Country Cutter, unknown maker, red body, gray tufted upholstered seat, rein rail, restored. 550.00

Hearse, unknown maker, bob runners. 850.00

Pony, unknown maker, "Manufactured for Wise Bros., Lewisberry, PA" tag, removable sleigh body, shafts.   700.00

Portland Cutter
  Blackhall & Co, Troy, NY, black and red body, red runners 700.00
  S B Wise & Sons, Orrstown, PA, shafts, late 1800s. 450.00
  Sturtevant & Larrabee Co, Binghamton, NY, Welsh pony size, black, red runners and shafts, lambs wool seat cover. 575.00

Racing, unknown maker, black body, maroon undercarriage, gold striping, maroon tufted upholstery, restored. 2,200.00

Squareback Cutter
  Charles Childs & Co, Utica, NY, black body, tan upholstery, yellow runners. 625.00
  John S Wilber, Sandy Hill, NY, black body, gold striping, red upholstery 550.00
  Unknown Maker, green, red upholstery, shafts, maker's tag . . .   400.00

Surrey, unknown maker, four passenger, bob runners. 550.00

Swell Body Cutter, unknown maker, dark green and maroon, striping, maroon mohair upholstery, shafts, restored. 3,000.00

Trap, unknown maker, oak, burgundy body, striping, gray wool upholstery, spindled sides, front seat moves back and forth for easy entry, fold-down back seat, shafts. 3,400.00

Victoria, panel boot, Brewster & Co, Broome St, NY, pole 3,400.00

Vis–A–Vis
  Heiko Wurhmann, six to eight passenger, burgundy, navy upholstery, hand carved lion heads both sides, brass trim, hand crank brake, brass heads on pole, restored. 2,900.00
  Unknown Maker, black body, yellow runners, two screens in front of coachman's seat, doors on both sides of passenger's seats 3,300.00

Wicker Cutter, unknown maker, dark green and yellow platform and runners, wicker body, restored . .   400.00

Sulky, unknown maker, cob size, natural finish, cane seat, shaft irons, black hickory shafts, c1891 . . . .   425.00

Surrey
  Michigan Buggy Co, pony size, four passenger, cut under with reach, canopy fringe top, whip holder, shafts.   1,600.00
  Studebaker, four passenger, auto top, black body, maroon wheels, striping on side enclosures, shafts, marked on step treads, new top and sides. 2,050.00
  Unknown Maker, four passenger, canopy fringe top, side spring, natural wood finish, tan upholstery, brakes, wheels on rubber, shafts.   1,500.00

Trap
  A T Demarest, side bar, natural wood finish, beige upholstery, rear seat reverses to face forward or backward, wheels on rubber, pole, yoke, restored 2,800.00
  Unknown Maker, back to back seating, black body, maroon undercarriage, natural wicker sides, striping on siding, cut under with reach, wheels on rubber, shafts, restored. 3,200.00

TRACTORS

Case
  1921, 10–18. . . . .   2,000.00
  1925, Cross motor, restored 6,000.00
  1935, model C, rubber, spokes 2,400.00
  1937, model L, on steel, runs 825.00
  1950, model SC 675.00

Farmall
  1930, Regular. 900.00
  1938, model F–14, rubber 1,750.00
  1940, model B, mower. 1,900.00
  1946, model M, restored. 2,300.00
  1949, model MD, complete, runs   600.00

Ford, 1953, model NAA	**2,250.00**	1953, model 50	**2,000.00**
Fordson		1955, model 80	**4,200.00**
1923, on steel, runs	**2,300.00**	Lawson, 1925, full jeweled	**1,500.00**
1936, rubber, runs	**1,100.00**	Mc–Deering	
Gray, 1916, three wheel	**15,000.00**	1936, model O–12, rubber, runs . . .	**2,500.00**
Hart–Parr, 1925, 28–50	**2,500.00**	1952, model WD–6	**600.00**
John Deere		M–H, 1936, Challenger, steel	**2,200.00**
1931, model GPWT, restored	**8,000.00**	M–M	
1935, model A, factory round spokes	**1,300.00**	1938, model KTA	**1,200.00**
1936, model B, on steel	**2,200.00**	1947, model GTA	**1,025.00**
1941, model AR	**1,350.00**	1953, model UT	**400.00**
1951, model AR	**1,950.00**	Oliver, 99 GM	**3,400.00**
1952, model 50	**1,075.00**	Silver King, 1946, runs	**1,800.00**

WOOD AND NATURAL MATERIALS

Rural America used wood because it was inexpensive and readily available. As land was cleared for settlement and farming, the wood from trees became fuel for heat or lumber for building or a host of products ranging from barrels to furniture.

Grain and tone explain the appeal of natural wood. Each piece exhibits individual characteristics. This aspect was understood and admired in an agrarian society. Natural wood has an earthy tone, strong yet subdued.

Over the years wood patinates and oxidates. These two forces create a feel to wood that is impossible to duplicate. Only time can accomplish the effect.

Many wooden forms were grained, painted, or stenciled. Because this was done by hand, they also exhibit strong individual characteristics. In the 1950s it was common practice to strip painted pieces and refinish them to expose the natural wood grains. The folk art revival of the late 1960s through the early 1980s focused interest on painted pieces, showing that the painting is an integral part of the piece.

Painted pieces now have strong appeal among Country collectors as well. Tastes range from ornately decorated blanket chests to the warm milk paint tones often found on pie safes. Painted wooden pieces have found a permanent home in Country.

BASKETS

History: The Country look focuses on baskets made of splint, rye straw, or willow, with emphasis on handmade examples. Nails or staples, wide splints which are thin and evenly cut, or wire bail handles denote factory construction which can date to the mid–19th century. Painted or woven decorated baskets rarely are handmade, unless American Indian.

Baskets are collected by (a) type—berry, egg, or field, (b) region–Nantucket or Shaker, and (c) composition—splint, rye, or willow. Stick to examples in very good condition; damaged baskets are a poor investment even at a low price.

References: Frances Johnson, *Wallace–Homestead Price Guide To Baskets, Second Edition*, Wallace–Homestead, 1989; Don and Carol Raycraft, *Collector's Guide to Country Baskets*, Collector Books, 1985, 1994 value update; Martha Wetherbee and Nathan Taylor, *Legend of the Bushwhacker Basket*, published by author, 1986;

Christoph Will, *International Basketry For Weavers and Collectors*, Schiffer Publishing, 1985.

Museums: Old Salem, Inc., Winston–Salem, NC; The Heard Museum, Phoeniz, AZ.

Reproduction Craftspersons: *General*—Darryl & Karen Arawjo, PO Box 477, Bushkill, PA 18324; Cheryl I Boyer, Berkshire Ash Baskets, PO Box 144, Lanesborough, MA 01237; Mr & Mrs J H Durham, Rte 2, Box 60, Cherokee, AL 35616; Richard & Christine Foster, Stannard Mountain Basketry, RD 1, Box 1385, East Hardwick, VT 05836; Bonnie & Jeffrey Gale, RFD 1, Box 124A, South New Berlin, NY 13843; Ross A Gibson, Day Basket Co, 110 W High St, North East, MD 21901 Barbara & Norbert Hala, 1641 Etta Kable Dr, Beavercreek, OH 45432; Sue Hahn, Old Times– Baskets, 41547 S R 558, Leetonia, OH 44431; Susan L Kelleher, 859 Iron Bridge Rd, Mount Joy, PA 17552; Jonathan Kline, Black Ash Baskets, 5066 Mott Evans Rd, Trumansburg, NY 14886; Susan Kolvereid, 834 Old State Rd, Berwyn, PA 19312; Dave Lewis Basketry, RD 2, Box 684,

Bedford, PA 15522; Martha Watson Lorentzen, 2 Jared Ln, Yarmouthport, MA 02675; Richard & Jodi McAllister, Red Bird Mission Crafts, HC–69, Box 15, Queen Dale Center, Beverly, KY 40913; John E McGuire, Baskets & Bears, 398 S Main St, Geneva, NY 14456; Deborah M Muhl, PO Box 513, Spinnerstown, PA 18968; Carol Nelson, Walnut Creek Baskets, 12018 217th St W, PO Box 84, Illinois City, IL 61259; Susi Nuss, Basket-maker, 5 Steele Crossing Rd, Bolton, CT 06043; Gary A O'Brien, Meadow Farm, Ruggles Hill Rd, Hardwick, MA 01037; Gwynne Ormsby, 415 W Market St, West Chester, PA 19382; Beth Peterson & Mark Kelz, Splintworks, PO Box 858, Cave Junction, OR 97523; Joyce Schaum Basketry, 2212 Reifsnider Rd, Keymar, MD 21757; Alvin & Trevle Wood, 2415 E Main St, Murfreesboro, TN 37130; Aaron Yakim, Rte 2, Box 314A, West Union, WV 26456; Stephen Zeh, Basketmaker, PO Box 381, Temple, ME 04984.

Indian—Rhonda N Anderson, Maine Abenaki Sweetgrass Baskets, 49 Ramsdell Rd, Gray, ME 04039; Gary O'Brien, Meadow Farm Baskets, PO Box 78, Hardwick, MA 01037; Donna Rohkohl, The Basket Barn, PO Box 138, Howell, MI 48844; Joyce Schaum, 2212 Reifsnider Rd, Keymar, MD 21757; *Nantucket Lightship*—Barbette & Richard Behm, Maine Island Baskets, 112 Euclid Ave, Portland, ME 04103; Barbara Bonfanti, 112 Ox-ford Dr, Lititz, PA 17543; Sue Gruebel, Log House Primitives, PO Box 206, Circleville, OH 43113; John & Holiday Hays, Holiday and Garshwiller, Rte 1, Box 34, Bloomingdale, IN 47832; Joe & Sylvia Hemphill, Heritage Baskets, PO Box 305, Britton, MI 49229; Virginia S Knight, PO Box 39575, Ft Lauderdale, FL 33339; Carol Lasnier, Country Companions, 35 Chittenden Rd, Hebron, CT 06231; Kathy & Robert Loring, Heirloom Bas-kets of Chatham, PO Box 1145, S Chatham, MA 02659; Carol S Lasnier, Country Companions, 35 Chittenden Rd, Hebron, CT 06231; Jack Nichols, 392 Schuylkill Rd, Birdsboro, PA 19508; Leslie Marshall Nutting, 32 Forest Hill Dr, Simsbury, CT 06070; Bill & Marilyn Rosenquist, Lightship Baskets, 342 Moose Hill Rd, Guilford, CT 06437; Ronald J Wilson, 1600 Westbrook Ave, Apt 633, Richmond, VA 23227; *Rye Straw*—Marie Stotler, 23 Frame Ave, Malvern, PA 19355; *Shaker*—Cindi L Bailey, Wilson Rd, Canterbury, NH 03224.

Reproduction Manufacturers: *General*—Adiron-dack Store and Gallery, 109 Saranac Ave, Lake Placid, NY 12946; American Folklore, 330 W Pleasant, Freeport, IL 61032; Anastasia's Collect-ibles, 6114 134th St W, Apple Valley, MN 55124; Bullfrog Hollow, Keeny Rd, Lyme, CT 06371; Checkerberry Hill, 253 Westridge Ave, Daly City, CA 94015; Chinaberry General Store, 1846 Win-field Dunn Highway, Sevierville, TN 38762; Country Loft, 1506 South Shore Park, Hingham,

MA 02043; The Country Stippler, Rte 2, Box 1540, Pine Mountain, GA 31822; Country Wicker, 2238D Bluemound Rd, Waukesha, WI 53186; Faith Mountain Country Fare, Main St, Box 199, Sperryville, VA 22740; Flying Pig Artworks, PO Box 474, Milford, MI 48042; Folk Art Emporium, 3591 Forest Haven Ln, Chesapeake, VA 23321; Gooseberry Patch, PO Box 634, Delaware, OH 43015; The Herb Cottage, Lincoln Way East, RD 2, Box 130, Fayetteville, PA 17222; Ingrid's Hand-craft Crossroads, 8 Randall Rd, Rochester, MA 02770; J M Brel, Rte 8, Box 246, Fairmont, WV 26554; Matthews Emporium, 157 N Trade St, PO Box 1038, Matthews, NC 28106; McClanahan Country, 217 Rockwell Rd, Wilmington, NC 28405; Mulberry Magic, PO Box 62, Ruckersville, VA 22968; Pure and Simple, PO Box 535, 117 W Hempstead, Nashville, AR 71852; Southern Man-ner, Inc, 106 North Trade St, PO Box 1706, Mat-thews, NC 28106; A Special Blend of Country, RD 1, Box 56, Fabius, NY 13063; The Vine and Cupboard, PO Box 309, George Wright Rd, Wool-wich, ME 04579; The Vinery, 103 Alta Vista, Waterloo, IA 40703; West Rindge Baskets, West Main St, Rindge, NH 03461.

Kits and Supplies—The Back Door–Country Baskets, 10 Batchellor Dr, North Brookfield, MA 01535; The Basket Barn, PO Box 138, Howell, MI 48844; Cane Bottom, 1 Park Dr, Roxana, IL 62084; The Country Seat, RD 2, Box 24, Kempton, PA 19529; Frank's Cane and Rush Supply, 7252 Heil Ave, Huntington Beach, CA 92647.

Apple

15″ d, 9″ h, oak staves, solid turned pine bottom, bentwood bail han-dle, overlapping rim strip, wire re-inforcement around lower section	**150.00**
16″ d, split wood, rounded bottom, bentwood swivel handle, hanging strap and hook, c1915	**68.00**
Bee Skep, rye, 17″ d, 17″ h	**230.00**
Berry, split wood	
5″ d, woven splint, round	**15.00**
7″ d, 5¾″ h, crisscross bands	**45.00**
8 × 9½″, 5″ h, woven splint, melon rib, old red paint and natural	**200.00**
10 × 10½, 6″ h, woven splint, but-tocks, good age and color, bentwood handle	**80.00**
10¾ × 11½″, 5½″ h, woven splint, buttocks, bentwood handle	**125.00**
Berry Carrier, turned handle, square tray, four stapled machine–cut soft-wood berry baskets	**24.00**
Burden, 14″ sq, 16″ h, woven splint, square bottom, round rim, old patina	**45.00**
Bushel, 18 × 11″, stave construction, wrapped with wire bands, wooden rim, bentwood rim handles, old var-nish finish	**150.00**

Buttocks, woven splint, weathered gray finish, some damage

12 × 14", 7½" h plus bentwood handle **50.00**

14 × 15", 7" h plus bentwood handle, square, some age and wear **85.00**

14 × 18", 8" h plus bentwood handle **95.00**

17 × 15", 9" h plus handle, worn black paint, some wear and damage **138.00**

17½ × 20", 11" h plus bentwood handle, stripped surface, traces of white paint and some damage. . . **60.00**

21 × 21", 11" h plus bentwood handle, some age and damage **72.00**

Cheese, hexagonal weave, woven splint, round

15" d **125.00**

21" d, 7" h, good age and color, minor damage **275.00**

21½" d, 8" h, gray scrubbed finish **275.00**

Clothespin, 14¼ × 12½", willow, early 20th C. **85.00**

Cotton Picking

18" h, woven splint, old worn blue paint, leather shoulder strap **310.00**

22" d, 20" h, split **115.00**

Dough Rising, 23" d, shallow, rye straw, hickory splint binding, PA, late 19th C **115.00**

Drying

11 × 15, 6¼" h, woven splint, open work bottom, open rim handles **55.00**

14½ × 15", woven splint, open weave wire bottom, bentwood handle branded "Dr. Webb" **70.00**

Egg

6½ × 9", 4" h, woven splint, buttocks, Eye of God design at bentwood handle **95.00**

7¼" d, 4½" h, woven splint, bentwood handle sgd "Haver," good patina **250.00**

7½ × 8", 4" h, woven splint, buttocks, bentwood handle **85.00**

8 × 10¾", 5" h, woven splint, radiating ribs, bentwood handle. **135.00**

8½" d, woven splint, old green paint **225.00**

Egg Basket, white oak splint, melon ribbed, 12½" l, 7½" w, 12" h, $150.00.

9 × 11", 4½" h, woven splint, melon rib, Eye of God design at handle **35.00**

10½ × 12", 6" h, woven splint, radiating ribs, bentwood handle, old varnish finish **60.00**

11 × 12", 6½" h, woven splint, buttocks, bentwood handle. **75.00**

11½ × 10½", 5½" h, woven splint, buttocks, bentwood handle **75.00**

15 × 17, woven splint, bentwood handle, weathered gray scrubbed finish **55.00**

Feather

20" d, 26" h, ash splint, New England, early 19th C **275.00**

21" d, 25" h, sliding lid, Shaker, New England, 19th C. **425.00**

Field, woven splint

15" d, 11½" h, wooden bottom, old natural patina, "H.S.B." painted in red. **60.00**

18" d, 12¾" h, round, good color, bentwood rim handles, minor damage **85.00**

28 × 17", 12" h, oval, oak splint, bow handles, ftd, carved oak runners reinforce bottom, c1875 . . . . **135.00**

29" d, ash and hickory splint, loosely woven, c1900 . . . . **325.00**

29½ × 17", oak splint, rib construction, wrapped bentwood handle, 19th C **265.00**

30" d, 15¾" h, oak splint, rib construction, carved handles, c1880 **225.00**

32" d, 16½" h, rib construction, bow handles, New England, c1850 . . . **275.00**

42 × 26", 12" h, rect, ash splint, CT, 19th C **350.00**

Flower

6" h, woven splint, bentwood handle **85.00**

10½" d, ash splint, tightly woven, extra long carved handle, 1800s, New England **110.00**

Fruit, 7¾" h, ftd, pierced, contrasting woods, attributed to North Andover, MA, 19th C **250.00**

Game, 21" h, woven splint, two part, loom crest, hanging. **195.00**

Garden, 11½" d, 6½" h, woven splint, carved handle continues to bottom, VA, 19th C **190.00**

Gathering

9½" d, woven splint, flat tray, bentwood handle, old green paint **145.00**

12 × 18½", rect, boat shaped, woven splint, shallow, high bentwood handle **55.00**

13½ × 10½", oval, woven splint, flared sides, traces of old red paint, some damage, 5" h plus bentwood handle **85.00**

14 × 22½", 6" h, woven splint, bentwood handle, sun bleached, minor damage. **45.00**

15" d, round, woven splint, weathered gray finish, minor damage, 8½" h plus well shaped bentwood handle. **105.00**

15½ × 20½", 10" h, woven splint, two bentwood rim handles, one perpendicular handle **145.00**

16 × 11", oval, woven splint, weathered gray finish, 8½" h plus bentwood handle **60.00**

16 × 15", oval, woven splint, radiating ribs, old varnish, 6 ½" h plus bentwood handle **210.00**

17" d, round, woven splint, scrubbed finish, 7¼" h plus bentwood handle **115.00**

18" d, 9" h, round, rye straw, rim handles, wear and one handle partially restored **105.00**

18¼ × 15½", oval, woven splint, 19th C.   **110.00**

Goose Feather, woven splint

16" d, 24" h, lid, bentwood handles   **95.00**

25" h, dome lid, good color, bentwood handles covered by lid, rim of lid broken, minor damage   **80.00**

Half, 11½ × 7", 5" h, woven splint, bentwood handle, good detail **175.00**

Herb Drying

16" d, 6¾" h, round, woven splint, open weave base, minor damage, bentwood rim handles **240.00**

20½ × 21", rect, woven splint. **355.00**

Hourglass Shaped

10½" d, 12" h, woven splint. **50.00**

12" d, 22" h, splint, two part. **70.00**

18½" d, 18½" h, Woodland, lid, woven splint, potato print designs, faded red, yellow, green, and natural **275.00**

Kitchen, 12 × 14, 6½" h, woven splint, buttocks, woven in three shades of splint **150.00**

Knife, 9 × 12", 3½" h, woven splint, divided interior, polychrome watercolor floral design, bentwood handle   **225.00**

Laundry, woven splint

18½" d, 12" h, round, bentwood rim handles, marked "OHW" **55.00**

19" d, 11¾" h, round, rim hand holds, copper wire woven in bottom **95.00**

19 × 31", 13½" h, bentwood rim handles. **100.00**

20½ × 25½", 10¾" h, rect, natural finish, bentwood rim handles . . .   **75.00**

21" d, 10" h, round, bentwood rim handles. **65.00**

22 × 27", 12½" h, oval, rim hand holds. **100.00**

24 × 20", 11" h, oblong, ribbed, open rim handles, damage **95.00**

26" d, 16" h, rim handles, dark finish, some damage **50.00**

31" l, 21" w, 10" h, rect **75.00**

40" l, 22" w, 12" h, minor damage   **60.00**

Loom

7½" w, 6¾" h, hanging, cane, faded curliqued ribbon, and string dec   **35.00**

10½" w, 17" h, hanging, woven splint, two section, traces of yellow paint. **375.00**

12" w, 13" h, hanging, woven splint, crest **100.00**

15" w, 17" h, hanging, woven splint, curlique designs, Eastern Woodlands. **40.00**

Lunch, 8 × 6", oval, woven splint, ash wrapped handle, two lift lids on crosspieces, tightly woven, 1800s   **165.00**

Market

8½ × 14½", 6¼" h, woven splint, natural, red, and black woven design, bentwood handle **85.00**

9 × 15", 8" h, rect, woven splint, bentwood handle **65.00**

11 × 20", 9" h, lid, woven splint, bentwood handle, damaged **75.00**

12" d, 7½" h, round, woven splint, wooden bottom, swivel handle   **125.00**

12½ × 17½", 6½" h, rect, woven splint, double swing handles **120.00**

16 × 14", woven splint, early 19th C   **70.00**

16 × 23", 11¾" h, woven splint, woven center brace, faded green bands, bentwood handle **195.00**

Melon Rib, 15" d, 7½" h, woven splint, round, cane wrapped wood handle **65.00**

Miniature

3" l, 3½" h, woven splint, buttocks, "one egg" size. **350.00**

3¼" d, 1⅝" h, woven splint, square base, round rim, old patina **85.00**

Market, rattan, painted rim and diamond design, 16½" w, 10¼" d, 15" h, $25.00.

$3\frac{1}{2} \times 7\frac{3}{8}$", 2" h, rect, woven splint, old patina, minor damage **115.00**

$4 \times 4\frac{1}{2}$", 2" h, woven splint, buttocks, bentwood handle, old patina, minor damage **250.00**

$4\frac{1}{4}$" h, melon rib, late 19th/early 20th C **330.00**

$5 \times 5\frac{1}{4}$", $2\frac{3}{4}$" h, woven splint, buttocks, bentwood handle **165.00**

Nantucket, Nantucket Island, MA, swing handle, early 20th C

6" d, 8" h, lightship type, swing handle. **1,100.00**

8" l, $4\frac{1}{2}$" h, oval, swing handle. . . . **245.00**

$8\frac{3}{4}$" d, $10\frac{1}{4}$" h, round, swing handle **330.00**

9" d, $4\frac{3}{4}$" h, incised base **550.00**

11" d, 5" h, incised base, varnished ext. **600.00**

11" l, $5\frac{1}{4}$" h, oval, swing handle. . . **265.00**

Native American

Algonquin, storage, $16\frac{1}{2} \times 24\frac{1}{2}$", 13" h, birch bark, negative scraped leaf designs, wear and breaks in bottom **200.00**

Apache, $20\frac{1}{2}$" d, $4\frac{3}{4}$" h, tray type, willow and martynia, eighteen figures, c1920, small rim breaks, 5" tear, painted rim **990.00**

Astugewi, Hot Creek, northern CA, $6\frac{1}{2}$" d, 5" h, turned base changes to full twist overlay of beargrass and redbud, lattice twined band, checkerboard design **250.00**

Cahvilla, southern CA, $11\frac{1}{2}$" d, $3\frac{3}{4}$" h, natural and dyed juncus design, rim wear **215.00**

Chemehuevi, $5\frac{3}{4}$" d, $4\frac{3}{4}$" h, polychrome basketry olla, brown and purple geometric design on natural ground, attributed to Ann Land, c1900 . . . . **3,500.00**

Native American, Apache olla, interlocking diamonds and checkerboard design, late 19th C, 21" h, $7,700.00. Photograph courtesy of W E Channing & Co, Inc.

Chippewa, 11" h, woven cane, multicolored **140.00**

Eskimo, $7\frac{1}{4}$" d, $7\frac{3}{4}$" h, knobbed lid, grass, polychrome design, c1900 **115.00**

Hupa, acorn storage, 10" d, $7\frac{1}{2}$" h, half and full twist twined beargrass and woodwardia design, heavy reinforced rim, two holes at base, one warp break at top spacing. . . **75.00**

Macha, 3" d, 2" h, lid, twined, whaling ships and birds, minor rim damage **115.00**

Makah, storage

$8\frac{1}{2}$" d, $5\frac{1}{2}$" h, brown, green, and natural stripes, wire supported rewrapped rim **25.00**

10×12", $4\frac{3}{4}$" h, leaf design between double bands. **105.00**

Mission, $9\frac{1}{2}$" d, $2\frac{3}{4}$" h, juncus design, rim damage **175.00**

Papago, bowl type, martynia and yucca

$7\frac{3}{4} \times 10$", $4\frac{1}{2}$" h, stepped zig–zag design **172.00**

$10\frac{1}{2}$" d, $6\frac{1}{2}$" h, stepped polychrome design, some rim damage. **325.00**

Pima/Papago, $7\frac{1}{2}$" d, 3" h, bowl type, martynia and yucca, woman design, some stitch damage **140.00**

Piute, seed storage, $9\frac{1}{2}$" d, $6\frac{1}{2}$" h, twined, jar shaped, plant cordage lugs **350.00**

Salishan, berry, 6" d, $4\frac{1}{2}$" h, bowl shaped, braided rim, beargrass spot design, loose rim end **85.00**

Western Apache, $11\frac{3}{4}$" d, $3\frac{1}{4}$" h, bowl type, willow and martynia, three circular bands of men and women figures, drips of green paint on rim and bottom . . **1,485.00**

Peanut Gathering, $19\frac{3}{4}$" l, $3\frac{1}{4}$" h, factory made, machine–cut wide splint, painted white, VA **75.00**

Pea Picking

10" l, splint, rect, red. **220.00**

16×11", 6" h, oval, wide overlapping split wood, attached feet, full circular bentwood handle **75.00**

Picnic

$7\frac{3}{4} \times 15$", 7" h, splint, double hinged lid, green and natural colored interior design, faded exterior, bentwood handle **100.00**

$9\frac{3}{4} \times 15$", 7" h, woven splint, red paint over earlier black paint, swivel handle **65.00**

16" l, $12\frac{1}{2}$" w, lid, woven splint, bentwood swivel handle **85.00**

Potato, round, ash splint **35.00**

Rye Straw, 12" d, $5\frac{1}{2}$" h **85.00**

Sewing, cov, woven, splint bottom, 9″ d, $30.00.

Sower's, 12 × 14½″, 7″ h, woven splint, bentwood handle **50.00**

Storage

10″ h, oval, rye straw **50.00**

12 × 15″, 9½″ h, rect, woven splint, red, black, and green painted dec **105.00**

12 × 16¼″, 6½″ h, woven splint, bentwood rim handles, dark patina **75.00**

13 × 15″, 10½″ h, woven splint, bentwood handle, minor damage   **75.00**

14″ d, 15¾″ h, woven splint, twill pattern, square base, round rim, old patina, c1910 . . . .   **145.00**

15 × 19″, 12″ h, rect, lid, woven splint, teal blue and pink watercolor designs, worn **135.00**

16″ d, 8½″ h, rye straw, rim handles   **85.00**

17″ d, 9″ h, woven splint, bentwood handle, misshapen **95.00**

17 × 18″, 9″ h, woven splint, bentwood swing handle, old mustard yellow paint **1,300.00**

17¼″ l, rect, lid, woven splint, alternating red potato print design and yellow paint, minor damage **250.00**

19 × 20″, 11″ h, rect, lid, woven splint, red, blue, and yellow watercolor designs, worn **170.00**

21″ d, 14½″ h, woven splint, rim hand holds, minor damage **145.00**

Storage, willow, two handles, 22″ d, 25½″ h, $65.00.

Table, 14″ d, white oak splint, loosely woven **45.00**

Tobacco, 38″ l, splint, open weave, shallow **75.00**

Utility

5¾″ d, round, woven splint, bentwood handle, old worn dark varnish **75.00**

7½ × 12½″, 4½″ h, oblong, bentwood handle **75.00**

8″ d, 5″ h, woven splint, hickory handle, weathered **105.00**

8½ × 9½″, 4¼″ h, woven splint, buttocks, bentwood handle **135.00**

9″ d, 5″ h, round, woven splint, bentwood rim handles, old patina   **175.00**

9¾″ d, 5½″ h, round, woven splint, faded red woven design **150.00**

10″ d, 4″ h, round, woven splint, scalloped rim, bentwood handle   **250.00**

10 × 14½″, 7″ h plus handle, oval, woven splint, double swivel handles, worn finish **100.00**

11 × 22″, 7″ h, rect, woven splint, buttocks, bentwood handle **25.00**

11½″ d, 6½″ h, woven splint, bentwood handle, old varnish . . .   **105.00**

12 × 12″ sq, 4½″ h, square, woven splint, natural patina, faded blue paint, 12 × 12″, 4½″ h **200.00**

12½ × 13½″, 10″ h plus bentwood handle, round, woven splint, faded green and purple **45.00**

13″ d, 6¾″ h, woven splint, curlique band, bentwood handle **155.00**

13 × 17″, 7½″ h, oblong, woven splint, radiating ribs, bentwood handle, old patina **65.00**

13½″ d, 8″ h, woven splint, bentwood handle **110.00**

13½ × 15½″, 9½″ h, woven splint, polka dot designs on red and black watercolor and natural ground, worn rim **85.00**

14½ × 18″, 8½″ h bentwood handle, oval, woven splint, dark varnish stain finish **62.00**

15 × 17″, 8½″ h, woven splint, bentwood swing handle, out of round, old varnish, old repair in bottom **130.00**

16½ × 18½″, 8½″ h, woven splint, buttocks, old patina, bentwood handle **65.00**

Vegetable, 18 × 14½″, 7¾″ h, rect, woven splint, bentwood handle attached lengthwise, c1880 . . . .   **120.00**

Wall Pocket

9″ l, woven splint, yellow over white and red, 19th C **110.00**

12 × 9″, 6″ h, poplar splint, New England, c1850 . . . .   **95.00**

Work, splint, 14" d, 8½" h, $75.00.

Wine, 21¾" l, willow, divided interior holds twelve bottles, factory made, early 20th C	**65.00**
Work, 11½ × 18", woven splint, bentwood rim handle, attached small woven oval basket interior corner, light blue paint	**110.00**

BOXES

History: Boxed storage was commonplace in the rural American home. Although pasteboard boxes (see Band Boxes) were available, most rural individuals preferred boxes made from wood. There simply was something sturdy and lasting about a wood box.

Boxes were designed for specific tasks. Among the most commonly found forms are: candle boxes, document boxes, jewelry boxes, and knife boxes. Everything imaginable was stored in boxes—clothing, salt, spices, and trinkets, just to name a few. Often the family Bible was kept in a Bible box.

The folk art collecting craze of the 1970s and 80s drew attention to the painted box. A grain painting revival occurred among contemporary craftspersons. The Country movement became enamored with "primitives," i.e., crudely constructed boxes. Completely overlooked were the high style and better constructed boxes, many of which were imported from abroad.

During the early American revival from the 1930s through the 1950s, a great hoopla was raised over Bride's boxes, ornately painted oval bentwood boxes, many of which featured a picture of bride and groom. Although many were passed as American in origin, research has proven that almost all originated in Europe.

In fact, there is a strong painted furniture tradition in a number of European countries—Norway, southwest Germany, and many Slavic countries. Although different in color tone and design, many novice collectors buy these items believing them to be American in origin.

Reproduction Craftspersons: *Bentwood and Pantry*—Donald Butler, 402 Lombard St, Philadelphia, PA 19147; E B Frye and Son, Inc, Frye's Measure Mill, Wilton, NH 03086; Charles Harvey, Simple Gifts, 201 C N Broadway, Berea, KY 40403; Bill Scherer, Shaker Carpenter Shop, 8267 Oswego Rd, Liverpool, NY 13088; Eric Taylor & Betty Grondin, Northern Swallow Tails, 13A High St, Danbury, NH 03230; Mary Travis, RR 1, Box 96, Fairbury, IL 61739.

Decorated—Donna W Albro, Strawberry Vine, 6677 Hayhurst St, Worthington, OH 43085; Carol Fankhauser, Heartwood, PO Box 458, Canfield, OH 44406; Petra & Thomas Haas, PO Box 20, Oley, PA 19547; *General*—Gary S Adriance, Adriance Heritage Collection, 5 N Pleasant St, South Dartmouth, MA 02748; Richard and Bess Leaf, Box 223, Rte 5, Jenkins Chapel Rd, Shelbyville, TN 37160; Jan Switzer, Painted Pony Folk Art, 8392 M–72 West, Traverse City, MI 49684; *Wall*—Tom Douglass, RD 1, Box 38, Hopwood, PA 15445.

Reproduction Manufacturers: *Bentwood and Pantry*—Chinaberry General Store, 1846 Winfield Dunn Highway, Sevierville, TN 38762; Country Lighting and Accessories, PO Box 1279, New London, NH 03257; Hofcraft, PO Box 1791, Grand Rapids, MI 49501; The Friends, Box 464, Frederick, MD 21701; Unfinished Business, PO Box 246X, Wingate, NC 28174; *Bible*—Conewago Junction, 805 Oxford Rd, New Oxford, PA 17350.

General—Classics in Wood, 82 Lisbon Rd, Canterbury, CT 06331; The Colonial Keeping Room 16 Ridge Rd, RFD 1, Box 704, Fairfield, ME 04937; Country House, 5939 Trails End, Three Oaks, MI 49128; Country Loft, 1506 South Shore Park, Hingham, MA 02043; KML Enterprises, RR 1, Box 234L, Berne, IN 46711; The Ohlinger's, PO Box 462, Gurnee, IL 60031; Our Home, Articles of Wood, 666 Perry St, Vermilion, OH 44089; Out of the Woods, 38 Pinehurst Rd, Marshfield, MA 02050; Pine Cone Primitives, PO Box 682, Troutman, NC 28166; South Bound Millworks, PO Box 349, Sandwich, MA 02563; Ye Olde Wood Smith, Box 300, Alliance, NE 69301; *Jewelry*—Honeybrook Woods, RD 2, Box 102, Honey Brook, PA 19344; *Pipe*—Five Trails Antiques and Country Accents, 116 E Water St, Circleville, OH 43113; *Salt*—Log Cabin Shop, Box 275, Lodi, OH 44254; Mulberry Magic, PO Box 62, Ruckersville, VA 22968.

Apple, 11¼ × 12¼", pine, primitive, canted sides, attributed to Shakers, some renailing	**125.00**
Apple shape, 3" h, turned fruitwood, mirror underside of cover, some losses at stem, 19th C	**425.00**
Ballot	
6" l, poplar, decorated, red and black graining, polychrome bronze powder stenciled eagle, shield, and vintage on lid, bird and foliage on front, gold striping, ballot slot in lid and bottom	**160.00**

14¼" l, walnut, dovetailed case, slot in lid, orig lock, red stained int., refinished exterior **125.00**

Bible, 17¼" l, pine, chip carved design on facade, rose head wrought iron nail construction, old dark patina, age cracks, replaced hinges **120.00**

Bird's Eye Maple, 12½" w, 9" d, 5½" h, brass bound, fitted int., lower drawer, imperfections **600.00**

Black Ball, 9½" h plus handle, walnut, turned handle, old finish, partial orig paper label "Parson & Co, Manufacturers of Regalia . . .", with marbles   **110.00**

Book, 12" l, walnut, int. slide out compartment, green gilt and red trimmed emb paper covering **200.00**

Bride's Box, pine, bentwood, oval

15" l, polychrome floral dec, light blue ground, insect damage **300.00**

15¾" l, polychrome buildings, house, and tree, white ground, damaged lid **225.00**

17¾" l, polychrome floral dec, black ground, lid dec with equestrian soldier with saber, German inscription, lid and base repinned, lid seam relaced **1,050.00**

18¾" l, polychrome floral dec, black ground, lid with couple holding hands and German inscription "Thou Goest with me and I with thee . . ." **2,300.00**

19½" l, polychrome floral dec and scene on lid with couple in park and German inscription, insect damage and wear, some edge damage, age cracks, lid seam relaced   **1,100.00**

20" l, polychrome floral dec, orange–red ground, top of lid with German inscription and découpage scene of Baker's, minor wear   **990.00**

20½" l, polychrome painted floral dec, blue ground, lid with couple and German inscription, bottom board and laced seams loose, age crack in side **1,300.00**

Bugle, 19¼" l, decorated, hard and soft woods, old black repaint over earlier blue, red striping, gold stenciled designs, initials, and polychrome bugle, repaired bottom board, missing handle **300.00**

Candle

9¾" h, mahogany, hanging, dovetailed, old finish, pine bottom with indistinct inscription "Manufactured by Uncle Daniel St– who died – 1824," old repair in end   **250.00**

10½" l, tin, hanging, horizontal cylinder, hinged lid, hanging tabs, old black paint **125.00**

14" l, pine, black and white striping and alligatored finish, orig red paint, sliding lid **200.00**

16½" h, hardwood, rounded crest, sliding front lid, old finish **275.00**

19¼" l, pine and poplar, three finger hole sliding lid, old red paint. . . .   **175.00**

Carved

3½" l, allover chip carving, sliding lid, made from one pc of wood   **100.00**

7¾" d, 5" h, round, cork, chip carved designs, leather trim, worn brown patina **55.00**

9" l

Mahogany, relief carved flower and foliage dec **85.00**

Pine, relief carved designs four sides and lid, four different eagles, foliage, crossed flags, and "U.S.A. Fort Hancock," homemade locking mechanism, old varnish finish, 7¾" h   **325.00**

12¼" l, walnut, dovetailed case, geometric chip carved and stamped designs, line inlay in base and lid molding, brass bail handle, old finish **400.00**

18" l, walnut, dovetailed, allover chip carving, engraved metal plate on lid inscribed "Desmond Fitzgerald 1877," ftd, lift–out int. tray, age cracks **225.00**

Decorated

7" l, poplar, lock and key, orig red flame graining **110.00**

8½" d, 8¼" h, round, poplar, red sponging on yellow ground, replaced lid finial **700.00**

9⅝" l, poplar, orig tan paint and gold stenciled designs on beveled edge lid **75.00**

10" l, 9" deep, 3" h, pine, gold stenciled floral dec and fruit compote on black ground, ftd, marbleized paper–lined int. **130.00**

10¼" l, poplar, rect, hinged lid, black and blue stenciled and freehand floral dec, red ground, wire hinges, old hard putty repair to bottom front edge **525.00**

11¼" l, tulip wood, imitation exotic wood graining, inlaid striping . . .   **105.00**

12¾" l, pine and poplar, dovetailed, turned feet, painted buildings, white, tan, and brown, green ground, replaced feet, one edge molding strip missing **350.00**

14" l, pine, red and black graining, applied base and lid moldings, brass handle and latch. **205.00**

14⅝" l, poplar, white striping and black edging, red stain, bluish–

green int., brass bail handle, alligatored finish **275.00**

14¾" l, pine, red and brown graining on yellow ground, paneled sides and lid, small porcelain button feet **95.00**

19¾" l, poplar, dovetailed, brown vinegar graining, wrought iron handles and lock, thistle design on emb brass handle, missing hasp and escutcheon **350.00**

24" l, pine and poplar, iron lock and hasp, brass keyhole cover, orig black and white graining **1,450.00**

28" l, 14" w, 11½" h, poplar, putty grained, dome top, New England, early 19th C **1,100.00**

Desk, 12¼" w, 10" deep, 7⅓" h, table top, pine, slant top lid, orig lock, emb brass escutcheon, dovetailed case, old refinish **200.00**

Document

7⅞" l, 4¾" d, 5¼" h, dome top, painted green, early 19th C **475.00**

13" l, 8¼" d, 6¾" h, shaped cov, smoke grained ext., New England, first half 19th C **450.00**

18" w, 9" h, pine, painted to resemble iron–bound trunk, black and yellow paint, natural finish, c1830 . . . .   **200.00**

Dome Top

7" l, pine, decorated, polychrome floral dec, blue–green ground, wire hinges and hasp replaced, small chip on front edge **300.00**

12¾" l, pine, decorated, dovetailed, brown vinegar graining, painted front panel with black, yellow, and olive initials and date "MAB 1822," staple hinges **350.00**

13" l, tooled leather cov, finely detailed wrought iron lock, hasp, and handle, worn wallpaper lined int., worn and split leather, hinges broken **55.00**

15" l

Hide covered, leather binding, brass tacks, brass bail handle, lock and hinges, lined with 1806 NY newspaper, broken hasp.   **80.00**

Pine and poplar, dovetailed, old black paint, gold stenciling over red, some wear, scraped band on back edge **110.00**

15¼" l, decorated, pine, dovetailed, red–brown paint graining, front panel with roses, German inscription, and date "1800," wrought iron lock with decorative escutcheon and key, replaced turned feet,

aged crack in lid, edge damage, paint wear **475.00**

20¼" l, 10" d, 9⅛" h, wallpaper covered ext., imperfections, New England, first half 19th C **200.00**

28" l, poplar, decorated, dovetailed, freely brushed black stippling and swirls, old brown patina, age cracks **475.00**

Dough Box, poplar, rect

33½" l, canted sides, heart cutout handles both ends, old red finish, age cracks, some edge damage **300.00**

36" l, 27" h, cov, whittled leg stand, old refinish **250.00**

42 × 19¾ × 27¾", cov, splayed base with turned legs, old worn red paint **825.00**

Hanging

12½" w, 13" h, walnut, high cutout swan's neck crest, dovetailed box **925.00**

13" w, 9½" d, 19½" h, pine, dovetailed, two drawers, open heart hanger, 18th C. **650.00**

14¼" h, 9" w, 8" deep, pine, carved, painted, pierced stylized figures crest, sloping lid on well above one drawer, polychrome stylized pinwheels and stellate design on sides and back, dark blue–green ground, Connecticut River Valley, New England, 1750–1800 . . . . . .   **8,750.00**

20½" h, walnut, inlaid dec, fiddle–back crest, shaped apron **245.00**

Hat, cov, bent laminated wood, leather strap handle, black painted label, int. paper label, 12" d, 16¼" h **65.00**

Inlaid, 13" w, 8¾" deep, 5¼" h, herringbone patterned sides, star dec on lid, 19th C. **150.00**

Jewelry

8" l, two drawers, gold painted cutout design with red cloth backing, white porcelain pulls, cigar box back board **35.00**

11¼" h, tramp art, miniature chest of drawers shape, traces of gold paint   **100.00**

14" l, tramp art, mirror and drawer in blue velvet–lined int., old varnish finish **195.00**

Knife

2¼" l, miniature, mahogany, dovetailed, cutout handle, early 19th C   **200.00**

11¾" l, bentwood, cutouts and wooden knob fasteners on laminate sides, old varnish finish **45.00**

13" l

Decorated, yellow striping, floral dec, and "Lizzie" on orig brown finish **200.00**

Pine, dovetailed, worn salmon and brown paint, cutout handle **115.00**

Poplar, scalloped edge and divider, orig red int., old green overpaint exterior **90.00**

Walnut, spurred cutout handle, old finish **135.00**

13½" h

Hardwood, turned handle, refinished, age crack **55.00**

Mahogany Veneer, upright, slanted lid, silver plated bail handles, tooled silver escutcheon, replaced int. **450.00**

14" l, walnut and ash, inlaid, chevron herringbone pattern, varnish finish **125.00**

14¼" l, mahogany, dovetailed, incised scrollwork, heart handle, early 19th C **350.00**

16¼" l, poplar and pine, dovetailed, hinged lids, cutout handle, old dark finish **250.00**

17¼" l, mahogany, dovetailed, scalloped ends, cutout handle, 19th C **225.00**

19" l, 12" h, pine, dovetailed, heart cutout handle, old worn patina, black painted handle **150.00**

Painter's, carved, central urn and flower surrounded by undulating border with ferns and flowerheads, PA, 19th C, 19½" l, 15¼" d, 4" h **500.00**

Pantry, cov, bentwood

Oval

4½" l, poplar, white and blue dec, salmon ground, worn paint, Lancaster County, PA **300.00**

4⅝" l, single finger construction on base and lid, worn red, traces of orange, minor edge damage **150.00**

7" l, single finger on lid, wrought iron tack construction, old patina, traces of bluish–gray paint **200.00**

9½" l, metal laced seams, old red paint **95.00**

12" l, metal laced seams, natural finish **75.00**

15¼" l, pine, laced seams, green repaint **225.00**

Pantry, bentwood, round, straight seam, 7¾" d, 3¾" h, $45.00.

Round

5½" d, old yellow repaint **55.00**

6½" d, old worn blue paint **95.00**

8¾" d, 4¼" h, copper tack construction, old green repaint over yellow varnish **175.00**

9½" d, old dark green paint **200.00**

11¼" d, 6¾" h, wire bail with turned wood handle, orange paint **375.00**

12½" d, 6½" h, pine, single finger construction, black, blue, and yellow stylized floral dec, orange ground **250.00**

13¼" d, pine, laced seams, black, yellow, blue, and white stylized floral dec, orange ground, minor wear, edge damage **875.00**

Pipe, hanging

12" h, 6½" w, 3½" deep, pine and hardwood, scalloped edge, dovetailed drawer, square nail construction **150.00**

16" h, pine, cutout top rim and crest, dovetailed drawer, old black repaint **2,200.00**

16½" h, oak, old green over red paint, 1720–50 . . . . **275.00**

17½" h, mahogany, replaced leather hinge, old finish, 19th C **100.00**

20" h, cherry, scalloped top edge, single drawer, brass knob, old refinish **220.00**

20½" h

Mahogany, truncated case, cutout crest, hinged lid, old finish **330.00**

Pine, hanging, primitive, circular crest with hanging hole, V–shaped cutout top edge, dovetailed drawer, old dark brown patina, edge damage to drawer, bottom board incomplete and loose **990.00**

22¾" h, curly maple, shaped crest, rect body, shaped sloping sides, small molded drawer, molded base, New England, 1770–90 . . . **1,650.00**

Saffron, cov, 5" h, Lehneware, poplar, turned, pedestal foot, painted dec and découpage, flowers and strawberries, multicolored on pink ground, glued break in foot, worn **250.00**

Salt, hanging, 9½" w, 7" d, 8¾" h, pine, dovetailed, cutout crest, lift lid, homemade hinges, old dark paint over green **150.00**

Scouring, 4¾" w, 18½" h, hanging, pine, primitive, high back with bentwood crest, old worn patina, minor edge wear **125.00**

Sewing, 10½" l, oval, very worn old gray paint, hinged lid **75.00**

Slant Lid
  10" l, pine and poplar, staple hinges, orig red paint, black stenciled dec on four sides and lid **475.00**
  14½" l, poplar, dovetailed, blue wallpaper lined int., traces of orig red finish **275.00**
Snuff, birch bark, oval, hinged lid, engraved designs with German inscriptions, 4" l **95.00**
Spice Box
  9" l, cherry, dovetailed, four compartment int., sliding lid, refinished **110.00**
  10" w, 25" h, hanging, hardwood, wire nail construction, shaped crest with hanging hole, nine small drawers over two long drawers, porcelain pulls, faded spice labels, repaired crack in back board. . . . **350.00**
  12½" w, poplar, dovetailed, scalloped crest with hanging hole, divided int., hinged lid **775.00**
Storage
  Cherry, 9" l, sliding lid, dovetailed, old soft finish, one edge of lid restored **75.00**
  Pine, carved, hinged lid, molded base, natural finish, punch work dec, front initialed "R.C.", New England, c1700, 24¼" w, 14" d, 12" h. **1,200.00**
Treen, round
  4" d
    Beech, polychrome floral dec, natural ground, threaded lid, age crack in lid **275.00**
    Poplar, polychrome geometric floral dec, brown ground, threaded lid **250.00**
  12" h, walnut, elaborately turned spire shaped finial, turned pedestal base, old soft finish, age cracks, some glued repairs **175.00**
Utility
  8" l, pine and poplar, sliding lid, old finish, scratch carved "P B Gaff" on lid **50.00**
  8⅝" l, beech, rect, floral dec, wood pin hinges, orig polychrome paint **550.00**
  12¾" l, pine, orig black paint, orange striping, stenciled "Deborah W Holway" **110.00**

BUCKETS, BARRELS, AND BOWLS

History: Wooden barrels, bowls, and buckets were a necessity in rural America. Barrels were used to store a wide variety of materials ranging

from fruits to flour to whiskey. Every medium–size village along a major transportation route had a cooper in residence.

Burl bowls were prized possessions. The individuality of the grain captivated the owners, and they wore like iron. Their major problem is that they were subject to cracking.

Like many other wooden objects, a number of specialized bucket forms developed. The pail is one example. However, the ones most sought by Country collectors and decorators are sugar buckets and firkins. Many sugar buckets eventually wound up inside the rural home as sewing baskets or storage containers for objects such as cookie cutters. Buckets with a manufacturer's mark or period paint bring a premium.

If not properly cared for, wooden barrels, bowls, and buckets will crack and fall apart. Keep them away from areas of high heat and low humidity. Barrels that were meant to hold liquid should be filled for a few days several times each year to keep the joints swollen tight. Do not oil bowls. Simply wipe them clean with a damp cloth.

Reproduction Craftspersons: *Bowls*—Carl Desko, PO Box 201, Willow Grove, PA 19090; Rip and Tammi Mann, Handhewn Bowls, PO Box 1584; Etowah, NC 28729; Don Mounter, Rte 1, Box 54, Fayette, MO 65248; John D Sadler, Wooden Bowls by John Sadler, Rte 1, Box 81, Bradyville, TN 37026.

Reproduction Manufacturers: *Bowl*—Lace Wood 'N Tin Tyme, 6496 Summerton, Shepherd, MI 48883; The Painted Pony, 8392 West M–72, Traverse City, MI 49684; Southern Manner, Inc, 106 North Trade St, PO Box 1706, Matthews, NC 28106; Unfinished Business, PO Box 246X, Wingate, NC 28174; *Buckets*—Chinaberry General Store, 1846 Winfield Dunn Highway, Sevierville, TN 38762; Conewago Junction, 805 Oxford Rd, New Oxford, PA 17350; Country Loft, 1506 South Shore Park, Hingham, MA 02043; Log Cabin Shop, Box 275, Lodi, OH 44254.

Barrel
  17½" d, 27" h, cov, pine staved, Lebanon, NY, late 18th C **360.00**
  19" h, stave constructed, laced wood bands, refinished **100.00**
Bowl
  8" d, 3⅜" h, ash burl, round, scrubbed finish **385.00**
  8" l, 5½" h, oval, stave constructed, chip carved edge, reed wrapped ext., old worn brown, red, and tan paint **55.00**
  10" d, 4¾" h, ash burl, round, old soft finish, minor surface and rim irregularities. **375.00**
  12½" d, 4¼" h, ash burl, round, mellow soft finish, plugged hole in bottom. **385.00**

13" d, 4¼" h, ash burl, round, scrubbed finish, age cracks and 1" notch in rim **500.00**

16¼" l, 11¾" w, 4¼" h, oblong, ash burl, cutout open handles **875.00**

19" l, treen, oval, orig seafoam green paint, Hudson Valley, NY, early 19th C. **175.00**

22½" d, round, chopping, carved, painted green, 19th C **525.00**

23½" l, 13¾" w, 4¾" h, boat shape, dark patina int., dark blue paint ext. **575.00**

24" d, round

Painted blue, chopping, imp "M.L. Goddard," 19th C, wear **525.00**

Poplar, 7½" h, turned, old red finish ext., edge wear, rim crack **350.00**

24¾" l, 15" w, oblong, end handles, worn patina. **180.00**

25" d, 6" h, yellow pine, octagonal, dovetailed joints with metal pins, old dark brown patina. **220.00**

Bucket

Grain Painted, 9¼" h, minor wear, 19th C. **275.00**

Miniature, 3¼" h, cov, turned wood, string handle, worn green paint **135.00**

Oyster, 12¼" h, cov, stave constructed, iron hoops, bail handle, and hasp closure, paint stenciled label "Boston Oyster Company" on front, sides taper from wider base to narrower top, New England, early 20th C **300.00**

Pickles, 13" h, cov, painted yellow, red bands, black stenciled label "Sweet Pickles," wire bail handle **110.00**

Sugar, firkin, stave constructed

5¼" h, sapling bands, swivel handle, green overpaint. **240.00**

9¼" h, old dark repaint. **110.00**

Oyster Bucket, stave constructed, iron hoops, bail handle, and hasp, painted, stenciled label "Boston Oyster Co," New England, early 20th C, 12¼" h, $302.00. Photograph courtesy of Skinner, Inc.

9½" h, cov, worn scrubbed finish **75.00**

9¾" h, worn blue paint **165.00**

11½" h, old red paint, missing handle **95.00**

12" h, light green repaint. **275.00**

13¾" h, 14½" d, swivel handle, age cracks in lid. **85.00**

Utility

9" h, cov, stave constructed, painted blue, porcelain knob finial on lid, late 19th C **225.00**

10¾" h, 14" d, primitive, stave constructed, iron bands, wooden side handles, varnish over worn orange and green paint **85.00**

13" d, cov, blue painted ext., yellow painted int., 19th C, wear **470.00**

Keg, 13" h, stave constructed, split sapling bands, worn paper label "Rifle Powder, Rustin Powder Co., Cleveland, Ohio". **125.00**

Piggin, 6¾" h, 9¼" d, stave constructed, bottom stamped "N. Corthell," old worn finish **160.00**

WOODENWARE

History: Many utilitarian household objects and farm implements were made of wood. Although they were used heavily, these implements were made of the strongest woods and well taken care of by their owners.

One of the elements that attracts collectors and decorators to woodenware is the patinated and oxidized finish on unpainted pieces. The wood develops a mellowness and smoothness that is impossible to duplicate.

Lehneware is a favorite with folk art collectors because of its polychrome decorations. It blends nicely with the stenciled decorated pieces of the mid–19th century. These collectors have chosen to ignore the fact that most of the pieces are mass–produced.

This category serves as a catch–all for wood objects that do not fit into other categories.

Reference: George C. Neumann, *Early American Antique Country Furnishings: Northeastern America, 1650–1800's,* L–W Book Sales, 1984, 1993 reprint.

Reproduction Craftspersons: *General*—Carl Desko, PO Box 201, Willow Grove, PA 19090; Tom Douglass, RD 1, Box 38, Hopwood, PA 15445; Robert P Emory, 115 Hickory Ln, Rosemont, PA 19010; Kevin Riddle, Mountainman Woodshop, PO Box 40, Eagle Rock, VA 24085; John D Sadler, Rte 1, Box 81, Bradyville, TN 37026; *Ladles, Scoops, and Spoons*—Virginia Petty, Whistlin' Whittler, 1684 Three Forks–Flatrock Rd, Oakland, KY 42159.

Reproduction Manufacturers: *Butter Churn*— Chinaberry General Store, 1846 Winfield Dunn Highway, Sevierville, TN 38762; *General*—Conewago Junction, 805 Oxford Rd, New Oxford, PA 17350; McClanahan Country, 217 Rockwell Rd, Wilmington, NC 28405; *Sock Stretchers*—Sock Stretchers, 112 SE Roza Vista Dr, Yakima, WA 98901.

Barn Vent, 42" h, pine, open cut nine-point star in triangle, traces of red, white, and blue paint on triangle, traces of gilt on star, wrought iron hinges and hasp on back **700.00**
Candle Drying Rack, 32" d, 40" h, hardwood and pine, wire hooks on eight removable disks, old patina **575.00**
Candle Stand, adjustable ratchet, iron socket with pushup, early 19th C, 29" h **40.00**
Canister, cov, 13" h, treenware, maple, barrel shaped, lathe turned, early 19th C. **275.00**
Clothes Tree, ball finial on turned standard, six turned pegs, four turned legs, ball feet, worn green paint, 68" h **225.00**
Compote, 5" h, 6¼" d, burl, varnish **250.00**
Cup, 3⅛" h, Lehneware, ftd, orig polychrome floral dec on blue ground **925.00**
Dipper, 10½" l, burl, well-shaped curly handle, curved hook and drilled hole for hanging, worn patina **250.00**
Dress Mannequin
  22" h, carved head and torso, jointed arms, conical frame base **1,155.00**
  48" h, female, carved, mid 19th C **2,750.00**
Drying Rack, poplar, three bars, chamfered posts, shoe feet, old black paint, 24" w, 30½" h **165.00**
Eggcup, turned, ftd
  2¾" h, Lehneware, orig red, green, black, and yellow strawberry dec on salmon pink ground **525.00**

Fish Line Dryer, maple, mortise construction, peg base, age cracks, 22¾" l, 24" h, $75.00.

3" h, Pease, old varnish **20.00**
3⅜" h, Lehneware, orig polychrome floral dec and decals, glued break on foot **205.00**
Finial, circus wagon, worn and weathered polychrome repaint, 7⅜" h, pr **165.00**
Frame, beveled, worn orig reddish brown flame graining, 13 x 16⅞" **100.00**
Grain Shovel
  37" l, carved maple, open D-shaped handle, early 1800s **150.00**
  36½" l, worn old surface, traces of gold paint **140.00**
Jar, turned, ftd
  2¾" h, Lehneware, polychrome floral dec on salmon ground **225.00**
  3" h, cov, Pease, wire bail and wooden handle, varnish finish . . . **75.00**
  3½" h, Pease, old varnish, replaced wire bail handle **85.00**
  3¾" h, Pease, old varnish, age cracks **105.00**
  4" h, cov, Pease, old varnish, age cracks in lid **100.00**

Eggcup, Lehneware, hand painted leafy stem and border, applied rose decals, pink ground, 3½" h, $200.00.

Jar, cov, turned urn shape, pedestal base, 2⅝" d, 6¼" h, $85.00.

4⅜" h, Pease, old varnish **100.00**
4½" h, turned hourglass shape, emb
brass button in lid, varnish finish   **25.00**
5¾" h, ftd, bottom stamped "Hand
Turned, J. C. Brown, Painesville,
Ohio," varnish finish **175.00**
6½" h, Pease, old varnish, wood and
wire bail handle **295.00**
9" h, stave constructed, porcelain
knob on turned lid, metal bands,
orig red graining, yellow, green,
white, and red floral vines painted
on black bands, alligatored sur-
face **2,000.00**
Jug, 3⅝" l, dog shape, removable head,
old finish, black spots **95.00**
Loom Light, hanging, ratchet type, dou-
ble, American, 19th C, 44" l ex-
tended **175.00**
Mantel, pine, Country Classical Re-
vival, old tan repaint, 62 ¼" w,
44½" h **190.00**
Match Holder, treen
3" h, beehive shaped, tartan découpage, ivory top socket holds burn-
ing match **75.00**
3½" h, wine glass shaped, two free
turned rings, black striping **55.00**
Measure, bentwood, round, turned
side handle, varnish over old finish,
age crack in bottom, some edge dam-
age, 5¾" d **50.00**
Mortar, burl, good figure, old soft fin-
ish, 7¾" h **275.00**
Mortar and Pestle, turned
3¼" h, miniature, turned, Lignum
vitae, worn **110.00**
6¼" h, burl mortar, chestnut pestle,
old finish **200.00**
7" h, maple **55.00**
7¾" h, light blue repaint **50.00**
Night Stick, curly maple, turned, good
curl, 16" l **45.00**
Noggin, 7¾" h, chamfered sides, old
patina **150.00**
Paddle, burl, soft finish, 4¾" l **335.00**

Plate
7½" d, treen, worn patina **225.00**
9¼" d, treen, deep rim, scrubbed
finish **250.00**
10" d, tiger maple, 19th C **525.00**
Saffron Jar, cov, Lehneware, ftd
4¾" h, polychrome flowers and
strawberries on yellow ground,
chips on foot **350.00**
5" h, polychrome flowers and straw-
berries on lavender ground paint
wear on lid, chip on foot **400.00**
Salt, Lehneware, 2⅞" h, ftd, poly-
chrome floral dec on pink ground,
chip on foot **275.00**
Sieve, round, late 19th C, 14" d **25.00**
Sock Stretcher, 14½" l **12.00**
Spoon
5" l, burl, soft finish **165.00**
6¼" l, carved, engraved design in
bowl, shaped handle with letter "K"   **60.00**
8⅛" l, treen, rope twist handle,
turned ivory finial **40.00**
17" l, curly maple, long handle **95.00**
Stocking Stretchers
16" h, child size, old patina **45.00**
23" h, adult size, old patina **35.00**
Swift, light and dark wood, 22" l **210.00**
Toothpick Dispenser, 6¼" l, carved,
bird tips into box, spears toothpick
with sharp metal beak, old red and
black paint, edge damage to tail . . .   **190.00**
Towel Rack
22¼" l, 2⅛" h, tiger maple, 19th C   **250.00**
17½" l, 15" w, 32¾" h, mahogany,
old finish, chamfered edge mem-
bers, mortised construction **275.00**
Trencher, 19 × 20", wear and age
cracks **200.00**
Tub Stand, three arms, mortised con-
struction, pencil post legs, old blue
paint traces, 28 × 36" **30.00**
Wall Pocket, 24" h, 18" w, 7½" deep,
poplar, treen, old blue repaint over
green and gold, serrated and scal-
loped edges, wire nail construction   **150.00**

INDEX